MW01624882

GRANVILLE'S LAST STAND

Secrets of the Stock Market Revealed

by
Joseph E. Granville

Hanover House
New York

A HANOVER EDITION

Published by
Hanover House
a division of the
Zinn Publishing Group
ZINN COMMUNICATIONS / NEW YORK

ISBN: 0-935105-12-0

Printed in the United states of America

Library of Congress Cataloging-in-Publication Data

Granville, Joseph E.
Granville's last stand: secrets of the stock market revealed / Joseph E. Granville.
p. cm
Includes index.
ISBN 0-935016-12-0
1. Stock-exchange—United States. 2. Speculation—United States.
HG4910.G756 1994
332.64'273—dc20 94-36453
CIP

For Dear Karen,
My Constant Inspiration

Acknowledgements

M.C. Horsey & Company, Inc.
"The Stock Picture" Chart Service
Salisbury, MD 21801
Tel: (410) 742-3700

Chart Courtesy of:
Arthur A. Merrill
Technical Trends
Chappaqua, New York

"Reprinted by Permission of the
Wall Street Journal

"Reprinted by permission of
Standard & Poor's, a division of
McGraw-Hill, Inc."
"For subscription information,
call (800) 221-5277."

"Reprinted by permission of
INVESTOR'S BUSINESS DAILY
Date of issue: 1-21-94

"There is nothing more difficult to take in hand, more perilous to conduct, or more uncertain in its success than to take the lead in the introduction of a new order of things."

Niccolo Machiavelli, *The Prince*

Contents

Section VII: The 1990-93 Bull Cycle

Section VIII: Earnings - The Worst of Indicators

Section IX: The Mystery Of the Bermuda Triangle

Section X: The Crash of 1994-95

Section XI: The Epilogue

Section XII: Appendix

Tables

The terms shown in the Glossary with the TM designation are proprietary terms, the property and trademarks of the author.

Preface

The French composer Georges Bizet said that "the composer gives the best of himself to the making of a work. He believes, he doubts, enthuses, despairs, rejoices, and suffers in turn." In the writing of this book, I did all of these things and more but through the passage of time in the further development of my stock market theory my beliefs strengthened, all doubts disappeared, my enthusiasm became boundless, all despair was without foundation. I rejoiced anew, and the only suffering that remained was in sympathy for those who have not yet encountered the great truths of the stock market and of life to be revealed here. I share these truths and discoveries freely and without reservation because I have observed that what you give away you truly acquire.

But the pursuit of knowledge when it comes to the stock market is a bit like greyhounds chasing a mechanical rabbit that is never caught. We technicians seek a final answer that always seems to elude us. Fascinated with the concept that an alien with a powerful enough telescope could see past events on the earth, reversing the process always tantalized me. Where would one stand in the universe to see future events on earth? But we do know that a valid technical stance in the market provides a view of the most probable market future.

This book is for students who truly love the market, who thirst for new knowledge. This book is for those who are willing to devote far more time to the subject, who are determined to not only succeed for themselves, but to make a lasting contribution for others. This book is designed to aid in creative thinking, not restricting the reader to hold to current restricting conventions. It is for those who are willing to toil for long periods of time though the yield be small. It champions the individual who in his quest for truth is immune to the critics born of the crowd.

Truth never dies. People die, but truth lives on forever. The stock market is an endless river. Regardless of our mistakes, the river continues to flow and will always give losers another chance .We can swim across the river or we can drown in it but our fate is not the river's fault. We make our own fate in the marketplace and whatever success we have, such success must be grounded in market truths that never die. The market is a continuous dance of life, the very nub of investigative inquiry.

Technical analysis of the stock market is an ever-expanding universe, reflecting an infinity of human thought. Recognizing this limitless reservoir of ideas and their yet-to-be discovered unique applications to the stock market, I have never stopped knocking on and opening new doors of market inquiry, challenged by new frontiers of technical discovery. To constantly tread worn paths of technical analysis, never risking unexplored detours, is to mentally stagnate and needlessly limit opportunities to restrictive past standards. Most contemporary stock market technicians tread known paths and make no original contributions to the literature. They are either lacking talent, inspiration, or simply afraid to embark on the unknown. They would rather follow known paths than be pioneers and risk failure. Thank God for the Thomas Edisons of this world. Suppose his thousands of failing experiments led him to give up on the light bulb? So if we are to expand the parameters of technical analysis, we must not let a failure or many failures deter us from that objective. We must make mistakes in order to learn. Leonard Bernstein said to teach is to learn and to learn is to teach.

So I seek to underscore what is correct regardless of my own record. The purpose of this book is to teach. The result of teaching is learning. But we best learn by our mistakes. I can maintain a quality of teaching by freely admitting mistakes and learning by them. If I can teach something about the market by one of my own mistakes then it has to be a lesson of high quality. To introduce new indicators I had to take risks. I had to risk being wrong in order to uncover the truth so that others can be right. So mistakes are positives, not negatives. Mistakes balance the equation of truth, proving that knowing what not to do is every bit as important as knowing what to do. Technical research and its development makes mistakes virtually certain.

So while the market's 1990-94 bull cycle looked like it was heading for a possible crash, my warnings of this in 1992 and 1993 were admittedly premature on the Dow-30, but not in terms of most stocks. There had been a brief entry into a market Bermuda Triangle of confusion in late 1992 which for awhile turned everything upside down but instead of being immediately followed by a bear market as I had expected, the Dow had another upleg to record in the 1992-94 period, what had all the characteristics of classic and final solitary walk. I had ignored the bullish early October 1992 reversal but the record showed that most stocks failed to recover on that rise. So I was wrong on the Dow but very correct that most stocks had seen their bull cycle highs. The experience told me that the next time we entered a Bermuda Triangle transition period, that we did in late 1993, it would be followed by a bear market that could no longer be avoided.

The market comes in two parts, the hidden market for the winners and the obvious market for the losers. It presents a new language fashioned from life itself, enlarging the spectrum of technical analysis to spread itself over a wider canvas, tools to determine every nuance of the market language. I also dedicate this work to the new generation of younger technicians who will be interpreting the market message long after I have gone. But alas, many of them will fall far short of their potential because talent without discipline is worthless. We have many devotees with genuine market talent who are lazy. They will not give themselves on the altar of work. If you want to always be on top of the market, you have to constantly work at it as would a concert pianist preparing for a concert at Carnegie Hall.

My own development rapidly fanned out from an initial curiosity that demanded freedom from the restrictions of fundamental analysis which had sadly entrapped so many for so long in its unimaginative measurements of price/earnings ratios, dividends, corporate earnings, and its overreliance on economic indicators, all those things which so often prove to be of worthless value. Quickly recognizing its uselessness, I was so anxious to purify that suffocating school of thought during my tenure at E. F. Hutton as their market letter writer (1957 to 1963) that I dashed off A Strategy of Daily Stock Market Timing For Maximum Profit in 89 nights, an iconoclastic work which made its first appearance in 1960. While that book was an anathema to fixed-thinking market fundamentalists, it became an instant bestseller and its success guaranteed a lifetime dedication to furthering the study and application of stock market technical analysis beyond all known frontiers.

But that pioneer work did not immediately take us out of the dark ages of market ignorance. I remember on many occasions during my widespread travels between 1977 and 1982 that any book on technical analysis was whisked out of sight at night by brokerage branch office managers, fearful of offending their clients. We have come a long way since then. Many of these managers, thankfully, have learned the error of their ways but far too many chose to remain in the dark ages of ignorance.

But we haven't come far enough. This is an angry book and rightfully so. Even after so many years of my challenging fundamental analysis, there are books still being written by self-appointed experts who seek to champion their stock selection formulas based on earnings. Nobody took the time and trouble to challenge these totally unreliable methods which have produced so many widespread losses for the naive investor. This writer took the time and trouble and the results contained here border on the scandalous. But I have to be charitable and consign it to ignorance. Tossing a coin presents far better odds for success than following any system of stock selection based on earnings.

I regard my invention of On-Balance Volume in 1961 as the cornerstone of all my future works on technical analysis. This single idea, like a mustard seed, was to become the mother of all later technical creative thought, embodying an all-inclusive new theory of technical stock market analysis. Its introduction made its appearance in 1963 in the book Granville's New Key To Stock Market Profits.

Nothing in my entire career matched the initial thrill of creating On-Balance Volume and my intense joy is best summed up by a quote from the mathematician Alfred Adler:

> A new mathematical result, entirely new, never before conjectured or understood by anyone, nursed from the first tentative hypothesis through labyrinths of false attempted proofs, wrong approaches, unpromising directions, and months or years of difficult and delicate work- there is nothing, or almost nothing in the world that can bring a joy and a sense of power and tranquillity to equal those of its creator. And a great new mathematical edifice is a triumph that whispers of immortality.

I updated my OBV theory in 1976 with the publication of A New Strategy of Daily Stock Market Timing For Maximum Profit and in 1988 published The Stock Market Teacher, introducing the important 4-column analysis which is developed further in this book. Here and there I borrowed small portions of those earlier works in this book.

The current work not only underscores my latest developments in OBV theory, but simultaneously is my boldest repudiation of fundamental analysis which has led so many down the primrose path to large losses and in too many cases to financial destruction. While so many books on technical analysis simply palm off nothing more than a collection of charts and very little text, I have sought to do the exact opposite, providing more than ample text and not consuming space by too many charts. Furthermore, I have always been more comfortable with tables rather than charts because tables can be more specific in denoting every little change. A table can be specifically marked with information regarding breakouts, OBV signals, trend changes etc. A chart, while always valuable as supporting evidence, cannot achieve the interpretive results derived from a table of numbers.

As I write these opening lines, a point I wish to particularly accent is the observation that the market is a fair game. It is not out to cheat you if you follow it. But it is a jealous god. It will not tolerate interference from fundamentalism and all its invalid artifacts of value, price/earnings, dividends, etc. And it proudly divorces itself from the diverting comments of economists as well as the so easily documented ignorance of the financial press.

The two things I most want to stress in this book is the earnings mirage and the market dichotomy. Nowhere is the public more severely deceived than when it comes to corporate earnings, a subject widely hyped by so many as to encourage the public to buy and sell stocks at the very worst of times. As for the dichotomy, every bull market develops an early internal cancer that eats away at it until it is terminal. The subject angers me because while the Dow (consisting of only 30 stocks) rose in 1993, attention to the growing technical cancer was especially ignored by the media which bore most of the guilt in spreading the fundamental gospel and gave the impression that the Dow is the market. Thus when the Dow peaked and the Street finally announces that a bear market has started, only then does it become painfully apparent to the public that most stocks peaked a long time before the Dow and that the public has been holding these stocks at large losses, most of those stocks bought at their highs based on widely hyped Earnings Per Share ratings, something that this book successfully challenges. The whole thrust of this book takes the reader through the technical steps that had to conclude with a crash.

Admittedly, many over the years have been offended by my writings and my market theory, offended because it threatened their own invalid foundations, such foundations of fundamental analysis proving to be the necessary antithesis of the truth that simply proved the existence and validity of that truth. That is technical analysis fulfilling its vital role.

And I take the opportunity in this book to present for the first time the daily readings of the Climax Indicator and the Net Field Trend indicator in 1929 both before and after the great crash, a perfect validation of my OBV theory and a stunning proof that human nature in the marketplace will never change.

I strived for total freedom in my methods of market analysis. The market has a message regarding the value of time. Once it is understood that the market never wastes time, we should extend those lessons to life itself. The country is increasingly fed sporifics which waste time, our most precious possession. If people would quit thinking about living to 80 and think of 80 years as 26,000 days, they wouldn't be so quick to waste so many of them.

In this book I do the same thing that caused my wrists to be slapped by my Russian piano teachers during my childhood. I improvise. Only in total freedom is there true creation and my stock market theory- condemned by Wall Street- is as fresh as tomorrow and at the same time as old as yesterday for it is truth and truth is eternal, never dies.

But one must be free from the clutches of misleading traditional ideas in order for the real truth of the market to be revealed and understood, otherwise there is no market success. Guiseppe Verdi put it this way: "Success is impossible for me if I cannot write as my heart dictates." Being a born iconoclast, I write as I please and freely condemn Wall Street for what it is, exposing it as the necessary contrast to the truth, vital to balancing the equation between winners and losers. Wall Street is the financial community and it is structured to make you a loser. It is the exact opposite of the stock market and that is what this book is largely all about-demonstrating that the only authority on the stock market is the stock market and thus it is vital to learn the language of the stock market and to go to no other source.

The language of the market is as beautiful and sublime as the finest piece of music. The market follows all the laws of harmony and embraces meter, melody, tempo, pattern, contrast, time and rhythm and then seeks variations which invert, reverse, contract, and expand in canonical fashion, always introducing the counterpoint between winners and losers. And, like music, the market is ever new, ever fresh, never boring. Joseph Machlis stated that "No two symphonies of Hayden or Mozart, no two sonatas by Beethoven are exactly alike. Each is a fresh and unique solution of the problem of fashioning musical material into a logical and coherent form." The stock market is totally logical and never without form and organization. Like music, the market gives us the dominant theme and develops it to a logical and predictable conclusion. Like a river, constantly seeking the sea, the literature of music is replete with references to this phenomenon of incompleteness seeking completion. Igor Stravinsky said "All music is nothing more than a succession of impulses that converge toward a definite point of repose." Joseph Machlis said "There is wisdom in the usage of language, that calls an individual part of a symphony a movement. For a piece of music is precisely that. It sets out from a certain point and moves inexorably towards the conclusion of the piece. When it gets there the music ends. Throughout its course we must feel the music as a progression toward a goal. Rhythm, melody, harmony, timbre, tempo, and dynamics unite to give us this impression. When they succeed, it means that the form is convincing." And Aaron Copland said, "A great symphony is a man-made Mississippi down which we irresistibly flow from the instant of our leave-taking to a long foreseen destination." And Arnold Schoenberg said, "The principal function of form is to advance our understanding. It is the organization of a piece which helps the listener to keep the ideas in mind, to follow its development, its growth, its elaboration, its fate."

So form is all-important. One of the key objectives in this book is to teach the reader how to organize his market material in order that he can always keep the uppermost idea of the market in mind. Ernest Toch said it so well "In any narrative, epic, dramatic or musical, every word or tone should be like a soldier marching towards the one, common final goal-conquest of the material. The way the artist makes every phrase of his story such a soldier, serving to unfold it, to support its structure and development, to build plot and counterplot, to distribute light and shade, to point incessantly and lead us gradually to the climax- in short, the way every fragment is impregnated with its mission towards the whole makes up this delicate and so essential objective which we call form."

Market analogies to all truths are infinite. We can talk about the market not only in musical terms, but we can be equally at home in physics. The markets follows all the laws of physics, easily explained in terms of momentum, gravity, attraction, acceleration, harmonics, time, space, energy, magnetism and even color as we deal with the entire spectrum of technical analysis, weaving a tapestry of infinite beauty. We never stray, however, from the cold and unemotional building blocks of truth- number. The mathematics of technical analysis are simple and quite precise and my entire theory of stock market timing lends itself beautifully to quantification.

Roger Sessions said, "The evolution of the harmonic idiom has resulted from the fact that musicians of all generations have sought new means of expression. Harmony is a constant stream of evolution, a constantly changing vocabulary and syntax." My stock market theory has evolved over the years, ever seeking that final state of repose. Relative to that evolvement, I would have to consider the theory as it now stands as being close to its pristine state.

My wife Karen, came to completely understand the finished work on my theory and was quick to always remind me through the tough times to trust my numbers. She told me in January 1993 that the Dow was headed higher. When it looked like the market was going against me in late 1993, Karen told me on October 30, 1993 that it does not matter what the market has done in the past but that only the future counts.

But my theory proved correct and stood the test of time. By April of 1994 the Wall Street Journal concluded that one was better off in cash in 1993 than in stocks and bonds, proving once again that the Dow is not the market. So, like the 1987-90 bull cycle, the 1990-94 cycle was also called correctly.

Section I

Concepts and Secrets

Concepts and Secrets

1. *The Game*

How does one describe life? In the physical sense life is breath. We inhale and we exhale. We are so used to doing it that we seldom think about it. It is not something that we have to ponder, whether it is time to inhale or time to exhale. We just do it. If you doubt the validity of this process you will be dead in four minutes. One part of the process is just as vital as the other part. By participating in both parts of the process, our life is sustained. I love the stock market because it follows every life process. The market goes up (inhales) and the market goes down (exhales). Yet most people actually think that the only way you can make money in the stock market is when it goes up. How stupid can one be? That is just like saying that the only way you can breathe is by inhaling.

Most people are attracted to the obvious, the familiar. When they buy stocks they want to feel the security of good news, good earnings ahead, a good economy. They would never feel comfortable buying a stock on bad news, lower earnings, or a sliding economy. *Yet people have to be trained to do virtually the opposite of everything they have been taught.* Most people will not find such a transition to be easy. In fact, most people will not be able to make the transition. For years most people who were airline passengers expected the propeller-driven aircraft to be the only way to fly. It took a little time to get over the shock of being up 35,000 feet and seeing no propellers outside the window. In the stock market one has to get used to walking on what would seem like an invisible foundation - buying and selling stocks without looking at news, earnings, or the economy. Remember Nicholas Darvas? He was a dancer who got interested in the stock market and in his 1962 book *How I Made $2 Million In the Stock Market* he said he could trade successfully anywhere (even in a locked room at the North Pole with no newspapers, radio or TV) as long as he had *Barron's* and a way of contacting his broker).

It would be a relief not to have to listen to economists, but the media, not fully understanding what really makes stocks tick, would never agree to removing all the economists they bore you with everyday.

Now, life is a game, a very serious game, but a game nevertheless. A game consists of winners and losers. The stock market, following every life principle, also consists of winners and losers. True to life, most people subconsciously opt in favor of following the losing side because they follow only one side of the coin, always attracted to the obvious. *The stock market is the exact opposite of human nature.* Until you learn that you will never be a winner in life or the stock market game. It isn't simply a case of doing the opposite of what most people are doing, or what is known as being a contrarian. It is simply a case of following the market. Sometimes the market is in harmony with what most people think and other times it is out of harmony with what most people think. How is one to know the difference? It is very easy. Learn the language of the market. Yes, there is a market language and it is called technical analysis. It is a beautiful language, unmarred by human frailties. It is as pure as a Bach theme or a beautiful Chopin melody. It cuts through all the Wall Street gibberish that is so totally inharmonious. Without this beautiful market language it is like having to find the bathroom in Tibet. You cannot ask the way simply because you don't know how to speak a word of that language.

So I see myself as nothing more or less than a language teacher. The true introduction to the magnificent world of the stock market is through its own language-technical analysis in its purest form. Never, ever, mix fundamental data with technical analysis. That is like putting water in your gasoline tank- your car won't go. Most people follow fundamental data (earnings, dividends, interest rates, money supply, etc.) and the record clearly shows that their car doesn't go. Since fundamental data has nothing to do with the stock market, most people end up losers in the market. How can you play the music of Bach, Beethoven, Brahms, or Chopin unless you can read it? How can you drive your car safely unless you can read the road signs? So the bottom line every time is language, the words of the market. Do you realize that you cannot acquire a license to drive unless you can read? Yet the financial highway is simply strewn with wrecks because most people cannot read the language of the market.

Some years ago I was doing a TV documentary down in Mexico and I stopped the TV crew at the top of a mountain overlooking a 300-foot drop to the blue Pacific below. The narrow road curved around the mountain sharply to the right. There was no guard railing. A little sign by the side of the road said TURN RIGHT. Suppose you didn't know how to read? You would go right over that cliff to a watery grave, a grave undoubtedly overcrowded with bank trust officers and economists, they being notoriously unable to read market signs. Market road signs are just as clearly illuminated as the road signs you encounter in your everyday driving. If you want to get on a highway you look for the word ENTRANCE. When you want to get off that highway you look for the word EXIT. You take those things for granted because you know the language. But suppose you couldn't read? You would wreck your car but the authorities would not have issued you a driver's license in the first place. *But Wall Street will accept your capital and never ask if you can read the market or not.* Wall Street is the exact opposite of the stock market. Wall Street is the financial community and it is structured to make you a loser.

2. *The Eternal Cleavage - The Auction Market*

Have you ever had the feeling that you are being set up in the market? That feeling is well-founded. You are always on the receiving end of every stock transaction you make. Sometimes you are part of the smart money and sometimes you are part of the dumb money. The trick is to learn whether you are being set up to be on the wrong side of the market. Nobody sets you up to be on the winning side. Only following the market will do that. Losers are always set up to be losers. So right at the outset you must be made conscious of the fact that the stock market is an *auction market.* Buyers and sellers come together and it is the pushes and pulls of supply and demand that sets a market price for the stock. The buyer buys because he thinks the price of the stock is headed higher. The seller sells because he thinks the price of the stock is headed lower. Obviously they both can't be right. One will make money and the other will lose.

I used to make the point that even prayer cannot help you in the stock market. Suppose 500 people are praying that the price of General Motors stock goes up. But it wouldn't be hard to imagine that another 500 people are praying that the price of General Motors stock goes down. Assuming it is the same god that they are all praying to, it is obvious that half of the prayers will not be answered.

The great economist John Kenneth Galbraith pointed out that in a competitive society somebody is bound to lose. He was simply expressing the winner/loser principle of an auction market.*

(Footnote) -

"Economist John Kenneth Galbraith, among others, has pointed out that large corporations cannot afford to compete with one another. Their survival is predicated upon cooperation and market segmentation. In a truly competitive system *someone* stands to lose. If General Motors, for example, were to lose, Ford would also. American big business has finally learned that everybody has to protect everybody else's investment. This is even more ominous when you consider that by 1980, seventy per cent of the productive capacity in the non-Communist world will be controlled by 200 corporations. These giant corporations, with their huge yearly media expenditures, are literally in control of American culture and its value systems. In 1974, U.S. ad expenditures totaled $26.7 billion. In 1975 $28.3 billion and 1976 volume might top $31 billion. Most of this advertising utilized subliminal techniques. These are not merely a few advertisements, but a mind-bending media saturation of the society. *Media Sexploitation*, page 15.

This type of market completely rests on the law of supply and demand. Half the equation is the supply of a stock and the other half of the equation is the demand for that stock. A seller cannot function without a buyer. A buyer cannot function without a seller. So the auction market automatically splits all buyers and sellers into two groups, these being winners and losers.

Always keeping this equation of buyer and seller in mind, one being right and the other being wrong, we then can become more aware of the tricks and subterfuges that one side will use against the other in order to make that side the losing side. This is a constant war, a battle as so accurately described by my late friend Gerald Loeb in his classic *A Battle For Investment Survival.*

Cruel as it seems, economists are recruited to populate the losing side of the market equation. It is immaterial as to what came first, the chicken or the egg. Either the economists were first there to confuse the public or the public was there seeking advice from the wrong source, the economists simply obliging and meeting the demand. Never was there a more glaring case of how disconnected economists were from an understanding of the stock market than during the 1991-92 period. In 1991 the Dow Jones Industrial Average rose 535.17 points while the U.S. economy got steadily worse. The public, sadly brainwashed to believe that economists were somehow classified as stock market experts, listened to and believed them in 1991 and didn't make a nickel. Then in 1992 economists stopped being negative on the economy and agreed that the recession was ending. The public, still blindly believing the economists, came back into the stock market like gangbusters after January 1992 just when the great *dichotomy* got started and most stocks had seen their highs, again being on the losing side of the market equation.

Economists are not alone in their misunderstanding of the stock market. Politicians can be identified as being in the same camp. Presidential candidate Bill Clinton in 1992 in a speech given in the Wall Street area bemoaned the sad condition of the economy *and said that the rise in stock prices was morally wrong.*

A constant conflict of interest exists in Wall Street and the bottom line of choice seldom opts in favor of the public. A front page *Wall Street Journal* headline on July 14, 1992 was this: *Under Pressure - At Morgan Stanley Analysts Were Urged To Soften Harsh Views- Bankers Told Them to Avoid Criticizing Firms Courted As Underwriting Clients.*

3. *Battle Between Smart Money and Dumb Money*

In the daily stock market battle being waged every day, all the deadly subterfuges and dirty tricks of warfare must assume to be present and can be more easily detected if one has been familiarized with the nature of the stock market game. Everything you see happening on television, everything you read in the newspapers, the very books you read, the rumors and stories that are circulated by journalists who know little or nothing about the stock market, all this and much more is designed to put you on the wrong side of the market. So you must be made aware of the various types of camouflage used to disguise what the real market is doing.

4. *Accumulation and Distribution*

Never forgetting the basic game-winning strategy of buy low - sell high, stocks are usually accumulated on bad news and low earnings and distributed on good news and high earnings. The smart money never forgets this principle, almost always at odds with the public. The public, on the other hand, forgetful or oblivious to their role in the stock market game, buys on good news and high earnings and sells on bad news and low earnings.

In keeping score on the high Earnings Per Share ratings published by *Investor's Business Daily* and documenting the high percentage of declines that followed, *it became increasingly apparent that stocks were being distributed in the 1992-93 period prior to the bear market that followed.*

5. *Camouflage For Bagholders*

The public has to be attracted to something that appears to be so obvious that it has to be right. But, like fly paper, it entraps more people on the losing side of the stock market than any other single thing. What is that dangerous camouflage? *It is corporate earnings.*

Playing on the public's ignorance of that key fact, *Investor's Business Daily* features a rating system every day, first citing corporate earnings per share and secondly reporting a relative strength rating.

Later on in this book I will demonstrate beyond the shadow of a doubt that any stock selection system based on *corporate earnings* creates more bagholders than any other single influence. Very few people like a bear market but somebody has to own all the stocks that are going down. In other words, the losers in a bear market were all caught holding the bag, now fulfilling the necessary function of balancing the equation between winners and losers. Some market players have played the role of bagholder so often that they have calluses. *Relying too heavily on corporate earnings is responsible for creating more market bagholders than any other single cause.*

6. *Market First - Stocks Second*

Human nature dictates that a person will give priority to the stocks he owns and will give the market second place attention. Let me remind the reader that *the market doesn't know you.* The market is going to do what it is going to do when it is ready to make its move. That action takes precedence over everything. If it is a topping action then *most stocks will be topping.* If it is a bottoming action then *most stocks will be bottoming.* I don't care how good a stock looks. It should not be bought if the technical indicators are underscoring a market top. Conversely, I don't care how weak a stock looks. It should not be sold if the technical indicators are underscoring a market bottom. And never, never base your buying or selling decisions on your tax situation. The market doesn't know your tax situation. Don't flatter yourself that you are that important. The market doesn't follow you. You have to follow it.

So *reverse your priorities.* Every stock you own is dominated by the market trend. Far too often the ownership of stocks blinds one to what the market as a whole is doing. If the technical condition of the stock market has turned negative, that is the dominant factor which determines whether further ownership of individual stocks is justified. One only has to listen to the TV question and answer sessions on stocks after the market trend has turned down to prove that most people got locked in by paying more attention to what they owned rather than on the market itself.

All actions should be guided by the market trend rather than by the substance of the action itself. An example of this was in 1992-93 when falling interest rates pushed owners of certificates of deposit into the stock market very late in the cycle when the technical posture of the market should have had first priority and tempered such action. Most stocks had already seen their highs and that stark technical fact explained much of what was to later take place.

It is easy to lay down rules and say this is what the public should or shouldn't have done in a particular situation but good advice will generally be ignored by the public when the technical evidence underscores a terminal phase of advance. Then the public will play their role of bagholder, buying stocks at the worst of times and fulfilling their function of balancing the market equation, buying their stocks from the smart money who is simultaneously distributing their stocks and taking profits.

7. *First You Have To Completely Change Your Thinking*

You must accept the fact that the only authority on the market is the market itself. There are only two things that can change the price of a stock and those two things are called *supply* and *demand*. That simple fact is what led me to invent On-Balance Volume, the measuring of supply and demand requiring that the answer had to come from the subject of volume measured a certain way.

Most people will never change their thinking about what causes changes in stock prices. Most will persist in being principally influenced by corporate earnings and news. Neither of those things are important. What is important is how the market *responds* to those things and a market response to anything is a technical function, belonging solely to the market technician and not to the market fundamentalist. Fundamental analysis is an anathema to the stock market technician. There are those who think they can successfully combine fundamental analysis with technical analysis. This writer maintains that mixing the two is like mixing oil with water- *your car won't go.* Thinking in terms of the market game, fundamental considerations are on the wrong side of the market equation. To mix that side of the equation with the other side is to immediately reduce the effectiveness of the analysis and relegate that analyst to the market losers, joining the bagholders.

8. *You Will Learn a New Language*

Your change of thinking following the discarding of such fundamental indicators as corporate earnings, price/earnings ratios, and dividends clears your mind so that you can now learn and embrace an entirely new market vocabulary.

The market can only speak to you in its own language. Technical analysis is the study of that language. What most people look at is not part of the market language. They are brainwashed into listening to economists and following the economy, they are told to put emphasis on corporate earnings and dividends, they are told to study companies and their products and sales. The market talks of none of those things. There are only two things that can change the price of a stock- supply and demand. That is what the market talks about. It talks supply and demand in terms of prices and volume. Nothing else matters. The market reacts to everything in terms of a market response. A market response is a technical function and fundamentalists do not know how to read the market and that is why so many of them have such poor market records.

9. *The Stupidity of the One Directional Concept*

We have heard it over and over so many times every day of our life. The comment might be "Well, we had a good day in the market today, the Dow climbing over 30 points." Or we might hear "What should have been a good day in the market turned sour in the afternoon and the Dow fell 20 points, giving us our first bad day this week." So there you have it, the perpetual assumption that up is good and down is bad. In the first case, the better than 30-point advance was a bad day for the shortseller and in the second case the 20-point decline was a good day for the shortseller. Since it takes two to tango, every day in the market is good for somebody and bad for somebody else. So we have to redefine the game here: *A good day in the market is being right and a bad day in the market is being wrong and it doesn't matter what direction the market takes.*

The great brokerage houses of Wall Street have never issued a sell signal. Think of it. Bear markets (down markets) follow bull markets (up markets) just as certainly as night follows day. Since this is just as basic and true as your constant breathing process, *then Wall Street is automatically structured to make you a loser everytime a bear market periodically comes along.* Since the market follows the laws of probability, I know from observation that 80% of all stocks rise following a market buy signal and I know that 90% of all stocks fall following a market sell signal.

The laws of probability show bear markets to be more profitable than bull markets and yet that is the side of the market that most people do not play. Throughout this book everytime I use the term "most people" you will find that it equals the losers in this game. Most people still look upon stockbrokers with a touch of awe, accepting the general belief that because they are stockbrokers they must know more about the stock market than most people. If a stockbroker does not understand the language of the stock market (and most don't) then he is worse than unknowledgeable because of the harm he can render in misleading his clients.

When the market gives a buy signal it always follows the laws of probability which says that most stocks will rise. Never go short in a rising market. If you go short on ten stocks in different industries the probability states that nine will be profitable and one will go against you. Since Wall Street never plays the down market you will see announcements during a bear market where the research department of some leading brokerage house will run an ad such as this: OUR RESEARCH DEPARTMENT HAS UNCOVERED THREE SPECIAL SITUATIONS WHICH THEY THINK ARE CAPABLE OF BUCKING THE TREND. Why buck the trend? Follow it. Wall Street, like most people, thinks that the only way you can make money in the stock market is when it goes up.

The way Wall Street analysts rate stocks is nothing short of abominable. In a weak market such as 1992 we would see a stock selling at 20 suddenly drop to 8. We would then hear that a leading analyst had cut his buy rating to a hold.

10. *What Everybody Knows Is Worthless*

The market is a *discounting* mechanism, always looking ahead. Thus current events are more often than not a trap. Since most people hang on the news, they more often than not seek to trade on things that the market has already traded in. So it can be said that news is a *lagging* indicator unless it comprises shocking news which the market could not possibly have discounted.

11. *The Market Anachronism*

I discovered one of the most intriguing secrets of the stock market by observing how often what the market is doing today suggests the kind of headlines we will see *nine months later.* Put another way, the market was acting on today's news nine months ago. I felt like Archimedes and shouted **EUREKA**. Of course there had to be a *time warp* between what the technicians see and what the fundamentalists see nine months later. If this market *anachronism* did not exist then everybody would want to buy and sell at the *same time* and that would be impossible.

12. ***The One Overriding Idea***

Prior to every major change of market direction there is discovered to be one *overriding idea.* The idea is always embraced by the dumb money and it contributes toward either the accumulation or distribution of stocks by the smart money depending on whether a bull cycle is ending or a bear cycle is ending. If a bull cycle is ending, the overriding idea will be a widely circulated popular belief bringing in strong demand for common stocks among the general public in order that the smart money can get back into cash and leave the public holding the bag with stocks about to go down. If a bear cycle is ending, the overriding idea will be a widely circulated popular belief that something very bad is about to happen and that the public would do well to sell their stocks. The smart money takes advantage of this and accumulates stocks on the public selling. So the time to identify that one overriding idea is late in the third phase of bull and bear markets.

The dumb money, after being the first to embrace the one overriding idea, unfortunately are the last to discover their very expensive error. The one overriding idea in early 1991 was that the Dow was about to fall 200 points, the public fearing the Persian Gulf war, the most widely advertised war in history. The world had its eye on January 15, 1991, the deadline for Iraq to get out of Kuwait. I was never more bullish and certain of what was about to come. The Dow rose about 700 points in the next couple of months. Yet on the first day of the war with the Dow up 114 points Bill Griffith asked me that night on the old *Financial News Network* whether the initial scud attack on Israel that night would turn me bearish. (No comment required)

Another widely disseminated overriding idea was the psychological response to the crash of October 19, 1987. It immediately planted such widespread fear that economists were predicting a *coming depression.*

13. ***Breaking the Continuity of Thought***

Usually following a time when the market is in the grip of believing the one overriding idea, *something unexpected happens that breaks the continuity of thought.* Following the all-time record inflow of money into the equity mutual funds in early 1992, it looked like nothing was going to upset the public's scenario which embraced lower interest rates, economic recovery, and the certain reelection of George Bush. Then came the Los Angeles riots and the emergence of Ross Perot as a serious third candidate for the Presidency. Joining this pattern of unpredictable disturbances, the worst earthquake occurring in the past 40 years took place in Southern California on the morning of June 28, 1992. Collectively, these disturbances took their toll on the 1992 stock market. The L. A. riots obviously affected real estate prices and travel plans, the Ross Perot image projected confusion and uncertainty, and the Southern California earthquake injected new uncertainties related to that area affecting real estate prices and travel plans. The public quickly discovered that the market was not a one-way street, coming in right after most stocks had seen their highs.

14. ***Market Problems***

Market tops are always more difficult to call than market bottoms. The reason for this is because bottoms coincide with concentrated fear while market tops come in waves with seldom a precise dividing line between a bull and bear cycle. *Most market tops are complicated by some glaring exception to a standard rule.* Such exceptions are easy to spot in retrospect but are seldom recognized at the time they are occurring *because at that time one expects the obvious to take place.* When CD rates collapsed in late 1991, most observers in January 1992 could only see a limitless rise ahead in the stock market. Instead, many stocks saw their bull cycle highs and a vicious dichotomy got started. So what was obvious to so many was wrong. Losing stocks began to be seen in what was thought to be a one way street to big profits.

Federal Reserve policy is important but it is capable of subtly changing during a market *transition* period which changes the market trend from bullish to bearish. Such a change is first seen in the stock market followed by the change in Fed policy. So what is vital, as always, is the market's reaction to any Fed move.

15. ***The Earnings Trap***

I consider corporate earnings as responsible for misleading most market players. Let us give this subject some serious thought. Corporate earnings are reported quarterly. Here is a question for those who lean on earnings. How do you follow a stock for ninety days with nothing to guide you other than that one earnings figure? I cannot conceive of being in a

90-day vacuum. I think of that song that went: "Is that all there is?" So we discard earnings immediately as an important factor. Earnings are nothing more or less than something for the stock to respond to. The stock may respond negatively or it may respond positively but it is the response that is important, not the earnings. And then we have something to watch each day, not having to be starved for information for 90 days. A new volume figure, a new price each day. So we are forced to learn how to read a chart, a picture of the technical action.

Since most TV commentators are not technically minded, they fill those 90-day vacuums by calling fundamental analysts on the telephone and then reporting to their viewers that is what they hear. They don't have a blessed notion as to whether the person they called is right or not but are quick to pass it on like it was the gospel. Nevertheless they are quick to announce that these are not the opinions of the network. But they are just as responsible for giving you bad information because they made it available in the first place.

Frankly, having started in this business in 1957, 1 don't recall ever having to call someone for a market opinion.

Perhaps the most revealing proof that earnings have little or no importance was forthcoming on September 25, 1992. A stock called *Medical Care America* tumbled from 58 to 25 on reported flat earnings. That not only dramatized the ridiculous Street overreliance on earnings as a smart indicator to follow, but it then signalled that nothing was safe from that type of price cascade.

16. *Keep a Diary*

If this turns out to be the only advice you follow from this entire book, you will have walked off with the key jewel of the crown. The human mind can hold just so much. Never is a perfect memory more richly rewarded than in the stock market. Since most people don't keep a diary, each market performance is a strange and new experience and one then has to needlessly retread old ground. They will become greedy at approximately the same wrong times they had become greedy in the past, buying at the top. They will panic with fear at approximately the same times they panicked in the past, selling at the bottom. There is nothing more instructive than being able to relive the past, tasting a replay of the emotions which had led one astray in the past.

Diary entries recording what one hears on the TV financial networks is particularly revealing. Those networks would never encourage their viewers to keep a diary because then it would become increasingly clear why the losers in the stock market game are always encouraged to be fundamental analysts. Furthermore, it would then reveal the identity of the network's usual stable of commentators to be the typically wrong people and thus comprising them to be the reliably contrary people indicators.

Now let us take a fresh look at some old indicators with a few new ones thrown in.

Section II
The Indicators - Old and New

THE INDICATORS-OLD AND NEW

1. *The High/Low Indicator*

I *consider this indicator as the most important of all indicators.* It is seldom given its proper due by the media because all the media cares about is how the Dow closes. To them that is the market and that concept will never change. The public will never be given the warnings this important indicator periodically records. This indicator is the soul of simplicity. It is simply the count of how many stocks are making new 52-week highs and how many are making new 52-week lows. *Positive and negative changes comprise the most important of all early warning signals.* The theory of the high/low indicator is sound. A technically genuine market rise is when we see new highs expanding and new lows contracting. A technically genuine market decline is when we see new highs contracting and new lows expanding. Conversely, a market rise that is not technically genuine will see new highs contracting and new lows expanding while a market decline that is not technically genuine will see an expanding number of new highs and a contracting number of new lows.

But what are the *parameters* of expansion and contraction? Are there limits which serve as technical guideposts of coming change? The answers to those questions comprise the very best estimates of where the market stands at that time. In bull cycles I have observed that anything over 300 new highs is dangerous and indicates a market top while in bear cycles I have observed that the area of 500-700 new lows indicates a market bottom. The 1,174 lows seen in October 1987 was so extreme that we may never see such a figure again. *So when these extremes on the upside and downside are again encountered, we have our most reliable evidence that the market is about to encounter a significant change and that we should also change our market posture.*

2. *The Great Stock Counting*

Outside of the discovery of On-Balance volume itself, I always felt that my technique of counting stocks within a point or less of their 52-week highs and lows is one of my most valuable contributions to technical analysis. If there are 50 actual new highs and 50 actual new lows and one knows that there are 350 stocks within a point or less of making a new high and 550 within a point or less of making a new low then we get a far more accurate picture of the direction money is flowing in as well as a very valuable look at the true technical posture of the market. In this example it would be very clear that money was flowing out of the market. In seeing the number of *potential* highs and lows before they became the *actual* numbers we then have a function of *range*. If we see a sharply expanding number of stocks within the one-point range of new highs then we know the market potentially is close to an upside explosion. Conversely, if we see an equally sharp escalation in the number of stocks within the one-point range of new lows then we know that we have the technical potential for a sharp decline ahead, or even a crash.

Years ago I would occasionally adopt the technique of counting big board stocks closing within one, two, and three points of making new 52-week highs and lows. It was a very effective technique and it revealed the true subsurface market strength or weakness and the direction of the money flow. That discipline, however, consumed a great deal of time. I recall only applying the technique when I was most concerned about the market and needed the best technical cutting edge possible.

After the 1987 market bottom I perfected a more practical solution, more accurate and less time consuming. Karen helped me by periodically counting the number of big board common stocks that traded within a point or less of their 52-week highs and lows. On some occasions I have even broken the one-point range down to eighths when I was particularly intrigued with the imminence of a major move. That involves a great deal of work but presents the most revealing picture of the internal condition of the market. So one can consider this technique of stock counting as an *advance high/low indicator.*

Our usual routine would be a weekly count by Karen. But then I adopted a quickie technique which could be easily done on a daily basis. We would count just the A stocks within a point or less of new 52-week highs and lows. Like an accurate poll of opinion, the percentage changes tended to duplicate the changes for the entire market.

Throughout the book I will be referring to the application of this indicator, identifying the critical parameters.

3. *Preferred Versus Common Stocks*

The stock count is done using *Investor's Business Daily.* We started that way because that paper was delivered to us on Saturdays two days before the *Wall Street Journal.* By so doing, however, we were only counting common stocks and omitting the preferred stocks inasmuch as that paper puts their preferred stocks in a separate section. The *Wall Street Journal's* high and low numbers include preferred stocks. But the two sets of figures gave us an advantage and another indicator. Each day I would subtract the figures from the *Investor's Business Daily* from those in the Journal and that would give me the number of preferred stock highs and lows, a very useful indicator when used against the background of high or low interest rates.

What more can I say about preferred stocks? These are income stocks because of their dividends which are higher than those paid on common stocks. So they tend to move with bonds and utilities, acting the strongest when interest rates are trending lower. But they comprise important market indicators. When they comprise 50% or more of the number of stocks making new highs that is a bearish indication because it then shows interest-sensitive stocks as being overbought and too popular. The opposite is equally true when the number of preferred stocks comprises more than 50% of the number of new lows because it shows that interest sensitive stocks are oversold.

4. *The Advance/Decline Line*

If a market rise is technically genuine, then it logically follows that more stocks should be rising in price than falling. Conversely, if a market decline is technically genuine it logically follows that more stocks should be falling in price. Thus every day we pay close attention to the daily number of stock advances and declines, what is popularly called the advance/decline line. Very seldom, if ever, is the Dow trend right and the advance/decline line wrong. Thus we always have to be on watch for any serious divergences between the two. When these occur, *always bet on the A/D line because most of the time it is underscoring reliable technical weakness.*

Has the A/D Line Ever Been Wrong?

Yes. It is capable of lagging as well as leading. While most of the cases have underscored the excellent record this indicator has in being a leading indicator of the market, it has seriously lagged on occasion. One such case the bearish divergence actually lagged the late 1968 peak and this wasn't apparent until the mid-1969 rally which was not confirmed. The actual A/D line peaked with the Dow on December 3, 1968.

5. *The New Advance/Decline Line*

I first introduced this indicator in 1988 in *The Stock Market Teacher.* I got so disgusted by hearing TV market commentators waxing enthusiastic on large advances in the Dow Jones Industrial Average on small rises in the orthodox A/D line or being too negative on large declines in the Dow Jones Industrial Average on small declines in the orthodox A/D Line. It was high time that one number could put the relationship in the proper perspective. I saw the problem solved by simply dividing the daily change in the Dow Jones Industrial Average into the daily change in the orthodox advance/decline line. That reduced the daily change to terms of *power-per point,* the A/D Line change for each point change in the Dow. The direction of the orthodox A/D Line always determined whether the power-per-point change was positive or negative.

A 10-point gain in the Dow with an A/D Line change of +400 is technically five times more powerful than a 10-point Dow gain on an A/D Line change of +40. In the first instance the power-per-point change is +40 while in the second instance the power-per-point change is only +4. By dividing the daily Dow changes into the daily changes in the orthodox A/D Line we therefore have a New Advance/Decline Line, one that shows a far more realistic indication than does the orthodox A/D Line.

By observing this New Advance/Decline Line since 1988, I discovered that changes of 100 or more in the New Advance/Decline Line provide significant forecasts of what lies ahead. And the more often we see those changes in a given direction the more significant the forecast becomes.

6. *How To Handle the Zero Changes*

After inventing this indicator, a problem soon arose that demanded a quick solution. How should an *unchanged* Dow industrial average be treated when there was a change in the orthodox advance/decline line?

Obviously we cannot divide by zero. If there was a change of .01 in the average we would then have a huge change in the New Advance/Decline Line. But such changes were very rare. I set forth the rule that when the Dow is unchanged *then the New A/D Line remains unchanged.* However, I discovered that an unchanged Dow produces a very strong signal based on the direction that the orthodox A/D line moves in.

Signals Prior To the 1989 Mini-Crash

Date	Dow	A/D Line	New A/D Line	Change	Change
Sept. 22	2681.61	-59,689	2400.8	+93	+70.0
Sept. 25	2659.19	-60,274	2374.7	-586	-25.3
Sept. 26	2663.94	-60,169	2397.0	+106	+22.3
Sept. 27	2673.06	-60,369	2375.1	-203	-21.9
Sept. 28	2684.91	-59,987	2392.6	+382	+17.5
Sept. 29	2692.82	-59,667	2545.7*	+320	+153.1*
Oct. 2	2713.71	-59,404	2558.2	+263	+12.5
Oct. 3	2754.56	-58,917	2570.1	+487	+11.9
Oct. 4	2770.90	-58,742	2580.8	+175	+10.7
Oct. 5	2773.56	-58,744	2580.8	-2	00.0
Oct. 6	2785.52	-58,631	2590.2	+113	+9.4
Oct. 9	2791.41	-58,583	2598.3	+48	+8.1

Here is a discovery: Gains of around 10 in the New Advance/Decline Line are considered to be technically weak rises. *Note here that we saw six consecutive such weak rises prior to the October 10, 1989 peak.*

Note that on October 5, 1989 we had a zero change in the New A/D Line. This was not considered to be a significant change inasmuch as in this case it was the almost unchanged A/D Line instead of an unchanged Dow reading.

7. *Time*

How could time itself be a market indicator? Not only is this fourth dimensional factor an indicator, but it could very well be THE indicator. When one is caught up in the day-to-day excitement of playing the market game it is very easy to forget about the market clock. But every game has its limit, and when that limit is reached the game is over *regardless of everything.* Football coaches constantly are aware of the game clock. Basketball players always know what time it is on the game clock. But in the stock market the tendency is to watch everything *but the clock.* Something happens (and there is always something happening), and the impact of that happening sends out a series of waves producing emotional responses. If it is the outbreak of war we normally respond with fear. If the President is assassinated we are numbed with immediate shock. If an enemy nation with which we are not at war attacks or confiscates U.S. property, or otherwise provokes a serious incident, we are normally gripped with anger. All these events would normally prod us into selling stocks. On the other hand, we normally respond with relief after a long strike is settled. We rejoice after a long war ends. We bask in a sense of new security when there is assured prosperity about us and we know the economy is strong. In these cases we normally respond by buying stocks.

When all those conditions are not related to what time it is on the market clock, they have all probably produced the wrong reactions on our part, and then it is like being called out of the game by the coach, forced to sit on the bench and ponder what went wrong. If we sold stocks when war broke out in Korea back in 1950, we did the wrong thing because the market clock said the bulls had plenty of time left in the game. If we sold stocks when President Eisenhower had a heart attack in 1955, we did the wrong thing because the market clock also said the bulls had plenty of time left on the upside. If we sold stocks when Treasury Secretary George Humphrey warned of a "depression that would curl your hair, back in 1957, we did the wrong thing since the market clock at that time showed the bearish game was practically over. If we bought stocks on the news that the long national steel strike of late 1959 had ended early in January 1960, we did the wrong thing because the market clock showed the bears in possession of the ball with time to go. If we sold stocks on the news that President Kennedy had been assassinated, we did the wrong thing because the market clock showed the bulls getting possession of the ball in 1962 with plenty of time left in the game to go. If we sold stocks when war broke out in the Middle East in June, 1967, we did the wrong thing because the market clock showed the bulls getting possession of the ball in 1966 with plenty of time left in the game. If we bought stocks in 1972 when the economy was strong and it looked like the U.S. was finally getting out of Viet Nam with a negotiated cease fire agreement, we did the wrong thing because the market clock showed that it was too late in the bull game, the bulls having had possession of the ball since 1970. If we smartened up and bought stocks on the next Middle East war in late 1973, we did the wrong thing because it was too early in the bear game, the bears getting possession of the ball in January 1973.

So then, *we learn that events are always secondary to the time in which they occur.* We cannot learn from the events themselves because they produce different responses at different times on the market clock. War is bullish early in a bull cycle. War is bearish early in a bear cycle. Peace is bullish early in a bull cycle. Peace is bearish early in a bear cycle. Prosperity is bullish early in a bull cycle (an unlikely occurrence). Prosperity is bearish early in a bear cycle. Recession is bullish late in a bear cycle or early in a bull cycle.

We had a strong bull market from 1942 to 1946 when the U.S. was at war with Germany, Italy, and Japan. The Viet Nam war involved the U.S. from 1961 to 1973, yet in that period the market carved out three bull cycles and three bear cycles, the market making the final peak at the end of the war. Similar comparisons can be made involving the long dollar crisis, inflation, and many other major problems stretching back an entire generation. Throughout it all the market game was played in isolation from all those outside events, *subservient only to the time factor.*

In my earlier books I had shown a close relationship of the time factor with a 4-1/2 year market cycle. Changes late this century have considerably bent the contours of that standard market cycle pretty much out of shape. In contemplating those changes, writing the 1976 *New Strategy* book was like doing so a hundred years ago. If I had entered a time capsule back then and returned today I would not recognize the background environment of the modern day stock market. Back then we were in the Cold War against the Soviet Union. We had no developed options market, no fully developed over-the-counter market, and no closely linked global market (no country funds), and the mutual funds industry showed no relationship to the 4,000 funds which were to mushroom later. No, one has to be far more pragmatic in embracing the modern day scene, but the current collection of technical indicators are expected to perform their functions every bit as well as they have in the past.

So the time indicator is there to answer the constant question: What time is it on the stock market clock? The question is still best answered when applying the market roadmap of the bull and bear phases which will be treated here later on.

8. *The Dow Theory*

This was the precursor of technical analysis, the first theory of markets wherein there was no requirement to answer the question of why. It described the market in terms of three trends: the primary, the intermediate, and the short-term. The favorite analogy was with that of the tides, the tide either coming in or going out. Charles H. Dow laid down various rules and over the years the theory was importantly added to by William Peter Hamilton, Robert Rhea, and in more recent times by Richard Russell.

The theory was the first to lay down the important technical requirement of confirmation, one average having to confirm the action of another. The two major averages used in Dow Theory was initially the Industrials and the Railroads, later expanded to today's Transportation Average. On upside breakouts Dow Theory required both averages to confirm on the upside, not necessarily on the same day, however. That would produce a Dow Theory buy signal. Conversely, downside breakouts required confirming action, but not necessarily on the same day. Such downside confirming moves would produce a Dow Theory sell signal.

That is an oversimplification but is at the heart of the Theory. Like all theories, this one had certain deficiencies. Having been formulated late in the 19th century, it was initially devoid of treatment regarding the advance/decline line, the high/low indicator, and the utilities. The subject of volume was treated with a broad brush stroke, simply describing rising volume on the upside and decreasing volume on the downside as bullish, with the opposite being bearish. The commonest criticism of the Theory relates to the timing of the buy and sell signals, these often occurring at or near critical turning points in the opposite direction.

9. *The Dow-Jones Industrial Average*

The Dow-Jones Industrial Average is the most widely watched of all market indicators. Because of this, it is notorious for playing tricks on those who fail to peer beneath this outer layer of the market. Being but one part of the entire market, the Dow industrial average moves most reliably when it moves in step with the entire market. It is when the Dow industrial average *walks alone* that an important reversal is in the making. Its movements must be confirmed constantly by the Dow-Jones Transportation Average, the advance/decline line, the high/low indicator and several other key indicators in order to maintain the trend then in progress.

Being so widely followed, it is natural to expect that in terms of the game tactics this is the indicator most responsible for keeping the majority in the market at the top and out of the market at the bottom. It does this by moving out into high ground without confirmation and into new low ground without confirmation. While the smart money is selling out in other market areas, the unsuspecting public largely senses no immediate market danger as the Dow industrials are working into new high ground. Conversely, as the Dow breaks to a new bear market low, the public is not likely to suspect that the smart money has been accumulating stocks elsewhere in the list for several months. This scenario has been replayed over and over with variations, important technical non-confirmations occurring involving, in varying combinations, the Dow Transports, high/low indicator, advance/decline line, the Standard & Poor 500 Index, the New York Stock Exchange Composite Average, the Nasdaq average and its advance/decline line, and the Mutual Fund Index. The disparity between the Dow Jones Industrial Average and the bulk of the broadest possible measurement is seen and explained here when describing the *Crack Index.*

10. *Weighting*

When the Dow industrial average embarks on one of those *solo walks*, either marching into new high ground or breaking into new low ground, it usually does so by concentrated buying or selling in two or three of the 30 stocks, thus creating a suspicious looking type of run-up or decline. This concentration in two or three of the Dow stocks heavily weights the move in the average itself, but the distortion is immediately spotted by comparing the swing in the industrials to the daily change in either the Standard & Poor 500 Stock Index or the New York Stock Exchange Composite Average. The old rule used to be to multiply the S & P 500 change by 10 so as to equate with the Dow change. Those measurements served very well to focus on any significant disparities.

11. *The Dow-Jones Transportation Average*

Like the Dow-Jones Industrial Average, the Dow-Jones Transportation Average is a vital segment of long, intermediate, and day-to-day market forecasting. Its major purpose as an indicator is to provide bullish and bearish signals based on confirmations or non-confirmations of strength or weakness in the Dow Jones Industrial Average. *No major forecast of stock market trends is complete without some reference made to what this indicator is saying.* The long record of the stock market is replete with instances of such important confirmations or non-confirmations occurring at the most critical times.

12. *The Role of Utilities*

Ironically, the Dow Utility Average was first presented on January

2, 1929, starting at the 85.64 level. It peaked at 144.61 on September 21, 1929. Now Dow Theorists pay as much attention to the Utility Average as they do to the Industrials and Transports. When the Utility Average is out of synch with the other key averages it is a market warning that must not be taken lightly. My own technical work is not complete without an analysis of the Dow 15 utility stocks.

13. *Important Utility Test*

Always check the Dow 15 Utility Average against the New York Composite Utility Average and the Standard & Poor Utility Average, those averages published every day in the Stock Market Data Bank on page C-2 in the *Wall Street Journal.* This is the standard technique of always comparing any average with a similar but broader average, the broader average always giving the true picture of what is going on.

14. *The Nasdaq Composite Average*

This average has been taking on much added importance, not only the average itself but that market's advance/decline line. The technical weight stems from the sheer breadth of the market represented. Later on you will see that this average has a great influence on both the Mutual Fund Index and the Crack Index, shaping two of the most important technical measurements we have to work with.

15. *The Mutual Fund Index*

Thanks to *Investor's Business Daily*, we have a Mutual Fund Index to consult each day. Their index is based on 20 major mutual funds and is charted. It provides an excellent tool whereby one can make a revealing comparison with the Dow-Jones Industrial Average and note any important non-confirmations.

16. *The 200-Day Moving Average Trendline*

Attention was first focused on this indicator in my 1960 stock market book and it saw the indicator later added to all major chart services. My contribution has now become generic and a whole generation has come on the scene totally unaware of where this indicator has come from. My buy and sell signals based on this indicator were republished in the 1962 Jiler book. But the discussion here is with the 200-day trendline on the Dow-30, not the same line on individual stocks. It becomes quite obvious that Dow crossings will always come considerably after Dow highs or lows. Suffice to say that such crossings will be after much time in a cycle has transpired. More on this in the discussion of *market phases.*

17. *Other Trendlines*

The *Trendline Daily Action Stock Charts* show two trendlines on the Dow-the short-term 10-week moving average and the longer-term 30-week moving average. The buy and sell signals will stem from upside and downside disparities from those trendlines as well as the more important crossings of those two trendlines.

18. *The Trendline Short Range Oscillator*

On the back cover of each issue of the *Trendline Daily Action Stock Charts* is a chart of their *Short Range Oscillator.* I find that their overbought and oversold readings are extremely important and when these record non-confirmations with the Dow it is very revealing. A big discussion of this is reserved for later.

19. *The Sentiment Indicators*

In a bull market all the indicators which show bearish sentiment to be increasing are correctly interpreted as being bullish. In a bull market the bulls are right. These contrary opinion sentiment indicators are shown below:

The Put/Call Ratio	When this ratio shows the heavy buying of put options in a bull market it comprises a reliable buy signal.
The Ansbacher Index	Is based on puts and calls and a reading under 1.00 in a bull market is considered to be a buy signal. The lower the reading the more bullish it is.
The Short Interest	In a bull market the shorts are considered to be wrong and thus a rising short interest in a bull market is always interpreted bullishly.

Short Interest Ratio	A high reading in a bull market is likewise always interpreted bullishly.
The Odd Lot Short Sales	The same theory holds true here. A sharp rise in the number of shorts in a bull market is a bullish signal. Some have contended that this indicator has lost its initial value since the advent of option trading. But its interpretation remains as it always has been.
Specialist Short Sales	Low numbers here are interpreted bullishly.
Advisory Sentiment	A high percentage of bearish market letters in a bull market always accompany buy signals.

Later on it will be shown that all these indicators get a reverse interpretation in a bear market.

20. ***Market Leadership***

It is always useful to keep track of the 15 most active stocks since these comprise the cutting edge of the daily trading, what the big money is doing. One should set up a daily advance/decline line based on the number of advancing and declining stocks in this table. One should also note the price mix, especially watching for an abundance of low-priced stocks denoting undue speculation.

21. ***The Crack Index****

This is a brand new indicator which I developed on the 1987-90 bull cycle. I think it is particularly reliable and revealing. Its great reliability rests on the fact that it embraces the broadest set of market measurements possible. Every day in the *Wall Street Journal* in the upper right hand corner of page C-2 is a set of market indices entitled STOCK MARKET DATA BANK. When I first developed my index there were 25 indices in this table. When the 400 Mid Cap was added later, I then had 26 indices to use in the computation of the Crack Index. Here is what comprises the table in the Journal:

Dow Jones Averages

30 Industrials
20 Transportation
15 Utilities
65 Composite
Equity Market Index

New York Stock Exchange

Composite
Industrials
Utilities
Transportation
Finance

Standard & Poor's Indexes

500 Index
600 Small cap
400 Mid Cap

Nasdaq

Composite
Industrials
Insurance
Banks
National Market Composite
National Market Industrials

Others

Amex
Value Line (geom.)
Russell 1000
Russell 2000
Russell 3000
Wilshire 5000

Each day I look at this table and count the number of indices that are up and the number that are down. I then have a simple advance/decline number for the day based on the broadest possible market measurement. After working with this measurement over a period of time, I came up with a divisor of 1.71 in order to correctly equate the *Wall Street Journal* Stock Market Data Bank with the Dow industrial average. If on a given day there were 15 rising indices and 11 declining indices then I would have an advance/decline digit of +4. I would then multiply 4 by 1.71 and that would give me a total of +6.84 to add to my cumulative Theoretical Dow level. I then subtract the actual Dow industrial closing from the Theoretical Dow and that gives me the Crack Index. A strong rising Positive number shows that the broadest market is outperforming the Dow and that is bullish. If the Crack Index is declining then the broadest market is underperforming the broadest market and that is bearish.

(Footnote) -

When I invented this indicator I was thinking of Humpty Dumpty. If the market was going to develop any serious cracks it would first show up in this the broadest of all possible market measurements. Thus it was a Crack Index and the name stuck.

22. *Insider Activity*

This indicator has a good record. In January 1992 when most stocks peaked the insiders were heavily selling anything to do with health: hospitals, medical care, health labs, drug shares etc. This entire general category collapsed. Yet William O'Neil's *Investor's Business Daily* was largely responsible for getting people to buy these stocks right at their peak prices, publicizing top Earnings Per Share ratings leading people to believe that that was a strong buying endorsement. O'Neil must have noted the heavy insider selling in these shares and to simultaneously publish peak Earnings Per Share ratings in January 1992 was not only irresponsible, but financially *immoral.* He was not alone. Hambrecht & Quist predicted that *US Surgical* would go to $200 a share right when that stock was peaking at 134-1/2 on an O'Neil peak Earnings per Share rating of 99. And the prediction was run in *Investor's Business Daily.*

Now on to On-Balance Volume, the best of all stock market indicators.

Section III
How I Discovered On-Balance Volume

HOW I DISCOVERED ON-BALANCE VOLUME

1. *Conception and Development*

In August 1961, while employed as the market letter writer for E. F. Hutton & Company, I conceived of the idea of On-Balance Volume. At that time much work among technicians had been done on the advance/decline line, the simple daily measurement of the net number of rising and falling stocks. But even then, the ordinary advance/decline line was little known or followed by the general public. Up until this time technicians didn't quite know what to do with the subject of volume. It was always treated as the major market enigma. It was generally recognized that rising prices on rising volume was bullish and that falling prices on rising volume was bearish. But nowhere did anyone bother to *quantify* that generality. To rectify the volume vacuum, I conceived of a volume advance/decline line which I named *On-Balance Volume.*

My conception was a very simple one. When a stock closed up in price I would assign the total daily volume to the upside. When it closed down in price I would assign the total daily volume to the downside. So each day I would either add or subtract a volume total from a running cumulative volume figure. When the stock closed unchanged, I would simply repeat the cumulative volume figure from the day before. I did that because *if the volume was unable to change the closing price of the stock then it wasn't worth recording.*

My favorite example is as follows: Suppose a $10 stock rises to 10-1/8 on the first day on a total volume of 50,000 shares. This first day of action would be recorded as follows:

Date	Price	Total Daily Volume	On-Balance Volume
Day One	10-1/8	50,000	+50,000

Now suppose the stock falls back to close at 10 on Day Number Two and the total volume is 25,000 shares. Closing down, we subtract all the volume traded that day from our OBV figure from the day before. Now our table looks like this:

Date	Price	Total Daily Volume	On-Balance Volume
Day Two	10	25,000	+25,000

Now you see two days of action in this stock. The stock went from 10 to 10-1/8 and then back down to 10. Most people are price conscious. They pay a price when they buy a stock and they get a price when they sell a stock. In the above example anybody seeing a stock go from 10 to 10 in two days would tell you that *nothing has changed in those two days.* But look again and you see that something has happened to the stock in those two days. There are 25,000 shares left over that weren't there two days before. Having added that net increment, the stock is technically stronger on Day Number Two than it was two days earlier at 10. That leftover increment is the *On-Balance Volume.* Eureka, I knew I had discovered something of great value. Unless one was following the volume figures, this two-day technical change would have been completely missed. What you have just seen is the very nub of my OBV Theory. *I discovered that volume precedes price as measured by my On-Balance Volume technique.*

Now I will extend the analysis so as to include OBV breakouts:

Date	Price	Total Daily Volume	On-Balance Volume	
Day 0	10	0	0	
Day 1	10-1/8	50,000	+50,000	
Day 2	10	25,000	+25,000	
Day 3	10-1/8	30,000	+55,000	Up
Day 4	10-1/2	40,000	+95,000	Up
Day 5	11	100,000	+195,000	Up
Day 6	10-1/4	75,000	+120,000	
Day 7	10-1/8	50,000	+70,000	

Day 8	10	50,000	+20,000	Down
Day 9	10-1/4	30,000	+50,000	
Day 10	10-1/2	65,000	+115,000	
Day 11	11	75,000	+190,000	
Day 12	10-3/4	50,000	+140,000	
Day 13	11	60,000	+200,000	UP
Day 14	11-1/4	75,000	+275,000	UP
Day 15	10-7/8	90,000	+185,000	
Day 16	10-3/4	50,000	+135,000	Down
Day 17	10-5/8	75,000	+60,000	Down
Day 18	10-3/4	35,000	+95,000	
Day 19	10-7/8	50,000	+145,000	
Day 20	10-3/4	40,000	+105,000	
Day 21	11	50,000	+155,000	Up
Day 22	10-3/4	60,000	+95,000	Down
Day 23	10-5/8	60,000	+35,000	Down

When the On-Balance Volume number goes above *the closest previous high* then it gets an up designation. On Day One the OBV stood at a high of +50,000. On Day Three we see the upside breakout to +55,000. Here I place the word Up to the right of the number.

Now note that I wrote the word Up in *lower case* type. Until proved otherwise, I have to assume that this is a *lower up* because I don't know what the OBV numbers were before I started the table. Being a volume advance/decline line, it can be started at anytime.

On Day Four and Five the OBV continues to rise and thus gets an Up designation on each day. On Day Eight we get the first down designation. This is because the OBV fell beneath *the closest previous low*. The closest previous low was the +25,000 reading of Day Two. Falling to +20,000 was a downside OBV breakthrough. But the down designation is a *higher down* because any OBV table always starts at zero and in staying above that number rates the higher down designation instead of a lower down.

Day Five gave us an OBV high at +195,000. That level was bettered on Day Thirteen with OBV rising to +200,000. Going above that closest previous high this time gives us an UP designation in *capital letters*. Anytime an OBV high goes above a previous high when separated by one or more down designations it gets the capital letters, a higher or true up. Conversely, anytime an OBV low goes below a previous low when separated by one or more up designations it gets the capital letters, a lower or true down.

Following through on the upside, Day Fourteen saw another UP designation at the +275,000 level. Since we are now seeing up designations, we want to refer to OBV *reference* levels. A reference level in this case would be the closest previous OBV low, a breaking of which would produce a down designation. The Day Twelve OBV +140,000 level is our reference level. Breaking down to +135,000 and +60,000 on Days Sixteen and Seventeen thus gave us higher down designations, higher because those levels stayed above the +20,000 low which was recorded on Day Eight.

Our next reference level was recorded on Day Nineteen at +145,000. A move above that level would produce an up designation. The upside breakout move was seen on Day Twenty One with OBV up at the +155,000 level. However, since that figure was well under the +275,000 level of Day Fourteen, it only got a lower up designation. Keep in mind that when designations are being recorded, new reference levels can always be ascertained. So we now see that our new reference level is the Day Twenty OBV +105,000 level. A move below that level will produce a new down designation. On Day Twenty Two OBV fell to +95,000 and gave us a higher down designation, OBV staying above the Day Seventeen OBV level of +60,000. However, on Day Twenty Three OBV fell to +35,000 and that gave us a lower down designation. Now shown as DOWN in capital letters. Going from down to DOWN comprises an OBV downside *abortion.*

2. *Accumulation and Distribution*

For many years there were many attempts which claimed to denote whether stocks were under accumulation or distribution. I found all of these methods of poor quality. Having conceived OBV over 35 years ago, I was naturally shocked to see at this late date that *Investor's Business Daily* palms off a crude formula which they claim denotes accumulation and distribution. Their Accumulation-Distribution rating on a stock is derived by multiplying daily volume by change and direction in the stock price. I discarded that option over 35 years ago. Not only is that method not valid, but it is a childish attempt to explain accumulation and distribution. Its shortcomings are of course obvious to trained market technicians. Multiplying volume and price change would signify strength and accumulation on big advances and more often than not bring in buyers at the worst of times, buying on the highs. Conversely, the big declines would more often than not bring in sellers right at the bottom, selling on the lows.

I will take Merck, for example, and show my OBV method computed in the column on the left and the *Investor's Business Daily* method computed on the right:

MERCK

Date	Price	Change	Volume	OBV	IBD's Volume
Mar. 3	154.00	-2.75	739,700	-739,700	-2,034,175
Mar. 4	151.25	-2.75	1,361,100	-2,100,800	-5,777,200
Mar. 5	151.25	Unch.	Unch.	-2,100,800	-5,777,200
Mar. 6	150.00	-1.25	844,900	-2,945,700	-6,833,325
Mar. 9	151.38	+1.38	644,800	-2,301,700	-5,944,605
Mar.10	152.13	+0.75	776,600	-1,525,100	-5,360,155
Mar.11	150.38	-1.75	575,300	-2,100,400	-5,978,600
Mar.12	147.50	-2.88	980,900	-3,081,300	-8,803,590
Mar.13	147.75	+0.25	871,100	-2,210,200	-8,625,815
Mar.16	147.38	-0.38	678,000	-2,888,200	-8,883,455
Mar.17	149.75	+2.38	630,000	-2,258,200	-7,384,055
Mar.18	148.25	-1.50	555,300	-2,813,500	-8,217,005
Mar.19	148.00	-0.25	458,100	-3,271,600	-8,331,530
Mar.20	147.13	-0.88	1,300,000	-4,571,600	-9,475,530
Mar.23	147.38	+0.25	591,700	-3,979,900	-9,327,605
Mar.24	150.00	+2.63	703,000	-3,276,900	-7,478,715
Mar.25	150.00	Unch.	Unch.	-3,276,900	-7,478,715
Mar.26	148.00	-2.00	530,500	-3,807,400	-8,539,715
Mar.27	145.88	-2.13	857,600	-4,665,000	-10,366,405
Mar.30	147.00	+1.13	566,000	-4,099,000	-9,726,825
Mar.31	147.13	+0.13	562,200	-3,536,800	-9,653,740
Apr. 1	149.63	+2.50	855,200	-2,681,600	-7,515,740
Apr. 2	147.00	-2.63	803,200	-3,484,800	-9,628,155
Apr. 3	147.88	+0.88	673,600	-2,811,200	-9,035,385
Apr. 6	149.25	+1.38	574,500	-2,236,700	-8,242,575
Apr. 7	146.50	-2.75	470,400	-2,707,100	-9,536,175
Apr. 8	146.38	-0.13	1,135,700	-3,842,800	-9,683,815
Apr. 9	150.13	+3.75	923,400	-2,919,400	-6,221,065
Apr.10	152.50	+2.38	721,300	-2,198,100	-4,504,370

3. *The Climax Indicator*

Back in 1961 the first encounters with my new theory were very simplistic. I did the daily homework of calculating OBV for each of the

Dow Jones industrial stocks. When I got an up designation I did not differentiate between lower ups and higher ups. I treated each OBV upside and downside breakout as having equal importance which describes how primitive my first efforts were with my new theory. After all, what I was doing had never been done before. Having to start somewhere, it was perfectly natural to treat all OBV ups and downs equally. So each day I faithfully counted the number of OBV up designations and subtracted the number of down designations. Theoretically, I had a full range of 60 to work with, +30 on the high side and -30 on the low side. My initial objective in doing this daily count of OBV upside and downside breakouts was in looking for extreme changes, climax highs or climax lows. Thus I called this daily count The *Climax Indicator.* I initially interpreted very low readings to be buy signals and very high readings to be sell signals. Little did I realize at that early time that every daily reading given by the Climax Indicator conveyed important technical intelligence.

Like so many indicators, the most effective application is seen when in conjunction with something else. Since the Climax Indicator was initially applied to the 30 Dow Jones industrial stocks, the most natural use of this new indicator was to compare it each day with the Dow Jones industrial average. Normal fluctuations in the Dow would generally see the CLX moving in the same direction as the Dow. In those early days, as I do now, I would be on the watch for *significant changes of pattern,* the CLX showing more strength than seen in the Dow alone or more weakness than seen in the Dow alone. Such deviations would be recorded as *non-confirmations* of either Dow downside moves or upside moves. Sometimes those non-confirmations took place in *repetitive clusters* which greatly added to the validity of a top or bottom formation at hand.

Undoubtedly the most famous stock market bottom of recent times was recorded on the day of the October 19, 1987 stock market crash. What did the Climax Indicator do on that unforgettable day? It did something it had never done before since I conceived of the indicator in August 1961. *It dropped to -30 on that day.*

Date	Industrials	CLX
10/ 7/87	2551.08	-7
10/ 8/87	2516.64	-14
10/ 9/87	2482.21	-20
10/12/87	2471.44	-16
10/13/87	2508.16	+1
10/14/87	2412.70	-19

10/15/87	2355.09	-25
10/16/87	2246.74	-29
10/19/87	1738.74	-30

That was the most extreme downside reading ever recorded. It is well to record that the market was a buy right at that point. Conversely, we never had a +30 on the Climax Indicator but did have a few occasions when the reading was as high as +28. The difference between market tops and bottoms in this regard is crystal clear. Market climactic bottoms are always easier to record and recognize than climactic market tops. Very seldom does a market top ever occur on a buying climax. Most tops are rolling affairs that can go on and on for a long period showing the progressive loss of upside momentum.

4. *Technically Worthless Advances*

I had stated that if volume is not sufficient to produce a price change, then that volume is not worth recording. Thus OBV remains the same when the price is unchanged. If an OBV advance does not produce an up designation then that rise is technically worthless. If an OBV decline does not produce a down designation then that decline is technically worthless. In actual practice I go still further in determining technically worthless advances or declines. If a price rise produces an OBV lower up designation then that is considered to be a technically worthless advance. If a price decline produces an OBV higher down designation then that is considered to be a technically worthless decline.

5. *The Cumulative Climax Indicator*

I also discovered that doing a cumulative reading on the Climax Indicator was very revealing. Generally swings of 100 or more proved to be significant.

6. *The Net Field Trend Indicator*

This is the second major indicator born in the constellation of the OBV galaxy. It was a natural outgrowth from ascertaining the worth of the up and down designations seen each day among the 30 Dow Jones industrial stocks. The key question was were those ups and downs forming positive or negative patterns? So I had to immediately define what comprised a positive pattern or a negative pattern. Being a stock market technician, we recognize upside price zig-zags as evidence of technical strength and downside price zig-zags as evidence of technical weakness. Since my theory proposed that *volume precedes price,* it then naturally followed that I would recognize upside OBV zig-zags as evidence of technical strength and downside OBV zig-zags as evidence of technical weakness.

So I had a ready-made formula here for technically weighing each of the 30 Dow Jones industrial stocks. An OBV upside zig-zag would be seen when the designations traced out a down, up, down and up series whereby the second down is higher than the first and the second up is higher than the first. These ups and downs can occur either singularly or in unbroken clusters. In tracing out the upside zig-zag formation, we have developed an OBV field and in this case a *rising field trend.*

Conversely, an OBV downside zig-zag formation would be the opposite. Here we would see the up, down, up, down series whereby the second up is lower than the first up and the second down is lower than the first down. And of course those ups and downs may or may not occur singularly or in clusters. In tracing out this downside zig-zag formation, we have developed an OBV field and in this case a *falling field trend.*

When no pattern of an upside zig-zag or downside zig-zag exists, then I stated that the stock was in a *doubtful field trend.* The use of the word doubtful did not necessarily denote technical strength or weakness in a stock. I later discovered that some of the strongest Dow stocks were in doubtful field trends and some of the weakest Dow stocks were in doubtful field trends. It simply meant that these doubtful field trends did not participate in the computation of the daily reading of the Net Field Trend Indicator. The Net Field Trend Indicator was thus computed by simply adding up all the Dow stocks in rising field trends and subtracting all those in falling field trends.

Like the Climax Indicator, the Net Field Trend Indicator which also tracks the 30 Dow Jones industrial stocks, has a theoretical range from -30 to +30. In actual practice, however, most of the time it is in a range from -18 on the low side to +19 on the upside.

7. *Is There Such a Thing As A False NFI Countertrend?*

Drawing first on the weekly readings shown in the 1976 *Strategy* book, I will examine each wide NFI swing to determine whether any of those swings was of a countertrend nature.

The first wide swing noted saw the NFI fall 25 fields from +8 to -17 between April 8, 1970 and May 27, 1970. That swing was accompanied by the Dow falling from 791.64 to 663.20 in this period of 7 weeks. Falling 25 fields in such a brief period of time proved to be a downside climax. And so this first examination saw the market trend and the NFI trend in harmony.

From that May 1970 bottom the weekly NFI soared 32 fields from -17 to +15 between May 27, 1970 and October 9, 1970. The Dow rose from 663.20 to 768.69 in this period of 18 weeks. And so this swing was also in harmony.

The NFI after peaking at +15, fell 27 fields to -12 between October 9, 1970 and November 17, 1971. The Dow, however, rose from 768.69 to 822.14 in that long period of over 58 weeks. I don't see that period as a major exception *inasmuch as it covered such a long period of time and traversed such a narrow band of 53 points in the Dow.* Here we also see the period in retrospect as the second year of a bull cycle and thus sharp drops in the NFI had no long-term bearish implications.

The next test is very interesting. The NFI quickly jumped 29 fields from -12 to +17 between November 17, 1971 and January 5, 1972. The Dow rose from 822.14 to 904.43 in that short period of 7 weeks. So the Dow and the NFI were back in harmony.

From there the NFI fell 28 fields from +17 to -11 between January 5, 1972 and July 19, 1972. The Dow actually rose from 904.43 to 916.69 in that period of 54 weeks. This out-of-harmony move takes on added significance because we now know that 1972 saw the beginning of an internal technical market cancer. It suggested that the next leg up would be the last one.

The NFI rose 28 fields from -11 to +17 between July 19, 1972 and December 6, 1972. The Dow rose from 916.69 to 1027.54 in that period of 18 weeks. It was again a period of harmony between the Dow and the NFI.

The next move saw the NFI fall 31 fields from +17 to -14 between December 6, 1972 and June 20, 1973. The Dow fell from 1027.54 to 884.71 in that period of 26 weeks. A vicious bear market was underway and the Dow was following the NFI.

The NFI then rose 28 fields from -14 to +14 between June 20, 1973 and October 10, 1973. The Dow rose from 884.71 to 960.57 in that 15 week period. It saw the Dow and the NFI in harmony on that first rally in the 1973-74 bear market.

The next NFI decline saw a loss of 31 fields from +14 to -17 between October 10, 1973 and December 5, 1973. The Dow fell from 960.57 to 788.31 in that 7 week period. Another rally in the bear market was at hand.

The NFI then gained 25 fields from -17 to +8 between December 5,

1973 and March 13, 1974. The Dow rose from 788.31 to 891.66 in that 13 week period. Again it was a period of Dow-NFI harmony.

The NFI then lost 27 fields from +8 to -19 between March 13, 1974 and September 4, 1974. The Dow fell from 891.66 to 647.92 in that 23 week period. The bear market was coming to an end, the -19 NFI level very terminal. Once again the Dow and the NFI were in harmony.

From that climactic level the NFI gained 39 fields from -19 to +20 between September 4, 1974 and January 29, 1975. The Dow rose from 647.92 to 705.96 in that 15 week period. This was the transition from bear market to bull market. But it could also be shown that during that transition period the Dow continued to decline between September 4, 1974 and December 6, 1974, falling from 647.92 to 577.60 while the NFI gained 6 fields from -19 to -13. And before the month of December 1974 was over, the NFI had gained 19 fields from -19 to 0 by December 31, 1974.

The NFI gained 29 fields from -15 to +14 between October 15, 1992 and March 10, 1993. The Dow jumped from 3174.68 to 3478.34 in that 21 week period. Once again the Dow was in harmony with the NFI.

Then came the biggest exception in the history of the NFI. The NFI fell 22 fields from +14 to -8 between March 10, 1993 and August 16, 1993. The Dow rose from 3478.34 to 3579.15 in that 23 week period. This was seen to be the exact opposite of the period when the NFI rose 25 fields from -17 to +8 between December 5, 1973 and March 13, 1974. That set the NFI up for the final dive to -19 because the rally to +8 was a failing NFI rally. In the 1993 exceptionary example the NFI had not seen it's low point.

8. ***How To Handle Changes Within Clusters***

In determining changes in the Net Field Trend indicator, I consider the lowest down reading in a cluster as determining whether a cluster of downs is a higher down or a lower down cluster. And of course I consider the highest OBV up reading in a cluster as determining whether that cluster of ups is a higher up or a lower up cluster. So before changing your NFI figures, make sure that you have strictly abided by these rules. Market students who are new to OBV usually stumble over this, thinking that the last designation in a cluster is the ruling one. The highest or lowest OBV designation is the ruling one that determines where that cluster belongs in the NFI zig-zag pattern.

Example:

Philip Morris

September 17, 1992	85.50	216,531,700	Up		Rising
September 18, 1992	85.88	219,031,700	Up		Rising
September 21, 1992	86.25	220,296,500	Up	Bullish Abortion	Rising
September 22,1992	85.34	218,745,600			Rising
September 23,1992	85.25	217,474,600			Rising
September 24,1992	86.25	218,724,900			Rising
September 25,1992	85.25	217,548,600			Rising
September 28,1992	85.38	218,682,500			Rising
September 29,1992	85.50	219,777,700	Up		Rising
September 30,1992	84.75	218,497,600			Rising

In the above example the key parameter OBV reading is the 220,296,500 figure of September 21st. When computing the Net Field Trend figures always use the highest up or the lowest down as the guide in judging a cluster. In order to maintain a rising field trend after getting a cluster of downs the OBV would have to go above the September 21st OBV, not the September 29th OBV.

More often than not, a cluster of higher ups followed by a lower up in the same cluster (as seen above) is a technical sign of weakness. A cluster of lower downs followed by a higher down in the same cluster is a technical sign of strength.

9. ***Abortions***

When a continued decline in a stock shows a series of higher OBV down designations followed by a lower or true down designation, that constitutes an abortion to the downside and is considered to be very bearish for that stock. Conversely, when a continued advance in a stock shows a series of lower OBV up designations followed by a higher or true up designation, that constitutes an *abortion* to the upside and is considered to be very bullish for that stock. Major turns in the stock market are detected by the number of these abortions. They constitute very reliable market indicators.

I consider up and down market swings to be more compelling if they follow a series of abortions. Consider the fact that after a series of lower downs the first ups encountered would be expected to be lower ups. Likewise, after a series of higher ups the first downs encountered would be expected to be higher downs.

Here is how this signalled the December 10, 1991 bottom and the rally that followed:

12/10	2863.82	-16	4	-12	-11	-3
12/11	2865.38	-9	6	-8	-15	-8
12/12	2895.13	+20	11	-4	-3	-16
12/13	2914.36	+21	11	-1	-4	-15
12/16	2919.05	+11	8	-7	-2	-12
12/17	2902.28	-5	6	-7	-8	-4
12/18	2908.09	+2	9	-6	-6	-5
12/19	2914.36	-7	10	-9	-12	-4
12/20	2934.48	+13	18	-3	-10	-8
12/23	3022.58	+35	23	-0	-0	-12
12/24	3050.98	+29	26	-1	-1	-5
12/26	3082.96	+31	26	-1	-1	-7
12/27	3101.52	+27	22	-3	-1	-9
12/30	3163.91	+52	41	-1	-0	-12
12/31	3168.83	+42	35	-0	-0	-7

Coming off the December 10th, 1991 bottom, we see the initial high number of lower up designations on December 12th, 13th, and 16th. Then, starting on December 20th, we see a very high number of higher up designations. So we can only conclude that we saw a high number of bullish upside abortions.

Now I present all the latest advances in my OBV theory.

Section IV
Advanced OBV Concepts

ADVANCED OBV CONCEPTS

1. *And Now The World of the Four Column Analysis*

For many years my followers hung on the daily readings of the Climax Indicator, each OBV up and down designation being treated equally. While always aware that higher down designations are potentially bullish and lower up designations are potentially bearish, I felt the need to formalize that observation. That was the major new contribution which I put in *The Stock Market Teacher* when it was published in October 1988. Instead of the old two-column analysis, OBV ups minus OBV downs, I could then introduce the new four-column analysis. The first number is the count of new OBV higher ups. The second number is the count of the higher down designations. The third number is the count of the lower down designations. The fourth number is the count of lower up designations. Now I automatically had two brand new daily indicators.

By adding the higher up designations in the daily series of four numbers and subtracting the lower down designations we have what I call *The True Climax Indicator*. That is treated as an *acid test indicator.* By employing all four numbers, adding the higher ups and higher downs and subtracting the lower downs and lower ups, we have what I call *The Early Warning Climax Indicator*. This indicator is aptly named because it includes the *potential* changes stemming from the number of higher downs and lower ups.

2. *The Quantum Leap*

The logic behind this quantum leap observation is best seen in the simple diagrams shown below.

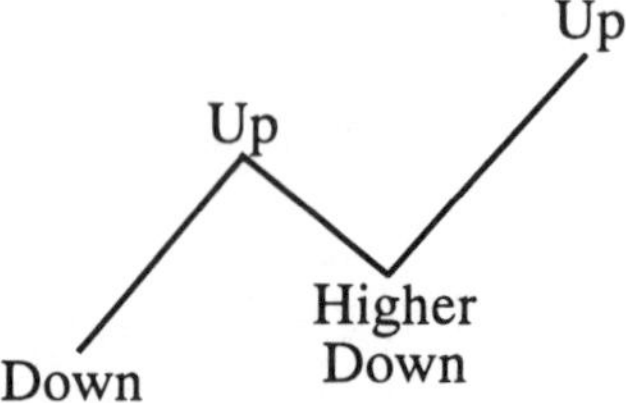

Here I show the simple upside zig-zag movement. Revealing a glaring truth, we see that the cornerstone of the rising zig-zag is the *higher down.* Since every upside zig-zag movement is bullish and since every upside zig-zag must include a higher down, *then it of course follows that higher downs have to be counted bullishly.* But since all higher downs occur on days when the price of the stock is *lower*, it underscores one of the most effective demonstrations of when to ignore any bearish implications of a price decline.

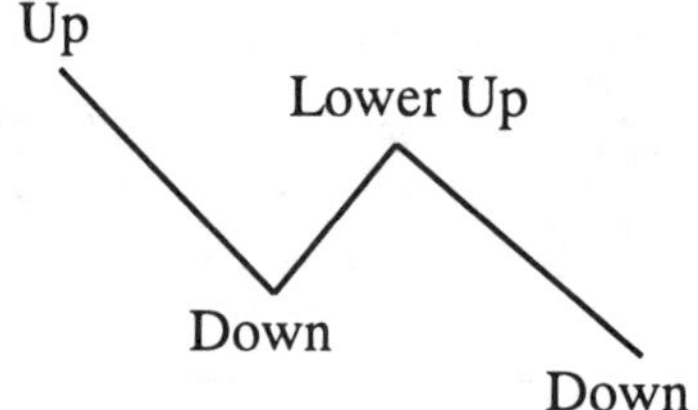

And here I show the simple downside zig-zag movement. Revealing a glaring truth, we see that the cornerstone of the downside zig-zag is the *lower up*. Since every downside zig-zag movement is bearish and since every downside zig-zag must include a lower up *then it of course follows that lower ups have to be counted bearishly.* But since all lower ups occur on days when the price of the stock is *higher*, it underscores one of the most effective demonstrations of when to ignore any bullish implications of a price advance.

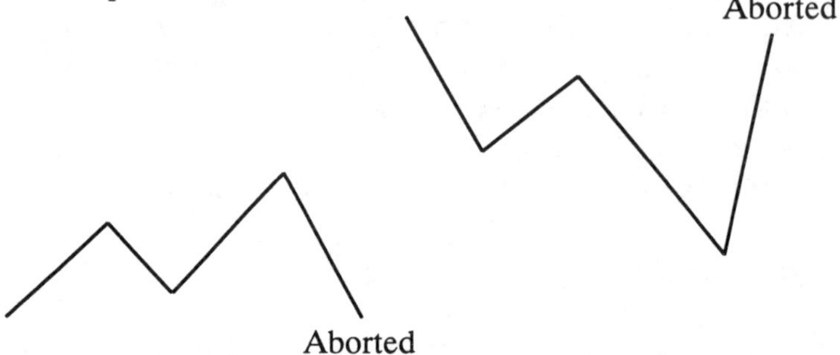

When upside zig-zags or downside zig-zags cannot be seen, then we are looking at stocks in *doubtful* field trends. Here we see the first diagram on the left showing the downside abortion which eliminated the upside zig-zag and the diagram on the right showing the upside abortion which eliminated the downside zig-zag.

3. *The Graded List*

I do the four-column analysis every day on the 30 Dow Jones industrial stocks, the 20 Transportation stocks, and the 15 Utility stocks. In adding my results, I automatically have the four column numbers on the 65 Dow stocks.

4. *Tracing the Flow- The Four-Column Analysis*

Following the flow of money into and out of the stock market can be documented in terms of the On-Balance Volume up and down designations. At a major bottom we will see a large number of true down designations. Initial market improvement will then favor a rise in the number of lower up designations. Coming off a major market bottom it is natural to expect that lower ups have to be seen before they abort to higher ups. Since it is assumed that a new bull trend has started, the first reactions following the initial upthrust will produce higher down designations. A resumption of the rise will then see major upside breakouts producing an expanding number of true up designations. Now we want to see the flow of money traced through this sequence of lower downs, lower ups higher downs, and higher ups.

5. *The Market Slot Machine*

I consider this four-column analysis technique as the single most important development in my On-Balance Volume theory. The idea of putting these numbers in a *Graded List* stems from an idea I had way back in 1942 when I was 19. I owned a slot machine, one of those three-dialed one arm bandits. I had the idea of recording what came up on every pull of the handle. My idea was that by putting all those results in a graded list I would then know what would likely come up on the next pull. For instance, if I came up with a plum, bar and lemon combination I would look up what happened after the last time I had the plum, bar, and lemon combination. Of course there was no validity to this system because each pull is totally independent of the previous pull of the handle, being a spring-operated device. But the idea of the graded list for the four-column analysis has total validity. I couldn't wait to use it, starting out with the 1991 figures.

I began to make a series of important discoveries from the graded list. The first revelation came from the January 1991 lows. I had the following four-column readings on January 7th, 8th, and 9th:

Date	Dow	Four Columns
Jan. 7, 1991	2522.77	1 -23 -11 - 1
Jan. 8, 1991	2509.41	7 -16 - 9 - 7
Jan. 9, 1991	2470.30	7 -18 -17 - 2

Here we see two important numbers: the 23 higher downs on January 7th and the 17 lower downs on January 9th. I will first list all the times we have had 18 or more higher downs:

Date	Dow	Higher Downs
Jan. 2, 1991	2610.64	18
Jan. 3, 1991	2573.51	19
Jan. 7, 1991	2522.77	23
Jan. 9, 1991	2470.30	18
Feb. 14, 1991	2877.23	20
Apr. 9, 1991	2873.02	26
May 14, 1991	2886.85	19
June 12, 1991	2961.99	20
Aug. 19, 1991	2898.03	20
Sep. 3, 1991	3017.67	27
Sep. 4, 1991	3008.50	22
Sep. 5, 1991	3008.50	20
Sep. 10, 1991	2982.56	23
Nov. 15, 1991	2943.20	21
Jan. 29, 1992	3224.96	22
Mar. 6, 1992	3221.60	21
Apr. 27, 1992	3304.56	18
Oct. 2, 1992	3200.59	18

Now I list all the times we saw 17 or more true downs:

Date	Dow	Lower Downs
Jan. 9, 1991	2470.30	17
Jan. 14, 1991	2483.91	17
May 15, 1991	2914.91	18
Jun. 19, 1991	2955.50	19
Aug. 19, 1991	2898.03	20
Nov. 19, 1991	2931.57	17
Nov. 20, 1991	2930.01	18
Nov. 22, 1991	2902.79	19
Apr. 2, 1992	3234.12	17
Apr. 3, 1992	3249.11	19
Apr. 7, 1992	3213.55	22
Apr. 8, 1992	3181.35	30
Jun. 17, 1992	3287.76	19
Jun. 18, 1992	3274.12	18
Jul. 22, 1992	3277.61	15
Aug. 12, 1992	3320.56	17
Aug. 13, 1992	3313.27	21
Aug. 21, 1992	3254.10	19
Aug. 24, 1992	3228.17	28
Aug. 25, 1992	3232.22	20
Oct. 5, 1992	3179.00	23
Oct. 7, 1992	3152.25	17
Oct. 9, 1992	3136.58	20

Now I combine all the above dates:

Date	Dow	Combined Higher Downs and Lower Downs
Jan. 2, 1991	2610.64	18 + 5 = 23
Jan. 3, 1991	2573.51	19 + 10 = 29
Jan. 7, 1991	2522.77	23 + 11 = 34
Jan. 9, 1991	2470.30	18 + 17 = 35
Jan. 14, 1991	2483.91	14 + 17 = 31
Feb. 14, 1991	2877.23	20 + 0 = 20
Apr. 9, 1991	2873.02	26 + 12 = 38
May 14, 1991	2886.85	19 + 13 = 32
May15, 1991	2914.91	10 + 18 = 28
Jun. 12, 1991	2961.99	20 + 8 = 28

Jun. 19, 1991	2955.50	17	+	19	=	36
Aug. 19,1991	2898.03	20	+	20	=	40
Sep. 3, 1991	3017.67	27	+	3	=	30
Sep. 4, 1991	3008.50	22	+	5	=	27
Sep. 5, 1991	3000.50	20	+	4	=	24
Sep 10, 1991	2982.56	23	+	12	=	35
Nov. 15,1991	2943.20	21	+	11	=	32
Nov. 19,1991	2931.57	15	+	17	=	32
Nov. 20,1991	2930.01	14	+	18	=	32
Nov. 22,1991	2902.79	14	+	19	=	33
Jan. 29, 1992	3224.96	32	+	7	=	39
Mar. 6, 1992	3221.60	21	+	16	=	37
Apr. 2, 1992	3234.12	14	+	17	=	31
Apr. 3, 1992	3249.11	10	+	19	=	29
Apr. 7, 1992	3213.55	17	+	22	=	39
Apr. 8, 1992	3181.35	14	+	30	=	44
Apr. 27, 1992	3304.56	18	+	10	=	28
Jun 17, 1992	3287.76	13	+	19	=	32
Jun 18, 1992	3274.12	9	+	18	=	27
Jul 22, 1992	3277.61	16	+	18	=	34
Aug 12, 1992	3320.56	11	+	17	=	28
Aug. 13,1992	3313.27	4	+	21	=	25
Aug. 21,1992	3254.10	12	+	19	=	31
Aug. 24,1992	3228.17	10	+	28	=	38
Aug. 25,1992	3232.22	6	+	20	=	26
Oct 2, 1992	3200.59	18	+	16	=	34
Oct. 5, 1992	3179.00	17	+	23	=	40
Oct. 7, 1992	3152.25	10	+	17	=	27
Oct. 9, 1992	3136.58	9	+	20	=	29

Totals of 40 or higher often coincided with important buying opportunities.

Using Graded Lists

6. *Exact Matches*

Since conceiving of the 4-column graded list, I have constructed a data bank containing these important numbers. New numbers are of course being added every day. The more often an exact match is recorded the more reliable is the next forecast. This forecasting technique will become increasingly accurate the more time that passes. Only the passage of time could eventually fill in all the gaps.

7. *Bottom Line Analysis*

At the bottom of every graded list we can look for the maximum high numbers. We have graded lists on the 4-column industrial, transport, utility, and 65-stock numbers as well as on the 4-column cluster numbers on the industrials, transports, utilities, and the 65 stocks. A quick look at the bottom line numbers reveals the date of the internal top action.

8. *Four Column Projections*

Now having tables of past 4-column readings, it then became possible to look ahead for any length of time and project not only future 4-column reading but also future Dow readings denoting the extent of the Dow swings for those time periods. This necessitated copying both the 4-column chronological lists and the graded 4-column lists and showing one month and three month projections for both the 4-column patterns as well as the Dow Jones Industrial Average as well as the extent of the Dow swings. While this involved a gargantuan effort, the yield it produced was well worth the additional labor.

65 Stock 4-Column Analysis

(1991)

Date	Pattern	1 Mo.Later	3 Mos.Later	Dow	Dow
11/29	2-12-12-8	9-16-2- 3	9-12- 5- 5	2629	2882
11/30	13- 0- 2-17	10-10-0- 7	9-12- 5- 5	2633	2882
12/ 3	21- 2- 4-12	6-19-10-4	10- 9- 4- 7	2573	2914
12/ 4	32- 1- 2-11	9-15- 9-5	10- 9- 4- 7	2566	2914
12/ 5	36- 2- 2-10	9-15- 9-5	26- 2- 0-14	2566	2972
12/ 6	25- 4- 6- 8	1-23-11-1	17-11- 5- 6	2522	2973
12/ 7	14- 5- 6- 2	1-23-11-1	8-13- 6- 4	2522	2963
12/10	12- 1- 8- 2	9- 5- 6-3	5- 9- 6- 4	2498	2939
12/11	8- 7- 7- 2	5- 9-10-5	5- 9- 6- 4	2501	2939

65 Stock Graded 4-Column Analysis

Date	Pattern	1 Mo.Later	3 Mos.Later	Dow	Dow
11/29	2-12-12- 8	9-16- 2- 3	9-12- 5- 5	2629	2882
12/11	8- 7- 7- 2	5- 9-10- 5	5- 9- 6- 4	2501	2939
12/10	12- 1- 8- 2	9- 5- 6- 3	5- 9- 6- 4	2498	2939
11/30	13- 0- 2-17	10-10- 0- 7	9-12- 5- 5	2633	2882
12/ 7	14- 5- 6- 2	1-23-11- 1	8-13- 6- 4	2522	2963
12/ 3	21- 2- 4-12	6-19-10- 4	10- 9- 4- 7	2573	2914
12/ 6	25- 4- 6- 8	1-23-11- 1	17-11- 5- 6	2522	2973
12/ 4	32- 1- 2-11	9-15- 9- 5	10- 9- 4- 7	2566	2914
12/ 5	36- 2- 2-10	9-15- 9- 5	26- 2- 0-14	2566	2972

9. *The True Climax Indicator and the Early Warning Climax Indicator*

The 4-column analysis technique was the precursor to creating the True Climax Indicator and the Early Warning Climax Indicator. The initial efforts concentrates on the 30 Dow-Jones industrial stocks. In my market letter I would record the daily reading for both of those indicators. It was a useful analysis but only part of the story. In the expanding development of my theory, I saw that it was going to be necessary to apply the same analysis to the Dow Transports and the Dow Utilities. That added analysis was largely responsible for keeping me bullish just prior to the explosive Persian Gulf war rally in January 1991. More than ever I saw how misleading it was to restrict attention to just the industrials. So the 65-stock analysis was born using these total CLX numbers. But one thing was MISSING. I needed the numbers that were best related to the trend of the market and that meant giving the cumulative True and Early Warning CLX numbers.

I explained their significance to new subscribers as follows in my October 1, 1992 market letter:

"Unless one has been with us for the past year or so, you are likely to miss the great significance of the current True and Early Warning Climax Indicator numbers as shown in the review table. The True Climax Indicator is the acid test indicator and in this case we have the cumulative differential between higher OBV highs and lower OBV lows on the entire 65 stocks (30 industrials, 20 transports, and 15 utilities). The Early Warning Climax Indicator also includes OBV higher downs and OBV lower ups. *On those two major indicators hang my entire theory of On-*

Balance Volume. New highs or new lows in those indicators have to be extremely significant and very reliable technical indications Of future Dow readings.

Analysts who largely rely on just price action are far more prone to making faulty technical interpretations which are short of the mark in their overlooking or lack of understanding of On-Balance Volume. The following is an excellent example: A Dow low was recorded on April 8th, 1992 at 3181.35. On that same day I recorded a reading of 1273 in the Cumulative 65-Stock True CLX and a reading of 1657 in the Cumulative 65-Stock Early Warning CLX. Now look at the review table and note that on September 30th, 1992 the True CLX stood at 1182 and the Early Warning CLX stood at 1455. Inasmuch as both of those readings were far under their April 8th levels, *I considered that to be very reliable technical evidence that the Dow would break under the April 8th level.*

10. *Four Column Analysis - Order of Notation*

I have designated an order of notation in the daily Four Column Analysis which records higher up designations in the first column, higher downs in the second column, lower downs in the third column, and lower ups in the fourth column. I found this order convenient because then the orthodox Climax Indicator was easily seen by adding the two outside numbers and subtracting the two inside numbers. All my tables consistently follow that order.

Suppose, however, that one was putting the higher ups in the first column, higher downs in the second column, lower ups in the third column, and lower downs in the fourth column. That order of notation is perfectly legitimate but it would of course change the graded list as well as the reciprocal readings.

Date	Columns	Reciprocal	Revised Columns	Reciprocal
1/16/91	7-5-8-11	8-11- 7-5	7-5-11-8	11-8- 7-5
1/17/91	24-0-0-23	0-23-24-0	24-0-23-0	23-0-24-0

But the revised reciprocals would provide the *identical signals*. For instance, the 8 - 11 - 7 - 5 reciprocal reading is identical with the 11 - 8 - 7 - 5 revised reciprocal reading. *Both readings would see the market the opposite of January 16, 1991 and be a powerful bearish signal.*

11. *Changing the Order*

All my initial researches on using the 4-column analysis had followed the pattern of OBV higher ups, higher downs, lower downs, and lower ups. I became so used to presenting that order that it didn't strike me until much later that using a pattern of OBV higher ups, higher downs, lower ups, and lower downs could be just as legitimate. There was of course no change in theory, but it could make important changes in forecasting results both from the new pattern and its reciprocal numbers. I got very used to the original series because the two ends of the series were opposites as were middle numbers. But the revised order also made sense because then one could see the logical pattern of money flow going from higher ups to higher downs to lower ups and finally to lower downs- the OBV downward zig-zag.

Here are some examples: I will first use my accepted original pattern of the 65-stock 4-column order in the example of August 30, 1993:

Original Order

Regular	11 - 5 - 2 - 6
Reciprocal	2 - 6 -11 - 5

Revised Order

Regular	11 - 5 - 6 - 2
Reciprocal	6 - 2 -11 - 5

This expanded the forecasting possibilities. Consulting the Graded List, the original regular order saw the two closest adjacent series being:

January 14, 1993	11 - 4 - 7 -13
November 7, 1991	11 - 5 - 4 -10

The two closest adjacent series to the regular order reciprocal was:

April 27, 1993	2 - 7 - 8 - 4
April 28, 1993	2 - 7 -10 - 5

But in using the revised regular order series of 11 -5 - 6 - 2 the closest adjacent series produced considerable changes.

12. ***Chain Forecasting***

My concept of *chain forecasting* is as follows:

1. Each day produces two forecasts, matching the date *above* the current 4-column daily series in the Graded List and the date below the current 4-column series in the Graded List. Those two forecasts then give rise to four forecasts which in turn can produce eight forecasts, then 16, 32, 64, 128 etc.

2.. Experimenting with various dates, I Will start here with the key day of *January 17, 1991*. On that day we had a 4-column series of 24 - 0 - 0 - 23

In the Graded List that produced the following adjacent 4-column series:

December 21, 1990	23 - 6 - 8 - 3
April 16, 1991	25 - 2 - 3 - 8

That then produced adjacent 4-column series of:

May 29, 1991	23 - 5 - 2 -14
January 17, 1991	24 - 0 - 0 -23
January 17, 1991	24 - 0 - 0 -23
June 3, 1991	25 - 3 - 4 - 6

Now I will take a different 4-column set of numbers and expand it into 14 4-column series, going from 2 to 4, to 8. Here is the actual 4-column series for December 26, 1991:

26 - 1 - 1 - 7

In the Graded List that produced the following adjacent 4-column series:

Date	Adjacent 4-Column Series	Forecasted Day
May 30, 1991	25 - 5 - 3 -13	December 27, 1991
Feb. 4, 1991	26 - 1 - 5 - 4	December 27, 1991

June 3, 1991	25 - 3 - 4 - 6	December 30, 1991
Feb. 4, 1991	26 - 1 - 5 - 4	December 30, 1991
May 30, 1991	25 - 5 - 3 -13	December 30, 1991
Mar. 5, 1991	26 - 2 - 0 -14	December 30, 1991
Apr.16, 1991	25 - 2 - 3 - 8	December 31, 1991
May 30, 1991	25 - 5 - 3 -13	December 31, 1991
May 30, 1991	25 - 5 - 3 -13	December 31, 1991
Mar. 5, 1991	26 - 2 - 0 -14	December 31, 1991
June 3, 1991	25 - 3 - 4 - 6	December 31, 1991
Feb. 4, 1991	26 - 1 - 5 - 4	December 31, 1991
Feb. 4, 1991	26 - 1 - 5 - 4	December 31, 1991
Apr.17, 1991	26 - 2 - 2 -13	December 31, 1991

December 31, 1991 turned out to be a powerful day. It showed a 4-column series of 35 - 0 - 0 - 7 and it so happened that on that day the bull market recorded the maximum number of new highs at 336.

3. When a date repeats in a forecast it is eliminated and this way we are always dealing with new numbers every day in our fore cast.

The above material appeared in my diary entry of December 27,1991. Now, almost two years later, I will project eight 4-column series to see how the numbers have changed in that period.

So I will start again with the 26 - 1 - 1 - 7 series of December 26, 1991:

Date	4-Column Series	Forecasted Day
May 30, 1991	25 - 5 - 3 -13	December 27, 1991
Feb, 4, 1991	26 - 1 - 5 -4	December 27, 1991
June 3, 1991	25 - 3 - 4 - 6	December 30, 1991
Dec. 26, 1991	26 - 1 - 1 - 7	December 30, 1991
Dec. 26, 1991	26 - 1 - 1 - 7	December 30, 1991
Mar. 5, 1991	26 - 2 - 0 -14	December 30, 1991
Apr.16, 1991	25 - 2 - 3 - 8	December 31, 1991
May 30, 1991	25 - 5 - 3 -13	December 31, 1991
May 30, 1991	25 - 5 - 3 -13	December 31, 1991

Feb. 4, 1991	26 - 1 - 5 - 4	December 31, 1991
May 30, 1991	25 - 5 - 3 -13	December 31, 1991
Feb. 4, 1991	26 -1 - 5 - 4	December 31, 1991
Dec.26, 1991	26 - 1 - 1 - 7	December 31, 1991
Mar. 5, 1991	26 - 2 - 0 -14	December 31, 1991

Not too much change in these numbers in a two-year period inasmuch as there were very few times when there were 25 or 26 higher OBV up designations.

So my concept of chain forecasting is an offshoot of the slot machine principle, the use of the graded list of the 4-column readings. Over a period of time the concept will become increasingly practical on the assumption that most combinations will have become seen, eliminating large skips in the numbers which would reduce the accuracy of the forecasts.

13. *Cluster Analysis*

An OBV cluster consists of three or more consecutive up or down designations. Every day I record the cluster power of the Dow 30 industrials, 20 transports, and 15 utilities. In the second column I record the total of all the clusters of OBV higher up designations. In the second column I record the total of all the clusters of OBV higher down designations. In the third column I record the total of all the clusters of OBV lower down designations. In the fourth column I record the total of all the OBV lower up designations.

We can now derive three vital indicators from these four totals of cluster power.

The first indicator is derived by adding up the cluster power of all the up designations regardless of whether they are higher ups or lower ups and subtracting all the down designations regardless of whether they are lower downs or higher downs. That is the orthodox measurement that ignores the zig-zag pattern, but simply recognizes all ups as ups and all downs as downs. That is the orthodox Cluster Climax Indicator. That was the technique employed every day to derive the original Climax Indicator based on the simple OBV ups and downs. That was a *horizontal* operation with each up or down designation a single numerical entity. With cluster analysis we have a *vertical* operation. Each consecutive up or down designation is in the form of increasing columns of numerical power. So now we have the construction of the orthodox Cluster Climax Indicator. That indicator is computed every day for the Dow Industrials, Transports, and Utilities.

The second indicator derived from our four columns of cluster readings is calculated by the simple operation of adding up only the clusters of higher ups and subtracting the clusters of lower downs. That gives us the Cluster True Climax Indicator. That is an acid test indicator. It is computed every day for the Dow Industrials, Transports, and Utilities.

The third indicator derived from our four columns of cluster readings is calculated by adding up the clusters of higher ups and the clusters of higher downs and subtracting the clusters of lower downs and lower ups. This gives us the Cluster Early Warning Climax Indicator. It is also computed every day for the Dow Industrials, Transports, and Utilities.

Having then computed the Cluster Climax Indicator, the Cluster True Climax Indicator and the Cluster Early Warning Climax Indicator for the Dow Industrials, Transports, and Utilities, we then simply add up all our cluster CLX totals and that gives us the very important Dow-65 stock cluster readings, these being the orthodox CLX reading, the True (or acid test) reading, and the Early Warning reading. Of course all these daily readings are added to continuing cumulative totals.

14. *Understanding Cluster Power*

Technical strength and weakness can very effectively be measured by Cluster power. If a stock is strong enough to record three or more consecutive OBV ups or downs then it is clustering. I have developed two cluster indicators. The first of these is the Current Cluster Climax Indicator. Here I use the 4-column analysis technique and it should be done each day for the Dow industrials, transports, and utilities. Here are the actual numbers for August 18, 1993, the day the Dow broke out to a new all-time record high at the 3604.8 level:

Industrials:	3	0	0	0
	3	0	0	0
Transports:	6	0	3	0
	6	0	3	0
Utilities:	0	9	5	0
			3	
	0	9	8	0
Totals	9	9	11	0

In the first column we put down all the clusters of OBV higher up designations. In the second column we put down all the clusters of OBV higher down designations. In the third column we put down all the clusters of OBV lower down designations. In the fourth column we put down all the clusters of OBV lower up designations. These numbers are then totalled for the three groups of stocks.

In this example we see that out of the 30 Dow industrial stocks, only one was able to record a Cluster of 3 consecutive OBV higher up designations despite the fact that the average had just recorded an all-time record high. It was the only cluster recorded. The 20 Dow transport stocks showed only one stock having a cluster of 6 consecutive OBV higher up designations and one cluster of lower downs. The 15 Dow utility stocks showed no clusters of higher ups, one large cluster of 9 higher downs, a cluster of 5 lower downs and a cluster of 3 lower downs and no clusters of lower ups. These numbers are now totalled, giving us 9 higher ups, 9 higher downs, 11 lower downs, and 0 lower ups.

The Current Climax Indicator reading for the 65 Dow stocks is computed the normal way, all the ups are added and all the downs are subtracted regardless of whether they are higher downs or lower ups. So we get a -11 reading. That then is the Current Climax Indicator reading for the 65 Dow stocks. Each day it should be computed in this manner and then added or subtracted from a Cumulative table. Two more computations must then be made. The True CLX is found by subtracting the third column from the first column, the acid test only involving the higher highs and the lower lows. Finally, the Early Warning CLX is computed by adding the first two columns and subtracting the sum of the last two columns. And those numbers are also added or subtracted from a Cumulative table.

The Current CLX Clusters is only concerned with current clusters, those only recorded on the current day.

Example:	Day One	UP
	Day Two	UP
	Day Three	UP
	Day Four	UP
	Day Five	

In this example the Current Cluster CLX records a +3 in the first column on Day Three. It records a +4 in the first column on Day Four. But since the OBV declined on Day Five the contribution in the first column on Day Five is zero. Only *current* numbers are counted.

Since only current clusters are counted each day, these numbers become the *cutting edge* of the Dow averages. A significant rise in the Dow averages should see several clusters of higher OBV up designations. I maintain that if this is not happening *then something is wrong.* A declining cumulative CLX would indicate a lack of staying power on a rally, fewer and fewer Clusters of OBV up clusters.

15. *The Effect of Abortions and Windows On the Cluster Indicators*

When a cluster of lower up designations is aborted by a higher up being recorded, *then the total numerical power of that cluster goes from lower ups to the technical equivalent of all higher ups.* That creates a large and significant technical positive change in the total cluster power and is a fair assumption of the technical positive change in the total cluster count.

When a Cluster of higher down designations is aborted by a lower down being recorded, then the total numerical power of that cluster goes from higher downs to the equivalent of all lower downs. That creates a large and significant technical negative change in the total cluster power and is a fair assumption of the technical negative of the larger negative change in the total cluster count.

The longer a cluster of higher downs or lower ups persists, the more significant becomes any abortion and that would also translate into a significant change in the Cluster indicators.

For instance, we see here a cluster of 10 higher down designations:

Down
Down
Down
Down
Down
Down
Down
Down
Down
Down

In the Current Cluster 4-columns we would see recorded 10 higher downs and that would contribute toward technical strength in the True CLX Cluster. Now, suppose the next OBV figure takes the total below the down designation of the *previous* Cluster of downs. That would then give us a *lower down* designation and our new cluster would look like this:

Down
Down
Down
Down
Down
Down
Down
Down
Down
Down
DOWN

But now the 10 higher down designations revert to the equivalent of 11 DOWN designations. That means that in the Current Cluster 4-columns what was once a 10 in the column of higher downs now becomes a zero and what was once a zero in the column of lower downs now becomes 11, the abortion producing a net drop of 21 in the Current Cluster count.

Stock A

Date	OBV	Designation	Cluster Power
June 7	3,982,700		
June 8	4,157,700		
June 11	3,989,700		
June 12	4,193,200	UP	
June 13	4,446,900	UP	
June 14	4,670,500	UP	3
June 15	4,983,600	UP	4
June 18	5,384,800	UP	5
June 19	5,890,800	UP	6
June 20	5,589,800		0
June 21	6,089,800	UP	0
June 22	5,789,800		0
June 25	5,429,800	Down	0

Translating the above numbers to a Cluster Table, we see that we have no cluster until June 14th. Thereafter, the power of the cluster grows until by June 19th we have a cluster power of 6. On June 20th we have no designation and that eliminates that large cluster of 6. On June 21st the OBV jumps to a new high but we have broken the continuity of an unbroken Cluster. So we have no Clusters as of June 20th and cluster power has dropped from +6 to zero.

Now assume the above example is a Dow industrial stock. Each day I would record the number of Dow stocks having up clusters and down clusters together with a cumulative power number (simply adding up the net number of designations). The technical reasoning here is very sound *and is pregnant with forecasting possibilities.*

In the above example each successive UP designation made it that much more difficult for the stock to record a down designation. It wasn't until the cluster was ended on June 20th that a change of pattern was suggested. Now the new UP designation on June 21st produced no cluster power but eliminated the previous Cluster count and then the stock was vulnerable to breaking under the June 20th *window* which it did on June 25th.

Now picture the technique of tracking the total number of 30 Dow Jones industrial stocks and recording the number of up clusters, the number of down clusters, and the cluster power reading each day. *There of course would have to be a correlation between the size of the cluster and the time it took the market to produce a move in the opposite direction.* Then I would note the number of windows (end of clusters).

16. *The Windows*

In our study of clusters these runs of up or down designations are terminated when a stock either has no designation or records a designation opposite to that of the cluster. When a cluster is terminated it usually creates a space. When a new designation is forthcoming the space then becomes an island or *window.* Now there is potential for change which wasn't there before.

To illustrate, suppose we have a long unbroken string of down designations in a stock. Since that run embraces a larger amount of downside OBV, it is more difficult for an advance to record an up designation. However, if that string of down designations is broken up into two runs of downside designations separated by a "window", then less upside volume is required in order to get an up designation. When the 30-Dow industrial stocks are observed in terms of how many of these windows exist, significant upside or downside potential can be determined. Obviously a large amount of existing windows shows the average to be vulnerable to significant change, either on the upside or the downside depending on the direction of the broken runs.

Examples:

36-7/8	1,281,500	DOWN	36-7/8	1,281,500	DOWN
36-1/2	1,005,900	DOWN	36-1/2	1,005,900	DOWN
36	861,300	DOWN	36	861,300	DOWN
35-5/8	598,400	DOWN	35-5/8	598,400	DOWN
35-1/2	375,200	DOWN	36	723,400	(window)
35-1/4	184,500	DOWN	35-1/4	552,700	DOWN
35-1/4	184,500	DOWN	35-1/4	552,700	DOWN
35	-56,000	DOWN	35	312,200	DOWN

In the first of the above examples, we see an unbroken run of eight lower down designations. Lower OBV downs are always capitalized (DOWN). The OBV fell from 1,281,500 to ---56,000. Having to clear a hurdle of eight DOWNS, no up designations are likely to occur here without some preliminary preparation.

Now look at the second example. Here we see two runs of DOWNS separated by a window. Looking at the average trading volume, it is far easier to clear the 723,400 OBV level on any rally than it is to traverse the unbroken drop seen in the first example. Now, being runs of lower OBV DOWNS, the probability is that the next up designation will be a lower up, (up). Windows between runs of higher downs increase the probability of higher UPS taking place. Conversely, runs of higher OBV UPS separated by windows increase the probability of higher downs while runs of lower OBV ups increase the probability of lower DOWNS.

Now we want to think about the relationship of clusters to windows. Since a window is a space between two clusters, it is easier to change an OBV designation once a window has been established.

Therefore, windows are *precursors of change* and thus it is important to keep track of the number of windows among the Dow stocks. The time to concentrate on tracking the number of windows is immediately following confirmed highs and lows.

It is also important to note what kind of clusters the windows are breaking up. For instance, is the window space between a cluster of higher ups or lower ups? Is the window space between a cluster of lower downs or higher downs?

I interpreted window placements as follows:

Higher ups separated by a window are most likely followed by higher downs

Lower ups separated by a window are most likely followed by lower downs

Lower downs separated by a window are most likely followed by lower ups

Higher downs separated by a window are most likely followed by higher ups

Windows enhance or reduce cluster power depending on whether they terminate an up cluster or a down cluster. Now, suppose the OBV after being interrupted by a window then records a higher up. Despite the higher OBV reading, there is a reduction of technical power because the thrust of the previous cluster is lost, having been terminated by the window.

<u>Example</u>

OBV Designations	Cluster Power
UP	
UP	
UP	+3
Window	0
UP	0

What we see here in this diagram are three consecutive up designations followed by a price decline that produces a window. Then another price rise produced a new up designation. What do we derive from this? Despite the higher price, the window cuts off the cluster count. Therefore, prior to declines we have to see up clusters separated by windows as producing a drop in the cumulative count of up clusters. A drop in the cumulative count of up clusters can only be produced by window separations or by a down designation. So despite the OBV strength seen in the last higher up designation, we have here the early warning of the cluster contraction due to the windows or an interrupting down designation.

The same phenomenon can be seen in reverse when we have the following:

OBV Designations	Cluster Power
DOWN	
DOWN	
DOWN	-3
Window	0
DOWN	0

Having shown the concept of how changes in clusters and windows precede important price changes, I now want to show how these changes are neutralized or exacerbated and how pressures can build up which then open up market fissures which can precede market crashes or parabolic advances.

17. ***Loss of Cluster Power Indicates Impending Price Decline***

The impact back to the 0 reading on cluster power due to window breaks and subsequent OBV higher ups having no cluster value will be relative to the size of the clusters that their windows and subsequent OBV readings neutralize. For instance, look at the technical negative impact of the following sets of clusters:

Cluster 1	Cluster 2	Cluster 3	Cluster 4	Cumulative Power
UP	UP	UP	UP	0
UP	UP	UP	UP	0
UP 3	UP 3	UP 3	UP 3	12
UP 4	UP 4	UP 4	UP 4	16
UP 5	UP 5	UP 5	UP 5	20
UP 6	UP 6	UP 6	UP 6	24
UP 7	UP 7	UP 7	UP 7	28
UP 8	UP 8	UP 8	Window 7	31
UP 9	UP 9	Window 8	UP 0	26
UP 10	Window 9	UP 0		19
Window 10	UP 0			10
UP	0			0

Note the sharpness of the drop from 31 to 0. That was based on the above example involving only four Dow stocks. By theoretically expanding this illustration to 30 Dow industrial stocks and extending the example to include expanding down clusters one can then visualize the type of early warning that might precede market crash action.

Actual Patterns Which Preceded Declines
1992

June Decline	August Decline	September Decline	October Decline
6/ 9 +15	8/ 5 +85	9/15 +41	10/2 - 22
6/10 - 1	8/ 6 +45	9/16 +16	10/5 - 69

6/11 -14	8/ 7 +29	9/17 +13	10/6 - 87
6/12 -47	8/10 - 7	9/18 - 9	10/7 -101

18. Using the Window Indicator As An Early Warning Net Field Trend Indicator

Now that we see the value of using clusters as an early warning indicator, we can also use cluster analysis to warn of impending changes in the Net Field Trend indicator.

Example:

Delta Airlines
1992

Date	Price	OBV	Designation	Field	Cluster Power	Signal
10/7	55-3/4	2,474,000		Rising		Up
10/8	56-5/8	2,698,800	UP	Rising		Up
10/9	55-3/8	2,361,600	Down	Rising		Up
10/12	54-3/4	2,162,500	Down	Rising		Up
10/13	56-7/8	2,574,100		Rising		Up
10/14	55-3/8	2,252,300		Rising		Up
10/15	56	2,483,300		Rising		Up
10/16	57-1/2	2,700,400	UP	Rising		Up
10/19	57-1/2	2,700,400	UP	Rising		Up
10/20	58-1/4	3,135,900	UP	Rising	+3	Up
10/21	59	3,530,100	UP	Rising	+4	Up
10/22	58	2,982,700		Rising	0	Down
10/23	58-1/2	3,394,300		Rising	0	Down
10/26	59-1/8	3,625,100	UP	Rising	0	Down
10/27	58-7/8	3,332,600		Rising	0	Down
10/28	58-3/8	3,080,700		Rising	0	Down
10/29	57-1/2	2,236,300	Down	Rising	0	Down
10/30	56-3/4	1,937,300	DOWN	Doubtful	0	Down
11/ 2	57-3/4	2,230,100		Doubtful	0	Down

In the above table we see the standard table showing the OBV readings and the field trend readings. I call your attention to the cluster of four higher ups which were recorded between October 16th and 21st. The third consecutive up produced a cluster power reading of +3 on October 20th. The next day the fourth consecutive up was recorded and that raised the cluster power reading to +4. No designations are seen on October 22nd and 23rd. The previous cluster of four consecutive ups retain their technical power and this keeps the cluster power reading at +4.

Then we see something strange and wonderful take place. The OBV jumps to a new high on October 26th. We then see October 22nd and 23rd as windows, days with no OBV designations. Here is the rule of thumb: *Anything that interrupts a cluster immediately by virtue of a new OBV designation eliminates the technical power of that cluster.* The single new higher OBV up designation of October 26th thus shows the break in the previous cluster. So the cluster power reading on October 26th is 0 on the higher OBV reading! *Now note how that loss of cluster power preceded the negative change in the Net Field Trend indicator which took place on October 30th.*

This new analytical technique presents an opportunity to not only retain the daily computation of the Net Field Trend indicator, but to ascertain the number of advance signals of change due to losses in cluster power readings.

19. *The Importance of Current Clusters*

If the market was on the verge of doing something important either on the upside or the downside, then it logically follows that the validity of technical strength or weakness would be reflected in the number of *current* clusters. Since it requires three days of consecutive ups or downs to get a cluster, the absence of clusters shows a market having no sustained moves, either up or down. So before one gets carried away with a swing in the averages, see if that upswing or downswing is supported in terms of rising or falling cluster power.

20. *Current Clusters As a Powerful New Indicator*

Besides showing cluster power in terms of totals, I elected to start recording the actual number of *current* clusters each day for the Dow Industrials, Transports and Utilities. By doing this the effect of undue weighting would be eliminated, wherein a couple of stocks were accounting for most of the cluster power thrust.

Example: Here I want to examine a number of *current* clusters among the Dow 30 industrial stocks prior to the November-December 1991 sharp break in order to judge the validity of advance signals from this technical source. Cumulative Cluster Power uses the 4-column analysis and thus the final power figure is tantamount to The Cumulative Climax Early Warning.

Here I show the Current Cluster CLX readings for the summer of 1993 as the Dow industrials were making all-time record highs:

Date	Dow	CLX	CC CLX	4-Columns	True Cum.	EW Cum.
8/4	3552.05	+3	+1745	15- 0 -15 - 3	+1839	+1932
8/5	3548.97	-26	+1719	8 -9 -25 - 0	+1822	+1924
8/6	3560.43	-5	+1714	18- 8 -15 - 0	+1825	+1935
8/9	3576.08	-9	+1705	13-11 -11 - 0	+1827	+1948
8/10	3572.73	-7	+1698	15- 9 -13 - 0	+1829	+1959
8/11	3583.35	+11	+1709	26-11 - 7 - 3	+1848	+1986
8/12	3569.09	-21	+1688	0-11 -14 - 4	+1834	+1979
8/13	3569.65	-13	+1675	3- 6 -15 - 5	+1822	+1968
8/16	3579.15	-12	+1663	4-16 -13 -13	+1813	+1962
8/17	3586.98	+7	+1670	8- 4 - 4 - 7	+1817	+1963
8/18	3604.86	-11	+1659	9- 9 -11 - 0	+1815	+1970
8/19	3612.13	+12	+1671	19-10 - 6 - 9	+1828	+1984
8/20	3615.48	0	+1671	0- 3 - 7 -10	+1821	+1970

The reason why I chose the minimum 3 OBV up designations to make a cluster is because I wanted to expose the weakness of new Dow highs recorded on an inadequate number of up clusters. Technically, genuine new highs would be required to show some technical staying power. Clusters of 3 consecutive OBV up designations posed a good technical requirement. And of course the reverse was true. By requiring clusters of lower downs I wanted to expose the strength of new Dow lows recorded on an inadequate number of down clusters.

A perfect example of upside exhaustion was seen in the current Cluster numbers for August 20, 1993 when the Dow recorded an all-time record high close at 3615.48.

We saw these numbers:

Industrials	0 - 0 - 0 - 0
Transports	0 - 0 - 0 - 10
Utilities	0 - 3 - 7 - 0
Totals	0 - 3 - 7 - 10

So an all-time record high in the Dow was unable to produce a single cluster of true OBV up designations. That told me that the new Dow high had no technical staying power.

And now we move on to the Supercluster Indicator. The main difference with the Current Cluster Indicator is that any cluster of 3 or more consecutive up or down clusters is required to be followed by a different designation in order to eliminate the previous cluster. Every cluster remains in force until so eliminated.

In the summer of 1993 the push to above Dow 3600 showed definite signs of technical weakness revealed by the Supercluster Indicator.

21. *Some More Observations on Cluster Power*

It logically follows that a cluster of three consecutive OBV higher up designations does not have the technical power of a cluster of four, five, or six OBV higher up designations or more. In other words, the bigger the cluster the more technical power is exhibited. The logic is quite apparent. An OBV down designation can only be recorded by the OBV going below the closest OBV low. The bigger the Cluster of consecutive ups the more difficult it is for the OBV to record a down designation. So we see rising cluster power as commensurate with the degree of technical insulation against a market decline. And of course there is a mirror image in all market analysis. So we can say that the bigger the cluster of consecutive downs the more difficult it is for the OBV to record an up designation. So we then see increasing negative cluster power as commensurate with the degree of technical insulation against a market advance.

22. *What To Conclude if Current Cluster Readings Match the Supercluster Reading*

This is rather rare, but when it does occur it brings all the readings up to the intensity of the cutting edge. Thus if the cutting edge is a very bullish combination then the matching numbers will intensify that bullish reading. A very bearish reading would be intensified by an exact match.

I only started doing cluster counts in March 1991 and did not have the numbers for the start of the huge rise that got underway in mid-January of that year. I had homed in on that huge advance before it got started. So after developing this technique of using clusters, I went back and calculated the Cluster Power readings for the critical January 1991 period to prove the validity of their power to predict. I wanted to demonstrate the huge upsurge following the outbreak of the Persian Gulf war and to show that the cluster indicators were significantly accurate in mirroring that great rise.

January 1991 Cluster Power

Industrials

Date	Up Clusters	Down Clusters	Cluster Power	
Jan. 2	1	3	-10	
Jan. 3	1	3	-8	
Jan. 4	1	12	-36	
Jan. 7	0	12	-46	
Jan. 8	0	13	-53	Low
Jan. 9	1	10	-42	
Jan. 10	1	10	-43	
Jan. 11	2	11	-41	
Jan. 14	2	9	-34	
Jan. 15	1	8	-34	
Jan. 16	1	8	-35	
Jan. 17	1	3	-14	
Jan. 18	3	0	+9	
Jan. 21	4	0	+13	
Jan. 22	4	1	+10	
Jan. 23	2	2	0	
Jan. 24	2	2	-1	
Jan. 25	3	2	+5	
Jan. 28	5	2	+11	
Jan. 29	8	2	+22	
Jan. 30	9	3	+24	
Jan. 31	12	2	+42	

Transports

Date	Up Clusters	Down Clusters	Cluster Power
Jan. 2	4	3	+7
Jan. 3	4	4	+4
Jan. 4	3	3	+7
Jan. 7	2	2	+3
Jan. 8	2	3	-5

Jan. 9	2	4	-8
Jan. 10	3	5	-7
Jan. 11	4	6	-6
Jan. 14	4	6	-5
Jan. 15	6	5	+4
Jan. 16	7	3	+17
Jan. 17	6	1	+23
Jan. 18	11	1	+42
Jan. 21	12	1	+50
Jan. 22	11	1	+48
Jan. 23	6	1	+32
Jan. 24	7	0	+39
Jan. 25	5	0	+19
Jan. 28	6	0	+16
Jan. 29	7	0	+24
Jan. 30	7	0	+24
Jan. 31	8	0	+29

Utilities

Jan. 2	2	2	+2
Jan. 3	1	2	-6
Jan. 4	1	2	-5
Jan. 7	0	5	-18
Jan. 8	0	6	-22
Jan. 9	0	3	-11
Jan. 10	2	3	-6
Jan. 11	2	5	-12
Jan. 14	1	5	-19
Jan. 15	1	7	-30
Jan. 16	1	9	-38
Jan. 17	0	8	-38
Jan. 18	1	6	-28
Jan. 21	3	6	-22
Jan. 22	4	5	-10
Jan. 23	4	4	-5
Jan. 24	3	4	-6
Jan. 25	2	4	-11
Jan. 28	3	4	-9
Jan. 29	4	2	+1
Jan. 30	4	3	-1
Jan. 31	3	3	0

Now give clusters some serious thought. The longer a trend persists the more extreme will become the up and down parameters.

23. *Cumulative Cluster Readings*

We have seen how individual CLX cluster readings have pinpointed upside and downside market extremes. *But what is the best trend indicator?* Here I return to a proven technique, recording a table of *cumulative* readings. I used the same technique employed in the construction of the extremely important 65-Stock True CLX and the 65-Stock Early Warning CLX, the two indicators most responsible for my success since the 1987 bottom.

Consulting this table of Cumulative CLX Cluster Readings (see Appendix) any questions regarding 1992's earlier downtrend were immediately dispelled. And we also saw a dramatic technical prediction of why the Dow had to break under the April 8, 1992 low of 3181.35. The numbers literally leaped off the page:

Date	Dow	Cum. CLX	Cum. True CLX	Cum.EW CLX
Apr. 8,1992	3181.35	-1237	-582	-35
Oct. 2, 1992	3200.59	-1804	-1531	-1074

24. *The True Dow and the Early Warning Dow*

Every day we see the Dow Jones Industrial Average ballyhooed all over the world as representative of the American stock market. Aren't you now curious as to what the Dow Average would look like each day if it was based purely on the daily OBV moves of those 30 industrial stocks? First of all, I had to make an assumption. I assumed that any daily change in a Dow stock that did not produce an up or down OBV designation was *technically worthless.* I then set up my four columns, adding all the true gains and higher downs and subtracting all the lower downs and lower ups. From those totals I could easily calculate both a True Dow Average and an Early Warning Dow Average. In calculating the True Dow, I simply subtracted the total of true downs from true ups.

25. *What Are the Parameters of Trend Change Using Clusters?*

Clusters indicate probable cumulative limits to a move which would then denote a changed trend. Nothing goes up or down forever.

The more parabolic a move becomes the more likely the move is ending. The maximum number of true up clusters on the entire Dow 65 stocks stood at 89 on January 9, 1992 with the Dow industrials at 3209.53. That was a good time to get out of the market.

Examining other extreme cluster parameters, I made up a table of all the Dow-30 cluster counts and then, using 4-column analysis, came up with three daily figures: the orthodox Climax Indicator (total of all up clusters minus the total of all down clusters), the True Climax Indicator (acid test of up clusters minus down clusters), and the Early Warning Climax Indicator (up clusters plus higher down clusters minus lower down clusters and lower up clusters).

From an examination of this chronological table on clusters, I noted all the extremes and their dates most likely to be identified with market tops and bottoms. Here were the findings to date in 1992:

High Readings:	Actual CLX	+62	January 9	3209.53
		+63	April 20	3336.33
		+65	May 12	3385.12
		+85	August 5	3365.14
Low Readings:	Actual CLX	-86	March 13	3235.91
		-98	August 26	3246.81
High Readings:	True CLX	+84	January 9	3209.53
Low Readings:	True CLX	-95	August 26	3246.81
High Readings:	EW CLX	+106	January 9	3209.53
Low Readings:	EW CLX	-92	August 26	3246.81

Looking at these 1992 high and low parameters, we see the tendency to peak in the +85 area for the orthodox CLX, the +84 area for the True CLX, and the +106 area for the Early Warning CLX. Since the True CLX is only counting higher ups and lower downs, the numbers are smaller than those seen in the Early Warning CLX which counts the higher ups, higher downs, lower downs, and lower ups.

As for the downside parameters, we see the tendency to make bottoms in the -98 area for the orthodox CLX, -95 for the True CLX, and -92 for the Early Warning CLX.

26. *Putting It All Together*

–1991–

Date	Industrials	Transports	Utilities	65-Stocks
Jan. 2	-10	+7	+2	- 1
Jan. 3	- 8	+4	-6	-10
Jan. 4	-36	+7	-5	-34
Jan. 7	-46	+3	-18	-61
Jan. 8	-53	-5	-22	-80
Jan. 9	-42	-8	-11	-61
Jan. 10	-43	-7	-6	-56
Jan. 11	-41	-6	-12	-59
Jan. 14	-34	-5	-19	-58
Jan. 15	-34	+4	-30	-60
Jan. 16	-35	+17	-38	-56
Jan. 17	-14	+23	-38	-29
Jan. 18	+ 9	+42	-28	+23
Jan. 21	+13	+50	-22	+41
Jan. 22	+10	+48	-10	+48
Jan. 23	0	+32	-5	+27
Jan. 24	- 1	+39	-6	+32
Jan. 25	+ 5	+19	-11	+13
Jan. 28	+11	+16	-9	+18
Jan. 29	+22	+24	+1	+47
Jan. 30	+24	+24	-1	+47
Jan. 31	+42	+29	0	+71

Another excellent case example is the first decline coming off of the April 17, 1991 Dow high of 3004.46. The bears were certain that April 17th was a very important market top. Thus when the Dow plunged over 33 points on April 19th they thought they were on the way toward fulfilling their extremely bearish projections. They couldn't have been more wrong. Their major error of calculation lay in the fact that *so many Dow stocks had built up clusters of up designations*. Thus the first large Dow decline produced virtually no down designations.

The reverse of that bullish situation is a market that has produced large clusters of down designations. The first large rally would usually fail because of the difficulty in producing up designations.

These conclusions will be significantly influenced as to whether the clusters consist of true OBV ups and true OBV downs or whether the clusters consist of higher downs and lower ups. Obviously clusters of higher downs hold more promise of bullish change ahead while clusters of lower ups potentially threaten to be followed by a bearish change ahead.

November-December 1991 Break

Date	Dow	No. of Clusters	Cluster PowerCum.	Cluster Power
Oct. 1	3018.34	6	-5	-5
Oct. 2	3012.52	2	+1	-4
Oct. 3	2984.79	4	-6	-10
Oct. 4	2961.76	7	-4	-14
Oct. 7	2942.75	10	-19	-33
Oct. 8	2963.77	2	+3	-30
Oct. 9	2946.33	4	-2	-32
Oct. 10	2976.52	1	+8	-24
Oct. 11	2983.68	4	0	-24
Oct. 14	3019.45	6	0	-24
Oct. 15	3041.37	9	+12	-12
Oct. 16	3061.72	6	+10	-2
Oct. 17	3052.00	6	+9	+7
Oct. 18	3077.15	3	+16	+23
Oct. 21	3060.38	2	+2	+25
Oct. 22	3039.80	4	+1	+26
Oct. 23	3040.92	1	+3	+29
Oct. 24	3016.32	5	+4	+33
Oct. 25	3004.92	5	+3	+36
Oct. 28	3045.62	0	0	+36
Oct. 29	3061.94	2	0	+36
Oct. 30	3071.78	3	+4	+40
Oct. 31	3069.10	2	+7	+47
Nov. 1	3056.35	2	0	+47
Nov. 4	3045.62	0	0	+47
Nov. 5	3031.31	1	-3	+44
Nov. 6	3038.46	2	0	+44
Nov. 7	3054.11	2	0	+44
Nov. 8	3045.61	2	0	+44
Nov. 11	3042.26	3	-10	+34
Nov. 12	3054.11	3	-10	+24
Nov. 13	3065.30	4	-3	+21
Nov. 14	3063.51	4	-8	+13

Here I got the proof of what I was looking at. The Cumulative Current Cluster Power fell *prior* to the November 15th 120-point break. I thought at the time that the drop came out of the blue with no early warning whatsoever.

Now I continue the table to show the early warning of the December bottom:

Nov. 15	2943.20	3	-6	+7
Nov. 18	2972.72	2	-3	+4
Nov. 19	2931.57	5	-19	-15
Nov. 20	2930.01	2	-12	-27
Nov. 21	2932.69	7	-15	-42
Nov. 22	2902.79	13	-24	-66
Nov. 25	2902.06	8	-33	-99
Nov. 26	2916.14	5	-32	-131
Nov. 27	2900.04	3	-17	-148
Nov. 29	2894.68	4	-17	-165
Dec. 2	2935.38	1	+4	-161
Dec. 3	2929.56	1	-3	-164
Dec. 4	2929.56	5	-4	-168
Dec. 5	2911.67	2	0	-168
Dec. 6	2889.09	6	-19	-187
Dec. 9	2886.40	5	-21	-208
Dec. 10	2863.82	6	-19	-227
Dec. 11	2865.38	3	-14	-241

Here we see the bottom and then the powerful opening days of the next 1991 rally:

Dec.12	2895.13	4	0	-241
Dec.13	2914.13	5	+10	-231
Dec.16	2919.05	6	-4	-235
Dec.17	2902.28	4	+10	-225
Dec.18	2908.09	6	+18	-207
Dec.19	2914.36	8	+15	-192
Dec.20	2934.48	8	+33	-159

27. *Doing the Daily Homework*

Every afternoon after 4:30 P.M. from Monday through Friday

(Missouri time) Karen gets all the volume readings and closings on the 65 DOW stocks: the 30 Industrials, the 20 Transports, and the 15 Utilities. I go to work on the 30 Industrial stocks right away because I need those numbers in order to compute the daily Climax Indicator and Net Field Trend indicator readings for my daily evening hotline *Commentary*.

The next morning I get up at 5 A.M. or earlier. I first listen to the CNBC business show, usually featuring Mark Haines on first. The first thing I want to hear are the market reports covering the Tokyo, London, Paris, and Frankfurt stock markets.

I then get out of bed, pick up my copies of *Investor's Business Daily* and *The Wall Street Journal* at the front door and move into my study. I turn on the TV in there to hear Debra Marchini and Stu Varney at 5:30 A.M. on the CNN Business Morning report. My first task is to compute and record the OBV numbers on the other 35 DOW stocks. I use the data Karen got out of the computer the night before and so my working day officially begins.

I rule out my **DAILY WORK SHEET** which looks like this:

January 10, 1994

Industrials

UP	Down	DOWN	Up	
XXXXX	XX		XXXX	
XXXXX				
XX				
12	2	0	4	CLX +14

Current Clusters

3			4
3			
5			
5			
16	0	0	4

Superclusters

3	3	3	4
3		3	3
5		4	
5		3	
		8	
		3	
16	3	24	7

Transports

UP	Down	Down	Up	
xxxxx xxx			xxxxx	
8	0	0	5	CLX +13

Current Clusters

3			3
3			
6	0	0	3

Superclusters

3			3
4			
3			
3			
13	0	0	3

Utilities

UP	Down	DOWN	Up	
	x			
0	1	0	0	CLX -1

Current Clusters

	6		
0	6	0	0

Superclusters

	3	7	
	6	10	
		5	
		6	
		4	
0	9	32	0

65-Stock Totals

4-Columns

12	2	0	4	
8	0	0	5	
0	1	0	0	
20	3	0	9	CLX +26

Current Clusters

16	0	0	4
6	0	0	3
0	6	0	0
22	6	0	7

Superclusters

16	3	24	7
13	0	0	3
0	9	32	0
29	12	56	10

Starting with the Dow industrials, we start out with the standard 4-column analysis. I show the higher OBV ups with the capital letters UP, followed by the higher OBV downs with the lower case letters Down, followed by the lower OBV downs with the capital letters DOWN, followed by the lower OBV ups with the lower case letters Up. I go through each Dow industrial stock and wherever I find an OBV up or down designation I record it in the proper column with the letter X. So on this particular day I had a 4-column series Of 12 - 2 - 0 - 4 giving me a Climax Indicator reading on the Dow industrials of +14.

The work continues.

I maintain in my data bank all the 4-column combinations in graded lists. I thus record the new daily numbers for the industrials, transports, utilities and the 65 Dow stocks. These graded lists are particularly revealing since they show the closest similar combinations. We can't expect an identical follow through performance on an exact match or even on a close match because there are offsetting factors which will always affect the outcome. Nevertheless, I always felt that using this slot machine technique is worth the effort, sometime revealing striking results.

The 65-stock analysis includes recording the True and Early Warning Climax Indicator numbers.

Then I *reverse* all the numbers on the legitimate theory that if I can find a reciprocal of a proven bottom that I then have a top and likewise if I can find a reciprocal of a proven top then I have a bottom.

Then I take the latest three 65-stock CLX readings and these go into a graded list so that the sequence can be compared with previous 3-number sequences on the assumption that the fourth number can be predicted.

The homework wrap-up includes updating all the Nasdaq statistics and finally I record the numbers to be seen in my weekly market letter: The Dow industrial CLX, the highs and lows, the advance/decline line and the New advance/decline line.

This daily homework exercise usually takes about 2-1/2 hours to complete.

Now we move on to Phase Analysis

Section V
What Time Is It On The Market Clock?

What Time Is It On The Market Clock?

1. *The Phases*

Here we present the bull and bear market phases. There are three bull market phases and three bear market phases. Theoretically, these phases are 9 - 11 months in length. I will show the probable posture of a number of key technical indicators in each of the phases.

There is a definite psychological background to each phase. In the three bull phases it is disbelief, belief, and overbelief. In the first phase which is accompanied by fear and bad news the public cannot believe that there is anything good about the market. They are selling their stocks while the smart money is buying. In the second phase the public is still fearful and selling stocks on balance but beginning to believe that the market can go higher.

The smart money continues to be heavy buyers of stock. In the third bull phase the public is so caught up on the market euphoria that their belief has turned to overbelief. The smart money, seeing the red flags, turns fearful and heavily distributes their stock holdings to the public's waiting hands. The public has gone from extreme disbelief to extreme overbelief.

In a bear market everything is the opposite. In the first phase of a bear market the public is still confidently buying stocks while the smart money is in cash and selling short. Here we also have the three psychological phases. This time it is disbelief that the market could go down, that changing to belief in a downturn, and finally that changing to overbelief in a downturn, extreme pessimism at a major market bottom. The smart money, always playing the other side, stays fearful through the first two phases of a bear market and then begins to accumulate stocks in the last phase of the bear market.

Sometime we will encounter periods in which the market refuses to go down in the face of bearish indicators or refuses to go up in the face of bullish indicators. When the market refuses to follow some technical indicators it is a warning that something is wrong. Either the indicators will have to turn around and confirm the market, or the market will reverse direction and get in line with the technical indicators. Later on it will be shown that the two indicators one should most rely on in these situations is the high/low indicator and the advance/decline line. When the market is out of step with those indicators it is more important than ever to trust the indicators and expect a market reversal.

2. *Bull Market*

A bull market is a rising market with the rise generally lasting at least 18 months. The length of a bull market is generally measured in terms of the Dow Jones Industrial Stock Average. Right at the very start the stock market neophyte is led to believe that the Dow average consisting of 30 industrial stocks is the market. While so many will deny this, the media is most guilty of keeping that notion alive.

There are so many examples of this. A typical one is the 1987-90 rise in the Dow. The true market, as measured by the high/low indicator and the advance/decline line, topped out in August 1989 but the Dow did not peak until July 1990. The advance/ decline line declined all the way from August 1989 to the end of October 1990. So the true bull cycle here lasted for 22 months while the bull cycle in terms of the Dow average lasted for 34 months.

3. *The Three Bull Phases*

Certain things characteristically act in a certain way in each phase of a bull cycle. Their actions help identify the phase the market is traversing. A bull cycle consists of three phases of 9 - 11 months each. Here are how the following major indicators are expected to act in each of those bull phases:

Bull Phase One

Indicator	*Characteristics*
Advance/Decline Line	Has traced out a previous longterm decline, has stopped going down and has moved above a previous interim high.
Highs and Lows	It can be shown that sometime during the previous nine months there was a climax in the number of new lows, some maximum number achieved in the 500 to 900 area, and since that time the number of individual new highs has been consistently out- numbering the number of new lows.
Dow-Jones Industrials	Sometime during the previous six to nine months made a major bottom confirmed by the Dow Jones Transports. Since then has either made an unconfirmed new low or a clear pattern of rising bottoms and tops.
Dow-Jones Transports	Some time during the previous six to nine months made a major bottom confirmed by the Dow Jones Industrials. Since then has either made an unconfirmed new low or a clear pattern of rising bottoms and tops.
Time Indicator	Check out all the market long-term cyclic bottoms, 1957, 1962, 1966, 1970, 1974, 1978, 1982, 1987, and 1990. Assuming a continued 4 to 4-1/2 year cycle, market should be within one to nine months after the recording of one of those cyclic lows.
Dow-Jones 200-Day Trendline	The Dow 200-day Trandline for a long time has been in a protracted decline. To insure against a mere rally in a bear market, the decline in

the line must have lasted longer than nine months. The Dow makes an upside penetration of that trendline roughly 4 to 4-1/2 years after a similar upside penetration in the first phase of the previous bull cycle.

The 50% Principle

If the Dow Jones Industrial Average has retraced more than 50% of the completed bear market decline then the evidence is most compelling that the market is in the first phase of a new bull cycle.

News

News is bearish in the main. The first phase of a cycle is never ushered in by good news because that would abort the market game principle. The fundamentalists would be buying along with the technicians and there would be no sellers. The news is most bearish during the first three months of the first phase, gradually lessening thereafter. As is so often the case, the country is in an economic recession during a bull cycle first phase, and the bad news stemming from it provides the necessary cover for technically inspired buying while the bulk of the fundamentally-oriented public worries over the daily headlines. The first phase of a new bull cycle always shows the market shrugging off the bad news, climbing on a wall of worry. It is the best evidence we have that expresses the degree of public disbelief that the market can rise in the face of such poor fundamentals.

General Motors

In the very earliest part of the bull cycle first phase, the price of General Motors stock drops to the lowest level seen in 4 to

4-1/2 years. When this occurs, immediately check out the technical evidence of a major market bottom having already been recorded inasmuch as General Motors, more often than not, has made its low after the Dow. Thereafter stock has no difficulty in effecting the bullish GM- four month rule, refusing to make a new low for four months. Once it records that bullish confirmation the market's first bull phase generally has three months remaining.

Sentiment As Measured By Money Market Assets

In the early months following the major bottom the trend of money market assets continues to rise as the public remains fearful. It then peaks and starts to come down while there is still widespread bearish sentiment.

Bull Phase Two

Indicator | ***Characteristics***

Advance/Decline Line

Advance/decline line made the first of two tops during the first bull phase. As Bull Phase Two gets underway, the A/D line is diverging, working temporarily lower, the strong first phase upswing being digested. In the middle of the second phase, the more extended downward corrective movement called the DECLINE THAT FOOLS THE MAJORITY carries the A/D line just low enough to make it difficult for the line to do more than recover that loss. That second top may or may not be higher than the first phase top, and it occurs very late in the second phase, practically at the dividing line between the second and third phases. Regardless of whether the line is moving up rapidly or not in the second phase, the general pattern calls for one top in the first phase and one about equal or higher in the second.

Highs and Lows

The number of new individual stock price highs may have topped out very late in the first bull phase if not reserved for a second phase peak. That largely depends on whether the first phase market movement was characterized by high or low volume. If first phase market volume was high and the advance in the Dow quite spectacular, then it is more probable that the number of new highs peaked late in the first phase. We never get as many new highs at one time in a bull as we get simultaneous new lows in a bear market. The usual peaking in the number of new highs is done in the 300-400 area while climax figures for new lows run as high as the 550 - 900 area and climaxed at a record 1,174 new lows on October 20, 1987, terminating that crash. Assuming the spectacular bull cycle first phase advance in the Dow on heavy volume, new highs now consistently run under the peak of the first phase, generally fluctuating in the 80 to 150 area. Following a more sluggish low volume bull phase one, new highs would not be expected to top out until late in phase two.

Dow-Jones Industrials

May or may not exceed first phase high prior to mid-phase sharp downward correction. Will make a new bull phase high very late in the second phase after a mid-phase correction.

Dow-Jones Transports — No serious divergences from the industrials are expected to occur during the second phase unless it precedes the mid-phase corrective move. A failure to confirm the industrial upswing after the mid-phase correction would be deemed to be serious.

Time Indicator — Ten to 20 months have gone by since a major confirmed market bottom has been recorded. An intermediate downtrend occurs approximately 15 to 18 months after such a major bottom.

Dow-Jones 200-Day Trendline — Trendline remains under the first phase peak throughout the second second phase of the bull cycle.

The 50% Principle — Has no major function during second phase other than helping to pinpoint extent of mid-phase secondary reaction.

News — While stock prices climbed the wall of worry during the first phase, news-oriented fundamentalists were stunned with disbelief. What usually starts the second phase of the bull cycle is a change in the news transforming that first phase public disbelief to belief. If the country was in an economic recession during the first phase, a reported end or near-end to the recession would usher in the bull cycle second phase, and such ushering in would probably coincide with a market reaction as the public comes in and pays top dollar.

General Motors	Trends higher through second phase, all reactions holding sharply above previous bear market low.
Sentiment As Measured By Money Market Assets	The trend of money market assets continues to fall as public confidence in the market improves, the falling trend here, reflecting money going into stock and bond funds.

Bull Phase Three

Indicator	***Characteristics***
Advance/Decline Line	Records major peak at end of bull second phase and generally diverges from the Dow industrials all throughout the bull cycle third phase.
Highs and Lows	There is one final attempt by new highs to scale the earlier bull cycle peak, but it fails. There is an increase in the number of new lows but the figure would seldom come up and pass the number of new highs.
Dow-Jones Industrials	The Dow industrials are in their glory during the third bull phase, pulling away from all the broader indices. A series of new highs for the bull cycle is recorded with the usual terminal move characterized by a sharp final perpendicular rise to a record high, a move lacking confirmation by a number of the major indicators.
Dow-Jones Transports	A serious divergence is expected during the third bull phase between the industrials and the transports, one of the two averages failing to

confirm the other. This is not absolutely required, however, to identify the third phase termination. It is possible that both averages could record a confirmed major top accompanied by a serious technical non-confirmation elsewhere, notably in the A/D line and the number of new highs.

Time Indicator

Twenty one to 33 months have gone by since a major confirmed market bottom has been recorded. By this indicator alone one would be warned that the bull cycle is aging, the time at hand to begin to look for the exits.

Dow-Jones 200-Day Trendline

Here we have what I have defined as a clear signal agent for the timing of the bull cycle third phase. When the trendline comes up after the phase reaction and zig-zags into new bull cycle high ground, that breakthrough signals the start of the bull cycle third phase. The bull cycle from that point usually has less, than a year to run and many times closer to six to eight months.

The 50% Principle

Has no important applications during bull third phase.

News

Economic news is glowing and the public is very bullish. Reflecting the industrial boom, all kinds of extremely bullish earnings forecasts are being published. The bulk of the market however, is not responding well to the very bullish news as seen in a slipping advance/decline line.

General Motors	General Motors has now topped out ahead of the Dow Jones industrial average.
Sentiment As Measured By Money Market Assets	Continues to decline rapidly as the public continues to pour money into the stock and bond funds. However, very late in the bull cycle money market assets bottom out and start to turn up as the smart money starts to leave the market.

4. *The Three Bear Phases*

Bear Phase One

Indicator	***Characteristic***
Advance/Decline Line	Breaks under the low recorded just prior to the final bull cycle in the blue chips and is a clearly defined downtrend.
Highs and Lows	The daily number of new lows climbs rapidly and surpasses the dwindling number of new highs. Consistently thereafter new lows outnumber new highs.
Dow-Jones Industrials	First sharp declines in the industrial average from the major peak recorded. Strong attempt to rally back 60 days later fails, the Dow then breaking the first important low point to record a very bearish looking downward zig-zag.
Dow-Jones Transports	Commensurate sharp decline from major peak with inability to recover on later rally attempt.
Time Indicator	Twenty two to 34 months have gone by since the last major bear market bottom. A market top having all the earmarks of a major bull market peak must have been seen within the past one to five months.

Dow-Jones 200-Day Trendline Previously rising 200-day line has flattened out and is just starting to turn down. The Dow Jones Industrial average has come down sharply and made a downside penetration of the trendline. Later the average might get back a bit over the line but promptly turns down again. This all usually happens during the first bear phase.

The 50% Principle The earlier this Principle is activated the more valid it is likely to be. If more than 50% of the previous completed bull market is retraced during the first bear phase, the record strongly points toward the previous bear market low being broken in this bear market. Previous 50% Principle signals showed that the bear signal was activated too late on the 1966 downswing to be effective, thereby setting up a fooler. It effected a breakthrough during the first phase of the 1968-70 bear cycle, thereby predicting that a bottom below that of 1966. It effected a breakthrough during the second phase of the 1973-74 bear market and that was also followed by a bottom below that of 1970. Summing up, if the Principle is activated during either the first or second phase of the bear cycle it is likely to be very valid and thus a very bearish indication.

News The news definitely remains bullish, very favorable to business. Most economic indicators support the continuation of prosperous times. While the market responded to favorable news during the second phase of the bull cycle with rallies, shrugged off the good news and went sideways during the third phase of the bull cycle, the market now goes into sharp declines in the face of continuing good news.

General Motors

General Motors is now in a very bearish looking downtrend. The price of the stock has made a downside penetration of its own long-term trendline, and the line itself has flattened out and is just starting to turn down.

Sentiment As Meassured By Money Market Assets

As the stock market moves lower in the first phase of the bear cycle money market assets now begin to climb rapidly, reflecting growing public fear of the market.

Bear Phase Two

Indicator	***Characteristics***
Advance/Decline Line	Turns up sharply on strong mid-phase rally and moves out of down channel, but the move turns out to be transitory, the A/D line soon thereafter breaking down even more sharply, breaking the previous low.
Highs and Lows	New highs temporarily outnumber new lows but soon gives way to the very bearish pattern of new lows consistently outnumbering new highs.
Dow-Jones Industrials	On a number of rally attempts since the major peak, one or two Dow Jones industrial stocks actually get back to the old high, deceiving many into thinking that

perhaps the previous decline was a secondary reaction in a bull market after all. Such spotty strength soon gives way to the primary bearish trend. Maximum deception occurs on strong mid-phase rally.

Dow-Jones Transports

Transports rally during mid-phase strength but fall woefully short of the peak and probably fail to confirm the industrial rise or visa versa.

Time Indicator

Anywhere from seven to 14 months have passed since the major bull market peak.

Dow-Jones 200-Day Trendline

The trendline is coming straight down hard which made it easier for the Dow to make the deceptive upside penetration on the mid-phase rally, the rally that fools the majority.

The 50% Principle

If the Principle is activated, and all the signs point to this being the second phase of the bear cycle, then the activation is very bearish, predicting a new low below that of the previous bear market.

News

The news has soured and market responds to the change in the news with further sharp declines. During the mid-phase rally market goes up on talk of recovery, but the talk proves to be premature. Public continues to buy on all reactions, still confident that bull market can be revived.

General Motors

General Motors is unable to tack on more than just a few points on mid-phase rally. The long-term trendline is trending sharply lower and upside penetration of the line by the stock

	proves very temporary, the stock breaking to a new low thereafter.
Sentiment as Measured By Money Market Assets	Stays at high levels pretty much throughout the second bear phase.

Bear Phase Three

Indicator	***Characteristics***
Advance/Decline Line	Continues to zig-zag to new lows with no let up.
Highs and Lows	List of new highs is running close to zero in number while new lows number in the hundreds, climaxing anywhere in the 500 - 900 range, but breaking all records with a climactic 1,174 lows on October 20, 1987.
Dow-Jones Industrials	Most stocks making new lows with a small handful of them accounting for a majority of the losses.
Dow-Jones Transports	Falling rapidly, keeping pace with industrials on the downside, recording new lows for the bear cycle.
Time Indicator	Market should be within 48 to 54 months since the last major cyclic bottom and within 14 to 21 months since previous market top.
Dow-Jones 200-Day Trendline	The trendline continues to come down hard and the Dow is now outpacing the trendline on the downside, dropping the maximum distance below it of any time during the entire bear cycle.

The 50% Principle	If the Principle is activated during this phase, the chances are very strong that the Dow is close to the bottom and that the activation of the Principle will result in a key bear trap.
News	Public has turned completely sour on the market and responds to every bit of bad news with heavy selling. Their previous misplaced confidence has now turned to extreme pessimism. The smart money, awaiting the collapse of the public confidence, shifts their stance from one of pessimism to one of confidence.
General Motors	This bellwether stock continues to make new lows, there being virtually no support for the stock.
Sentiment As Measured By Money Market Assets	Continues to move higher, reaching new peaks.

5. *More On the 50% Principle*

This is something that should always be in mind when following the market. Some people apply intra-day highs and lows when applying this principle to the Dow. I always apply it on closing prices. The theory on better than 50% retracements is that when the halfway point is bettered then the Dow will make a 100% retracement. Inability to better a 50% retracement on the upside is bearish and inability to better a 50% retracement on the downside is bullish.

6. *The Market Must Always Climb a Wall of Worry*

Every significant rise in market history has always had a wall of worry upon which to rise. The worry must be rooted in something fairly widespread and obvious to all. But this is most evident during the first two phases of a bull cycle. In the third and final phase of the bull cycle the wall of worry becomes more difficult to define and increasingly becomes a slippery wall.

7. *Bull Market Declines*

What we have to determine here is whether the decline will remain within the framework of a continuing bull market or whether it is the start of something far more serious. That is ascertained in a number of ways. The best method of determination is to check out the current posture of the major indicators to see which market phase is most probable. But here, and I cannot accent it enough, the Dow is not the market. As I review various market highlights of the past several years, knowing what every individual stock has done is the only technical intelligence that is superior to all other market insights. While that requirement at first glance might appear to be a gargantuan task, I have presented stock and chart counting methods that simplify the task and bring the results within reach of everybody willing to make the effort.

8. *Bull and Bear Traps Always Occur At Market Extremes*

Bull and bear traps tell us a great deal about where the market is headed. We see the great bear traps at market bottoms when it looks like a decline will never end. Always the key indicator to watch is the high/low indicator. When we see very negative market sentiment accompanied by hundreds of new lows then we know the market is ripe for a major reversal to the upside entrapping all the bears. While market bottoms are generally easier to identify than market tops, *to call for a bullish reversal to the upside too early in a proven bear market could see such a call quickly backfire. Make sure the bottom was accompanied by widespread fear rather than the simply widespread complacency that is characteristic of Bear Phase One.*

But it is a different story with identifying market tops and bull traps. The reason is simply that most major bottoms are characterized by widespread fear and thus a concentrated and climactic terminal move. But a market top is formed over a period of time by waves of euphoria and greed and thus there are many false starts to the downside. The several requirements for a major bull trap include what would appear to be a fundamentally strong market characterized by low interest rates, virtually no inflation, an improving economy and rising earnings. Major bull traps see the market fundamentalist as the most vulnerable. Everything has to look good without a cloud in the sky. But the trap must include a worsening technical picture underscored by the fact that an increasing number of stocks have topped out. The key word accompanying all bull traps is technical upside exhaustion. So once again our attention is always directed to the high/low indicator. The key warning of all bull traps is a declining number of stock highs.

We now move on to some recent market history, starting with the 1987 bottom.

Section VI
The 1987-90 Bull Cycle

The 1987 - 1990 Bull Cycle

1. *The 1987 Crash - A Study in Fear*

Every skill of modern day technical analysis is brought to bear here in order to clearly show that there was only one predictable market outcome following the 1987 crash, an outcome that without deviation was clearly shown right from the outset. It cut through all the thick layers of misplaced gloom and doom psychology, proved that the media was not the public's friend, showed up the economists, and otherwise revealed the value of stock market majority opinion as worthless.

The October 19, 1987 stock market crash was unique. There was nothing comparable in the entire history of the stock market. Most market observers tried to relate the event to the 1929 crash *and therein lay their greatest error.* They assumed that the crash was signalling a great bear market ahead. Technical analysis did not square with that popular assumption. Right from the birth of post-crash action, the market deviated from the 1929 scenario. But the majority could not be swayed. When I announced a major buy signal on October 26, 1987, my view was not only the minority view of a technician, but considered that of a madman, someone totally unaware of the fact that the world is flat.

Seeing the crash as an ending rather than a beginning of market trouble, my initial assumption was totally contrary to the thinking of the public, the media, the economists, and the overwhelming majority of stock market advisors. While the crash was unique, technical analysis provided the tools to cut through all the confusion at the outset, enabling followers of those signals to march to a different drummer.

I saw October 19, 1987 as a tremendous blessing in disguise. The super climactic nature of that historic day immediately put all post-crash market action in a different light. All post-crash action was seen to be technical preparation for a much higher market starting with the construction of major base patterns. While many complained that after the first ten months of post-crash action the Dow was only rising at a low key 22 degree angle of ascent, I saw that as being an exceedingly bullish portent for the future. Rather than trace out a sharp but shortlived rise typical of a rally in a bear market, it was this extended low key rising trend that indicated a new bull phase ahead. Even the bears had never seen a 10-month rising trend in a bear market and their earlier calls for new lows in the Dow below the 1738 level had long since been silenced. With Dow Theory having produced so many buy signals since the crash, only a closing below the 1738 level could support the bear market thesis according to that theory.

It was of course not easy to go in one direction when all the traffic appeared to be going the other way. I trusted my charts and, above all, I trusted what I saw in my new indicators.

The stock market crash of 1987 drove the public out of the market. People had become disillusioned and apathetic. The volume of trading steadily fell. Brokerage house stocks fell and brokers began to lay off personnel. So programmed was the public to believe that the bear market was going to steadily get worse and culminate in a very severe recession or even a great depression, that some even began to question the very life of the brokerage industry. The universal belief was that anything good in 1988 was nothing more than a rally in a bear market and that things would get very bad in 1989 after the election and that everything said in Ravi Bhatra's *The Depression of 1990* would inevitably come to pass. The public wanted no part of the stock market.

It was all very remindful of the time when I was writing the 1976 *New Strategy* book in the early months of 1975. The 1973-74 bear market had ended in the fall of 1974 and I vividly recalled the background problems that were associated with that important market bottom. I had written the following in the introduction:

"A great deal of this book was written against one of the most disturbing backgrounds the market has ever had. In the 1973-74 bear market, Wall Street was so buffeted by crises that it was thought by a growing number of people to be dangerously incapable of defending itself from total collapse and possible extinction. The brokerage industry was hobbling along as best it could, seeking to serve a totally disillusioned public, a people caught up in the daily struggle to stay ahead of a mounting inflation that threatened to tear away at the basic fabric of our democratic society.

A growing doubt as to the future of the economy was whipped up to a national frenzy of fear and was reflected by a major slide in stock prices. That fear syndrome had done its work again, effectively, ironically blinding the public at the point of maximum investment and speculative opportunity. By late 1974 the down cycle correlating with maximum fear had reached its extreme. Inasmuch as the stock market game is played on a field bounded on each by these goalposts of fear and greed, once an extreme has been reached, the action reverses itself and heads back in the opposite direction toward the other extreme. The market is constantly in the process of working toward one of those extremes and is seldom static.

Unable to maintain a continued uptrend or downtrend at the point of these greed and fear extremes, the market makes a long-term reversal at the most illogical of times, completing one cycle and embarking on another of generally similar length. But, now stressing the anachronism between the market and fundamental data, what would appear to be illogical market action to the uninformed becomes very logical to the informed. Months after one of those seemingly illogical market moves, fundamental data confirms the market logic. At that point, however, the market may be marching to a different drummer, a new tune to be played by the fundamental band perhaps nine months later.

Writing against the storm of controversy in late 1974 that perhaps the market had gone too far, perhaps beyond the point of return, some very astute thinkers contended that there was no way out of the 1974 inflationary dilemma except via a depression. They maintained that the market had not seen its bearish extreme."

At the time that was the parallel I was looking for. Nobody could dispute the maximum fear produced by October 19, 1987. That maximum fear *changed the timetable.* The public is not supposed to get fearful about the stock market until the transition from bear market to bull market. In my 1976 *Strategy* book I had laid down the indisputable rule that if you are going to beat the market you must accumulate stocks while the public is fearful and distribute them while the public is confident. That is the name of the game. The following diagram became a cornerstone in the 1976 *New Strategy* and in the 1988 *Stock Market Teacher*:

	Bull I	Bull II	Bull III	Bear I	Bear II	Bear III
The Public	Fearful	Fearful	Confident	Confident	Confident	Fearful
The Smart Money	Confident	Confident	Fearful	Fearful	Fearful	Confident

I maintained that due to the extremity of the crash and the fear it produced that an entire bear cycle was capsuled into the brief period from August 25th to October 19th in 1987. But, looking at the historical parallels, the bears were certain that all post-crash action was typical of the first phase of a bear market. But now you see that something was wrong with that analogy. If the market was traversing the first phase of a bear market in the post-crash period the public should have been confident according to the above diagram. But, instead of being confident, the public was in the *reverse* posture, extremely fearful, *an attitude that is associated with new bull markets.* The public wanted nothing to do with the stock market, *their precise attitude at the end of the 1973-74 bear market.*

But this raised a very important question. How could the 1987-88 market action equate with coming off the 1974 bottom if the 1973-74 bear market lasted for 23 months while the 1987 bear phase only lasted for less than 2 months? So this was the argument that this observer stated was solved by the severity in the 1987 period as equating with the longer time period of the 1973-74 period. This writer took the position that both down periods *were terminated with maximum fear.**

The 1987 post-crash market offers the most compelling opportunity to examine the full spectrum of technical analysis in a new light. Inasmuch as nobody had ever before seen the Dow Jones Industrial Average drop 508 points in one day, the crash of October 19, 1987 naturally produced instant fear, confusion, and general consternation.

(Footnote) -

*In making my point about comparing the 1973-74 bear market with the downturn between August and October of 1987, one market was stretched out to a two year bear market and the other was shortlived but even more devastating. Thus we can equate both markets legitimately because the severity of the shorter period produced the same bottom line results as the longer but milder period. I make this legitimate comparison because in both cases the upturn in the Dow 200-day trendline which ultimately followed those two periods several months later ushered in an extensive rally that lasted for a long time.

It produced the sharpest division of market opinion this observer had ever seen. The majority opinion was the one dominated by fear and following the obvious. This opinion cleaved to the Dow Theory sell signal of October 15th, taking place two days before the climactic market bottom. The belief was that a major bear market was underway. Those who held to that opinion were certain that the crash was signalling major trouble ahead. The minority opinion, on the other hand, saw the crash as an ending by virtue of its totally climactic nature. The majority saw the crash as a broad warning to get out of the market while the minority saw the crash offering a major buying opportunity.

Ironically, the safest time to fly is immediately after a major plane crash. But when the stock market crashed it created so much fear that it blinded the majority to the opportunities which were at hand. Financial advisors told their clients to go out and buy a parachute when they should have been telling them to buy an airline ticket. In one day the market did something that it ordinarily would have taken one to two years to accomplish. It produced a parabolic plunge which showed up in all stock charts as a straightline vertical drop. Chartists had never seen anything like this before. It left them confused. But they heard the term *parabolic* before and should have known that it terminates a move. The bear had thrown his worst punch. The bear won and the fight was over just when most thought the fight was just beginning.

2. *Picking the 1987 Bottom*

Some years ago Vincent Price appeared in a thriller called *The Tingler*. The thing represented the isolation of human fear into an object that had shape and substance.* It existed independent from the body. It was horrible and very real. It made quite an impression on me when I first saw it. It wasn't until October 19, 1987 that I could relate *The Tingler* to the stock market. On that unforgettable day in stock market history one not only encountered raw naked fear but saw the shape of it, something that could be drawn, charted, and forever preserved in the market psyche, just as real as the Hollywood brainchild called *The Tingler*.

(Footnote) -

There was a very interesting article in the *Wall Street Journal* on September 23, 1991 about the research done by Manfred Clynes of Australia on emotions. He said that emotions have shapes that one can see and reproduce. He found distinct patterns in music as well as life. He used his program to manipulate phrases, amplitudes, individual note shapes and infinitesimal pauses. This writer has related the stock market to music, medicine, and physics. But I found my work covering the emotion of fear to be most rewarding, both developmental triggering and accidental triggering. Technically I picture the shape of such emotions in terms of market extremes.

Such an extreme drop had to be terminal. It created a total fear which blinded market observers to the virtually guaranteed buying opportunity at hand. The classic formula for making money in the stock market is to *buy low/sell high.* But the irony of it was that accompanying the opportunity was a total paralysis brought on by the abject fear which blinded one to the opportunity to buy low.

The 508-point drop in the Dow on October 19, 1987 was an *accident*. An accident is not *predictable*. Accidents comprise complete surprises. When they occur in the stock market the market seeks to quickly correct what it was unable to see. That was true following other market accidents such as the Eisenhower heart attack in September 1955 and the Kennedy assassination in November 1963. More recently, the Russian coup of August 19, 1991 served as an additional example.

These accidents comprise the safest time to buy because the extremity of the stock drop convincingly suggests that most people have done their selling. That was dramatically evident in the 1987 bust when 1,174 stocks fell to new 52-week lows. That number was so extreme that we may never see such a figure again in the future.

3. *On Feeding the Birds at Emile's*

Some years later, my wife Karen noted the duplication of this important principle while feeding the birds at Emile's, a famous German deli restaurant in Kansas City. We often ate there at an outside table under the trees so we could feed the sparrows. Karen would line up pieces of bread on the limb of the tree above her. She quickly noticed that the more courageous birds went directly to the tree limb and got the most food *without any risk.* The more timid birds waited for pieces of bread to fall to the pavement below. So even in the world of birds there are the technicians and the fundamentalists. The technically minded birds kept their eyes on the dot and were not afraid of the people sitting close by. They thus ate the best. On the other hand, the timid birds of fundamental persuasion, demanding security, ate last and were getting only the crumbs.

And so it was at the October 1987 stock market bottom. While it appeared to most that the stock market was a terrible place to be, the courageous technicians swooped in without fear, knowing it was the safest time to buy. They were the first to be rewarded. The majority however, blinded by fear, waited until the technical early buyers had their fill and only seeked to buy much later. Like the birds of fundamental persuasion, they of course got the crumbs. It is a beautiful lesson: *to the courageous belong the spoils.* The smart little sparrows, having no fear, saw their opportunity, and pounced on it.

Yet in the face of this extreme buying opportunity at the October 1987 bottom, *economists and the media proved to be the public's worst enemies.* On October 19, 1987 Pierre Rinfret, an economist, was a guest on the Larry King show. The Dow had fallen 508 points that day to close at 1738. Rinfret predicted that the Dow would see the 1000 level before it ever saw the 2000 level again. As it turned out, the Dow crossed above 2000 within two days and never saw the 1738 level again.

4. *October 30, 1987*

"In this letter last week I said that we could be but hours away from a buy signal. My eyes were constantly on the one key indicator that was telling us ever since the October 19th crash that *most stocks had seen their lows.* That indicator was the number of stocks making new lows, a number that saw a climactic reading of 1,174 the week of the crash. October 19th was Blue Monday, what I called Big Blue. Then on October 26th we saw Little Blue, the Dow dropping 156 points but with a clear indication that this was not only typical post-crash action but that we were not going to make new lows. *It wasn't even necessary to wait until the close to see that the market was flashing a major buy signal.* I immediately sent out an Early Warning buy signal with the calls commencing at 11:30 A.M. New York time on October 26th with the Dow at 1815. That was almost precisely the moment that Arthur Kane (Katz) committed murder and suicide at the Merrill Lynch office in Miami, another omen of the market bottom. A similar buy signal bulletin was mailed out to letter subscribers on the afternoon of October 26th.

Since no two cycles are ever exactly alike, I felt that many people were going to miss this buy signal because the 1929 scenario had been too widely publicized by the media. Virtually everybody was expecting new lows because the Dow made a new low nine market sessions after the 1929 crash. Now we are seeing a very bullish *change of pattern.* As I write this (October 29th) we are in the eighth day after the October 19th crash and instead of threatening the Dow 1738 low, the market has told us that the testing phase is over and *now the Dow is free to advance by several hundred points.*

When I did my regular weekly telecast on Wednesday, October 28th, for the *Financial News Network* I said that we were looking here at a MAJOR BOTTOM and, like all major bottoms, catches most people bearish at the bottom, something well attested to by the latest figures from *Investors Intelligence* which showed bears far outnumbering the bulls.

I told Bill Griffeth on the FNN show that I have a bone to pick with the media and I was singling nobody out but directing my observations about all the media. When they get a big story they try their best to keep it on the front page as long as they can. Earlier this year the PTL scandal, the Contra and Irangate hearings were excellent examples. Now the story of the year is the stock market crash. I told Bill that technically the stock market crash is old news and the efforts to keep it on the front page is typical of the media because they love a good story. I said that the stock market has been telling us for over a week in every way it can that the crash is DEAD news, dead as a dodo. So, when you read the newspaper, listen to the radio, and watch TV, *keep in mind that they want to keep the crash story alive as long as possible.* It is good for their business and that is why they will keep beating the negative drums long after the market has turned for the better. The stock market, however, is not in the media business and has been proving every day that it is in the recovery mode. That should be the #1 story, but the media have their teeth so deeply embedded in the crash story that they are completely missing the real #1 and that is that *we have seen the worst and most stocks have seen their lows and that we may be looking at one of the best stock market recoveries on record.* On one of my many telecasts, I told viewers on October 26th right after the close that they could now spit into the wind and come up with a dry face.

By riffling through the pages of the *Trendline* chart book we see something that comprises one of the rarest of all technical phenomena. It is so rare that you may never see this again in your lifetime. We see that the crash action of earlier October took virtually every stock straight down in a parabolic collapse, all the chart lines going absolutely due south. It was almost as if a giant magnet was put under all the stocks at the same time and, like iron filings, they all quickly lined up in a vertical row. The conclusion, going completely against the grain of public opinion, was that most stocks became an automatic buy, or, by turning the charts upside down, they would have all looked like an automatic sell. The rare phenomena (and you can prove it to yourself by looking at all the charts) is that *simultaneously all charts look alike.* It is that rare time when you can blindfold yourself and throw darts into the *Wall Street Journal* stock pages and buy whatever the dart hits and the odds are strongly weighted in your favor that you will make money with your new purchases. The first order of technical business is the reflex rallies in each stock back to their trendlines and that means that you are looking at a large number of potential doublers right now.

So now let us put a microscope on the very earliest phase of post-crash action and look at the numbers as the bloodless verdict of the marketplace-no bias, no emotion, but simply what the market was saying:

Date	Dow	CLX	Market Comment	NFI	High/Low	A/D Line
10/19	1738.74	-30	Classical selling climax	-14	4 - 542	-70,913
10/20	1841.01	- 9	Start of reflex bounce	-15	1 -1174	-71,849
10/21	2027.85	0	End of the bounce	-15	2 - 108	-70,309
10/22	1950.43	- 3	Lows to be tested	-15	1 - 172	-71,488
10/23	1950.76	- 5	One more good hit needed	-15	1 - 144	-71,866
10/26	1793.93	-15	MAJOR BUY SIGNAL	-16	2 - 467	-73,523
10/27	1846.49	+ 1	Bullish CLX upside breakout	-16	0 - 341	-73,403
10/28	1846.82	- 4	Recovered from sharp drop	-16	0 - 477	-73,965
10/29	1938.33	+12	Getaway breakout	-14	2 - 169	-72,196
10/30	1993.53	+21	Very strong showing	-14	1 - 39	-71,539
11/ 2	2014.09	+18	CLX signal for pullback	-14	1 - 34	-71,075
11/ 3	1963.53	+ 2	Extremely bullish pullback	-14	1 - 37	-71,793
11/ 4	1945.29	+ 1	Extremely bullish pullback	-14	2 - 39	-72,013
11/ 5	1985.41	+ 3	Sharp rise as expected	-12	2 - 45	-71,182
11/ 6	1959.05	- 1	New pullback underway	-12	0 - 21	-71,189
11/ 9	1900.20	-13	Further weakness	-12	2 - 46	-72,061
11/10	1878.15	-16	Another rising button	-14	1 - 75	-72,193
11/11	1899.20	- 4	Market anticipating	-15	2 - 39	-72,515

The market spoke with total authority on October 19th and said with no reservations that you were looking right at the bottom. It wasn't a bottom. It was THE bottom, a bottom so powerful *that it would now hold up under all conditions*, holding in the face of all the gloom and doom, the dire forecasts by economists, and the extreme bearishness of practically every big name analyst in the business. What was the first technical indicator to proclaim the certainty of the bottom? It can be seen here on the day of the crash. It is the -30 reading in the Climax Indicator.*

That was immediately followed the next day by the highest number of individual new stock lows ever recorded in one day in stock market history! So this is all you had to see and know that an historic market bottom had been put in place.

* Since there are only 30 stocks in the Dow Jones Industrial Average, the Climax Indicator, which is the net count of up and down OBV breakouts, cannot ever drop below a -30 reading by definition. I created this indicator in August 1961 and the indicator had never recorded a -30 reading until October 19, 1987. Obviously it could only improve from that level.

5. *The Economists*

Why does it appear that most economists give the impression of being stupid when it comes to relating their work to the stock market? The explanation is simple and logical. Economists follow the economy and the economy is a lagging indicator. The stock market is a game of futures. It looks ahead and is only concerned with tomorrows. The economy, being a lagging indicator, can only allow economists to make projections which are late by definition. Thus is was no surprise following the 1987 stock market crash to hear most economists predicting an imminent recession, with some going further and predicting an economic depression. So they were certainly harming the public with their off-the-mark wild statements. After the crash the economists were telling the public to buy a parachute. That poor advice was totally irrelevant to what had happened. The plane had already crashed. It was the time to buy an airplane ticket.

6. *The Media Mind*

The media was equally harmful, but even more so, having control over the widest circulation of their off-the-mark views. Every day the media was spewing out the news to a news hungry public, a public gripped with fear. But never is the public more impressionable that when a single event takes place, especially one as exciting as a full blown stock market crash. At such times the public is totally dependent upon the media to quickly report what is happening. For a very brief period the media functioned as expected. But then something strange takes place and becomes harmful to the public, especially in the arena of financial reporting. *The media becomes caught up in the importance of their own story and stops looking at the stock market in response to the news.* With the national spotlight suddenly on them, young financial news commentators visualized themselves as young Walter Cronkites, basking in the glow of this new-found national attention. Being reporters, they had sunk their teeth into the biggest story of the year, loved the taste, and was loathe to let this meal of the gods come to an end. So they constantly regurgitated the morsels of this headline-grabber long after the stock market was looking ahead to better days. In other words, the media was hugging the big story long after the stock market was writing a new story, the story of tomorrow. While watching TV at that time, one could literally see how much these reporters were enjoying the excitement of the crash. Obviously, they did not want the Dow to stop dropping. Their excitement over the big story transcended their function of properly serving the public and noting that the market was signalling a major bottom. But major bottoms are no fun to these reporters. Bottoms don't make the front page. Market crashes are far more fun to watch and report. So it was with great regret when the media saw their big story no longer on the front page. They didn't give a damn that a great buying opportunity was at hand. That doesn't sell papers or make for instant fame.

And the 1987 crash is not an isolated instance. The media mind is the same today as it ever was or will be, When CNBC took over FNN in 1991, I was hoping it would be different, that perhaps for the first time the public would be introduced to intelligent financial reporting wherein the stress would be where it belonged, on market response rather than on market input. But CNBC, choosing to remain in the typical non-productive mode, reproduced every known mistake in financial reporting. Numerous interviews with economists cluttered up their program. Most of time such output being totally irrelevant to the stock market. Then they reported the news, putting the stress on the news rather than the market's response to the news. They were particularly guilty of doing interviews with various analysts with absolutely no reference to their track records, the viewing public exposed to information that more often than not was not productive.

Without exception, these financial programs are always heavily weighted by the fundamental school of thought. Stress is on such things as corporate earnings, the price/earnings ratio, dividend yield, book value, management, the product, and the economy. I had hoped that those things would be downplayed in favor of reading the market in terms of technical analysis. To give the impression that their reporting was balanced, they presented what they called their resident technical analyst. But that person so totally hedged his opinions and frequently changed his mind that the public was left everyday in general confusion, offset from time to time with slivers of clarity.

Perhaps the most damaging exposure the public was subjected to is a syndicated columnist who by his own admission doesn't understand technical analysis. Instead, all his time is spent circulating rumors and stories. Being so available, he of course would be reporting much garbage put upon him by those with a motive and knowing he is a sucker for a story. The public, of course, got the worst of this, many market losses being generated by a reporter more interested in spreading a rumor or story than in the welfare of the viewer exposed to this type of cheap sensationalism.

Probably the biggest single mistake CNBC makes is accenting the negative when they should be accenting the positive (as in 1991) and in accenting the positive when they should have been accenting the negative (as in late 1993). But I don't point a finger at that since that simply documents my game theory.

* * * * * *

By early 1989 my stock counting technique was a regular exercise and had stood me in good stead throughout the 1987 - 89 bull cycle. In May of 1989 I saw an excellent example of how misleading the actual number Of stock highs and lows can be at times and why it is so necessary to dig beneath the surface to see what is really happening.

May 4, 1989

7. *The Pause That Refreshes**

Most people are lazy by human nature and thus I am certain that the figures I am about to give you were never known to others until presented here. First of all,

I want to quote something from a bearish market letter in order to demonstrate that the bears *are totally misled by surface indications* when it comes to analyzing what they see as a dwindling number of stocks making new 52-week highs. The bearish market letter writer made the following statement on *April 14th:*

> "On each of the three assaults above 2300, there were fewer daily new highs each time: Feb. 8 peak, 144; March 16 peak, 120; and April 12 peak, 102. This market isn't strengthening, it's weakening Watch out below!"

In direct contrast, here is what I said on April 13, the day before:

"The market is about to go into orbit and will be at new post-crash highs in the next few days. Most people will be astonished with the new power coming in to this market as the Dow readies to scale new post-crash highs."

Now obviously the writer of the bearish April 14th statement had not taken the time to count the number of big board stocks within a point or less of making new 52-week highs. If he had *he would have seen that that number was steadily growing*, not dwindling. So while the casual observer saw 69 stocks make new highs on April 5th, I reported on *Financial News Network* to Richard Saxton on that day that big board stocks within a point or less of new highs had grown to 432 in number. So of course it was no surprise to see new highs make a new post-crash high of 173 on April 18th. But now the casual market observers are repeating their earlier mistakes. They are alarmed because they see a dwindling number of new highs since April 18th. But they are lazy. They still refuse to count up the number of stocks within a point of making new highs. If they had done so, *they would have detected a tremendous surge of power beneath the surface.* Just between April 5th and April 28th the number of big board stocks within a point or less of new 52-week highs grew at the astonishing rate of 432 to 643. So on April 28th the casual observer sees 120 stocks at new highs and thinks the indicator is breaking down when on the same day *the subsurface strength showed those potential 643 new highs.* So obviously I was very upset when I heard a technician on FNN say on April 24th that *strong stocks were dwindling in number.* That was an out and out lie and was simply the result of failing to take the time to count the stocks within a point or less of making new highs.

So when I see the same people citing technical weakness in the high/low indicator which is simply not there, it is time to again stress this recent research and to update it and go a step further. You have heard these big name analysts tell you that the market is brain dead and that the market is going nowhere, making such statements just before the market went into orbit last month as predicted. Now I want to extend this counting technique a step further. The technique comprises *the most valid advance indications of what lies ahead for the high/low indicator.* So I sat down and counted all the big board stocks within 2 points to 1-1/8 points of new 52-week highs and added that number to the number of stocks within a point or less of new highs.

Here are the numbers as they stood on April 28th: 606 stocks within a point or less of new highs and 544 stocks within the 2-point to 1-1/8 point range of new highs. So now I can make an amazing statement: AS OF APRIL 28 THERE WERE 1150 BIG BOARD STOCKS WITHIN 2

POINTS OR LESS OF NEW 52-WEEK HIGHS! That is almost HALF THE ENTIRE BOARD!

The extreme bullishness recorded here saw the actual new highs continue to expand until they peaked at 306 on August 1, 1989.

August 19, 1989

8. *Racing Toward a Climactic Top*

As I pointed out here last week, this is the first time in the entire post-crash period going back to October 1987 *when traders have to seriously prepare in advance for an important market top.* So I repeat here the famous Boy Scout motto: BE PREPARED. So while I am not yet pulling the switch, I have instructed subscribers to keep raising stops, grab any call option profits when they hit 100%, and plan to be mostly in cash *by the end of this month.* Last week I called for increasing cash reserves to 25%. *This week cash reserves are raised to the 50% level.*

Frankly, I would like to be out of the market now but my technical work tells me that we still have a rendezvous with destiny at higher Dow levels. As long as my indicators are going up the Dow has not reached the top of this move. And my indicators are continuing to go up. But there isn't much time left and the top of this move could come even sooner than I first projected. A simple glance at the Dow Transport Average tells one that we are looking at *a major parabolic rise*, something that smacks of being terminal.

One by one the pieces are falling into place *which should compel looking at the other side of the coin on everything.* So here goes:

1. While everybody was looking for a crash in the Japanese market back in late 1987, I saw that that was not only impossible at that time *but championed the Tokyo market all the way up to the recent crossing of the Nikkei Dow 35,000 level.* I saw a particular chart pattern in the Japanese market that our market was destined to follow. So while the Japanese market astounded all the bears by not reacting negatively to many disturbing political changes and a string of scandals, now we have come full circle to dangerous complacencies. Many months ago I predicted that the Nikkei Dow would rise to the 35,000 level. I now no longer have the confidence of a further significant rise in the Nikkei Dow.

2. When the stock market crashed on October 19, 1987, *gold peaked at $500 an ounce on the same day.* Just when the market was saying that the worst was over, the public got out of the market *with many going into gold at the worst of times.* The other side of the coin would be *gold bottoming and stocks peaking.* This is another opposite coming into play.

3. I don't know why they insist on doing this but they do. It would make a lot more sense if brokerage firms hired brokers at an important market bottom in order that their clients could profit from the rise that followed. *But they do the exact opposite.* They fire at the bottom and hire at the top. They are forced to do that because they don't have enough customers at market bottoms to pay their brokers. Astute market observers do the exact opposite of the brokerage firms. While brokers were being fired and laid off, this writer was acting on the major buy signal of October 26, 1987 at Dow 1793. *Now, after a rise of 967 points since the 1987 crash,* the brokerage firms now have enough customers to again be hiring new brokers. So I repeat the fact that they fire at the bottom and hire at the top. It is another side of the coin to keep in mind, another case of an important opposite being seen.

4. Back in May 1988 I told Bill Griffeth on my weekly *Financial News Network* telecast that the upside breakout then in *Fannie Mae* stock at 33 signalled not only a much higher market for that year and 1989, but that *Fannie Mae* was the most reliable forecaster of interest rates. So, thinking in terms of *opposites*, we see that *Fannie Mae* recently went to the 100-5/8 level. The simple line chart shown in the *Trendline* chart book shows a parabolic upswing which looks *terminal.* So while I was the champion of lower interest rates all through the entire post-crash period, I have to recognize the important technical fact that *Fannie Mae* is not telling us about a soft or hard landing. It is telling us that there is no landing. I have been telling you for a long time now that *the economy is neither too hot or too cold.* It is continuing to *oscillate* between inflationary and deflationary fears. So, again observing these opposites, *Fannie Mae* now does not justify optimism over the current outlook and the ability of the Dow to cross the 3000 level without some *important detours* first.

9. *The August 15, 1989 Sell Signal*

Having seen new highs peak on August lst and the advance/decline line peak on August 8th, it was believed that most stocks had seen their highs. Again I underscored what I believed were four important opposites. One of the parabolics most strongly supporting my sell signal was unknown to everybody. While we had a published figure of 306 stocks at new 52-week highs, *we had 800 big board stocks within a point or less of new highs.* That was an extreme parabolic rise and it looked very terminal.

August 16, 1989

SELL SIGNAL IS VALID

Reaching an intra-day high of 2747.53 on August llth, the market recorded a major reversal to the downside. Traditionally, we wait until the Dow makes a non-confirmed new high and then we get a sell signal. This time, however, I would not bank that strongly on the ability of the Dow to make a new high and don't believe there is that much time left to clear the 2747.53 intra-day high. You will see the evidence here that most stocks have peaked. That evidence was so emphatic in terms of the shrinking number of stocks making new 52-week highs that my Early Warning subscribers received the following message after the close of August 15th:

"This is the call to liquidate stocks, August 1989 top signals too clear now to ignore. The Dow could rally in late August but it is clear that most stocks have seen their highs and the risks of a very sharp decline in the September - October time frame are too high to ignore. Gold stocks can be held but everything else is suspect."

Last week I pointed out four major opposites which have now come to pass which led to the following conclusions: (1) The Japanese market has peaked, (2) Stocks are a sale and gold stocks are a buy, (3) Brokerage firms in a position to hire brokers thus coinciding with a market top, and (4) Fannie Mae has signalled that the low in interest rates has been seen. Now I can add another key opposite coming to pass. *The most vehement bears of 1987-88 are now becoming bulls at the worst of times.* A new Dow high will produce potential whipsaws of great magnitude. One who has featured the bear in his letters and ads since the crash says that the picture of a bull will be restored in his letter and his ads when the industrials better the 2722 level. Here is another picture of a significant opposite at work. Another vehement bear now says that if the Dow goes simply above the 2700 level that a new upper target of 3584 in the Dow can be projected. Of course having missed the last 1000 points in this market, they have no audience. Then there are those bulls who hope you don't remember how bearish they were for so long after the crash. They want to make doubly sure that you don't know they are in the bull camp. *It is from this group that most of the current forecasts of Dow 3000 are coming.* I have not said that we can't eventually see 3000 or higher in the Dow. What I have said is that *I see no move to 3000 without first seeing a significant downside detour.*

The August 14th issue of *Barron's* will be an issue long remembered. The cover alone is as good a sell signal as you would ever want. The headline is **3000 ON THE DOW THIS YEAR?** Then in a huge box is one word: **WOW**. How quickly they forget the **POW** of October 1987. If **POW** can produce such a genuine buy signal, WOW has to be a sell signal. The **POW** of October 1987 was against the background of bad news. The **WOW** of August 1989 is against the background of good news. That's another opposite coming full circle.

10. *Parabolics, Tsunamis, Airpockets and Other Shocks*

A parabolic rise is one in which the price steadily rises and the angle of rise becomes increasingly acute on the upside until it is almost vertical. *When something is in a vertical rise it is seen to be terminal.*

Here are some outstanding examples of parabolic rises:

On January 21, 1980 the price of gold reached $875 an ounce and silver reached $50 an ounce. The fever of speculation was rampant and it served to blind most people to the utter stupidity of what was going on. It was a perfect example of the parabolic curve. The final months of advance saw the price of gold rising almost perpendicularly. The day before the top I was in Minneapolis and saw my prediction of collapse for the precious metals headlined in *The Minneapolis Tribune* as follows: ANALYST SAYS GOLD AND SILVER ABOUT TO TURN TO DROSS. The very next day was the top, both gold and silver embarking on a 12-year bear market.

On August 15, 1989 after keeping my subscribers 100% fully invested since October 26, 1987, I turned bearish and recorded a sell signal on that date. Two days later I was interviewed by Dan Dorfman regarding my sell signal. He asked me what my favorite short sale was. I told him that UAL without question was the perfect short sale on the big board and was set to plunge. That night on the August 17th *Moneyline* show on the Cable News Network, Dorfman told Lou Dobbs that UAL was my favorite short and didn't I know that UAL was a done deal on a takeover deal? He then said that he would judge me in the future based on what UAL stock did. UAL collapsed as predicted and led the market down in the October 13, 1989 mini-crash. Here is the chart of UAL showing the parabolic rise that culminated in the 1989 crash.

11. *The UAL 1989 Parabolic Curve and Collapse*

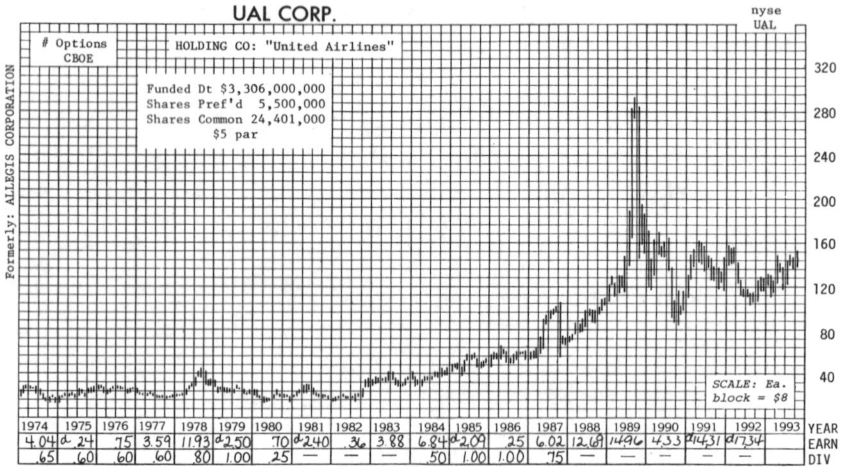

Now I want to show the reader the great significance of a sharp expansion in the number of stocks within a point or less of making new 12-month lows. In October 1989 the market suffered a 190-point mini-crash which was blamed on a collapse in the price of UAL stock. So the technical warnings coming from the stock count were followed by an *event.* Technical analysis cannot identify what the event will be other than stating that there will likely be an event.

Here I show my warnings of this based on what I saw in September 1989:

September 21, 1989

Last week I underscored the fact that no market has ever recovered following an 80% drop in new highs coming off of an August top. There is no exception to that observation. Yet so many commentators blindly extend their bullish outlook *and make absolutely no reference to the high/ low indicator.* By definition it is *impossible to be bullish* in the face of these numbers. You have seen the almost total destruction of the new highs, dropping from 306 on August lst top the recent low of 14 on September 14th. While we were witnessing this 95% drop in new highs since August 1st, *our attention is now focused on the increasing number of new stock lows.* Here I applied the same counting technique that had kept me so bullish all the way to my recent August sell signal. Instead of counting the number of stocks within a point or less of making new highs, I now count the number of big board stocks within a point or less of making new lows. AND HERE I MADE A MAJOR DISCOVERY! I was so excited that I called John Dorfman of the *Wall Street Journal* and he saw that my findings were published in the *Journal* on September 18th. I discovered that on September 14th we had 359 big board stocks within a point or less of recording new 12-month lows! You will note that we recently saw the first crossing in the high/low indicator since March 27th. However, back then we didn't have the huge negative back-up number of 359 stocks about to make new 12-month lows.

So what we have here is the *imminent move above 50 new lows which will then signal a radical acceleration toward literally hundreds of new stock lows.* This is why it is a laugh to hear so many born-again bulls talking Dow 3000 or better when at best, *the market is giving you the best technical evidence possible of a severe detour to the downside.*

September 28, 1989

12. *WATCH THE EXPANDING NUMBER OF NEW LOWS*

The market is following a very definite bearish pattern to a T. Market *momentum* peaked in early August when the number of individual 12-month stock highs reached 306. Since then the destruction in the number of stocks making new highs has many times exceeded a shrinkage of 80%. Especially coming off of an August peak, *we know that the market has never recovered from such a shrinkage without either going into a massacre or crashing downside price movement.* Last Spring when there were still so many bears, I called attention to the fact that we had *hundreds of big board stocks* within a point or less of making new 12-month highs. Because of this valuable analysis I was able to keep my subscribers bullish right into the August top. Now I am giving you the same very valuable analysis *but this time am telling you about the hundreds of stocks currently within a point or less of making new 12-month lows!* When I first did the count I called up John Dorfman of the *Wall Street Journal* to tell him that we had 359 big board stocks within a point or less of new lows. He was amazed and saw the significance of this right away, putting the figure in the *Journal* the next morning. Since that initial count, *the number has grown closer to the 400 level.* So as bullish as I was this past Spring when I saw similar numbers working toward new highs, *I am equally bearish today.*

Anybody who has the *Trendline* chart book can turn it over and see the high/low indicator charted. There you will see the giant downside zig-zag in the number of new highs, *such a zig-zag last seen just prior to the 1987 crash.* Many market observers call me up and tell me that they see no dangers in this market. One could have made a similar observation in September 1978 just prior to the October massacre that year. The number of stocks making new lows was slow to expand and it wasn't until the number reached 56 that everything then promptly fell apart! Within 7 market days the number of new stock lows expanded dramatically to 583. That is what one can expect to see in a market massacre.

So at this writing we have almost 400 big board stocks within a point or less of recording new 12-month lows! That piece of information is so bearish that it cuts through everything else and *renders any opposing information as virtually worthless.* Now, I have underscored the probability that when we see more than 50 new lows then we can expect the market to *accelerate on the downside.* The imminence of breaking out above 50 new lows is further dramatized by the fact that we *now have almost 100 big board stocks within a quarter point of making new lows.* So the market cannot technically tolerate any further weakness *without triggering a waterfall effect in the expanding number of new lows.* This technical deterioration underscores the *game of musical chairs* currently being played in the market. The high/low numbers prove that every day chairs are being steadily removed from the game as the powers that be increasingly *try to talk the market up.* Closely study the indicators reviewed on page 3 and you will quickly see why any bull on this market should be very concerned. There is no technical basis for any significant recoveries from current levels.

Two weeks later the market crashed.

The 1987-90 bull cycle ended in mid-July 1990 with the Dow at 2999.75. Question: How effective was the stock counting technique in warning of the 635-point decline in the Dow that followed that peak? You be the judge.

13. *Third Phase of 1987 - 90 Bull Cycle*

After the October 1989 smash the Dow bottomed and entered the final upleg of the 1987-90 bull cycle. True to form, many stocks failed to keep up with the Dow between November 1989 and July 1990 and thus a *dichotomy* could be identified which served as a technical precursor of the 1990 bull cycle peak. The cycle ended in July 1990 with the Dow at 2999.75.

The very bearish changes in Karen's stock count took place right at the very peak of the bull cycle:

The July 1990 Stock Count

Date	12-Month Highs*	12-Month Lows*
July 13	351	475
July 20	167	500
July 24	142	582

*Within a point or less

14. *Pre-Top Frustration May to July 1990*

As we approach every market top there is always a degree of frustration because every top embraces the *dichotomy syndrome*, the internal technical disease which sees the solo walk in the Dow masking the internal technical destruction of the general market which is soon to surface and be seen by all. It is awfully hard to convince the media that one is right on the market when the Dow makes it look obvious that one is wrong on the market. That was my predicament prior to the July 1990 peak.

Prior to all cyclic tops the dual market threatened the demise of the Dow blue chips, the blue chips being the last segment to give way to a bearish trend. The following letter appeared in the May 21, 1990 *Barron's.* It correctly warned of the consequences of the market dichotomy, the Dow peaking in mid-July and then followed by a drop of 635 points.

Gloomy Outlook

"The April 16 Up and Down Wall Street column by Alan Abelson was worth the price of admission. For one thing, the information imparted was in complete agreement with my own thoughts, and I always like that. More important, the column provided an enlightening discussion of the economy and its effect on the financial markets.

I make no pretense of being a great economist (two mutually exclusive words). However, common sense dictates that slowing auto and housing sales, coupled with large quantities of vacant commercial real estate, an increasing rate of bankruptcies, cutbacks, layoffs, etc. forecast trouble downstream for the equity markets.

While many of the underlying factors may differ, the similarities to the 1972-74 bear market are striking. Those years produced a slow, agonizing decline with occasional rallies. Portfolio losses of 50% were quite common. Portfolios with Amex and OTC issues suffered even greater losses. By the time the bear market ended in December 1974, many investors were wiped out.

As for the similarities between the early 1970's and the current situation, they are quite striking. At that time, the Nifty Fifty, the wonderful companies deemed to be impervious to economic downturn, held up the overall market. It seemed as if this would go on forever, but it did not.

In the current situation, the DJIA holds up the overall market but the advance/decline line ratio and the high/low list indicate that the rest of the stocks are headed down. The odds are high that the Dow will join the rest of the market in a downturn as the economic situation worsens." - Robert A. Hauslen, Mahwah, New Jersey.

One could sense my frustration in my pre-top interviews at that time with Richard Saxton and also in my weekly market letters.

June 6, 1990 FNN Telecast

"Richard, I missed the recent rally as you know, but I saw it as a very dangerous blowoff, an upswing having no bullish long-term significance whatsoever. I see it as more likely kicking off a bear market in the 1990-92 period.

In my May 31st letter I drew attention to a number of amazing technical parallels with the January 11, 1973 major peak, a peak that saw the beginning of the worst bear market since 1929.

The bull trap was set on the Monday morning approach to the 2950 Dow level. Now the rug is being pulled from under all the latest buyers as the DOW stocks plunge beneath their most recent intra-day lows.

We have seen a dangerous loss of upside momentum since the mid-May momentum peaks and because of that I could not let my subscribers get caught up in this euphoria.

What we are seeing here is a *rupture in the continuity of bullish opinion.* The real technical tests will come on the next attempt to rally and thus one cannot automatically expect that this correction is offering new buying opportunities. Everyone is telling you that a move down to 2850-2875 is a buying opportunity. Once we get down there you may not want to buy.

Everything I am seeing here duplicates the same technical traps recorded late in the 1972 market.

The average person hasn't the remotest awareness of the fact that right now the market is giving the precise technical warnings that had served as the foundation for Roger Babson's famous warning of *September 5, 1929.* While the Dow had soared into the wild blue yonder back then, *52% of the big board stocks had already been in a bear market for nine months.* You know what happened next. So I underscored this in the *Barron's* piece. I got people out of the market last August while new highs, the advance/decline line and the Transport average were peaking. Despite recent all-time record highs in the Dow industrials, those key indicators aren't even remotely close to their highs of last summer.

So Richard, *I am betting on technical analysis, history, and human nature. This market has had it and we could be headed for a summer bust.*

Anybody telling you to buy stocks now in the face of this technical and historical evidence is, in my opinion, irresponsible.

In my June 14th letter one could sense my frustration with the rising Dow but at the same time my faith in the time tested indicators that pointed to a near-term market fall.

June 14, 1990

15. *WHAT WAS THE GIST OF BABSON'S WARNING?*

The Dow-Jones Industrial Acerage peaked at 381.17 on September 3, 1929, ending at that time the longest and strongest bull market Wall Street had ever seen. The Dow would not see that level again for twenty five years. Just two days off the top, Roger Babson made a speech predicting that the Dow would drop to the 300 level. The Dow fell almost 10 points on September 5th which would be roughly equivalent to a drop of 73 points in the current market. By November 13th the crash had dropped the Dow to 198.69 and by July 8, 1932 the Dow came to rest at the unbelievably low level of 41.22. As history showed, Roger Babson was not bearish enough. But the point here is to get a handle on what had bothered Babson? If our market merely duplicated Babson's prediction the Dow would fall to approximately the 2289 level. Well, in a nutshell, Babson had noted that the previous nine months of advance was concentrated in the blue chip stocks. He noted that most stocks had peaked the year before and he was particularly alarmed over the small number of stocks making new highs while the Dow Jones Industrial Average was soaring into the wild blue yonder. On the very day of the high on September 3, 1929 54 stocks made new highs while 19 made new lows.

From time to time the *Wall Street Journal* would allude to some of the things that were bothering Roger Babson but those items were mostly buried in a sea of optimistic statements which were so common just prior to the great crash.

My closing advice was as follows:

You are witnessing the last throes of a Dow parabolic upswing. You want to take advantage of this and move into at least 75% cash. If I am right about the 1990-92 bear market, there will be plenty of time for shorting and buying puts. We are not short and we have no puts at this time. I want to see what bothered market students back on September 25, 1929 and when you see this then you go short and buy puts:

(Quoted from the *Journal*)

> "Those who study the Dow-Jones average chart closely are somewhat disturbed by the action of the market recently. *Every rally has been halted slightly below the previous peak, while each decline has taken the average into new low ground. This in considered indicative of lower prices by these students."*

At this time the media began to poke fun at the bears:

June 18, 1990 - Barron's Cover Headline

ENDANGERED SPECIES: BEARS IN A BULL MARKET

I had told Kate Welling in the interview that while I had called the entire 1000-point advance of 1987-89, this latest rally was the last hurrah, a major bull trap, the rally that fools the majority.

June 20, 1990 FNN Telecast

"Richard, I last spoke with you on June 6th, saying then that the rally was seen as a very dangerous blowoff, an upswing having no bullish long-term significance whatsoever. That rally is over, almost an exact double top of June 4th and June 15th The June 15th high had reflected almost total *technical exhaustion.*

June 21, 1990

16. *The Wheels Are Coming Off*

The very fact that the Dow could immediately drop 54 points following my technical warnings summarized in the June 18th issue of *Barron's* reflected an impaired position. Here I borrow a phrase from the September 10, 1929 *Wall Street Journal:* "Many observers felt that the market's sensitiveness to the Babson prophecy indicated an *impaired position.*" I refer again to Babson's famous warning of September 5, 1929. My technical concerns in this regard rest on the fact that *Babson's warning could be made today because it rests on precisely the same technical evidence.* Babson was particularly concerned with the *high/low* indicator and the *advance/decline line.* He stressed the fact that these two indicators peaked in 1928 and that while the 1929 upswing was concentrated in the blue chips, *52% of the big board stocks had been in a bear market for the previous nine months*. Now subscribers can begin to see why I have kept them in 75% cash since last August. *Last August marked the true top of the bull market.* After all, most stocks topped out in that month, new highs peaking at 306 on August 1st. The advance/decline line peaked a week later on August 8th. Completing the technical top, the Dow Transport average peaked on September 5th. Now keep this in mind: despite the recent series of all-time highs in the Dow industrials, those three major technical indicators are not even remotely close to their 1989 highs. I will say it again. *Anybody telling you to buy stocks under these conditions is technically irresponsible as were the analysts back in 1929 who told their followers to keep buying stocks.*

Subscribers know I keep a detailed diary. Everytime the market is at a top the predictions for a higher market become more numerous and *the bulls become increasingly arrogant.* This has been the case *and especially so in June.* So we know this is a *major top* and can only be followed by a further decline, then a failing rally, and then collapse. All this will be taking place this summer. The close bunching of these bullish forecasts are mostly identified with people who have been telling you now for the past nine months that we are about to pass the Dow 3000 level, what I call my *people* indicators. Some of these even predicted Dow 5000 this year.

**Optimistic Comments I Have Heard
So Far in June Taken From My Diary**

June 7	-	I think the stock market is headed higher. I feel the Dow has good support at 2900. I think the market could begin moving higher later this week.
June 7	-	3000 - 3100 by end of June
June 7	-	Will see 3250 sooner than we expect
June 7	-	(On the *Guru Revue* - FNN) - Extensive list of *rabid* bulls were quoted
June 8	-	Dow support at 2880
June 8	-	Sees 3250 over the next 12 months
June 12	-	Is very bullish (missed the 1000 point rise in 1987-89)
June 13	-	Extreme upside projections on Dow stocks and Dow 3100 in July
June 15	-	Dow headed for over 3000
June 16	-	Sees Dow 3200 ahead
June 16	-	Market will make a run to Dow 3000
June 16	-	Sees Dow 3400 ahead
June 16	-	August-September top foreseen
June 16	-	10% to 15% higher over next 2 - 3 months
June 16	-	Sees 3200 this year
June 16	-	Sees Dow 3150 and then 3500 long term
June 18	-	3000 in next two weeks
June 18	-	Bottom by Wednesday and then month-end strength
June 19	-	Sees Dow 4000 in next 18 months

Obviously the market has thrown a monkey wrench into the predictions of a near term move to Dow 3000. If one will do their homework they will note that it is pretty much a hard core of the same analysts who keep telling you that the Dow will cross 3000 this quarter. So another quarter is about to end with no Dow 3000. Obviously those analysts are not technicians because the current market breakdown is similar to October 1989 and January 1990. But this time it is far worse because the broadening top is being completed.

The Dow has a far worse downside projection *if a pattern of declining tops can be recorded.* Thus I wouldn't be surprised to see a drop this month to around the 2820 level followed by a *failing rally in early July.* A failing rally means a rally that does not take the Dow to a new high. Thereafter, *I am looking for crash action.* But the market technically looks so bad, *I will add some shorts and puts now just in case the Dow lacks support at the critical 2800 level.*

I would hope that all subscribers have read the June 18th lead article in *Barron's* entitled *Endangered Species: Bears In a Bull Market.* I had capsuled the following highlights of my analysis to Kathryn Welling in my interview:

Technical Warnings

1. Virtually exact parallels with the 1929 and 1973 peaks
2. Exact 9-month lead time on intervals
3. Broadening top
4. Flagrant upside non-confirmations
5. Extreme weighting by 5 stocks accounting for half the rise
6. Excessive number of stock splits
7. Major warnings stemming from:
   (a) Contraction in new highs
   (b) Major A/D line warnings on all exchanges
   (c) The Transports
   (d) The Utilities

Conclusion and Forecast:

Latest rally was the last hurrah
No shorting until pattern of declining tops seen
Crash action highly probable

Bear market stretching from 1990 to 1992, Dow bottoming in April 1992

Recommendations:

Get quickly into 75% cash. If I am correct on the 1929 and 1973 parallels then we can look for an upturn in gold to accompany the 1990-92 bear market.

Since our internal indicators had all peaked in mid-May, the Barron's covers thereafter had provided some reliable indications of the market top. Their covers of May 28th and June 4th will serve as classics in that regard. The May 28th cover was headlined **Why Everything Is Fall-**

ing Into Place For IBM. Those who bought IBM based on that cover story have barely covered commissions. Then on June 4th the headline was **The Big Boys Still Love That Bull:** So their love affair is hot at the top.

June 28, 1990

17. *IN A BEAR MARKET THE BEARS ARE RIGHT*

Right now we have a record high short interest. In a bull market that would be a very bullish technical support for the market. But since we are not in a bull market, *it provides no technical support whatsoever.* Note that the Dow has dropped almost 100 points since that record high short interest report was published. The explanation is very simple. This is not a bull market. It is a bear market and *in a bear market the bears are right.* In my June 14th letter *I gave you proof that the short interest was very large just before the 1929 crash.* I provided quotes from the September 16th, September 26th, October 9th, and October 25th issues of the *Wall Street Journal* which related to the very high short interest.

Right now we have a majority of bearish market letters. In a bull market that would be a very bullish technical support for the market. But since we are not in a bull market, *it provides no technical support whatsoever.* The almost 100-point plunge in the Dow since June 15th saw a majority of bulls become a majority of bears. Some market commentators immediately jumped on that fact seeing it as signalling a market bottom. But they overlooked that critical difference. In a bear market the bears are right. I didn't ask subscribers to take my word for this. In the June 14th letter I quoted from the September 24th, September 26th, and October lst issues of the 1929 *Journals*. These quotes referred to the large number of bears that existed just a few weeks before the great crash. Of course, *in a bear market the bears are right!* Our current commentator who referred this week to the large number of bearish market letters also referred to the fact that this was a complete flipflop from a month earlier. The bells rang again. I saw in that another parallel. I will quote the October 1, 1929 Journal once again to stress that new point:

October 1, 1929

"Reading the market letters of forecasters, I find that 75% of them are bearish. They cannot see anything but lower prices. Most of these same forecasters were telling how much higher the market was going when stocks were at peak prices and optimism was filling the air".

Another commentator said this past week to not get concerned over these short term moves. He said that the way to play the market is to simply buy the quality stocks and put them away for the long term. Those familiar with 1929 pre-crash commentary will immediately recognize an exact parallel in that statement. Several statements were made to that effect in the *Journal* in 1929 just before the great crash.

Another interesting parallel is found in the current consensus opinion that when this current correction is over that the Dow will go to new highs. That opinion was published frequently in the *Journal* in 1929 just before the great crash.

I have made it as clear as possible in these letters that the June 15th Dow high was the last hurrah and *following that high are only failing rally attempts and then a total collapse.* My technical numbers have become progressively so weak that I couldn't wait for the completion of a failing rally in order to recommend going short and buying put options. Too much publicity of a market crash this fall is being circulated. From this I can only draw one conclusion. *It will happen sooner rather than later*, I have to see it that way because right now I am seeing too many parallels with September 1929 for collapse action to be delayed until September or October this year. With what I see ahead, nobody will want to complacently hold their stocks through the summer because somebody is looking for Dow 3249 in September while technically the market is already deteriorating too rapidly to lend any credibility to that type of forecast.

July 5, 1990

18. *FAILING RALLY*

We have now entered what the consensus believes will be an outstanding summer rally. *One of the more popular forecasts is for Dow 3249 by September*. I have a very different opinion and it is based on the market. I had forecasted an initial thrust to the downside following the June 15th Dow high, then a failing rally, then a total collapse. This forecast is based on technical warnings stemming from the high/low indicator, the advance/decline line, the Dow Transports, and the Dow Utilities. Most recent indications underscore the contention that time has run out on the Dow. I had first looked for a May-June decline. Those who only look at the Dow say it didn't happen. But those who look at the market see that it peaked in mid-May and that was followed by the expected June downturn. The very fact that the important Net Field Trend indicator peaked at +15 on

May 18th is technical proof enough underscoring the accuracy of the May-June downturn technical expectation. Now the stage is set for the Dow to follow those earlier indications of technical weakness, collapsing this summer instead of holding up until after Labor Day as so many expect.

A correct interpretation of the Climax Indicator sees not only that the Cumulative CLX topped out over a month ago, *but that the indicator is signalling an imminent break.* This is being written on July 4th and thus we could even be into it by the time you receive this letter on July 9th. You will see that the CLX rose to +12 on July 3rd as the Dow completed the fifth day of rally. However, what is less apparent is that on July 3rd the +12 CLX reading included *eight lower up designations*. To lose field trend strength the OBV designations must give us a true Up, a down, a lower up and then a lower down. Each day I record the true ups, the higher downs, the lower downs, and the lower ups. On July 3rd we had the highest number of lower up designations since June 15th, a total of eight. On June 15th we had six lower ups. The next day the Dow fell almost 54 points. So I see the stage as set for another sharp break.

Then noting some changes since the June 21st letter. We see large losses of strength in *American Telephone, Exxon, and Goodyear.* We see depressed stocks such as *Bethlehem Steel, Sears, and Union Carbide* showing bearish patterns and about to roll over to still lower prices. We note that *General Motors* is in a falling field trend. We see that only 3 Dow stocks made it to new OBV highs this past week.

Note once again that with full knowledge of the new record high in the short interest I am predicting a market collapse. This is one of the best of the 1929 parallels at work. As I underscored it last week, *in a bear market the bears are right*. Those who are banking on bearish sentiment to support their bullish outlook are doomed to failure for the same reason. Now here is another parallel with the 1929 market: As the market progressively broke down from the September 3, 1929 high, the *Journal* pointed out that *investors increasingly sought to buy those firms that had the proven earnings.* That was the exact headline in the *Journal* on June 29th. Then in the July 5th *Investor's Daily* (before paper changed name) appeared a subheadline: *Investors Sought To Buy a Piece of Companies That Were Posting Strong Earnings.*

When in doubt as to what to do, *try the mirror test*. Turn to the charts in the *Wall Street Journal* in the C section. Turn them upside down and look at them in a mirror and ask yourself if you should be buying or selling. Upside down in the mirror the charts look extremely bullish. The industrials are breaking out from a strong base, the transports are about to break out above a double top, and the utilities are also seen headed for a double top breakout. Now back in the real world the industrials are in a major top formation, the transports are about to break a double bottom and the utilities are likewise about to break a double bottom.

With all the talk about how powerful the rally was between April 27th and June 15th, note that the advance/decline line has only gone up a measly 586 since May 14th. That small increment of change accompanies the 90-point rise since May 14th and so obviously something is very wrong.

Probably the best evidence that something is very wrong is the new bear market lows being recorded every day in the *bank stocks.* I would remind my critics that the sell signal last August *coincided with the exact highs in the bank* stocks.

July 12, 1990

19. *And Give Us Our Daily Breadth*

According to the bulls, this is supposed to be a very hot summer market. One of them headlines his July letter **Firecracker Month! Upside Explosion Is In the Stars.** The most famous astrologer in America back in the 1920's was Evangeline Adams. Her fame was extraordinary and much of it stemmed from her stock market predictions. Probably her most famous forecast was given on Labor Day, September 2, 1929. When asked where the market was headed in the coming months, she replied that "the Dow Jones could climb to heaven." The very next day the Dow closed at a new record high of 381.17, *a figure not to be seen again for twenty five years!* Of course we live in a different time. The key question here is what did Evangeline Adams see in the stars right at the top that made her forecast a market climb to heaven? And the second question is: are the current astrologers seeing the same formation of the planets that fooled Evangeline Adams right at the top? I love to stare at the stars at night. While I can detect no heavenly forecast, I am getting some pretty stiff market warnings right here on earth from such mundane things as the high/low indicator, the advance/decline line, the Transports, and the Utilities. Those indicators give no hint of a runaway summer rise to such widely advertised levels as Dow 3249 by September. On the contrary, they warn of collapse.

After Richard Russell expounded on a number of weak technicals in this market, Bill Griffeth of FNN (later merged with CNBC) last week asked him why the Dow was still going up. I was dying to give the answer but there wasn't enough time on my segment. The correct answer is this: The identical question could have been asked of one in August 1929, January 1973, August 1987, or October 1989. The very fact that the Dow was still rising at those times *produced absolutely no market bullish proofs.* The technical warnings were already in place and those *warnings prevailed.* In retrospect, everybody would have gotten out of the market at those times if they had trusted the technical indicators and simply said "the hell with the Dow." *So we are at one of those key technical junctures where the indicators are telling you to tell the Dow where to go.*

I don't ask much of the market. I simply demand it to tell me the truth. I trust it in this regard and am doing my best to interpret it one day at a time. If a day is technically positive I want to see the industrials, transports, and utilities go up on good breadth and volume. Is that asking too much? So while the media is telling you every day about the great bull market in stocks, I am not seeing many positive days. *Do you realize that we have only seen the Dow industrials, transports, and utilities simultaneously close higher only four times since June 4th?* This is being written on July 11th before the close and so we might see the fifth in-gear day on the upside since June 4th.

There is a discipline to technical analysis. The very indicators that put me into the market in October 1987 for a 1000-point rise are the very same indicators that told me to get out of the market in August 1989. Those indicators are the high/low indicator, the advance/decline line, and the Dow transports. For the past ten months those indicators have trended lower despite the higher Dow! For those who insist on calling this a bull market, turn to the C section of the *Wall Street Journal.* There you will find the Stock Market Data Bank consisting of 25 indices (later became 26). *Now note that 16 out of the 25 are down on the year!* I am an old fashioned technician. I was taught that a bull market demanded that there be an expanding number of stocks making new highs. That was no longer true after August 1, 1989. I was taught that more stocks should be rising. That was no longer true after August 8, 1989. I was taught that the transports should confirm the industrials on new highs. That was no longer true after September 5, 1989. So every night when I say my prayers I always end with "and give us our daily breadth." That prayer has gone unanswered since last August.

On my hotline on Saturday, July 7th, I said, *"This coming week is most critical for the bulls because they must take the market up sharply because I see this coming week as their last chance to catch the brass ring. After July 13th the market heavily favors the bears."*

20. *Headlines*

In early July of 1990, a few days before an important cyclical Dow top, there were two references to investors concentrating their stock purchases in companies that were posting strong earnings and in stocks they hoped would be safe from negative earnings surprises.

Then we saw this same change of emphasis just prior to the peak in the 1990-93 cycle. Investors were looking for firms that perform well in a down market.

In the 1987-90 cycle the most intriguing question I had to answer is why could I so effectively have been bullish from October 1987 to August 1989 for a 1000-point advance and then justify my bearish posture from August 1989 to the summer of 1990? What went wrong? Technically nothing went wrong. The indicators that put me into the market in October 1987 at the bottom were the very same indicators that took me out at the true top in August 1989. But after the 1989 summer high, those indicators never remotely approached the 1989 highs and would not allow for market reentry.

The nub of the problem was simply this: As the Dow Jones Industrial Average was at the 2935.89 level on June 15, 1990, I asked: Does one bend a little and acknowledge a record market high and be bullish or does one cleave to the discipline demanded by technical analysis and correctly describe the Dow as masking the start of a bear market?

The discipline of technical analysis would accept only one answer. As I wrote in early July 1990, the major technical indicators would have had to record a dramatic improvement in order to change that bearish scenario. Here was the problem: A rising market logically demands that the number of stocks making new highs continue to expand. Such a required expansion ended on August 1, 1989 with 306 highs. A rising market also demands that more stocks go up than down. That was no longer happening after August 8, 1990. A healthy market also demands that the Dow Jones Industrials and Transports remain in gear on the upside. After September 8, 1989 those two averages were no longer in gear on the upside.

I would wager that not a single bullish analyst is even remotely aware of this startling fact that *582 big board common stocks are within a point of new 12-month lows!* If he was aware of this fact he couldn't possibly be a bull. *These numbers were last seen just prior to a stock market crash.*

Now keep in mind that while the Dow was thought by most to be a cinch to cross the 3000 level there were *475-500* stocks at new bear market lows! I simply bet on the latter. When I saw the number of stocks within a point of their highs drop over 50% on July 20th it was very easy to predict some kind of crash action dead ahead.

The numbers didn't lie. As expected, we were looking at the July Dow peak dead ahead.

July 19, 1990

21. ***Coming Down To Earth***

My advice to the market astrologers is to forget what is happening out there in outer space and concentrate on what is happening right here on planet earth. While they told you to expect a firecracker month this July, the advance/decline line is screaming NO WAY. In fact, as this is being written on July 18th, the advance/decline line is only up 100 on the entire month so far and that could be lost before the market closes. In other words, this month, which was supposed to record an explosive rise according to the astrologers, *is about to show more declines than advances and the month is over half over.* The advance/decline line, more than any other indicator, *is strongly suggesting a summer collapse in stock prices.*

When I was bullish from October 1987 to August 1989, *that was a technically genuine rise.* But when I told people to get out of the market in August 1989 after enjoying a 1000-point rise I was widely disbelieved. Yet there hasn't been a confirmed rise in this market for the past eleven months. This letter told you to sell when the advance/decline line was at the peak so there is no question that the peak in most stocks was reached last August. So I do not have to apologize about missing the obvious bear market rally since late April *because my followers have avoided far greater losses in most stocks since last August.* After all, this letter told you to get out of the bank stocks, for instance, at their exact highs last August. So I have to take strong exception with anyone who is proud of being bullish right through the period since last August. *Most stocks have gone down since last August so what is their pride based on?* Internally this market entered a bear market last August and now the 1990-92 *external* bear market is about to start.

So many of the bulls have tried to give you the impression as to how strong the market technically has been in 1990. *Nothing could be further from the truth.* I am going to show you here the advance/decline line comparisons with 1989. I show the month, the Dow points gained or lost, and the A/D line gain or loss. Then I show all of this for the year to date. The 1990 numbers will absolutely shock you!

Advance/Decline Line Comparisons

1989			1990		
January	+174	+4,322	January	-63	-5,793
February	- 84	-1,479	February	+37	- 44
March	+ 35	+802	March	+80	+651
April	+125	+2,221	April	-51	-4,263
May	+62	+2,418	May	+220	+4,471
June	-40	-569	June	+ 4	-550
July so far	+104	+2,612	July so far	+100	+123
1989 so far	+386	+10,515	1990 so far	+227	-5,405

Using technical analysis we don't seek to predict events. *But the technical condition of this market warned to expect sudden jarring news.* The bulls were so convinced that their scenario was correct that they thought they could sweep several technical discrepancies under the rug and get away with it. But the persistent warnings stemming from the advance/decline, new highs, and the transports have gone on for too long to be flagrantly ignored. *Don't ever go against the advance/decline line. It is still the most important of all indicators. That advice is based on painful experience, the deep regrets when I ignored A/D line warnings.* Not only is the big board giving A/D line warnings but the NASDAQ and Amex A/D lines are in similar bad shape. The Amex A/D line is about to make a new bear market low. This past week the sudden jarring news was the new budget deficit projections. It was so bad that the message is finally getting through. The time for fun and games is over and some tough decisions must be made in a hurry. And there is no room for error. So the key word of the 1990-92 bear market is out-of-control DEBT, our fiscal situation caught between a rock and a hard place.

July 26, 1990

22. *A MIDSUMMER DREAM*

The bulls had dreamed of Dow 3000 for so long that it never occurred to them that it was just that - *a dream.* Soon they will wake up screaming, jarred into the realization that it was a nightmare and time had run out on their projections of Dow 3100, 3200, 3249 etc. *How long did they think they were going to fool their followers into thinking that the technical condition of the market could support those sugarplum visions?* Any technician worth his salt knew the bearish implications of a trend of contracting highs since August lst, an advance/decline line that had been trending lower since August 8th, a declining trend in the Dow Transports since September 5th, a declining trend in the bank stocks since last August, and a Dow Utility average trending lower all this year. Any failure to recognize those proven technical guideposts, guideposts that have defined the market to have been in a bear market since last August, would label the observer as something other than a stock market technician. Tell somebody holding a bunch of bank stocks that we are in a major bull market and the Dow is about to explode and he won't even provide the courtesy of an audience, the numbers being so ludicrous. When I told people to get out of the market last August *Bank of New England* stood at $24 a share. Now it is 2-7/8. *Any analyst who has stayed bullish after August 1989 has taken his followers through a bloodbath-bank stocks, autos, defense stocks etc.* They have hidden behind the facade of the Dow-30 *while the bulk of the stocks trend toward new bear market lows.*

August 2, 1990

23. *AUGUST CATASTROPHE**

Just in case you have forgotten, here is the series of new stock lows leading up to the crash of October 19, 1987:

Date	12-Month Lows
October 7	54
October 8	78
October 9	89
October 12	112
October 13	88
October 14	123
October 15	189
October 16	327
October 19	542
October 20	1174

With a current number of 74 stocks at 12-month lows (July 31st), the reader may not appreciate the concerns of this writer. The reason for such complacency, of course, is that most people would never take the time and trouble to count the number of big board common stocks within a point or less of making new 12-month lows. This service does take the time and trouble and with 570 big board common stocks right now within a point or less of making new 12-month lows the extremes of mid-October 1987 are very attainable and could be very close, even just days away. We saw 118 new lows on July 23rd. Top that number and see 189 new lows, then 327 new lows, and then 542 new lows, *then you won't need any signals from here that a crash is imminent.*

Now think of this: You could never see a 3-day series of 189 new lows, then 327 new lows, and then 542 new lows *without many hundreds of stocks coming within that one-point range first.* Now the reader can begin to appreciate why I think *we could even be just days away from a major debacle, a meltdown, a catastrophe. With 570 stocks within a point of new lows, that is a bigger number than the actual number of new lows on October 19, 1987.* **SO WE ARE POTENTIALLY CLOSE TO DISASTER.** But what a buying opportunity such a collapse might offer. *So, be on your toes if you ever see that 189/327/542 combination show up for the new lows.*

NOTE - The very day after this letter was written **IRAQ INVADED KUWAIT** and the Dow extended the decline in the Dow to 635 points. So once again the sharp escalation in the number of big board common stocks within a point or less of new 12-month lows not only correctly preceded a major market decline, but one again associated with a **MAJOR EVENT**.

On September 6, 1929 the *Wall Street Journal* published the Babson warning. Babson stated that most stocks were not following the leaders. He cited about 40 leaders and then said that *out of the 1,200 listed stocks, 614 of them had declined in value since the first of the year.* That was reflected by the poor high/low indicator numbers.

On September 30, 1929 the following paragraph appeared in the *Journal:*

"We are now beginning to hear queries as to whether this is the start of a bear market. The people who ask this question seem to forget that *60% of the issues on the Stock Exchange have been in a bear market for nine months.*"

On October 5, 1929 the following paragraph appeared in the *Journal*:

"A writer has taken the trouble to compile statistics which show that if you purchased one share of each stock traded in on the Stock Exchange in the latter part of 1928 and sold out today you would be out of pocket."

So this is the very nub of Babson's famous warning. *If Babson was alive today he could underscore the precise things that bothered him back in 1929.* He would tell people that most stocks peaked nine months ago as measured by the high/low indicator and the advance/decline line, and he would tell you about the large number of stock splits. He would explode the myth attached to cash on the sidelines and the short interest. In short, since Babson is not alive, I will resurrect his warnings and show why I am repeating them now.

The bulls love to tell you how much cash is sitting around awaiting investment and they like to remind you that we are seeing the highest short interest in history. They also like to tell you that there are too many bears. I will now explode those myths by again turning to the *Wall Street Journal.* All those conditions existed just prior to the great crash.

On the subject of the high short interest

(Direct quotes from the *Journal*)

September 16, 1929

Because of the big short interest which is believed to exist in the stock market, it is the growing view that a good technical recovery is in prospect. So many of the traders turned bearish recently and out of stocks that the internal market structure is probably stronger than in some time.

September 26, 1929

Brokers who keep in touch with the situation tell you that the short interest is larger than usual. It has been the kind of market that induces short selling. The largest short interest is in the motor stocks.

October 9, 1929

Of course, the operations for a rally were aided by the technical position of the market which had become oversold in many directions by the bears, with the short interest larger than in some time.

October 25, 1929

Every important student of the market expresses the opinion that there is a substantial short interest in the market.

On the Subject of Cash Awaiting Investment

September 18, 1929

Everybody is buying. Can anyone expect anything else than a rising market with corrective reactions?

September 19, 1929

The public appetite for securities continues unabated.

October 2, 1929

But no one can say that industry is not on a very solid foundation, in better condition, in fact, than at any time in history. Corporations and individuals have more cash than ever before.

October 4, 1929

We are richer than ever before, with more surplus cash for investment purposes than ever before. The foundation for a prosperous 1930 is even stronger than it was a year ago.

October 22, 1929

There is a vast amount of money awaiting investment. Thousands of traders have been waiting for an opportunity to buy stocks on just such a break as has occurred over the last several weeks, and this buying, in time, will change the trend of the market.

On the Subject of Too Many Bears

September 24, 1929

There are many bears in the financial district. The so-called information services are strongly advising liquidation.

September 26, 1929

There are plenty of bears but many of them are temporary bears.

October 1, 1929

Reading the market letters of forecasters, I find that 75% of them are bearish. They cannot see anything but lower prices. Most of these same forecasters were telling how much higher the market was going when stocks were at peak prices and optimism was filling the air.

I could go on and on. The last point is especially interesting. When the market is at the top that is when most of the rosiest forecasts are made. Without mentioning any names, of course, we have the same people telling you right now with such authority why the Dow is going to 3250 and higher. A widely read columnist tells us on television why the Dow will be at 3100 in July and then tells you that he hears that Merck is going to 100, Procter Gamble is going to 100, General Motors going to 65, IBM going to 140-150, and General Electric going to 90. This type of TV coverage is irresponsible. The Wall Street Journal referred to this type of thing on September 20, 1929: "Price Projections - These forecasts are tame compared with those of the more rampant bulls."

Phase Analysis

24. *Reviewing the 1987-90 Bull Cycle*

Here we review the entire 1987-90 bull cycle to see how closely the market followed the standard phase descriptions.

This bull cycle began with a crash bottom on October 19, 1987, most indicators all bottoming simultaneously. Crash bottoms violently turn all sentiment indicators negative and thus we saw instant widespread *disbelief* that the market could go up. Crash bottoms comprise the most certain evidence that the market is starting a new bull phase, ready to climb the wall of worry triggered by the market smash.

The standard phase analysis was closely adhered to throughout the first bull phase. I saw that first bull phase as lasting from October 1987 to November 1988, a period of 13 months. That was a bit longer than the time I had assigned to most phases. I had used the 9-month phase as being standard but in later years saw an 11-month period as being closer to the norm.

Assuming that the second bull phase began in November 1988, that was in line with the time indicator that had stated that 10 to 20 months had passed since the last major bottom was confirmed. In this case 13 months had passed. Now I underscore here the most reliable phase identities as being tied to the high/low indicator. While there are some rare cases of individual new highs peaking in the first bull phase, I always felt more comfortable with the more common evidence of new highs peaking late in the second bull phase. So when I saw the very strong indications in May 1989 stemming from my stock counting technique which revealed 643 stocks within less than a point of new 52-week highs while the actual number was a mere 80, I knew we were then getting to be late in the second bull phase. The public was coming back into the market and the psychological background had turned to one of *belief.*

Having then seen a *potential* 643 new stock highs, I knew that we wouldn't see the peak in new highs until the *actual* number was at least above the 300 mark. Mentally I would then mark such a peak as the end of the second bull phase. I didn't have to wait very long. On August 1, 1989 we saw the peak in actual new highs at 306. Simultaneously the number of stocks within a point or less of new 52-week highs rocketed to over 800. One might have argued at that point that this was an indication that the number of actual new highs would keep rising, reaching maybe 400, 500, or even 600. But I quickly ruled that out because (1) crossing 800 stocks within reach of new highs was a *parabolic blowoff* and (2) crossing the 300 mark on actual new highs had in most cases signalled the peak. But the further proofs that we had seen the peak in new highs were quickly forthcoming. The very next day new highs contracted sharply from 306 to 156 and by August 14th had shrunk to 54, recording a contraction of more than 82%, triggering my 80% contraction rule.

The advance/decline line peaked on August 8th and now with my two major indicators as having peaked, I went on record with a sell signal on August 15th, 1989. The Dow made one final non-confirmed runup to the 2791 level followed by the mini-crash of October 13th. I saw that event as having officially ended the second bull phase.

The third bull phase lasted from October 1989 to July 1990, a period of 9 months. That saw the entire bull cycle as lasting 33 months, matching the number as described by the time indicator. In that final bull phase the market closely adhered to the standard bull phase three descriptions. The advance/decline line diverged throughout this phase, never getting back to the August 8, 1989 peak. The high/low indicator also exactly adhered to the standard bull phase three description. It never surpassed the 306 highs of August 1, 1989. It did match the description by making one final attempt to scale the earlier peak, getting back up to 159 on July 13, 1990.

The Dow Jones industrials adhered perfectly to the bull phase three description. Those blue chips were in their glory as they pulled away from all the broader indices. The final Dow peak came on July 16, 1990 at 2999.75. The entire bull cycle of 1987-90 was complete.

Not realizing this, the public in typical fashion remained bullish throughout bull phase three, responding to the psychology of *overbelief.* The smart money had turned bearish after October 1989, selling all their stocks to the bullish public.

Section VII
The 1990-93 Bull Cycle

The 1990 - 93 Bull Cycle

1. *Turning Bullish on December 4, 1990*

I had stated in November 1990 that if the Dow could better the 2580 level that I would turn bullish. On December 4th the Dow closed at 2579.70. Reliable internal measurements had turned overwhelmingly bullish. I saw the orthodox Climax Indicator jump to +18 with the Net Field Trend Indicator soaring to +17. The advance/decline line closed at the highest level seen since October 2nd, having rallied vigorously off the October 31st low. The A/D line had been declining from August 8, 1989 to October 31, 1990. I had stayed bearish through that long decline. On December 4, 1990 it was time to turn bullish.

Just a few days earlier, on November 29th, the United Nations had set the date of January 15th as the deadline for Iraq to get out of Kuwait. That date turned out to be the most publicized date in recent history. I had stated in the September 3, 1990 edition of *NEWSWEEK* that *when war broke out in the Persian Gulf that the stock market would soar*. Now the die was cast. The 15th deadline made war look inevitable by mid-January and *I made an unhedged prediction of a soaring U.S. stock market at that time.*

It is awfully difficult to change a market position. Having seen the maximum number of new stock lows recorded on August 13, 1990 and the Dow bottom on October 11, 1990, my staying bearish until December 4th had gotten uncomfortable. By then in my heart of hearts, I knew I was getting into difficulty. The advance/decline line had continued to fall until October 31, 1990 and so I was actually a little over a month past the point when I would have preferred to have turned bullish. *But always better late than never.*

John Liscio (then with *Barron's*) described my December 4, 1990 return to the bull camp in the December 17th *The Trader* column as follows:

"Joe Granville has also just recently shifted into the bullish camp, and the details of his dramatic Saul-like conversion make an interesting read. Back on Tuesday afternoon, December 4, with the DJIA down nearly 30 points just a half hour before the close, Granville was as happy as a honey bear. Suddenly, as you may recall, stocks turned violently positive, rallying more than 40 points to close 14 points higher on the day. Granville was storming about in a fury. The market had been tumbling even in the face of the Fed's decision to trim reserve requirements, now they had soared on a report on a British cable station that Saddam Hussein was ready to make a deal on moving out of Kuwait. To top it off, this British cable channel was owned by Rupert Murdoch, the Aussie media mogul who brought headlines like 'Skylab Misses Son of Sam' to the *New York Post*.

"No, I smell a rat," Granville wrote in his diary that evening in a white heat. "Just like I did in early August when Shevardnadze said Iraq would remove their troops from Kuwait on Sunday afternoon, Aug. 5. Well, they didn't and the Dow fell as much as 123 points during the next day. Like then, I think we are looking at the end of a bear market rally and I wouldn't trust any strength seen this month. I think we will look back in January to what is now happening and see it for what it is - a major bull trap."

"Yet when Granville's rage subsided enough for him to review his charts, he, too, had to admit he was looking at unquestionable technical power. The thrust that day had volume and breadth. Granville's Climax Indicator revealed that the number of volume breakouts on the upside far exceeded the downside tally, his Net Field Trend indicator showed that a total of 17 of the 30 Dow stocks were locked into an upward zig-zag pattern, the highest level since the Dow flirted with 3000 back on July 16. And something Joe calls his Crack Index which is the net count of the advances and declines among the 25 key indices printed every morning on page two of the "C" section of the *Wall Street Journal*, had risen steadily from a low of plus 11 on October 11, 1990, when the Dow stood at 2430, to plus 178 on Dec. 4. (The Crack Index also peaked, at plus 376 (back on July 16)"

2. *The January 1991 War In the Persian Gulf*

Preceded By a Countertrend
From the *Commentaries*

(Author's Note: January 15, 1991 was probably the most publicized date in recent history. That was the day of the ultimatum requiring Iraq's withdrawal from Kuwait. There was a growing fear of that date, a fear that war was inevitable. Technical analysis proved that such a fear was ill-based.)

January 2, 1991 - Wednesday Evening

The new year opened with a decline of 23.02 points in the Dow. This was seen to be a very bullish start for the new year. Most people have very short memories when it comes to the stock market. In the 1989 market we started the year with a decline of 23.93 points. Then immediately the market went up to new highs and kept trending higher for many hundreds of points until I got a major sell signal the following August. So obviously we need more evidence before anything troubling can be predicted.

The small drop in the advance/decline line neutralizes any downside sting.

The Climax Indicator fell to -11 and amazingly fell precisely to -11 in the opening decline of 1989. Not only that, but we had 12 higher down designations today so once again internal action was very positive.

The Net Field Trend indicator fell to +13, losing a field in *Merck* and a field in *Philip Morris*. Now hold your breath. On January 3rd, 1989 we lost four fields and got them all back two days later.

Most of the bank stocks rose today, responding positively to the lowering of the prime rate by several money center banks.

Reports of behind the scenes efforts to bring about a peaceful settlement of the mideast crisis saw bonds soar, and oil and precious metal prices plunge. I reported caveats on the golds despite the recent upside breakout.

So nothing happened today to change the current bullish opinion.

January 3, 1991 - Thursday Evening

The sharp pullback today to the Dow 2575 area failed to threaten the rising channel that has been in force since October. Only a move below the 2500 level would break that channel. The high/low indicator is the best existing evidence that the October lows will not be threatened. We saw this on Wednesday when a 23-point drop in the Dow only produced 11 new lows. *The advance/decline line presents good evidence that the current decline won't be serious.* For instance, Monday saw the A/D line rise by 422. Since then the Dow has dropped almost 60 points but the combined two-day drop in the A/D line is approximately 482 points. So the A/D line has only fallen a net 60 in the past three days.

I would still maintain that the market has a bullish surprise in store this month. Yes, we sustained some technical damage today but nothing that threatens the overall recovery. I could cite a number of examples of breaks that appeared to end the 1988 upswing: the 140-point break of January 8, 1988 and the 100-point break of April 14, 1988. Those breaks only presented rising bottoms and this is what I see following today's downswing.

The Climax Indicator fell to -16 with 11 higher down designations. The Net Field Trend Indicator fell to +11, losing a field in *Alcoa* and a field in *Coca Cola.*

I would sit tight here and await what I suspect will be a very strong recovery to spring from the 2500-2575 area.

January 5, 1991 - Saturday Afternoon

In an extraordinary demonstration of a technically strong and brief three-day market pullback, the high/low indicator and the advance/decline line are the best technical bets that Friday saw a probable bottom. First, the number of new lows showed an 11 - 16 - 21 series, great internal strength for a 67-point decline in the Dow. The advance/decline line was equally impressive, rising almost 100 on Friday and putting the line higher than an December 28th when the Dow stood at 2629. The Climax Indicator also supported the probable bottom, rising from -16 to -10 to record a key downside non-confirmation. Then the Dow itself traced out a bottom formation, falling to almost the 2550 level for a drop of over 20 points to only close down 7.42. The Net Field Trend Indicator remained unchanged at +11, gaining a field in *Exxon* but losing a field in *General Electric.*

The earlier drop and the strong attempted recovery following Iraq's agreement to meet with James Baker on January 9th underscored all current moves as more or less directly tied to war jitters as the key date of January 15th is approached. The now agreed upon date for a talk is the first time Iraq and the U.S. has agreed upon anything since the crisis began.

Once again, *my numbers strongly point to a bullish outcome this month.*

I am recommending the purchase of *Panhandle Eastern* April 10 calls.

As for the bank stocks, note that the *Bank Stock Index* has gone up every day this year so far.

January 7, 1991 - Monday Evening

The market today was a small essay on a great fear, everything underscoring the fear of war. The dollar, oil, and gold soared while the stock market tanked. So it is *a completely news-driven market*. Being so, *it is equally capable of being quickly reversed also on a piece of news.* But to quickly draw conclusions as to the ultimate outcome is a dice shoot. It would seem silly to panic on a 43-point decline *with only 40 stocks making new lows.* That is a far cry from the better than 700 new lows of last August.

Most stocks right now look better than the external market averages would imply.

The Climax Indicator fell to -19 *with 10 of these being higher down designations.* The Net Field Trend indicator fell to +9, losing a field in *Procter & Gamble*. Friday's adjustment for the loss of a field in *Woolworth* is included.

It may be difficult to avoid breaking the Dow 2500 level, *the level which represents the 50% retracement of the recent rally*, but if such a move lacks confirmation by the high/low indicator and the A/D line it will be a big positive.

Aside from the fear of war, concerns regarding the bank stocks are technically seen to be overdone. Now most of the bank stocks have bottomed, only Bank of Boston making a true down designation today. Since these make up the bulk of the current portfolio, today was not a bad day at all.

January 8, 1991 - Tuesday Evening

With one day before the critical Geneva meeting, the Dow could have fallen far more than the 13 points it did lose. But the decline was orderly and 13 of the industrial stocks actually rose while 1 was unchanged, a far different market than the one seen on Monday. This enabled the Climax Indicator to rise from a revised -18 reading to -10 today on the lower Dow.

The Net Field Trend indicator fell to +8, gaining a field in *Chevron* but losing a field in IBM and a field in *Sears*.

Also unlike Monday, the Transports rose 3.76 and the Utilities rose 1.26. In the final half hour of trading, there was a noticeable improvement in the advance/decline line as it cut a better than 500 deficit to roughly 366.

These improvements coming on the high side of the Dow 2500 level suggests that support at that level has been strengthened. However, if the Dow breaks under the 2500 level *it is well to remember that we are seeing here a very small number of new 12-month lows.* Today we only had 54 new lows. Stacking that up against the better than 700 new lows seen in August, one can make a case that the market is in a transition from bear to bull.

Bank stocks are still giving us trouble but that is typical of a group that is mostly seen to be in a bottoming formation. Today we were stopped out of Bank of Boston. New OBV lows were also seen on *Banc One, Bankamerica* and *Wells Fargo.* But we only lost *Bank of Boston.*

The market is longing to see what is on the other side of January 15th. I'm not sure I know, but I call your attention to the article in the *Journal* this morning headlined: *When Wall Street Says Sell It's Usually Too Late.* That certainly applies to bank stocks.

January 9, 1991 - Wednesday Evening

What a day, but nevertheless no surprises. Nobody expected any decision to be made today in Geneva. The real showdown is yet to come.

But hope springs eternal, the Dow rising about 45 points on hope *and then cruelly reversing 84 points on reality.* Nevertheless, the market is doing a job here. *It is turning virtually everybody bearish on this move under Dow 2500.* The majority was already bearish before today's reversal to the downside and *this decline sets up a major bear trap.* The big picture shows over 700 new lows in August, 375 in October, and 53 now. *It is incredible that today's large decline actually saw a contraction in new lows from 55 to 53.*

The Climax Indicator fell sharply to a climactic -22 while the Net Field Trend indicator fell to +5, losing fields in *American Express, Exxon* and *Primerica.*

The market would appear to be *very oversold* and may be about to give us a very bullish *selling climax. In any case, the market is seen to be soon to end the slide in as dramatic and sudden a fashion as it began on January 2nd and it all seems to tie in with the widely advertised date of January 15th.*

With this in mind, I would sit tight and not do a thing. *I am betting on a near-term market change for the better on or about that date, war not withstanding.*

January 10, 1991 - Thursday Evening

Capitalizing on an *oversold market* not facing any bothersome news, the Dow was able to rise over 28 points. Being on very light volume, there was very little that could be read into the day's action other than it broke the string of declines. But the pattern in the Climax Indicator underscored *a definite bottoming formation now at work.* This was seen in the sharp improvement from the -22 level to the -1 level. That lessens the likelihood of any lower CLX readings than -22, *a very interesting observation when facing an imminent war.* So the market is again suggesting that a collision may be avoided.

The Net Field Trend indicator fell to +4, losing a field in *Westinghouse.*

Fannie Mae acted well today and would consider purchasing the June 35 call options. *Merrill Lynch* jumped 1-5/8 today and there I am recommending the April 20 call options.

Half of our bank stocks rose today but these require great time and patience.

I liked the way *Bethlehem Steel* acted today, it moving out to a new OBV high for the year, a refreshing statement to make.

January 12, 1991 - Saturday Afternoon

The moment of truth is quick approaching and the market technically says it is capable of withstanding any major shocks without undoing the good work being done by the high/low indicator, the advance/decline line, and the Dow Transportation Average. The Dow surprised many by withstanding an afternoon decline on Friday only to close up, the second consecutive advance *and within four days of what would appear to be imminent war.* So regardless of which side of the aisle our emotions would lean us in these critical days, the bloodless verdict of the marketplace will dominate which way prices are headed.

The Climax Indicator declined slightly from -1 to -4 and against the background of Wednesday's -22 reading, *a bottoming formation appears to have started.* Once again, this market's ability to withstand new lows in the face of the most critical phase of the Persian Gulf crisis may be the market's most important message, *telling us that if there is war it is mostly already in the market.*

No field trends were lost on Friday, the NFI remaining at +4.

Again half the bank stocks rose and half declined. I am most impressed at this point by Friday's rise for *Bank of New York* and *Chemical Banking.*

January 14, 1992 - Monday Evening

One day away from Armageddon and we only got 66 stocks making new lows. That is incredible technical strength. Bullish change of pattern seen today. The Dow was down 43 at the worst but cut that drastically to close down only 17.58 points at the 2483.91 level.

The Climax Indicator only fell back to the -9 level and the Net Field Trend Indicator remained unchanged at +4. Last week's rise from an oversold -22 level to the -1 level on Thursday set up today's *classic bottoming formation.* Couple that with the relatively small number of new stock lows and the market is dictating technical strength right in the face of imminent war. *Maybe the market knows something.*

In any case, continue to hold all long positions but obey the stops. I expect a higher market by the time I get to Portland in two weeks.

January 15, 1991 - Tuesday Evening

The market largely marked time today, mesmerized by seeing the hours tick away toward the war deadline in the desert. Rather than prompting a wave of selling, the market did a perfect imitation of a market that is exhausted, very oversold. It seems like anybody who wants to sell has already done his selling. It also appears that if there is a war it is largely already in the market. These are all very positive observations and, fully in keeping with these, here we are on the verge of war and the market recorded only 59 stocks making new lows today. *That is incredible technical strength.*

The Climax Indicator rose from -9 to -5 while the Net Field Trend indicator fell to +3, losing a field in *Eastman Kodak.*

The bank stocks continued to pass through their baptism of fire but escaped all stop out levels. *Bank of New York* is showing price weakness but maintains a positive OBV trend. Believe it or not, the best acting bank stock so far this year is *Chase Manhattan.* It hasn't lost a penny, closing today right where it did on December 31st. *Manny Hanny* was down again but has enough OBV strength to avoid making a new low. *Wells Fargo* got hit and we missed getting stopped out by a quarter of a point.

Merrill Lynch rose to 21 today, the chart looking increasingly attractive. I had recommended the April 20 calls.

January 16, 1991 - Wednesday Evening*

The U.S. is now officially at war and that removes a big market uncertainty. Now the market is only concerned with how quick the war will be until victory is achieved. Sensing this, the market rose today, anxious to get the conflict over with. So the nervous market with a gain of 18 points underscores my scenario of better things ahead, the war notwithstanding. It underscores the validity of the Dow bottoming a week ago at the 2470 level when the CLX fell to a climactic -22 reading. Now any breaking of the 2470 level because of any initial selling wave based on emotion will lack confirmation by the high/low indicator. Today the CLX rose from -5 to zero. The Net Field Trend indicator fell to +2, losing a field in *Exxon.*

New stock lows came in at just 54, continually underscoring the current period as an excellent buying opportunity, war or no war.

Got stopped out on *Wells Fargo* today but most of the other bank stocks closed up. We are retaining the call options on these since there is time for some good recoveries.

New buy recommendations include *Alaska Airlines* and *Southwest Airlines*. Call options are the Alaska Airlines April 20 and Southwest Airlines June 17-1/2.

Fannie Mae had a nice upswing today and I am predicting new highs on that one.

The smart money is seen waiting for the start of the war to coincide with a buying opportunity. The war has now started.

(Footnote) -

The war in the Persian Gulf started at 7 P.M. Eastern Standard Time on January 16th. Early that evening Iraq launched a scud missile attack. Bill Griffeth (then with the *Financial News Network*) interviewed me that evening *and asked me if the scud attack turned me bearish on the market*, revealing a complete ignorance of technical analysis and so typical of media announcers who lack qualification to intelligently discuss the stock market)

3. *The December-January Explosion of 1991-92*

Preceded By a Countertrend
The Commentaries

November 14, 1991 - Thursday Evening

Today is considered to again be a technical victory for the bulls. The Dow cut a 17-point loss to less than 2 points which was equivalent to a gain for the day inasmuch as *Caterpillar Tractor* had fallen 3-1/8 points, accounting for approximately 6-1/4 points. *Without that one stock the Dow would have been up almost 4-1/2 points.* The A/D line was down by such a small amount that this key indicator remained within easy reach of another high.

The Climax Indicator fell back from +4 to zero. While there was some internal weakness in the industrials which showed four true downs, the Transports and Utilities easily promised enough technical strength to more than offset that and continue to push the internal CLX numbers to new highs. The Net Field Trend indicator reflected some of the industrial weakness by falling to zero. While *Merck* gained a field, *Boeing* lost a field and *Caterpillar Tractor* lost two fields.

Shoney's, still enjoying the technical fruits of the recent breakout above 18, forged ahead strongly today to 22. There is no key upside resistance until 32.

Favored*Marion Merrell Dow* moved up strongly to 32. Stock made a key bottom a month ago under 28. Dan Dorfman's advice to dump it yesterday coincided with my buy signal. I recommend the January 30 calls. In the same vein, favored *US Air*_today rose to 10-3/8. Dan Dorfman's advice to dump the stock triggered my buy signal, the chart showing a nice bottoming formation. Go for the March 10 call options.

No change in my very bullish outlook. I am looking for Dow 3200 by the end of this year and 3600 next summer.

November 16, 1991 - Saturday Afternoon

If it's obvious, it's obviously wrong. This was the fifth worst Dow decline in market history *but the more I saw of the Friday market the more I liked what I saw.* Here is the bullish technical evidence:

1. We got a new high in the *Early Warning Climax Indicator* by virtue of the high number of higher down designations.

2. We got a wide downside nonconfirmation by the A/D line. The Dow went 61 points under the October 25th low but the A/D line closed 1,019 higher.

3. My OBV numbers showed almost a perfect fit with the August 19th bottom.

4. Since so many Dow stocks showed either no designation or a higher down, over 77% of the total decline was seen to be *technically meaningless.*

5. The Standard & Poor 500 did not confirm the drop in the Dow.

6. The NYSE Composite did not confirm the drop in the Dow.

7. And amazingly, we saw 78 highs and 37 lows on this 120-point break.

So I would have to say that Friday's sudden plunge sets the market up for strong rebounds ahead. Friday was either THE bottom, or just an hour or so away from a Monday climax and reversal to the upside.

By always adhering to our rule of selling half our call options on a doubling and selling all the call contracts on a tripling, our followers have automatically been taking some huge profits prior to Friday's break, always forced to take some money off the table. We are not perfect. We took some big hits on Friday's plunge, stopping us out in a number of places, but this has happened before during this bull cycle and in each case we have weathered the storm and come out on top.

Now we move on to the second key call I made in 1991, preceded by brief *countertrend* action.

November 18, 1991 - Monday Evening

The Dow made the expected strong turnabout, closing up 29.52 points at the 2972.72 level on high volume. While the advance/decline line was negative on the day, all previous comments regarding the wide downside nonconfirmation remain true. The high/low indicator showed weak readings but those simply reflected the lows of the day and those figures did not bother me.

The Climax Indicator rose sharply from -17 to -2, in line with previous strong recoveries. The Net Field Trend indicator rose from Friday's

-3 to -2, gaining a field in *International Paper.*

The first message transmitted by the market today was the technical proof that this is not another 1987. There are far too many differences and that message was clear on Friday prior to the Monday opening.

Some of the better acting stocks in our portfolio today included *Elscint, Fuqua, Santa Fe Pacific, Pier One, Shoney's,* and *Marion Merrell Dow. Mr. Coffee* acted well today and I will write that stock up in the coming letter.

I expect the Dow to make new highs over the next two or three weeks and go on to 3200 by the end of the year and much higher next year.

I believe the 120-point break on Friday got rid of the corrective move that was scheduled for mid-November, taking place in the middle of the second phase of the current bull cycle. *Now it should be clear sailing for the rest of the year.*

November 19, 1991 - Tuesday Evening

Today looked like a carbon copy of the January 9th bottom. While down about 78 points at the low of the day, the Dow rallied in the final hour and a half to cut the deficit to 41 points with the Dow closing at the 2931.57 level. That closing rally ended at the highs of that rally with ticks well above the 500 level. The deficit in the advance/decline line was cut sharply from about 1400 to 1080, thus enabling that indicator to close well above the August 19th level, the level the Dow encountered support at today.

Not only did the late strength look good, but the Climax Indicator recorded a key downside nonconfirmation. It fell from -2 to -12 *but closed well above the Friday low of -17.*

So today we saw the low of this move and I would doubt if today's lows will be broken. *I think we have clear sailing for the rest of this quarter.*

So the three things that most impressed me today was the late rally, the Climax Indicator downside nonconfirmation, and the continuing downside nonconfirmations recorded by the advance/decline line, that indicator staying well above the August 19th level. Other areas of technical strength stemmed from specialist buying, the TRIN, and the put/call figures.

Like the first week of January 1991, as the market is falling the internal early warning numbers are making new highs and thus we can soon expect an early resumption of the higher market.

Excellent strength was seen in *Amgen* today as it closed at 56-1/4 after being down at 52-12. I would suggest the April 55 calls for risk accounts.

November 20, 1991 - Wednesday Evening

The 6-point rise in *Merck* today failed to adequately offset the weakness in most of the other Dow stocks. Nevertheless, the CLX fell from -12 to -14 but stayed well above Friday's -17 reading. The Net Field Trend indicator fell to -4, gaining a field in *Alcoa*, but losing a field in *General Motors* and losing a field in *McDonalds.* This time there was a *beneficial change of pattern,* gains being recorded by the Transport and Utility averages. We also saw gains in the American Stock Exchange Average as well as the NASDAQ.

There was a contraction today in the number of new lows from 70 to 35 and that was a positive.

The advance/decline line, while down moderately, nevertheless persistently stayed above the August 19th level. I would call attention to the chart of the A/D line shown in the current issue of *Barron's*. It points up this positive divergence very well.

I think the damage in the biotech stocks has been overdone. Today *Biogen* had a strong move, jumping from 38-1/4 to 41-1/4. I would suggest the *Biogen* April 40 calls for risk accounts. *Chiron* should be the next to move, it closing down today at 62-1/8.

I noted the firmness in such favorites here as *Elscint, Fuqua*, and *US Air.*

November 21, 1991 - Thursday Evening

I liked the action today because we are getting good sidehelp now from the Transports and Utilities. Better yet, *something big is about to happen sometime over the next four days.* I base that statement on the fact that we are following the same pattern I saw in early January just before the big upside explosion. Best expectation would be for another cut in the discount rate the day before Thanksgiving so as to encourage more Christmas buying.

Whatever it turns out to be, the current bottoming formation is classic and I look for an early resumption of heavy buying.

I noted that odd lot short sales were the heaviest since August 19th. *Latest poll shows two thirds of Americans looking for no gains in the economy next year.* A similar poll in the fall of 1987 had the same figures.

The Climax Indicator rose from -14 to -11. It wasn't a big improvement but seen to be enough to maintain downside nonconfirmations on any new weakness. The Net Field Trend indicator stayed unchanged at -4.

More firmness was seen in low-priced *Elscint* as it moved ahead today to 4-3/4. Low-priced *Mr. Coffee* was firm and looking good at 6-1/2. Favored *Chrysler* had a good day. *Marion Merrell Dow* rose to 31-1/8 and has had superior action during this market break. Low-priced *US Air* rose to 10-3/8 and I am banking on that stock to be one of the biggest surprises when least expected.

So I say we saw the lows on Tuesday at around the 2895 level in the Dow. Those waiting around for lower levels will be left at the gate.

November 23, 1991 - Saturday Afternoon

There is no doubt that my technical work detects a near-term upside explosion. I see it as *January - Deja Vu.* It is highly probable to start sometime between now and Thanksgiving. I see Friday's action as a successful test of the Tuesday low with support in evidence in the 2890s. However, if we don't hold here, there is more than enough evidence supporting the belief that the trading range will not be broken, Dow 2850 holding sacrosanct. *In any case, we will be released from bondage by Wednesday.* A bull cannot be held hostage for long with what I see ahead.

The media continues to expand on the negative news, CNBC-FNN all day on Friday featuring the Christmas Bust. We haven't even gotten to Thanksgiving yet and already they are out to kill Christmas. After this is all over, I will remind you who played SCREW-ge.

So we have the negative media, the successful test of Tuesday's lows, and a replay of January's numbers.

The Climax Indicator closed at -19 with the Net Field Trend indicator falling to -6, gaining a field in *Coca Cola*, but losing a field in *DuPont* and two fields in *Minnesota Mining*.

You will recall that on Thursday night I remarked about the firmness in *Elscint, Marion Merrell Dow,* and *Mr. Coffee.* Now check your papers. All three of those stocks moved up on Friday's 40-point market break. *Elscint* closed at 4-7/8. *Marion Merrell Dow* closed at 31-1/2, and *Mr. Coffee* closed at 6-5/8. These are among a select group of Arnold Schwartzenegger stocks, stocks showing strength in the face of weakness elsewhere.

So sit tight. *We will soon see some bullish fireworks.*

November 25, 1991 - Monday Evening

Technically, we saw a full court press today, successfully avoiding a rout. The Dow was down around 19 in the early trading and up over 12 in the afternoon. A late slide was scary with the Dow falling back to an 11-point deficit, but late firmness cut the loss to a mere 0.67. The down close was important because the Climax Indicator rose from Friday's -19 reading to today's -12 reading, recording a key downside nonconfirmation.

The Net Field Trend indicator fell to -7, losing a field in *Eastman Kodak.* While that looks like key weakness, it is well to keep in mind the NFI fell to -11 in July 1988 in that continuing bull cycle.

The Transports were down but continued to avoid breaking the October low. Utilities showed strength and thus the overall imprint of Monday's market showed some successful downside tests, the Dow once again closing above the 2900 level after being considerably lower in the morning hours. *So once again strong support was forthcoming in the Dow 2890's.*

Today's Arnold Schwartzenegger stocks included *Bank of Boston, Chrysler. Computer Associates. Fuqua, Panhandle Eastern, Santa Fe Pacific,* and *U.S. Air.* Strong upmove seen in newly recommended *Biogen.*

Elscint, Marion Merrell Dow and *Mr. Coffee* showed minor and normal declines.

If the Dow can close up tomorrow with supporting advances in the Transports and Utilities, the pre-Thanksgiving bottom formation will be complete and no more significant declines will take place this year.

This entire November correction has offered an excellent buying opportunity.

November 26, 1991 - Tuesday Evening

Further successful probing of the lows saw the market once again pass a very important test. For awhile it looked like the bullish validity of the Monday Climax Indicator had gone by the boards when the Dow temporarily plunged to a loss of 33 points. But the up closing of over 14 points at the 2916.14 level not only fulfilled my technical forecast of a significant change to the upside before Thanksgiving, but it is no longer necessary for any further downside tests of the extent seen today. The market tells us that the Dow 2850 level still poses maximum support.

The Climax Indicator rose from -12 to -5, an excellent rebound from Friday's -19. The Net Field Trend indicator jumped from -7 to -3, seeing a gain of two fields in Exxon and a gain of two fields in Sears. Note the change in Sears right in the face of today's weak numbers on consumer confidence.

I had said here Monday night that if we could close up today with sidehelp from the Transports and Utilities that the pre-Thanksgiving bottom formation would be complete *and no further significant declines will be seen this year.* So I officially proclaim a completed bottom formation.

These kind of market turns in the face of obvious bad news underscore very important advances to follow.

Again I cite a growing number of Arnold Schwartzenegger stocks, those issues which have strongly stood up in the face of the November correction. Today we saw stability in our favored *Bank of Boston, Chrysler, Computer Associates, Elscint, Fuqua, Marion Merrell Dow, Mr. Coffee, Panhandle Eastern, Santa Fe Pacific,* and *U.S. Air.* And I look for new strength in *Amgen, Biogen, and Chiron.*

I want to devote most of December to detecting the new market leadership, so stand by.

November 28, 1991 - Thursday Afternoon

The four market days I had assigned to something big taking place before Thanksgiving are now up *and a major turn for the better has been seen.* The technical signals currently being flashed are extremely bullish. The Wednesday market produced classical strength. Here are just a few of the technical proofs:

1. The Climax Indicator actually rose from -5 to -4, recording another key downside nonconfirmation.

2. IBM accounted for almost half of the 16-point decline and yet couldn't even record a down designation.

3. The Utility strength more than offset weakness in the Transports, eight of the Dow utility stocks recording true up designations. That hasn't been seen since August 6th.

The Net Field Trend indicator remained unchanged at -3.

Appearing on CNBC - FNN's *The Insiders* Wednesday night, I proclaimed the completed bottom and buy signal and called for a resumption of the uptrend with strength having the upper hand for the next nine months.

So with what we have here, *I would look for a rather dramatic rally dead ahead.* I don't know what news item will specifically trigger it other than the technical evidence for an upside explosion shown here.

Referring to the Arnold Schwartzenegger stocks, here are four selected issues culled from my list: *ARCO Chemical, Apple Computer, Biomet,* and *Cadence Design.* I would recommend purchase of the *ARCO*

Chemical April 35 calls, the *Apple Computer* April 50 calls, the *Biomet* April 45 calls, and the *Cadence Design* February 20 calls. If I could only go for one, my top pick would be the *Cadence* calls.

November 30, 1991 - Saturday Afternoon

This has been an incredibly bullish week from the technical standpoint. The news got steadily worse and the Dow industrials only dropped 8 points for the entire holiday-shortened week. The great strength in the Dow Utilities went a long way toward offsetting weakness elsewhere. *The net result was a completed bottom formation and a buy signal.* A week ago the Climax Indicator stood at -19. This past week with the Dow closing lower the CLX traced out the bullish pattern of -12, -5, -4, and -7. The very light holiday volume of 77 million shares on Friday contributed toward the bullish readings, avoiding a number of down designations.

So the small pullback in the Climax Indicator from -4 to -7 recorded another downside nonconfirmation *and sets the market up for a very strong rally ahead.* The Net Field Trend indicator remained unchanged at -3.

The advance/decline line almost drew even on Friday after being down sharply in the morning.

All day on Friday CNBC-TV kept reporting a string of bad news stories, especially highlighting the rumor of another Russian coup to start next week. The bears tried to draw a parallel with Friday August 16th.

But this was the quietest Friday seen in a long time and not one seen to precede a bad Monday. On the contrary, *a very strong upturn appears to be imminent.*

I was again impressed with the action in favored *Panhandle Eastern* on Friday, my favorite utility. Favored *US Air* rose on Friday in an otherwise weak Transport group. But to get this current market buy signal right in the face of the Dow Transport Average breaking under the October low is impressive indeed.

December should be a good month for the market.

December 2, 1991 - Monday Evening

Now the rewards come. Capitalizing on the buy signal recorded here, I stated on Saturday that *December should be a good month.* Not wasting anymore time, the Dow saw the lows for the day in the opening minutes and reversed from a 30-point loss to close up 40.70 points at the 2935.38 level. This was another test of the lows and a very successful one. It also underscored the fact that the breaking of the October low in the Transport average set up a *bear trap,* a trap that snapped shut today with authority. Again underscoring a very bullish signal, the Dow Jones Utility average scored a major upside breakout to a new high for the year and pulled the rug out from under most bearish arguments.

The Climax Indicator rose from -7 to +8. *While the majority of up designations among the industrials were lower ups, the momentum of the current upturn is expected to continue and that should produce some bullish abortions from lower ups to higher ups.* The Net Field Trend indicator remained unchanged at -3.

Numerous features underscored today's strong market. Among the utility stocks, my favorite *Panhandle Eastern* broke out to a new high for the year at 16-1/4. our January 12-1/2 calls jumped to almost 4 for a gain of 166%. Remember to clean out that position for a 200% gain at the 4-1/2 level. *Santa Fe Pacific* made a nice turn to 10-3/4 after being down to 9-7/8. We are in the December 10 calls, our biotech stocks did well, nice gains in *Amgen, Biomet ,and* others. *Cadence Design* looked good as it rose to 21.

Mr. Coffee firmed up to 6-1/2, one of the better looking low-priced stocks.

No further tests of the Dow 2850 level are in sight. A new rally is underway and it looks good.

December 3, 1991 - Tuesday Evening

The media doesn't have the remotest idea of what is actually happening now in the market. This market has registered a completely bona fide buy signal. Some have talked about going down again to test the 2850 level. The market never wastes time repeating something that is no longer necessary. The market has already tested the 2850 level twice and will not do it again on this move. The economy is slowly and subtly improving and 6 - 9 months from now will be roaring.

The market action today was very bullish, a well taken industrial pullback with the Climax Indicator only falling from +8 to +5. We haven't seen two back to back positive CLX numbers since the end of October.

The Net Field Trend indicator stayed unchanged at -3.

But the top feature today was the almost 24-point gain in the Dow Transport average. *That provided further technical proof that the recent move in that average below the October low was a bear trap.*

While the Dow Utility average fell a point, that average has been so strong that no down designations are possible on this pullback.

So all in all, the December 2nd upturn was not a bounce. It was the start of a very strong rally that will prove to be very painful for the bears.

Our star performer today was highly favored *Marion Merrell Dow.* The stock closed up at 33-1/4. I have an initial upside objective of 38. I have suggested the April 30 call options which are currently scoring nice gains.

The announcement of John Sununu's resignation after the close will be treated very bullishly by the market tomorrow. Whatever it takes to put this market up will take place.

December 4, 1991 - Wednesday Evening

I loved the market today. *I doubt if the market is capable of giving out more bullish technical signals than currently being seen.* The new high in mutual fund cash is a major bull signal. The put/call ratio numbers are going off the page along with the McClellan Oscillator and Aarms Index oversold signals. Besides all this, *Investors Intelligence* now records 36% bulls and 39% bears. These are exceedingly bullish numbers.

Today the Climax Indicator fell back to -5, seen to be a very normal pullback. The Net Field Trend indicator rose from -3 to -2, gaining a field in *Merck*, gaining a field in *Procter & Gamble,* and losing a field in *Westinghouse.*

With the 17.89 point drop in the Dow today, it is well to note that *Boeing* accounted for a third of the entire decline. Also it is noted that the advance/decline line only fell by a paltry 84, an exceedingly small decline for an almost 18-point drop in the Dow.

The Dow Transports fell 3.92 points but this was mostly caused by UAL.

I have a whole bunch of new stock and option buy recommendations. Here are the new options and of course the stocks are also recommended: Limited February 25, Lowes April 25, Mirage Resorts February 25, Molex April 30, Teledyne April 20, and Varian Associates February 35.

I am adding *Zenith Electronics* to the low-priced stock portfolio.

Biomet rose to 50 in the hot biotech group. *Cadence Design* jumped to 21-1/2. *Panhandle Eastern* rose to 16-3/8, a powerhouse stock and *US Air* starred in an otherwise weak airline group today, rising to 11-1/4. These were all hot stocks today.

So look for a quick resumption of the rally.

December 5, 1991 - Thursday Evening

The numbers today were much better than what they appeared to be. The Dow closed down at a new closing low on this move but the internal numbers showed wide downside nonconfirmations, *leading me to believe that the Dow 2850 level will hold.*

The number of new stock lows failed to go above the 74 figure recorded on November 22nd. These numbers have to be very closely watched now because if my market outlook is correct, we should soon see a further contraction of new lows and an expansion in the number of new highs.

The Climax Indicator fell to -9, a far cry from the -19 figure recorded on November 21st. The 65-Stock CLX showed a still more dramatic downside nonconfirmation, closing at -8 as compared with the -32 figure of November 15th. Despite what looked like a serious drop for the Transport Average, the almost 6-point drop in UAL accounted for the lion's share of the decline. Furthermore, all our most favored rail stocks rose, stocks like *Burlington Northern, Norfolk & Southern,* and *Santa Fe Pacific.* This strength, as well as a continued favorable mix for the Dow utility stocks, accounted for the better overall numbers.

So the decline today changed nothing in the positive outlook I have for this month.

Marion Marrell Dow continues to show independent strength, withstanding today's decline, closing unchanged at 33-1/8.

December 7, 1991 - Saturday Afternoon

The technical power of the current buy signal and market bottom is absolutely unmistakable. This was further confirmed on Friday when the Dow industrial average dropped 21 points to once again encounter strong support in the same area that checked the declines of November 26th and December 2nd. While the small decline in the Dow did see a new closing low on this move, the frequent downside nonconfirmations are nothing short of dramatic. On Friday the Climax Indicator rose from -9 to -6 while on the Dow 65 stocks the CLX rose from -8 to -3. This can best be appreciated by noting that on November 15th it stood at -32 while now at the lower Dow level it has improved to -3.

The Net Field Trend indicator fell to -4 on Thursday, losing fields in *International Paper* and *McDonalds* and fell further on Friday to -6, losing fields in *Goodyear* and *Union Carbide.*

The great side help coming from the utilities has contributed toward these significant downside nonconfirmations and has increased the validity of the current market bottom formation.

So this is the time to step back and again view the big picture. *A market that refuses to drop in the face of bad news is a market readying for a significant advance. The news on the economy has steadily worsened since June and yet the advance/decline line stays above the June 26th low.*

Stocks getting the banner headlines on Friday saw the holy trinity of the biotech stocks in the forefront, Amgen rising to 62-1/4, Biogen rising to 42, and *Chiron* rising to 63-3/4. *Biomet* closed unchanged at 48. Our Amgen April 55 calls have now almost doubled. Our Biogen April 40 calls are up 64%, and our Chiron April 60 calls are up 27%, all in a matter of days.

But the current darling of the drug stocks is our *Marion Merrell Dow*, rising on Friday to 33-5/8 and pushing the recommended April 30 calls to 4-3/8 for a gain of 46%.

December 9, 1991 - Monday Evening

The market will toy with you, tease you, twist you, and then give you pain, and then torture, and then enough of a case of sweats to make you consider changing your religion. Then it changes after you are limp as a rag and devoid of any more feeling or thought.

Today was that day. It was a day of many wide downside nonconfirmations. The Climax Indicator closed down at -7. The Net Field Trend indicator rose from -6 to -5, gaining a field in *DuPont*.

Once again I believe we can expect support in this area where the Dow has been three times over the past several days.

Believe it or not, *both the New York Stock Exchange Composite and the Standard & Poor 500 indices failed to confirm the drop in the Dow*, closing higher than on Thursday.

General Motors and *IBM* made new lows today and the decline in those two stocks accounted for 72% of the decline in the Dow. Both of those stocks are seen to be hooks, a smokescreen diverting attention from accumulation elsewhere.

Now again look at the big picture of what is happening here. On Friday we had terrible economic news and this morning we got the report of the breakup of the Soviet Union. *On those two days we see the NYSE Composite and S & P indices moving higher.*

Many favorites held firm today- stocks like *Marion Merrell Dow, Panhandle Eastern,* and *US Air.* Many of the biotechs continue to do well.

The Aarms Index or TRN is the highest I have seen in four years. I see the lowest block ratio in four years and I see the specialist ratio down 31% which is extremely bullish.

I would seriously doubt is there if much downside action left in this market.

December 10, 1991 - Tuesday Evening

I am pleased that we closed well off the low today. I don't know how many times the Dow has to test the 2850 level. Apparently today was the 4th test. It had to be considered successful since we closed at 2864.04, well above the 2852 level that the Dow had dropped to earlier.

The two stocks that had spearheaded the decline up until now reversed today to close up, General Motors rising 7/8ths to 28-1/2 and IBM rising 1-3/8ths to 86-1/2 on very heavy volume.

Such recoveries enabled the Climax Indicator to once again record a downside nonconfirmation, again seeing a -7 recorded today. *This now gives us a cluster of four consecutive downside nonconfirmations.*

I see additional evidence that the smart money is taking advantage of this decline while the public, as shown by the sharp rise in money market fund assets, is fearful.

The economy is not as bad as the media tells the public it is. In any case, the stock market is radically oversold and should have great difficulty in moving any lower this month.

As for stocks, newly recommended The Limited had broken out above the 27 level and is a continuing immediate buy for a near-term move to the 32 level. I am recommending the February 25 calls. Probably my favorite stock at this time continues to advance, *Marion Merrell Dow* rising 1/4 point today to close up at 34-1/8. There we are in the April 30 calls. Next resistance in the stock is the 38 level.

December 11, 1991 - Wednesday Evening

Since November 22nd we have seen no less than seven CLX downside nonconfirmations, four consecutive nonconfirmed downside moves ending on December 10th. So the reversal to the upside today comes as no surprise. It was technically clearly indicated. In the middle of the day the Dow got socked for a 24-point loss, dropping the average to around the 2839 level with the intraday low well below that. This was the bear trap that was so well signalled, the move well below the critical Dow 2850 level with a full recovery thereafter with the Dow closing up on the day at the 2865.38 level. This was the fifth testing of the Dow 2850 level and the most successful test of them all. No better proof than seen today completely validated the oversold nature of the market *as well as the imminent probability of a large move to the upside.*

Despite all the bearish sentiment, *the New York Stock Exchange Composite Average continued to close up on the month.* It stood at 207.75 on November 29th and closed on December 11th at 208.53. It puts the technical lie to the 31-point drop in the Dow so far this month. Something else I want to underscore: The entire decline so far in the NYSE Composite average is only 4.7%. That average reflects the prices of every stock on the New York Stock Exchange.

The Climax Indicator rose today from -7 to -1 while the Net Field Trend indicator rose to -3, gaining a field in *Coca Cola* and a field in *United Technologies.*

So we have seen enough technical evidence to say that no further significant declines are expected this month.

Recommended *Lowes* fell to 25-5/8 earlier today but closed strong at 27-1/4. Continue to buy the April 25 calls. Favored *Biomet* fell to 47 in the early trading but closed strong at 48-1/8. There I have recommended the April 45 calls.

December 12, 1991 - Thursday Evening

Based on the strong Wednesday reversal to the upside, I was looking for a large move to the upside today. I wasn't disappointed. As mentioned here on Wednesday, the New York Stock Exchange Composite Average stayed positive in December and was putting the lie to the decline in the Dow. While the Dow exploded higher today as expected, closing up almost 30 points at the 2895.13 level, the NYSE Composite average closed at the 210.45 level, almost bettering the 210.65 level recorded on December 2nd when the Dow stood at 2935.38. *So we have clear indications here that the Dow will continue to rally for the rest of the year.*

The Climax Indicator rose from -1 to +10 with the Net Field Trend indicator falling back to -4, losing a field in *Eastman Kodak.*

The Transport Average soared almost 40 points to close up at 1199.74, this move having very bullish implications. The Dow Utility average fell a minuscule .07, reflecting the drop in Arkla, irresponsibly bashed by Dan Dorfman and thus underscoring the stock as an important buy. I would recommend the immediate purchase of the February 10 call options. I think we will do as well in *Arkla* as we did in *Panhandle Eastern*, buying it while Dorfman bashed it.

The precious metals tanked today and I warn against a long involvement. I have methodically kept subscribers out of the precious metal stocks and continue to do so.

I liked the action today in *Bank of Boston* which rose 1/2 at 11-3/8. Keep your eye on *Computer Associates* at 9. It looks like a winner. *Chrysler* looked good at 11-1/2, jumping 1/2 point today. Biotech stocks again took on some technical muscle, *Biomet* and *Chiron* making feature advances today.

4. *The Trailblazers*

A review of the critical January 1991 and November-December 1991 markets reveals a definite pattern in the indicators. *Both periods saw indicators leaving a trail leading to an inevitable conclusion.*

1. A bullish conclusion always starts with weakness
2. Large number of higher down designations
3. Bear trap break below widely watched support level
4. Rising bottoms in key indicators
5. CLX downside nonconfirmations
6. Well defined fear
7. Relatively small number of new lows
8. CLX bottoms in -19 to -22 area
9. Bearish sentiment is widespread
10. Market very oversold
11. I take some heat
12. Must feel anger and frustration
13. Reversal to the upside

The above indications blazed a trail to a bullish conclusion following the January 1991 and November-December 1991 periods.

Trailblazers

1. A bearish conclusion always starts with strength
2. Large number of lower up designations
3. Bull trap breakout above widely watched resistance level
4. Declining tops in key indicators
5. CLX upside nonconfirmations
6. Well defined greed

7. Relatively small number of new highs
8. CLX tops out in the +19 to +22 area
9. Bullish sentiment is widespread
10. Market very overbought
11. I take some heat
12. Must feel anger and frustration
13. Reversal to the downside

The January 1992 Market Peak

The public came rushing into the stock market in January 1992. I was enjoying the huge rise coming off of the December 1991 bottom and by mid-January was telling my followers to take their huge profits. There had to be a single day that took me out of the bull camp. Most people would expect that day to be a big down day. Wrong. Market peaks are almost always signalled by a *loss of upside momentum.* What I saw on January 22, 1992 took me out of the bull camp. Here is what I sent out that night:

January 22, 1992 - Wednesday Afternoon

Today the Dow rocketed up 32 points to more than offset yesterday's 30-point decline. I saw no problems yesterday and thus the sharp rise today was *in keeping with what I expected. Today, however, is different.* I did not like what I saw in the market today. Not only did the Climax Indicator fall to zero on the rally, but I was shocked to see a contraction in the number of new highs to 76. We are getting close to an 80% contraction in new highs and that will produce a sell signal a couple of months from now. I think what bothered me the most is that I have loved this upswing for so long that I am not used to seeing some things I don't like. They are premature in their significance now, but nevertheless they are early warnings which must be dealt with down the road.

I think, at least over the short term, *that you are going to detect some changes in my attitude.* I am going to be very careful with any new buying and I am going to be *increasingly conscious of opportunities to take profits.* We had some gorgeous opportunities to do exactly that today. These are formula moves which have nothing to do with the trend of the market but if we get enough of those opportunities it will become a trend. Today my favored *Computer Associates* exploded for a large gain of 3-1/4 points to close at 15-1/8. That pushed our recently acquired April 10 calls to 6 for a 200% gain which now calls for liquidating that entire option position. The recently acquired April 12-1/2 calls jumped to 3 for a 200% gain which now calls for liquidating that entire option position. So by simply following the formula of taking excessive profits has automatically seen us taking a ton of money out of this market this month. *Excessive profits become an indicator.*

5. *The Widely Touted Summer Rally of 1992*

Virtually the cream of Wall Street analysts went on record looking for a big summer rally in 1992.

The Warning Given By Lower Up Designations

Prior to the onset of sharply lower markets, it is technically required that we see a large number of OBV lower up designations. Such evidence then sets the market up for a plunge toward a maximum number of lower down designations, thus completing giant downward zig-zag formation.

In the 1992 bear market we saw the following record of extreme OBV ups and downs:

December 30, 1991	41 higher ups
January 29, 1992	22 higher downs
July 1, 1992	24 lower ups

Seeing the large number of lower up designations occurring on July 1st, 1992, that technically bearish piece of evidence killed off any summer rally before it could even get started. My daily *Commentaries* got increasingly bearish:

July 1, 1992 - Wednesday Evening

The Dow closed up 35.58 points today at the 3354.10 level *in what appeared to be a classic bull trap advance.* And the Dow Transports soared 25.60 points to close at the 1341.37 level. These moves look like the completion of the return moves to the upside *and thus I see no further significant advance.* On the contrary, my OBV numbers are revealing *major internal failures.* We had a nice upswing in the high/low indicator today as well as in the advance/decline line but when measured against earlier highs, *these upswings are also seen to be terminal.*

The Climax Indicator rose to +10 on the new Dow high and thus that constitutes an upside non-confirmation. Of that number we had no less than 8 lower up designations and that has been the major technical characteristic underlining recent strength. Because of that, I see today's action as constituting a *classic bull trap.*

If a Dow stock goes up in price and there is either no designation or a lower up, then I consider that advance *technically worthless.* Today the better than 35-point gain in the Dow industrial average *was technically 76% worthless.*

The Net Field Trend Indicator fell today to -5, losing two fields in Exxon. Seeing that change on a day when the surface appearance of the Dow looked flawless, *also points to the bull trap.*

Fannie Mae closed at 62-3/8, thus stopping us out at 61-1/2. Rather than seeing this as the start of a new and significant upswing, it is interpreted as part of the anticipation of the Fed soon lowering rates, a move that could very well be followed by a market disappointment.

Bank stocks mostly rose again but there were no stopouts.

Gold stocks mostly did better again and this time we had some features. *Pegasus Gold* advanced to 15, bringing percentage gains to 20%. Our September 10 call options rose to 5-1/2, ballooning our percentage gains to 340%.

July 4, 1992 - Saturday Afternoon

The final hopes for the bulls were shot down in flames on Thursday. The Fed, quickly reacting to the surprisingly weak June employment numbers, cut the discount rate from 3-1/2% to 3%. The initial response was a 19-point gain in the Dow but that quickly gave way to a closing loss of over 23 points. The Fed would not have acted unless the economy was in deep trouble. That is what produced the later decline in the Dow, the bulls finally waking up to the realization that there will be no significant rise in corporate earnings. That was their last hope for new highs in the Dow. *The night before the employment report I warned of a major bull trap.*

The Climax Indicator fell from +10 to +1. The Net Field Trend Indicator rose to -4, gaining a field in *J. P. Morgan.* Greater strength was seen in the Utilities. The Dow Utilities saw *American Electric Power, Detroit Edison,* and *Houston Industries* all gain field trends bringing the Utility NFI to +4. But this is seen to be defensive action as investors are attracted to anywhere they can get a satisfactory yield. It has no bullish significance because we also had a strong utility contingent in December and the market was about to peak.

The price of gold is effecting a good looking upside breakout.

Equity mutual funds are down for the second quarter. Money market funds are up and gold shares are up. So we have our followers in the perfect posture, being in the money market funds and in gold stocks.

I think the implications of Thursday's shock to those leaning on earnings will carry through this coming week on the downside. It will dash the hopes of those looking for a summer rally.

The financial stocks were strong on the news but *I see the banks as in a major top formation.* I draw the same conclusion on *Fannie Mae.*

July 6, 1992 - Monday Evening

Foraging through a haystack of data, my internal numbers did not technically justify the better than 8-point gain in the Dow. Each segment had a message of its own. Industrials were so closely mixed, best seen in terms of the Climax Indicator which only rose from +1 to +2. So we have here the +10 reading of last Wednesday, the sharp drop to +1 on Thursday and the feeble recovery today to +2. As for the Transports, that average dropped more than 3 points and that put the market out of gear. Utilities were strong. I drew attention to that strength on the Saturday message but it reflects a defensive position and the struggle to acquire higher yields. I do not believe that that strength has any important staying power. The current strong readings for the utilities were also seen last December just as they were about to top out.

The Net Field Trend Indicator rose to -2 today, gaining a field in *Eastman Kodak* and gaining a field in *Exxon.* Offsetting numbers among the transport stocks rob these numbers of any particular bullish significance.

For a change, most of the bank stocks declined today. However, we were stopped out on *J. P. Morgan* but will retain the September 55 put options.

Gold stocks had another good day, the Newmonts looking particularly strong, *Newmont Gold* at 48-5/8 and *Newmont Mining* zooming to a new high at 51-1/4. That pushed our Newmont Gold August 40 calls to 9 for a gain of 177% and our Newmont Mining September 40 calls to 12 for a gain of 152%. *Pegasus Gold* closed up at 15-1/8, pushing our August 12-1/2 calls to 2-3/4 for a gain of 175%.

All in all, the market's response to the economic summit was practically a non-event.

July 7, 1992 - Tuesday Evening

I am on record that there will be no summer rally. Today the implications of last Thursday's reversal to the downside following the discount rate cut and the terrible employment report, brought home the message that without economic recovery there will be no earnings recovery and so the key plank in the bull's argument collapsed. Today the Dow rose about 12 points in the early trading and then encountered one selling program after another, dropping the Dow over 44 points to close down at 3295.17. I tried to make it clear that it didn't matter whether rates were cut last week or not. In either case, my numbers called for a market disappointment. Today put the month of July in the red.

The Transports reversed from a 6-point gain to a 6-point loss.

The strength is in the utilities but I would remind those who are impressed that we had similar strength in the utilities in late December.

The collapse of the U.S. dollar today is seen to be related to the implications of the parabolic curve in U.S. credit expansion. And the second day of the Munich G-7 meeting ends with no significant progress.

The advance/decline line cut the spread from the low and thus far no significant technical gains have been seen coming off the June low. The number of new highs bounced back to 102 today but that does not reflect the sharp decline following the recording of those highs. Thus we can expect another immediate sharp contraction.

Most of the bank stocks declined today but mostly by fractions.

Gold stocks did not act poorly today in the face of the normal retreat in the bullion price.

The Climax Indicator fell sharply from +2 to -10 and that looks very bad. The Net Field Trend Indicator stayed unchanged at -2.

Today we saw that persistent characteristic of this bear market, big name stocks taking big hits. *I look for more downside action immediately ahead.*

July 8, 1992 - Wednesday Evening

A late industrial rally cut an earlier 21-point loss to less than 2 points. However, that recovery carried with it no bullish implications whatsoever. The Transports got slammed for a loss of almost 25 points. Continued strength was seen in the utilities but that strength is seen to have limited life, similar to what was seen in late December.

The advance/decline line deficit was cut to 88 but nevertheless a downner. The high/low indicator reflected weakness, new highs contracting to 80 with new lows expanding to 53.

The Climax Indicator showed a meaningless improvement from -10 to -9. The Net Field Trend Indicator stayed unchanged at -2, *International Paper* losing a field and *Union Carbide* gaining a field.

Most of the bank shares we follow fell today while most of the gold shares we follow rose. Downside objectives on the banks see *Banc One* at 38, *Bank of Boston* at 16, *Bank of New York* at 26, *BankAmerica* at 31, *Bankers Trust* at 50, *Barnett Banks* at 26, *Chase Manhattan* at 20, *Chemical Banking* at 29, *Citicorp* at 14-1/2, *Mellon* at 31-1/2, *J. P. Morgan* at 40, and *Wells Fargo* at 52.

The Munich G-7 Summit concluded today. The market *response* to that Summit had to be classed as a negative.

This market is in a financial Bermuda Triangle and everything that the bulls think are pointing upward are actually pointing downward. I see no bottom in this market and no summer rally.

July 9, 1992 - Thursday Evening

Keeping the sharp rise in the Dow industrials today in the proper perspective, we must remember that we were up 12 points on Tuesday morning only to close down over 44 points, a 56-point reversal to the downside. Therefore I am not overly impressed simply because the Dow rose 42 points today to close up over 30. *This simply puts the Dow up 5 points for the month so far.* That is perspective. The Transports closed up almost 12 points but that is measured against a loss of almost 25 points yesterday. That is perspective.

If you will study the list of daily new highs you will note that *half of them are either preferred stocks or utilities*. Such a large defensive contingent is seen to be a bearish omen.

The Climax Indicator was only able to rally to a +5 reading and that is not impressive on a 30-point rise in the industrial average. Furthermore, out of 30 industrial stocks there are only 7 capable of recording true OBV highs. The other 23 stocks are all a technical drag, like a heavy anchor.

The Net Field Trend Indicator rose to -1, gaining a field in *General Electric.*

The late $1 rise in Comex gold to $349.40 was impressive. Should cross $350 tomorrow.

Bank stocks mostly moved higher, the only decliners today being *Banc One* and *BankAmerica.* But there were no further stopouts.

All in all, the market was not as strong as it looked on the surface.

What we are seeing here are simply return moves within the declining trend.

There are very few strong groups left and much of the strength seen today were bounces having no staying power. The evidence dictates remaining defensive.

6. *Alignment For Disaster*

Completely contrary to Wall Street's erroneous thinking, the important Net Field Trend Indicator in September 1992 traced out a pattern very similar to the one seen just before the 1987 crash.

Date	Dow	NFI	Date	Dow	NFI
10/ 7/87	2551.08	11	9/14/92	3376.22	-1
10/ 8/87	2516.64	0	9/15/92	3327.32	-3
10/ 9/87	2482.21	-2	9/16/92	3319.21	-5
10/12/87	2471.44	-3	9/17/92	3315.70	-6
10/13/87	2508.16	-2	9/18/92	3327.05	-5
10/14/87	2412.70	-5	9/21/92	3320.83	-4
10/15/87	2355.09	-12	9/22/92	3280.85	-4
10/16/87	2246.74	-13	9/23/92	3278.69	-7
10/19/87	1738.74	-14	9/24/92	3287.87	-6
10/20/87	1841.01	-15	9/25/92	3250.30	-7

But, aside from the NFI, other key indicators such as the Climax Indicator, Highs and Lows, and the Advance/Decline Line had yet to get into alignment. But what was lining up was foreshadowing a very bad market ahead.

Always dancing around in my head are the wild children of unrelated patterns looking for a home. I try to store away every statement, every idea, every theory I am exposed to. My diaries bulge with material of incredible value as well as bits of trivia which could prove valuable at some future date. Then comes the thrill when during a very critical period these jigsaw pieces simultaneously fit together to reveal a very clear picture of what lies ahead.

Let us examine a few of these jigsaw pieces and see the technique of how I fit them together prior to the October 1992 crash:

I remembered that Lou Ehrenkrantz made an interesting statement on CNBC-TV prior to the great downturn. He said that the next 100 points would determine the direction of the Dow for the rest of the year. Between

September 14th and 25th the Dow fell 126 points and the mold for the balance of the year was set.

Some years ago Ned Davis referred to a pattern that ended most bull markets. He talked about six weeks up, three weeks down, and two weeks up. That pattern was seen in September 1992.

Then in September 1992 George Lindsay's 3 Peaks and the Domed House pattern was seen to be a vain warning of trouble dead ahead. I had correctly attacked those who were using that pattern the year before. But now my numbers pointed to trouble ahead that wasn't there the year before. The Lindsay pattern called for a break to Dow 2900 and ultimately to 2350. That exactly fit my projections which called for the Dow to break 3000 by election day.

Then an ominous event took place on September 25th which signalled an imminent major stock market slide. *Medical Care America* fell almost 57%, collapsing from 58 to 33 on flat earnings. *What that single event was saying was that no stock in the market was safe any longer, especially the higher priced stocks.*

That event, more than anything else at that time, justified my sharp criticism of those TV market correspondents who would spend their time talking on the telephone every day with analysts who leaned so heavily on corporate earnings projections. That was a practice that had questionable value in bull markets but was a total waste of time in bear markets.

So these were some of the wild children jig saw pieces which came together in September 1992 to reveal the deep price chasm ahead, an alignment for disaster.

7. *MAJOR BUY ON THE GOLD STOCKS*

A Warnings of Things To Come

December 1, 1992 - Tuesday Evening

Today was seen to be decisive. It was a solid down day with no excuses. The morning trading saw a steep decline in the Dow of around 19 points before rallying back to the black. The afternoon saw an inability to rally, the Dow closing down 10.80 points at the 3294.36 level. Transports bucked the trend with a 7-point rise but loss of cluster power there equates with topping action. Utilities closed down. The advance/decline line stood practically unchanged but internal weakness among the Dow industrials was seen to be critical.

Further internal weakness was seen, more internal Up clusters being shot down. *General Electric* closed down and lost 6 ups, IBM closed down and lost 4 ups, and *United Technologies* closed down and lost 6 ups. That dropped the current cluster power indicator on the industrials from +27 to +17. Total losses in this indicator on the full 65 Dow stocks over the past two days is seen to be decisive.

The Climax Indicator fell sharply from +12 to +3, underscoring the warning value of the three consecutive CLX upside non-confirmations just recorded. The Net Field Trend indicator fell to a revised +4, losing *Coca Cola* yesterday and *Disney* today. The numbers today equated with June 2nd, one day off the high. With today being one day off a high, the numbers are pretty exact in saying this is very definitely a market top.

Watching the movements in the gold stocks very carefully these past few days, I am impressed. This time strength is coinciding with the strongest seasonal period of the year for the precious metal stocks. I am reinstating buy recommendations on the entire group of stocks. I doubt if this time we will be thrown off the horse.

December 2, 1992 - Wednesday Evening

Today the market fell again, the Dow declining 8.11 points to close at the 3286.25 level. Transports had a small 3 point rise and utilities fell again. So far December has been a down month with the Dow off 18.91 points from the recent November 30th rally high.

Stock highs contracted to 91, still a troublesome indicator.

The Climax Indicator fell from a revised +1 to -1. The Net Field Trend indicator rose to +7, gaining a field in *Allied Signal* and two fields in *Philip Morris*. The current OBV cluster power indicator fell again, declining from Tuesday's +17 reading to today's +7 reading. *Alcoa* declined, losing a cluster of five ups, and *Union Carbide* declined, losing a cluster of four ups. Significant changes were seen in *Coca Cola* and *Procter & Gamble*, each of those stocks recording three consecutive OBV lower down readings and thus the gain of 3 OBV ups in *General Motors* was lost in the shuffle. The trend is seen to be increasingly on the downside now among the Dow stocks. It is the general scarcity of these OBV up clusters among the Dow stocks which showed how quickly upside momentum evaporated.

The play now is definitely in the precious metal stocks. Most of these rose today. I am especially impressed with the action in recommended ASA. The stock advanced to close at 34. Next upside resistance is at 40.

Dow is now retreating back toward the 200-day line which was recently bettered. I will consider a closing back under the trendline as very bearish and that would increasingly underscore the recent November 30th Dow rally high as the pinnacle of a very important bull trap. The battle cry is sell into strength. The smart money is rapidly heading for the exits.

December 3, 1992

8. *CAVEAT EMPTOR*

As I look over my diary notes I detect a subsurface buildup of evidence pointing toward a significant decline ahead. My work supports all the bearish conclusions, all of them coming from quarters I respect. But first I want to list all the characteristics of the current market top formation and bull trap, what I had called in the last letter the Clinton bull trap. *Here are the current characteristics of that trap:*

Here Is What the Public Hears

1. *The Era of Good Feeling* - Under the impression that President-elect Bill Clinton will meet his obligations to keep all pre-election promises, there is a feeling in Wall Street and across the nation that good times lie ahead.

2. *The Economy Is Improving*

3. *The Public Is Pouring Money Into the Stock Market* - That is seen in money pouring into the stock mutual funds

4. *Experts Tell the Public to Buy the Low-Priced Stocks*

5. *Fear of Inflation is Virtually Non-Existent.* That explained the poor performance in the precious metals prior to their December 1992 bottom.

6. *Earnings Expected to Rise as Economy Improves*

7. *Short Interest At Record High*

8. *Strong Year-End Rally Expected and Spilling over Into January.*

Now these are the things the public sees and hears about every day on TV. They understand these things because they are spelled out in simple terms of apples and oranges by the economists. It is all boiled down to the one - two - three step conclusion of (1) The Economy Improves, (2) Earnings Rise, and (3) Stock Prices Rise. It is an easy concept to sell to the public and Wall Street is going all out in packaging the products attractively as possible.

Well, what is wrong with all this? Nothing if the timing was right, but the timing was not right.

December 17, 1992

9. *TECHNICALS SAY SOMETHING IS RADICALLY WRONG*

Once again Wall Street coaxed the public into the market right at the top of the rally, the invitation to buy reproduced on a wide scale by the media. The media made sure you heard all the good news of low inflation, the good looking producer price index, the good looking consumer price index, the good looking retail sales, the strong number from the University of Michigan, and the rave reviews coming out of the two-day Clinton economics conference in Little Rock as well as our early success in Somalia. But we don't read the market that way. Anybody who attempts to read the market in terms of news is doomed to disappointment and frustration. The market can only be read technically because that is the only language the market can communicate in.

Here is what the market is saying:

1. Rally started too soon to extend through December
2. Technical strength collapsed in late November
3. November-December rise was a countertrend rally
4. Trading pattern is up in the morning and down in the afternoon
5. This kind of weakness in December is not typical
6. Parabolic rise in the Nasdaq is terminal and it borrowed strength from January
7. Recent rally ended in a classic bull trap
8. Again breaking below the Dow 200-day trendline spells major trouble

(*Author's Note*)

My later research revealed that this era of good feeling which the heavy public buying of stocks the very next month *saw most of those January 1993 purchases showing a loss by January 1994.* So what the public heard in December 1992 was essentially correct, it nevertheless entrapped the majority into buying stocks just prior to their declines. What I was seeing at that time was the beginning of the identical technical sickness that was to later collapse the 1929 market, most stocks topping out while the public was blinded by the late bull market blue chip strength. The only way I could rationalize this confusing dual market response to the December 1992 technical indications was to show that the market was speaking with a forked tongue, correctly warning that the majority of stocks were headed lower while the blue chips would move higher in this bull cycle third phase.

10. *The Dyki Letter*

In March 1993 I received the following letter dated March 19, 1993 from Joe Dyki of Dearborn, Michigan. I reprint it here because not only does it exhibit a rare insight into the future of the market at that time, but the reference to a "once in 30 years occurrence" clearly implied that the market was heading for a serious blind spot, a distortion so serious that it could only be experienced in a transition period likened to my Bermuda Triangle example, the posture of the market just prior to a crash when everything turns upside down.

March 19, 1993

Dear Joe Granville,

"You may not remember me but I'm the guy who wrote you about two years ago with my thoughts on fundamental reasons why the economy would benefit from the Gulf war. (You were gracious enough to publish my thoughts with full credit.)

This time I believe you are right in your technical indicators that the market "should" go down but are too early. You are too early in that huge amounts of money are pouring out of money market funds into mutual funds (into stocks from there). As long as this continues the picture will be distorted and the market will go sideways or up; a market that "needs" to go down for technical reasons.

This is a "once in 30 years" occurrence that gives technicians grey hairs. The indicators you use are true but are subject to this gross phenomenon.

I have received many good ideas from you and now wish to share one with you. Watch the number of new lows on the NYSE. When we get to 60 to 70 it's all over and the "true" direction will reestablish itself (down).

How long? One week? 10 Months? I don't think anyone knows in that this is a once in 30 year type of distortion that does not lend itself to pure technical analysis. There may be 10% to the upside left (I don't think so but maybe). The point you make about reward/ risk says to me that I want to sidestep the market now and not try to make money either way. Preserve my capital, wait it out and make your money when the market breaks. It might happen so fast that you can't get aboard on the down side but at least you will not be one of the suckers left holding the bag as the market tanks. They never said market analysis was easy. Yes! The smart money is selling into this strength. I think you are one of the smartest technicians I know of.

Joe Dyki

11. ***Phase Analysis***

Reviewing the 1990-93 Bull Cycle

Here we review the entire 1990-93 bull cycle to see how closely the market followed the standard phase descriptions.

According to the Dow, the bull phase began following the October 11, 1990 bottom at the 2365.10 level. But the true internal bottom was recorded in August when the number of actual new lows skyrocketed to over 700. In that regard it was likened to a crash bottom. Certainly the 635-point drop in the Dow being squeezed into the very brief period of three months between July and October described the period as a violent correction rather than a bear market. Seen in retrospect, it was simply a brief break between two bull cycles.

The high/low indicator was the first to move in typical bull phase one fashion. My standard description had called for a climax in the new lows to have taken place sometime during the previous nine months with the number climaxing between 500 and 900. I was slow in responding to that indicator, having seen so many 1929 type indicators at work in the summer of 1990. But by December 4, 1990 I saw that the bull phase one identity was certain. The industrials and transports had both bottomed on schedule and the advance/decline line was acting in a very bullish fashion. Even the time indicator was on target, fitting the 4 to 4-1/2 year cyclic pattern.

But whatever market doubts I might have had prior to December 4,

1990, these all disappeared in plenty of time in order to fully benefit from the great Persian Gulf war rally that was triggered in January 1991. Prior to the war, it was easy for the public to be bearish, war fears having been generated after the August invasion of Kuwait.

General Motors did not adhere to the typical phase pattern. It showed a bottom around the 30 level in very early 1991 but didn't make its final bottom until it fell to 27 the end of 1992. By then the bull cycle was in the early part of phase two. The stock made one more higher bottom at 29 and then proceeded to go due north in the typical bull phase three pattern. The stock illustrated the wisdom of never completely relying on any one indicator. In this case one would have missed the start of the 1990-93 bull phase.

Having seen the typical bullish public *disbelief* throughout the 1990-91 bull phase one which lasted 15 months, it appears that January 1992 saw the start of bull phase two. The public acceptance of the rising market saw public *disbelief* becoming *belief* That change coincided with the peaking in a number of key stock groups, notably drugs and HMO's. So what was to become a great *dichotomy* and bring the entire bull cycle to its knees, saw this technical cancer getting its start in early 1992.

The major indicators continued to adhere to the normal bull phase two patterns. Serious upside non-confirmations were reserved for bull phase three. I didn't expect bull phase two to come to an end so soon, terminating at the October 1992 bottom. So while the public *belief* of bull phase two quickly translated to the start of public *overbelief* as bull phase three got underway in October 1992, my attention was increasingly focused on the worsening dichotomy which began to put so many stock portfolios underwater despite a rising Dow.

The serious terminal non-confirmations occurred late in bull phase three but the public *overbelief* in this highly speculative terminal phase blinded them to the mounting evidence that the smart money was heading for the exits.

The advance/decline line peaked late in bull phase three and that may have been a factor in extending that terminal phase beyond normal phase length. The high/low indicator followed the expected third phase pattern, consistently recording a substandard series of numbers for the new stock highs.

What was seen as the most serious loss of technical strength in that bull phase three followed the peaking of the Utility Average in early September 1993. The Utility Average began a serious declining trend from which it never recovered.

Fulfilling their typical bull phase three description, the Dow industrials were truly in their glory in the extended 1992-94 third bull phase. There were many occasions when it looked certain that the bull cycle was over, only to see the Dow industrials keep getting a new lease on life. That kind of action, while atypical in a normal bull phase three, was far more remindful of the more memorable peaks of 1929 and 1987. The common denominators of those highs were the solo walk by the Dow and the serious dichotomy which had captured so much of my analytical attention.

As the market entered 1994, bull phase three had kept going since October 1992, a long 15 months. That extended the full bull cycle since October 1990 to 39 months, a final peak long overdue.

When the Dow persistently keeps rising in the face of virtually certain bearish technical evidence, I describe that phenomenon as *blocked indicators*. Rather than validating a continuing bullish trend, it merely postpones the inevitable beginning of a bear market, but not for long.

Moving on, I want to talk about earnings and the great dichotomy so as to more clearly explain the dual nature of the market and how these subjects misled the public at the most crucial times.

Section VIII

Earnings - the Worst Of Indicators

Earnings - The Worst of Indicators

1. *Use Your Common Sense*

The tried and true basic method of success in the market is to buy low and sell high. Common sense dictates that that should also apply to earnings. One should buy on low earnings and sell on high earnings. But what do most people do? They predictably do the opposite. They are attracted to high earnings and generally come in at the high water mark in the stock. They continue to hold until they see bad earnings and then sell. Since it takes two to tango, the smart money sells their stocks to the public on high earnings and then buys them back after the public tires of holding them in the face of worsening earnings.

The earnings hook perfectly fits the three-phase market cycle. In a bull cycle the public doesn't get strongly bullish until the second phase. By the time the first phase of a bear market gets started, the public is buying right at the peak because of the high corporate earnings.

If I can prove that earnings are totally unreliable as a market indicator, then it logically follows that I can also prove that anything based on earnings is equally unreliable. The overused price/earnings ratio immediately comes to mind. Common sense dictates that the popular price/earnings ratio is a totally worthless gimmick, another tool designed to attract the public to buy stocks, and usually at the worst times. If there was a good correlation between corporate earnings and the price of the stock then it follows that all price/earnings ratios should remain stable. Instead, however, price/earnings ratios bounce up and down like ping pong balls. Yet the public accepts this indicator as having some validity when it is so easy to punch a fatal hole in it.

My anger regarding the subject is well anchored to the views of some of the most respected names in market history. I had the great privilege of working with Gerald Loeb back in my days at E. F. Hutton between 1957 and 1963. The first book I read after starting with Hutton was Loeb's great book *The Battle For Investment Survival.*

Here is Loeb's little essay on earnings taken from that literary gem:

2. *The Earnings Mirage*

It is revealing to look back at previous earnings forecasts and add up the score in light of subsequent actual results. A useful source for such information is *Standard & Poor's Earnings Forecaster*, published weekly. Much can be learned about the precarious nature and unreliability of such predictions by taking a hard look at the earnings forecasts made at the close of 1968 for the full year 1969. Naturally, estimates changed as quarterly figures were released, but an investor who pinned his hopes on some of these annual forecasts was very much disappointed with the outcome. As unsatisfactory 1969 earnings were made public, they caused some extremely sharp market moves- mostly down.

As an example of how very far from the actualities some of these forecasts turned out to be, note Penn Central. Analysts doing field research late in 1968 publicized 1969 estimates of $4.25 to $5.50 a share for Penn Central. The actual figures turned out to be earnings of just 16 cents a share. There were Chrysler estimates of from $5 per share to $8. The final figure was $1.87.

These two were especially wide of the mark. Likewise some analysts were talking of $3 a share earnings for MGM in 1969. The actual figure turned out to be a loss of over $6 a share. Time, Inc., earned $2.45 a share compared to estimates as high as $4.50. There were disappointments in many directions, including companies like American Smelting, Armco Steel. Certain-Teed and TWA.

A few declines in individual stocks occurred as some companies publicly announced changes in their method of reporting. The actual results were the same- they were merely reported more realistically to stockholders. One such example was Career Academy, which announced a retroactive change in accounting methods that reduced prior earnings by 50 percent. The stock declined over 50 percent.

Substantial market declines occurred in Astrodata, Memorex, Control Data, and others on disappointing earnings results. Astrodata dropped from 32 to 18 and later to 11. Memorex was down 24 points between sales.

Investors should learn from these figures how difficult it really is to forecast earnings correctly a year in advance. Yet some analysts and corporate officers attempt to forecast three to five years ahead.

It is almost as difficult to be right in a year of rising earnings as in one of falling earnings. In 1965, a year before the major TV networks went into all-color, I found corporate officers giving me projected profits that were sharply under the final results achieved.

A further hazard for the investor is that in too many cases the bottom line fails to report the actual operating profits for the period covered. The quality of earnings varies, depending on the degree of leverage in a corporation's capital structure. You need to look at the footnotes of the statements for the year and for previous years to make up your own estimate of what really happened. In some cases you will find nonrecurring capital gains. In cases where mergers have occurred, there may be many accounting loopholes. Often where management changes occur or where companies experience a bad year, they take excessive write-offs that will be written back up again as "profits, in a future year.

Ronello B. Lewis, well known financial counselor to management, in his book *Management Control Techniques For Improving Profits* comments on recognizing these accounting practices for what they are. He concludes: "Investors are to blame when they willingly purchase the shares of such companies without even noting the annual report or the footnotes in which some of the 'pseudo' elements are revealed."

The accounting-principles board of the American Institute of Certified Public Accountants issues a publication, "Opinions," for the purpose of correcting these misleading statements. The SEC and the NYSE also endeavor to correct misleading statements but the corrections come slowly and late. Some corporate managements have excellent forecasting records. Some have just the opposite. We know this, because much of what they expect is put into writing. Just keep a file and look back a year or so or check with your broker or investment counselor. It is worth the effort to check history.

The price actions of stocks are often warning signals. If the figures publicized suggest higher prices and if instead you see a sluggish or weak market, be doubly careful. We also know this because of the big blocks of stock liquidated after the release of disappointing figures. Control Data once lost practically half its market value in six weeks when earnings expectations were scaled down. On the other hand, big blocks of a company's stock are often bought at higher prices after unexpectedly good figures come out. The important thing to realize is that wide price movements, up or down, accompanied by high volume, usually indicate that earnings are, or shortly will be, more favorable or more disappointing than generally expected.

The price/earnings ratio has come to be a popular method of stock appraisal. Before you accept it, think over the unreliability of both factors. We have shown here how little dependence can be placed on the earnings portion of the ratio. The multiplier used, whether it be 10, 20, 50 or whatever, is even more unreliable. There are theorists and mathematicians who will tell you what the multiplier ought to be; but in the market it rarely is. The multiplier is more likely to be the product of investor psychology, and its swings are as wide as the difference between the mini and the maxi-skirt.

Earnings are the dominant influence on the actions of individual stocks. As Ron Lewis says, "Pseudo profits are a disgrace. And their existence is a weakness in our free enterprise system."

As for the investor, forewarned in forearmed!"

So that was Gerald Loeb's effective condemnation of earnings, stressing their unreliability and low forecasting value. What is particularly interesting here is that Loeb refers specifically to the rosy earnings forecasts which appeared in late 1968, an important market top taking place on December 3, 1968. Over the next few years mutual funds virtually collapsed by 1974.

In the 1990-93 bull cycle we saw the repetitive evidence of this. Zacks always prided their earnings rating service, stating that there was nothing more important than changes in corporate earnings. But if one will take the time to check out the relationship of earnings to the bull and bear market phases they will find that the market was the best buy on poor earnings and a sale on high earnings. I noted in my diary that Zacks was lowering earnings estimates on September 14, 1991 when I was so extremely bullish on the market. But then those who follow Zacks were getting more bullish on September 30, 1993 while profits had been surging in the third quarter of 1993. I was extremely bearish.

And now I move on to my friend Arthur Merrill who was keenly aware of what a poor indicator earnings are. He published one of the most amazing charts I had ever seen at the time, showing the strong tendency for the market to go down on rising earnings and to go up on falling earnings. I got his permission to reprint that chart in my 1976 *New Strategy* book. It best explains the market game, the battle between the smart money and the public. Here is that chart:

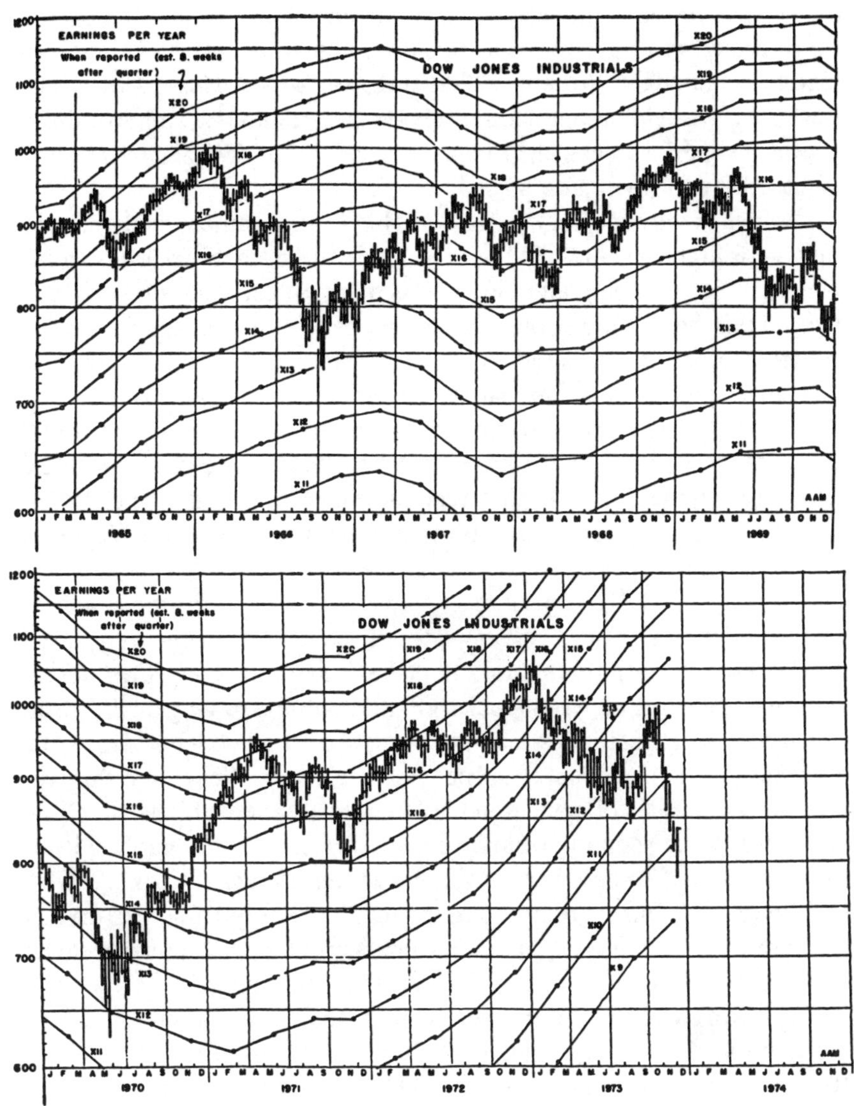

Chart Courtesy of Arthur A. Merrill, Technical Trends, Chappaqua, New York

3. *The O'Neil Propaganda*

Having proven that earnings provide no reliable indication of what future prices will be, never was this better illustrated than in the propaganda circulated by William O'Neil and *Investor's Business Daily*. They preach the gospel that one should rely on their ranking system for the selection of superior stocks. In O'Neil's book *How To Make Money In Stocks* appeared the following on page 172:

"Most of the superior stocks available for investment will generally rank 80 or higher on both EPS and Relative Strength. Since one is a fundamental measurement and the other is marketplace valuation, insisting on both numbers being strong should, in positive markets, improve your selection process compared to the old, unscientific methods of faulty opinions, academic theories, stories, promotions, tips, and touts."

Putting such undeserved stress on earnings not only attracts the public to buy at peak prices, but triggers smart money selling of those stocks, always the winners because they recognize the earnings trap and its function of seeing the public part with their money, always attracted to that poor indicator.

Here are the O'Neil peak ratings in January 1992 for the stocks we sold at those peak prices. What you will see here is a shocking revelation of the questionable claims that these extremely high ratings are helpful in selecting superior stocks. On the contrary, relying on E.P.S. and Relative Strength statistics is an illegitimate method which is dangerous, misleading, and irrelevant to proper stock selection. Never was this truer than in the internal collapse from the January 1992 stock highs which saw no helpful advice coming from *Investor's Business Daily* enabling investors to get out of *Amgen, Biomet, Choice Drugs, Circon, Datascope, Fifty Off Stores, U.S. Surgical* and so many hundreds of other stocks that had superior O'Neil ratings right at their January 1992 peak, precisely when those stocks should have been sold rather than bought.

U.S. Surgical most dramatically underscored the faulty O'Neil rating method, having been rated with a superior 99 on E.S.P. and 95 in Relative Strength on January 15, 1992, the stock responding to those superior ratings with a collapse from almost 135 down to 15-7/8 over the next two years, a crash of almost 119 points.

Stock	Jan. 15, 1992 O'Neil Rating E.P.S.	Rel.St.	We Sold In Jan.1992 At	Last	Decline Since Jan. 1992
Allied Clin Labs	99	91	40	20-1/8	-49%
American Claims	99	99	24	3-1/2	-85%
Amgen	95	93	80	35-5/8	-55%
Astro-Med	96	92	24-1/4	14-1/4	-41%
BMC Software	99	90	75-1/4	44-5/8	-40%
Ballard Medical	98	90	46-1/2	12-1/4	-73%
Biomet	97	93	32	10-1/4	-68%
Cambex	99	97	40-1/2	7-1/4	-82%
Cannon Express	96	96	24-1/4	7-1/2	-69%
Choice Drugs	94	99	11-3/8	3-1/8	-72%
Circon	90	97	50	15	-70%
Clearly CD Bv	94	94	27-1/4	8-1/4	-69%
Comprsn Lab	96	93	35-1/4	10	-71%
Cyber-Optics	99	98	14-1/2	4-5/8	-68%
Datascope	96	95	33	12-1/2	-62%
Deprenyl Research	91	94	19-5/8	2-7/8	-85%
Easel Corp.	99	93	41	9	-79%
Electromedics	95	92	9-5/8	4-1/8	-57%
Fifty Off Stores	99	97	27-3/4	7-7/8	-71%
Hauser Chemical	94	99	27-1/2	13	-52%
Healthcare Comp.	99	97	44	10-1/2	-76%
Healthinfsn	97	97	27-1/4	8-1/4	-69%
ILC Technology	99	92	23	13-1/4	-42%
Isco	98	93	25-3/4	14-1/4	-44%
Laser Precision	96	93	16-1/2	6-7/8	-58%
Merit Medical	94	96	21-1/2	5-1/2	-74%
NView Corp.	99	97	27	4-3/4	-82%
OI Corp.	97	94	17-5/8	6-1/8	-65%
U.S. Surgical	99	95	134-1/2	31-3/8	-76%
Value Merchants	97	92	38	4-3/8	-88%

And since these numbers were published, most prices worked still lower, notably *U. S. Surgical,* falling to 15-7/8, a percentage fall of over 88% in a stock that William O'Neil assigned a peak Earnings Per Share rating of 99 and a Relative Strength Rating of 95 right at the January 1992 peak price of 134-1/2.

But to prove the validity of the buy low - sell high concept when applied to earnings, I had to not only show that the majority of O'Neil's highest Earnings Per Share ratings were followed by declines, but that the majority of his lowest Earnings Per Share ratings were followed by advances. I presented that evidence in May 1993.

May 13, 1993

4. *The Dark Side of the Moon*

In the interest of educating my subscribers to the fact that there is very little validity in using corporate earnings and relative strength as an effective tool in determining where stock prices are headed, I demonstrated in my April 15th letter that many of the highest earnings and relative strength ratings published in *Investor's Business Daily* in January 1992 were followed by huge price declines. Now adding to the proof of my findings, I now look at the dark side of the moon and show what happened following the worst O'Neil earnings and relative strength ratings. My conclusions are simple and logical. Since I showed that the best O'Neil ratings often led to severe price collapses, it logically follows that the worst O'Neil ratings should often lead to worthwhile price advances. Here is the proof that that is precisely what happened:

The Worst O'Neil EPS Ratings In January 1992

Stock	EPS*	Price	Later High	Gain
ADT	34	7-1/8	9-7/8	+38%
Acme Electric	42	4-7/8	9-1/4	+89%
Arco Chemical	36	35-5/8	47-1/4	+22%
ARX Inc.	23	1-1/2	2-1/4	+50%
Affiliated Pubs.	18	9-3/8	14-1/2	+54%
Airlease Ltd.	42	9-7/8	14-3/8	+45%
Alex and Alex	29	22-1/4	28-7/8	+30%
Alexanders	11	24-7/8	59-3/4	+140%
Allied Irish ADR	42	18-3/4	24-3/8	+30%
Allied Product	12	3	9-3/4	+225%
Alcoa	41	62-1/2	80-5/8	+29%
AMAX	29	18-1/2	23-3/8	+26%
Amoco	43	48-1/4	59-1/4	+22%
Amrep	3	3-1/2	6	+71%
Anadarko	48	21-3/4	40-1/2	+86%
Ann Taylor	30	18-1/8	25	+36%
Applied Magnetics	18	5-3/8	14-1/2	+169%
Aquarian	41	22-1/2	27-7/8	+23%
Armco	21	4-3/4	8-3/8	+76%
Armstrong World	29	27-3/4	37-1/2	+35%

Asarco	36	20-5/8	31-3/4	+54%
Atlantic Richfield	46	108-3/8	127-3/4	+17%
Augat	14	8-7/8	15-1/8	+70%
BRT Realty Trust	48	2-1/4	4-1/4	+80%
Bairnco	34	6-5/8	9-1/2	+28%
Baltimore Bancorp	17	5-5/8	9-3/8	+66%
Bany Mtg Inv Fund	27	9/16	7/8	+63%
Berkshire Realty	18	9-1/8	12-1/8	+32%
Bethlehem Steel	20	13-5/7	20-3/8	+49%
Biocraft Labs	25	16-1/2	25-7/8	+56%
British Steel	9	12-1/2	15-3/8	+23%
Browning Ferris	43	23-1/4	28-5/8	+23%
Brush Wellman	30	12-7/8	18-1/4	+41%
Burger King	42	12-1/4	15	+22%

*E.P.S. is Earnings Per Share. The highest rankings possible according to William O'Neil are 99. In my *April 15th* letter I documented the fact that many of O'Neil's highest ratings on both E.P.S. and Relative Strength led to the most severe stock price collapses. Now here I show that many of the worst O'Neil ratings were followed by worthwhile stock price advances. The only reason why his faulty rating system is allowed to continue to be circulated is simply that nobody went to the trouble to successfully challenge it, which is now done here. *If the O'Neil rating system was valid then I have no technical stock market theory.*

What the O'Neil rating record shows is that stocks with superior earnings ratings and relative strength are often largely overbought and ready for a fall while stocks with poor earnings ratings and relative strength are often largely oversold and ready for a rise. I have so many examples of this that space does not permit a full review. A good example is *Synergen.* The stock topped out at 75 in *January 1992.* Right at the top *Investor's Business Daily* gave the stock a superior relative strength rating of 99. I got investors out of the stock at 71-3/4. The stock then collapsed all the way down to 8, a drop of almost 90%. *Now readers can understand why I never look at relative strength.* I do not consider it a technical indicator. It is a favorite indicator followed by fundamentalists. So much for fundamentalism. *It is not the way to read the market.*

So there is the evidence that the O'Neil rating system is highly unreliable. According to his book, he said to buy the stocks with the highest ratings and avoid those with low ratings. Well, many of the stocks with the O'Neil low ratings should have been bought and many of the stocks with the O'Neil high ratings should have been sold.

I get so upset when I see investors and traders get constantly misled by earnings. Brokerage firms actually have analysts for various sectors. For instance, an auto analyst, a drug analyst etc. Since earnings are published quarterly, what in the world do those analysts do to earn their salary for the next 89 days? And some of those analysts only follow 3 or 4 stocks. In stark contrast to this, *a technician has to cover the waterfront.*

Out of the 122 big board stocks beginning with the letter A, 74 advanced and 48 fell. Of the stocks having the highest O'Neil earnings ratings in January 1992, 62% of these declined. Of the stocks having the worst O'Neil earnings ratings in January 1992, 77% of these rose in price.

Out of the 151 Nasdaq stocks beginning with the letter A, 81 advanced and 70 declined. Of the stocks having the highest O'Neil earnings ratings in January 1992, 53% of these declined. Of the stocks having the worst O'Neil earnings ratings in January 1992, 75% of these rose in price.

And that of course completely invalidates such a ratings system as being no better than tossing a coin.

While I wrote these lines, Novell was again under pressure, falling to 18-1/8. But how many people will go to the trouble to discover that this stock peaked at 65 in January 1992. In the January 15, 1992 *Investor's Business Daily* it was shown that Novell closed at 63-1/4. It was also shown that the stock was given a superior rating at the top.

I constantly reminded my followers that most of their bad choices on stock selection could be traced to following corporate earnings, what I had always considered to be the worst of all indicators. Therefore, any rating system based on earnings is a very poor system indeed.

I wanted to show how *Investor's Business Daily* is usually unduly influenced by strong earnings reports, certainly no surprise inasmuch as the publisher of that newspaper is wedded to the importance of earnings, an indicator which I have proven here is of such dubious value. A classic example of this was *Apple Computer,* that stock peaking on maximum earnings expectations and optimism at 64-1/2 in January 1992 with earnings expectations being slashed amidst lowered ratings in July 1993 at 27-1/2. 1 covered this as follows in my July 22, 1993 market letter:

Since most people are told to buy stocks when the earnings look the best, I had completely documented that fact in my 1976 Strategy book that earnings are the worst of indicators. *Nothing has proven that to not be the case.*

Here I put *Investor's Business Daily* quotes regarding *Apple Computer* side by side. One will see how enthusiastic was the coverage by that paper at the top and how grim was their coverage at the bottom. One will note the comparative comments on earnings.

What *Investor's Business Daily* said about Apple Computer:

July 15, 1992
Price 64-1/2

"Apple, which has been trending higher for the past few weeks, is expected to report strong earnings next Thursday after the close."

"I think most people are expecting a good quarter because business trends remain very Positive," said Brown Brothers Harriman & Co., analyst Walter Winnitzki. He's looking for Apple to earn as much as $1.20 a share, compared with a year earlier's $1.28 a share."

"Demand for Apple's products has remained strong and the company's product mix is richer than people expected," said Winnitzki. The fall in the U.S. dollar should also contribute to higher earnings, he noted."

July 16, 1993
Price 27-1/2

"Several analysts slashed estimates following the disappointing earnings report. Citing a 16% decline in Apple's gross profit margin, analysts said it needs to cut costs further. They also doubt whether new products will have much of a bottom-line impact until 1995.

Walter Winnitzki of Dillon, Read & Co. sliced his 1993 earnings estimate to $2.45 from $3.95 a share, and lowered his 1994 projection to $2.50 from $4.25 a share. In fiscal 1992, Apple earned $4.33 a share. The stock should hover in the mid-20 range for the next few months, Winnitzki said. Technology stocks going through major transition periods normally trade at about 10 times earnings, he added."

It doesn't require a Sherlock Holmes to make some startling conclusions here. First of all, proving again the invalidity of basing buy and sell recommendations on earnings, we see *Investor's Business Daily* in January 1992 citing the expectation of strong corporate earnings while the stock is making a major top. So the fundamentalists were buying in at the top, impressed by earnings. In the second place, Holmes would have drawn attention to the fact that they were projecting higher earnings at the top and slashing earnings at the bottom. That explains why William O'Neil's rating system has put so many people in at the top since it is based on earnings. As here in the case of *Apple Computer*, earnings proved to be the flypaper that caught so many at the top. Thirdly, Sherlock Holmes would have noted that not only did *Investor's Business Daily* interview the same fundamental analyst again who was so wrong in January 1992, but it was apparent that Winnitzki *changed firms*. One can only speculate whether he was fired by Brown Brothers Harriman. That would be quite logical in the face of the Apple collapse. Fundamental stock analysis cannot compete with technical analysis. And finally, I suspect that *Investor's Business Daily* wasn't aware of the fact that they had chosen Winnitzki to interview on both occasions, *revealing their lack of memory*. In short, one should always keep a diary. But *Investor's Business Daily* would discover that by not keeping one, their most frequently quoted analysts were caught recommending key stocks in January 1992 right at their top, stocks that later collapsed.

5. ***Most Stockbrokers Are Fundamentalists and Follow the Herd***

Now to prove that most stockbrokers are fundamentalists and follow the herd, I want to demonstrate again how expensive stockbroker's buy recommendations can become. Here is a list of stocks most favored by 412 stockbrokers for large gains by mid-1993. The poll was conducted by the Rivel Research Group in April-May 1992. The table below also includes the William O'Neil Earnings Per Share and Relative Strength numbers at their 1992 peak and the July 1993 numbers for comparison. (EPS is William O'Neil Earnings Per Share rating and RS is the O'Neil Relative Strength rating).

6. ***Stocks Most Favored By Stockbrokers in May 1992***

(Table In Order of Preference)

Stock	Their 1992 Buying Price	July 7, 1993	Change	EPS	RS	RS	EPS
Philip Morris	85	48-1/8	-43%	96	68	87	8
Merck	52	34-1/2	-33%	96	82	86	16
Glaxo	31	16-1/2	-46%	96	88	62	10
IBM	100	48-1/2	-51%	27	18	22	11
Coca Cola	45	42-3/4	- 5%	91	81	84	85
Disney	41	40-3/4	- 0%	50	59	86	43
Telefonos de Mexico	52	47	- 9%	99	66	91	93
Walmart	30	25-5/8	-15%	96	79	91	17
AT & T	44	62-1/4	+41%	77	60	56	75
Boeing	40	36-3/4	- 8%	83	45	50	32
Microsoft	75	87-1/4	+16%	99	90	96	47
Pepsico	37	36-1/4	- 2%	62	66	66	24

Bristol-Myers	72	56-5/8	-21%	90	56	55	22
Syntex	40	18-1/8	-55%	80	80	41	11
Home Depot	40	43-5/8	+ 9%	98	90	96	43
Amgen	78	35-3/8	-54%	95	93	95	7
General Motors	44	43-5/8	- 0%	18	15	58	70
Pfizer	84	63-1/2	-24%	85	86	86	29
Nike	75	54-5/8	-27%	85	87	79	8
Abbott Labs	33	25-1/4	-23%	91	74	84	23

The average share price when recommended by stockbrokers in 1992 was $54.90. A year later in the early summer of 1993 the average share price was $43.30, showing an overall loss of 21%. Out of the 20 most favored stocks, 85% turned out to be losers. As for using the O'Neil Earnings Per Share rating as a guide, 75% of the EPS ratings on these 20 stocks were 80 or higher at time of purchase. Average Relative Strength ratings at time of purchase were 69. At the end of the comparative period with the lower share prices the EPS ratings were 13% lower and the Relative Strength ratings collapsed from 70 all the way down to 28, proving again beyond a doubt that both the William O'Neil Earnings Per Share ratings and Relative Strength ratings both proved to be totally unreliable.

Now let us see what the charts of those 20 stocks looked like at the time those 412 stockbrokers recommended them:

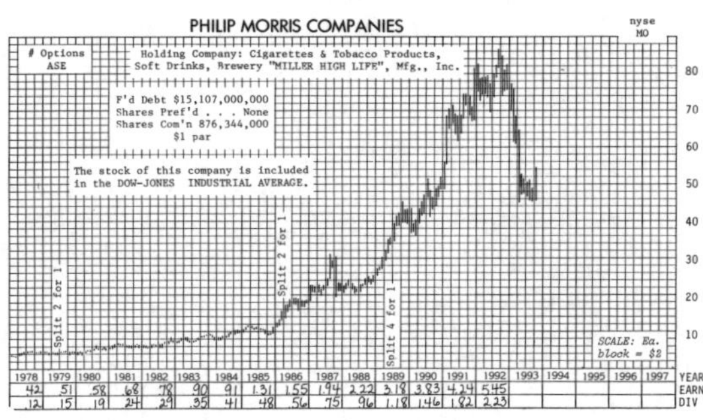

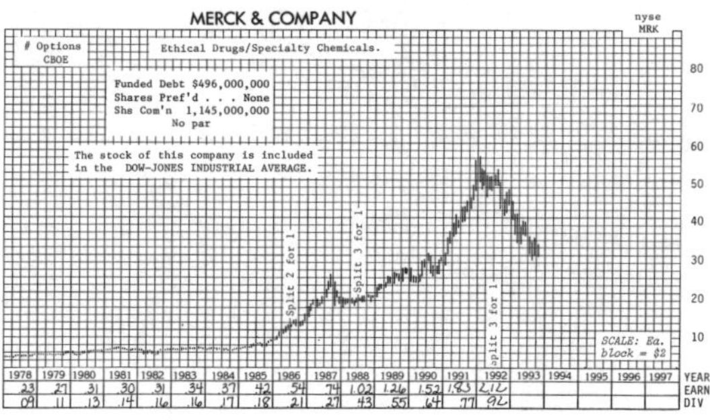

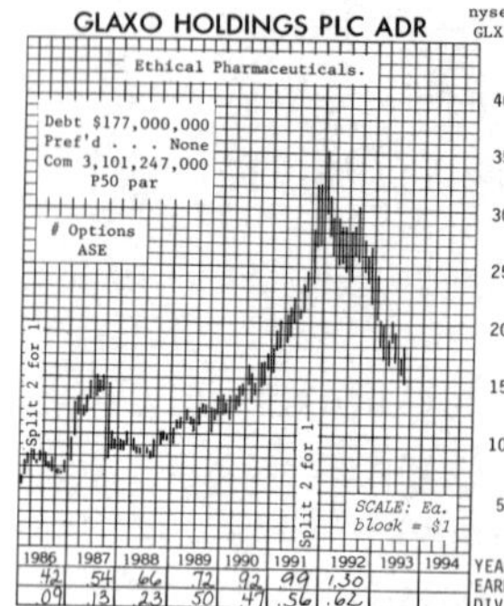
GLAXO HOLDINGS PLC ADR
nyse GLX
Ethical Pharmaceuticals.
Debt $177,000,000
Pref'd . . . None
Com 3,101,247,000
P50 par
Options
ASE
Split 2 for 1
Split 2 for 1
SCALE: Ea. block = $1
YEAR
EARN
DIV

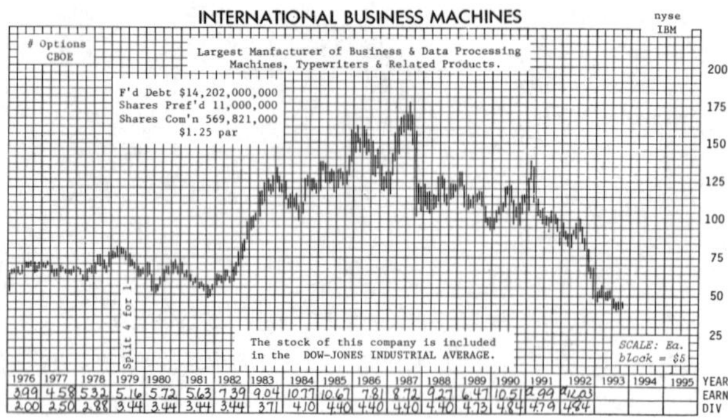
INTERNATIONAL BUSINESS MACHINES
nyse IBM
Options
CBOE
Largest Manfacturer of Business & Data Processing Machines, Typewriters & Related Products.
F'd Debt $14,202,000,000
Shares Pref'd 11,000,000
Shares Com'n 569,821,000
$1.25 par
Split 4 for 1
The stock of this company is included in the DOW-JONES INDUSTRIAL AVERAGE.
SCALE: Ea. block = $5
YEAR
EARN
DIV

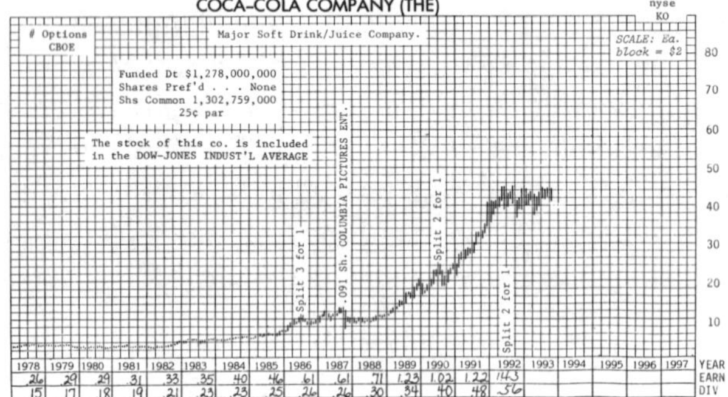
COCA-COLA COMPANY (THE)
nyse KO
Options
CBOE
Major Soft Drink/Juice Company.
SCALE: Ea. block = $2
Funded Dt $1,278,000,000
Shares Pref'd . . . None
Shs Common 1,302,759,000
25¢ par
The stock of this co. is included in the DOW-JONES INDUST'L AVERAGE
Split 3 for 1
.091 Sh. COLUMBIA PICTURES ENT.
Split 2 for 1
Split 2 for 1
YEAR
EARN
DIV

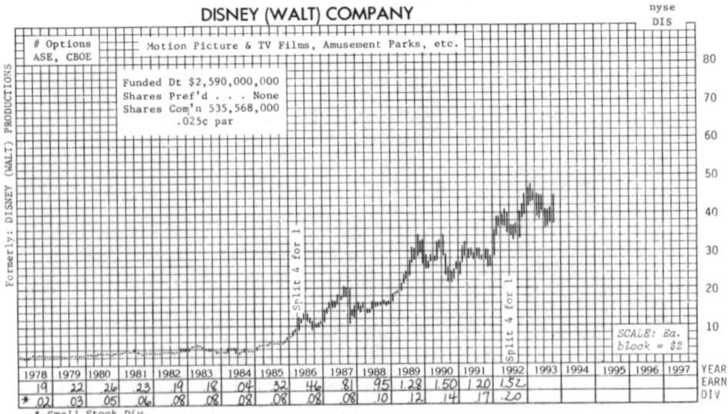
DISNEY (WALT) COMPANY
nyse DIS
Options
ASE, CBOE
Motion Picture & TV Films, Amusement Parks, etc.
Funded Dt $2,590,000,000
Shares Pref'd . . . None
Shares Com'n 535,568,000
.025¢ par
Formerly: DISNEY (WALT) PRODUCTIONS
Split 4 for 1
Split 4 for 1
SCALE: Ea. block = $2
YEAR
EARN
DIV
* Small Stock Div.

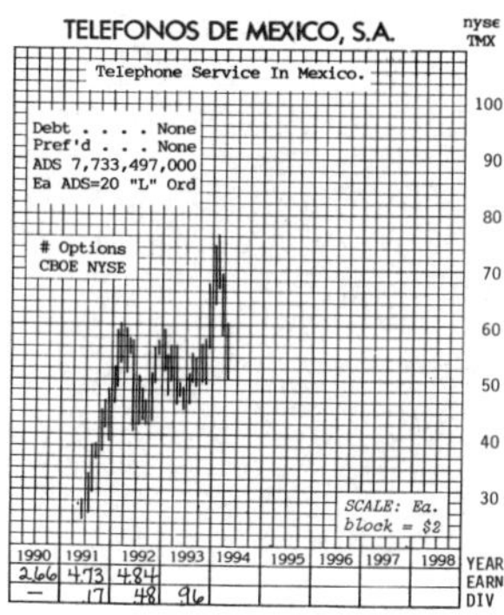
TELEFONOS DE MEXICO, S.A.
nyse TMX
Telephone Service In Mexico.
Debt . . . . None
Pref'd . . . None
ADS 7,733,497,000
Ea ADS=20 "L" Ord
Options
CBOE NYSE
SCALE: Ea. block = $2
100
90
80
70
60
50
40
30
YEAR 1990 1991 1992 1993 1994 1995 1996 1997 1998
EARN 2.66 4.73 4.84
DIV — .17 .48 .96

WAL-MART STORES, INC.
nyse WMT
Options
CBOE
Operates Discount Stores.
SCALE: Ea. block = $2
Funded Dt $5,579,000,000
Shares Pref'd . . . None
Shs Common 2,300,020,000
10¢ par
Split 2 for 1
Split 2 for 1
Split 2 for 1
Split 2 for 1
Split 2 for 1
Split 2 for 1
Split 2 for 1
SCALE: Ea. block = $1
40
35
30
25
20
15
10
5
YEAR 1976 1977 1978 1979 1980 1981 1982 1983 1984 1985 1986 1987 1988 1989 1990 1991 1992 1993 1994 1995
EARN .01 .02 .02 .02 .03 .04 .06 .09 .12 .15 .20 .27 .37 .48 .57 .70 .87
DIV NIL NIL NIL NIL .002 .003 .005 .008 .012 .016 .02 .027 .037 .051 .065 .08 .10

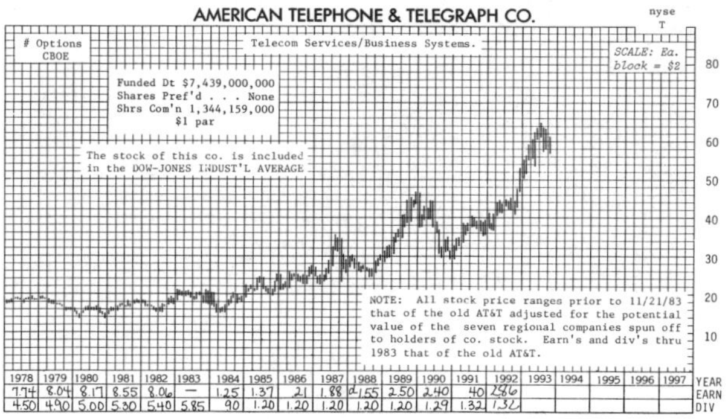
AMERICAN TELEPHONE & TELEGRAPH CO.
nyse T
Options
CBOE
Telecom Services/Business Systems.
SCALE: Ea. block = $2
Funded Dt $7,439,000,000
Shares Pref'd . . . None
Shrs Com'n 1,344,159,000
$1 par
The stock of this co. is included
in the DOW-JONES INDUST'L AVERAGE
NOTE: All stock price ranges prior to 11/21/83 that of the old AT&T adjusted for the potential value of the seven regional companies spun off to holders of co. stock. Earn's and div's thru 1983 that of the old AT&T.
80
70
60
50
40
30
20
10
YEAR 1978 1979 1980 1981 1982 1983 1984 1985 1986 1987 1988 1989 1990 1991 1992 1993 1994 1995 1996 1997
EARN 7.74 8.04 8.17 8.55 8.06 — 1.25 1.37 .21 1.88 d1.55 2.50 2.40 .40 2.86
DIV 4.50 4.90 5.00 5.30 5.40 5.85 .90 1.20 1.20 1.20 1.20 1.20 1.29 1.32 1.32

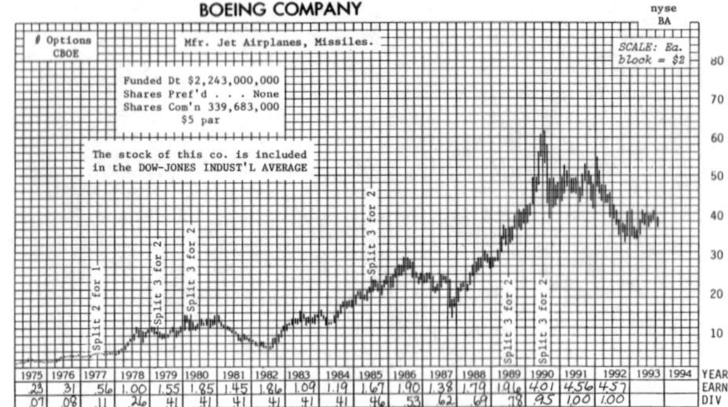
BOEING COMPANY
nyse
BA
Options
CBOE
Mfr. Jet Airplanes, Missiles.
SCALE: Ea.
block = $2
Funded Dt $2,243,000,000
Shares Pref'd . . . None
Shares Com'n 339,683,000
$5 par
The stock of this co. is included
in the DOW-JONES INDUST'L AVERAGE
Split 2 for 1
Split 3 for 2
Split 3 for 2
Split 3 for 2
Split 3 for 2
Split 3 for 2
80
70
60
50
40
30
20
10
YEAR 1975 1976 1977 1978 1979 1980 1981 1982 1983 1984 1985 1986 1987 1988 1989 1990 1991 1992 1993 1994
EARN .23 .31 .56 1.00 1.55 1.85 1.45 1.86 1.09 1.19 1.67 1.90 1.38 1.79 1.96 4.01 4.56 4.57
DIV .07 .08 .11 .26 .41 .41 .41 .41 .41 .41 .46 .53 .62 .69 .78 .95 1.00 1.00

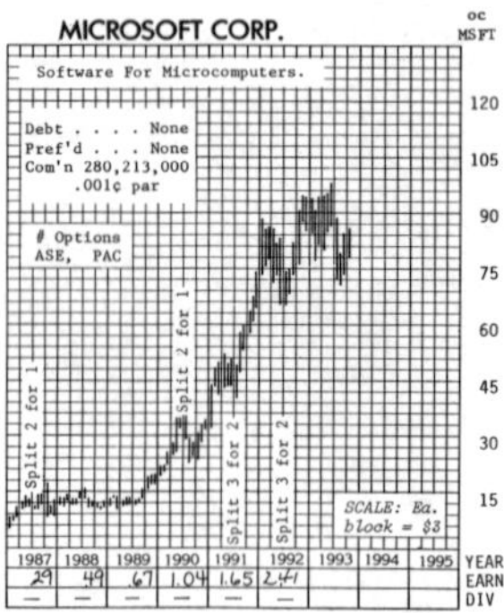
MICROSOFT CORP.
oc
MSFT
Software For Microcomputers.
Debt . . . . None
Pref'd . . . None
Com'n 280,213,000
.001¢ par
Options
ASE, PAC
Split 2 for 1
Split 2 for 1
Split 3 for 2
Split 3 for 2
SCALE: Ea.
block = $3
120
105
90
75
60
45
30
15
YEAR 1987 1988 1989 1990 1991 1992 1993 1994 1995
EARN .29 .49 .67 1.04 1.65 2.41
DIV — — — — — —

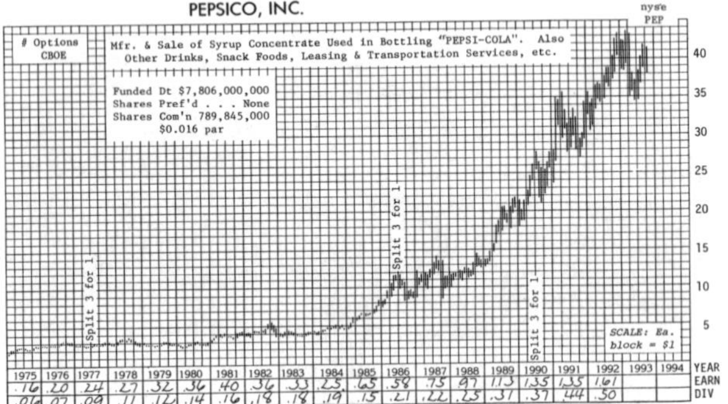
PEPSICO, INC.
nyse
PEP
Options
CBOE
Mfr. & Sale of Syrup Concentrate Used in Bottling "PEPSI-COLA". Also
Other Drinks, Snack Foods, Leasing & Transportation Services, etc.
Funded Dt $7,806,000,000
Shares Pref'd . . . None
Shares Com'n 789,845,000
$0.016 par
Split 3 for 1
Split 3 for 1
Split 3 for 1
SCALE: Ea.
block = $1
40
35
30
25
20
15
10
5
YEAR 1975 1976 1977 1978 1979 1980 1981 1982 1983 1984 1985 1986 1987 1988 1989 1990 1991 1992 1993 1994
EARN .16 .20 .24 .27 .32 .36 .40 .36 .33 .25 .65 .58 .75 .97 1.13 1.35 1.35 1.61
DIV .06 .07 .09 .11 .12 .14 .16 .18 .18 .19 .15 .21 .22 .25 .31 .37 .44 .50

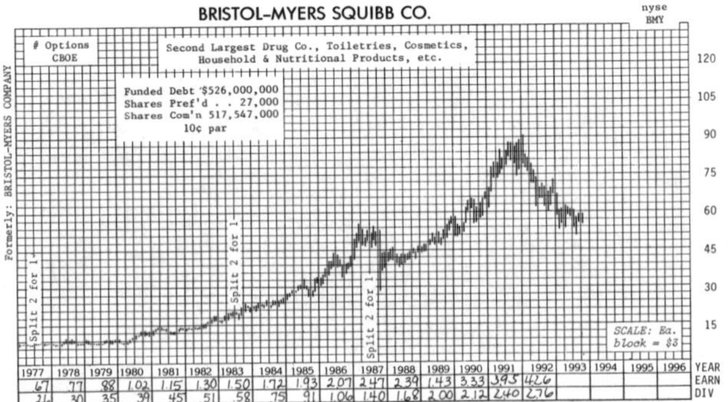
BRISTOL-MYERS SQUIBB CO.
nyse
BMY
Formerly: BRISTOL-MYERS COMPANY
Options
CBOE
Second Largest Drug Co., Toiletries, Cosmetics,
Household & Nutritional Products, etc.
Funded Debt $526,000,000
Shares Pref'd . . 27,000
Shares Com'n 517,547,000
10¢ par
Split 2 for 1
Split 2 for 1
Split 2 for 1
SCALE: Ea.
block = $3
120
105
90
75
60
45
30
15
YEAR 1977 1978 1979 1980 1981 1982 1983 1984 1985 1986 1987 1988 1989 1990 1991 1992 1993 1994 1995 1996
EARN .67 .77 .88 1.02 1.15 1.30 1.50 1.72 1.93 2.07 2.47 2.39 1.43 3.33 3.95 4.26
DIV .26 .30 .35 .39 .45 .51 .58 .75 .91 1.06 1.40 1.68 2.00 2.12 2.40 2.76

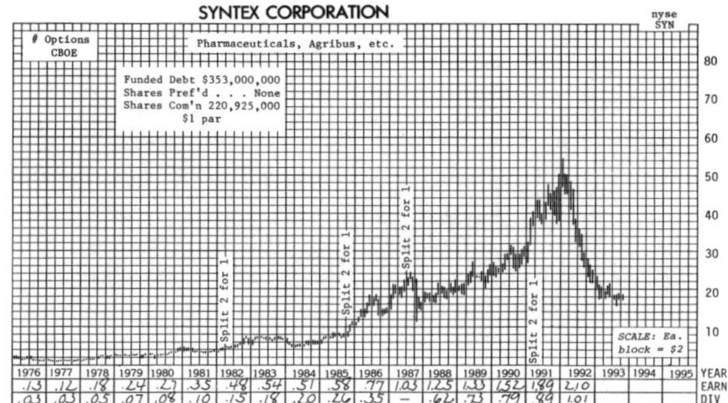
SYNTEX CORPORATION
nyse SYN
Options CBOE
Pharmaceuticals, Agribus, etc.
Funded Debt $353,000,000
Shares Pref'd . . . None
Shares Com'n 220,925,000
$1 par
Split 2 for 1
Split 2 for 1
Split 2 for 1
Split 2 for 1
SCALE: Ea. block = $2
80 70 60 50 40 30 20 10
YEAR 1976 1977 1978 1979 1980 1981 1982 1983 1984 1985 1986 1987 1988 1989 1990 1991 1992 1993 1994 1995
EARN .13 .12 .18 .24 .27 .35 .48 .54 .51 .58 .77 1.03 1.25 1.33 1.52 1.89 2.10
DIV .03 .03 .05 .07 .08 .10 .15 .18 .20 .26 .35 — .62 .73 .79 .89 1.01

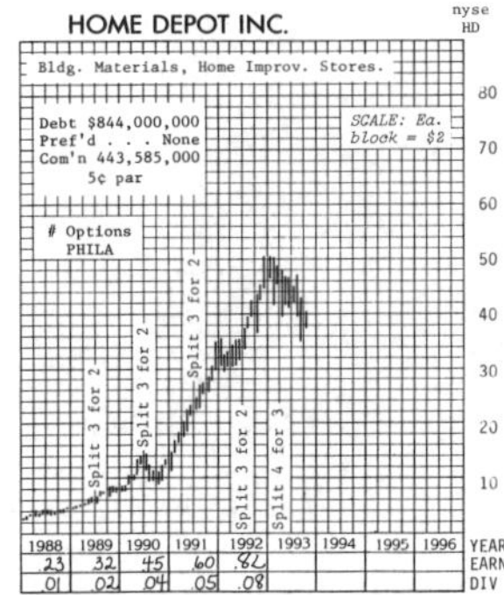
HOME DEPOT INC.
nyse HD
Bldg. Materials, Home Improv. Stores.
Debt $844,000,000
Pref'd . . . None
Com'n 443,585,000
5¢ par
SCALE: Ea. block = $2
Options PHILA
Split 3 for 2
Split 3 for 2
Split 3 for 2
Split 3 for 2
Split 4 for 3
80 70 60 50 40 30 20 10
YEAR 1988 1989 1990 1991 1992 1993 1994 1995 1996
EARN .23 .32 .45 .60 .82
DIV .01 .02 .04 .05 .08

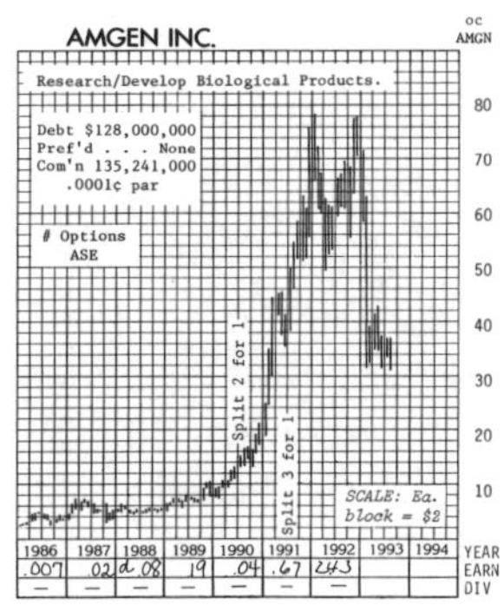
AMGEN INC.
oc AMGN
Research/Develop Biological Products.
Debt $128,000,000
Pref'd . . . None
Com'n 135,241,000
.0001¢ par
Options ASE
Split 2 for 1
Split 3 for 1
SCALE: Ea. block = $2
80 70 60 50 40 30 20 10
YEAR 1986 1987 1988 1989 1990 1991 1992 1993 1994
EARN .007 .02 d.08 .19 .04 .67 2.43
DIV — — — — — — —

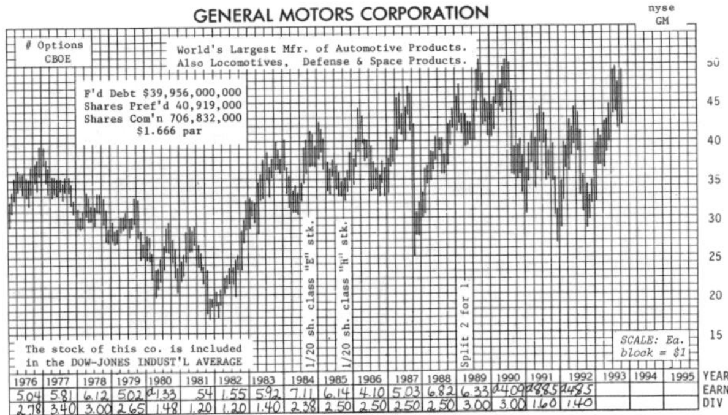
GENERAL MOTORS CORPORATION
nyse GM
Options CBOE
World's Largest Mfr. of Automotive Products.
Also Locomotives, Defense & Space Products.
F'd Debt $39,956,000,000
Shares Pref'd 40,919,000
Shares Com'n 706,832,000
$1.666 par
1/20 sh. class "E" stk.
1/20 sh. class "H" stk.
Split 2 for 1
The stock of this co. is included
in the DOW-JONES INDUST'L AVERAGE
SCALE: Ea. block = $1
50 45 40 35 30 25 20 15
YEAR 1976 1977 1978 1979 1980 1981 1982 1983 1984 1985 1986 1987 1988 1989 1990 1991 1992 1993 1994 1995
EARN 5.04 5.81 6.12 5.02 d1.33 .54 1.55 5.92 7.11 6.14 4.10 5.03 6.82 6.33 d4.09 d8.85 d4.85
DIV 2.78 3.40 3.00 2.65 1.48 1.20 1.20 1.40 2.38 2.50 2.50 2.50 2.50 3.00 3.00 1.60 1.40

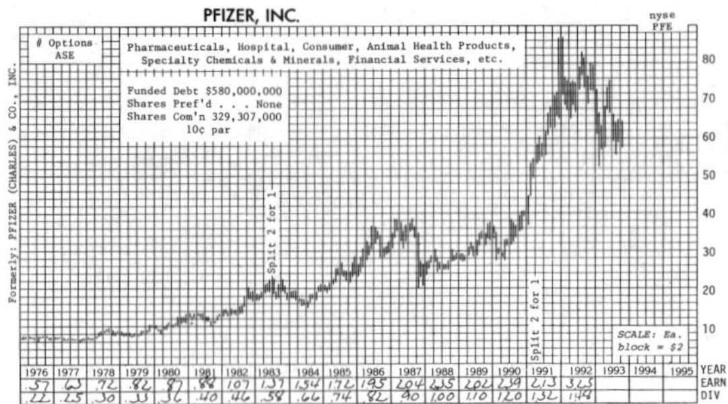
PFIZER, INC.
nyse
PFE
Options
ASE
Pharmaceuticals, Hospital, Consumer, Animal Health Products, Specialty Chemicals & Minerals, Financial Services, etc.
Funded Debt $580,000,000
Shares Pref'd . . . None
Shares Com'n 329,307,000
10¢ par
Formerly: PFIZER (CHARLES) & CO., INC.
Split 2 for 1
Split 2 for 1
SCALE: Ea. block = $2
80
70
60
50
40
30
20
10
YEAR 1976 1977 1978 1979 1980 1981 1982 1983 1984 1985 1986 1987 1988 1989 1990 1991 1992 1993 1994 1995
EARN .57 .63 .72 .82 .87 .88 1.07 1.37 1.54 1.72 1.95 2.04 2.35 2.02 2.39 2.13 3.25
DIV .22 .25 .30 .33 .36 .40 .46 .58 .66 .74 .82 .90 1.00 1.10 1.20 1.32 1.48

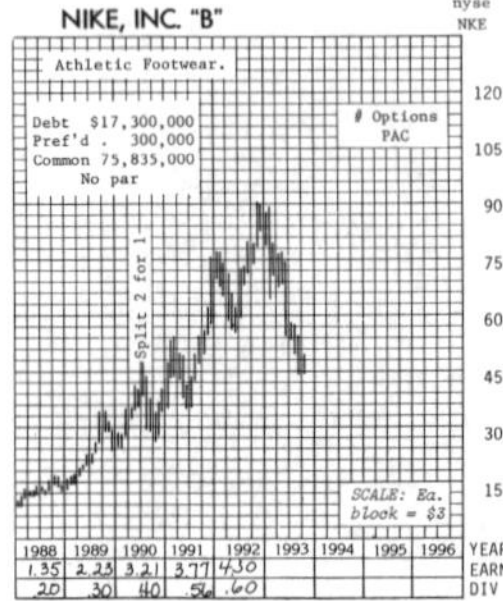
NIKE, INC. "B"
nyse
NKE
Athletic Footwear.
Debt $17,300,000
Pref'd . 300,000
Common 75,835,000
No par
Options
PAC
Split 2 for 1
SCALE: Ea. block = $3
120
105
90
75
60
45
30
15
YEAR 1988 1989 1990 1991 1992 1993 1994 1995 1996
EARN 1.35 2.23 3.21 3.77 4.30
DIV .20 .30 .40 .56 .60

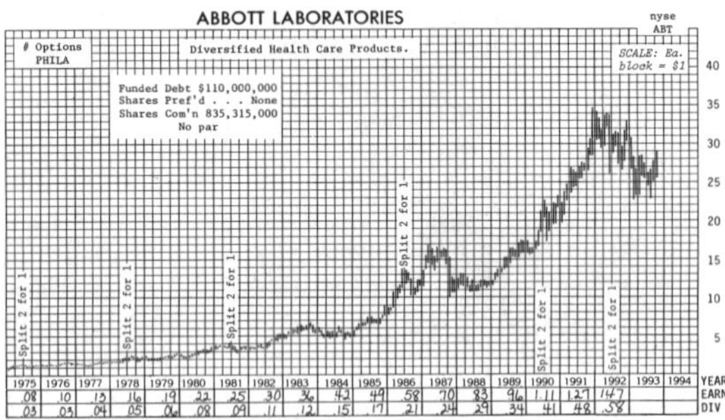
ABBOTT LABORATORIES
nyse
ABT
Options
PHILA
Diversified Health Care Products.
Funded Debt $110,000,000
Shares Pref'd . . . None
Shares Com'n 835,315,000
No par
SCALE: Ea. block = $1
Split 2 for 1
Split 2 for 1
Split 2 for 1
Split 2 for 1
Split 2 for 1
Split 2 for 1
40
35
30
25
20
15
10
5
YEAR 1975 1976 1977 1978 1979 1980 1981 1982 1983 1984 1985 1986 1987 1988 1989 1990 1991 1992 1993 1994
EARN .08 .10 .13 .16 .19 .22 .25 .30 .36 .42 .49 .58 .70 .83 .96 1.11 1.27 1.47
DIV .03 .03 .04 .05 .06 .08 .09 .11 .12 .15 .17 .21 .24 .29 .34 .41 .48 .58

7. *EPS Ratings Failed to Spotlight Huge Gold Rise*

The year 1993 was the year of GOLD. Gold Mutual Funds soared over 82% on the year, far outdistancing all other funds. But, since *Investor's Business Daily* showed lackluster Earnings Per Share ratings on the gold stocks, they missed out on highlighting the hottest stock group of the year, a group that had begun a major bull market in December 1992 after a 12-year decline.

Now I am going to again prove how worthless the O'Neil rating system is. I am going to take all my precious metal stock recommendations and give the O'Neil Earnings Per Share ratings and Relative Strength ratings in January 1992 and the ratings in July 1993. My purpose in doing this was to show why *Investor's Business Daily* missed the precious metal stocks when those stocks bottomed in 1992, the simple reason being that *they did not have favorable O'Neil ratings.* I also want to show that the changes were virtually the *opposite* of the changes shown in the stocks that had been most recommended by stockbrokers in 1992. Here you will see that the earnings continued to show lackluster O'Neil ratings and that the Relative Strength soared from an average 33 rating to a huge 87 rating. So once again I proved that the best moves so often spring from the worst O'Neil ratings and the worst moves so often develop following the highest O'Neil ratings. The answer is very simple and it underscores what has always been an anathema to this stock market technician: *The subject of earnings is a fundamental indicator of something that has already taken place. It doesn't tell you a blessed thing about tomorrow.* The market is a game of tomorrows, not yesterdays. Thus I avoid anything related to earnings like the plague. Now look at these O'Neil numbers on the precious metal stocks:

	Jan. 1992		July 1993	
Stock	EPS	RS	EPS	RS
ASA	0	43	–	77
American Barrick	98	70	99	90
Battle Mountain	21	27	19	89
Echo Bay Mines	37	17	27	96
Hecla	23	25	13	87
Homestake	22	20	60	87
Horsham	43	38	74	81
Lac Minerals	61	24	35	89

Newmont Gold	52	53	30	67
Pegasus	36	41	16	89
Placer-Dome	22	9	42	92
Sunshine Mining	67	8	52	99

So here is the hottest stock group of 1993 but O'Neil assigned an average Earnings Per Share rating of 43 to the stocks at their bottom. To a fundamentalist they won't buy unless they see good earnings and the precious metal stocks left them cold. Now note at the 1992 bottom the O'Neil average Relative Strength rating for the group was 33. O'Neil's system wouldn't recommend stocks with such low EPS and Relative Strength ratings and thus *his system goes completely against the most basic money making law of all markets: buy low, sell high.*

But note that after the group had a major rise by July 1993 that the O'Neil average Earnings per Share rating still suffered, staying virtually unchanged at 42 but that the O'Neil average Relative Strength rating had shot up to 87. So that ratings system missed the bottom but still couldn't warm up to the group because they couldn't see impressive earnings.

The stock market fundamentalists missed the 1993 upturn in the golds because, seeing no signs of inflation, they saw no reason for the gold stocks to go up. This writer, however, made the following observation in July 1993:

Most of the commentators are still in the dark as to the real reason behind the great rise in the precious metal stocks. You have heard many reasons other than the major reason. The major reason is that *the smart money has been selling into strength all this year and switching into gold stocks as their hedge against a developing bear market.*

People think they are buying earnings when they buy a stock and that is why they have this strong tendency to buy at or near a top when earnings are strong. They then belatedly discover that they still have the stock they bought which has since collapsed. My study of the William O'Neil ratings system of stock selection proves that his highest ratings based on earnings led to the most stock collapses and his lowest ratings led to the most stock advances.

8. *The Great Dichotomy of 1992-1993*

Typical of all bull cycles, the market tops out internally long before the Dow makes its final gasp. But the media is always so focused on the Dow that it glows like a Christmas tree every time the Dow closes at a new record high. There's nothing new under the sun. Three of Aesop's

Fables deal with the stock market when it is at a cyclic top, when everything looks so terrific to the uninitiated. The first of these is *The Leopard and the Fox*. The lesson there is that *Beauty is Only Skin Deep*. When I read that fable I can only think of the 30 Dow industrial stocks that so many refer to as the "market" at the worst of times. The second fable that refers to the stock market is *The Vain Jackdaw*. That fable teaches us that *Fine Feathers Do Not Make Fine Birds*. Anybody who bought *Amgen* at 80, *Glaxo* at 38, *Merck* at 58, *Philip Morris* at 82, and *U. S. Surgical* at 134-1/2 in 1992 quickly found out that they owned no fine birds. And lastly, Aesop was very specific on this stock market fable: This one is called *The Fox and the Mask*. The lesson taught here is that *A Fine Appearance Is a Poor Substitute For Inward Worth.*

By July 1993 we were in the midst of a new batch of earnings and it provided a fine opportunity to again review the *Apple Computer* example. By then most people had forgotten how enthusiastic analysts were at the top when the expectations on improving earnings were running so bullish. I drew attention to similar examples. We had seen fantastic earnings reports on *Sears, Compaq Computer* and others but it was important at that time to home in on the strong reports on the bank stocks, the key symptom that those stocks had peaked. On July 20, 1993 all the *bank stocks* declined.

So many stocks had topped out in January 1992 that it occupied many pages in my letters to list them all. Wall Street didn't want you to know that the core of the market was beginning to go bad and so analysts continued to like stocks such as *Amgen, Apple Computer, Glaxo, Merck, Philip Morris, Synergen, U.S. Surgical* and so many others that later were taken out and shot. Of course I never got any credit from the media for identifying the dichotomy and guiding so many people to avoid some terrible losses. Many months after rescuing so many at the internal January 1992 peak, others in our industry finally gave me credit by belatedly recognizing that so many stocks had left the party. But their recognition was not much solace for those people who were locked into those losing stocks. Richard Russell of *Dow Theory Letters* did a wonderful little piece on the subject in his July 7, 1993 letter, though long after the fact:

"Question: Remember the movie, *Who's Killing the Great Chefs of Europe?* Well, we have its sequel. It's called *Who's Killing the Great Stocks of America"* Answer: Darned if I know, but one by one they're getting knocked off. *Walmart, Procter & Gamble, Johnson & Johnson, U. S. Surgical, Amgen, IBM, Apple, Merck, Eli Lilly, Bristol-Myers, Haliburton, Gilette, Digital Equipment, Waste Management*- the list goes on and on.

And, of course, you know where the public is. They're loaded, *super loaded in mutual funds.* So what's happening there? *Investor's Business Daily* runs their index of 20 leading mutual funds. This is interesting -- their Mutual Fund Index is now only slightly above its peak recorded back in January 1993, *so my perception is that the typical mutual fund has gone nowhere in 1993, despite the incoming billions of dollars from a semi-frenzied public.*"

And then Russell further referred to the *dichotomy* again in July 1993:

"*Late Notes*:

What's happening in the market is becoming increasingly clear. As I've written many times before, 38% of all the stocks on the NYSE are now extremely interest rate-sensitive (these include the numerous preferreds, the many bond funds, the bank stocks, the S & Ls, the brokerage stocks, etc.) With interest rates dropping persistently lower, this 38% of the market has been creeping higher. But under the guise of declining interest rates, a great many 'regular" common stocks have been hit and hit hard. Thus, many portfolios holding a variety of common stocks (including top grade issues) are now under water, and investor's can't understand why (why, with the stock averages moving higher).

Is a bear market operating, hidden by the 38% of interest-sensitive stocks? I've been wondering about that, and it's making me very uneasy."

So by the summer of 1993 the cracks began to be increasingly recognized. Jeff Bower finally acknowledged the technical sickness many months after those stocks had peaked, stating in his newsletter *The Guru Revue* that "Most people right now are holding stocks at a loss." James Dines referred to the situation as *an invisible crash.*

This subsurface technical quicksand opened up criticism of the more visible TV technicians who were seldom present to provide advance warnings prior to so many individual stock collapses. Their less than satisfactory performance is described by the term *technical pathologist.* This is one who performs technical autopsies long after the stock is dead. They love to tell you how badly *Apple, Glaxo, Liz Claiborne, Picturetel, Storage Technology, T-2 Medical, U.S. Surgical* and so many others are performing now but where were they in January 1992 when those chart patterns were flashing major sell signals?

Here is just a few of the hundreds of stocks that peaked in January 1992:

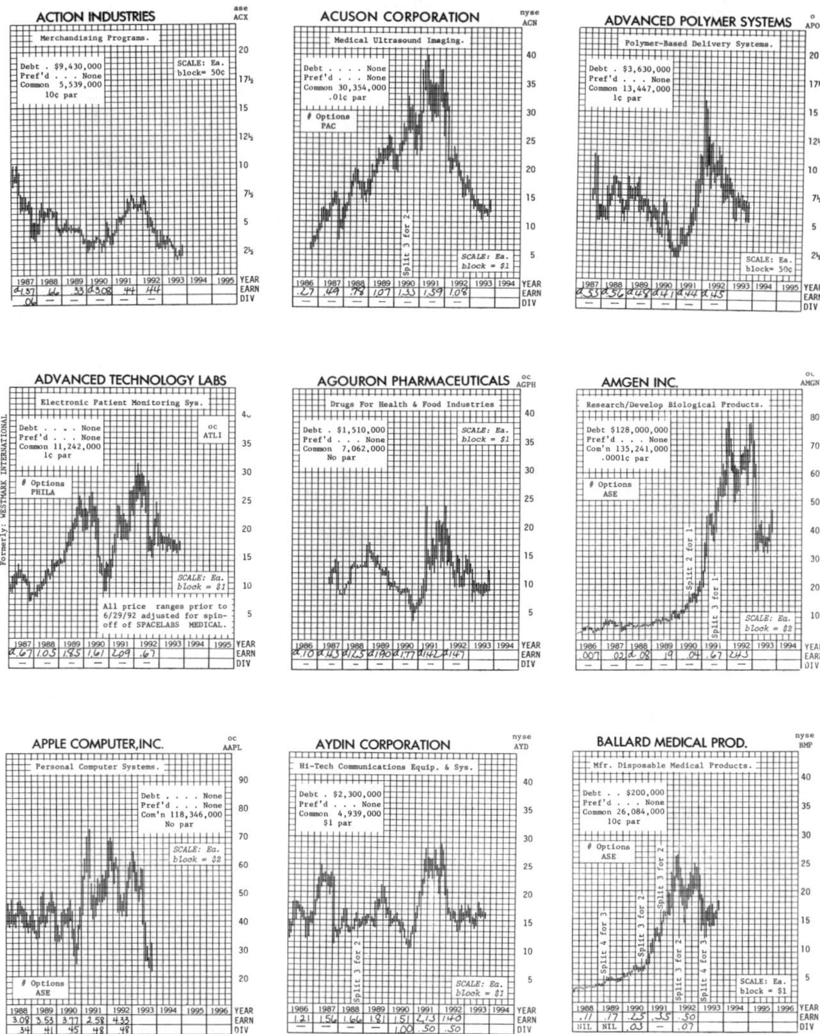

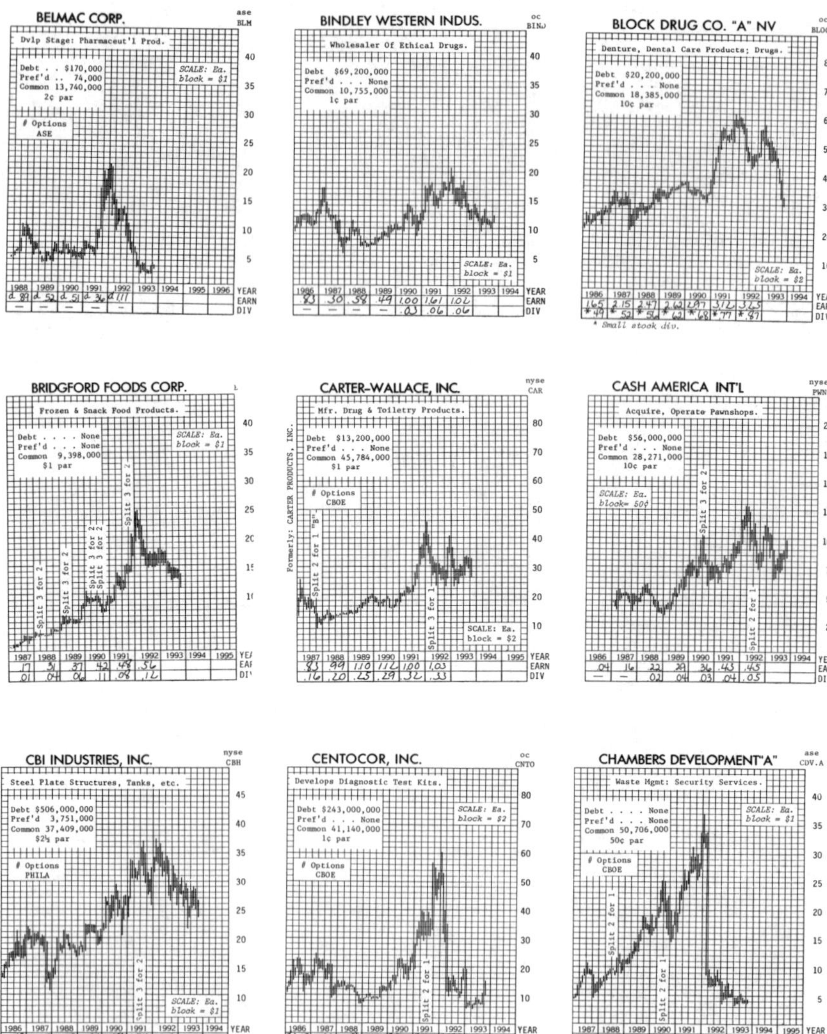

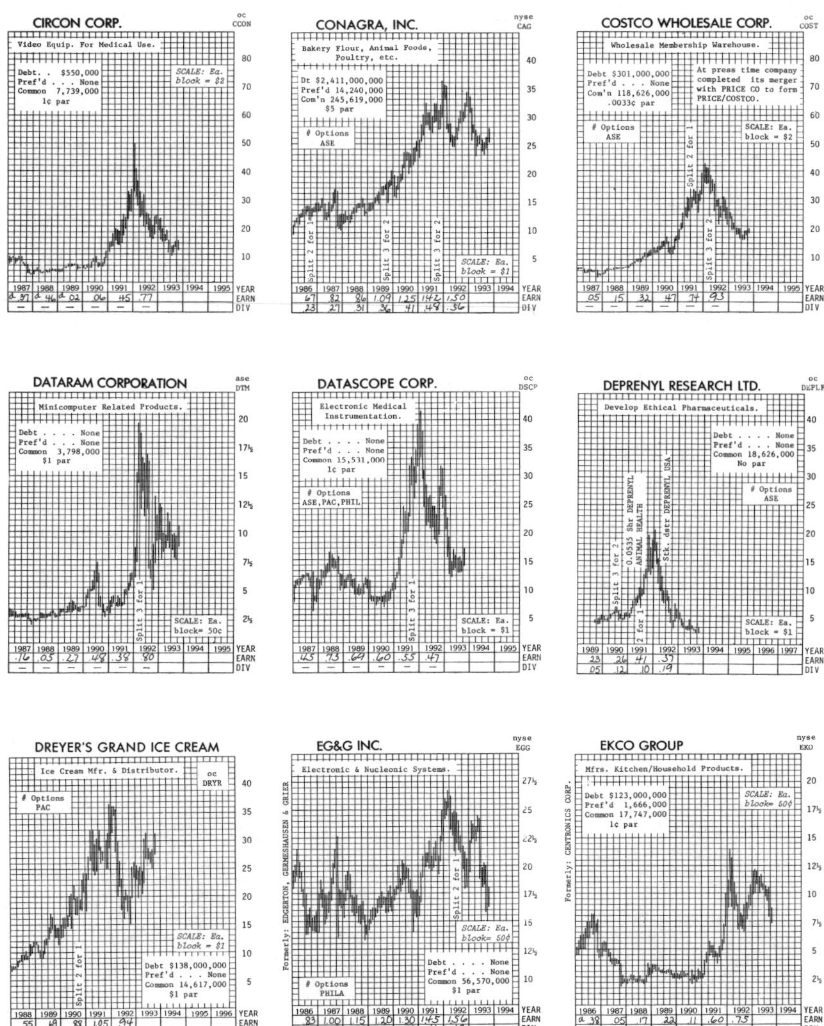

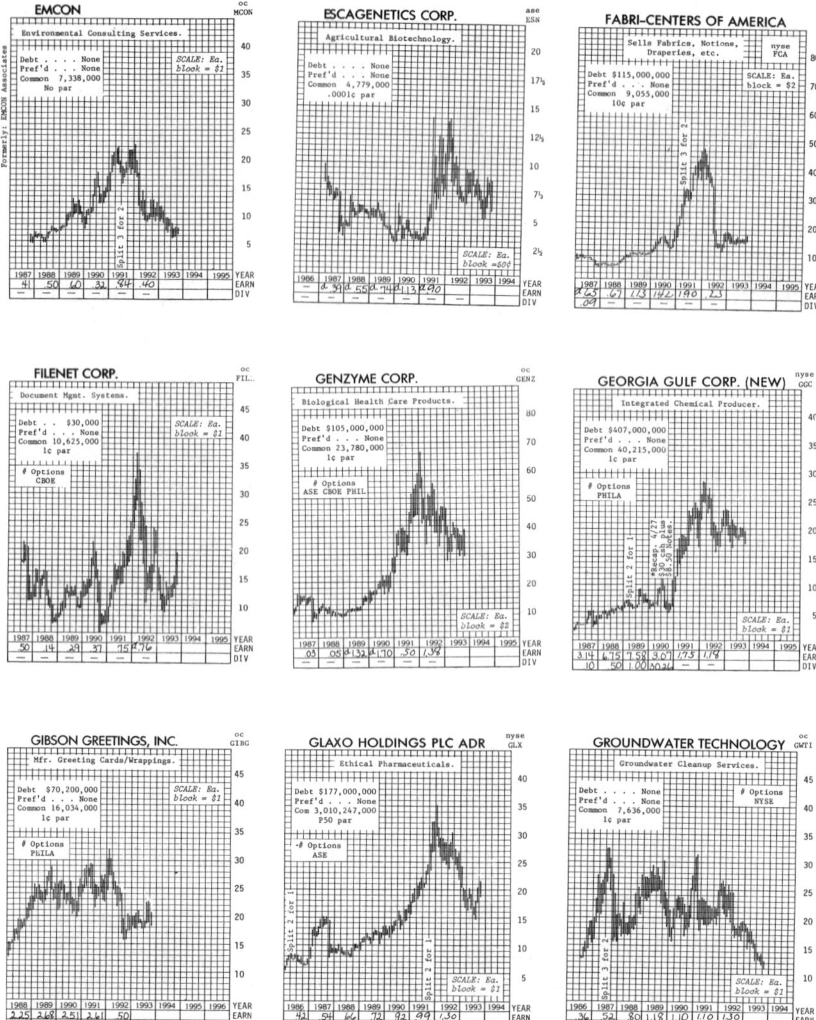
EMCON
Environmental Consulting Services.
Debt . . . . None
Pref'd . . . None
Common 7,338,000
No par
ESCAGENETICS CORP.
Agricultural Biotechnology.
FABRI-CENTERS OF AMERICA
Sells Fabrics, Notions, Draperies, etc.
FILENET CORP.
Document Mgmt. Systems.
GENZYME CORP.
Biological Health Care Products.
GEORGIA GULF CORP. (NEW)
Integrated Chemical Producer.
GIBSON GREETINGS, INC.
Mfr. Greeting Cards/Wrappings.
GLAXO HOLDINGS PLC ADR
Ethical Pharmaceuticals.
GROUNDWATER TECHNOLOGY
Groundwater Cleanup Services.

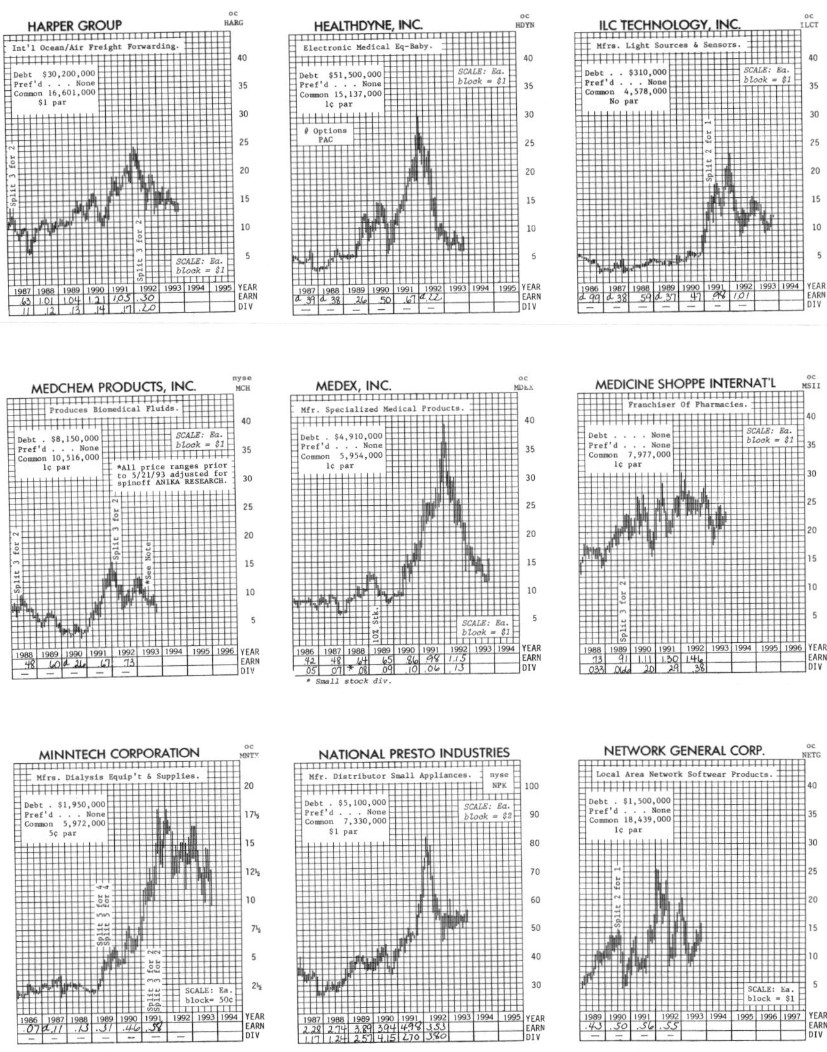

The next period may go down as one of the most fascinating periods in market history. Certainly with more stocks going down than up in the face of a Dow that looked like it was going to go up forever, it had to be correctly described as a Bermuda Triangle. What I wanted the reader to see here is how wrong on the surface I looked to so many people prior to the great fall that was to lie ahead. If ever there was a period to stick to your guns, it was this one.

Section IX

The Mystery of the Bermuda Triangle

The Mystery of the Bermuda Triangle

1. *The Riddle of the Time Warp*

By the late summer of 1993 I felt that we were entering one of the strangest periods in market history. I could only accurately describe it in terms of the Bermuda Triangle, an enigma that still baffles science. Back on December 5, 1945 five Navy torpedo bombers left the Fort Lauderdale Naval Air Station, never to return. This flight was under the command of Charles C. Taylor of Corpus Christi.

Here is how Taylor's ground communication went:

"Calling tower, this is an emergency. We seem to be off course. We cannot see land ... repeat ... we cannot see land."

"What is your position?" the tower radioed back.

"We are not sure of our position," radioed Lieutenant Taylor. "We can't be sure just where we are. We seem to be lost."

The tower operators were startled. How could five planes with experienced crews be lost with fair to good flight conditions? "Assume due west," the tower radioed.

Taylor replied, "We don't know which way is west. Everything is wrong... strange. We can't be sure of any direction. Even the ocean doesn't look as it should." (The Devil's Triangle, Richard Winer, Bantam Books, 1974).

Then there is the well documented case of the an expert US Air Force pilot flying a jet built by General Dynamics who crashed into the side of a mountain. Due to an instrument malfunction he was flying upside down and did not know it. When he pulled the joystick toward himself to gain altitude, he instead put the nose of the plane down and crashed.

There is a mysterious time warp in the stock market, this Bermuda Triangle stretch of time wherein a number of key market indicators malfunction, breeding mass confusion among investors and traders. This strange phenomenon most often takes place when markets go through a transition period between bull and bear markets. When the stock market ends a bull run, it doesn't immediately flip over into a bear market. It first enters that transition period wherein *all the bearish sentiment indicators malfunction.*

Why the bearish sentiment indicators? Because while in a bull market all the bearish sentiment indicators are correctly relied upon to give bullish *contrary opinion* signals. In a bull market shortsellers are wrong and thus a rising short interest is a bullish *contrary opinion* indicator. In a bull market those who buy put options are wrong and thus an increasing number of put buyers is a bullish *contrary opinion* indicator. And in a bull market increasing bearish sentiment is a bullish *contrary opinion* indicator. But what happens to all those bearish sentiment indicators in a bear market? They are the first to malfunction because in a bear market *the bears are right.* In a bear market the shortsellers are right and thus a rising short interest is no longer a bullish contrary opinion signal. The bearish market opinion is the correct opinion. In a bear market buyers of put options are now on the right side of the market and thus a rising number of put buyers is no longer a bullish contrary opinion signal. And finally, in a bear market increasing bearish market sentiment is no longer a bullish contrary opinion signal.

In late 1993 we saw a rising short interest, an increasing number of put option buyers, and a decided increase in bearish market sentiment. The bulls at that time were flying upside down and didn't know it. They thus continued to get erroneous bullish signals from that evidence, not realizing that they had entered a period of great confusion linking the bull cycle to a bear market, meaning that the bears were to be increasingly right.

2. *Turbulence, Wind Shear, and Downbursts*

By August of 1993 I was increasingly disturbed by what I saw as increasingly erratic market action. The dictionary tells us that turbulence means the state or condition of being violently disturbed, restless, or confused. In physics it is the irregular eddying flow of a gas or other fluid, generated by varying pressures and velocities, especially as caused by an obstacle or by friction, as of a ship or airplane in rapid motion. In the language of meteorology, it is a disturbed condition of the atmosphere due to irregular wind. Another definition is simply that it is disorder.

The mechanical definition of shear is an internal force tangential to the section on which it acts: shearing force.

From this we use the wind shear as a perfect example of conflicting forces that are capable of resulting in aeronautical disasters. Of course there is an excellent analogy here with On-Balance Volume whereby we can visualize a force and an equal and opposite counterforce which results in the market getting temporarily locked into a very narrow range. After seeing that narrow range persist for awhile, complacency is seen at the worst of times. For what usually follows next is crash action.

These technical conditions by late 1993 were pointing toward an inevitable severe decline. The final conflict would see the heavy public buying of stocks offset by the equally strong counterforce of the late bull cycle smart money selling, the market pulled apart by this deadly shearing force, culminating in a crash.

In the annals of the weather bureau we often hear the term downburst. This comes very close to what I thought was getting closer, a sudden technical bust.

3. *The Transition Periods*

Listen to the weather reports and note the next time comments are made about the clash of hot and cold air currents. This contact creates the kind of turbulence just described. Translated into stock market terms, the air currents would be likened to bull and bear influences which now increasingly clash and create high market *volatility.* This condition is usually observed in a market transition period between market phases, a sort of no man's land most common when the market is shifting from a bull market to a bear market. This very subtle market change creates much confusion.

Market observers are first alerted to these confusing crosscurrents when they see that a number of widely accepted indicators are *malfunctioning*. Those are the periods I have described as a technical Bermuda Triangle wherein everything seems to be going into reverse. Fortunately, however, these confusing periods have a short life of only a few months. Indicators that appear to be malfunctioning are actually not malfunctioning but are *prepositioning* for the change of market phases soon to be seen. Once these clashing indicators are resolved into a single direction, the view then becomes clearer and it is generally one of an emerging bear market.

September 23, 1993

4. *Bearish Sentiment Is the Correct Sentiment*

I have contended that when the Dow is traversing the very difficult and confusing period that separates the end of a bull cycle and the beginning of a bear cycle *then the market is entering a technical no man's land or Bermuda Triangle.* The reason why these transition periods defy normal analysis is because during this technical blackout most of the standard indicators malfunction.

That is analogous to a serious instrument failure on a plane which so often proves to be fatal. There are documented cases of instrument failures whereby the pilot is flying upside down but doesn't know it. Thinking himself right side up, he pulls the joystick toward himself to gain altitude, but instead heads the plane lower into a fatal crash.

So as the stock market approaches a cyclic top it is seen to enter one of these Bermuda Triangle periods and to avoid the fate of the pilot who thinks he is flying right side up just before crashing, we have to start to seriously read our indicators in reverse. Like Alice, we are about to go through the looking glass.

So when I hear an analyst talk about how strange the market is while we are going through one of these confusing transition periods, I am not only fascinated, but tempted to completely reverse his market stance on the assumption that the market has turned upside down and must be read correctly in reverse.

Being totally convinced that the summer of 1993 saw the market enter such a critical Bermuda Triangle period, I was intrigued by the market column which appeared in *Investor's Business Daily* in the September 20, 1993 issue. Dennis Jarrett made an intriguing market observation that I just could not stop thinking about. Here is what he said:

"In all the years I have followed the market, this is one of the strangest. *The higher the market goes the more pessimistic people get.* My feeling is that the market will have to go much higher to generate the over-optimism needed to make a top."

If that was a valid observation in an up market then the reverse would be equally true in a down market. *But by reversing Jarrett's statement we see that it doesn't make sense:*

"In all the years I have followed the market, this is one of the strangest. The lower the market goes, the more optimistic people get. My feeling is that the market will have to go much lower to generate the over-pessimism needed to make a bottom."

So, having established by logic that Jarrett's observation wasn't valid, the correct conclusion was that while Jarrett thought pessimism was increasing the higher the market went, indicators had reversed and higher pessimism was bearish and not bullish. The bears are right. This was analogous to a pilot thinking he was flying straight up into the sun and not realizing that his instruments had to be correctly read in reverse. Instead of flying straight up he was flying straight down and didn't know it until it was too late. So Jarrett was thinking that the constantly rising pessimism in the summer of 1993 was bullish when actually it was a very bearish omen.

I concluded that the first indicator to seriously malfunction as we entered these Bermuda Triangle transition periods was *sentiment.* In a bull market the bulls are right and the bears are wrong. But in a bear market the bulls are wrong and the bears are right. So there has to be a transition period wherein bearish sentiment is no longer a useful technical tool because the bears are no longer a contrary opinion indicator. This key change in correctly reading market sentiment is what trips up bulls at market tops more than any other single thing.

My conclusion was further fortified by seeing another Jarrett quote in June 1990 shortly before the July peak of that year which was followed by a drop of 635 points. In an *Investor's Business Daily* article during that critical 1990 summer transition period, Jarrett referred to the positive implications of bearish sentiment a couple of weeks before that key Dow cyclic top.

5. *Sudden Changes in Sentiment Precede Key Market Turns*

On Monday, June 25, 1990 Jeff Bower reported on the old *Financial News Network* that 59% of the advisory letters he reads were bearish. He thought that high percentage presented a buy signal. Since I saw the market at that time at a cyclic top, I interpreted the high Bower bearish sentiment reading as very bearish for the market because I strongly suspected that the bears were going to be right on the market. I saw it as a clear parallel to when the *Wall Street Journal* reported on October 1, 1929 that 75% of all market letters were bearish. Then Bower revealed a significant change in his sentiment figures. He said that only a month earlier

60% of the letters he followed were bullish. Instantly I saw that as another parallel with 1929 when the *Journal* also referred to how fast sentiment went from bullish to bearish before the crash.

And on the tailend of the 1990-93 bull cycle Mark Haines of CNBC remarked how fast his bearish sentiment figures were rising.

Peter Eliades in a very timely study noted near the 1993 top that he was seeing a major exception in his study of sentiment figures:

"One of the potentially strongest arguments against a major top or even any kind of top occurring in this time period is newsletter sentiment as measured by *Investors Intelligence.* The highest percentage of bullish advisors over the past several weeks has been between 40 and 42%. It is not the kind of outright bullish sentiment that usually precedes or accompanies major market tops. We say "usually" because there was a time period where, one could argue, a major top was reached without extreme bullish sentiment and in many ways it was similar to the current time period. We are referring to the major top in December 1968. At that time the *Investors Intelligence Survey* was published only every two weeks, but here are the percentage of bullish advisors around the time period of that major top:

November 13, 1968	33.3%
November 27, 1968	40.9%
December 11, 1968	44.8%
December 25, 1968	49.3%
January 10, 1969	29.7%

I had identified the December 3, 1968 major top right to the very day. My method was almost solely based on the Climax Indicator and other OBV measurements which were not fooled by the sentiment numbers at that time. They were also not fooled by the advance/decline line.

September 30, 1993

6. *Through the Looking Glass*

Every market top is a Bermuda Triangle of mystery and confusion. The market is in that tricky transition period going from bull market to bear market. This is the period when the bulls will see their favorite indicators malfunction. This is a hall of mirrors wherein just about everything reverses. So, like Alice, we will now go through the looking glass into a Humpty Dumpty market.

Current action is duplicating the reverse of the two periods which led up to the huge advances that started in January 1991 and December 1991. Thus current signals warn of an approaching Dow drop of 500-700 points and that will probably be only the first leg down in the new bear market. Subscribers will recall how this letter homed in on both of those huge bull market *first phase* rallies. Now we are in the transition from *Bull Phase Three to Bear Phase One. By Bear Phase Three* in 1995 or later we could easily be down to Dow 2000 or lower.

Logic dictates that the mirror test can always be relied upon. If the current Dow charts are bearish as I contend, then *upside down* they should look bullish. Take the three Dow charts shown on page C-3 of the *Wall Street Journal*, turn them upside down and look at them in a mirror. Seen upside down, they look technically attractive.

Smart money buys on low earnings and bad news and sells on high earnings and good news. Therefore, *the smart money is currently using high Earnings Per Share figures to distribute stocks.* I credit Arthur Merrill for the magnificent chart he presented years ago which I reprinted in my *1976 New Strategy* book. That chart showed the Dow going up on declining earnings and going down on rising earnings, *the very opposite of what most people think.* Subscribers will recall how bullish I was all through 1991 while the media and economists were so bearish. *My diary noted that Zacks lowered earnings estimates on September 24th, October 4th, and October 10th in that year.*

I also noted in my diary that Europeans left the U.S. market in 1990 just when they should have been buying. Now in 1993 they have *reentered* the U.S. market. The record shows that Europeans have a habit of falling in love with U.S. stocks when our market is peaking. So this is another *opposite* of note.

Back in 1991 I was asked on more than one occasion what it would take to turn be bearish. Readers will recall that I reported in early September that I was asked what it would take to turn me bullish. Ironically, the Dow had already seen its August 25th peak. So this was another opposite to take note of.

Everyone thinks that current bearish sentiment is very bullish for the market. The following letter appeared in *Barron's* in their August 13, 1990 issue. Evidently the letter was written as the Dow was just coming off of the 3000 level in July 1990:

"From 15 years of being a broker, I have learned almost nothing. That admitted, I do know that the philosophy and stock market indicator that is the rage of Wall Street will only be effective in the short term and will fail miserably in the longer-term.

The one true fact I ascertain from reading the research of technicians, money managers and brokers is that the market cannot go down because sentiment, measured in the intermediate term by market advisors and in the short term by the revered "put/call ratio," is too negative.

When an indicator reaches maximum acceptance, its effectiveness is significantly diminished. Therefore, I suggest that sentiment-following is now worthless because everyone practices it. As Yogi Berra said, "Nobody goes there anymore, it's too crowded."

That letter is a gem. Unfortunately, I cut off the bottom which named the author of the letter. It underscores the flip-side of key indicators at a major market top. Yes, those who think current bearish sentiment is bullish are in for a rude awakening.

In going through my diaries, I noted articles just before the 1990 top that increasingly revealed that investors were looking for firms that would do well in a down market. Now I see similar references, an omen of a near-term downturn.

In further discrediting high Earnings per Share numbers, I was curious as to what the *insiders* were doing when *U. S. Surgical* was topping out in January 1992 at 134-1/2 with peak *Investor's Business Daily* Earnings Per Share ratings of 99 and Relative Strength ratings of 95. I called up Norman Fosback of *Market Logic* and asked him what his data showed at the time of the *U.S. Surgical* peak. He told me that there was very heavy insider selling in *U.S. Surgical* right at the top in January 1992.

The 1992-93 period in the market was the strangest I ever encountered. I had already gone on record in early 1992 that a bear market was getting started. I had detected an internal technical cancer that was destined to ultimately terminate the bull cycle that had gotten started in late 1990. Strangely enough, a number of stocks having been assigned the largest earnings ratings numbers by William O'Neil, the publisher of *Investor's Business Daily,* peaked in the face of their optimism and started to move importantly downhill. This generally went unnoticed by the Wall Street crowd and the media. *Investor's Business Daily* certainly wasn't going to call attention to it and since they were the largest advertiser on CNBC, that TV station wasn't going to be about to embarrass their largest financial benefactor. Nevertheless, one key stock after another began to fall apart, stocks having the highest O'Neil earnings ratings. It included such previous Wall Street darlings as *Amgen, Glaxo, Merck, Philip Morris,* and *US Surgical* and the believing public became hopelessly locked in with huge losses on these stocks and so many others like them that had peaked on those high William O'Neil Earnings per Share ratings.

But since the Dow industrial stocks had not yet been affected by this internal technical cancer, the Dow Jones Industrial Average continued to rise into the summer of 1993. I was looking at the most vicious market dichotomy I had ever seen. When I got complaints from those I had put into the money market funds in early 1992, I tried hard to accent the fact that they had also been spared the suffering from the sharp breaks in the many stocks that had been breaking down since January 1992.

Everybody follows the Dow industrial average. But suppose there was an average based on the money saved by avoiding all those huge individual price breaks? In other words, what is more important, *General Motors* going up 5 points or *US Surgical* going down 119 points? Suppose their roles were reversed and *US Surgical* had been a Dow industrial stock. Then that one stock would have dropped the Dow by 238 points.

At the outset of a bear market we encounter one of the most fascinating series of changes in the market. The longer the preceding bull market, the more people are blinded to the transition. This is because they have adopted a series of habits that have grooved them to think and react a certain way for a number of years. They are now so inflexible to change that they are going to continue to think and react as they always have. They are now completely unconscious of the fact that not only is a bear market the opposite of a bull market, *but all indicators have to now be read in reverse.*

But the initial changes are very subtle and only detectable to the trained eye of a good technician. The changes are internal and are not quickly noticed by those who don't know how to read the market. Failing to diagnose the market as a terminal case, those who are still bullish during this critical transition from bull market to bear market will still have the opinion that the market complexion is healthy. But internally there is now a technical cancer that is growing.

The first thing to recognize and accept in a bear market is that the bears are right. Now that immediately demands an *opposite* interpretation of advisory sentiment, the short interest, the put/call ratio, odd lot indicators, mutual fund cash and the money market. Even the interpretation of news has to be handled differently.

Advisory Sentiment - All through a bull market it is consistently shown that the bears are wrong. Thus whenever there was a rise in bearish sentiment the market followed that with a rally. But a bear market demanded a reverse interpretation. In a bear market a rise in bearish sentiment is bearish because the bears are right in a bear market. In the October 1, 1929 *Wall Street Journal* it was stated that 75% of all market letters were bearish.

The Short Interest - Now the short interest is no longer a contrary opinion indicator because the shorts are right. Very few people are aware of the fact that there was a very big short interest in the market back in October 1929 just before the great crash. Those who were bullish at that time thought that the large short interest would provide a strong technical support for the market. But they were soon to learn that the shortsellers were correctly betting on the collapse that followed.

The Put/Call Ratio - In a bull market the buyer of put options is betting on a down market and will lose. So when it is noted that there are heavy buyers of put options that is followed by a rally in a bull market. But in a bear market all bets on the downside will be winners and thus the put/call ratio has to be read in reverse in a bear market.

Odd Lot Indicators - Prior to the advent of widespread option trading, market followers relied heavily on the odd lot numbers for clues pointing toward future market trends. Their favorite bullish indicator was a sharp rise in the number of odd lot shorts, the theory being that the little market players who are generally wrong were looking for a down market and that meant the market was headed higher. But such numbers in a bear market would point toward a further market decline, the odd lot shortselllers being right in a bear market.

Mutual Fund Cash and the Money Market - Being in cash in a bear market is the correct posture. Thus high mutual fund cash reserves and money pouring into the money market are no longer bullish indicators. Just prior to the 1929 crash it was stated several times in the *Wall Street Journal* that the public was holding a great deal of cash.

The News - All through the preceding bull market the market tended to climb a wall of worry. The market responded positively to good news and also responded positively to bad news. But everything changes in a bear market. Now the market responds negatively to good news and also responds negatively to bad news.

But it is very important to know that the internal market indicators turn bearish before any of the above.

The transition from a bull market into a bear market comprises a number of indicators that appear to the bull to be *malfunctioning.* Picture a jet pilot who is now flying upside down at low altitude but who thinks he is flying right side up. Alarmed at his very low altitude, he pulls the stick forward, thinking that he will now go up. Instead, he crashes. So during the critical transition from bull market to bear market in late 1993, I was particularly alert to anything that appeared to be malfunctioning. I felt that there was far too much attention on the Dow and not enough on the increasing number of individual stock disasters.

While all the CLX numbers related to Dow forecasting, there was no magic bullet here homing in on identifying individual disasters, the technical seeds of future market cancers. There I had to turn to the number of new stock highs as the best single source of technical information relating to a degree of internal market weakness not identified by all the Climax Indicator and Net Field Trend numbers. I knew I was on the right track when, despite the new Dow highs in 1993, I could identify a growing number of individual stock collapses which began to show up as early as January 1992. I could therefore correctly claim that I got people to sell when most stocks were making their highs. But to convince people of that I had to break through a wall of mental resistance, an effort that never fully succeeded until after the January 31, 1994 Dow peak.

My evidence of this market dichotomy was very convincing and very complete. It was easy to go through any chart book and cite the hundreds of instances of January 1992 stock price peaks. But a bigger picture began to unfold. I had the additional evidence that this market dichotomy was a feature of every bull cycle. It showed up as early as the *second* phase of the bull cycle and in every case proved to be ultimately fatal, ushering in the next bear market.

So this was a newer concept, a problem requiring analytical solutions. Much of these were to stem from exhaustive research on the high/low indicator. Probably the most classic case of this internal growing cancer about to terminate a solo walk in the Dow was the 1929 market. While the Dow Jones Industrial Average soared for most of that critical year, peaking in the wild blue yonder on September 3rd, the high/low indicator on that fateful day showed 54 new highs and 19 new lows. The internal cancer had set in the year before. In more recent bull markets, the market was technically deteriorating in 1972 prior to the January 1973 Dow peak. And in the 1987-90 bull cycle which terminated in July 1990 it was easy to document the true internal peak the year before in August 1989 when new highs peaked at 306 on August 1st of that year. So when I saw new highs peak at 336 on December 31, 1991 in the 1990-93 bull cycle I was already aware that the cycle of internal technical destruction was about to start.

7. *Frustration At Key Turning Points*

There are many times when a technician is tormented with indecision. The 1993 period was a particularly trying time because the primary Dow indicators pointed upward while the market as a whole was breaking down internally. If I had to pick a single day of maximum frustration it would have been December 23, 1993. The Dow had previously recorded an all-time record high on December 13th at 3764.43. Standing at 3762.19 on December 22nd, it was obvious that any new high would be widely non-confirmed by the advance/decline line since that key indicator stood 3,245 under the October 15th peak. Now, we had already seen no less than a dozen A/D line non-confirmations since October 18th and yet the Dow kept making new highs. By late December I felt that another A/D line non-confirmed new high followed by no sizable decline was intolerable. So the afternoon of December 23rd reached a point of maximum frustration. The Dow for awhile was up over 12 points putting the Dow at a new record high of 3774, but the Dow solo walk can only endure just so many key A/D line upside non-confirmations. Needing only 2 points to make a new high, the Dow fell from 3774 and closed down over 4 points at the 3757 level.

The Late 1993 A/D Line Upside Non-Confirmations

(1)	10/18	3642.31	-48,942	Next day	-6.99
(2)	10/20	3645.10	-49,588	Next day	-8.94
(3)	10/22	3649.30	-49,769	Next day	+24.31
(4)	10/25	3673.61	-49,925	Next day	-1/12
(5)	10/28	3687.86	-49,811	Next day	-7.27
(6)	11/ 1	3692.61	-49,305	Next day	+5.03
(7)	11/ 2	3697.64	-49,548	Next day	-35.77
(8)	11/16	3710.77	-51,389	Next day	-6.14
(9)	12/ 7	3718.88	-51,509	Next day	+15.65
(10)	12/ 8	3734.53	-51,445	Next day	-4.75
(11)	12/10	3740.67	-51,844	Next day	+23.76
(12)	12/13	3764.43	-51,909	Next day	-21.80

8. *A Paradox*

I had previously stated that an established rising trend or an established falling trend in the 65-Stock True Climax Indicator and the 65-Stock Early Warning Climax Indicator were two of the most reliable indicators that the trends would continue in their given direction. That is true up to a point. While in some cases there is an advance warning that the trends are about to change, we also find that both indicators often peak or bottom at the same time as the Dow. Therefore, *a given trend is capable of ending at any given time with the advance warning coming from another source.*

Seeing many 1929 parallels, I felt that it would be instructive to go back and review all the daily market commentaries as far back as August 1993 in order to get the feel of the Bermuda Triangle analogy.

August 17. 1993 - Tuesday Evening

The Dow walked into a record high today at 3587.26 under very questionable technical credentials. The gains in *IBM, Merck, Philip Morris,* and *Procter & Gamble* were equal to a rise of 12-1/2 points in the Dow and without the weighting effect of those four issues the Dow would have closed down 4 points instead of up 8.11.

The Climax Indicator showed a very weak rise from +3 to +4 on the new Dow high and this represents a very significant CLX upside non-confirmation, a signal that the market will retreat. The Net Field Trend indicator could gain no fields and stayed unchanged at the -8 level. It is the NFI current trend that signals a major decline ahead inasmuch as it is duplicating what was seen prior to the crash of 1987.

The Nasdaq scored another high today, closing up 4.11 at the 731 level. But nobody is calling attention to the fact that the A/D line is about 2000 below the February 4th level for a very wide upside non-confirmation. So that average could be a very significant CLX upside non-confirmation, a very weak showing on a Dow record high. The Net Field Trend indicator continues to tell a very bearish technical story. Final figures yesterday saw Minnesota Mining avoiding a field trend change adding two fields. Likewise today, this same stock still avoided adding two field trends. And so the revised NFI on Wednesday was -4 instead of -2 and despite the 7-point rise in the Dow today the NFI remained unchanged at -4.

I am adding 7 new short sale recommendations in the new letter, these being Adaptec, Advanta, Albertsons, American Power Conversion, Analysts International, Apache, Applied Materials, and Arrow Electronics. These all have parabolic rises and high *Investor's Business Daily* earnings ratings, the proper combination for a collapse.

Golds had a normal decline and are strong buys right here.

August 18, 1993 - Wednesday Evening

With what I saw today, I have to consider the sharp 17.88 point upswing to the 3604.86 level as a hook, not destined to remain long at these lofty levels.

Once again the bond market was very strong, the long bond rising 21/32nds and dropping the yield to 6.26%. But all these moves look terminal.

New highs expanded to 169 but that is only half of what we saw last February. Despite another high today in the Nasdaq, its advance/decline still remains under the high of last February. Transports closed down and that average still hasn't confirmed the industrial rise. Those things don't appear important now but when the industrials turn down, a move increasingly imminent, then all non-confirmations will look very important, even the fact that the S & P 500 missed making a new high today by just a third of a point.

The Climax Indicator shot up from +4 to +11. The Net Field Trend Indicator scored a sharp jump from -8 to -2, gaining a field in *Boeing,* a field in *Coca Cola*, a field in *Goodyear*, a field in *International Paper*, and two fields in *Minnesota Mining*. Before one gets carried away with those numbers, it is well to note that a month before the 1987 crash the NFI rallied from -8 to -2, getting up to +3 by October 5th, 1987, and then crashing ten sessions later, the NFI dropping to -14.

I am in favor of rebuying all the precious metal stocks, the Gold Stock Index acting very well today with a 2.92 point rise to the 114.10 level.

Despite the rise in the Dow today, the auto group is breaking down and *General Motors* was again under pressure today.

Several bank stocks moved lower today despite the Dow rally. *Bank of New York, Barnett, Chase*, and *Wells Fargo* retreated.

Our latest short sale *Promus* broke again today, closing down at 64-3/4. It was at 70 this past Monday when we went short.

August 19, 1993 - Thursday Evening

The Dow rose 7.27 points to a new all-time record high of 3612.13. The Dow Transports rose 14.53 points to the 1654.63 level, only 29 points away from a new high. Utilities gave back more than what they gained on Wednesday.

The Nasdaq fell 4.35 points to the 730.48 level, also giving back more than what they gained on Wednesday. Once again, the A/D line here never confirmed the new highs.

The long bond soared 25/32nds to put the yield down, to a new low of

6.20% This parabolic collapse in yields is no longer getting a similar response in the stock market.

The number of new highs contracted from 169 to 116. This was a contraction of over 31% and added to the probability that we are seeing the Dow highs right here.

The Climax Indicator dropped sharply from a revised +8 to +1. This is seen to be more bearish than if the Dow had fallen today because it records what is seen to be a very significant CLX upside non-confirmation, a very weak showing on a Dow record high. The Net Field Trend indicator continues to tell a very bearish technical story. Final figures yesterday saw Minnesota Mining avoiding a field trend change adding two fields. Likewise today, this same stock still avoided adding two field trends. And so the revised NFI on Wednesday was -4 instead of -2 and despite the 7-point rise in the Dow today the NFI remained unchanged at -4.

I am adding 7 new short sale recommendations in the new letter, these being Adaptec, Advanta, Albertsons, American Power Conversion, Analysts International, Apache, Applied Materials, and Arrow Electronics. These all have parabolic rises and high *Investor's Business Daily* earnings ratings, the proper combination for a collapse.

Golds had a normal decline and are strong buys right here.

August 21, 1993 - Saturday Afternoon

Unraveling the mystery of Friday's options expiration session, several interesting technical quirks were revealed, obvious last minute weighting by *Chevron, General* Electric, and *International Paper* was responsible for the Dow turning around in the last hour from a 15-point loss to a gain of 3.35 points, putting the Dow at a new record closing high of 3615.48. Without the help of those three cited stocks, the Dow would have closed down about 7 points. As it was, 20 of the Dow industrial stocks closed unchanged to lower.

Transports, after coming within about 29 points of a record high, were trampled with a loss of 21.37 points and put the deficit from the high at about 50 points.

The number of new highs contracted again, down to 110. But we are of course watching the number of common stock highs and these are at 85 and far short of the level of last February despite the new Dow industrial highs.

The Nasdaq edged fractionally higher, the A/D line still far short of the February high level.

I was surprised to see volume contracting 5% on an options expiration day.

Bonds were down 7/32nds and I am looking for a break in the bond market as the major excuse for the coming severe stock shakeout.

The Climax Indicator showed a very weak rise from +1 to +2. The Net Field Trend Indicator rose sharply from -4 to zero, Chevron gaining one field, *Exxon* gaining one field, and *Texaco* gaining two fields. While that may look like an impressive change for the better, *the NFI did precisely the same thing back in 1987 just before the crash.* A review of those numbers will appear Monday in the new letter.

If one will check out the gold and silver charts in *Investor's Business Daily* I think they will be pleasantly surprised to see excellent base formations taking place with silver moving out on Friday.

August 23, 1993 - Monday Evening

The Dow fell 9.50 points to close at 3605.98. Transports and utilities edged lower. The advance/decline line only showed a very moderate decline and new stock highs expanded to 144. The Nasdaq also showed a small fractional decline and its advance/decline line fell by about 126.

Bonds stayed little changed with the long bond up 2/32nds.

Among the 30 Dow industrials stocks today there were no upside clusters. That is a sign of very important technical weakness. A cluster is a minimum of three consecutive OBV up designations.

The Climax Indicator fell from +2 to -2 with the Net Field Trend indicator remaining unchanged at zero. Despite recent new Dow highs, the Cumulative CLX this year peaked on June 2nd.

The Gold Index rose 0.72 to close at 115.12. The path of least resistance appears to be the upward one. All the precious metal stocks we follow were unchanged to higher. Better looking moves included *American Barrick* at 25-7/8 and Placer-Dome at 20-5/8. *American Barrick* has apparently found good support at the rising 10-week trendline at 24 and looks headed for new highs on this move. Likewise *Placer-Dome* is in a similar technical Position and I expect a new high here shortly. We are in the October 20 calls on Barrick and in the September 27-1/2 calls on *Placer-Dome.*

Off to a good start on our new shorts. *Advanta* fell to 51-1/2, *Albertsons* dropped to 56, *Analysts International* fell to 34-1/2, *Applied Materials* fell to 72-1/4 and *Arrow Electronics* fell to 40-3/8.

Half of our bank stocks edged lower.

August 24, 1993 - Tuesday Evening

The Dow responded strongly to the note auction today which saw the long bond rise 11/32nds to put the yield at 6.19%. That brought in program buying late in the day which helped put the Dow up 32.98 points to the new record high closing of 3638.96. Seeing this many record highs in such a brief period of time is *symptomatic* of a *blowoff top*, one that definitely should be sold into. The bond market could reverse at any time with no further warning and the drop in yields there looks parabolic.

The number of new highs should have been way above the 142 reported. So that also looks like an upside non-confirmation.

The Climax Indicator rose from -2 to +10 and that +10 number included five lower OBV up designations. The Net Field Trend rose from zero to +1, gaining a field in *Union Carbide.* The sharp advance positioned several Dow industrial stocks to lose fields on the next leg down. *American Express* could lose a field, *American Telephone* could lose a field, *Caterpillar* could lose two fields, *General Electric* could lose a field, *Sears* could lose two fields, and *Texaco* could lose a field. One should be very suspicious of this big a rise in the Dow that only produced the gain of a single field in the NFI.

We have the experience of August 1987 to fall back upon here. I showed that the Dow had a sharp rally between September 21st and October 2nd that year, the NFI rising from -8 to +3. Currently the NFI has risen from -8 to +1 against the same technical background.

Gold stocks again acted very well, the Gold Stock Index rising a strong 2.3 points to the 117.48 level.

If the Dow opens strong tomorrow morning I would then look for it to quickly run into a reversal.

August 25, 1993 - Wednesday Evening

The Dow rocketed ahead to another new record high, closing up 13.13 points at the 3652.09 level. Transports were also very strong, closing up over 14 points. And utilities scored a good advance. The advance/decline line added another 240 to another high and the individual stock highs expanded sharply to over 190.

This time the Nasdaq declined.

The Climax Indicator fell from +10 to +9, marking an upside non-confirmation. The Net Field Trend indicator rose from +1 to +2, gaining a field in *Allied-Signal*. Again, tracking the 1987 pre-crash pattern, the NFI rose from -8 to +3 back then and the current pattern shows a rise from

-8 to +2. The only conclusion possible is that this is the final rally, the completion of what the Elliot Wave theorists call the important fifth leg, such a move to be followed by a devastating decline.

Our recent short sales performed very well today in the face of the Dow rally. Albertson's fell again, declining to 54-7/8. We have the December 55 puts*American Power Conversion* fell to 46-1/8. There we are in the December 45 puts.

Analysts International fell to 34-3/8. There we hold no put options. *Applied Materials* fell to 70-1/2. We are in the October 80 puts. And *Arrow Electronics* edged down to 40-7/8. There we are in the December 40 puts.

And gold persistently creeps higher, the Gold Stock Index today rising 0.64 to 118.12. The better moves were in*American Barrick, Echo Bay Mines, Newmont Gold, Pegasus,* and *Placer-Dome.*

And I continue to view the general market in a highly precarious state.

August 26, 1993 - Thursday Evening

Going into the last hour, the Dow was up 10.90 at the 3662.99 level with the intraday high just above the 3684 level. Those magic numbers almost precisely equated with the exact completion of the Elliot Wave final fifth leg. Once hitting that level, the Dow retreated and closed down 3.91 points at the 3648.18 level. Transports were hard hit with a 13.25 point decline at the 1651.42 level. The A/D line maintained the series of new highs but the number of new stock highs contracted sharply from 189 to 139, a drop of almost 27%. And Nasdaq fell again.

Bonds soared again today, this time rising 1 and 1/32nds to put the yield down to 6.08%, another record low. But there are two things now that are bad here. First of all, *the collapse in yields is parabolic and when the reverse comes it is going to be severe.* Secondly, the soaring bonds failed to prevent the Dow from dropping almost 15 points in the last hour.

I noted that the majority of the big name Nasdaq stocks that fell today had peak William O'Neil earnings ratings at their highs.

The Climax Indicator fell from +9 to +3. The Net Field Trend indicator lost three fields, dropping from +2 to -1. *International Paper* lost a field and *Sears* lost two fields. The poor showing in the NFI is the most reliable precursor of crash action.

Gold took a hit today, the Gold Index dropping 3.57 points to the 114.55 level. The price of the metal took a big hit but even there gold closed sharply above the low of 367, closing at 370.8. I see nothing significant in the pullback there today.

Among our most recent short sales, *Applied Materials* fell over 3 points to close down at the 67-3/8 level. We are in the October 70 puts.

I think the market arrived today at its most critical juncture, ready now for a severe decline.

August 28, 1993 - Saturday Afternoon

For awhile the Dow was down over 22 points and threatening a possible rout inasmuch as the bond market had turned very weak. Both markets improved from the morning lows, the long bond down 14/32nds putting the yield at 6.12% and the Dow closing down 7.55 points at the 3640.63 level.

The Climax Indicator fell from +3 to -2. The Net Field Trend Indicator stayed unchanged at -1, losing a field in *American Express* but gaining a field in *Disney*.

While the overall decline was quite restrained, it left a worst case scenario for Monday at a potential CLX -15 level, out of range of any crash action. Once the potential falls to the low -20's then it comes within range. This is something to watch very closely every day now that we are about to enter the critical September/October time frame. The market cannot crash until it first comes within technical potential range. We are not there yet but could be soon.

The debacle du jour today was *KCS Energy*, dropping 8 points to 49. The point I wish to stress here is that the stock has a *double 99* rating on earnings and relative strength according to William O'Neil, the highest possible fundamental recommendation.

National Medical Enterprises fell 3-3/8 to 7-3/4. Our followers sold the stock in January 1992 at 17-3/8. The move here is typical of the *dichotomy* in this market, so many key stocks peaking in early 1992 and never fully recovering.

Apache Corp fell a full point to 31-1/2. Downside objective in that stock is first support at 28 and next support at 25. Breaking 25, it could fall all the way to 20. I have recommended the purchase of the October 35 puts.

August 30, 1993 - Monday Evening

The Dow was up over 14 points for awhile today but suddenly plunged for no apparent reason late in the day to a loss but was able to retrieve some of this for a small gain of 3.64 points, closing at 3644.27. But the sudden loss of over 70% of the gain is interpreted as an omen of coming weakness. And keep in mind that the Dow intra-day high is 3681.71 as recorded on August 26th.

The bond market has traced out an acute parabolic and that appears to be where the major trouble will come from this fall.

The Nasdaq still shows some punch but I am aware of the fact that the A/D line this year peaked on February 4th.

The Climax Indicator recorded a weak rise from -2 to +1. The Net Field Trend indicator advanced from -1 to +1, gaining a field in *Sears* and a field in *Woolworth*. The NFI has been showing technical storm clouds over this market for some time now, *having peaked at +18 in March, 1993.*

Many analysts are again bad mouthing gold and I think the rise of 2.14 in the Gold Index today was very impressive. That brought the index back up to the 117.55 level, just under the 118.12 level of August 25th seen the day before the one-day plunge to the 114.55 level. Every precious metal stock we follow rose today, especially good gains seen in *Battle Mountain Gold, Homestake,* and *Placer-Dome.*

American Power Conversion took an earlier hit but cut the loss on the close to 3/4, closing at 42-3/4. This looks like one of the most vulnerable of the recent short sale candidates. *Analysts International* fell a point to 34-1/4, another featured short sale.

August 31, 1993 - Tuesday Evening

The market move today was almost to the point of being boring, lulling the bulls to sleep. But it was a very revealing day technically. The Dow added 7.26 points to close up at the 3651.25 level. But there was a failure to better the 3652.09 closing high of August 25th, needing less than a point while the Dow was running higher on the close. But what was particularly significant was the fact that 14 of the Dow industrial stocks closed lower with one unchanged. But despite the 15 stocks that closed higher, the volume figures were so weak that the mix at the end of the day saw only 2 Dow stocks make higher OBV highs. And despite the 7-point closing rally, the Climax Indicator actually fell on the day from +1 to -5 and I am sure that that technical weakness was lost on the bulls. The Net Field Trend indicator remained unchanged at +I.

The advance/decline line was strong with another new high recorded and the Nasdaq was especially strong with a wide upswing in its advance/decline line. But strength in these indicators, like the strength in bonds, increasingly smacks of ending moves rather than significant beginnings of new uplegs. In fact this whole period is very similar to the end of the previous bull cycle, the July 1990 top.

Major source of future weakness should stem from bonds. This morning bonds opened up 19/32nds and lost all of it but then managed to end up 8/32nds with the yield at 6.09%. Expect increasing volatility there and then a sudden air pocket.

I think the stock market started a reversal pattern on Monday. Certainly the rise today carried no bullish credentials.

Watch for upside breakout in Gold Stock Index above the 118.12 level. We closed up today at the 117.87 level.

9. *All Parabolics Are Followed By Collapse*

By the summer of 1993 it was apparent that as much as a third of the market was considered interest-sensitive. It was the last segment of market support. It was giving way. Having already cited the parabolic rise in bond prices (collapse in yields), this was the technical sword of Damocles hanging over the bond market. It was certain to break. It did so immediately following the Israel-Palestine September 13, 1993 accord which was formalized in Washington on that date. I didn't attempt to connect the two events other than to remind my followers and students that often a major news event will take place and deflect attention from a key market at a critical time. The final warning was the negative bond closing following an earlier rally on that peak day. The very next day saw all hell breaking loose in the bond market and that was followed by a *key change of pattern*, another downside followthrough the next day, something the bond market had refused to do the week before.

10. *The Pullback Syndrome*

In Frederick Lewis Allen's *Only Yesterday* is a very interesting observation which especially related to the stock market in the summer of 1993:

"As people in the summer of 1929 looked back for precedents, they were comforted by the recollection that every crash of the past few years had been followed by a recovery, and that every recovery had ultimately brought prices to a new high point. Two steps up, one step down, two steps up again- that was how the market went. If you sold you had only to wait for the next crash (they came every few months) and buy in again. And there was really no reason to sell at all: You were bound to win in the end if your stock was sound. The really wise man, it appeared, was he who "bought and held on."

I call this the *pullback syndrome*, wherein every pullback is seen to be healthy and temporary. I used three pertinent quotes from the *Wall Street Journal* in my 1985 book *The Warning.*

September 26, 1929

"Market sentiment is very much mixed again. You will find, however, that bulls are still in the majority. There are plenty of bears but many of them are temporary bears. They believe the market will do little on the bull side until there is some contraction in the brokers' loan item."

September 28, 1929

"The Street terms it the type of healthy reaction from which there is always a substantial recovery."

September 30, 1929

"This house-cleaning had a salutary effect on technical conditions within the market."

A month later the market crashed.

A striking parallel was noted in the *Wall Street Journal* on June 28, 1993

"Since the crash of 1987 individual investors have learned the fundamental lesson of stock investing- buy on price declines. Now, she says, mutual fund buyers are likely to search for bargains during a downturn, which will provide support for the market.

"People are becoming more sophisticated," Ms. Brown says. "They know they're better off to buy when prices are low, so they keep investing whether the market is up or down."

September 1, 1993 - Wednesday Evening

The Dow deviated from its recent pattern of showing strength on the close. This time there was a backtracking and the Dow closed down 6.15 at the 3645.10 level. The Transports lost the entire Tuesday gain of 14.32 points, losing 14.75 points today and dropping that average to the 1650.75 level. The Utility average gave back almost as much as was gained on Tuesday. So this time all three averages closed down and there was nothing technical to save the industrial average from extending the current pattern which suggests further retrenchment. We have a smart looking little pattern recognition picture here that would call for lower prices.

The Climax Indicator rose from -4 to -2 while the Net Field Trend indicator remained unchanged at +1.

The worse case scenario expanded to a potential CLX of -22, not within crash range but another down day tomorrow could do it, thus setting up Friday for a very critical market session.

If one will take the time to examine the May - July 1990 top formation, he will see that we are showing a remarkable symmetrical pattern suggesting a similar top formation. Even the news stories are similar.

The commentators were bad mouthing gold today, only looking at the bullion price. The Gold Stock Index showed a good rebound off the earlier lows and managed to only close down 1.25 at the 116.2 level.

I expect a further pre-Labor Day decline in the general market.

September 2, 1993 - Thursday Evening

Change of pattern seen today which had to disturb the bulls. The long bond rallied sharply for a gain of 20/32nds which dropped the yield to 6.04% but it proved to be no help for stocks, the Dow falling 19 points to close down at the 3626.10 level. Transports, seeing the same handwriting on the wall, collapsed again, falling over 19 points to close down at the 1631.98 level, extending the two session drop to almost 34 points. The Utility average fell a sharp 1.71 points to drop that average to the 253.63 level, extending the two session loss to 2.83 points. The logic behind today's divergent markets is that the economy is not responding to the lower interest rates and thus attention is increasingly to be focused on lower earnings and a downturn in cyclical stocks. With the Dow down to the 3626.10 level and in perfect symmetry with the July 1990 top, the *August 26th intra-day high of 3681.71 takes on added significance now that the Dow is 55 points under that level in just one week.*

Lacking any help from the Transports and Utilities today, undoubtedly the 65-stock Climax Indicator was down sharply and traced out the very bearish large downward zig-zag formation. So this top formation we are in looks increasingly important.

The Climax Indicator today fell from -2 to -7. While the Net Field Trend indicator remained unchanged at +1, the drop today positioned *Caterpillar, DuPont, General Electric* and *General Motors* to each lose a field and drop the NFI from +1 to -3. The market will not be able to withstand any bad news tomorrow. You see, as we are about to enter a bear market, *bad news is bad news.* The days of rallying on bad news are seen to be over.

The price of gold took a hit today but we saw the close well above the earlier lows. The Gold Stock Index was not hit as hard, falling 3.94 points. Every precious metal stock we follow closed comfortably above their stop-close only levels.

I look for an equally critical day tomorrow.

September 4, 1993 - Saturday Afternoon

The Dow rose 7.83 points in the late trading to close at the 3633.93 level. It was down 6.70 points for the week. The Transports fared a great deal worse, falling an additional 8.12 points to the 1623.86 level and down 31.20 points on the week.

The Climax Indicator rose from a revised -8 to -3 in a very weak show of late strength. Twelve Dow industrial stocks recorded technically worthless advances which were equal to a 12 point swing in the Dow. A worthless advance is one showing either no OBV designation or an OBV lower up designation.

The Net Field Trend indicator fell from +1 to -1 and Friday saw the gain of a field in *American Express*, but the loss of a field in *Caterpillar Tractor, General Electric,* and *General Motors*. I had indicated the risk in those stocks the day before. The downtrend in General Motors and the other auto stocks typifies the current distaste for cyclical stocks and the impending further downturn in the economy.

The Dow was seen to have made a very important top on August 25th at the 3652.09 level with the intraday peak recorded the next day at the 3681.71 level. My numbers are duplicating those of mid-July 1990 and thus there is a big risk of a huge loss of several hundred points dead ahead. You will recall the loss of over 600 points in August 1990 following the July peak at the 3000 level. *This market technically threatens to return to that Dow level.*

The price of gold got hit again but the bullion price closed $1 off the low and above the critical chart support levels. While the Gold Stock Index retreated to the 109.97 level, all the precious metal stocks closed above their stop close only levels. *Pegasus* came close to being stopped out at 21.

September 7, 1993 - Tuesday Evening

Last week a major bear market signal was rendered when bonds exploded on the upside but the Dow closed down on the week. Those two diverging markets pointed toward a worsening economy and corporate profits and the cyclical stocks took it the hardest as expected. The market was left in such a weakened state on Friday that there was little left to turn to for support.

Today the Dow broke 26.83 points to close down at the 3607.10 level.

That was about 75 points below the intra-day high of August 26th. And Transports got hit again, closing down 10.47 points at the 1613.39 level. While the Utility average recorded a fractional gain of 0.39, the inability to show a stronger response to the huge gain in the bond market is suspicious. And perhaps it is because with this latest rise of 24/32nds dropping the yield to 5.88%, this *parabolic collapse of yields is signalling an imminent reversal.* Certainly the performance of *Fannie Mae* is telling us that. And the sharp drop in that interest rate bellwether stock is also telling us that something isn't right with the soaring bond market. *Fannie Mae* is a short sale. Buy the December 75 puts.

The Climax Indicator fell from -3 to -10 while the Net Field Trend indicator remained unchanged at -1. *Allied-Signal* and *DuPont* are now positioned to lose field trends. The NFI trend right now is ominously similar to what it was in 1987 a few days before the crash.

Breaking the key support today in the gold chart, we were stopped out today on the entire precious metal portfolio with the one exception of *Newmont Mining.* Since most of the call options have lost so much of their value, they might as well be held until expiration. The only September calls are on *Hecla, Newmont Mining,* and *Placer-Dome*. I don't buy the idea that golds are through. So I have told investors to hold their gold mutual funds.

September 8, 1993 - Wednesday Evening

The market continues on a crash course. After being off as much as 33 points, the Dow settled for a loss Of 18.17 points at the 3588.93 level, 93 points below the intra-day high of August 26th.

Bonds continued to soar, the long bond up 18/32nds to yield 5.86%. But the parabolic collapse in yields increasingly suggests an imminent reversal and that would exacerbate a stock market collapse.

Significant changes of pattern here are all bearish. We had horrendous declines in both advance/decline lines. We have now had two large back to back declines in the Nasdaq and the collapse in the A/D line there definitely shows that the previous rally formation has been killed. And another huge decline of over 20 points in the Transports adds to the bearish appearance of this market.

The high/low indicator is soon to flip over. Today we had 64 highs and 35 lows and that is a very bearish change of pattern.

The Climax Indicator rose from a revised -12 to -8. The Net Field Trend Indicator rose from -1 to +2, reflecting the gain of a field in *Coca Cola* and the gain of two fields in *Procter & Gamble*. Technically the market cannot take a big down day tomorrow because we have worse case scenario for tomorrow of a -26 CLX reading, well within technical range of a crash. But we could be temporarily saved from disaster by the fact that we had a CLX downside non-confirmation today, a higher CLX on a lower Dow.

New short sale recommendations are on *Autotote, Cohu, DSC Communications, IDP Communications, Plum Creek Timber*, and *Pogo Producing.*

The debacle du jour was *Structural Dynamics,* dropping 5-3/8 points to the 13-5/8 level. We got out at 28 in January 1992 when there was an O'Neil Earnings Per Share rating of 97 on the stock.

I have stated my policy on the gold stocks. Short-term we are out but holding call options until expiration. Long term bullish on gold. Hold the mutual fund shares.

September 9, 1993 - Thursday Evening

It finally happened, the inevitable break in the bond market. The long bond today fell 1-12/32nd, pushing the yield up sharply to 5.96%. Judging by the angle of the parabolic, I think today was merely the beginning of a far more extensive break which will add to the bearish appearance of the stock market.

The Dow Jones Industrial Average, after trying to put together a decent earlier advance, succumbed to much of the internal weakness and only managed to close up 0.56 points at the 3589.49 level. That was seen to be very unreliable holding action and leaves the Dow wide open for further extensive declines. When considering the fact that the Dow dropped 45 points in the first two sessions this week, it certainly was entitled to a bounce of more than a fraction of a point.

In relation to what was lost on Tuesday and Wednesday, what the market regained today was very unimpressive. The Transports, for instance, tried to get back what was lost yesterday and an earlier 18-point gain melted away to just a 10-point gain. The Nasdaq put on a better show but I doubt very much that it can fully recover. We had a continued sharp contraction in the number of new highs.

The Climax Indicator rose from -8 to -5. The Net Field Trend Indicator for Wednesday was revised to +1, *Coca Cola* not gaining a field. But today *Coca Cola* did gain a field and *Disney* lost a field and thus the NFI remained unchanged at +1. The market responded to the CLX downside non-confirmation reported here yesterday. That allowed the market to avoid an otherwise technical debacle. But the performance was merely a very unreliable holding action.

I was glad to see the entire list of precious metal stocks rebound today inasmuch as I have recommended continued holding of the precious metal mutual funds as well as all the call options. I was most impressed with the rebound to 2-1/2 in *Sunshine Mining*, still my best pick for long-term gains.

11. *Psychology At Major Market Tops*

Right near the 1993 bull peak one of my subscribers asked me what it would take to turn me bullish. I immediately accepted the question as perfect psychological proof that the market top was at hand. I then answered the question in detail in the September 9, 1993 market letter:

WHAT WOULD IT TAKE TO TURN ME BULLISH?

A subscriber asked me this question this past week. That is the kind of question I would expect to be asked right as the market is about to crash. In my August 19th letter I described the current conditions as *those most likely to precede the crash of 1994.* Now I will answer that gentleman's question. The most simplistic answer to the question would be that *everything that makes me bearish would have to reverse.* Let us look at a few of those things:

A Market Crash - Ironically, *nothing would turn me bullish more rapidly than a market crash.* At least it would, as in October 1987, produce a major buy signal. Since I have carefully documented the current technical signals as likely to be followed by a better than 600-point decline as in August 1990, a crash of that magnitude or worse is highly probable. A crash produces the perfect oversold bottom, completely reversing the overbought conditions at the August 25th Dow high.

Time- This subject alone would make it virtually impossible to turn bullish. Since we cannot turn the clock back, to reverse the time indicator would be like trying to put the toothpaste back into the tube. In other words, if we could put the market back to where it was in late 1990 I could then turn bullish. That was the *first phase* of the current bull cycle and it turned me bullish. After January of this year the market was skating on increasingly thin technical ice since we were then about to go past the typical 27 months of a bull cycle. Thus a significant downturn in 1994 is far more probable than starting a new extension of the bull cycle which is already overextended.

New Stock Highs- The peak date and level in this important technical indicator is December 31, 1991. On that day the number of new stock highs on the New York Stock Exchange stood at 336. *It has never seen that level since.* Obviously, if I thought there was any chance of seeing that figure again I would have to turn bullish because I could no longer hang my hat on declining highs.

The Dichotomy - So many stocks topped out after*January 1992* that those can never fully recover during this cycle. Let me put it this way: I will turn bullish when*Amgen* closes above 80, when*Apple Computer* closes above 65, when*Glaxo* closes above 38, when *Merck* closes above 53, when *Philip Morris* closes above 86, when T-2 Medical closes above 65, and when *US Surgical* closes above 134-1/2. I could go on and on and on. I have kept repeating it over and over that this market has become afflicted with an internal technical cancer. *It then becomes increasingly obvious that there is nothing the Dow can do to make me turn bullish.* How can one manipulate 30 stocks so as to cover up and repair the extensive damage I have correctly cited since January 1992? This is a game of musical chairs. Too many chairs have been removed from the game. Put all the chairs back and start over again and I will turn bullish.

I just received a letter from a Kansas City gentleman who periodically makes recommendations. The opening lines say a mouthful and further bear out my contention that we are dealing with two markets here:

"I have always felt that credit should be given when it is due. And I think my last (June 8, 1993) stock letter sent to some of these stations should be cited for what it was: one of the worst list of stocks ever touted. For one thing, the list was too long- the longer the list of stocks- the less selective one can be.

By our count, as of the Friday September 3, 1993 closing, only 18 of our 47 stock selections had net gains. That's a batting average of only .382. That would be a good baseball average-but it's terrible as an advisor average."

The Transportation Average - Close the Transports above 1683.08 and that would make me think about turning bullish. You notice, it is no one thing that could turn me around. It would require a collection of things and at this writing nothing is even remotely in sight that could suggest a gargantuan and improbable market change.

The Nasdaq Advance/Decline Line- As the Nasdaq Composite Average roared ahead to new highs this past week, the media loved to tell you about those new highs but I don't recall anybody warning of the fact that the Nasdaq advance/decline line peaked last February 4th and that all those new highs were non-confirmed. On September 3rd the A/D line almost made a new high but failed. The declines immediately thereafter were awesome. I would want to see new highs in the Nasdaq Composite confirmed by its advance/decline line.

New OBV High On the Dow Industrials - I want you to look at the table of Dow industrial stocks shown on the bottom of page 3. There you will see the On-Balance Volume highs for each stock and when those highs were recorded. If you put all those OBV high dates in chronological order you would see a *table of technical upside exhaustion.* A third of all the Dow industrial stocks saw their OBV highs last year. Now we have reached the pinnacle of upside exhaustion, no Dow stocks recording OBV highs. Inasmuch as my contention that volume precedes price gave birth to my development of On-Balance Volume, one will now see that any remaining upside momentum in the Dow industrials has totally collapsed. I couldn't possibly turn bullish again until that upside momentum is restored.

September 11, 1993 - Saturday Afternoon

Highlighting this holiday-shortened week, the surprising turn based on Friday's producer price index prevented what could have been a very bad week, cutting a Dow weekly loss of about 45 points to just 12.30 points at the 3621.63 level. Adding to the Friday euphoria was the Israel-Palestine accord, to be signed in Washington on Monday.

The bond market followed the Thursday collapse by almost recouping the entire loss, the long bond rising almost 1-1/4 points with the yield falling back to 5.88%.

But the equity markets had some technical caveats. While the steep drop earlier in the week entitled the market to some rebound, the number of new highs rebounding on Friday from Thursday's low 61 number to 132, nevertheless saw this new number as far short of the 189 highs of August 25th which in turn was far short of the bull market high of 336. That is still the biggest technical problem area.

The Climax Indicator rebounded from -5 to +6, not a very big move for a Dow rally of 32 points. In fact, the highest CLX number seen going back to last May was the +10 reading of August 24th, making the entire summer season pose a big technical question mark. The Net Field Trend indicator rose to +3, gaining fields in *Disney* and *Goodyear*. Here we have the NFI parallel with the 1987 pre-crash period. In the 1987 market we went from -8 to +3 between September 18th and October 2nd. In this market the NFI went from -8 to +3 between August 17th and September 10th. So these numbers certainly foreshadow a very critical few weeks ahead.

Golds have to rebuild a new base. They don't have much time to do this in order to save the October and November call options but since I feel we have seen the worst on this move we have no choice.

September 13, 1993 - Monday Evening

The eyes of the world were on Washington to witness the incredible event of the Israel-Palestine accord. Many would argue, of course, that the market should have done better in the face of such an historic spectacle. As it was, the Dow was up 17 at the best but that was cut back to a closing gain of 12.30 points at the 3633.93 level. The Transports did much better, closing up 23.30 points at the 1634-76 level but now running into a very strong upside resistance area. Utilities only added a fraction of 0.40 while the long bond actually closed down 1/32nd, well below the morning high.

The high/low indicator improved with 156 highs and 25 lows but well under the 189 highs of August 25th. The advance/decline line was most restrained with only a positive spread of 65 and so it was apparent that there was much selling today, taking advantage of the great event in Washington to hide their intention.

This restraint was reflected by a decline in the Climax Indicator from a revised +5 to +2, recording a CLX upside non-confirmation and a signal of fresh declines ahead. The Friday numbers were revised to show that *Goodyear* did not gain a field and that *Procter & Gamble* lost a field. Thus the NFI was unchanged on Friday at +1. Today *Goodyear* did gain a field and the NFI now stands at +2. That remains a very substandard performance and one that promises future trouble.

And Nasdaq took an almost 4-point tumble today.

Gold stocks had their own troubles, tumbling again sharply today. The very speed of the decline may be its best hope to produce a new buy signal. I am convinced that gold will not make a new low on this move but will shortly trace out a pattern of rising bottoms above the low of last December. We hold to the long-term bullish outlook, investors told to continue holding their mutual fund shares.

Despite the Dow rise, our short positions in *Adaptec, American Power*

Conversion, Analysts International, Apache, Applied Materials and *Arrow Electronics* prospered.

September 14, 1993 - Tuesday Evening

The Consumer Price Index came in at three times higher than the economists predicted and the long bond, looking for any excuse to decline, fell 1-11/32nds to push the yield up to 5.97%. The stock market, already technically weakened by the sell signal recorded here yesterday by the Climax Indicator upside non-confirmation, promptly declined and the damage was wide and across the board. The Dow fell 18.45 points, Transports got hit over 22 points, and the Utility Average fell 1.32 points.

The advance/decline lines an both the big board and the Nasdaq took very big hits and underscored how genuine the decline was. New highs contracted sharply to 69.

The Climax Indicator fell from +2 to -1, not a wide move for an 18-point Dow decline but the market cannot afford another down day tomorrow. It could do a great deal more technical damage. The Net Field Trend Indicator remained unchanged at +2 but could easily lose fields tomorrow on *Allied-Signal, Union Carbide,* and *United Technologies.*

The current decline in the Nasdaq underscores the importance of the inability to score a new high in its advance/decline line.

Gold stocks, now down in the areas of major technical support, had an up day. I want to see a new base form here before taking any new aggressive buying stance.

Our short sales again prospered, declines today in so many of these. Biggest declines were in *American Power Conversion, Applied Materials, Autotote, DSC Communications, Fannie Mae,* and *Plum Creek Timber.*

Fannie Mae looks like the best short sale.

The market is seen to be on a crash course.

September 15, 1993 - Wednesday Evening

The Dow exhibited great resilience today, bouncing back strongly from a steep morning drop from well under the 3600 level to post a gain of 17.89 points at the 3633.65 level. Transports were up over 11 points but much of that was from a better than 3-point rise in *Federal Express.* Utilities couldn't join the party, posting a fractional loss, reflecting another drop in bonds. But bonds cut a huge earlier loss of well over a point to just a loss of 6/32nds with the yield at 5.99%.

While the Dow recovery looked impressive on the surface, there were a few technical caveats worth mentioning. For one thing, the number of new highs contracted from 72 to 66. So while the Dow stood at the 3634 level on Monday with 157 new highs, the Dow today at 3633 only saw less than half that number at 66. Secondly, the almost 18-point rise in the Dow was accompanied by a loss in the advance/decline line. Though it was only a small loss, it means the A/D line is 697 below the Monday level when the Dow was at 3634. So the market did lose a few spots.

The Climax Indicator is revealing. The rally today saw the CLX jump from -1 to +7. *But we had 10 lower up designations today and that sets us up for some fresh declines.* The Net Field Trend Indicator rose to +3, gaining a field in *Exxon.*

Again I draw attention to the fact that in 1987 the NFI fell from +14 to -8, rallied back to +3 by October 2nd and then crashed two weeks later. In this market we have a carbon copy. The NFI peaked at +14 in March, fell to -8 by August 17th and has now rallied back to +3.

So I am very suspicious as to the implications of today's comeback. Keep those technical caveats in mind.

Gold stocks mostly rebounded today. My advice remains the same. I want to be sure they are forming a new base before resuming aggressive new buying. I suspect that we are starting the second leg up but I want to be sure. We are staying with the mutual funds. The call options need a miracle but most of them don't expire until October and November.

September 16, 1993 - Thursday Evening

A late smash in the bond market produced a drop of 25/32nds in the long bond, sending the yield up to 6.03%. Apparently the stock market didn't see that number, only falling 2.80 points to the 3630.85 level. But the technical action was not strong, there being 10 Dow industrial stock gains that were technically worthless. A worthless rise is when the stock either posts no designation or records a lower up designation. The Dow got no side help either, transports only up 1.06 points and the utility average again showing a fractional decline.

Again the advance/decline line fell. It wasn't by much but now that indicator is down over 1000 since the September 3rd high. If the Dow suddenly shot up over 22 points into new high ground it would lack an A/D line confirmation. I missed the final number of new highs but we only had about 50 with half an hour to go until the close. So that was not impressive, again being far under the Monday figure.

The Climax Indicator fell from +7 to +2 while the Net Field trend indicator remained unchanged at +3.

Albertsons fell to 52-1/8 today. A break under 49 would look very bearish and send the stock down to the next support at 47.

Gold had a big day. The Gold Stock Index closed up a huge 5.83 points at the 103.68 level. But most of the stocks are coming back to key resistance levels and thus we have to see more before aggressive new buying can be recommended. But there is enough evidence here to proclaim the second leg advance underway. Now the stocks have to back and fill for awhile so as to build a reliable base.

I continue to see the general market technically on a crash course.

September 18, 1993 - Saturday Afternoon

The Dow fell 17.60 points to the 3613.25 level *for the third consecutive weekly loss.* Transports managed to rise on the week but the individual stocks making up the Transport average look technically weak, especially the airlines.

The high/low indicator showed a definite change toward weakness this past week.

Triple witching days are always a technical risk because whichever way the market goes the volume is assigned in that direction. The bears won on Friday because the very heavy volume of 370 million shares saw most of that assigned to the downside in the Dow industrial stocks.

The Climax Indicator fell from +2 to -6, not low enough to be climactic but low enough to detect further troubles coming. The Net Field Trend Indicator showed a bearish mix on balance. *Caterpillar, DuPont,* and *General Electric* all gained fields but *Eastman Kodak* lost two fields, *Exxon* lost a field, *McDonalds* lost a field, and *United Technologies* lost a field. This net loss of two fields dropped the NFI back to +1.

Apache fell to 27-5/8. We went short at 30-7/8. First support is at 24-1/2. I have recommended the October 35 puts. *IDB Communications* fell to 50. No real support until 37. There I have recommended the November 50 puts. These look very attractive.

Gold seen to have a normal pullback. We have a good bottom in place now and near-term action expected to be constructive backing and filling as a new reliable base is formed. Stay with mutual funds and call options but I feel new aggressive buying is still premature. I want to see more backing and filling.

September 20, 1993 - Monday Evening

Making the expected downside followthrough on the parabolic curve in bond prices, the long bond cracked 22/32nds bringing the yield up to 6.09% and that was accompanied by a break of 37.45 points in the Dow dropping that average to the 3575.80 level. After three weeks on the downside, the Dow is off to a good start on a fourth week of decline. The Dow is now 106 points below the 3681.71 intraday high of August 26th. There was no sidehelp to act as a technical shock absorber, Transports and Utilities also falling, utilities down a sharp 1.32 points.

The advance/decline fell by approximately 277 while the high/low indicator showed 80 highs and 23 lows. But the big decline today will see a sharp contraction in the number of new highs to be reported tomorrow.

I think the big decline took most people by surprise today because it extends the losses for those who bought on Rosh Hashana and it failed to reverse the Friday triple witching option expiration, a pattern many were probably counting on.

The Climax Indicator fell to -12 while the Net Field Trend indicator remained unchanged at +1.

Gold prices rose along with the price of oil, a double negative for bonds.

CBS's *60 Minutes* presented an expose on *National Health Labs.* That stock fell 1-7/8 points to 15-1/8. William O'Neil assigned a top earnings rating of 97 on the stock in January 1992. I got people out of it at 28-1/2. NIKE fell 1-3/4 points today to 46-1/2. I got subscribers out of the stock at 74-3/4 in January 1992. O'Neil gave it a high earnings per share rating of 85 at that time.

Fannie Mae fell 1-1/8 points today to 75-3/4.

The Dow closed at the exact low of the day and that suggests another slide tomorrow.

September 21, 1993 - Tuesday Evening

Looking for another slide in the market today, the Dow broke 26 points in the morning trading. Bonds attempted a rally and for awhile were actually up on the day. But then all hell broke loose. Word hit the Street that Boris Yeltsin had dissolved the Russian parliament and called for new elections in December but the Supreme Soviet Council stripped Yeltsin of all powers and appointed a new President. This crisis saw the Dow down as much as 67 points for awhile but then recovering to close down 38.56 points at the 3537.24 level. There was no offsetting side help, Transports down

18.38 at the 1598 level and utilities down 1.51 at the 251.19 level.

The Dow has now fallen 76 points so far this week and is down 144 points under the August 26th intraday high. It appears virtually certain that this is the fourth week of decline in the Dow.

The long bond fell 13/32nds to yield 6.12%. Now the extreme bearish significance of a parabolic rise is being well demonstrated.

In parallel with the July 1990 cyclic top and ensuing decline, the market was warning of a shocker as it had back then with the invasion of Kuwait.

The huge declines in both the NYSE advance/decline line and the Nasdaq warns of further steep declines. Most analysts are misreading the A/D line, thinking that only a very short-term correction is taking place. Those analysts have forgotten that the A/D line was a coincident indicator on December 3, 1968.

The high/low indicator showed 68 highs and 38 lows. Today's steep decline points toward even weaker numbers tomorrow.

The Climax Indicator today fell to -17. The Net Field Trend indicator fell to -2, losing fields in *Alcoa, Caterpillar*, and *International Paper*.

Gold responded to the Russian crisis with a steep rise of $9.50 an ounce. This was a great help to those maintaining their gold mutual fund shares as well as those still holding their call options. Hold all gold instruments but I still have some reservations as to chasing the shares at this point.

September 22, 1993 - Wednesday Evening

The Russian situation calmed down overnight and Wall Street was looking for a big rebound today. As it turned out, the Dow peaked right after the opening with a gain of better than 18 points but that was cut in half by the close with a gain of 9.78 points at the 3547.02 level. We have to keep that in perspective, having seen the Dow fall over 75 points on Monday and Tuesday. So it was not an impressive rebound. The same could be said for the Transports and Utilities.

The advance/decline line gained about 658, a good portion of what was lost the day before. The high/low indicator with only 77 new highs was not impressive, having seen over double that number last week.

The Climax Indicator rose from -17 to -6 and that was certainly not a show of strength. The number of technically worthless gains today among the Dow industrial stocks equalled 16 points. So with the Dow up less than 10 points, the market today was the technical equivalent of a loss of 7 points.

The Net Field Trend indicator remained unchanged at -2.

Good news for gold traders. As I said yesterday, I did not want to chase the stocks on that sharp Tuesday runup. That was emotional and on news and of course was ripe for the decline today. But you will now see that the gold chart shows a perfect reverse head and shoulders bottom. I was impressed today by the fact that gold closed $3 off the bottom and the Gold Stock Index cut a better than $5 loss to $2.91 at the 106.40 level. So I see a green light on for new buying in the gold and silver stocks.

New short sale recommendation is *Motorola*, closing today at 94-3/4. Stock is a perfect parabolic curve and has an O'Neil Earnings Per Share rating of 94. So the stock is ripe for a major decline. Buy the December 95 put options. Use Stop loss on the stock at 105.

September 23, 1993 - Thursday Evening

The Dow fell 7.27 points today to close down at the 3539.75 level. Now being down 73.50 points on the week so far, we are about to see the fourth consecutive week of decline. Transports rose 11.11 today but failed to turn in any significant technical numbers. Utilities fell a sharp 1.91 points and the weakness there could nullify what otherwise would be a downside CLX nonconfirmation today.

The internals were better than the Dow today and new highs rose to 115 with lows contracting to 19. So we do have an excuse here for at least some short-term recoveries. But both the NYSE and the Nasdaq advance/decline lines are under their highs and the higher number of new highs last week proved to be temporary and thus it is too early to talk about anything significant on the upside.

The Climax Indicator today rose from -6 to -3 on the lower Dow reading and this signalled some new technical strength. The Net Field Trend indicator again remained unchanged at -2.

Gold rose $4 as expected while the Gold Stock Index closed up 1.97 at the 108.37 level. So this index has almost made up what it lost yesterday. I think technically we are again on solid ground with the gold and silver stocks.

Adobe and *Storage Technology* got hit today. Those stocks had *Investor's Business Daily* peak Earnings Per Share ratings of 86 and 96 respectively at their highs.

So the big picture remains the same. I think we are in the first phase of a bear market. One has to be very defensive.

September 25, 1993 - Saturday Afternoon

The Dow closed out the week with mixed Friday performance, but further featured weakness in the Dow Utility Average. The net decline of over 70 points in the Dow industrials underscored this as being the weakest of the four weeks of consecutive decline.

It *reversed* the traditional rise that usually takes place between Rosh Hashana and Yom Kippur. It also *reversed* the traditional rise that usually follows a triple witching option expiration. What was seen to be particularly significant was that after it was quite apparent that Yeltsin had the upper hand in the Russian crisis, the Dow still closed down 70 points. The inability to rebound more off the low identifies the presence of other deep seated technical deficiencies.

The Climax Indicator rose from -3 to -1. However, the 65-stock CLX fell from -9 to -10. Industrials and Transports were a standoff *and the entire net decline stemmed from the drop in the utility average.* That average has now fallen over 8 points under the high of 250.53, closing down 1.05 on Friday at 248.42. That is underscoring new warnings for the general market.

The Net Field Trend indicator rose to zero, gaining two fields in *Bethlehem Steel.*

The Nasdaq closed at a new high of 754.65 but nobody draws attention to the fact that the A/D line remains well under the February 4th high.

Perrigo collapsed 4-1/2 points to 29-1/4. This stock was featured in a recent inside back cover full page recommendation by *Investor's Business Daily* right near the high of 34-1/2. The stock was assigned a peak Earnings Per Share rating of 98 and a Relative Strength rating of 91. *I have concluded that stocks are being distributed under the guise of these high O'Neil Earnings Per Share ratings.*

After being down most of the day, the Gold Stock Index managed to close up.

Under the present technical circumstances it will be difficult for the market to mount a meaningful rally.

September 27, 1993 - Monday Evening

Bonds took the ball right from the opening and ran with it as far as they could, pushing the gain to 1-12/32nds with the yield falling back to 5.95%. The Dow tried to draw a carbon copy but there the hype was far greater than the technical results. By mid-afternoon the Dow was temporarily up over 30 points but the final 45 minutes of trading saw no gain and the Dow closed up 24.59 points at the 3567.70 level, over 20% down from the peak.

Transports and utilities were strong but nowhere near strong enough to make an impression in cutting previous losses.

New highs, the advance/decline line, and the Nasdaq were all turning in good performances but the immediate test is the ability to followthrough.

The Climax Indicator rose from -1 to +7. While one might consider that a good advance, one has to look at the fact that we had only 3 higher OBV up designations, 1 higher down designation, 3 lower down designations, and no less than 8 lower up designations. The Net Field Trend indicator remained unchanged at zero but looking at those 8 lower ups, any fresh downturns will see a large loss of field trends.

Keep the Dow in the proper perspective. Despite the rally today, that average is 114 points under the August 26th intraday high.

The golds took a big hit today *but fell back into attractive support areas.* For instance, ASA fell from 43 to 41-5/8 but that is *a rising bottom. American* Barrick performed in the same constructive manner as did *Homestake* and other key precious metal stocks.

September 28, 1993 - Tuesday Evening

The Dow was unable to followthrough on the upside today, closing down 1.68 points at the 3566.02 level. The side help was stronger, both Transports and utilities closing higher. We remain 116 points under the August 26th intraday high.

The A/D line again improved, rising a net 186. New highs remained in the 150 area. Over on the Nasdaq another new high was seen at the 763.66 level but the advance/decline line still persistently failed to confirm the high.

The Climax Indicator fell from a revised +6 to +3. Once again the number of OBV lower up designations was larger than the CLX, a telltale indication of important technical weakness. The Net Field Trend indicator remained unchanged at zero.

Motorola continued to rise, jumping today to the 104-1/2 level. I had assigned a stop loss level at 105. If we get stopped out it doesn't change the outlook. The stock has traced out an extreme parabolic rose. Six months from now I wouldn't be surprised to see the stock back to the first important chart support at 45.

Gold stocks were firm to higher today and again I stress the attractiveness of current levels. These stocks are ripe for important reaccumulation.

The popular view now is that this market has another leg on the upside before an important decline. Having already seen the 3650 level and the higher intraday high of 3681, I suspect that we have already seen the last upleg. In a bear market the bears are right and my work underscores our current entry in a bear market and thus bearish sentiment is the correct sentiment.

September 29, 1993 - Wednesday Evening

The Fat Lady was singing today. The Dow was up 10 points in the morning, fell back to a deficit of 11, and then climbed back up to close up 0.28 at the 3566.30 level. The key word today was oil but it carried with it a price tag. The XOI soared over 7 points as OPEC made some production cuts. *Chevron* rose 2-1/2 points, *Exxon* rose 1 point, and *Texaco* rose 1-1/2 points. Those three gains represented a Dow rise of approximately 10 points. But nobody would have seen that to look at the practically unchanged average. I therefore have to conclude that stocks were distributed under the guise of the strength in the oil issues. *We may be seeing the last missing link in this bull cycle.* Most such cycles end with a flurry in the oil stocks and thus the Fat Lady is singing her most important aria.

The rise in oil prices bombarded the Transport Average, Bending it down 16.25 points to the 1637.53 level. Utilities got hit for a drop of 1.65 points, practically wiping out Monday's large gain.

And the oil rally socked bonds for a loss of 26/32nds bringing the yield back up to the 6% level.

The Climax Indicator fell from a revised +4 to -1. Once again the number of lower up designations far exceeded the CLX which was again a bearish signal. Despite the oil strength, the Net Field Trend indicator remained unchanged at zero.

With the complete lack of any side help today, the 65-Stock CLX showed significant weakness. Again I underscore the weakness in the utility average. I believe what we are seeing here is the end of the line for the interest-sensitive stocks.

I think the new high today in the Nasdaq A/D line is a bull trap. Take advantage of the current pullback in the gold stocks.

September 30, 1993 - Thursday Evening

The Dow fooled the pundits again and fell 11.18 points to the 3555.12 level. Many had expected and predicted a strong closing on end-of-the-quarter window dressing. While some oil stocks still showed strength, the flareup seen yesterday died today, even *Exxon* falling 1-1/8 points. Again, conspicuously absent, there was no offsetting sidehelp in the averages.

Transports fell again while utilities were flat.

But the advance/decline line did well on both the New York Stock Exchange and on the Nasdaq. The high/low indicator showed a loss of strength, new highs contracting to 106.

The bond market retreated again, losing 12/32nds and putting the yield up to 6.02%. With several key economic statistics due tomorrow, bonds could be in for another large retreat. The stock market cannot afford a big drop tomorrow. It would only require a drop of 12 points to see the market declining for the *fifth* consecutive week.

The Climax Indicator fell from -1 to -3. The 65-stock CLX did a great deal worse, reflecting the Dow Transport stocks in major retreat. Out of 20 stocks, 13 declined today with 3 unchanged.

What we have to watch now is the number of preferred stocks making new highs. I expect a significant contraction as it becomes increasingly apparent that interest rates have bottomed and are now headed higher. Once the interest-sensitive contingent goes into full retreat the advance/decline line will collapse.

I think August 25 marked the high and that we are in the first phase of a bear market. The fat lady is still on stage.

Golds did better today.

October 2, 1993 - Saturday Afternoon

The Dow avoided a fifth declining week by turning in a rally prompted by new quarterly buying and an extension of strength in the oil group. The Dow rose 25.99 points to close at the 3581.11 level. Transports had a bounce but volume statistics showed that group as having no significant technical strength. A typical example was UAL rising 2-5/8 points on a volume of only 67,300 shares. Like examples elsewhere tagged the Friday rally as having no technical staying power, a rally to definitely sell into.

A reliable method of gauging the technical strength of a Dow advance is to only count the number of higher OBV highs and subtract the number of true or lower OBV down designations. All advances not producing higher OBV highs are deemed to be technically worthless. Friday saw no less than 13 worthless advances as well as a large number closing unchanged to lower. Despite the 38-point gain in the Dow for the week, such measurements as all the Climax indicator readings for the industrials, transports and utilities were lower for the week.

The Climax Indicator on Friday rose from -3 to +4 but the 65-stock CLX only showed a feeble +2 reading, a far cry from the +19 reading at the August high. The Net Field Trend indicator rose to +1, gaining a field in *Alcoa*. Nevertheless, that Dow stock was still 11 points under the all-time high and those are just some of the statistical tricks that averages play.

Motorola fell a point to 100 and I think we made a good call on that stock as a completed parabolic rise. It looks like an excellent short. It went against us for awhile but now the January 95 puts should soon be back in the money. Summing up, early October strength is deemed to be meaningless as was the early October strength in 1989.

October 4, 1993 - Monday Evening

Despite the generally positive response abroad to the Russian crisis, the Dow closed down 3.35 points at the 3577.76 level. Transports were seen to have a meaningless rise *while the Dow Utility Average again sounded a clarion call of coming trouble, 14 out of the 15 Dow utility stocks closing unchanged to lower.* That average fell 1.85 points to the 247.56 level. I have gone on record that bonds have peaked and the drop in the utility average is in keeping with that trend. The long bond fell 7/32nds to push the yield back up to 6%.

The advance/decline line moved out to a new high today while the number of new highs contracted to 134.

Last week's 38-point rise in the Dow was heavily weighted by the gain in *Chevron*. All the Dow oil stocks retreated today. *Chevron* has shown a parabolic rise and is a stock that can be shorted. *Chevron* fell 2 points today.

The Climax Indicator fell from +4 to +1. The Net Field Trend Indicator fell from +1 to -1, losing two fields in *DuPont*.

Gold stocks were pretty much higher across the board and I think they would have gone up regardless of the attention on the Russian crisis.

So this week starts off with a Dow decline although internal strength still looked impressive today. But the Dow stocks on balance look increasingly vulnerable. *Minnesota Mining* was weak today.

Chevron looks vulnerable for a move back down to 80 over the next three months. *DuPont* should drop to 42 over the next term on a closing under 46. *Minnesota Mining* should drop to 97 for an important test of long term support.

Summing up, the Dow has been dropping over 80% of the time since August 25th. Continue to sell into strength.

October 5, 1993 - Tuesday Evening

The technical features seen today were negative on balance. The most disturbing feature was that of weighting. While the Dow closed up 9.50 points at the 3587.26 level, the 2-1/8 point rise in *Minnesota Mining*, the 1-5/8 point rise in *Procter and Gamble*, and the 1-3/4 point rise in *Sears* accounted for about an 11-point rise and thus 10% of the Dow stocks accounted for more than the entire rise.

So this was not a strong response to the large gains today in the European market. Early strength saw the Dow up more than 20 points, losing all of this in the late afternoon before a late technically meaningless attempt to make the list look good.

Again we got another warning from the Dow Utility Average as it closed down 1.45 points and produced its own Climax Indicator -9 reading, more than enough to wipe out the industrial Climax Indicator +8 reading.

The Net Field Trend indicator returned to the +1 level, *Union Carbide* and *Woolworth* each gaining a field.

One will note the chart resistance at Dow 3600. Coming within 3 points of that level on the early rally was enough to stop the advance.

Bonds were unchanged with the yield at 6.01% and again I stress the top formation there.

Today we saw quite a few big hits, a definite day of selective liquidation, breaks *in Advanced Micro Technology, Micron Technology, Verifone,* as well as a drop of 2-1/8 points in *Motorola* to the 98-3/4 level, our best bet short sale.

Golds were firm to higher, *Placer-Dome* looking particularly good at 20-1/2.

October 6, 1993 - Wednesday Evening

Once again the Dow floundered at the 3600 level. Early strength gave way to afternoon weakness as the industrials reached for supporting help and found that it was again lacking. President Clinton's afternoon remarks on Somalia simply injected further uncertainty.

If a Dow advance is going to be technically significant, *side help is required.* By side help I mean the Transports and the Utilities. Today such side help was again lacking. So the gain of 11.73 points in the Dow was not convincing, again closing under the 3600 level. The Transports closed down 3.85 and the Utility Average posted a fractional gain of 0.33.

Bonds showed nothing, closing unchanged with the yield at the 6.01% level. The inability of the utilities to rally left that segment forecasting further trouble down the road.

The Climax Indicator fell from +8 to +5 and with the lack of side help produced a weak 65-stock CLX number.

The Net Field Trend indicator rose from a revised +2 reading to +3, reflecting the loss of a field in *General Electric* and the gain of two fields in *McDonalds.*

Those who have followed my Climax Indicator for a number of years find it to be nothing short of incredible that the CLX never bettered the +10 level after August 24th, the last major peak at +18 on May 19th. Equally, the inability of the Net Field Trend indicator to put on any impressive show of strength also raises legitimate technical questions.

You will notice that *US Surgical* reached a new low today of 20, having fallen all the way from 134-1/2 since January 1992. Silence. No apologies from those earnings enthusiasts who gave it their top rating right at the peak price.

Gold stocks continued to attract buying well past the peak of the Russian crisis. The Gold Stock Index rose strongly to 111.67, effecting a trendline breakout and further validating the bottom that was recorded last month.

October 7, 1993 - Thursday Evening

The market was on the defensive all day. The Dow got steadily weaker on balance as the day wore on and closed at the low of the day, losing 15.36 points at the 3583.63 level. This technically reflected the inability to rise above the 3600 level on this return move rally attempt since September 21st. Anybody comparing the internal action of the market on this latest rally attempt with the action from August 10th to the August 25th high will see a tremendous loss of upside momentum which made the technical failure at Dow 3600 virtually certain to occur. Now the Dow should drop rapidly and quickly break under the September 21st low at the 3537 level.

The drop today almost eliminated all of the rise this week and if the bond market gets bad news tomorrow on a large number of new jobs then we will be looking at the fifth down week for the Dow out of the last six.

New highs contracted to 106 today and since the market fell, the number is expected to contract sharply on Friday.

The 4-3/8 point rise in *American President* was responsible for the gain in the Transport average. But the chart of that stock underscored the rise as a selling opportunity. Most Transport stocks fell.

Again the real focus of the market was on the steady show of weakness in the Utility average as it fell again to a new low on this move. 11 out of the 15 Dow utility stocks closed down today and that promises another low CLX reading for that group as well as on the 65-stock Climax Indicator.

The Climax Indicator fell from a revised +6 to zero. The Net Field Trend indicator fell to +1, *Coca Cola* losing a field and a downward revision in *DuPont* dropping another field.

I had mentioned the new low in *US Surgical* yesterday against a background of silence. Typically, the stock rallied today, maximum media attention at the top and few if any rooters at the bottom.

The Gold Index moved up to the 113 level today, still headed higher.

October 9, 1993 - Saturday Afternoon

Friday put on a fireworks display in the bond market, exploding the long bond 1-1/4 points with the yield dropping to 5.92%, responding to the latest monthly employment report. Analysts immediately projected a sharp Dow rise. Instead, the Dow went into a brief collapse of 27 points but late afternoon strength saw it recover to a gain of 1.11 points at the 3584.74 level.

Gaining 3.63 points on the week, the large drop of over 5 points in the Utility Average grabbed the technical headlines. Industrials have a dubious future in the face of this fast developing weakness and will feel the loss of sideline support.

The Climax Indicator rose from zero to +3 while the Net Field Trend indicator remained unchanged at +1. The 65-Stock Climax Indicator improved from -6 to zero and there was no net improvement in field trends. *Consolidated Freight* and *UAL* each gained a field in the Transports but earlier in the week we saw losses of fields in *AMR, Roadway,* and *Xtra* so there is no strength worth noting in the Transports. We saw *American President* rise another 2-1/8 points, stretching the 2-day gain to 6-1/2 points with no accompanying OBV up designation. That is an incredible show of technical weakness, not strength. We saw *Federal Express* on Friday jump 3 points and yet only could attach an OBV lower up designation to the move. Despite those obvious examples of weighting, the Transport average could only rise 0.43 points.

The gain in fields in the Transports on Friday was offset by the loss of two fields in *Pacific Gas & Electric* in the Utility section and thus the 65-stock NFI again was down on the week. *It is the steady loss of strength in the Dow Util-*

ity Average that underscores the cutting edge of current technical concern.

ASA moved out to 45-5/8, a typical leader in the current rebounding gold stocks. Chartwise, the old highs are coming into sight again on stocks like *American Barrick* and *Placer Dome.*

October 11, 1993 - Monday Evening

Today was a holiday market. The Dow closed up 8.67 points at 3593.41, still trading half a dozen points under last Thursday. There was no teeth in the advance, light volume and only a small rise in market breadth.

The bond market was closed for Columbus Day, futures giving up 1/32nd.

The Transports rose 11.54 points.*American President* added another 1-1/2 points to stretch the gain to 8 points in three sessions. And still there is no OBV up designation, making the entire upswing extremely suspicious.

But technicians continued to focus on the continuing weakness in the utilities, the Dow utility average dropping 0.59 points.

New highs contracted 15% to 95 but if we assume that we still had 27 preferred stocks on the new high list, then the number of common stock new highs fell 21% to 68. This indicator, more than any other, most seriously questions any further significant extension of strength in this market.

The Climax Indicator fell from +3 to +2, very suspicious for a gain of over 8 points.

The Net Field Trend Indicator jumped from +1 to +4, gaining a field in *General Electric* and two fields in *Merck.* Not too much can be read into this improvement in the NFI inasmuch as the NFI showed a sharp jump in October 1989 just before the mini-crash.

Intel came in with double earnings and the stock got hit by 4-3/4 points, closing down at the 65-1/2 level. *Motorola* reported double earnings and that stock dropped 2 points to the 98-1/2 level. One commentator referred to earnings as history, something I have always contended. An earnings report is a statement of something that has already taken place. It has no relationship to tomorrow. The market deals in tomorrows.

Golds continued to act well, ASA advancing to 45-7/8.

October 12, 1993 - Tuesday Evening

The Dow started out on the upside with a better than 6 point gain but again encountered resistance in the Dow 3600 area, closing fractionally lower at the 3593.13 level. Transports did not fare well, closing down

10.69 at the 1636.25 level. But the focus remained on the sliding utility average as it again fell.

The Climax Indicator rose from +2 to +5 but this minor strength was more than offset by the declines in the Transports and Utilities. Again I underscore the observation that without the necessary side help, the industrials are hamstrung.

The failure to gain anymore field trends also downplayed the industrials, the NFI remaining unchanged at +4.

I was under the impression yesterday that the earnings on *Motorola* were already released while the stock was still trading. That of course was not the case and the stock soared 5 points. We are using a stop at 110. But we are seeing such euphoria at advanced levels. Today the brokerage house stocks soared on big earnings gains and that looks like the end of the line for that group.

Gold was up $7.50 today and there was no specific news event to account for this great strength and that is especially bullish for the group. The Gold Stock Index jumped 3.91 to the 118.16 level and further strength should see traders adding more December and January call options here. The strength in gold spells trouble ahead and it seems to be aimed at bonds, preferreds and utilities. It also senses that the readings on the Producer and Consumer Price Indexes to be reported later this week will send the gold stocks still higher and knock the general market which is now so vulnerable to bad news.

October 13, 1993 - Wednesday Evening

The Dow managed to close up 10.06 points at the 3603.19 level. Transports gained 8.98 points but once again the utility average fell, dropping another 1.25 points. The industrial gain disguised the fact that there was extreme internal weighting. *Disney* rose 4-3/8 points and *Philip Morris* rose 3 points. Those two stocks accounted for a rise of almost 15 points in the Dow industrial average. So without those two stocks the Dow would have been down about 5 points. Both those stocks remained in doubtful field trends and today's sharp advances did nothing for the NFI.

That effect also was reflected in the Climax Indicator falling sharply from +5 to -3, the drop revealing the fact that 19 out of the 30 Dow industrial stocks closed unchanged to lower.

The drop in the utilities produced a utility CLX reading of -8 and that combined with the -3 reading for the industrial CLX virtually guaranteed a fresh drop for the 65-stock CLX, despite the better than 8 point rise in the Dow Transport average. *The Utility Average is now so weak that even unchanged readings produce OBV down designations.*

It is amazing that we have seen only one industrial CLX reading above the May 27th +10 reading, that being the +11 reading of August 18th. This is a very rare pattern, the absence of double digit readings on the upside for such a long period. I interpret that as another warning that should not be disregarded. When we get a *weighted* advance such as seen today, it is unlikely to generate a positive double digit CLX figure.

There was a slight contraction in new highs at 140 while the advance/ decline line showed a moderate decline. Most of the strength was concentrated in the Nasdaq which barreled ahead to a new high with a better than 6-point gain.

The Net Field Trend indicator remained unchanged at +4.

The gold stocks recorded normal consolidating moves following the sharp October 12th advance.

October 14, 1993 - Thursday Evening

Today the Dow rose 18.44 points to the 3621.63 level in what looked on the surface to be very important strength. A closer look, however, again revealed very heavy individual stock weighting. Wednesday saw *Disney* and *Philip Morris* account for the equivalent of a 15-point rise in the Dow. Today saw a 3-point rise in *American Telephone,* a 2-point rise in *Coca Cola*, a 1-1/2 point rise in *McDonalds*, and a 2-1/4 point rise in *Procter & Gamble.* So that was the equivalent of a 17-1/2 point gain the Dow, representing almost the entire net advance. Looking at the last two days combined, we see that six stocks accounted for the equivalent of an almost 33-point gain in the Dow. Offsetting much of that strength, the Dow Transports fell 9.19 points, erasing the entire Wednesday gain. The Utility Average, reacting to the huge 28/32nd gain in bonds, rose a sharp 3.03 points but that did nothing for the technical action of that average. After the steady decline that average has had since early September, the rise today had to be classified as a bounce.

New highs came in at 149, introducing no new strength. While the advance/ decline line rose, it was not commensurate with the better than 18-point gain in the Dow industrials.

The weighting in just a few Dow stocks saw the Climax Indicator only rise to the +6 level, again avoiding a positive double digit figure. The last time we had such a figure was the +10 reading of August 24th.

The Net Field Trend indicator did better, jumping to +7, seeing the gain of a field in *DuPont* and two fields in *Minnesota Mining. It had also rebounded to the +7 level in October 1989 just before the mini-crash.*

Again gold stocks consolidated in a positive manner.

I see the strength today as a miasma, posing a trap as so much strength was too obvious. Be very careful now.

October 14, 1993

12. *The Double Masks of Halloween**

Looking over the many market opinions published each week by *Barron's*, I noted a common thread of dangerous complacency mostly based on the current interpretations of *sentiment*. Based on current readings of sentiment, one analyst saw the market in no danger of a free fall. Another saw sentiment as too negative for a major market top. Still another said the market could not fall in the face of current negative sentiment. The curious quirk here is that the negative sentiment that everybody thinks is so bullish constitute the first mask, the one everybody sees. But there is another layer on the cake to be considered. Since everyone sees the high negative sentiment as the *consensus*, they have overlooked the widespread *recognition* of that consensus as *another consensus*, the one that counts. That is the *double mask.* So I underscore one of the great market verities: *What everybody knows is worthless.* So two widespread opposites neutralize each other and we find ourselves back to square one: The bears are right and bearish sentiment is the correct sentiment as it always is in a bear market. The bulls have simply not yet recognized that the market is in a *transition period* from bull market to bear market.*

*(footnote)-

Charles Biderman, writing in the January 10, 1994 edition of *Barron's*, countered the traditional contrary opinion bearish sentiment indicator and saw it instead as currently existing bullish sentiment which would be rated as being bearish. This may be confusing to the novice but he was basing his analysis on *what people did rather than on what they said.*

That was the exact gist of my *Double Masks of Halloween* letter of October 14, 1993 wherein I saw such widespread references to the then existing bearish market sentiment as proof that those overseers were actually bullish and that the underlying *correct* market sentiment was bullish and therefore, as a contrary opinion indicator, was drawing a *bearish* conclusion.

In order to best reveal the very serious loss of technical upside momentum, I have compared two very recent periods using my unique cluster analysis. Instead of using the simple up and down designations of OBV, I am concerned here with only the *net cluster power.* An up cluster is three or more consecutive OBV up designations and a down cluster is three or more consecutive OBV down designations. A cluster remains in force until a new cluster replaces it. I am employing the simple CLX technique wherein any kind of an up is an up and any kind of a down is a down. The two periods to be compared best reveal the current loss of technical power in this market. The first period is the rally from August 10th to the August 25th top. The second period is the return move rally from September 21st to October 6th, indicating why that second rally attempt had to fail at the Dow 3600 level.

Date	DowCum.	Cluster CLX	Date	Dow Cum.	Cluster CLX
8/10	3572.73	+1616	9/21	3537.24	+1540
8/11	3583.35	+1621	9/22	3547.02	+1473
8/12	3569.09	+1611	9/23	3539.75	+1392
8/13	3569.65	+1614	9/24	3543.11	+1320
8/16	3579.15	+1590	9/27	3567.70	+1257
8/17	3586.98	+1572	9/28	3566.02	+1209
8/18	3604.86	+1562	9/29	3566.30	+1167
8/19	3612.13	+1569	9/30	3555.12	+1131
8/20	3615.48	+1576	10/1	3581.11	+1103
8/23	3605.98	+1573	10/4	3577.76	+1098
8/24	3638.96	+1566	10/5	3587.26	+1086
8/25	3652.09	+1573	10/6	3598.99	+1082

So here we see that between August 10th and August 25th the Dow rose from 3572.73 to the rally peak of 3652.09. The Cumulative Cluster CLX showed a very small decline from +1616 to +1573. Then we see the comparison with the Dow *return move* rally which started at the September 21st low of 3537.24. Now we see a steady loss of technical power and by the time the Dow is threatening to go back above the 3600 level, the Cumulative Cluster CLX has dropped sharply to the +1082 level. That shows a dramatic loss of power with the rally that culminated on August 25th.

But that is only a small part of the story. First of all, *my record of the Cumulative Cluster CLX starts at zero in January 1992.* Secondly, the most recent peak in the indicator was recorded on September 3rd at the +1747 level. Now hold your breath. As of October 11th the indicator has fallen to the +991 level. *That is a steep drop of 756 points just since September 3rd.* A similar drop in the next five weeks would sink the indicator to the 235 level by around November 8th and to the -521 level by December 8th. A drop to -521 will have returned the indicator to the December 28, 1992 level, *wiping out more than the entire 1993 rise.* So, as this indicator plummets, keep in mind the following important parameters:

Date	Dow	Cumulative Cluster CLX
January 9, 1992	3209	Zero
December 28, 1992	3333	-564

With the projection to -521 by around December 8th, and noting that the last time we were down to these numbers was last December with the Dow at 3333, *then a near term break below the key Dow 3500 level is a given.*

13. ***The High/Low Indicator Using the Preferreds***

Readers of *Investor's Business Daily* will note that they do not combine the number of common and preferred stock highs and lows into a single figure as does the *Wall Street Journal.* This provides us with a valuable exercise. In one column I place the *Investor's Business Daily* count of common stock highs and lows. I have two other columns showing the *Wall Street Journal* count of highs and lows. The difference thus comprises the number of *preferred* stock highs and lows. Since I had underscored the worsening Dow Utility stock numbers, it logically followed that there would be fewer preferred stock highs and an expanding number of preferred stock lows which turned out to be the case.

Keep in mind that the maximum number of new highs was recorded at the 336 level on December 31, 1991. I have stated it many times in my books that if a market rise is technically genuine then it logically follows that *there should be a steady expansion in the number of new highs.* Not only has the number dropped to 17, but the total number has recently dropped from 189 just since August 25th, contracting over 90% since then.

October 16, 1993 - Saturday Afternoon

The meteoric strength in the bond market spilled over in stocks and saw the Dow rise 44.99 points to the 3629.73 level. For awhile the Dow was up almost 21 points on Friday and for awhile lost all of it in the final hour, but bounced back in the final minutes to post an 8.10 point gain. Volume was heavy due to option expiration. Final hour selling was seen to be significant.

Only four Dow industrial stocks are able to close at their high of the day while the other 26 closed under their highs, many of them qualifying as key reversals to the downside.

Note that several of the stocks that so pointedly weighted the Dow on the upside this week ran into resistance on Friday. *American Telephone* declined, *Coca Cola* declined, *Disney* declined, and *McDonalds* declined.

Despite what looked for awhile on Friday like a runaway move on the upside, the Climax Indicator again closed at +6 and that counts as an upside nonconfirmation. We are seeing numbers now that correspond with market tops, as last seen in August. The Net Field Trend Indicator again had a big day, jumping to +9. *Exxon* gained a field and *United Technologies* gained two fields while *Woolworth* lost a field.

Note the identity of the new winners in this market. They are stock *retreads*, stocks that had previously topped out in this 1990-93 bull cycle. For instance, *Apple Computor* jumps 4-1/2 points to the 28-1/4 to boost the Nasdaq. But I was recommending the stock as a short sale last January at over 60. *Kellogg* bounced ahead 3-1/4 points on Friday to the 56 level. But my followers got out at 68 in January 1992. *Philip Morris* is breaking out of a long flat base, having a big week as it closed up on Friday at 53. But my followers got out at 82 in January 1992. So I see these moves as not capable of having sustained strength leading to new highs. They have all seen their highs in this current bull cycle.

There is no doubt that the smart money is taking advantage of the current rally, not willing to play the last hurrah.

October 18, 1993 - Monday Evening

It would seem as if everything under the sun is being tried now to keep the market up. But today saw no victories for the bulls. On the contrary, the Dow industrials and transports were about the only averages to rise outside of a big up day for the gold stocks. The *Dow* industrials closed up 12.58 at the 3642.31 level. Transports had a good day with a better than 14-point rise but the Dow utility average fell 2.18 points, giving back over a third of the strong Thursday-Friday gains of last week. But all the broader indices closed lower and the bond market took a sizable hit and there seemed to be much selling on the news of a prime rate cut. There was heavy selling in several of the key bank stocks.

Individual stock highs contracted from 174 to 155 and the advance/ decline line on all markets declined .

Once again we saw flagrant stock weighting to make the average look good. *Minnesota Mining*, the easiest Dow stock to move on light volume, rose 2-3/4 points to the 107-3/8 level and that was equal to a rise of 5-1/ 2 points in the Dow, that one stock accounting for over 43% of the entire Dow rise. As a matter of fact, six Dow stocks accounted for a rise of 19 points but the Dow only closed up 12.58points, thus indicating much weakness elsewhere.

Again we saw heavy volume which increasingly suggests a blowoff and the drop of over 4 points in the Nasdaq today suggests that the speculative bubble is starting to break.

For the third straight session the Climax indicator closed at the +6 level, underscoring another key upside non-confirmation. The Net Field Trend indicator managed to move up to +10, *General Motors* gaining a field Again I draw attention to the fact that the CLX hasn't had a positive double digit reading since August 18th.

The Gold Stock Index was strong, closing up at the 119.80 level, large advance seen in *American Barrick, Homestake,* both the *Newmonts, Pegasus* and *Placer-Dome*, the latter breaking out to a new high at 23-1/8.

As for the general market, a major break looks imminent.

October 19, 1993 - Tuesday Evening

The Dow met overwhelming upside resistance as it approached the old August 25th high at the 3652.09 level and then translated a better than 8-point gain into a closing loss of 6.99 points at 3635.89 level. Transports continued strong again with a gain of 8.98 points at the 1664.89 level while utilities continued to give back some of the gains of last week, losing 0.59 points at the 243.28 level.

The number of new stock highs contracted by almost 34%, falling from 157 to 104. The advance/decline line fell a sharp 449 and we can expect further significant declines in that key indicator as it is increasingly apparent that interest sensitive stocks have topped out.

Today the Nasdaq recorded a major break, the Nasdaq Composite falling by 14.18 points with the average down to the 768.73 level. The advance/decline line fell a huge plurality of 843 net decliners. This decline today in the OTC will go far in breaking the current continuity of bullish opinion.

All the important indicators were down today, the S & P 500 off over 2, the Amex Value Index off over 4, the Mid-Cap off. Monday saw the Bank Index break a huge 7.66 points and that cuts the heart out of the last of the previously strongest sectors.

The Climax Indicator which had recorded two consecutive upside non-confirmations was stronger today at +7. But the broad general market countered anything the Dow was doing and while the Dow improved in the final minutes of trading, the general market failed to join in.

The Net Field Trend indicator rose to +11, gaining a field in *DuPont.*

Again the gold stocks continued their rise, The Gold stock index rising 1.96 to the 121.76 level, now within sight of a new 1993 high.

October 20, 1993 - Wednesday Evening

Once again we are seeing the *solo walk* in the Dow. The industrial average rose 9.78 points in the final minutes of trading as it had done on Tuesday. Transports were up 3.42 and utilities closed unchanged. But elsewhere there was little doubt as to what was going on. Everything that was wrong with the market yesterday was repeated today. Both advance/decline lines fell, the Nasdaq closed down, and there was a further contraction In the number of stock highs, falling from 97 to 90. So in three days we have seen new highs go from 174 to 90, a drop of almost 50%. But it is far worse over on the Nasdaq. Over there highs contracted from 329 to 139 in two days. The last important top also showed the break after new highs had expanded over 300.

The Bank Stock Index on Tuesday fell another 7 points and that 14-point break in two days technically signals the death warrant for the bank stocks.

There were many air pockets today and looking at most of the numbers one could never guess that the Dow industrials could be up over 9 points. We are getting a very interesting dichotomy here. Certainly without the general market the Dow cannot go very far. So I would again tell subscribers to keep selling into this kind of strength. I think we will look back on this period and see that the third quarter earnings provided a smokescreen to deflect attention from the approaching market top.

The sharp break in *Circus Circus* today signals the beginning of the end for the casino stocks.

The Climax Indicator rose from +7 to +9. There is little doubt that the Dow is being bulled again but without the general market behind it it looks very dangerous and terminal. The Net Field Trend indicator rose to +11, gaining a field in *Sears.*

The gold stocks continued their strong rally and that is a warning for the general market.

October 21, 1993 - Thursday Evening

Like a drowning man, the Dow industrial average tried three times to close above the August 25th high of 3652.09 and failed. I don't expect a fourth attempt. The Dow was up over 10 points in the morning, fell to down 13, tried one more afternoon attempt to rally and then closed down 8.94 at the 3636.16 level. Transports fell 4.70 and Utilities, up all day until the close, fell 0.33.

The day was again mostly like previous sessions this week wherein the broad market was down across the board. Again both advance/declines fell despite a 3-point rise in the Nasdaq Composite. The NYSE advance/decline line declined for the fourth consecutive session.

Again the number of new highs contracted, dropping to 82.

Going generally unnoticed, the intraday high in the Dow has dropped on every session this week.

The Climax Indicator today fell sharply from +9 to -1. Despite gains of 2-3/4 points in *Caterpillar* and 1-3/8 points in *IBM*, equating with a rise of over 8 points in the Dow, the Dow ignored such weighting and that indicates how weak the market was.

The Net Field Trend indicator today fell from +12 to +10, losing a field in *Texaco* and losing a field in *Union Carbide.*

A real story is unfolding here and it is certainly not bullish. On Monday the prime rate is lowered and bank stocks collapse. This morning Germany lowers the discount rate and our bond market collapses, falling 1 and 12/32nd points with the yield rising to 5.91%. The drop in the number of new highs reflects the further developing weakness in the interest sensitive stocks.

So we are seeing here significant news stories setting up key traps. And again a stream of earnings reports deflected attention away from the important topping action in the general market.

Gold stocks took a hit today, the Gold Index falling back to the 121.06 level. This was a natural place for a pause and all pullbacks are seen to be fresh buying opportunities.

October 21, 1993

14. ***Setting Up Safety Zones***

Negative Sentiment Is Bullish

This week I want to introduce a new angle on market psychology. My theory is simply that everything that is being touted today as being "safe" is setting up a dangerous trap wherein these safety zones will in actuality turn out to be the exact opposite. Last week I talked about the two masks of Halloween showing that two superimposed majority opinions neutralize each other and then the original premise becomes the correct one. The example given was the fact that the market bulls based much of their bullish posture on what they contended was widespread negative sentiment. Contrary opinion then saw that as being bullish. But I contended that what everybody knows is worthless and since the consensus was reading negative sentiment that way it thus presented widespread positive sentiment rather than negative sentiment and contrary opinion thus says that the correct market posture is bearish, not bullish.

The 1987 Crash Cannot Repeat

So let us look at all the things that make the bulls say that the market cannot go importantly lower. They put on the blinders and hide in their "safety zones". This past week presented the perfect example of what I mean. CNBC-TV presented a program on October 19th since it was the sixth anniversary of the 1987 crash. Jimmy Rogers made a classic statement that gave me the whole idea of safety zones. He told Ron Insana that as long as we had CNBC programs like the one being conducted that the market cannot crash. So the recognition and review of October 19th is a *safety zone*. It eliminates all fears of a crash. So we have been told that we cannot have a crash. I therefore contend that *we can have a crash*. I say this because the theory here is that everything that looks safe is actually not.

Interest Rates and the Bond Market Are Supporting the Stock Market

The first thing you heard on the October 19th crash anniversary is that the bond market was going down back then while it is now going up. So I see the bond market as another one of those safety zones which will catch the bulls bullish on bonds and interest rates right at the worst of times - like now. The low interest rates have lulled the majority into a very dangerous complacency that the stock market simply cannot go down. Go back through your market history. *Every single one of the important tops were prefaced by a widespread opinion that the market cannot go down.*

Low Money Market Rates Guarantee the Steady Exodus Into Mutual Funds

Mutual funds are treated as a safety zone and I contend that just the opposite is soon to take place- the exodus out of stock funds back into the money market funds. Current government awareness of the mutual fund safety problem is a new warning.

Market Cannot Fall With a Strong Advance/Decline Line

I have pointed out that the advance/decline line can peak simultaneously with the Dow as it did on December 3, 1968.

So we have here a technical safety zone which the bullish technicians have based much of their bullishness on.

You Have To Be In Stocks Because There Is No Other Place To Go

So just when cash looks like the last thing you would want to be in, that is when cash becomes king. Stocks will no longer be a safety zone.

Summing up, the start of a bear market makes mincemeat of all indicators, reversing every single one of them, what I have described as the Bermuda Triangle.

October 23, 1993 - Saturday Afternoon

The Emperor Wore No Clothes. The Dow rocketed higher on Friday for a 40-point gain and somebody must have noticed that not a single indicator was confirming the rise. The Dow was caught technically naked and immediately became a sitting duck for an important reversal to the downside. For most of the day it looked like a new Dow closing high was a given, but even there, closing below the August 25th high of 3652.09 after being about 25 points above that high was seen to be a very bearish outcome. So the Dow closed up 13.14 points at the 3649.30 level. For awhile it looked like all the forces of nature were determined to get a confirmed high. Even the Transports came within 10 points of confirming with a 10 point rise but soon gave up with only a fractional rise of 0.85.

Pulling the rug out from under the market, the bonds collapsed with a drop of 27/32nds with the yield jumping sharply to 5.97%. The Dow Utility average recorded a sharp drop of 2.44 points to the 240.51 level which recorded an exact double bottom with the October 13th closing.*A major downside breakout is now imminent.*

The impact on the interest sensitive segment has many interesting sidelights. We had 81 common stock highs and only 9 preferred stock highs. So, as expected, the sunset for the interest sensitive stocks will tear the heart out of the advance/decline line. We see this now happening, *the A/D line declining every single day this past week.* It has dropped enough now so as to make certain a key upside nonconfirmation should the Dow try for another high. But I think the Friday technical failure sees the bulls as no longer having the heart to fight the bond market.

The Climax Indicator in the face of the 13-point rise closed unchanged at -1, a very poor showing. The Net Field Trend indicator, still enjoying a run in the blue chip cyclicals, rose to +11, gaining a field in *International Paper.*

The Gold Stock Index, throwing off early weakness, made excellent late trading gains, another concern for the interest sensitive segment.

October 25, 1993 - Monday Evening

Homing in on a handful of Dow industrial stocks, the Dow industrial average zoomed up 24.31 points to close at a new bull cycle high of 3673.61. Technically, it was a complete no-no. Like Rudyard Kipling's cat that walked alone, the Dow executed a *solo walk* today, absolutely nothing confirming the rise. So on the close the Dow industrial average was technically naked, a sitting duck for important selling. The Transports closed up 13.25 at the 1677.71 level and that average is within 5.37 points of confirming the industrials but the technical action today was so bad that I doubt if the market will wait for the Transports tomorrow.

Bonds fell 14/32nds with the yield rising to 6.01%. That was an improvement from earlier levels but the Dow Utility Average fell and stayed near the lows, breaking the key double bottom as I had expected. The demise of the interest sensitive stocks was reflected in a further contraction in the number of stock highs, falling today from 91 to 67. The Climax Indicator on the utilities stood at -6, offsetting a good portion of the industrial and transport scores.

For the sixth session the advance/decline line fell. It also fell on the Nasdaq.

The Climax Indicator again gave an extremely weak performance, only rising from -1 to +1 on the new Dow high. The Net Field Trend Indicator actually lost a field, falling to +10, losing a field in *Boeing*. Two thirds of the Dow rise was seen to be technically worthless.

The Gold Stock Index closed down 0.94 at 122.53, this seen to be a very constructive performance.

So again I underscore the fact that today the Dow broke out above the August 25th high with nothing confirming, a major sell signal. That is like the Dow making a new low with no confirming declines when looking at the opposite mirror image.

October 26, 1993 - Tuesday Evening

Today the Dow-Jones Transportation Average rose over 19 points to reach a new record high and confirm yesterday's rise in the industrials. But the session was strangely similar to Monday's rise, the transports making the solo walk and widely lacking simultaneous confirmations elsewhere. Industrials were down 1.12 at the 3672.49 level.

The core of continued technical weakness remained in force. The Utility Average was able to close unchanged but the downtrend in that average that has been in force since early September shows no hope of being reversed. It is a major deepening shadow looming over the entire market. Bonds were able to close up 5/32nds today with the yield back down to 5.98% but there are too many signs pointing toward lower bond prices to read anything positive into this.

Technical concerns continued to grow today as we saw declines in both advance/decline lines. The drop today was the 7th consecutive decline on the NYSE and has gone on long enough so as to make certain key upside non-confirmations should the Dow make another record high. The demise of the interest sensitive stocks is showing up in the steady contraction in the number of new stock highs. That number contracted further today to 65. That number was 174 as recently as October 15th. The Nasdaq took another hit today and there were numerous airpockets. So we have strong evidence now that not only have the utilities topped out, but so has the Nasdaq. The Bank Stock Index took another hit today and that is another important negative. *I see a red flag warning on the Paramount battle.*

The Climax Indicator stayed unchanged at the low +1 reading of yesterday while the NFI rose to +13, gaining two fields in *IBM* and one field in *Westinghouse*.

Comex gold cut an earlier loss of close to $3 to just 20 cents. But the stocks weren't waiting and were heaven bound with the Gold Index rising a sharp 3.99 points to the 126.52 level.

October 27, 1993 - Wednesday Evening

Today was a sort of in between day. There were some improvements but nothing that particularly stood out. The Dow fell 7.83 points to close down at the 3664.66 level. Transports edged up to a new high with a gain of 1.07 points while the Utility Average for a change posted a small fractional rise of 0.26. Even the advance/decline line showed a very small rise. The Nasdaq index was up over 6 points while its A/D line posted a decent plurality of 316.

The number of individual stock highs improved slightly to show 71 highs and 34 lows. But a great deal of damage has been sustained in the past few days and today's numbers indicate no change in the current negative trend.

The Climax Indicator today fell from +1 to -2 but the Net Field Trend Indicator rose to a new bull cycle high of +15, seeing a gain of one field in *General Motors* and a field in *Procter & Gamble.* We have to view this indicator as not only reflecting the concentration in the blue chip stocks, but now the mirror image of key market bottoms. Thus the NFI smacks of a Dow top. Market students will find it of great interest that the Net Field Trend indicator peaked at +15 in July 1990 just prior to a drop of 635 points in the Dow. *Therefore today's +15 reading is bad news for the bulls.* It signifies a top.

After the close *Eastman Kodak* soared to 62 but still was able to only record an OBV lower up designation.

I am recommending some new short sales. *Autodesk* and the January 45 puts, *Bankers Trust* and the January 80 puts, *Merrill Lynch* and the January 95 puts, *Whirlpool* and the March 65 puts, and *Worthington Industries* with the March 20 puts.

Bonds fell 8/32nds bringing the yield back up to 6%.

Gold stocks acted well today, pretty much holding their own. The Gold Stock Index fell 1.45 to the 125.07 level, seen to be a perfectly natural pullback.

October 28, 1993 - Thursday Evening

From many technical standpoints today looked like the a very probable end of the line for the Dow averages. The public heard many commentators carelessly slip and say that stocks soared to new highs today. Nothing could be further from the truth. The Dow Jones Industrial and Transport Averages did go to new highs but a closer examination revealed the deficiencies. The industrials closed up 23.20 points at the 3687.86 level *but down about 20 points from the earlier rally high.* Gains of over a point in five Dow industrial stocks accounted for a Dow gain of 21-1/2 points and thus the other 25 stocks had to be accounted for. We see that 13 out of the 30 stocks closed unchanged to lower. The weighting on the upside by *Eastman Kodak* and *General Motors* alone accounted for almost 14 points of the Dow gain, or about 60% of the entire Dow gain.

Of course obvious upswings on news are weak plays. So I am not impressed with the *Eastman Kodak* and *General Motors* rallies today.

And keep in mind that we recorded another key upside non-confirmation by the important advance/decline line.

That resulted in a highly unsatisfactory Climax Indicator reading of +3, a very bearish reading for a new high in the Dow. The Net Field Trend indicator fell to +14, losing a field in *Goodyear*. And again I remind listeners that the NFI peaked at +15 in July 1990 prior to a drop of 635 points in the Dow.

Paramount Communications fell to 80-3/8. I consider this a critical bubble stock and would look for a collapse following any five-point decline from a high. Of related companies in the takeover battle, QVC has the worst chart and has been declining since early September.

The Gold Stock Index today at 124.04 remains close to new breakout highs.

October 30, 1993- Saturday Afternoon

Despite a day that showed a mixture of pluses and minuses, the late Thursday reversal to the downside that saw a Dow rise of almost 44 points cut to a gain of 23.20 points, saw the gain reduced on Friday by another 7.27 points to the 3680.59 level. I think the proper perspective here is not that the Dow closed up 31.29 points on the week, but that the average closed 27 points under the Thursday afternoon high and considerably under the intra-day high. For instance, on the Thursday close five of the industrial stocks closed over a point under their highs and on Friday that number had grown to 13 from 1-3 points under their highs, many of these marking significant reversals to the downside. True to form, stocks that had previously weighted the average most on the upside joined the biggest decliners. Now *Eastman Kodak* is 2-1/8 under its high and *General Motors* is 2 points under its high, the two stocks that accounted for 60% of the Thursday rise in the Dow.

Even some stocks that closed up showed large reversals to the downside under their intraday highs, notably *Philip Morris* falling from 55-3/4 to 53-3/4 even though it closed up.

With 13 of the Dow stocks now well under their intraday highs, any new high in the Dow should be dangerously non-confirmed.

The Climax Indicator fell from +3 to +1, having shown substandard numbers on this entire recent rally. The Net Field Trend indicator fell from +14 to +13, losing a field in *American Telephone.* That now gives us a three-day series of 15-14-13 in the NFI, the exact series last seen at the July 1990 bull cycle highs.

Federal National Mortgage fell to 77-7/8, closing at the low of the day. A significant break looks imminent and an expected move under 75 should drop the stock rapidly to 70. We are in the December 75 puts and these look like an excellent buy right now.

The Gold Stock Index continues to consolidate in a positive manner.

November 1, 1993 - Monday Evening

I said on Saturday that any new high in the Dow would be dangerously nonconfirmed. That is precisely the kind of new high that we saw, the Dow rising 12.02 points to close at a new record closing high of 3692.61. Transports were strong again. But closer examination revealed considerable weighting. Strong gains in *IBM* and *International Paper* accounted for 8 points of the Dow gain, or 66%. All recent examples of stock weighting in the Dow saw those stocks then become the targets of important selling pressure afterwards. Last month we saw such examples in *American Telephone, Coca Cola,* and *Disney*. Then last week we saw two more key examples being *Eastman Kodak* and *General Motors.* Now we have these new examples to contend with.

New highs expanded today to 122 but remained well under the recent higher reading of 174 seen on October 15th. Once again the advance/decline line failed to confirm a Dow high, showing a very small positive plurality for a 12-point rise in the Dow. Despite a strong Nasdaq, its A/D line declined today.

The Climax Indicator rose to +2, again staying well under the +9 reading of October 20th. The Net Field Trend indicator fell to +11, losing two fields in *Merck.*

Federal National Mortgage fell 5/8ths to 77-1/4, a good looking short sale.

Barron's devoted their *Striking Price* column to *Paramount Communications* and exposed their readers to the validity of a possible break to 60. Readers of my market letter saw that I suspect a Paramount bubble. Today the stock fell 7/8 points to the 79-3/4 level. Remember, I consider a move of 5 points or more under the high as the technical signal for a bust.

The price of gold took a hit today, Comex gold closing 7.50 lower at 362.10. Our followers know that we don't play the gold price. But I call attention to the superior performance of the gold stocks, the Gold Stock Index only falling 2.57 to the 120.88 level, a far better commensurate performance.

November 2, 1993 - Tuesday Evening

Very strong economic figures smashed the bond market today, the long bond dropping 21/32nds with the yield rising to 6.07%. What we are seeing here was well signalled in advance. The entire interest sensitive segment is at risk. We had dangerous speculation in the bond market, a sharp better than 19-point drop in the Bank Index, the early September warnings from the utility average, and most recently the report that third quarter corporate profits surged. I believe that from here on out earnings have been fully discounted and thus stocks are vulnerable. If the Dow can rise 800 points on a worsening economy why can't it fall 800 points on an improving economy?

The Dow turned around from an earlier loss of over 24 points to post a gain of 5.04 points at the 3697.64 level. But all of that gain was due to a better than 3-point rise in IBM. Transports fell 5.13 and Utilities took a big hit of 3.36 points. The decline in the Utility Average is serious and cannot be talked away.

The number of new highs contracted to 112 while the advance/decline line showed a negative plurality of 257 and is once again failing to confirm the new high in the Dow today.

The Climax Indicator rose to +3. The Net Field Trend indicator is revised to the +12 level, *Merck* only losing one field yesterday and not two.

Fannie Mae reflected the weakness in the bond market and fell again, down 5/8 at the 76-5/8 level. Banks and brokerage house stocks were down, *Merrill Lynch* which we are short on falling 2-3/4 points today to 93-1/4.

Paramount Communications fell to 79-1.8, now 3-1/8 points away from the break point, five points under the high. *Once stock closes under 76 I would look for break back to 60.*

The Gold Stock Index was down 1.95 at 118.93 but each break is at higher levels and the trend is up.

November 3, 1993 - Wednesday Evening

Hitting the market like a Malibu fire, the Dow broke 35.77 points to close down at the 3661.87 level. Transports were down over 14 and the Dow Utility Average broke a sharp 6.19 points, *a clarion call warning to everyone still holding interest sensitive stocks to divorce themselves from that segment of the market immediately.* The market break today was heavily confirmed with several outstanding signals that more market carnage is to soon follow.

The extensive sweeping declines in both the NYSE advance/decline and the Nasdaq advance/decline line left no question as to the extensive breadth of the declines. The high/low indicator looked very weak with a sharp contraction in the highs to 88 and a very sharp rise in the number of new lows to 56. *These numbers strongly suggest a near-term crossing which would be very bearish.*

The Climax Indicator fell to -6 while the Net Field Trend indicator showed the loss of three fields taking the NFI down to +9, losing two fields in *Chevron* and one field in *General Electric.*

Significant breaks were seen in three of our best looking short sales *Bankers Trust* breaking 2-1/4 points to 77-1/8, *Merrill Lynch* breaking 2-3/8 points to 90-7/8, and *Motorola* breaking 3-7/8 points to 99-3/8. Downside objectives are 68 for *Bankers Trust*, 78 for *Merrill Lynch*, and 80 for *Motorola.*

It was a very good day for the gold stocks as these are now beginning to get a whiff of the coming inflation.

Summing up: The bond market is finished along with preferreds, utilities, bank stocks, Fannie Mae, brokerage house stocks, and insurance stocks. That blows a big hole in the stock market outlook.

November 4, 1993 - Thursday Evening

Expecting more carnage to follow the Wednesday hit, today was almost a duplicate performance, the Dow collapsing another 36.89 points to close down at the 3624.98 level *to put the Dow down 100 points under Tuesday's intra-day high of 3724.75.* Transports took another hit and the utility average broke over 5 points, reflecting panic conditions and the broad-based willingness to jettison such stocks at any cost.

Last night I predicted an imminent crossing in the high/low indicator and this took place today- only 40 highs but 73 new lows. One will see that a strong contributing factor to this very bearish switchover was a sharp jump in the number of preferred stocks as these reflected the carnage among the interest-sensitive stocks.

Both advance/decline lines totally collapsed again and it is that factor that so strongly suggests another repetition of the freefall again tomorrow.

The Climax Indicator fell to -10 while the Net Field Trend indicator fell to +6, losing two fields in *Minnesota Mining* and one field in *J. P. Morgan*. The sharp drop of 9 field trends in the past week is symptomatic of a collapsing market.

Again a number of key stocks we are short in hit air pockets today. One of particular interest is *Fannie Mae* which fell today to 74-3/4, breaking the key 75 support level. We are in the December 75 put options. Now the stock is technically free to make a wide open break. *Merrill Lynch* fell to 89-3/8 and our January 95 put options soared. *Motorola* fell to 97 and has much further to go on the downside. The January 95 put options are shaping up to be big winners. *Bankers Trust* fell to 74-3/4, breaking under the key 75 support. Seen headed for the 68 level.

I think we are headed for a 3-day blitz this week. Tomorrow looks very bad for the bulls who so complacently walked right into what should be the biggest break of the year.

Our strong buying recommendations on the gold stocks are paying off. Bond yields made a key upside breakout today, the yield rising to 6.20%.

November 6, 1993 - Saturday Afternoon

This past week was well prefaced by the October 28th reversal to the downside which so well signalled the break that followed. The Dow experienced a technically worthless bounce of 18.45 points on Friday but was down 37.16 points on the week at the 3643.43 level. The Transports and Utilities also bounced on Friday but none of these moves could hide the devastating internal market damage suffered this past week. As expected, we had a further downside three-day blitz in the advance/decline line which almost returned it to the September 21st level when the Dow stood at 3537, *over 100 points below the current level.*

The key technical change this past week was the important crossing in the important high/low indicator, Friday breaking down despite the Dow to show 12 new highs and 99 new lows. *The worst showing in over a year.* This ripped off the worthless surface veneer of this market revealing the technical rot within.

The Climax Indicator improved on Friday from -10 to zero but the fact that the Net Field Trend indicator stayed unchanged at +6 underscored it as a bounce. We had more evidence of technically worthless stock weighting, *Philip Morris* and *Procter & Gamble* accounting for almost half of the Dow rise and neither stock could record an OBV up designation. Our *war indicator* (based on the NFI) is within four days of being activated and a drop in the NFI to +2 or lower could trigger this.

Headline evolution saw the sharp September drop in fund sales evolve to the current sharp drop in the Mutual Fund Index, the September warning being quite valid.

It was a very profitable weak for shortsellers, cleaning up in *Bankers Trust, Merrill Lynch,* and *Motorola* and then the Friday break in Autodesk a pleasant surprise.

The sharp continuing break in bonds saw the long bond yield climb to 6.21%. Gold stocks followed through on our buy recommendations this past week and these all look higher.

November 11, 1993

15. *Catastrophe*

Those who have been with me for awhile will remember that the title for my August 2, 1990 letter was **AUGUST CATASTROPHE.** Since we always write the letter the day before we mail it, and since we always date the letter on the day it is mailed, then it is clear that I could not possibly know that Kuwait would be invaded on August 2nd and exacerbate a decline of 635-points in the Dow. I don't know anything about catastrophe theory but I can tell you that the market right now is where it was a few days before the August 2, 1990 Kuwait invasion and that a catastrophe could very well lie directly ahead. Technical analysis cannot be specific in describing future events but it can underscore dangerous parallels with previous catastrophes. So, until proved otherwise, the parallels with the July 1990 market top could even be justified as a war indicator.

I will show a comparison of the Net Field Trend indicator readings at the July 1990 top and the current market:

Then (1990)			Now (1993)		
July 18	2981.68	+15	October 27	3664.66	+15
July 19	2993.81	+14	October 28	3687.86	+14
July 20	2961.14	+13	October 29	3680.59	+13
July 23	2904.70	+9	November 1	3692.61	+12
July 24	2922.52	+6	November 2	3697.64	+12
July 25	2930.94	+6	November 3	3661.87	+9
July 26	2920.79	+5	November 4	3624.98	+6
July 27	2898.51	+4	November 5	3643.43	+6
July 30	2917.33	+4	November 8	3647.90	+7
July 31	2905.20	+3	November 9	3640.07	+7
August 1	2899.26	+4	November 10	3663.55	+6
August 2	2864.60	+2	November 11	....	

So some kind of shocking news looks imminent. The critical NFI level is the +2 reading. Breaking under that level, you will note that we lost 7 fields on August 3, 1990, the day after the invasion.

I cannot rule out a military shock. One will note that just before Desert Storm all the defense stocks were rapidly moving up. One will note that currently we have recently seen parabolic advances in *General Dynamics, Grumman, Martin Marietta, McDonnell Douglas, Rockwell Manufacturing,* and *United Technologies.* And it is interesting to ponder the fact that cutbacks in defense spending had no negative effect on the stocks.

The current decline got its impetus from the October 28th reversal. On that day the Dow was up 44 points but was cut back to close up 23 points. Internally, the Dow stocks never recovered from that important reversal to the downside. By October 29th we saw 5 Dow industrial stocks close at multi-point distances below their intra-day highs. On November 1st the number had grown to 13. On November 2nd the Dow rose to an all-time high but we still had 12 Dow stocks at multi-point distances below their intra-day highs of October 28th. On November 3rd the number grew to 15 stocks. On November 4th the number grew to 21 stocks. On November 5th the number stood at 23. On November 8th the number stood at 21 and on November 9th the number stood at 22. Individually, the distance under the October 28th intra-day highs ranged to as high as 4-3/4 points on *Chevron* and 4-1/4 points on *General Electric.* Looking at all these numbers, the chances of coming back to make a new Dow high are remote. But if the Dow did make one more new high the break expected to follow would be even sharper.

The two most important technical indicators are the *high/low indicator* and the *advance/decline line.* Let us first look at the high/low indicator. The maximum number of new stock highs seen in the bull cycle since 1990 was 336 recorded on December 31, 1991. That number was never exceeded. I always contended that a genuine rising trend is one that is accompanied by a constantly expanding number of stock highs. But something went wrong in 1992 starting with the healthcare and drug stocks which we got our followers out of at their exact highs. New highs kept contracting until by last week highs and lows actually crossed, more lows than highs. Now I want to briefly talk about *the mystery of the two black Pyramids.* This will have the most meaning for subscribers to the *Trendline Daily Action Stock Charts.* On the back is a chart of their *Short Range Oscillator.* There one will see a huge black pyramid which corresponded with the great Desert Storm rise which pushed the Dow up about 500 points. Then we see a second black pyramid in the December-January 1991-92 period. That was good for another 500 points in the Dow. Subscribers will recall that we caught the full extent of both of those 500-point rises. *But now the mystery:* Knowing that the Oscillator is based on the A/D line and volume, *why didn't the Dow highs in 1992 and 1993 produce a third black pyramid?* And we know the answer. It is because of the *dichotomy* in this market that sees so many market participants not making any money on balance. And the situation is worsening. The latest issue of their chart book shows the oscillator bearishly turning down and entering the beginning of the oversold territory.

(See the further discussion of this in the Appendix)

Now for the advance/decline line. It peaked at -48,915 on *October 15th.* The evidence of the July 1990 top showed that once the A/D line fell more than 2,000 then there was no turning back. Currently the A/D line broke under the 2,000 decline barrier on November 4th and efforts to recover have been unsuccessful. The main reason why the A/D line has seen its high is that *one third of the entire market consists of interest sensitive stocks.* Since interest rates have bottomed, interest sensitive stocks are now a drag on the market and that knocks a gaping hole in the advance/decline line. The latest rally attempts in this market are led by the cyclical stocks but once again I see much evidence of stock weighting which removes much of the technical shine of the current rally attempts.

An interesting way to read the news is to see it as an evolution toward the events that follow, what I would call *headline evolution.* Here is a recent example: A headline in the October 29th issue of *Investor's Business Daily* was **FUND SALES DECLINED SHARPLY IN SEPTEMBER.** Then a few days later we saw a headline in the November 8th issue of *Investor's Business Daily* which read **MUTUAL FUND INDEX SUFFERS A SHARP DIVE.** The relationship between the two headlines is intriguing and one will find that very often one headline will be clearly forecasting what will soon follow. Other examples which can be related were the stories about the extreme speculation in bonds which was soon followed by a major break in bond prices. Still another example was seen when the*Journal* ran a story on September 7th telling their readers that it was a great time for stocks four days before the Utility Average peaked.

November 11, 1993 - Thursday Evening

Sometimes the market saves it most effective messages for semi-holiday markets when not too many people are watching. Today was one of those days. With some belated celebrating of the Tuesday Gore-Perot debate, the Dow was up over 15 points in the early trading. On the Wednesday message I said that the market was set up for a resumption of the slide. The resumption set in today, the Dow closing down 1.12 points at the 3662.43 level with accompanying weakness in the Transport and Utility averages. Most importantly, *it is the 1.71 point drop in the Utility Average today that poses the greatest danger for the future of this market.* With the Dow Utility Average closing today at 223.97, it has now come within a mere 10 points of reaching a 17% decline, the precise position that average was in just prior to the October 1987 market crash.

The bond market was closed today but bond futures tumbled 20/32nds today and that sets the market up for a still further slide tomorrow which will not bode well for stocks, and especially the utility stocks.

The CRB Index had a big day on the upside and despite the sharp rise in gold stocks on Wednesday, the Gold Stock Index only gave up 0.45 today at the 129.90 level, overcoming some early weakness. *American Barrick* was the key feature as it jumped 2 points to close up at 29-3/4, pushing our January 25 call options ahead to 6 for a gain of 200% since purchase. Move the stop loss on the stock up to 27-3/4 and stay long.

The Climax Indictor fell from +3 to -1 while the Net Field Trend indicator stayed unchanged at +6, gaining a field in *Eastman Kodak* but losing a field in *Goodyear*.

So we are set up for a probable Friday slide led by lower bond prices.

November 8, 1993 - Monday Evening

Attempting to build on Friday's run-up in the Dow, the Dow was up over 17 points going into the last hour but since it was obvious that the 2-day rise still saw a net decline in the A/D line, the Dow rise was quickly cut to just 4.47 points at the 3647.90 level. Transports lost part of their gains and the utility average closed down. *So the Dow is ready now for a resumption of the downtrend tomorrow.*

The market faces much news this week: first the Gore-Perot debate on Tuesday evening and the Producer and Consumer Price indices on Tuesday and Wednesday. *But only the market's response is important, not the news itself.*

As expected, the large price rise in *Philip Morris* on Friday encountered profit-taking today. The next target of selling following these weighted moves will be *Procter & Gamble.*

The Climax Indicator fell from zero to -1 while the Net Field Trend rose from +6 to +7, gaining a field in *Minnesota Mining.* The NFI is maintaining a close correlation with the pattern seen on the July 1990 top and a move down to the +2 level would be critical. Anything under that would trigger the *war indicator* as was done on August 2, 1990. The defense stocks had runups just prior to Desert Storm. Now the defense stocks are very strong and show no signs of cuts in defense spending. But I wouldn't buy them inasmuch as they have all traced out parabolic advances.

The two most important indicators are bearish. Today the high/low indicator showed 30 highs and 39 lows. While the advance/decline line rose today, it could not eliminate the Friday loss and thus the past two market sessions which showed a Dow rise of roughly 23 points was accomplished on a net decline in the A/D line. Coming off the July 1990 top, once the A/D line was down more than 2000 off the high there was no turning back. Coming off this top, the A/D line broke below the 2000 decline barrier on Thursday and Friday of last week.

The Gold Stock Index today pulled back slightly to 124.62 and looks ready again to surge higher this week.

November 9, 1993 - Tuesday Evening

Fully aware that the Producer Price Index number was going to be released today, *I nevertheless predicted a resumption of the market decline and cautioned to lean on the market response to the news rather than the news itself.*

The Producer Price index was a surprise and was down .2% instead of up. That immediately electrified the bonds and in minutes gained 1-

10/32nds with the yield dropping to 6.10%. *But that was the sucker play.* New bond buyers came in at the top of the day and on the close the gain was cut to 25/32nds with the yield at 6.14%. The effect on stocks was even more acute. The Dow was pushed up over 20 points shortly after the opening but closed at the worst level of the day, falling 7.83 points to the 3640.07 level. I see today as a key reversal to the downside.

Transports were likewise dealt a reversal as well as the Utility Average. Underscoring the lack of significance attached to the bond rally, the Dow Utility Average closed at the low of the day, off 2.04 points at the 225.09 level, a new closing low on the current decline.

Also ignoring the bond rally and the Producer Price Index report, gold stocks rallied today, the Gold Stock Index jumping 2.09 points to the 126.71 level.

The Climax Indicator fell to the -3 level while the Net Field Trend indicator stayed unchanged at +7.

We had 49 highs and 19 lows, still seen as weak numbers.

Tomorrow we get the Consumer Price Index and again I say lean on the market response and not the news. You learned that lesson today in spades.

Today's market sets us up for another important decline tomorrow, the Producer Price index notwithstanding.

November 10, 1993 - Wednesday Evening

The Dow rose 23.48 points today to the 3663.55 level. It was seen as a market celebration of the Gore victory according to the polls in the Tuesday Gore-Perot debate. That led many to predict that NAFTA would pass next week and thus the rally today must be passed off as one based on news, a rally expected to have a very short life.

Despite the rise today, there are far too many Dow industrial stocks at multipoint distances under their October 28th intraday high to expect that the rise can continue. On the contrary, the continued decline in the interest-sensitive stocks contributed to a substandard rise in both the high/low indicator and the advance/decline line. Bonds suffered a sharp drop of 26/32nds putting the yield back up to 6.20%, underscoring the foolishness on the part of those who bought bonds right at their highs on Tuesday morning.

The rise in the Consumer Price Index of .4% and the higher core rate today as well as an upside breakout in the CRB Index triggered soaring gold stock prices, the Gold Stock Index breaking out to the 130.35 level, up 3.64 points. Many of our call options have doubled and so I remind holders to sell half of their holdings on all doublings.

The Climax Indicator rose today from -3 to +3, a suspiciously small move for a Dow rise of 23 points. Something is obviously wrong with this market when the last positive double digit reading on the CLX hasn't been seen since the +10 reading of August 24th. There was much weighting among the cyclical Dow stocks but far too many Dow stocks declined to be impressed with the rise.

The Net Field Trend indicator fell to +6, losing a field in *Disney.*

Based on what I saw today, I think the market is set up today for a very important resumption of the slide.

16. ***Bedtime Story***

Once upon a time a group of powerful financiers decided that they would rig the stock market to their advantage and the public be damned. So they adopted the strategy of concentrating all their buying into those stocks that comprised the market average and selling off most of the other stocks so as to finance their objective. So what did the market look like at the top? *Just as it looks like today in the Nasdaq.* The media loved to announce the new highs in the Nasdaq Composite Average in a fashion that is typical of all their announcements. Their reporters simply read something that is handed to them and they do not question the material. They are blinded by the disease I call *averagitis.* I suspect that we have been witnessing serious internal market deterioration for months which was cleverly disguised by the "averages". Here is the evidence:

Preliminary research reveals that 66% of all the Nasdaq stocks are down double digit percentages under their highs. That is a far cry from the impression one would get listening to the TV financial commentators who were so anxious to report the recent record highs in the Nasdaq which were so far off the mark from the true condition of the market. Apparently nobody on those programs was even remotely aware of what was actually taking place. Seeing the actual numbers makes it very clear that very few have done the right research on the Nasdaq. And that reveals the vacuum that exists among these media financial teams that simply do not have the time to break the market down and report the true complete picture to the public. So the public today is left with an erroneous impression that everything is all right with the Nasdaq when in reality we are getting numbers that are strangely reminiscent of 1929 when the averages said that we were at all-time record highs when nothing could be further from the truth.

So the Nasdaq bubble is about to burst and reveal the internal technical rot.

Subscribers know I first identified the internal *dichotomy* in this market, getting out at the highs in *U.S. Surgical, Apple Computer, Merck, Philip Morris* and so many others in 1992. Now the topping process is seen to be fully mature.

Now the economy is getting stronger. Last January I asked Ron Insana on CNBC the following question: *If the Dow can rise 800 points on a weakening economy why can't it fall 800 points on an improving economy?*

Besides the developing internal weakness, *investors are divorcing the entire interest sensitive segment of the market.* The advance warning signs were there for all to see:

1. Speculation in bond market
2. Latest prime rate cut was a hook
3. Early warnings from the Bank Index
4. Early warnings from the Utility Average
5. Surging third quarter corporate earnings

Looking at each of these points, the bond market has recorded a major top and a recovery is highly remote. I had reported that the last cut in the prime rate on October 18th was a hook and that move was accompanied by a break in the bond market and a sharp fall in the bank stocks, an excellent warning of things to come. The breaks in the Bank Index and the Utility Average were too important to ignore. Then the recent announcement that corporate earnings were surging in the third quarter put the icing on the cake. Future earnings have already been discounted and thus there is nothing further from that area to support the market.

I have made much of the earnings mirage, *what I have always considered to be the biggest hook in the market.* If there was a good correlation with earnings then price/earnings ratios would be stable. Instead, these bounce up and down like ping pong balls. I have referred to such authorities as Gerald Loeb and Arthur Merrill to puncture the myth. I have proven that the majority of the highest Earnings Per Share ratings as published by *Investor's Business Daily* were assigned to stocks just prior to declines and the lowest Earnings Per Share ratings were assigned to stocks just prior to advances. A classic example was the 99 EPS rating given *U.S. Surgical* right at the peak price of 134-1/2 in January 1992. Another was the 99 given *T-2 Medical* at its peak.

So the biggest props are being removed from the market: rising bond prices and rising earnings. Removing the entire interest-sensitive spectrum from this market sounds the technical death knell for bonds, preferreds, utilities, bank stocks, insurance stocks, Fannie Mae, and brokerage house stocks.

November 13, 1993 - Saturday Afternoon

Thanks to a dramatic rise in the bond market out of the ashes of the Thursday decline, there was no anticipated Friday slide. On the contrary, the Dow made a pass at a new high but gave up in the afternoon, cutting a 28-point rise to 22 points at the 3684.51 level. Transports did make a new high and Utilities had a rare rise of almost a point, but the pattern of rising bond yields underscores the Friday rally as having a short life.

Strangely, new highs scored a small 5% expansion but new stock lows showed a 100% expansion, doubling from 23 to 46 on the Dow rally. While the advance/decline line did show a normal rise, the line is still down 2000 from the high and thus any new Dow high would be widely non-confirmed and set the market up for a still more serious slide.

The Climax Indicator rose from -1 to +5 but the lack of good strength in that indicator is also a perpetual mystery because we haven't seen a positive double digit reading since the +10 reading of August 24th.

The Net Field Trend indicator fell to +5, losing a field in *Exxon*. We are getting down to critical levels in the NFI, levels that sparked major declines in the past having peaked at +15, a parallel to the July 1990 market peak. There are possible near-term field losses of 2 fields in *Bethlehem Steel*, 2 fields in *McDonalds,* and 2 fields in *United Technologies*. Any drop under the NFI +2 level would signal a technical crisis.

Most stocks have seen their highs and recent strength is running on stock retreads. *Philip Morris* jumped 2-1/4 points on Friday to 59 but I got subscribers out at 82 in 1992 and now the stock runs into a wall of upside resistance at 60 and I would be a seller.

The market spotlight continues to focus on the gold stocks, *American Barrick* and *Horsham* breaking out to new highs this week. Continue to raise the stop levels and take partial profits as previously indicated.

November 15, 1993 - Monday Evening

Today the market was far weaker than the Dow average indicated. The Dow closed down 6.99 points at the 3677.52 level and, while this was not all that far under the November 2nd high, the high/low indicator, advance/decline line and utility average set up technical roadblocks threatening more than a normal retreat ahead.

The high/low indicator showed 52 highs and 43 lows and that is a weak showing. The advance/decline line recorded a negative plurality of 409, putting the A/D line beyond reach of any hope of confirming a new Dow high. And the focal point of current technical weakness was again the utility average, dropping a sharp 2.43 points today to the 222.45 level, expanding the loss since September 13th to over 34 points, a drop of 13.2%. That average is now critical, getting down close to the 17% decline level the day before the October 1987 crash.

The Nasdaq took a 6-point hit on a large drop in its advance/decline line.

The Climax Indicator fell back from +5 to +1 while the Net Field Trend Indicator stood at a revised +4.

The key feature today was a sharp break in *Paramount Communications,* closing down 2-7/8 at the 80-1/8 level. The new high in the stock on Friday had been accompanied by a key OBV upside non-confirmation. The recent high of 83-1/2 in the stock now focuses attention on a close at 78-3/8 or lower as the technical signal for a bust in the stock to 60.

The Gold Index edged higher, rising 0.34 to the 129.61 level. No change in the bullish outlook there.

This is an extremely critical week for the market and if today poses a hint of what kind of a week it is going to be, it looks bad.

November 16, 1993 - Tuesday Evening

Monday night I said here that this looks like a bad week for the market. One would expect the 33.25 point rise in the Dow to a new record high at the 3710.77 level to cause a retraction of that statement. On the contrary, *the market today simply exacerbated the technical problems and increased the odds favoring a significant decline dead ahead.*

Again I underscore the two most important of the standard technical indicators, these being the high/low indicator and the advance/decline line. Today's record Dow high saw 71 stocks at new highs and 48 at new lows. *That is about 80% fewer highs than the peak in that indicator.* As for the A/D Line, here we have a Dow high on an A/D line down about 2,400 from its high, a major upside non-confirmation.

And I draw attention to another sharp drop today in the Nasdaq advance/decline line.

But the rise today was in anticipation of the news tomorrow on NAFTA, the word being passed today by the White House that it will pass tomorrow. But the technical condition of the market more strongly suggests that this is a set-up for a sharp decline, heavy selling on the news on Thursday.

The OBV indicators cannot be fooled. Today the Climax Indicator showed a rise from +1 to +9, short of a significant breakout. The Net Field Trend indicator rose to +5, gaining a field in *General Electric,* but that is a far cry from the +15 reading of October 27th. And of course the big rise in the utility average today was a bounce from a temporarily oversold condition. And that was a wide upside non-confirmation of the Dow high.

For the second consecutive session *Paramount Communications* took a hit, falling 1-3/8 points to the 78-3/8 level. Closing over 5 points under the 83-1/2 high, *we now have the anticipated signal for a collapse which should take the stock down to 60 or lower.*

Looking at everything, *this is the market one should love to sell into.*

The Gold Index took a hit today but we have a good picture here of rising bottoms. All this week I had accented the taking of some profits.

November 17, 1993 - Wednesday Evening

Selling enveloped the market today before the NAFTA vote. I see this as an anticipation that regardless of which way the vote goes, the market has put together a major bull trap, the Tuesday record high in the Dow accompanied by far too many technical non-confirmations to avoid a significant selloff ahead.

After being hit for over 24 points earlier in the day, the Dow cut the loss to 6.14 points at the 3704.63 level. The improvement was due to large gains in the oil stocks as well as a gains in *Boeing* and *General Motors.* Despite these gains amounting to a rise of 19 points in the Dow, the Dow still closed down reflecting the large breadth of the decline.

The effects of the strength in oil had the manifold effect of reversing bonds from +20/32nds to down 8/32nds, the yield at 6.18% on the close. The higher oil prices knocked the Transports down over 27 points and the utilities gave back about a third of the Tuesday rise. The price of gold jumped about $8 off the morning low, maintaining the bullish appearance of the charts. I was very impressed today by how rapidly gold turned up from the morning lows.

But the collapse of the advance/decline lines on both the NYSE and the Nasdaq preached the bearish sermon technically, pulling the rug out from under both markets. Once again the high/low indicator recorded a very bearish number: 60 new highs and 55 new lows.

This morning the *Journal* and *Investor's Business Daily* had bearish warnings for those who noticed them. The *Journal* headlined the fall in small stocks despite the large Dow rise. The other paper showed the Mutual Fund Index as standing still on the Tuesday Dow rally.

The Climax Indicator fell from +9 to -3 and the Net Field Trend Indicator rose to +7, gaining a field in *Boeing*.

I think regardless of how the NAFTA vote goes tonight, this market has had it and the way of least resistance is down, the pockets of strength seen today notwithstanding.

November 18, 1993 - Thursday Evening

Capitalizing today on the Wednesday bearish signals and set to sell on the news of the NAFTA winning House vote, the Dow fell 19.01 points to the 3685.34 level. Down as much as 35 points in the final hour, selective improvements cut the loss considerably. At the same time, however, the advance/decline line showed little ability to reduce the large earlier loss and the final loss was approximately a negative plurality of 491. The A/D line on the Nasdaq mirrored that loss and these large daily A/D line declines cut the heart out of any bullish arguments.

The high/low indicator again showed the bearish switch, 34 new highs and 62 new lows. Nothing underscores the bearish case more than this key indicator.

The very fact that *Chevron* and *Boeing* could turn right around after Wednesday's sharp run-ups highlights the weakness in this market. There are no strong follow throughs. When strength is recorded it immediately becomes a selling target.

The Climax Indicator fell to -5. The Net Field Trend indicator fell to +6, losing a field in *Westinghouse.* Stocks close to losing fields are *American Express, Bethlehem Steel, Sears,* and *United Technologies,* threatening a potential drop in the NFI to +I, possibly as early as Monday.

Paramount Communications fell again, closing down at 77. This stock is undergoing a collapse, On-Balance Volume falling over 13,000,000 since November 8th. I have designated a drop to at least the 60 level.

Golds consolidated constructively today.

November 18, 1993

17. ***Bull Trap Supreme***

The day before the crucial House vote on NAFTA the Dow rocketed ahead 33.25 points to post a new all-time record closing high of 3710.77. Transports also closed at a new record high. Now what does this prove? Dow Theory claims it is a new confirmed high. But let me refer to perhaps the most famous Dow highs of them all, the September 3, 1929 high which also saw a simultaneous new high in the Transports. That confirmation by the Transports proved to be worthless. Today the same two indices are accompanied by imminent danger. On the 1929 high there were 54 new stock highs and 19 new stock lows. The advance/decline line had peaked the previous December. On the November 16, 1993 high we had 73 highs and 49 lows and the advance/decline line stood 2,400 under the October 15th high. Making a new Dow high with these technical red flags flying comprises a *supreme bull trap.* And to spring the trap on the NAFTA vote underscores a touch of irony reserved for this most classic of bull traps.

This latest high in the Dow was a product of clever stock rotation which showed the Dow high as being virtually meaningless inasmuch as *most of the Dow industrial stocks had already seen their highs a long time ago.* Look at the record on page 3 of the Dow industrial stock OBV highs and the dates recorded. Despite all the hoopla about the record Dow highs, *you will see that one third of all the Dow industrial stocks saw their OBV peaks in 1992.* On this latest Dow high of November 16th you will see in the page 3 table that *only three Dow stocks made new OBV highs.* To keep the strength going it was necessary to start running *the retreads like IBM and Philip Morris*, showing that Wall Street was having a hard time coming up with new ideas. When they start going back to those Dow stocks that have already had their best bull cycle runs, the entire cycle is then judged to be terminal.

The reason why the public is so slow to recognize when it is time to sell their stocks is largely because their attention is constantly diverted from the true market by the Dow. Thus by the time the Dow seriously turns down, most stocks have been declining for many months and the public sells long after the peak percentage gains have been seen. *So the Dow itself is the final trap.*

The only ingredients lacking on the late August market alert was the downturn in bonds and the decline in the advance/decline line. These ingredients are now very much a part of the current sell signal. One third of the market consists of the interest sensitive stocks. Since these have now peaked, it explains why the advance/decline line has been unable to recover since peaking on October 15th. Relating the current market peak to that of July 1990, I said that once the A/D line was down 2,000 from the top there *was then no recovery.* I had also drawn parallels with the action in the Net Field Trend indicator in the two periods and saw alarming similarities, both numbers peaking at +15 and thereafter dropping sharply.

November 20, 1993 - Saturday Afternoon

Overcoming one of the most overhyped events of the year, the Dow failed to better the Tuesday pre-NAFTA high of 3710.77, closing the week out at 3694.01. Seeing the earlier high in the Dow as a major bull trap, this was well borne out with probably the weakest technical internal readings of the year. Option expiration on Friday saw the Dow close up 8.67 points, but everything else fell and fell decisively. The continued collapse in the advance/decline lines on both the big board and the Nasdaq is setting the stage for a major market decline ahead.

And once again new lows outnumbered new highs on all exchanges, a key technical requirement for all bear markets.

The bond market got smashed on Friday, the long bond plummeting 1- 11/32nds to boost the yield from 6.23% to 6.33% in a single day. The widespread declines in all interest-sensitive stocks is what is contributing the most to the great weakness in the advance/decline lines.

The Climax Indicator rose on Friday from -5 to zero but the Net Field Trend indicator fell from +6 to +4, losing a field in *Sears* and a field in *United Technologies*. We almost lost *American Express* but it closed unchanged. However, we missed losing two fields in *McDonalds* by a hair. New candidates to lose fields now include one field in *Allied-Signal* and the two fields in *McDonalds*. And so a break to the NFI +1 level still looks imminent.

Bearish sentiment is very strong and my numbers tell me that this time the bears are right as they always are in a bear market.

Fannie Mae is breaking now, closing down Friday at 74-3/4 Now breaking a triple bottom, stock is a candidate now for a plunge to 58-60 for first support. *Merrill Lynch* at 90-1/4 on Friday, heading for 68 (34 on new stock). *Motorola* seen headed for 80.

Paramount Communications down every day this past week, OBV in huge collapse.

Outlook the same: *Market collapse ahead and strong upside in the golds.*

November 22, 1993 - Monday Evening

As expected, the market took another large hit today, extreme weakness seen in all advance/decline lines. The long bond dropped 20/32nds which pushed the yield up to 6.38%. The Dow was down over 40 but cut the loss to 23.76 points at the 3670.25 level.

The advance/decline line today took another huge hit of 1,201, dropping the line to -54,140, the lowest level since July 28th when the Dow stood at 3553. The Dow tends to catch up with the A/D line and thus today predicts that the 3553 level will soon be seen. More importantly, the A/D line is now only 654 away from the July 7th level when the Dow stood at 3475. That could be seen tomorrow. But more importantly, the Dow 200-day trendline stands at 3560 and thus the market today is already predicting that the Dow will soon go under its major trendline.

The high/low indicator showed 20 highs and 109 new lows, another upside breakout in the number of new lows.

Our best looking short sale candidates took some more big hits. *Fannie Mae* fell to 73-7/8, Motorola dropped to 93-1/2, and *Merrill Lynch* collapsed to 87.

And once again *Paramount Communications* fell, falling to 75-1/4 and recording the sixth consecutive decline. The collapsing On-Balance Volume in this stock cuts through all the side drama. Postponed decisions announced today only feeds uncertainty and markets hate uncertainty.

The attempts to support the Dow by pushing a handful of stocks in that 30-stock average is of little avail against the extreme breadth of the decline. The A/D lines have fallen too far to look for any meaningful recoveries.

The Gold Stock Index closed at 127.41, off only 0.20.

November 23, 1993 - Tuesday Evening

I said here on Monday night to not look for any meaningful recoveries in the face of such weak market breadth. The market today simply recorded a bounce in the bond market and the utility average from a temporarily oversold condition. But the other Dow averages were mixed to sharply lower. The Dow industrials closed up 3.92 at the 3674.17 level after turning down in the final hour from a better than 13 point gain. The Transport Average fell a sharp 17.95 points, most of the airline stocks getting slaughtered. Here was a perfect example of technical analysis having the upper hand over the news. The strike by airline stewardesses at *American Airlines* was settled yesterday and today the stock fell 3-1/2 points.

Technical weakness was not confined to just the U.S. market. Great Britain cut its bank rate this morning and all European markets closed down.

The advance/decline line showed a moderate rise but well within the range I pointed out yesterday that would project the Dow down to 3475 and well under its 200-day trendline.

The high/low indicator continued to reflect the current technical weakness, showing 17 highs and 81 lows. The Nasdaq showed a sharp rise but well within the parameters of expectation noting its recent sharp slide.

Monday saw the Climax Indicator at -3, only recovering to zero today. The Net Field Trend Indicator fell to +2 on Monday, losing a field in *American Express* and two fields in *McDonalds*, but gaining a field in *Eastman Kodak*. *Bethlehem Steel* is within range to lose two fields tomorrow. The NFI remained at +2 today.

Paramount Communications bounced to 79 yesterday on the close but gave most of that decline back today, falling 2-3/4 points to 76-1/4. No change in outlook there, any statements tomorrow notwithstanding.

The Gold Stock Index closed well above the earlier lows.

November 24, 1993 - Wednesday Evening

The market ran along traditional lines today, making a pre-Thanksgiving Dow advance of 13.41 points with the average closing at 3687.58. Transports celebrated by reversing the almost 18-point decline recorded on Tuesday. Utilities rose 0.46 and it is important to point out that the Dow utility stocks showed five lower up designations on Tuesday, technically a very weak advance.

The advance/decline line posted a strong advance of 427 putting the reading at -53,453. It was last at that reading on August 6th when the Dow stood at 3560 so keep this in mind. The A/D line tells us where the Dow is headed. Thus we cannot read anything positive into today's advance. *This indicator is running 127 points ahead of the Dow on the downside despite today's rally.* As for highs and lows, this is where the true trend is best reflected, 26 highs and 34 lows.

The Climax Indicator rose to +3, far short of the +9 reading of November 16th. The Net Field Trend indicator rose to +3, gaining a field in *Goodyear*, but remains far under the +15 reading of October 27th.

Paramount Communications remained an enigma, the market waiting all day for word from the judge in the case. The stock closed strong, up 3-3/4 points at the 80 level. It is important to remind subscribers that we were not playing the stock as a short sale, but observing it as the possible trigger of a major market decline. Having previously shown the stock down on a huge On-Balance Volume loss, the rise today as well as any new high will of course be widely non-confirmed. Today saw the stock recording a lower OBV up designation and that sets the stock up for a renewed slide. I am reading the stock technically, completely independent of developments in the merger case.

Many observers are counting on a year-end rally and a downturn in early 1994. The market may come up with a surprise and ignore the seasonal strength.

November 27, 1993 - Saturday Afternoon

Very interesting week containing what was hyped as two of the strongest days of the year, the day before and after Thanksgiving. But as it turned out, the Dow was not only down 10.06 points on the week, but fell 3.63 points on Friday to close down at the 3683.95 level on what was looked for by so many to be a big up day for the Dow. But it was only the oil stocks that messed up the day for the Dow industrials. The rest of the market looked all right but the extremely low volume of 90 million shares neutralized so much of the otherwise positive action. For instance, UAL rose a huge 5-5/8 points but did so on such low volume that the stock couldn't even make an OBV lower up designation. Moves like this cut down the importance of the almost 29-point rise in the Transports on Friday.

The high/low indicator switched to the positive side with 32 highs and 17 new lows but the improvements have been coming from a temporary contraction of the lows rather than a significant expansion of the highs.

The Climax Indicator remained unchanged at +3. The Net Field Trend indicator rose to +4, gaining a field in *International Paper*. But the big picture here is the decline from the +15 level since October 27th. An excessive number of OBV lower up designations on the Dow Transport and Utility stocks sets those averages up for later declines just when the industrials will need all the help they can get.

Despite the recent ruling in the *Paramount* case which apparently opened the way for higher bids, the stock declined on Friday to 79-7/8, *the OBV having dropped over 11 million shares since peaking on November 8th.*

I look for further declines dead ahead.

November 29, 1993 - Monday Evening

Looking for immediate further declines in the market, the Dow recorded a reversal to the downside today after temporarily being up over 15 points and meeting significant upside resistance at the 3700 level. The close saw the Dow off 6.15 at the 3677.80 level. Transports were up 19.23, benefiting from the drop in oil prices. The Utilities made a significant reversal to the downside, up over 2 points in the morning but closing down 0.60 points. Wall Street called the market wrong and the media took their cue from Wall Street leading many to think the market would make a large rise today.

The morning gain in the A/D line was completely eliminated and the high/low indicator showed poor numbers, 54 highs and 35 lows. But that was a small improvement while the Dow was up 15 earlier. Thus the numbers will worsen tomorrow.

The Climax Indicator fell to +2, once again falling far short of its best case scenario. The Net Field Trend remained unchanged at +4, gaining a field in *McDonalds* but losing a field in Texaco.

Some individual stocks took big hits today. *DSC Communications* fell to 53-7/8. expanding the gain to 13% and the gain on the January 65 put option to 12 for a gain of 100%. and *Motorola* dropped sharply to 93-1/4.

Paramount Communications fell to 78-1/2 on over a million shares.

November 30, 1993 - Tuesday Evening

Once again the Dow was turned back as it encountered the 3700 level, reducing a 20-point gain to 6.15, the Dow closing at 3683.95, precisely where it closed on Friday. But it failed to regain everything. The Dow gain was almost completely traced to the rebounding oils. For the month the Dow was up 3.36 points but the advance/decline line in the same period was down significantly and the high/low indicator has been disintegrated.

The advance/decline line fell again, this key indicator in a decisive downtrend since October 15th.

Today saw 43 stocks at new highs and 42 at new lows. Now here is a number that will blow your socks off: Yesterday there were 432 big board stocks within a point or less of new 52-week lows. That means that this market technically cannot afford any significant declines because that would see that statistic break out into the open with several hundred new lows.

The Climax Indicator rose from +2 to +6 while the Net Field Trend indicator remained unchanged at +4.

I am so impressed by the bearish implications of the stocks near 52-week lows that I cannot visualize the market making any significant December advance.

Paramount Communications closed up at 78-3/4 but the huge OBV loss persists and I would seriously doubt that this stock can avoid the decline that the OBV loss so clearly implies.

Section X
The Crash of 1994-95

Crash

All through the 1992-94 period I kept pounding away that something was very wrong with the market. Since most people are lazy by human nature, it was far easier to adopt the Wall Street party line and agree with the averages that the market was making record highs. Yet the dichotomy that started like a cancer in January 1992 was so damaging to the big picture that most people who bought stocks in January 1993 were holding those stocks at a loss by January 1994. It not only paralleled the 1929 performance but it was statistically worse. I was so angered after recording my secret findings that I sat down and wrote the following in January 1994:

1. ***Wake Up And Smell The Coffee***

Every morning I tune in to CNBC-TV and listen to the Buy-Hold-Sell program. Each day a different analyst takes the calls giving advice on what to do with a given stock. After awhile I would write down the names of all the stocks covered. Almost without exception, the reason for the calls was because the stocks covered were under water and giving the caller trouble. At first I thought it was just stocks like *Amgen, Apple Computer, Borden, Fruit of the Loom, Glaxo, Marion Merrell Dow, Syntex,* and *U. S. Surgical* where everybody is under water and everybody knows it. But after several weeks of recording the stocks covered on the show, a general pattern became increasingly apparent: *Most people were losing money in the market.* With the Dow having risen over 600 points just since January 1993, how could such a statement possibly be true? But the persistent listing of *losing stocks* on the CNBC show every morning intrigued me. I could understand if most of the questions every day were on the same stocks. But my lists told me that it was a far more widespread sickness than seen at first glance. **SOMETHING WAS VERY WRONG.** While the Dow kept telling everybody we are in a bull market, *I was getting a strong whiff of something that smelled much more like an approaching bear market.*

In 1929 Roger Babson made a discovery that was followed a few weeks later by the great crash. He announced in early September of that fateful year when the Dow stood at an all-time record high that of the 1,200 stocks listed on the New York Stock Exchange that 612 of them were down on the year. With the current Dow also at an all-time record high, *I wondered how many stocks were showing a loss since January 1, 1993.* I was determined to find out. No newspaper was going to give you such vital information.

What you are about to see here cuts through all the worthless mish mash you hear on the TV financial shows about stocks at record highs. Nothing could be further from the truth. My research centered on the *M.C. Horsey* chart book. There I could see the charts of close to 2,000 stocks and I could record how many of them were under water since January 1, 1993.

I started my count with the November 1993 edition. I would record the page number, how many charts on the page, the number of charts showing a stock loss since January 1, 1993, then the percentage of losers. To perfectly equate with the evidence revealed by Babson in September 1929, I would have to show at least 50.5% of all stocks showing a loss. *The results were absolutely astounding.* The November 1993 *Horsey* chart book showed that 56% of all the stocks in that book were down since January 1, 1993. But hold your hat. It gets even more revealing. I just received my January 1994 edition of the Horsey chart book. I haven't finished my study yet but so far (almost halfway through the book) *58% of the stocks covered are down since January 1, 1993.*

(*Author's Note*)-

My later research revealed that this era of good feeling which prompted the heavy public buying of stocks the very next month saw most of those January 1993 purchases showing a loss by January 1994. So what the public heard in December 1992 was essentially correct, it nevertheless entrapped the majority into buying stocks just prior to their declines. What I was seeing at that time was the beginning of the identical technical sickness that was to later collapse the 1929 market, most stocks topping out while the public was blinded by the late bull market blue chip strength.

In the interests of continuity, I felt it to be important to preface the early 1994 market action with the December 1993 *Commentaries*, convinced that clues to later market action could be detected there in retrospect.

December 1, 1993 - Wednesday Evening

The stunning revelation about the 432 stocks within a point of new lows in one blow cuts straight through the entire facade of meaningless technical mish mash, making it crystal clear that the bears can relax and comfortably get through anything the market has in store for the month of December. Today the Dow rose 26 points but this was cut in half by the close, the Dow closing up 13.13 points at the 3697.08 level. This was significant because it showed a brick wall of technical resistance at the November 16th high of 3710. So we are seeing more evidence now of selling into strength.

New highs were 56 and new lows 25, very substandard action with the Dow so close to new highs. The Dow was turned back at the old high when it became apparent that any new high would lack an advance/decline line confirmation.

The Dow Utility Average fell 2.18 points to the 223.17 level, closing just 0.72 points above the November 22nd low of 222.45. This average has almost duplicated what it did just before the crash of 1987 and so it bears especially close watching now.

New put options are the *Charles Schwab* March 35, *Shoneys* January 20, *Upjohn* January 32-1.2, and *Wells Fargo* January 120. The underlying stocks are all short sales.

The Climax Indicator rose from +6 to +9 but there were 9 OBV lower up designations, underscoring today as a dangerous technical failure. The Net Field Trend indicator rose to +6, gaining a field in *American Express* and a field in *General Electric.*

Gold stocks showed excellent strength today.

December 2, 1993 - Thursday Evening

The day didn't have much to recommend it, the Dow closing up 5.03 points at the 3702.11 level. Transports and utilities rose but there was no teeth in the advance. Volume was moderate and one could again sense the distribution characteristics that continue to show up among the most active stocks.

The technical evidence continues to mount up, making it increasingly unlikely that we won't be able to get through the month of December without seriously stumbling. The bulls are counting on seasonal strength but there are too many stocks close to making new lows, far too many to expect a significant further advance.

The advance/decline line rose again but is too far away for a confirmation of any new Dow high and that would bring in heavy selling. There were 62 highs and 21 lows but that disguises the true condition of the market, 432 stocks within a point of new lows.

The Climax Indicator fell from +9 to +7 on the Dow rise and once again there was a plethora of lower OBV up designations, 8 of these seen today. The Net Field Trend indicator remained unchanged at +6.

The Limited collapsed to 18, making a five-year low. Very few noticed that the stock had peaked at 33 in January 1992 with so many others in that particular month.

Paramount Communications edged up to 79 but retains a very bearish pattern of heavy liquidation as evidenced by its OBV trend.

Gold stocks retained their positive patterns despite a $1 pullback in the gold price.

December 2, 1993

2. *COUNTDOWN TO DISASTER*

Probably nobody in the world is aware of what I am about to reveal to you. The information is invaluable and it will knock your socks off. As I write this, the Dow has made a stab at a new record high but at the same time **THERE ARE 432 BIG BOARD COMMON STOCKS WITHIN A POINT OR LESS OF NEW 52-WEEK LOWS!** This number has been getting bigger all year and now predicts a market disaster within 2 to 4 weeks or less. *(Memo to CNBC's Roy Blumberg: I noted Roy's recent surprise when new lows suddenly expanded to 105 on November 22nd. If he knew how many stocks were within a point of new lows then of course he would not have been surprised. Now he can expect to see several hundred actual new lows in the weeks ahead.)

Counting stocks within a point or less of new 52-week highs and lows accents the subject of *range.* This counting technique which I introduced has homed in on every significant market change of direction. It corresponded with my October 26, 1987 buy signal, my August 15, 1989 sell signal, the predicted UAL collapse and mini-crash of October 13, 1989, the July 1990 top, the August 2, 1990 Kuwait collapse, the 635-point drop in the Dow, the late 1990 bottom, the huge Persian Gulf war rally of January 1991 and the equally powerful rally of December 1991. Now the high/low indicator is calling the Dow top and imminent collapse going into 1994 but most people will miss the signal until it is too late, following merely the actual high/low numbers rather than the count of the NYSE stocks coming within those important one-point ranges.

The maximum number of stocks within a point or less of new highs was seen on April 6, 1993 when the number reached 777 stocks. That was the climactic internal peak in the high/low indicator.

Then more numbers to knock your socks off: Karen counted the big board common stocks within a point or less of new 12-month highs. As of Monday, November 29, 1993, *there were only 389 stocks within a point of new highs.* So we have seen the very bearish 50% contraction there since April, so like mid-July 1990, we have more stocks about to make new lows rather than new highs. We are thus sitting on a technical mine about to explode.

3. *NOW WE HAVE TO LOOK FOR A BIG EVENT*

We saw how effectively the 1989 break was identified with the OCTOBER UAL COLLAPSE and we saw how the 1990 Summer break was identified with the KUWAIT INVASION. Now having the identical technical warnings on the high/low numbers, what will be the BIG EVENT identified with the coming collapse? Technical analysis tells us there will be a collapse but the big triggering event could come from anywhere. I speculated that it might be a collapse in *Paramount Communications* or a military shock. I had talked about my war indicator and the parallels with the condition just prior to the Kuwait invasion of August 1990. It is interesting to note that the price of oil had dropped all the way back to where it was just before the Kuwait invasion.

So I felt very sure of my ground when I closed out the December 2, 1993 letter by stating that the stunning revelation about the 432 stocks within a point of new lows in one blow cuts straight through the entire facade of meaningless technical mish mash, making it crystal clear that the bears can relax and comfortably get through anything the market has in store for the month of December.

December 4, 1993 - Saturday Afternoon

Blockbuster economic news greeted the scene Friday morning, the *biggest drop in monthly unemployment figures in ten years!* Bonds took the numbers in stride and shrugged them off. Encountering this extraordinarily strong economic news, the Dow had only to hurdle a mere 8.69 points in order to easily record a new high. Instead, however, the Dow's popularly-expected huge rally was a mere 1.96 points. Instead of fireworks, it was all suspiciously quiet on the western front. *Any trained technician had to conclude that something was very wrong.*

Transports and utilities sat it out, both refusing to participate in any bullish charades. The advance/decline line, however, put on a good show but still ended up 3000 away from the October 15th high and thus provides no lasting technical help.

But the month of December is expected to benefit from seasonal strength, although technically in serious doubt. Nobody expects any serious December disturbances and that is why they are increasingly probable. Besides possible triggering events of war or a *Paramount* collapse, the strong Friday economic news now positions the Fed to make a surprise tightening move sooner than generally expected.

The Climax Indicator fell from +7 to +5 on the higher Dow reading, a further indication of technically increasing upside exhaustion. A further good portion of strength was neutralized by the declines in the Transport and Utility averages.

But the gold stocks continued to forge ahead in a more convincing manner.

December 6, 19993 - Monday Evening

The Dow missed a new high by a fraction, closing up 6.14 at the 3710.21 level. Transports fell 7.69 points to the 1756.35 level while utilities had a strong rise. But it was a mixed day, the Nasdaq falling, reflecting a 4-point drop in the price of *Intel.* Both the high/low indicator and the advance/decline line had a good day but both those indicators are so far under their highs that they simply serve to remind us that *the only thing going for the market right now is year-end seasonal strength.* We had 100 new highs today, the highest since November 2nd when we had 115.

The Climax Indicator rose from +5 to +9 and again it is important to know that we had 6 lower ups today. The Net Field Trend indicator, however, jumped to +8, reflecting gains of a field in both Merck and *Union Carbide.*

Tomorrow night we will have the new count of common stocks within a point of new 52-week highs and lows. The last count showed a definite trend toward important weakness and I do not expect any significant improvements. We will try to get these numbers to you every Tuesday night.

I would draw your attention to the John Dorfman article in the *Jour-*

nal this morning as well as the fine article in the current *Barron's* by David Rocker before getting too impressed with the December strength. It smacks too much of the last hurrah rather than signalling a significantly higher market.

Looking at the *Intel* chart, this is a stock that has definitely seen its high. It broke today to under 60. If it breaks 56 it won't hold at 50 but will trace out a bear market decline to 42.

December 7, 1993 - Tuesday Evening

The Dow scored another record high *with virtually nothing confirming the advance.* The rise of 8.67 points put the Dow at 3718.88. Transports and Utilities also rose. But the advance was technically very suspect, with large gains in *Boeing* and *Sears* accounting for roughly half the advance. Previous records of Dow stocks weighting a rise then saw those stocks as no longer rising.

The number of new highs contracted from 100 to 78 on the higher Dow with the new lows coming in at 24. The latest count of stocks within a point or less of new 52-week highs and lows showed 529 stocks within a point of a high and 405 stocks within a point of a low. If the market was coming off a bottom then these numbers would be very bullish. But coming down from a top as we are now doing shows the high number well under the peak of last April and the low number over 400 being very bearish. This underscores the direction of the flow of money as it steadily leaves this market.

I would say that the most important technical event today was that *we finally got a Dow high widely non-confirmed by the advance/decline line.* The market tomorrow will quickly reveal how sensitive it is to such bearish signals. *My guess is that it will be very sensitive and give us a significant decline.*

The Climax Indicator fell from +9 to +5 on the new Dow high while the Net Field Trend indicator rose to +9, gaining a field in *Boeing.*

Paramount Communications closed down at 79-1/4.

Gold stocks were impressive today. Later this week we get the inflation numbers coming from the Producer and Consumer Price indices.

December 8, 1993 - Wednesday Evening

In still another technically unconfirmed move, the Dow today rose to another record high at the 3734.53 level, up 15.65 points. *The upswing was not confirmed by anything*. Europe was celebrating GATT but their celebration may be premature.

The key word today was **GOLD.** A massive breakout above the 380 level was accompanied by an almost 7-point rise in the Gold Stock Index. This is highly significant because tomorrow and Friday we get the Producer and Consumer Price indices. It is highly likely that the gold runup today could be traced to a leak of the Thursday and Friday inflation numbers. That is the most obvious reason for the gold upside explosion today. The second reason has even bigger implications. Since I have underscored the technical signals that imply the near-term emergence of an event that will trigger a major market break, the sharp gold advance today adds to the probability of such a break and such a triggering event. The triggering event could be any of a series of things such as a *Paramount* Collapse, a Federal Reserve tightening move, a failure to see GATT passed next week, or a military crisis. And it is interesting to note that all *US nuclear weapons were withdrawn from South Korea a year ago.*

The Climax Indicator advanced from +5 to +8 on the new Dow high, another key *upside non-confirmation.* The Net Field Trend indicator remained unchanged at +9.

Remember to adhere to the rule of selling half your gold stock call options on all doublers. We have a large number of doublers as of today.

Paramount Communications closed unchanged at 79-1/2, But we are moving close now to the denouement and the collapse in the OBV is expected to indicate the expected decline.

I think we are sitting on an imminent surprise.

December 9, 1993 - Thursday Evening

The Dow reversed from an earlier advance of over 13 points to close down 4.75 points at the 3729.78 level. The Dow was succumbing to broad weakness which was already in evidence. An advance can go on just so long on its own and this advance had no help to keep it going. The morning high in the Dow just might be a key rally peak. Nobody expects that and that makes it more likely. Today was a down day across the board.

Highs and lows came in at 98 and 31, still showing relative weakness and the advance/decline lines on both the big board and Nasdaq took large hits.

The Climax Indicator still showed a positive reading but fell from +8 to +7. Transports and Utilities provided no side help, both with rather significant declines. The Transports showed 75% of the stocks unchanged to lower while 80% of the Dow utility stocks were unchanged to lower.

The Net Field Trend indicator rose to +10, gaining a field in *Caterpillar.*

Virtually every index declined today.

Paramount Communications rose 2-3/4 points today to 82 following the morning hearings on the merger case. But I maintain that the sharp OBV drop has an ultimate negative message.

After rising almost 7 points yesterday, the Gold Stock Index was down in the morning but was able to close up 0.79 points at a new high of 131.07, very bullish action. The Producer Price Index this morning showed a doubling of the core rate, justifying the strength in the gold stocks that anticipated it. Perhaps the late strength today in the gold index is anticipating a Producer Price index change tomorrow that will push the golds still higher. Else, the rise in gold is a harbinger of bearish stock market news.

December 11, 1993 - Saturday Afternoon

The Dow turned higher in the late trading to post still another record high at the 3740.67 level, rising 10.89 points. It scored a gain of over 36 points on the week. On the week Transports closed down 0.21, Utilities closed up 0.86, the Nasdaq closed down 11.48, the advance/decline line inched higher by a mere 72, while the A/D line on the Nasdaq closed down 556. The NYSE Composite was up a mere 0.19, while the Standard & Poor 500 was down 0.96. The Friday Dow gain was virtually a solo walk.

For the week new highs contracted and new lows expanded in number. On Friday new highs contracted sharply to 67 while new lows expanded sharply to 43. The advance/decline line again fell on the Dow rise and Friday's level equated with September 22nd when the Dow stood at 3547. So right now the A/D line is moving 190 points ahead of the Dow on the downside. The theory here is that the Dow goes to where the A/D line says it will go. This implies that the coming drop will take the Dow below its 200-day trendline.

The last three Dow highs were all accompanied by extremely bearish Climax Indicator upside non-confirmations. Friday saw the CLX fall to +4 on the Dow high. The Net Field Trend indicator fell on Friday to +9, losing a field in *Merck.*

After the Thursday hoopla of the *Paramount Communications* hearings in a Delaware courtroom opening the way for new and higher bids on the stock, *Paramount* closed down 7/8 at 81-1/8 on Friday on 2.6 million shares, not a bullish response to what most people thought was an action that signalled sharply higher prices.

And again the Gold Stock Index moved to new highs after being off in the morning, closing up 0.62 at the 131.69 level. Roll over the Hecla December 10 calls to the March 12-1/2 calls.

So we are seeing here the extremely dangerous Dow solo walk to new highs, virtually supported by nothing. Having no net, the coming fall should be technically fatal.

December 13, 1993- Monday Evening

The Dow solo walk continued today but if it was dangerous on Friday it was far more dangerous today. The Dow scored a typical blowoff rise of 23.76 points, closing at the 3764.43 level. Transports and utilities rose but the fly in the ointment was again market breadth.

The New York advance/decline line fell 85, putting the line down to the -51,929 level, the lowest level seen since September 21st when the Dow stood at 3537. That means that as of today the A/D line is moving 227 points ahead of the Dow on the downside. *Ascending so sharply this early in the month increases the odds of a sharp decline before the month ends.*

There were 80 highs and 45 lows, not good numbers. While everybody was watching the Dow, the Nasdaq A/D line fell sharp a 486.

We have not shorted any Dow stocks in many months and so the rise today affected none of our followers.

The Climax Indicator rose to +6, marking another upside non-confirmation, the fourth in the past five sessions. That traces out a cluster of non-confirmations. The Net Field Trend indicator stayed unchanged at +9.

Motorola broke under 90 today, typical of a wide range of stocks breaking while the Dow average goes up. Typical of the sheer idiocy of this latest Dow rise, *Minnesota Mining* today rose 2-7/8 points to the 110-7/8 level, accounting for over 25% of the total Dow rise. Yet the stock couldn't even get an OBV up designation. That is technical weakness.

Paramount Communications fell again, dropping to 80-5/8. The real test is tomorrow when open bidding should start.

The Gold Stock Index today soared to 135.14, up 3.45 points. Our gold stocks were outstanding. We will be raising the stop levels in the next letter. *Take advantage of these huge option gains and take some partial profits.*

December 14, 1993 - Tuesday Evening

Capitalizing on the sheer idiocy of the technically worthless blowoff rise in the Dow on Monday, selling moved in today as expected and took the Dow down 21.80 points to the 3742.63 level. Transports and utilities followed suit. The authenticity of the across-the-board decline today was punctuated by broad collapses in both the NYSE advance/decline line and the Nasdaq advance/decline line. The advance/ decline on the big board fell 674 to push the line down to the -52,583 level, equating with August 16th when the Dow stood at 3579. So the A/D line is running 163 points ahead of the Dow on the downside. The Nasdaq A/D line was down about 873, a technical disaster. That will have a very negative effect on the Mutual Fund Index which is carving out a very bearish chart pattern.

The high/low indicator showed 50 highs and 57 new lows but just under the surface was another shocker. The latest stock count of stocks within a point or less of their 52-week highs and lows showed a contraction to 501 highs and a huge 20% expansion to 481 stocks within a point or less of new 52-week lows. Those were the Monday numbers. Obviously the big drop in the A/D line today means that we had much more negative numbers today. We are seeing here a duplication of the numbers seen just before the August 1990 invasion of Kuwait.

The Climax Indicator fell from a revised +7 to -7. The Net Field Trend Indicator fell to +8, losing a field in *Caterpillar.*

The break of 31/32nds in the long bond provided a very bearish backdrop for stocks.

Paramount Communications rose to 81-1/8 but with the maintained bearish OBV numbers here as well as the immediate very bearish outlook for the market, I don't think the stock is going to have a run on the upside.

December 15, 1993 - Wednesday Evening

Expecting Tuesday's break to be the beginning of something important on the downside, the expected December bust continued today with the Dow plummeting 25.71 points to close down at the 3716.92 level.

This market is so prone to go lower that even the President's afternoon press conference announcing the done deal on GATT couldn't give the market a lift, the Dow doubling its loss after the conference. After the close it was announced that Les Aspin is resigning effective January 20th. Whatever the news now the market will react with a negative response.

The biggest damage continued to be inflicted in terms of market breadth. Today the big board advance/decline line gave up another 286 dropping the line to -52,875. That equated with August 13th when the average stood at 3569. So the A/D line is forecasting a drop to the 3569 level, that indicator currently running 147 points ahead of the Dow on the downside.

Once again the high/low indicator came in with weak numbers- 47 highs and 51 lows. *But I now estimate that there are over 500 big board common stocks within a point or less of new 52-week lows.*

The Climax Indicator rose to -5 inasmuch as Kodak was accounting for about 60% of the Dow decline. The Net Field Trend indictor fell to +7, losing a field in *Eastman Kodak.*

I continue to like all the recommended precious metal stocks and I was impressed to see *Sunshine Mining* close up at 2-7/8 today. I still see this stock as having the least downside risk of all the gold/silver stocks.

December 16, 1993 - Thursday Evening

Today the market recorded a weak bounce which pushed the Dow up 9.22 points to the 3726.14 level. Typical of the mixed market today, the Transports closed down 13.51 points at the 1750.95 level. Today caught a piece of the unwinding action prior to tomorrow's triple witching option expiration session. It is difficult to see what the market will do on Friday but everything I have said about this market for the month of December stands.

The market today did little for the breadth numbers and the advances were small enough so that they could all disappear tomorrow.

The high/low indicator continued to show weak numbers today, 51 highs and 61 lows. Now that the numbers have flipped over, it is very difficult to again see a significant expansion in the number of new highs.

The Climax Indicator was only able to get back to zero on today's advance. The Net Field Trend Indicator fell to +6, losing a field in *Procter & Gamble.*

Every day now there are some huge casualties in the over-the-counter market. This is a Dorian Grey market, the healthy looking stocks allowed to be seen in the parlor while most issues have been trundled off to the attic, old and ugly and far under their earlier highs.

The golds continue act very well, the Gold Stock Index today only down 0.52 at the 132.44 level, holding close to their highs.

So today was an in-between day. Tomorrow could be critical.

December 18, 1993 - Saturday Afternoon

Friday's triple witching session saw the Dow rise a sharp 25.43 points to close at 3751.57. After the bulls finished celebrating and the smoke cleared, a technical evaluation of what actually happened was quite sobering.

Curiously, the high/low indicator showed 70 highs and 40 lows, a sharp contraction from earlier December levels, the key indication that not much bullishness can be read into Friday's rally. The advance/decline line took a sharp leap with almost 800 net advances but remained well under required breakout levels. The current reading equates with September 22nd when the Dow stood at 3547. So the A/D line is running 204 points ahead of the Dow on the downside. And the A/D line was down on the week.

But the main technical warnings are coming from the Nasdaq. Friday saw a small rise in its A/D line bringing the current reading to +753, a small rise from Wednesday's recent low of +483. Keep in mind that the low of the year is -1888 of last April and the high was +5969 on October 15th so we have seen much deterioration and right now is in easy range to make a significant breakout on the downside to a new low for the year. That would have significant negative implications for the early 1994 market. And the message here is directed at the mutual funds since the Mutual Fund Index so closely correlates with the Nasdaq. Note that that index hardly budged on Friday.

The Climax Indicator showed no quantum leap on Friday, showing a very small rise from zero to +3, certainly not in keeping with a better than 25-point Dow rise. Close analysis revealed the reasons. (1) *Allied-Signal, General Electric,* and *IBM* accounted for almost half the entire advance. (2) We actually saw declines in *Alcoa, American Telephone, Coca Cola, DuPont, Goodyear, Minnesota Mining, Sears, Union Carbide,* and *United Technologies.* So this was no across-the-board Dow blitz.

The Net Field Trend indicator improved with a jump to +8, gaining two fields in *Disney.*

So as good as the numbers might have looked to some on Friday, this observer was not impressed.

December 20, 1993 - Monday Evening

The Dow failed to build on early gains, only able to close 3.64 points higher at the 3755.21 level. Transports fell over 5 points while utilities were almost unchanged.

While there was a small improvement in the high/low indicator to 93 highs and 38 lows, market breadth was negative on both the big board and the Nasdaq. The big board advance/decline line fell back to the pre-October 15th level of -52,.046 equating with September 21st when the Dow stood at 3537. So as of today the A/D line is moving a steep 217 points ahead of the Dow on the downside.

The situation is far worse on the Nasdaq. Today the A/D line there fell to 512, giving back almost all of the gains for the past two days. The A/D Line on that market is within 2400 of a new low for the year, the breaking of which would then constitute a technical catastrophe.

The Climax Indicator fell from Friday's small +3 reading to +1, The Net Field Trend indicator gave back the Friday gain, dropping back to +6, losing a field in *Alcoa* and a field in *Minnesota Mining.*

Motorola still looks like an outstanding short sale. The stock chart is tracing out a classic bear market pattern and looks like it could decline all the way to the 60 level. New players in the stock can go short here and play the April 85 puts. Stops should be no closer than 97.

The Gold Stock Index continues to edge higher, this the hottest group of the year.

December 21, 1993 - Tuesday Evening

The Dow fell 10.06 to the 3745.15 level. But once again the big story was again the growing internal weakness.

The high/low indicator came in at 76 highs and 50 lows. A sharp contraction in the new highs from yesterday.

The NYSE advance/decline line fell 340 and the indicator remained at the lowest pre-October 15th level since September 21st, currently running 208 points ahead of the Dow on the downside. Over on the Nasdaq the situation was far worse. There the advance/decline line fell a sharp 518 bringing the line down to +47, the lowest level since July 28th when the Nasdaq Composite stood at 705. Now the A/D line there is only 1935 away from the low for the entire year. At the rate that market is falling, *it is even conceivable that a new low could be seen before the year is out.* And don't forget that this market correlates very closely with the Mutual Fund Index, that index tracing out a very bearish pattern.

The Climax Indicator fell to -2 while the Net Field Trend indicator stayed unchanged at +6.

Paramount Communications was the feature today, the stock beginning to unravel now as it fell 1-3/4 to 80-1/4 on 3,140,900 shares. When the bidding finally ends then the stock will become a short sale or a fall of 5 points off the top, whichever takes place first. The whole affair is a classic example of stock distribution, proven by the sharp drop of over 9 million in the OBV since the November 8th peak. I maintain that the stock is headed down to the 60 level. The OBV clearly implies that the stock is seriously overpriced.

The Gold Stock Index fell sharply today but the chart underscores this as normal profit-taking after the recent run.

December 22, 1993 - Wednesday Evening

It is difficult to break tradition and the market tried to act jolly three days before Christmas. But try as it did, there wasn't enough buying power around to significantly lift the advance/decline line after the usual concentration on the Dow stocks. The Dow industrial average closed up 17.04 points at the 3762.19 level and the Transports joined in and closed up points 14.15 points.

New highs came in at 71 and new lows stood at 41. This was the dead giveaway that the large rise in the Dow industrial average was technically worthless. There was virtually no expansion in the new highs.

On Karen's stock count stocks within a point of new 52-week highs fell significantly, dropping from 501 to 463. Stocks within a point of new 52-week lows showed little change, dropping from 481 to 478.

Again the key feature to keep our eyes on in this market are the two advance/ decline lines- the NYSE and the Nasdaq. First of all, the NYSE advance/decline line made a technically weak showing for a Dow rise of 17 points. It was only up a net 182. Secondly, the Nasdaq advance/decline line fell by 142, dropping the reading to -55, now only 1833 away from a new 1993 low. This indicator could still make a new low before the year is out. In any case, both advance/decline lines urge one to keep the blinders on and completely ignore the Dow stocks which are nothing more than a smokescreen to deflect attention away from the very weak technical picture of the entire market.

The climax indicator rose to +8 while the Net Field Trend indicator rose to +7, gaining a field in *Philip Morris.*

The Gold Stock Index came back significantly from the morning lows, only being off 0.11 at the 129.33 level.

December 24, 1993 - Friday Evening

The Dow broke a long standing tradition in closing down on Thursday, the pre-Christmas session. Up over 12 points in the afternoon, the Dow fell in the final hour to post a loss of 4.47 points at the 3757.72 level. Transports and utilities followed suit, all closing lower. But the internal action was positive with gains in both the NYSE and Nasdaq advance/decline lines.

Most of the day the Dow was in new record high ground but the late selloff avoided what would have been the 13th A/D line upside non-confirmation since October 18th. Thursday's session underscored the probable fact that new Dow highs will no longer be technically tolerated.

The Climax Indicator fell from +8 to +5 with the Net Field Trend indicator closing unchanged at +7. *Coca Cola, Goodyear, J.P. Morgan, Union Carbide* and *Woolworth* are all close to losing field trends.

Looking through the charts of the Dow stocks, strength is no longer accepted as a defense against sharp declines. *Allied-Signal* and *General Electric* are both excellent examples, both stocks extremely overbought and now vulnerable to sharp decline with no further warnings necessary.

Paramount Communications continues to unravel, falling a full point on Thursday to 78-5/8. The OBV has fallen a sharp 7 million just since last Monday and the stock is now in a falling field trend. I had previously stated that the stock is a short sale on any closing more than 5 points off the high. Since the price high was 83, breaking 78 will put us short.

No change in outlook. Stay long on the golds, be selectively short, but continue to avoid shorting any Dow stock.

December 27, 1993 - Monday Evening

The Santa Claus rally saw the Dow rocket 35.21 points higher to close up at a new record high of 3792.93. Both Transports and Utilities went along for the ride.

As good as everything looked today, there were technical potholes limiting the rise to what could be described as a good day having no follow through implications. A technical critique would home in on the high/low indicator and the advance/decline lines. Despite the 35-point advance, new highs only expanded from 102 to 104, virtually no improvement whatsoever. The advance/decline line showed a strong rise of 540 but even with that rise the line stands at the September 24th level when the Dow stood at 3543. So now the A/D line is running a huge 249.82 points ahead of the Dow on the downside. So the internal pressures for a sharp correction continue to build.

Two other factors get poor reviews. The late rise was purely on buy programs. Ticks rose from 81 to 412 in the closing ten seconds of trading and overall volume was the lightest of the year for a full day of trading.

Dow gains were very uneven this month so far, *Allied-Signal, Boeing, Disney, General Electric,* and *IBM accounting for over 82% of the entire Dow December rise.*

The Climax Indicator rose from +5 to +11, not an outstanding rise considering the fact that there were five lower up designations. The Net

Field Trend indicator rose to +8, gaining a field in *Woolworth.*

Paramount Communications fell again, closing down 1/2 at 78-1/8. Will only short on a close under 78.

The Gold Index was very strong, rising 1.51 points today to 130.53.

December 28, 1993 - Tuesday Evening

The Dow closed at another record high thanks to a fractional rise of 0.56 at the 3793.49 level. Volume was light.

The high/low indicator again flashed technical warnings, only able to expand to 108 with over a third of the highs being foreign stocks and funds. The advance/ decline line had a nice rise but the indicator recorded the 14th non-confirmation of a new Dow high. And I figure new highs will continue to be non-confirmed.

The Climax Indicator fell from +11 to +8, a key CLX upside non-confirmation. The Net Field Trend indicator rose to +9, gaining a field in *Chevron.*

Paramount Communications closed down 1/4 at the 77-7/8 level. Having broken more than 5 points off the high at 83, we are now officially short the stock. Today is the fifth consecutive daily decline, the OBV today collapsing to the -12,650,300 level. Now the stock is within easy distance of breaking under the November 19th level when the OBV stood at a low of -14,847,900. With both *Paramount* and QVC collapsing, I am beginning to suspect that Viacom plans to walk away from the deal and leave QVC holding the bag, a bag that is progressively worth less and less each day. So QVC will be winning a vastly overpriced asset and Viacom will have the last laugh. The decline in QVC from 72 to 37-7/8 tells you that they are the fall guy, caught holding the bag. The stock has fallen over 47% since July and that is not too smart for a reputed sharp operator. The OBV told the true story right from the beginning.

Buy the *Paramount Communications* April 75 put options.

December 29, 1993 - Wednesday Evening

The Dow eked out another record high with a fractional rise of 0.56, closing at 3794.33. Transports and utilities fell.

New highs expanded to 119 and new lows stood at 21. Both the advance/decline lines rose but I consign that strength to the calendar and don't see it as likely to continue next month.

On the latest count of stocks selling within a point or less of their 52-week highs and lows, we had 559 on the high side and 471 on the low side. It was expected that the stocks on the high side would expand in light of the recent strength but it is incredible that in the face of the record Dow high we have 471 within a point or less of new 52-week lows. That retains a hard core of internal weakness which will be more fully released in January.

Yesterday's weak stocks rose while yesterday's strong stocks fell. That phenomenon produced a severe CLX upside non-confirmation of the new high, the second CLX non-confirmation this week. The CLX fell from +8 to a very weak looking +3 on the new Dow high. The Net Field Trend indicator fell to +8, losing a field in *J. P. Morgan.*

Paramount Communications closed unchanged and remains within easy reach of new OBV lows. We are now officially short.

Gold made a strong move today, the Comex up 3.30. The Gold Stock Index moved up to 131.69, up 1.39. Bonds declined again.

December 30, 1993- Thursday Evening

Following through on the strong sell signals recorded by the Climax Indicator, the precipitous downturn in the bond market reflecting a sharp drop in job claims triggered a drop of 18.45 points in the Dow, closing at the 3775.88 level. It appears that the hopes by the bulls for a move above the 3800 level this month has been dashed. The long bond fell 1 8/32nds, driving the yield up to 6.34%.

The high/low indicator came in at 100 highs and 17 lows. But that number will be considerably changed tomorrow, a sharp contraction in highs expected. The advance/decline line fell by 131, not a very big drop but enough to lead one to expect further non-confirmations should the Dow turn up again.

The Climax Indicator fell to -3 and we have seen this week the +11, +8, +3, -3 series, comprising a clear technical picture of upside exhaustion in the Dow. The Net Field Trend indicator remained unchanged at +8.

Few expect a serious downturn at this point, much less one starting in the Santa Claus month of December. However, the number of stocks that have gone down this year has masked a major technical problem and the internal cancer is expected to soon be fully revealed. Every important decline in the Dow has been preceded by a severe dichotomy, just as many stocks declining as advancing and the dichotomy this year has been especially severe.

Paramount Communications fell again, closing down 3/8 at the 77-1/2 level. Note how high the prices on the put options are on this stock. For instance, the March 60 puts are over $2. Betting on the downside for a stock almost 18 points out of the money has got to be significant, telling you where the sentiment lies. A drop tomorrow on over 1-1/2 million shares will put the stock at a new OBV low.

And gold stocks continue to advance as expected, the Gold Stock Index up 0.42 at the 132.11 level.

January 1, 1994 - Saturday Afternoon

We have to consider the reversal to the downside on Friday as important for several reasons. First of all, it was a surprise to most market observers because they had already consigned the month of December to be a safe month. My numbers had pointed to an imminent downturn. In my Friday morning CNBC interview with Ron Insana he referred to my prediction of a December downturn as turning sour *but I told him the month wasn't over yet.* That might have sounded like a ridiculous thing to say with the Dow up 15 points in the late afternoon, but as it turned out, the Dow plummeted in the final hour to close down 21.79 points at the 3754.09 level, some 36 points under the earlier Friday high.

What is fascinating is that the Dow *went 100% counter to tradition*, closing down on the week, a week that had begun with a 35-point gain on Monday. I offer the explanation that we have been in a bear market since October 15th and that everything is now going into reverse. And note that we are going down now in the face of a record high short interest, just as we did in July 1990.

The Climax Indicator fell sharply from -3 to -8. During the week the 65-Stock CLX had recorded the sharpest drop ever recorded on a record Dow high and that set the stage for the iconoclastic Thursday and Friday declines. I think those declines are going to continue into the new year.

This past week we were treated to a string of strong economic numbers and here is the stock market *response* to those numbers. Some of the most important market declines germinate from a strong economic background, something the market has now already fully discounted.

January 3, 1994 - Monday Evening

The Dow eked out a small gain of 2.51 points at the 3756.60 level. Technically the move was virtually worthless since it was a down day with the exception of the precious metal stocks.

Keep in mind that we use the S & P to determine whether we get a bull signal out of the first five days of January trading. The bears won today on this first trading day of the year.

New highs contracted sharply from 116 to 55 while the advance/decline line was down on both the NYSE and the Nasdaq.

The Climax Indicator rose from -8 to -4 while the Net Field Trend indicator fell from +8 to +6, losing a field in *McDonalds* and a field in *Union Carbide.* The extensive weakness today in the Dow Transport and Utility averages when added to the negative reading in the industrials pushed the 65-Stock CLX into another sharp decline.

But the applause today was all for the highly recommended gold and silver stocks, the Gold Stock Index recording the sharpest daily rise since I first recommended these stocks at the exact December 1992 bottom. This key upside breakout today carries with it not only the warning for the bond market, *but a warning that the Fed may be led to raise rates sooner than most expect.* In any event, it all fits with my expectation for a coming major stock market break. Rising gold prices spell trouble.

Bonds got socked for a 31/32nd point drop with the yield soaring to 6.42%.

Paramount Communications edged up to 78 on light volume. I am betting that OBV is the ruling reason that the stock is headed for a sharp fall.

January 4, 1994 - Tuesday Evening

It seems like the powers that be are doing everything possible to keep the Dow rising and to deflect attention away from the rest of the market. Today a sharp rise in bonds triggered a late buy program, sending the Dow industrials up 27.30 points to the 3783.90 level. We are not short any Dow stocks and thus none of our followers are being hurt by the Dow rise. But the rest of the commentary reveals the huge technical potholes showing up in this market.

Everybody is watching the so-called January effect. With the Dow now up 29.81 points so far this year, the S & P 500 is only up 0.44 and the all-inclusive New York Stock Exchange Composite average is actually down 0.21 on the year.

That is the first shocker. The second shocker is the fact that despite the sharp rise in the Dow, the high/low indicator showed 56 highs and 29 lows. So this key indicator virtually stood still today. Besides that, 12% of the highs are gold stocks.

The Climax Indicator was +6 and the Net Field Trend indicator was at a revised +8, gaining a field in *United Technologies.* Today was seen as a technically failing rally.

The third shocker is *Merrill Lynch*, breaking today to the 39-1/2 level.

This bellwether stock is reliably signalling the coming bear market. We went short at 48-7/8. *Motorola* fell to 88-1/4, another very bearish looking chart. We went short at 100-1/8.

The fourth shocker was *Paramount Communications,* falling to 77-1/2 on heavy volume. That dropped the OBV to -12,651,400.

Golds stocks consolidated in a very bullish fashion.

January 5, 1994 - Wednesday Evening

The Dow made it to another record high today at the 3798.82 level on a rise of 14.92 points. I warn here to not mistake that strength for being a genuine exhibition of the January Effect. So far on the three sessions this year, the Dow is up 44.73 points. But the Standard & Poor 500 is only up 1.10 points on the year and the more inclusive New York Stock Exchange Composite average is only up a measly 0.23 points. So looking at those far more representative numbers there has been no evidence as yet of any January Effect.

Market observers put a great deal of emphasis on what the market does in the first five days of the new year. With two days to go, the outlook does not look promising. Bonds fell 21/32nds today pushing the yield back up to 6.40% and the strong outlook for employment statistics to be announced on Thursday and Friday could collapse the bond market, making it very difficult for stocks to make much headway.

The high/low indicator improved along with the advance/decline line but both readings comprise non-confirmations of the Dow strength.

The latest stock count showed 548 within a point of new highs and 403 within a point of new lows. The remaining hard core of over 400 on the low side is seen to be a ticking technical time bomb.

The Climax Indicator revealed great weakness among the Dow stocks. Today 15 rose and 13 fell. The Climax Indicator actually fell sharply from +6 to +1. The Net Field Trend indicator fell to +7, losing a field in *Union Carbide.*

Merrill Lynch and *Motorola* took a breather today, both offering fresh shorting opportunities. The same goes for a bounce in *Paramount* to 78-1/4.

January 6, 1994 - Thursday Evening

After being up over 13 points in the early trading, the Dow cut its gain to 5.06 points, closing at another record high at the 3803.88 level. The game of damn the torpedoes full steam ahead with the Dow is seen coming to an end. The lag is so bad in the broader indices that as of today the

Dow is up 49.80 points on the year while the Standard & Poor 500 index is up 0.67 and the all-inclusive New York Stock Exchange index is now DOWN 0.08 on the year. The NYSE index embraces all the stocks on the big board. Being now down on the year puts the big lie to the January Effect, that phenomenon being hard pushed in order to facilitate the distribution of stocks from strong hands to weak hands.

New highs came in at 117 and at market tops this figure makes failing attempts to get back to the peak. So the number of 117 is a distinct technical failure. The advance/decline line today was a virtual wash and so this is recorded as another non-confirmation of this latest Dow rise.

Despite the rise of 25/32nds in the long bond, dropping the yield to 6.34%, the Dow Utility Average again recorded a sharp drop, falling to the 221.20 level, breaking the entire November-December shelf.

The Climax Indicator rose to a weak looking +4, recording another upside non-confirmation. The Net Field Trend indicator remained unchanged at a revised +8.

Once again the gold stocks proved their tremendous resilience. The gold price had fallen $7 early in the day but regained $5 to only be off $2. Gold stocks acted as if they didn't know about the earlier price drop, closing strong.

The market is now technically positioned for a steep Friday selloff.

January 8, 1994 - Saturday Afternoon

This past week presented as perfect a picture postcard view of technical upside *exhaustion* I have ever seen. Looking solely at the Dow, it was a perfect week with another record close at the 3820.77 level, up 66.08 points on the week. But that was the end of a good report.

The number of new highs contracted sharply to 87. The advance/decline line was strong but nevertheless both of these indicators recorded serious upside non-confirmations.

Despite the strong Dow rise, the January Effect was left in serious doubt with the Standard & Poor 500 recording a substandard weekly rise of 3.45 points. A comparison between the Dow and the New York Stock Exchange Composite average revealed the extreme internal technical weakness with the latter recording a measly rise of only 1.26 points. So while the Dow has carved out what looks like a final parabolic blowoff, the index reflecting the action of all stocks virtually sat it out for the week, going sideways.

That exhaustion was well reflected by the Climax Indicator tracing out a 5-day pattern of -4, +6, +1, +4, and +3. The all-inclusive 65 Stock CLX saw five readings of -14, +3, -3, +I, and a zero on Friday. A great deal of the weakness was traced to a sharp decline in the Transport CLX from +10 to +3 on Friday.

The January 5-day indicator should not be confused with the January indicator, the latter comprising the record of the entire month. Because of the poor performances by the S & P 500 and the NYSE for the week, the Dow advance looks terminal.

The sharp drop in the Gold Stock index is seen to offer new buying opportunities.

January 10, 1994 - Monday Evening

All parabolic rises end in crash action. The current market rise is seen to be no exception. While there is no end in sight to the Dow industrial rise, parabolics seldom require warnings that they are about to reverse. Today the Dow tacked on 44.74 points to put the Dow at the 3865.51 level. The S & P 500 and the New York Stock Exchange Composite tried to make up for lost time and overcome the lag seen in the earlier sessions this year. Having risen 111.42 points so far this year, the large gains today saw the S & P make up most lags and extend the gain for the year to 8.72 points and close at a new high. The NYSE Composite also made a new high for the year and extended the gain for the year to 3.66 points. But despite the new high, that is seen to be a small rise when compared with the 111 point rise in the Dow.

The number of new highs only expanded to 131, maintaining its substandard action. The A/D line was strong but still lacked a confirming new high although now very close.

The Climax Indicator rose sharply to +14. Market students should be reminded that the CLX rose to +19 in mid-July 1990. So we will continue to look for technical parallels with that peak period. The Net Field Trend indicator surprisingly stayed unchanged at +7. *Westinghouse* lost a field on Friday.

Paramount Communications fell 1-7/8 points today to 77-3/8 so here was the market *bearish response* to the Viacom Friday bid. The OBV fell to -9,788,200 and is in range to break a key OBV support. I reiterate that this stock is headed for 60 or lower.

The gold price acted very well today, rising $6.20 off the low. The Gold stock Index rose 0.04 to 136.42, an excellent performance considering the earlier plunge in the gold price.

I look for a highly probable decline tomorrow in the Dow which could turn out to be significant.

January 11, 1994 - Tuesday Evening

Assuming that Monday saw a completed parabolic upswing, the decline ahead is expected to be severe and unrelenting. The Dow fell 15.20 points today to the 3850.31 level. Transports also fell as well as the Dow Utilities. The Dow Utility average lost 2.24 points, giving back more than was gained on the Monday advance. The Dow Utility Average persists in flashing a persistent warning that the general market will take a big spill in 1994. My guess is sooner, rather than later.

The advance/decline line showed a moderate loss but it is significant that it was robbed today of a possible new high. Tomorrow we will count the big board common stocks within a point or less of new highs and lows. The results will be given here tomorrow night.

The Climax Indicator fell sharply today from +14 to -3, the 65-Stock CLX falling even more sharply, validating the belief that Monday was the probable Dow peak. Once again the Net Field Trend indicator remained unchanged at +7. As I pointed out here on Monday night, the parallels with the July 1990 peak are too close to be disregarded.

While supposedly the best brains in Wall Street haven't the foggiest notion as to where *Paramount Communications* is headed, the OBV numbers leave no doubt as to the future of this stock. It is seen to be headed sharply lower.

Merrill Lynch is providing the most reliable technical arrow as to the kind of year the brokerage industry can expect. It's going to be rough and that outlook is similar for the equity mutual funds. The bears should love 1994.

I was very impressed with the gold stocks today. The Gold Stock Index rose 3.25 points to the 139.67 level. This again proves that every single pullback in the golds is a new buying opportunity.

January 12, 1994 - Wednesday Evening

The Dow showed a sharp recovery from earlier lows, only recording a minor loss of 1.68 points at the Dow 3848.63 level.

New highs today fell to 100. The advance/decline line improved but was still short of a new high. The true A/D line remained down on the year.

Bonds broke out on the upside today but lagging utilities pose an increasing technical problem.

The Climax Indicator rose from -3 to -2 but the numbers are so far below the Monday level that efforts to improve will be insufficient. The Net Field Trend indicator fell to +6, losing a field in *Eastman Kodak*.

Yesterday the 65-Stock Climax Indicator plunged from +26 to -8, making it very difficult now to achieve any meaningful technical recovery.

Instructions for option players is to buy the following new gold call options: American Barrick April 30, Battle Mountain April 10, Echo Bay April 12-1.2, Homestake April 25, Horsham April 15, and Lac Minerals April 7-1/2.

New put options to be bought include Bankers Trust April 80, Merrill Lynch April 45, Motorola April 95, and Upjohn April 30.

Paramount Communications fell again. Heavy insider selling in the stock was reflected in the falling OBV numbers. The *Wall Street Journal* this morning mentioned that arbitragers own over half the company. That unstable ownership shows how vulnerable the stock is. I am projecting 60 and lower.

January 13, 1994 - Thursday Evening

The Dow closed down 6.20 today at the 3842.43 level. Transports showed a small rise but the Dow Utility Average fell sharply by 1.71 points to the 220.87 level, a new low. You will recall that the strong rally in bonds on Wednesday could hardly make the utilities budge. That was a warning for bonds. Today bonds collapsed by 1 point and 6/32nds to raise the yield to 6.26%, putting egg on the faces of those who were cheering an upside breakout for bonds yesterday. The Dow Utility average has fallen by a sharp 8.43 points so far this year, throwing a wet blanket on the market and a major warning for the future of this market.

General Motors made a new high today at 60-1/4 but the OBV was almost 2 million shares under the January 11th level.

So far the Dow has fallen on every day of the Clinton Summit.

New highs contracted again, falling to 79. The advance/decline line pulled away further from the opportunity of making a key upside breakout.

The Climax Indicator fell today to -4. The Net Field Trend indicator rose to +7, gaining a field in *Exxon*, gaining a field in *Minnesota Mining* but losing a field in *Procter & Gamble.* Today belonged to the gold shares. The Gold Stock Index jumped 3.25 points to the 141.11 level. We need a turnabout in oil prices to push gold well above the $400 level. Other commodities are not waiting. The CRB was very strong today and I think the move above 400 gold is getting very close. Once above 400 I see that we could make it to $800 gold in two years.

In the meantime, the general market is getting close to a major plunge.

January 15, 1994 - Saturday Afternoon

Friday offered a gourmet delight for technicians, a veritable cornucopia of priceless intelligence. First of all the Dow rose 24.77 points, clearing the Monday hurdle by a mere 1.69 points to post a technically worthless new high at the 3867.20 level. Transports scored another new high and the Utility Average posted a fractional rise. Instead of thinking of Friday's rally, concentrate on the fact that the Dow has only gone up 1.69 points in the past four sessions.

The Utilities are a veritable technical sinkhole and their severe warning of what lies ahead persists.

Despite the high volume seen so far this year, the New Advance/Decline line is down on the year signifying the bulk of the strength in the Dow blue chips and not enough in the general market, also dangerous churning action in evidence. And once again the standard A/D line again failed to confirm the Dow.

New highs expanded but were well below Monday's level and thus Friday is recorded as a day of very serious upside exhaustion.

The Climax Indicator rose to only +3, recording a wide upside non-confirmation and well below Monday's +14 reading. The 65-Stock CLX also recorded a major upside non-confirmation, rising to only +6 and sharply below Monday's +26 reading. And once again the Net Field Trend index showed no gain, still at +7 on Friday's new Dow high.

Paramount Communications rose for the second day but again on light volume, the OBV failing to get any up designations. A very weak numbers pattern.

Again the golds deserved much bullish comment. They were down all day until a late push in oil prices saw the Gold Stock Index rise 0.95 to the 142.06 level.

Summing up, Friday exhibited overwhelming technical upside exhaustion and the stage is set for an extended slide.

January 17, 1994- Monday Evening

America woke up to the terrible news of a strong earthquake in Los Angeles. It nevertheless had a limited effect on stock prices, though most of these were down. The Dow was up almost 10 points in the final hour but that was sharply cut in the closing minutes to a small gain of 3.09 points at the 3870.29 level. Transports, hit by rising oil prices, fell 12.23 points. Utilities gave back the small Friday gain to close down 1.18 points at the 220.21 level, down 36 points since September and at another new low today.

New highs at 115 again failed to expand and both advance/decline lines declined.

The Climax Indicator was unchanged at +3 and the 65-stock CLX was far weaker due to the drops in the transports and the utilities. The NFI was unchanged at +7. This is another weak showing for a Dow record high.

Rising oil prices filled in an important missing link in the across-the-board commodity support for gold and thus it was no surprise to see the Gold Stock Index jump 3.23 points to the 145.29 level. Some of this may have been due to the earthquake but I think it was mostly the oil prices.

Paramount Communications rose for the third day but still at insignificant OBV levels on the upside, getting no OBV up designations. It closed at 78-3/4.

Among the recommended gold and silver stocks these were mostly higher across the board. *Echo Bay* broke out to a new high close at 14-7/8. Next resistance is at the 20 level.

The Dow continues to build a top formation while the general market has already peaked. We are short no Dow stocks but heavily committed to gold stocks.

January 18, 1994 - Tuesday Evening

Expecting an imminent Dow top, it was very interesting that the Dow closed unchanged today at the 3870.29 level, interesting because when the Dow peaked in July 1990 it made the high on July 16th and the Dow was unchanged on July 17th. Thereafter the Dow went south. Two weeks later was the Kuwait invasion and in a matter of weeks the Dow was down 635 points.

Transports also closed unchanged and utilities showed a small fractional rise.

The Climax Indicator rose to +4 while the Net Field Trend indicator fell to +6 losing a field in *IBM*.

The bidding war erupted again on *Paramount Communications* with the stock rising to 80. Despite this, the OBV only rose to -6,400,700, posting a lower up designation and remaining far under the December 20th level when the OBV stood at -2,954,300 and the price was 82.

The unchanged Dow was in the face of a large rise in the bond market.

Some softness in the oil price and a downturn in the CRB resulted in the gold stock index making a normal retreat.

In order to maintain an exact parallel with the July 1990 top, we might get an 18-point decline in the Dow tomorrow. In any case, the January rise appears to be at an end.

January 19, 1994 - Wednesday Evening

The Dow put on a late show to close up 14.08 points at the 3884.37 level. Having no Dow stock short sales, we can watch the Dow rise totally devoid of emotion as it closely parallels the July 1990 top formation. With my new evidence that most stocks right now are under their January 1, 1993 levels, that dramatically underscores the solo walk in the Dow and how far removed that average is from the reality of what is actually going on in the market. Very quietly and with no fanfare the Dow Jones Utility Average edged into new low ground, closing down 0.52 at the 220.08 level.

The real market was far removed from the Dow. 80% of the most active stocks were down with most of the drops being multi-point declines. *Pfizer* down 5 points.

The auto stocks looked very toppy today and the bank stocks took big hits.

The Dow-30 is a far cry from legitimizing the new record high seen today. Nine of the stocks saw their OBV highs in 1992, twelve peaked in 1993, and on this 1994 rally only nine Dow stocks made new OBV highs.

The Climax Indicator came in at +6, recording another upside nonconfirmation. The Net Field Trend indicator rose to +7, gaining a field in *American Telephone*.

New highs contracted from 151 to 136 on the higher Dow. The A/D line rose again but the gain wasn't commensurate with the 14-point rise in the Dow. That was well seen with the S & P 500 index only up 0.05 points.

The Nasdaq took a hit today, reflecting big declines in *Intel, Microsoft* and others.

Not wanting to be left out of the subsurface deterioration, bonds fell 14/32nds to push the yield back up to the 6.30% level.

Best shorts are in banks and brokerage house stocks.

January 20, 1994 - Thursday Evening

The Dow rose over 7 points to record still another record high. But it is paying a great technical price for doing this. It is forming a dangerous parabolic vertical rise and there is nothing under the average once it starts down. All the strength in the industrials was taken away by the Transports.

Once again the most active stocks told a story. Out of the top 10 there were only two stocks that rose. The number of new highs contracted to 129 and so we are seeing many telltale signs of upside exhaustion.

The Climax Indicator fell back to a +4 reading and that recorded the fifth consecutive CLX upside non-confirmation. Only a major top could produce a cluster that large.

The Net Field Trend Indicator rose to +8, gaining a field in *Procter & Gamble.*

While many market observers think the market is giving out very bullish signs, what we are seeing is almost an exact match of the terminal July 1990 run-up which was followed by a drop of 635 points in the Dow.

New short sale recommendations are as follows: *Bank of New York* and buy the April 55 put, *Chase Manhattan* and buy the March 35 put, *Chemical Bank* and buy the March 40 put.

On the stock count this week stocks within a point of new lows shot up from 365 to 401.

So all the pieces are rapidly falling in place for a major break which will start any day now.

The new letter contained a warning on the gold stocks. Stops were sharply raised and we got stopped out on *Pegasus* at the new stop of 23. The warning was to only do new buying on dips such as that seen today. The new stops are very close now to the market. Sit back and let the market do the talking.

January 22, 1994 - Saturday Afternoon

The Dow solo circus act continued this week, climaxed by a thrilling rise of 22.52 points putting the average at still another record high at the 3914.52 level. But the cheering is set to soon fade away as it became increasingly apparent that we were looking at a virtually completed parabolic advance.

The Friday option expiration day was replete with technical failures all the way from the glaring weighting of an almost 5-point advance in *Caterpillar* to the fact that for the third straight day there were only two advancing stocks among the 10 most active issues. The Friday Dow rise was as hollow as a baby's rattle. Just about everything went down except the Dow.

Once again the Dow Utility average fell to another new low and is very close now to the percentage decline which was followed by the crash of 1987.

But nothing says it better than the Climax Indicator which fell sharply to zero on the record Dow high. The Dow 65-stock CLX was even worse, falling to -4 on the record Dow high. These declines produced a cluster of six CLX upside non-confirmations and that is a major warning that crash action is close at hand.

Following my warning on the gold stocks, the Gold Stock Index took another drubbing as expected. We had tightened our stops so as to get stopped out with our large profits pretty much intact. On a closing basis we have been stopped out now on *American Barrick* at 29, *Echo Bay* at 13-1/2, *Homestake* at 22-1/2, *Newmont Mining* at 56, and *Pegasus* at 23. Hold off on new buying and continue to obey the new stops.

Summing up, the market appears to be at the maximum level of upside exhaustion. This is as good a time to sell out everything, get on a boat for a marvelous cruise, and leave all your troubles behind.

January 24, 1994 - Monday Evening

Technically, the market had no other way to go except down today. It was left Friday at a point of virtually 100% upside exhaustion. So it was no surprise to see a 20-point gain in the Dow get blown away in the late afternoon trading, closing down 1.69 points at the 3912.79 level. Transports held on to a gain of 4.51 points but sharply under earlier highs. The Dow Utilities captured the spotlight with a large decline of 2.64 dropping the average to still another new low at the 217.11 level. This key average is fast overtaking the level it was at just prior to the 1987 stock market crash. It is the most dangerous of all indicators at this time. The divergence between the utilities and the industrials is so serious that it underscores the probability that there is too little time left before a major market bust.

Once again new highs contracted, falling to 114 while new lows expanded to 34. All advance/decline lines got hit hard today.

The Standard & Poor 500 Index took a large hit of 2.75, driving it back down to the 471.97 level and that makes it a little more apparent that the market as a whole has not made much progress in this new year.

TV commentators were gushing over the 3-3/8 point rise in IBM today. It was a technically worthless advance, rising against a large cluster of lower OBV down designations.

The Climax Indicator rose to +3. The Net Field Trend indicator, after losing *Alcoa* on Friday, returned to +8 today on a rise in *American Express*.

I want to observe the gold stocks a bit longer before flashing the all clear for new buying.

But the first order of business is to sidestep the plunge which looks increasingly imminent.

January 25, 1994 - Tuesday Evening

The Dow followed through today on the Monday bearish reversal, falling 17.45 points to close at the 3895.34 level. Transports followed suit, falling 10.30 points while the Utility Average went up 0.86 to the 117.97 level, a move having no bullish significance whatsoever. I stated here on November 11th when that average had closed down at the 223.97 level that it had come down to within 10 points of reaching a 17% decline, the precise position that the average was in just prior to the October 1987 stock market crash. *Now with the utility average at the 217.97 level today, it is only 4 points away from where it was the day before the crash.*

I had stated here that the sharp rise in the Dow so far this year was a technical farce. It was the classic solo walk. Now the broader measurements show virtually no gain this year and the true market is heading south with a vengeance.

The high/low indicator told a big story today, new highs contracting sharply to 65 while new lows rose dramatically to 52. Of course that should come as no surprise to those aware of the fact that over 400 big board stocks are currently within less than a point of new lows. We will have a new count tomorrow.

The A/D lines again took big hits. The media had suckered many into thinking IBM would rise today on the good earnings news. Yesterday I warned here that the better than 3-point rise was technically worthless. Those who bought calls lost half their money while the puts doubled.

The Climax Indicator fell to -2. The Net Field Trend indicator remained unchanged at +8.

Gold stocks consolidated today, being closely mixed. They are being held here unless stopped out.

January 26, 1994 - Wednesday Evening

The Dow farce continues, the industrials up 12.66 points putting the average at the 3908.00 level. Transports moved moderately higher while the Dow Utility average jumped over 3 points. But that same average jumped a huge 3.95 points on November 16th and the large number of lower up designations then pointed toward the further collapse that materialized.

The bearish response to the IBM earnings report is typical of the underlying bearish condition of this market. That stock fell to a new lower down designation today. The chart looks very bearish.

While the advance/decline line today showed a normal rise commensurate with the Dow advance, the number of new stock highs contracted again, falling to 61. We are getting similar warnings with our weekly count of stocks within a point or less of new highs and lows. The latest count shows a contraction in the stocks within a point of new highs from 651 to 617 while the number of stocks within a point of new lows expanded from 401 to 427. A move back above 500 in that number is considered critical.

Besides the revealing small number of new highs, the Climax Indicator today barely moved on the Dow 12-point advance. It showed a feeble rise from -2 to -1, a dead giveaway that something is wrong. Furthermore, the Net Field Trend indicator fell from a revised +7 to +5, losing two fields in *Boeing*.

While we are stopped out on most of our gold stocks, we retained the call options and these were helped today by today's rise. I simply want to observe the action awhile longer before deciding to reenter the market and buy the stocks.

So once again the late upswing in the Dow left the market very vulnerable.

January 27, 1994 - Thursday Evening

In all my years I have seldom seen a Dow high as technically weak as the one we saw today. It was almost an insult to one's intelligence to say that the Dow was up 18.30 points at the 3926.30 level. Of the 30 industrial stocks we saw 17 up, 3 unchanged, and 10 down. But so few of the gainers were able to record an OBV up designation that the Climax Indicator came in at a very weak +1. To see a +1 reading on an all-time Dow record high underscores how weak the Dow technically is at this juncture but it also extends the string of substandard readings we have seen since January 10th, which was the date of the internal high. It sets the Dow up for a very large one-day decline which is now imminent.

The Dow Utility average was very strong for the second day. But I don't think we see enough strength there to reverse the downtrend since early September.

Further underscoring the internal shortcomings, the number of new highs today could only expand to 98, well under the 151 highs recorded on January 18th when the Dow stood at 3870.29.

The Net Field Trend indicator fell to +4 today, losing a field in Exxon.

Paramount Communications rose to 80 today and the On-Balance Volume on the stock has shown little change. So it appears that the stock is waiting until the last day of bidding by Viacom and VSQ. Thereafter, a big spill is expected.

The Gold Stock Index was shattered today with a drop of 7.08 points, putting the index down to the 129.54 level. I still think it is too early to rush back into these stocks. Simply sit tight.

I think the +1 reading in the Climax Indicator today is enough of a warning to look for imminent weakness. It isn't wise to sit around and wait for more warnings.

January 29, 1994 - Saturday Afternoon

Traders and investors Friday morning were confronted by a double whammy of news that sent stocks and bonds soaring. First was the report of the record $14.5 billion going into mutual funds in December and second was the blockbuster news of the Gross Domestic Product more than doubling in the 4th quarter to 5.9%. Many commentators after the close said that it doesn't get any better than this. Ironically, that is the best market forecast that I heard. Things always look the best at the top and Friday certainly was a picture postcard. Fundamentalists love this market.

There was no disputing the surge into the wild blue yonder but few will question anything until they see obvious weakness.

New stock highs rose to 148, still short of the 151 of January 18th. But the advance/decline line continued to explode to new highs. The new high in the Nasdaq however, was non-confirmed, the A/D line there having peaked on October 15th.

Only the indicators based on On-Balance Volume saw beyond the rose colored glasses, seeing Friday's high as a trap. The Climax Indicator only rose to +7 with most of that number being 6 lower ups. The CLX is measured against the +14 of January 10th and thus Friday saw another upside non-confirmation. Looking at all 65 of the Dow stocks, we have the +26 of January 10th to measure against. Friday's +14 couldn't cut it, and most of that number consisted of lower ups. A study of clusters also shows the Dow has lost the cutting edge. Friday saw *McDonalds* make the only cluster of OBV higher ups. Several forward compartments are getting flooded, volume signals looking bearish on *Telephone, Boeing, Coca Cola, General Electric* and *General Motors* for instance. And *Caterpillar* is now too far above its trendline.

While bulls look the worst on bottoms, bears look the worst on tops. The heavy volume of trading suggests that many bears are throwing in the towel. So while I can't give you the precise day of the Dow high, the Friday signals certainly tell us that we are close- very very close. Now all the good news is out.

January 31, 1994 - Monday Evening

The Dow roared ahead to close up 32.92 points at a new record high of 3978.35. Transports kept pace, also scoring another record. The high/low indicator saw highs soar to 206 and the advance/decline line also made another new high. It was difficult to find anything wrong.

But there were some things. It was found in a comparison with previous highs, and some similarities in the action of the Climax Indicator and the Net Field Trend indicator. The CLX rose to +13 on the new high and, in staying under the +14 reading of January 10th, comprises still another upside non-confirmation. We saw what looked like a runaway market in July 1990 when the Dow marched uphill to the final high in four advances totalling 110 points, stopping at the 2999 level. The CLX peaked at +19 and the NFI jumped sharply from +9 to +15 between July 11th and 17th but it was the top. Today the Net Field Trend indicator rose from Friday's +5 to +9, gaining a field in *Alcoa*, two fields in *J. P. Morgan*, and one field in *United Technologies.* But there we have the lesson Of July 1990 so don't get carried away.

The biggest factor working against the market now is the time factor. We are so overextended into the third and final bull phase that the alarm is set to go off regardless of where the indicators stand. That is the symptom indicating a *climactic blowoff.* So I will stick to my guns and point out the continuing dangers that show the major top to be at hand.

Most of the precious metal stocks are still below where we took our profits and I would wait a bit longer to be sure that we are back on solid ground. But we retained all the call options and today's rise helped many of these.

February 1, 1994 - Tuesday Evening

Seeing Monday as a *climactic blowoff*, technical exhaustion took its toll today and the Dow fell 14.35 points to close down at the 3964.01 level. Turning the Dow chart as seen in the *Journal* upside down and looking at it in the mirror brought into view an average ready to go up. And so saw the actual market as radically overbought and ready to collapse. The excesses are too numerous to dismiss. We have the IPO's, the mutual fund mania. We have the heaviest margin buying since September 1987 and the heaviest volume since October 1987. Besides this, the market peaked on the large jump in the Gross Domestic Product as it has on all previous jumps in that fundamental indicator. Today's strong fundamental statistics took the bonds down and that cast the chill everywhere except in the golds.

So the whistle blew yesterday and it was game time regardless of the posture of any indicator.

Today was a broad based downturn embracing most stocks and the number of new highs showed a sizable retreat from Monday's 209 figure.

The Climax Indicator fell sharply from +13 to +2. The NFI remained unchanged at +9.

Alan Greenspan's Monday's remarks were met with a negative market response, bonds down a point with the yield jumping to 6.32% and gold stocks up sharply. The response there was strong enough to no longer delay in rebuying all the precious metal stocks that we previously took profits in. We retained all the call options in that group and of course those strongly benefited today from the gold stock rally. So we are back with a 100% commitment in the precious metal group.

Like the July 1990 market failing to close above the 3000 level without first experiencing a sharp detour, the current market should have difficulty in bettering the 4000 level and the detour could stretch itself out to a full blown bear market.

February 2, 1994 - Wednesday Evening

It looked for awhile like the Dow was up to it old tricks, making the run for the roses in the last hour. It rose 11.53 points to close at 3975.54. But with this seeming magic wand that can produce buying at will, the powers that be failed to get the 2.83 points required for another record high.

Then it was revealed why the Dow failed. The Climax Indicator actually fell from +2 to +1 on the Dow rise. A number of technical failures were revealed. For instance, *General Electric* jumped 2-1/4 points and couldn't get an OBV up designation. *General Motors* rose and again no OBV up designation. But the sharp 2-1/2 point drop in *Sears* on huge volume of over 6 million shares saw the loss of a field, dropping the NFI to +8 on the lower down designation.

Two features today worthy of comment: The battle is over for *Paramount* and the stock broke to 78 on huge volume of over 3 million shares. This is only the first shot in the predicted collapse. I still underscore 60 as the initial downside objective. I have recommended the purchase of the April 75 put options.

The gold stocks retreated today and I view it as a buying opportunity. The new stop loss levels on our new stock purchases is 49 on *ASA*, 25 on *American Barrick*, 9-1/2 on *Battle Mountain Gold*, 12-1/4 on *Echo*

Bay, 19-1/2 on *Homestake*, 42-1/2 on *Newmont Gold*, 51-1/2 on *Newmont Mining*, 19-1/2 on *Pegasus*, and 23-1/2 on *Placer-Dome*. I still favor all new buying on weakness.

February 3, 1994 - Thursday

As we get deeper into February, market concerns are mounting. The President's health plan received a major setback today as a cornerstone of American business rejected it. The market was made nervous by the meeting of the Open Market Committee, increasingly convinced that the Fed will boost the discount rate to 3-1/2%. The Dow fell 7.88 points to the 3967.66 level. Dreams of a near-term rise above Dow 4000 are rapidly becoming pipe dreams. Always seen at major market tops, high Dow projections become very numerous. There was no side help, Transports down over 9 points and a drop of almost a point in the utilities.

New highs contracted to 136 and the A/D line fell.

Volume was very heavy today at 320 million shares. I do not consider that to be a bullish indication. That reflects the added volume with many bears throwing in the towel and turning bullish at the worst of times.

The Climax Indicator fell to zero, a dramatic loss of strength in just three days. The Net Field Trend indicator fell to +6, *Woolworth* losing two fields.

We had an across the board rise in the precious metal stocks, the Gold Stock Index jumping 2.32 to the 136.46 level. The advance off the lows of the day were quite impressive. I especially favor *Hecla*, *Lac Minerals*, and *Horsham,* stocks we were not stopped out on when we raised our stops a couple of weeks ago.

Tomorrow is a very critical day since the Fed is ready to act should it see something that it doesn't like.

February 3, 1994

4. *IT'S GAME TIME*

A useful exercise at all market extremes is to do the mirror test. Take the chart of the Dow Industrials as seen on page C-3 in the *Wall Street Journal*. Turn it upside down and look at it in a mirror. If the market looks overbought and is a sale at the top, it should look oversold and a buy at the bottom. *You will agree with me that the reversed chart you see here sure looks like a market that is ready to start a major rally.* So the real market is about to collapse. The most important of all indicators is now signalling that it's game time. That is the time indicator. It is the only indicator that is capable of rendering all other indicators meaningless regardless of their posture. It is just like a football game or a basketball game or any game played by the clock. When the whistle blows or the bell rings there is nothing more the players on the field can do to influence the score in any way. What the market has just seen is a *climactic blowoff.* It ends the upswing *and now renders all indices worthless as market indicators.*

Climactic Blowoff As Seen With the Mirror Test

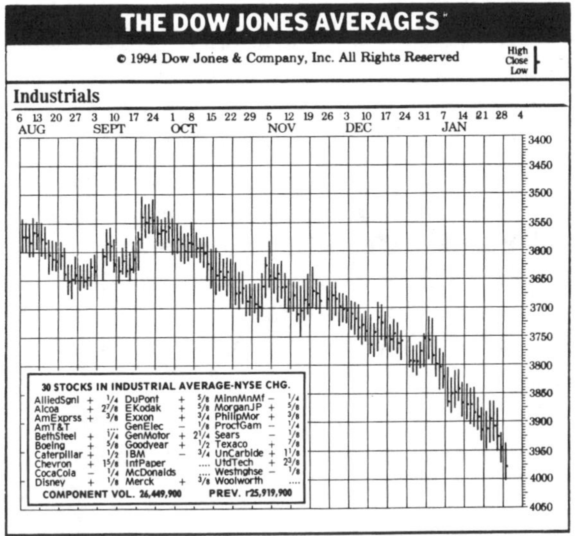

30 STOCKS IN INDUSTRIAL AVERAGE-NYSE CHG.

AlliedSgnl	+	1/4	DuPont	+	5/8	MinnMnMf	–	1/4
Alcoa	+	2 7/8	EKodak	+	5/8	MorganJP	+	5/8
AmExprss	+	3/8	Exxon	+	3/4	PhilipMor	+	3/8
AmT&T		....	GenElec	–	1/8	ProctGam	–	1/4
BethSteel	+	1/4	GenMotor	+	2 1/4	Sears	–	1/8
Boeing	+	5/8	Goodyear	+	1/2	Texaco	+	7/8
Caterpillar	+	1/2	IBM	–	3/4	UnCarbide	+	1 1/8
Chevron	+	1 5/8	IntPaper		....	UtdTech	+	2 3/8
CocaCola	–	1/4	McDonalds		....	Westnghse	–	1/8
Disney	+	1/8	Merck	+	3/8	Woolworth		....

COMPONENT VOL. 26,449,900 PREV. r25,919,900

Quoting from the new edition of *Technical Analysis of Stock Trends* (Robert D. Edwards and John Magee), "The market will continue to go up and down in the future as it has in the past. Your technical knowledge will save you from buying at the top in the final climactic blowoff, and it will save you from selling everything in a fit of depression and disgust when the bottom is being established."

The very heavy volume toward the end of the rally strongly suggested that many stock market bears were throwing in the towel and joining the bulls right on the Dow highs. Putting everything together, there are simply too many excesses to read the market any differently. The key fits too many locks and opens too many doors to the coming bear market. I will touch on a few of these.

I am very concerned with the sheer number of mutual funds. Too many cooks spoil the broth. The current danger is well described in the following quote:

"Much has been written about panics and manias, but more than with the most outstretched intellect we are able to follow or conceive; but one thing is certain, that at particular times a great deal of stupid people have a great deal of stupid money... At intervals, from causes which are not the present purpose, the money of these people - the blind capital, as we call it, of the country- is particularly large and craving; it seeks for someone to devour it, and there is a "plethora"': it finds someone, and there is "speculation"'; it is devoured; and there is "panic"." (Walter Bagehot "Essay on Edward Gibbon")

So my concerns with the future of this market include the future of those thousands of stock mutual funds which sprang up like weeds and attracted countless billions of the public's money, a public seeing their stake now locked into a growing number of stocks held at a loss. Do you think it is any different with the funds? If most people are now holding stocks at a loss, why shouldn't most funds begin to mirror the same dilemma?

I think the public became so enamored with the economic strength in 1994 that they perhaps did not recognize the signs of excess all about them. In December 1993 new issues hit a record of over $1 trillion. Money continued to pour into stock mutual funds at an unprecedented rate. Stock mutual funds took in $14.5 billion in December 1993 and fund executives were expecting even a bigger inflow in January. Last week *The Wall Street Journal* said that mutual funds now rank among the dominant buyers and sellers in the stock market. The huge cash inflow into stock funds in December capped the biggest year in history for mutual fund sales. Stock funds attracted a record $128 billion in 1993, far above the prior record of $78 billion set in 1992. But stock market bulls were blinded to the implications of this tidal wave of cash, momentarily forgetting that they were viewing the peak of an acute *parabolic curve.* And that peak was seen *when individual investors most depended on and trusted these stock fund managers to do their thinking for them.*

John Kenneth Galbraith wrote the following in his excellent book *The Great Crash - 1929:*

"As 1929 wore along, it was plain to see that more and more of the new investors in the market *were relying on the intellect and the science of the trusts.* This meant, of course, that they still had the formidable problem of deciding between the good and the bad trusts."

The fantastic growth in the number of funds also poses a potential problem that psychologically threatens their future just at the time when the public is most enamored with them. On January 21, 1994 *Investor's Business Daily* in a front page article said that the government was eyeing the funds as a possible source of untapped revenue to finance the credit needs of the communities in which they are based. What caught my eye was the chart that accompanied the article. It showed the parabolic rise of mutual fund assets to $2 trillion, a potential bubble of dangerous proportions.

It was reported this past week that we are seeing the *heaviest buying on margin since September 1987* and *the heaviest volume of trading since October 1987.* Then we saw the large market rise last week when it was reported that the Gross Domestic Product leaped from $2.9 trillion to $5.9 trillion in the fourth quarter. But if one took the time to study the chart that accompanied the report *it would be seen that the market peaked on all previous sharp GDP runups.*

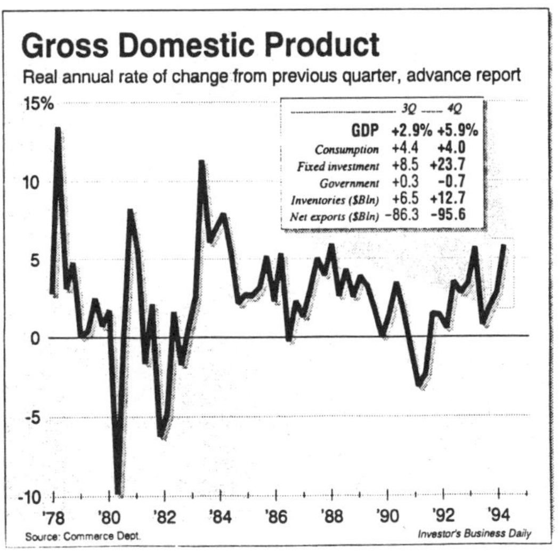

Sharp GDP peak in early 1981 corresponded with Dow top in April 1991 and proved the validity of my famous January 6, 1981 sell everything signal. The next runup corresponded with the January 1984 market top. We saw other peaks in 1987 and 1990 corresponding with stock market tops. Why should the current GDP advance be different?

5. *THE RANGE INDICATOR*

As we moved into the early part of 1994, I was especially cognizant of the technical requirements for crash action. Foremost among these was the *range indicator.* This indicator fails to get the credit it deserves. A target cannot be hit unless it is in range. For instance, if a 16-inch gun can lob a shell 20 miles it can never hit a target until that target comes within a range of 20 miles. This is why I have developed the technique of best case and worse case scenarios for the Climax Indicator. From my own records of market past performance, *no market is going to crash unless we get a worse case scenario of -20 or lower, and preferably lower.* If a crash requires a CLX reading of -26 or lower and we have a worse case scenario of -16 based on our range of potential OBV designation changes, then a crash cannot take place the next day. In other words, all potential measurements have to be within range of a crash the day before.

So to technically attain a certain objective, range must be easily attainable. This is true whether it be in terms of advances and declines, highs and lows, the Climax Indicator, field trends, clusters, etc. But rather than wait for the actual numbers, it is very helpful to measure *potential* changes. One indicator coming within crash range isn't enough. Getting a double barreled confirmation by the important Net Field Trend indicator, for instance, would make crash action much more probable.

February 4, 1994

Below is a review of indicators the way they looked just before the early 1994 debacle:

Review of Indicators

Date	Industrials	CLX	True CLX	EW CLX	NFI	Highs/Lows	A/D Line	New A/D Line
1/12	3848.63	-2	2377	2803	+6	99-13	-49,282	10,300.8
1/13	3842.43	-4	2376	2807	+7	78-14	-49,488	10,267.6
1/14	3867.20 NC	+3	2377	2803	+7	117-11	-49,114	10,282.7
1/17	3870.29 NC	+3	2378	2805	+7	113-13	-49,191	10,257.8
1/18	3870.29 NC	+4	2381	2806	+6	151-19	-48,873	10,257.8
1/19	3884.37 NC	+6	2389	2816	+7	135-18	-48,712	10,269.2
1/20	3891.96 NC	+5	2398	2826	+8	127-15	-48,562	10,288.9
1/21	3914.48 NC	0	2400	2834	+7	126-22	-48,668	10,284.2
1/24	3912.79	+3	2404	2842	+8	105-34	-48,940	10,146.2
1/25	3895.34	-2	2406	2850	+7	64-49	-49,259	10,128.0
1/26	3908.00	-1	2410	2855	+5	61-30	-48,675	10,150.4
1/27	3926.30 NC	+1	2420	2864	+4	102-12	-48,067	10,183.6
1/28	3945.43 NC	+7	2429	2868	+5	148-10	-47,513	10,211.9
1/31	3978.36 NC	+13	2451	2879	+9	209-13	-46,850	10,232.0
2/1	3964.01	+2	2464	2892	+9	137-14	-47,037	10,219.0

2/2	3975.54	+1	2471	2895	+8	158-15	-46,623	10,254.9
2/3	3967.66	0	2475	2905	+6	136-20	-46,881	10,222.5
2/4	3871.42	-17	2462	2910	+4	96-51	-48,604	10,204.6.

We see in the above numbers a whole series of CLX upside non-confirmations. (NC) The string of six consecutive non-confirmations was the most compelling of signals and that large a cluster has never been wrong. It allowed the smart money traders to walk away from the market in unruffled condition, avoiding the crush to get out on February 4th.

Next we note something that had escaped everybody's attention. While the Dow was screaming higher through all of January, *The New Advance/Decline Line stopped going up after January 12th.* You will recall how it is computed. The change in the Dow industrial average is divided into the change in the orthodox A/D line. The result is either added or subtracted from a cumulative total depending on whether the orthodox A/D line is positive or negative. The inability to go up after January 12th was one of the most reliable of the technical warnings of major trouble ahead at that time.

The sharp drop to -17 in the Climax Indicator on February 4th brought that indicator in range of crash action.

The February 4th crash saw not only the sharp drop in the actual highs to 96 and the upside breakout in new lows to 51, but employing the technique of counting stocks within a point or less of 52-week highs and lows, we knew we were duplicating the technical action of late July 1990, a week before the Kuwait invasion of August 2, 1990. You will recall the July 1990 numbers when I showed the count of stocks within a point of new highs contracting sharply:

The Stock Count

July 1990					February 1994				
Date	Highs	Change	Lows	Change	Date	Highs	Change	Lows	Change
July 13	351	475			Feb. 1	734	352		
July 20	167	-52.4%	500	+5.3%	Feb. 4	481	-34.4%	419	+19.0%

The market dropped on February 4th on high volume of roughly 380 million shares. Some thought the high volume was a bullish sign but I differed with that conclusion, seeing the high volume as reflecting the fact that many bears had thrown in the towel and turned bullish right on the Dow highs. Many observers said at this time that bear markets do not start this way. Apparently they had forgotten 1929 which began in early September of that year with the Babson break from which it never recovered.

So while this looked like the logical place to end the story, the opening saga of the initial 1994 decline demanded an epilogue.

Section XI
Epilogue

Epilogue

1. *Daily Commentaries*

Now I present my Daily Commentaries for the post high period of February to April 1994, detailing the technical stock market deterioration as it progressed day by day. Perhaps the most telling indicator that so accurately forecasted the market destruction that followed the January 31, 1994 Dow peak was the counting of the big board common stocks selling within a point or less of their 52-week highs and lows. On December 14, 1993 with the Dow at 3742.63 there were 405 stocks within a point of new 52-week lows. On March 11, 1994 with the Dow at 3862.70 there were 633 stocks within a point of new 52-week lows. So while the uninformed thought the Dow was still acting in a healthy manner in March 1994 because it was 120 points above the mid-December level, stocks within a point of new lows had shown a 50% escalation.

As you read these early 1994 Commentaries, keep in mind the losses that were later to be reported, especially by the mutual funds, that were horrendous. That was expected following the fact that they had all painted themselves into a corner, their extreme proliferation in number reflecting greed rather than need.

On April 1, 1994 the *Wall Street Journal* ran a large story relating how legendary Michael Steinhardt was selling heavily after suffering the loss of $1 billion in the first quarter, seeing about 25% of his $4.9 billion under management go up in smoke. Another headline on the same day stated that brokerage houses faced new pressure. Reminiscent of Herbert Hoover, President Clinton on March 31st sought to soothe the nation by saying that the economy was healthy and sound.

The Dow Jones Industrial average had fallen 342.40 points between January 31 and March 31, 1994 and for awhile had been down close to 400 points. The chart patterns were very similar to the opening weeks of the great 1929 decline and the public, while beginning to show some concerns, were largely too complacent.

The *Journal* reported the case of Susan Siegel:

"Like millions of investors around the country, she has watched the value of her stock portfolio skid since January.

Dr. Siegel, a dentist in the Riverdale section of New York's Bronx borough, is standing pat.

"I won't sell at the low," she vows. Besides, the stock market downturn doesn't make any sense to me. Things seem a whole lot better than they did a year ago."

They just don't get it. That was proof positive that the market was headed much lower in 1994. When the public doesn't sell, the market will go much lower. A panic bottom is when everybody is selling. Having the public mind, the White House was caught up in the same psychological trap.

In the Appendix you will see the piece about the two black pyramids. The forecast was that the next one of these would be a major one on the downside. Of particular interest is the fact that by the end of March 1994 my reciprocal readings showed the Dow at the exact opposite of where it was on the great Persian Gulf upside breakout of January 17, 1991.

February 5, 1994 - Saturday Afternoon

We were well prepared for Friday's crash which toppled the Dow 96.24 points to the 3871.42 level. The tightening action by the Fed had a far more severe response than most had expected.

Once again I reiterate that the high volume of 380 million shares on the Friday crash has to be seen as bearish.

The cataclysmic net drop of 1,723 in the advance/decline line fully equated with the numbers seen in a stock market crash. Stocks within a point or less of new highs and lows were especially revealing. Karen's count showed a huge 34% contraction from 734 to 481 on the highs and a 21% expansion in the lows from 352 to 429. Like the July 1990 market top, it is the sharp contraction in the highs that prefaces much more market trouble to come.

Actual highs and lows showed 96 highs and 51 lows. Those numbers are expected to reverse on Monday, more lows than highs.

Now it is significant to know there are 429 big board stocks within a point of new 52-week lows. That number will escalate on Monday as it did a week before the Kuwait invasion of August 2, 1990.

The Climax Indicator plunged to -16. The 65-stock CLX plunged to -32. Those numbers brought the market within range of having a blue

Monday crash. The Net Field Trend indicator only fell to +5, losing a field in *Goodyear*, but further losses of two fields in *Chevron*, and a field in *DuPont* and *General Motors* is probable on Monday. Elsewhere we lost fields in *Carolina Freight, Norfolk & Southern, Ryder*, and *American Electric Power.*

Paramount Communications fell 1-5/8 to 76-1/2, dropping the OBV to -13,128,200 and within easy reach of breaking the

November 19th low on Monday. The recommended April 75 put options jumped to 18-3/4. Subscribers paid 11-1/4 for these.

Best shorting opportunities now are in *Caterpillar, Chrysler* and *General Electric*. The handcuffs are off the Dow stocks.

Gold stocks offer buying opportunity.

February 7, 1994 - Monday Evening

Most observers disbelieved the implications of the Friday break just as they had done following the September 5, 1929 Babson break. Like then, the Dow recorded a rebound that had no technical significance. Today the Dow rebounded 34.90 points to 3906.32, recovering 36% of the Friday loss. But elsewhere the rebounds were pitifully small. Transports recovered 13%, Utilities closed down, the S & P 500 recovered 17%, the New York Stock Exchange Composite recovered 13%. and the Nasdaq recovered less than 4%. Both advance/decline lines fell and the high/low numbers were extremely bearish, showing 18 highs and 64 lows, making the expected crossing I referred to here on Saturday.

Like 1929, the public has been brainwashed into believing that every pullback is a buying opportunity. Some observers say that bear markets do not start this way. They couldn't be more wrong. This is the way the 1929 drop started, the initial break producing disbelief similar to the reaction today.

Gold stocks took a hit today, ASA a stop out at 49. Best looking charts in the group still include *Battle Mountain, Hecla, Homestake* and *Lac Minerals.*

Ironically, the market might have been better off if it had had a sharp decline today. Instead, a patently weak rebound in the main indicators today left the market that much more vulnerable. The focal point of weakness is best proven by those very weak high/low numbers.

The Climax Indicator rose from a revised -17 to -3, not good action at all for a 35-point rebound in the Dow. *Union Carbide* lost a field on Friday and that lowered the NFI to +4.

Today *Caterpillar* gained a field and *Chevron* lost two fields and so the NFI is now down to +3. Strength today in stocks like *Alcoa, General Electric, General Motors* and *IBM* showed very poor OBV responses. Poor CLX numbers in the Transports and Utilities underscored the entire day as a technical failure.

February 8, 1994 - Tuesday Evening

Falling back from a better than 11-point rise in the morning, the Dow couldn't maintain much interest, falling back to close down 0.29 at the 3906.03 level. Transports and Utilities also closed down. Long bond yields reached a 5-month high on the close on a sharp drop of 24/32nds putting the yield up to 6.44%. That kept a lid on most stock prices. But with rates rising, the big story continues in the utility average, dropping 1.32 points today to the 118.03 level, less than a point away from the January 24th low of 217.11 and only 4 points away from where it was the day before the 1987 stock market crash.

The Standard & Poor 500 fell 0.70 today to 471.06, cutting the gain since the Friday break to a mere 1.25, reducing the recovery of the Friday break to a mere 11%. The all-inclusive New York Stock Exchange index did not fare much better.

While the advance/decline line rose today by a net 216, it was only the first rebound since the Friday break. We saw 68 stock highs and 36 stock lows.

The Climax Indicator fell to -4. The Net Field Trend indicator remained unchanged at +3.

Sears got hard hit for 3-1/4 points down to the 47-3/4 level, the lowest close since last July. It has fallen a huge 11-1/2 points since it peaked last October at 59-1/4. Like most Dow stocks now, they are vulnerable.

Nothing new on *Paramount*, edging up today to 76-3/4.

The Gold Stock index managed to hold on to a small gain and there were no stop outs on most recent purchases.

The market remains very vulnerable and now we are again getting signals that a key event is very close, one that will drop the market sharply.

February 9, 1994 - Wednesday Evening

The Dow rose 25.89 points today to close up at the 3931.92 level. While Transports and Utilities rose, their gains were far more subdued. Utilities, in rising less than a point, could easily give all of that back on any resumption of weakness in the bond market.

Highs and lows showed 98 highs and 46 lows. Karen's latest count of stocks within a point of 52-week highs and lows showed the highs expanding moderately from Friday's sharp drop. They moved up from 481 to 516. But the real story is coming from the lows. There we see the numbers going from 352 to 429 to 459. So while we saw 46 actual lows today, there are 459 stocks within less than a point of recording new 52-week lows. This market simply cannot afford another February 4th break but I have to report here that another one looks very close.

The Climax Indicator rose from -4 to +6. While that showed a little more technical muscle than we have seen for awhile, the inability to change the Net Field Trend indicator indicates that the rise will have no staying power.

Gold stocks held their ground in a critical session, most of these very close to their stop out levels. Comex Gold rose over $5 off the morning low while the Gold Stock Index rose 1.42 points to the 127.56 level and well above the morning lows.

February 10, 1994 - Thursday Evening

The Dow plunged 36.58 points to the 3895.34 level, also taking down the Transports 19.20 points and a huge decline of 3.58 points in the Dow Utilities. The break in the utility average to the lowest level in two years has particularly bearish implications for the market. It is 2 points away from the percentage decline it was at the day before the 1987 crash.

The sharp drop in the advance/decline line today underscored the increasing importance of the recent February 2nd high. Today's decline increases the drop in the A/D line to almost 2,000 under the recent high.

The high/low indicator accents the worst of the technical omens of a crashing market ahead. Today there were 80 highs and 56 lows and it is the steady rise in the number of lows that predicts triggering hundreds of lows in the days ahead. I documented that yesterday by showing that there are 459 stocks within a point or less of new 52-week lows.

The Climax Indicator fell from +6 to -4 and the weakness was extreme in the Transports and Utilities, bringing the market back into range for crash action. The New York Stock Exchange Composite Average today closed under the low of last Friday, documenting the industrial rally after Friday as being technically worthless.

The public was bored with *General Motors* earnings news with little said about the decline in all the auto stocks. Like most stocks, auto stocks should be sold immediately.

Bonds down sharply today. But tomorrow is the most critical day of the week and I again look for a sharp drop.

February 12, 1994 - Saturday Afternoon

New York snow put off what would have been another technical bust, now postponed until Monday, fittingly coinciding with what could be the St. Valentine's Day Massacre. When news spread that the market was about to be closed, shorts were quickly covered, giving the false impression of some genuine market strength. A normal closing hour would have more fully revealed that the rug has been pulled out from under this market. The Dow closed at 3894.78, down 0.56 points. Transports stayed weak and the bounce in utilities was not impressive.

The high/low indicator showed the true marks of an early bear market, reversing to show 36 highs and 50 lows. But Karen's count of stocks within a point or less of new 52-week highs and lows reveals far more. Friday showed stocks on the high side contracting to 478, recording a downward zigzag. Stocks within a point of new lows expanded to 500, this the major technical sword of Damocles hanging over this market, signalling not only a bust at hand, but a key event that will trigger the slide.

The Climax Indicator showed a weak rise to zero while the Net Field Trend indicator rose to +4, gaining a field in *Boeing*.

The Gold Stock Index was on the way to full recovery on Friday until cut short by the exchange closing.

Answering the question which will collapse first, the market or *Paramount*, the market will cross the finish line first. *Paramount* will then follow with a good imitation.

Our shorts in *Caterpillar, Chrysler*, and *General Electric* are working out. These were not in the latest letter, that being an oversight. Bank stocks continue to break down and these are still among the best shorts.

February 14, 1994 - Monday Evening

Up 25 points in the morning, the Dow fell back to close up 9.28 points at the 3904.26 level. Transports and Utilities were a wash and were of no technical significance, Transports up 0.44 and Utilities down 0.52. Sentiment rapidly cooled as the repercussions of the failed Friday trade talks with the Japanese spilled over today with a steep collapse in the dollar which dropped the long bond 18/32nds with the yield rising to 6.45%. The latest concern is that the Japanese will start dumping U.S. Treasuries. Once again the Dow was practically meaningless with the S & P 500 up a mere 0.05 and the all-inclusive New York Stock Exchange Composite Index down.

The advance/decline line showed a substandard rise of 81 while the high/low indicator showed 61 highs and 36 lows, again a substandard reading. Friday we had a revised reading of 520 big board stocks within a point or less of new 52-week lows.

The Climax Indicator rose from zero to +2 in a very weak showing dominated by OBV lower up designations. The NFI remained unchanged at +4.

Paramount was smashed to 76-1/8 with the OBV plummeting to a new low of -16,479,500. *Viacom B* collapsed to a new low well under 30 to post a decline of over 52% from the high of 61-1/4. So while *Viacom* had their eye on *Paramount*, they had no regard for their shareholders who took a bath.

I would use last Wednesday's market as a blueprint to indicate that we probably face a stiff decline in the Dow tomorrow. Last Wednesday we rose 25.89 to the 3931.92 level in a sub-standard session and today's market was far weaker. Remember that we fell 36 points on Thursday.

The dollar slide is serious and implies a worsening of inflation, a much lower bond market and higher gold prices. It alerts the Fed to further tightening.

The Gold Stock Index continued improving from where it left off on Friday, rising 1.37 points to the 127.49 level.

So look for a sharp decline tomorrow which could match the 36-point decline of last Thursday.

February 15, 1994 - Tuesday Evening

The expected break did not materialize, but what did take place was pretty disconcerting for the bulls. We saw a major technical failure on the upside. Here are the technical shortcomings: (1) The Dow industrials closed up 24.21 at the 3928.27 level but failed to move out above the February 9th 3931.92 level and thus we have a repeating pattern here of declining tops. (2) Both Transports and Utilities closed down and thus the industrial rise was out of gear. The Utility Average closed at 215.46, missing a new low by 0.07. (3) There were 82 stock highs today, considerably below the 209 of January 31st and also below the 98 highs of February 9th. (4) The advance/decline line showed a substandard rise for a 24-point Dow gain, another set of declining tops.

The Climax Indicator rose from +2 to +6 but we had 8 OBV lower up designations and that underscored technical weakness. The Net Field Trend indicator rose to +5, gaining a field in *Minnesota Mining*. But the CLX +6 reading failed to move above the February 9th level and that was a technical negative.

Bonds and gold were put on hold today, bonds unchanged and the Gold Stock Index down but a small fraction.

Paramount rebounded but the move is seen to be technically meaningless in the face of the new OBV low recorded yesterday. *Viacom B* collapsed to 28, widening the drop to 33-1/4 points from the 61-1/4 high. The many *Viacom* shareholders paid a terribly high price for the greed of a few. All participating stocks in this game are down.

The longer a steep drop is postponed, the worse the drop is expected to be.

There was little comfort in today's rally in the industrials.

February 16, 1994 - Wednesday Evening

Plenty of technical bombshells to report. The Dow showed late strength to close up 9 points at 3937.27. Gains in *Boeing* and *United Technologies* accounted for the entire rise. And once again Transports and Utilities fell. The drop of 2.70 points in the Dow Utility Average dropped it to a new low at 212.76. That puts it down over 17% since peaking last September 13th and duplicates the percentage decline the day before the October 1987 crash.

Karen's new count reveals 519 stocks within a point a new highs and 528 within a point of new lows. Now look at the market again. What is more important, two Dow stocks that accounted for the Dow rise today or almost a quarter of the entire big board within a point of new lows?

The Climax Indicator fell from +6 to +1, recording a key upside nonconfirmation. The NFI stayed unchanged at +5. With Transports and Utilities down again, the 65-stock CLX will show far weaker numbers.

New shorts being added here are *Allied-Signal, General Motors, McDonnell-Douglas*, and *United Technologies. McDonnell-Douglas* is the best looking short sale since seeing a similar parabolic curve in UAL back in 1989. Recommended put options are *Allied-Signal* June 80, *General Motors* June 60, *McDonnell-Douglas* May 120, and *United Technologies* May 70.

I urge those who have the Horsey chart book to look at the *McDonnell-Douglas* chart and note that the good news on the Saudi sale was announced by the President right at the top of the chart. I suspect that the Saudis were buying the stock all the way up from the 33 low of a year ago. Like UAL, the public is being told that it is a done deal.

No change in outlook. *Serious break dead ahead.*

February 17, 1994 - Thursday Evening

Humpty Dumpty took a great fall today, bonds busting a key support, reversing from a morning rise of 20/32nds to close down 1 and 4/32nds to see the yield climb sharply to 6.54%. Some observers were surprised by this. The Utilities have been constantly warning of this, the Dow Utility Average breaking today to still another low. The Dow industrial average did well to restrict the loss to 14.63 points, closing at the 3922.64 level, but another break tomorrow is highly likely.

Highs came in at 107 today but that merely reflected the morning strength which quickly dissipated. So we can look for a sharp contraction in highs tomorrow. The advance/decline line made a major reversal from a morning surge of +600 to a closing loss of almost 400.

The Climax Indicator fell from +1 to -4 while the Net Field Trend Indicator fell sharply to +2, losing a field in*American Telephone* and two fields in *J. P.Morgan*. Among the 65 Dow stocks, we have now lost 18 fields so far this year.

Blockbuster broke a double bottom, falling 7/8 to 23-5/8. Shareholders will not support *Viacom* on the *Paramount* deal and that spells out a serious collapse in*Paramount* stock. That stock fell to 76-1/4 today with the OBV making a new low at -17,112,600. Now the arbs will quickly liquidate and run for the hills.

U.S. Surgical collapsed to 18-5/8 today. William O'Neill gave this stock the highest possible rating when it was priced at 134-1/2 in January 1992. Fundamentalists recommended the stock all the way down.

With the long bond yielding 6.54% the stock market is ready for a very serious fall.

February 19, 1994 - Saturday Afternoon

The collapsing bond market sets the stage for a stock market crash. The long bond on Friday fell over a point again and sent the yield up to 6.64%. The Dow recorded a sharp 35.46 point fall to the 3887.18 level. A time comparison shows Friday equating with September 17, 1929 and the current market is only 11 points away from an exact percentage decline comparison measured from the September 5th Babson break in 1929 and the February 4th crash this year on the Fed interest rate boost. If that comparison is to remain valid, then we can look, for a better than 100-point break in the week ahead.

The ferocity of the Friday decline was well reflected by the flip flop in the high/low indicator which showed 42 highs and 96 lows. But what was happening beneath the surface was far more revealing. Karen's latest count of stocks within a point of new 52-week highs and lows showed the highs contracting from 519 to 433 while those on the low side expanded from 528 to 547. So don't be surprised to see hundreds of actual new lows in the days directly ahead.

The Climax Indicator fell sharply from -4 to -13 while the Net Field Trend indicator fell from +2 to zero, losing a field in American Express and a field in Merck.

As predicted here, Paramount Communications is disintegrating as the arbs increasingly desert the stock. It closed down 1-1/4 at 75 on Friday with the OBV falling to another new low of -20,662,000.

Both the Viacom stocks broke to new lows as the Redstone empire showed further decay, leftover fragments of one man's ambition to control a company which is now a wasting asset.

My main message today is to place conservation of capital as the number one priority. If you can maintain your current bottom line without making or losing a penny you will be ahead of most everybody by the end of this year.

February 22, 1994 - Tuesday Evening

The Dow recorded a technically weak bounce of 24.20 points to put the average at the 3911.66 level. Transports and utilities also rose and all three averages continued to trace out the weak pattern of declining tops. One didn't have to be a rocket scientist to see how technically weak the market was, most Dow stocks either tumbling or recording worthless advances. The Dow closed today 12 points under the close of last Thursday.

The weakness in the Dow stocks was well exhibited by the very weak showing of -9 in the Climax Indicator which was a technical no-no for a rise of over 24 points, a rise obviously traced to gains in *Caterpillar, IBM, Minnesota Mining* and *Procter & Gamble*, four stocks that could only record a single lower up designation on *Caterpillar*. Only *Union Carbide* was able to record a single genuine OBV up designation. So the weak volume figures today revealed the Dow rise as a probable one-day bounce.

That was borne out by the very weak advance/decline line showing of less than a 140 rise. And if there were still any lingering doubts, the Dow bounce could not erase the fact that we had 61 highs and 86 lows, the first time we have seen two consecutive days of more lows than highs in a long time.

Paramount Communications broke to 74-5/8 on the close today, extending the predicted collapse.

Gold stocks remained on a slippery barber pole, some getting a short-term haircut. We purposely kept our stops very close so as to minimize any damage. We were stopped out on *ASA, American Barrick, Echo Bay, Horsham, Pegasus* and *Placer- Dome* with minimal damage. As for the call options, we sold half of most of these when they doubled and thus there is no damage there, the remaining half with most of those expiring in April costing nothing.

No change in general market outlook.

February 23, 1994 - Wednesday Evening

Bearing out my Tuesday evening warning that the rise that day was nothing more than a one-day bounce, the Dow fell 19.98 points today to the 3891.68 level. This brought the average into easy range of breaking the February 4th Dow low of 3871 because the break in the bond market to a new low is sending a bearish message regarding the Thursday market. The long bond broke 17/32nds to break the yield out to a new high on this move of 6.64%. Everything reversed from the early morning attempts to put on a show of stability which at best had a very short life. The Transports fell from an early 10-point rise to post a loss of over 5 points. Utilities, rising yesterday against a wall of down designations, never had a chance to extend any gains.

Highs and lows showed 79 highs and 64 lows but right beneath the surface was the more important count of stocks within a point or less of new 52-week highs and lows. Karen's latest count showed 466 stocks on the high side and 560 on the low side. This equates with a few days before the August 1990 Kuwait invasion.

The Climax Indicator fell to -10 while the Net Field Trend indicator fell back to zero, losing a field in *Bethlehem Steel* and a field in *United Technologies.*

Seeing technical weakness in *Blockbuster* a symptom of the collapse of the Redstone empire, the stock looks good as a short sale. I would buy the June 25 put options.

I have advised letting the gold move exhaust itself, obeying stops but holding off on any buying. The reversal today from early weakness may have been the turn for the better but I would take no new action as yet.

February 24, 1994 - Thursday Evening

Bear market technical signs abounded as the Dow plummeted 51.78 points to close down at the 3839.88 level. Transports crashed almost 35 points and utilities again took a very serious slide, dropping over 3 points to another new low. Bulls who completely missed this decline were quick to blame it on anything. The obvious villain was the bond market as it fell 1-3/32nds to push the yield way up to 6.74%.

But others blamed it on Bell Atlantic, breaking up a multibillion dollar merger with TCI. A quick look at the chart of Bell Atlantic would have alerted anybody last October that the stock was a blowoff on news at 69 and shouldn't be touched with a 50-foot pole. Calling off huge mergers is a symptom of bear markets and apparently the smart money was quick to get the message.

The total collapses in the advance/decline line and the high/low indicator were key bear market characteristics. We had 38 highs and 148 lows and you can imagine that we probably have about 600 stocks less than a point from new lows.

The Climax Indicator fell out of bed, dropping from -10 to -19 while the Net Field Trend indicator dropped sharply to -3, losingfield in *Exxon, Goodyear*, and *Union Carbide.*

The Nasdaq was roughed up along with the big board. Nothing escaped the net of the grim reaper as each day evidence mounts that the market is on a crash course.

The fun begins when selling completely envelops the mutual funds. And remember, nothing is safe. Bonds and stocks are equally vulnerable.

What was especially deadly was the degree of complacency before this plunge. The bulls point to bearish sentiment and have completely forgotten that in a bear market the bears are right. This is a bear market. Make no mistake about that.

February 26, 1994 - Saturday Afternoon

Following Thursday's 52-point drubbing, it was clear that the market was going to try to put together some kind of a bounce. All eyes were on the bond market since that area has been calling all the shots. But there wasn't much happening and that kept stocks mostly under wrap, the Dow easing 1.12 points to the 3838.78 level. Dropping almost 50 points in a 4-day week, is merely the opening move in a major bear market and again I stress capital conservation over profit since most people are averse to short selling and playing the option market.

A key feature of these Saturday Commentaries is Karen's count of stocks within a point or less of new 52-week highs and lows. Friday saw the stocks on the high side contract sharply from 466 to 369 while stocks within a point or less of new lows escalated to another new high from 560 to 577. This is the best single proof I have that we are in a bear market.

The Climax Indicator rose from -19 to -12 but there are far too many technical negatives to look for any legitimate bullish signals this early in the downturn. The current posture of the advance/decline line, the high/low indicator, the time indicator, General Motors and several other cornerstone indicators validates my conclusion that we are in the first phase of a bear market. Perhaps one of the clearest indications of this is the arrogant complacency on the part of the bulls who have such difficulty in accepting the fact that in a bear market the bears are right. That invalidates their reliance on such things as bearish sentiment, the put/call ratio, and the short interest to support their case. The Net Field Trend Indicator fell to -4, losing a field in *Minnesota Mining.*

This was a great week for subscribers with large declines in most of our most recent short selling candidates: *Allied-Signal, Caterpillar Tractor, Chrysler, General Motors*, and *United Technologies.*

February 28, 1994 - Monday Evening

After several repeated efforts during the day to make earlier gains stick, the Dow closed at the very low of the day, off 6.76 points at the 3832.02 level. The Dow collapsed 18 points in the final half hour of the day. This brought the total February decline to over 146 points, a far cry from the euphoria of January 21st.

But the general market was far stronger than the Dow but seen to be nothing more than a temporary rebound following last week's smash.

While the high/low indicator reversed to show more highs than lows, it did nothing to change the fact that there are 577 stocks within a point of new lows.

The Climax Indicator rose to -10 on the lower Dow. There was still little to recommend the market as a turnaround situation. The Net Field Trend indicator fell to -5, losing a field in *Philip Morris.*

Tobacco stocks got smashed as the government redefined the industry as selling drugs, particularly accenting that the companies are selling poison to children and lacing the product with extra doses of nicotine to enhance the addiction, the major target being minors. While earlier attacks on the industry have been rebuffed in the past by an army of industry lawyers representing probably the strongest of all lobbies, current government statements pose the strongest of all attacks, and also the most justified against an industry having very few morals.

Philip Morris broke to 56 on heavy volume and technically appears headed for an easy break under 50. Buy the June 55 puts.

Gold stocks responded well to the early news of shooting down the 4 Serbian jets, the Gold Stock Index rising 2.70 to the 128.39 level. This helped our April call options but we are still holding off for awhile on aggressive new buying in the stocks.

March 1, 1994 - Tuesday Evening

We are seeing the results of the warnings I flashed here last September when utilities were peaking and again in October when bonds were peaking. Nowhere did the media flash the major warnings that these segments were also flashing for the stock market. Now stockholders cannot switch to bonds for safety and bondholders can't switch to stocks for safety. There is virtually no guaranteed escape from the financial slaughter that is signalled to increasingly envelop all markets.

Bonds painted a black stripe across the market today as the long bond collapsed by 1-15/32nds to see the yield rocket up to 6.78%. One doesn't have to wait on the Fed for the next tightening move. The bond market is calling the shots and the immediate future looks bleak, a far cry from the arrogant optimists who tell you that we will soon be making new highs. But their cries are becoming fainter and their conviction is quickly entwined with hedging their bets.

The one-day breadth improvements seen on Monday were more than given back today while the Dow fell 22.79 points to close down at the 3809.23 level. There was no relief elsewhere, Transports down 13.46 and utilities down 1.05. Bulls were still pinning some hopes on the Nasdaq after seeing the strength there on Monday. However, the Nasdaq fell 3.88 and the breadth was weak, 1284 up and 1973 down.

The high/low indicator is sour but not nearly as bad as it will soon be. Tomorrow I will report here Karen's new count and it will probably curl your hair. We are getting numbers now that have always been followed by a crash.

The Climax Indicator fell to -13 as the OBV lower downs predominated. The Net Field Trend indicator fell to -6, losing a field in *DuPont.*

Golds still haven't formed a guaranteed base and so we are waiting there before adding to our previous advice.

March 2, 1994 - Wednesday Evening

The Dow put a temporary bottom in place, translating a 50-point loss to a gain of 22.51 points at the 3831.74 level. I purposely did not use the word reversal because it is not legitimately used unless there is a corresponding reversal in tbe advance/decline line. There the market displayed its true technical colors, the big board A/D line falling 656 to a new low on the 1994 decline. Even weaker action was seen on the Nasdaq. The decline looked moderate at 5.15 points, but the A/D line was down a steep 998. Therefore, seeing no legitimate reversal, today's blue chip rally should be heavily sold into tomorrow and Friday.

The high/low indicator today showed very negative figures, only 29 highs but 177 lows. That is a reflection of the early trading when the Dow was down about 50. But the blue chip turnaround in the late trading could not change the figures much and that was proven by the sharply lower advance/decline line.

Here are Karen's latest numbers: We contracted to 356 on the high side and expanded to 611 on the low side. Such numbers in the past have always been followed by a stock market crash.

Because of the technical damage inflicted by the huge OBV changes to the downside seen in most of the 30 Dow industrial stocks, the blue chip rally today was what I see as a positioning move. The strongest Dow stocks mostly were only able to record lower up designations and that technically sets the market up for the next slide.

The Climax Indicator stayed in minus territory at -1 on the blue chip rally. The Net Field Trend indicator fell to -7, gaining a field in *Goodyear,* but losing a field in *Allied-Signal* and a field in *IBM.*

Gold stocks were soft but there were no further stop outs. The gold price closed well above the lows of the day.

March 3, 1994 - Thursday Evening

The bond market continues to call the shots. The long bond collapsed 25/32nds to push the yield up to 6.84%. That kept stocks under wrap, the Dow closing down 7.32 points at the 3824.42 level. Expectations are very strong that a high figure tomorrow morning on non-farm payroll jobs will trigger another Fed hike in interest rates. It was quite bearish that the Dow could not followthrough today on the Wednesday bounce.

On the surface it looked like the high/low numbers improved in showing 56 highs and 65 lows. But one has to remember that there are 611 stocks just under the surface within a point of new lows and that the advance/decline line today fell again, closing at a new bear market low.

The CLX on the Transports is so weak that it more than offsets any strength in the industrials. This is the reverse of the situation a week before the huge Persian Gulf rally back in January 1991. I have other evidence strongly suggesting that there is a huge market break about to take place.

The Climax Indicator fell back to -5 while the Net Field Trend indicator rose to -6, gaining a field in Exxon.

Paramount Communications fell another 2 points today to the 46-3/8 level. I will have more on this tomorrow.

New short sale recommendations and put contracts are as follow: *Airborne Freight* May 35, *Burlington Northern* July 60, *CSX* May 85, *Roadway* July 70, and *UAL* May 130. Because of the very weak Transport numbers, I drew all these new recommendations from that source.

Gold stocks very quiet and mostly lower today with no stop outs. As long as the gold price can stay above 370 a new base is being built and we could get another strong go on the group.

March 5, 1994 - Saturday Afternoon

Again we saw a continuation of the pattern of declining tops, the Dow rising about 22 points at the top of the Friday rally but only closing up 7.88 points at the 3832.30 level. We saw another reason why we never lean on government statistics, the January non-farm payroll jobs revised from +60,000 to -2,000. That averaged out far less than the huge 217,000 February figure and that reversed the initial downward impact on the bond market. Nevertheless, while cutting earlier losses, bonds still closed down on the day and the Dow closed down on the week. Only the Nasdaq boasted a rise but the advance/decline line there remains very weak looking.

Since the advance/decline line only enjoyed one day off the 1994 low, no bullish implications could be read into the Friday rally attempt. Certainly the high/low indicator only underscores the bearish trend. For those who measure the market in terms of the Dow, I have a simple question for them. We saw 167 new 52-week lows on March 2nd. When do you think those 167 stocks made their highs? Right, many months ago, underscoring the severe dichotomy which preceded the Dow top. On Karen's latest count, we have 362 stocks on the high side and 604 on the low side. Now when do you think those 604 stocks made their highs? Now you see why the smart money moved out of this market long before the Dow peak.

The Climax Indicator was only able to rally to a -2 reading on the Friday rally. We did see some strength in the utilities and noted that *American Electric Power, Consolidated Edison*, and *Pacific Gas & Elec-*

tric all gained a field. But these gains were tempered by the fact that the 4-column mix was the same as on February 3rd, the day before the 96-point break on the Fed interest rate hike.

Golds again were lacklustre, but no further stop outs were recorded.

More steep declines in the general market seen to be dead ahead.

March 7, 1994 - Monday Evening

The Dow rose 23.92 points today to the 3856.22 level. Technically, the rise was full of potholes. When the Dow broke to 3871.42 on February 4th, that level then became the upside resistance on any rallies. So the rise today went above no significant resistance levels.

While the advance/decline line posted the second consecutive rise, it fell short of the February 28th level when the Dow stood at 3832.02. So this was a serious technical upside failure with the Dow at 3856.22.

The high/low indicator showed 96 highs and 48 lows but that was well under the February 17th 114 new highs. With over 600 stocks within a point of new lows, the market cannot afford any technically failing rallies, but it got one today.

The low volume was partially responsible for the Climax Indicator today recording a very weak looking +1, with only one Dow industrial stock recording a true OBV up designation. Elsewhere we had 2 higher downs, 3 lower downs, and 5 lower ups. The Net Field Trend indicator remained unchanged at -6. Today's lower ups sets the Dow up to lose some more field trends.

Late in the day the Dow fell from a gain of over 29 points but one of the more significant late changes was the S & P 500 Index falling from +3.06 to +2.17, an almost 30% contraction.

Not a single Dow stock made a new OBV high today and another significant late move was seeing *General Motors* close down after being up all day.

We were stopped out today in *Homestake* at 19-1/2 and *Newmont Mining* at 51-1/2. That reduces our gold and silver stock holdings to just five stocks- *Battle Mountain, Hecla, Lac Minerals, Newmont Gold*, and *Sunshine Mining*. We are obeying stops and waiting to see how far this burnout carries.

March 8, 1994 - Tuesday Evening

The bond market hit an air pocket late in the day dropping the long bond 24/32nds with the yield right back up to 6.86%. The Dow fell 4.50

points to the 3851.72 level. The drop would have been more had it not been for a 2-1/2 point rise in IBM which had no technical value whatsoever, coming off a string of down designations.

While the Transport average rose over 10 points, there was nothing there to alter the bearish pattern of declining tops. An almost 2 point drop in the Utility average reflected the weakness in the bond market.

I think what we have here is a breadth problem which is quite apparent in both the New York Stock Exchange statistics as well as the Nasdaq. Today we see the big board advance/decline line only some 900 off the bottom, something that can be easily taken out in two days.

The Climax Indicator fell back to zero. The drop would have been greater if it hadn't been for a number of lower up designations. The Dow stocks are now vulnerable to lose one field in *Alcoa*, one field in *Boeing,* two fields in *General Electric*, one field in *General Motors*, two fields in *International Paper*, one field in *Minnesota Mining*, one field in *Philip Morris*, one field in *Procter & Gamble*, and one field in *United Technologies*. That is a total immediate vulnerability of 11 fields. Seldom is there such a large short-term vulnerability. That much smoke spells fire. The current Net Field Trend indicator was unchanged at -6.

So I look for the imminent start of the next significant downleg in the Dow.

March 9, 1994 - Wednesday Evening

The long bond had a partial rebound today and that helped the Dow reverse an early 20-point decline. But the powers that be couldn't get more than a small gain of 1.69 points at the 3853.41 level. Transports fell 8.39 points and the utility average fell 1.25 points and thus the overall numbers were negative. The advance/decline line fell 130 and that means that the A/D line is only about 770 off the low of the year.

The high/low indicator showed 68 highs and 89 lows. The new count shows 399 stocks within a point of new highs and 583 within a point of new 52-week lows. So despite the 43-point rally off the March 1st low, the number of stocks on the low side remain significantly high.

The Climax Indicator rose today to a very weak looking +4, there being as many as 7 lower up designations. That keeps the Dow very vulnerable.

The Net Field Trend indicator was unchanged at -6.

I have five short sales in the upcoming new letter. Here they are along with the recommended put options: *Foster Wheeler* April 45, *W. R. Grace* May 45, *Great Lakes Chemical* June 75, *ITT* June 85, and *Scott Paper* July 45.

Gold stocks executed what looks like a good reversal to the upside. The group became radically oversold and the turn today may be in time to materially help our April call options. I was very impressed and see this as a general reentry signal. The index was down over 2 points in the morning but closed up 3.79 for a 6-point turnabout. We have advocated no selling for those in the precious metal mutual funds.

So the overall market was impressive today and looks ready to slide.

March 10, 1994 - Thursday Evening

The market executed a perfect followthrough on the signals reported here yesterday. The market took a big slide while the price of gold soared.

Again bonds were the culprit, the long bond crashing 1-12/32nds to push the yield all the way up to 6.95%. So the 7% is almost a done deal.

The Dow fell as much as 37 points today but cut the loss to 22.79 points. Transports collapsed 18.54 points and utilities fell a sharp 2.24 points, now less than a point away from a new bear market low.

The advance/decline line fell over 700, now about 100 away from a new bear low. The high/low indicator showed 46 highs and 113 lows but the internal action was far worse. Our count of potential new lows tells us that the Dow is headed sharply lower.

The Climax Indicator fell from +4 to -5. Knowing we could lose a large number of fields, the Net Field Trend indicator fell sharply today to -10, gaining a field in IBM but losing two fields in *General Electric,* two fields in *International Paper*, and 1 field in *Procter & Gamble.* These are bear market numbers.

Gold was the star today, rising over $8 with the Gold Stock Index posting a gain of 3.27 at the 326.53 level. We are on record as being long again in all the gold stocks along with the call options. The gains today were excellent, especially sharp gains in *Echo Bay, Homestake, Placer-Dome* and *Pegasus*.

News by itself is not important but the way the market responds to the news means everything. So the market's response to Whitewater developments is extremely bearish. It has broken the continuity of bullish opinion.

March 12, 1994 - Saturday Afternoon

Some recovery move in bond prices after the long bond touched a 7% yield sent the Dow up 32.08 points to the 3862.79 level. It was a very weak move technically. Seeing a rise in price on a Dow industrial stock without an OBV designation or on a lower up designation as technically worthless, the Friday rise showed that 82% of the rise was technically worthless. Besides this, Transports fell again and the rise in the utility average did nothing to prevent the 65-Stock CLX from closing in the minus column.

So while the Dow industrials recovered over 100% of the Thursday loss, the important advance/decline line only recovered about 21%, and thus this market continues to have a serious breadth problem. Because of this, the Mutual Fund Index hardly moved on Friday. The funds have painted themselves into a corner.

The high/low indicator continued to show negative numbers, Friday showing 43 highs and 120 lows. But Karen's latest count shows 377 stocks within a point of new 52-week highs and a sharp rise to 633 big board common stocks within a point or less of new 52-week lows. Keep in mind that we had 582 on July 24, 1990 just prior to the crash on the Kuwait news. Also keep in mind that our count of lows has expanded to a new high right in the face of the Dow 32-point Friday rally. With 633 stocks about to make new lows, restricting the Dow to a 5% correction is impossible.

The Climax Indicator rose to a very weak looking +2. The Net Field Trend indicator fell to -11, losing a field in *Minnesota Mining.*

Gold stocks acted very well on Friday, consolidating following the meteoric $8 rise on Thursday. Our letter subscribers will be coming in on the Monday openings.

March 14, 1994 - Monday Evening

Bonds took a late slide of 13/32nds, pushing the yield back up to 6.94%. The Dow maintained a fairly narrow range throughout the day, up 7, down 7, up 8, and then declining in the final half hour to +0.28 at the 3862.98 level. Another member of the Clinton administration resigned and that cast a pall over the market. The bonds were nervous over the inflation numbers to come out over the next two days.

While the advance/decline line did show a moderate gain of 202, it was not enough to significantly alter the breadth problem. The Nasdaq was also having a problem, a small gain of 100 in the A/D line despite the 3-point rise in the index.

The high/low indicator showed 67 highs and 82 lows but just beneath the surface was a potential 633 new 52-week lows.

Strength in the Transports was transitory, being only the first gain while the drop of better than a point in the Utilities kept that average within easy distance of new lows.

The Climax Indicator edged up to a very weak looking +3 because there were 8 lower up designations. The Net Field Trend indicator remained unchanged on the very weak looking -11 level.

Letter subscribers reentered the gold stocks today at slightly lower levels. Today subscribers went short on *Foster Wheeler* at 44, *W. R. Grace* at 44-3/4, *Great Lakes Chemical* at 74-7/8, *ITT* at 87-3/4 and *Scott Paper* at 44-7/8.

March 15, 1994 - Tuesday Evening

Bonds responded positively to the rise in the Producer Price Index because most of the rise was in heating oil, the last dregs of the effects of winter. For awhile it looked like stocks were following bonds, the Dow up 8 in the early trading. Then something went wrong. For the second day running, the Dow met predictable upside resistance at the 3871 level, the bottom of the February 4th 96-point decline. Bonds continued to rise to a gain of 24/32nds but stocks got steadily weaker. Then bonds peaked and cut their gain to 17/32nds but the Dow ended a double digit loser, losing 13.39 points at the 3849.59 level. Transports hung on to an 8-point gain but the Dow Utility Average fell 1.58 points to a new bear market low at 207.03 and did that despite the rise in bonds.

The high/low indicator showed 90 highs and 79 lows, disguising the fact that there are 633 common stocks within a point of new 52-week lows.

The Climax Indicator edged lower to +2 but it is important to again point out that there were 6 lower up designations, a focal point of current technical weakness. The Net Field Trend indicator rose to -10, gaining a field in *Goodyear*.

I was impressed by the turnabout in the Gold Index today which offset early weakness to close up 0.50 at the 125.57 level. Tomorrow we get the Consumer Price Index and the weak closing today suggests more trouble, this also being an option expiration week.

March 16, 1994 - Wednesday Evening

Today proved to be a conversation piece, bonds closing up 31/32nds to push the yield down to 6.80%. That spread to stocks and there was no question the market was up, what with 550 net gainers. Transports zoomed ahead almost 18 points and utilities threw off early weakness to close fractionally higher. Right up to a minute before the close the Dow was enjoying a large double digit advance but in one fell swoop gave back more than the entire advance to close down 1.44 points at the 3848.15 level. Those who might have left a few minutes before the close to go home had to be in for a surprise when they listened to the evening news. While the internal action of the market was positive today, the sudden flim flam in the Dow on the close is judged to be a negative. Whatever the cause for the instant sell program, it was inexcusable and underscores a disturbing volatility that does not sit well.

The high/low indicator came in showing 88 highs and 59 lows but Karen's count of stocks within a point or less of 52-week highs and lows showed 434 on the high side and 636 on the low side, a disturbingly high number close to 52-week lows.

The Climax Indicator edged higher to +4 but the mix was again unfavorable, showing as many as 8 lower up designations. The Net Field Trend indicator improved to -8, gaining two fields in *Sears.*

McDonnell-Douglas took a hit of 4-5/8 points, falling to 114-1/2. We went short at 120 and have recommended the May 120 puts. The first chart support is at the 94 level.

Gold stocks continued to consolidate in narrow ranges but I see no serious trouble for that sector.

March 17, 1994 - Thursday Evening

Selected blue chip strength pushed the Dow up 16.99 points today to the 3865.14 level. But again the closing was well short of the critical 3871 upside resistance level where the Dow had closed on February 4th. Transports retreated, most of the airlines lower and the utility average while up, could only add a small fraction and thus remained within easy distance of new lows.

The market definitely had a better tone to it today but lacks staying power. I judge staying power in terms of On-Balance Volume up clusters. Without these, all rallies are transitory. *Right now my cluster indicators are all making new lows.* For instance today, not a single Dow industrial stock had a single up cluster, a cluster being three up designations or more. This signifies that there is no followthrough on the upside on rallies. That will be interesting to watch now that tomorrow is a triple witching session.

The Climax Indicator moved up to +6 today and the Net Field Trend indicator showed some technical power, *Alcoa, Texaco* and *Union Carbide* all gaining a field and *Boeing* losing a field. That reduced the NFI negative reading from -8 to -6.

While the media was extolling the virtues of the Nasdaq's new high, nobody was talking about the fact that the A/D line on the Nasdaq peaked at over 6000 last October and today stood around 2000 on the new high in the average.

Airborne Freight, W. R. Grace, ITT and *UAL* took some hits today and so it wasn't all pink lemonade.

Gold stocks continued to consolidate.

March 19, 1994 - Saturday Afternoon

Option expiration days often have very little relationship with the true trend of the market and Friday was no exception. The triple witching session saw the Dow sprint ahead 30.80 points to close up at the 3895.94 level. But the technical negatives were not hard to find. The Dow was practically a loner, the strength failing to spill over into the Transports and Utilities. The Dow Utility Average fell to a new bear market low of 206.24 and this segment of the market has had the most accurate record of foreshadowing the peak in the stock and bond markets.

The Nasdaq average eked out a new high, widely non-confirmed by its advance/decline line. Despite the Dow industrial rise, the big board A/D line was down on the day and with the Dow up 63 points so far in the month of March, the A/D line is down for the month.

The high/low indicator remains substandard on Dow rallies.

The Climax Indicator rose to +11 but the fact that the 65-stock CLX fell sharply from +9 to +2 shockingly revealed the heavy negative effect of the Transports and Utilities. The Net Field Trend indicator rose sharply from -6 to -1, gaining two fields in *Coca Cola*, and a single field in *General Electric, Merck*, and *Procter & Gamble*. But it is important to point out that the NFI often experiences misleading bubble moves just prior to big downturns, the NFI rising from +2 to +15 between June 27th and July 17th in 1990, just prior to the 635-point drop in the Dow.

The Dow rise did not prevent further declines in *Airborne Freight, Chrysler, Foster-Wheeler, General Motors, W.R. Grace, Great Lakes Chemical, ITT, McDonnell-Douglas, Merrill Lynch. Roadway*, and *UAL*, virtually our entire portfolio of short sales.

Gold stocks had a strong day, every one of our stocks up on the day with many closing at the high of the day.

Summing up, I suspect that we will soon see all of the Friday Dow gain given back, the general market saying nothing has changed. The trend is down.

March 21, 1994 - Monday Evening

I had stated here on Saturday that the large Friday gain was about to be taken back. Today the industrials fell 30.80 points to close down at the 3864.85 level. Once again persistent weakness in the Transports and the Utilities robbed any strength left in the industrials, knocking the 65-stock readings sharply lower.

Bulls have maintained that it is very important that the Dow Utility Average remain above the 206 level. But the Dow Utility Average closed down 0.27 at the 205.97 level, a legitimate downside breakthrough and carrying with it very bearish implications for the days ahead. This is another bear market low.

Of paramount importance today, the advance/decline line fell about 982, putting that key indicator within less than 200 of recording a new bear market low. This tells us that the Dow rise thus far in the month of March is worthless.

The high/low indicator was very weak, showing 54 highs and 115 lows.

The Climax Indicator fell sharply, dropping from +9 to +1. The Net Field Trend indicator remained unchanged at -1.

Auto stocks were weak again today. *McDonnell-Douglas* fell to 113-1/8,*Airborne Freight* was again a casualty, falling to 35-1/2,*Roadway* fell again and *UAL* declined.

Gold stocks were generally lower following Friday's strength. However, this is seen to be a normal consolidation and no stops were triggered.

Bonds took another drubbing, the long bond falling 17-32nds to push the yield up to 6.95%, again within sight of the 7% level. Tomorrow is another critical day.

March 22, 1994 - Tuesday Evening

The Fed played games today, no early announcement and that knocking the market down. Then later in the afternoon they announced that they will raise short term rates a quarter point tomorrow. The long bond soared 1-5/32nds on that news but the Dow lost strength in the final hour, closing down 2.30 points at the 3862.55 level. Transports also lost strength, closing unchanged. Utilities hung on to a nice gain of better than 2 points but coming off a bear market low, will not show significant numbers.

The advance/decline line showed a nice rise but this indicator remained within one-day distance of a new bear market low.

The A/D line had a positive spread of 77/67 but that is nothing to crow about.

The Climax Indicator rose to +6 while the Net Field Trend indicator fell to -3, losing a field in *Goodyear* and a field in *Philip Morris*. *Merck* fell to 30-1/2. One brokerage house lowered their rating from hold to sell.

I got subscribers out at 57 in January 1992. Sharp break not confirmed by OBV. Shortsellers should cover the stock here, it now looking very oversold. *Novell* took a big hit today, falling 3-3/4 to the 20 level. That is another stock we got out of in January 1992 near peak levels.

Despite the strength in bonds today, gold continued to get stronger and the Gold Stock Index topped a 5-point rise. Every precious metal stock we follow rose today. Silver was especially strong, almost reaching a 4-year high. *Sunshine Mining* was under heavy accumulation at 2-1/4. Still an outstanding buy.

March 23, 1994 - Wednesday

Like Tuesday, there was a significant loss of strength on the close, the Dow closing up 6.91 at the 3869.46 level after coming down from an earlier almost 19-point rise. Transports bounced over 10 while the Dow Utility Average fell 1.45 to the 206.50 level, now close to another bear market low.

The advance/decline line rose about 195, keeping that indicator close to bear market lows. Highs and lows showed 81 highs and 42 lows but that disguises the presence of over 600 within a point of new lows. People should ask when those stocks made their highs.

The Climax Indicator fell from a revised +5 to zero, a very flat finish for a day that saw the Dow at one time up almost 19 points. The Net Field Trend indicator stood unchanged at -3.

Glaxo fell to 18-3/8 today, another of the many stocks we got out of at their exact high in January 1992. William O'Neil gave *Glaxo* a peak EPS rating of 96 at the top. *Novell* fell again today, dropping to 19, another that peaked in early 1992.

Again the prime inflation indicators put on a show, the Commodity Research Bureau index showing a breakout to the 130.10 level, a 3-year high. Again gold and silver stocks responded on the upside. *Hecla* made a nice move to 13-7/8, *Homestake* to 21-1/2 and *Newmont Mining* up strongly to 57-1/4. Hotliners got in on *Newmont Mining* at 50-3/4 on the March 10th opening on that important gold/silver buy signal. The Gold Stock Index exploded on the close for a gain of 3.25 points. This was especially bullish in view of the fact that the price of gold fell to 387.40 on the Comex.

The long bond fell 10/32nds to put the yield at 6.88%. Several banks raised their prime rate *from 6% to 6-1/4%* prime rate from 6% to 6-1/4%.

March 24, 1994 - Thursday Evening

The market had no other place to go today except down. The technical bearish signals have been unmistakable. Any excuse would be enough to trigger a landslide. Since the bears are right in a bear market, note that the bearish sentiment has no bullish implications, nor has the record high short interest or the heavy buying of put options. Those three things are the biggest trip wires for the bulls.

Since all March rallying attempts were a sham, it was no surprise to see the Dow shed 48.37 points, dropping to the 3821.09 level. Transports fell over 19 points and the Utility Average dropped sharply to a new bear market low at the 204.06 level, severely busting the 206 level that some bulls thought would hold. The long bond fell 26/32nds to push the yield up to 6.96%

The important advance/decline line tumbled by almost 1200 to another bear market low and the high/low indicator showed 31 highs and 119 lows but that didn't even begin to adequately describe the internal collapse. The Nasdaq mirrored the big board weakness.

The Climax Indicator collapsed from zero to -15 without a single Dow stock recording an up designation of any kind. The Net Field Trend indicator fell to -4, *Sears* losing a field.

Auto stocks got trounced today, *Chrysler* falling to 56-1/8 and *General Motors* falling to 58-1/8. We are short both of them and there is no better evidence than this of the developing bear market.

But again the honors went to the precious metals. The Gold Stock Index rose 2.54 to the 135.66 level. Best looking stocks today included *American Barrick, Battle Mountain, Echo Battle Mountain, Echo Bay, Hecla, Homestake, Horsham, Lac, Nemont Gold, Newmont Mining, Pegasus and Placer-Dome.* In other words, most of them.

March 26, 1994 - Saturday Afternoon

The Dow suffered the worst weekly loss since 1989, falling 120.92 points to the 3774.73 level. So obviously the technicals warning of this bear market have been right for a very long time. Black Friday saw the Dow drop 46.36 points and that was a back-to-back loss of 95 points in two days. That was the change of pattern signalling the almost total inability of any meaningful rebounds from here.

The most decisive warnings were always coming from our count of stocks within a point of new 52-week lows. Having demonstrated that 636 stocks are within a point of new lows, one can picture that most of those stocks made their highs 12 to 20 months ago and longer, at the time we got subscribers to correctly clean house and were most widely criticized for having done so.

Friday saw new bear market lows for the advance/decline line as well as the Dow Utility average, decisively moving under the 206 level, falling to 202.15. That was a more than adequate reflection of the collapse in the long bond which now yields a fat 7%.

Typical of major declines, most analysts were caught bullish at the top, tripped up mainly on sentiment indicators, their forgetting that in a bear market the bears are right.

The Climax Indicator fell from a revised -11 to -15. The Net Field Trend indicator fell from -4 to -5, losing a field in *General Motors.*

The S & P 500 closed under its 200-day trendline and that best shows that there is no room for complacency in this market.

A great week for the precious metal stocks.

The bulls have little or nothing to look forward to as we go into the new week.

March 28, 1994 - Monday Evening

After hitting 7% on Friday, the long bond rose today and gave the stock market a little relief from what earlier had been a smash of 44 points. The Dow cut the loss to 12.38 points at the 3762.35 level, now 216 points under the January 31st high.

While the break in the oil price gave the Transports a little better action relative to the industrials, there were no excuses capable of turning the breadth indicators. Both the big board and the Nasdaq sported horrendous breadth losses pushing both A/D lines to new bear market lows and while some were hoping for a meaningful reversal to the upside in the Dow, don't ever forget *there are no reversals unless also seen in the A/D line.*

The high/low indicator recorded 15 highs and 134 lows and beneath the surface last week saw 322 stocks within a point of new highs and 607 within a point of new lows, very weak numbers showing money leaving the market.

The Climax Indicator rose from -15 to -12 while the Net Field Trend indicator fell to -6, losing a field in *Disney.*

Allied-Signal took a hit today, dropping to 37. Our June 40 puts rose to 3, now showing a 50% gain. *Merrill Lynch,* having a terribly weak chart pattern, fell to 39-1/8, pushing our April 45 puts to 6-1/2 for a gain now of 44%.

Gold stocks showed normal consolidations following the sharp runups seen last week.

March 29, 1994 - Tuesday Evening

Fully exposed to terrible technical indications, the market could only repeat in spades what it has been doing. Today the Dow not only broke 63.05 points to the 3699.30 level, but also broke under the important 200-day trendline in the process. Transports broke to the 1675 area and the Dow Utility Average broke over 4 points to a new bear market low.

Again breadth indicators suffered horrendous bear market breaks and the high/low indicator showed 5 highs and 223 lows. That was simply the inevitable reflection of what our counting technique has been predicting all along, that actual new lows would soon be counted in the hundreds.

Typical of all panic markets, the media features all those who missed the decline.

The Climax Indicator today fell from -12 to -21 while the Net Field Trend indicator fell sharply from -6 to -10, losing a field in*Allied-Signal,* two fields in *McDonalds,* and a field in *United Technologies.*

This market is no longer handling bulls with kid gloves. After having had so many warnings, bulls are now being rudely shaken, paying a steep price for their unwillingness to bend with the trend. Now they are being broken with no mercy.

Our entire list of short sales prospered along with our put options. Only a panic bottom will stop this waterfall decline. Watch the space required in the *Journal* to list all the lows. When it reaches a foot we will be at the bottom. This market looks so weak that one can pick out short sales by merely throwing darts.

Precious metal stocks are OK, simply having a nice consolidation.

March 30, 1994 - Wednesday Evening

Twice today the market mounted failing rallies, the Dow coming within 4 points of zero only to get murdered on the close with the Dow dropping 71.69 points, falling to the 3627.61 level. Transports fell 37.08 points while the Dow Utility Average broke to another bear market low, closing down 3.23 points at the 198.00 level.

Yesterday the Dow broke the important 200-day trendline and the Mutual Fund Index also broke under its 200-day trendline. Under these circumstances no meaningful rallies having any staying power are likely.

The high/low indicator showed 4 highs and 429 lows so obviously we are getting close to some kind of a bounce.

Again the breadth indicators plunged deeply to new bear market lows.

The Climax Indicator fell from -21 to -23 while the Net Field Trend indicator fell to -11, losing a field in *Merck.* These are extremely bearish numbers and show that we are in the very eye of the storm with no bottom in sight.

Again our shorts prospered, huge declines seen in *Allied-Signal, Burlington Northern, Chrysler, General Motors, McDonnell-Douglas, Motorola* and many others.

Golds fell again but no stops were triggered.

With a long weekend ahead the bulls will get no relief tomorrow. Also, any window dressing this time will comprise the jettisoning of weak stocks and there are certainly plenty of these.

April 2, 1994 - Saturday Afternoon

The Dow turned around from an earlier drop of over 60 points to close up 9.21 points at the 3635.96 level. Nevertheless, Thursday was another down day, both advance/decline lines again plunging to new bear market lows. Some even talked of a reversal in the Dow but those only count if matched by reversals to the upside in the A/D lines. Even among the Dow industrial stocks there were more declines than advances.

Again the high/low indicator was showing climactic numbers *but the public is slow to panic.*

The Climax Indicator rose from -23 to -17, very weak numbers for a Dow rise. The Net Field Trend indicator fell to-13, losing a field in *American Express* and field in *Union Carbide.*

Investors were greeted with a shocking bulletin Friday morning, the economy generating 456,000 new jobs, double what economists expected. That put the bond market into an immediate tailspin, the 30-year long bond falling almost two full points and skyrocketing the yield to 7.26%. I was already projecting a drop of 100 points in the Dow for Monday before I heard the Friday morning bulletin on jobs. Now another ratcheting up of interest rates by the Fed is a foregone conclusion, a probable boost in the discount rate on Monday. As I have said so many times here, whatever it takes to put the market down will take place.

The Rukeyser *Wall Street Week* program didn't mention a word about the plunge in the bond market, a shocking omission of such an important piece of news. I think most people were uninformed and thus that will add to the Monday selling.

Gold stocks scored nice comebacks and these along with the silver and platinum stocks are set to go much higher.

April 4, 1994 - Monday Evening

Dropping about 83 points in the early trading, the Dow cut the loss to 42.61, putting the Dow at a new bear market low of 3593.35. Transports took large hits as well as the Dow Utility Average.

The Climax Indicator fell back to -20 but stayed above the -23 reading of last Wednesday. That is a downside non-confirmation. The Net Field Trend indicator was unchanged at -13.

Dropping almost 400 points since January, it is very late right now to do any selling, that best reserved for the bounce that I see ahead. Today we had 4 stocks at new 52-week highs and 643 at new 52-week lows. I had constantly warned a few weeks ago with over 600 stocks within a point of new lows that soon we would see many hundreds of stocks at actual 52-week lows. Well, today is that day and with 643 stocks at new lows that is too close to climactic levels not to take some profits on our short sales. So the call now goes out to cover all shorts. I expect a near-term rally but that should be followed by new Dow lows later in April or in May. If that Dow low is accompanied by important downside technical nonconfirmations, then a buy signal might be issued. But for now we can only cover shorts, taking advantage of the climactic numbers in the stock lows. Also having some very large profits in the put options, all of these should be liquidated.

On the precious metal stocks, the index was down sharply today but the closing prices again threatened no stop outs.

April 5, 1994 - Tuesday Evening

Traders were rewarded with a huge Dow gain of 82.06 points today, putting the average back up to the 3675.41 level. Transports zoomed ahead by over 40 points and the Dow Utility Average soared over 5 points. Having seen this coming on the Monday closing, the entire group of shorts were covered at the opening as well as total liquidation of all the put options.

As pointed out on Monday, reasons for the covering move were manifold. First of all we had excessive profits, then we had an excessive number of actual new stock lows, then we had a significant Climax Indicator downside non-confirmation. That was a clear indication that a bottom was at hand. I said a bottom, not *the* bottom. I expect this brief rallying move will be followed by a renewed slide to new Dow lows. If we can get a contraction in the number of new lows then we will have a tradable rally and a buy signal for a bear market rally.

The Climax Indicator rose sharply today from -20 to -1, thus setting the stage for significant downside non-confirmations on a test of the lows. The Net Field Trend indicator remained unchanged at -13.

What I surmise now for the future of this market over the next several weeks is a resumption of the decline from around the Dow 3750 level with a bottom sharply lower in the May-July time frame. I will be selecting a new string of short sales when I think this bounce has exhausted itself.

Most stocks are expected to be sharply lower this year and I look for a bear market bottom late this year or during the first quarter of 1995.

I have faith in the precious metal stocks, the index today closing up.

April 6, 1994 - Wednesday Evening

Today was a mixed day but definitely a technically favorable one. The Dow managed a positive closing with a gain of 4.32 points at the 3679.73 level. Transports also had a small rise but utilities were weak, reflecting a fresh downturn in the bond market.

The two technical positives of significance were the rise of about 315 in the advance/decline line and a high/low reading of 20 highs and 79 lows. That is a dramatic improvement from Monday's 637 stock lows and increases the probability that fresh lows in the Dow will trigger a tradable buy signal. But for now traders are out, having liquidated all their shorts and put options.

The Climax Indicator fell from a revised +1 to zero while once again the Net Field Trend indicator remained unchanged at -13. The OBV numbers continue to show no up designations other than the technically weak lower ups.

I'm concerned about the gold stocks and see this current weakness as an important test. If we can avoid triggering any stops over the next few days we should have a fresh upturn.

April 7, 1994 - Thursday Evening

There is enough technical power here for a further rise before heading south. The Dow industrial average, after several feints to the downside in the early trading, managed to put on a fairly good show with a rise of 13.53 points to the 3693.26 level. I have cited the 3750-3800 area which stakes out the maximum upside technical resistance.

Again the two strongest indicators at this juncture are the advance/decline line and the high/low indicator. The advance/decline line rose a strong 655 today. The high/low indicator revealed great strength, showing 31 highs and 56 lows. These technical things again underscore the correctness of our covering all shorts at the exact lows two days ago. But current strength is already showing the technical limitations recorded by the On-Balance Volume numbers.

The Climax Indicator showed a rise from zero to +3 but with 5 lower up designations, there was no sustainable technical strength. The Net Field Trend indicator again remained unchanged at -13. Putting all this together, it validates our scenario that the upside is limited and that a test of the lows lies ahead *General Motors* rose to 60-1/8 today on a string of lower up designations, the stock back up into a chart area of maximum upside resistance. Stock requires almost 5 million shares on the upside to gain a field.

The gold shares looked like they met good support today. It is very important that they hold since they are all testing their trendlines.

April 9, 1994 - Saturday Afternoon

As stated here on Thursday, the upside is limited and a test of the lows lies ahead. Friday saw the Dow retreat 19 points to the 3674.26 level, the Transports and Utilities giving ground.

Right now traders are held in check by a glass that is both half full and half empty. On the one hand, traders cannot buy because all the technical indications clearly point to new Dow lows coming. The upside is impeded by the fact that all trendlines have been broken on the downside with rebounds encountering upside resistance as prices approached those lines on the market bounce. One can see that while the Dow almost got back to the 3700 level where the 200-day line is, the S & P 500 is far short of the trendline. Now on the other hand, the high/low indicator makes it increasingly likely that new Dow lows will trigger some kind of a buy signal. Friday saw the new lows at only 77, a far cry from the 637 lows of April 4th. Thus traders must not go short in the face of that one glowing technical positive indication. So we are temporarily deadlocked, awaiting new signals. Investors are out of the market and traders are temporarily neutral.

The Climax Indicator fell back on Friday to -2 from +3, a far cry from the -23 reading of March 30th and so that is a positive. The Net Field Trend indicator remained unchanged at -13.

Precious metal stocks remained in a narrow trading band of support just above key trendlines.

April 11, 1994 - Monday Evening

A trendless mixed market is the best we could come up with today, the Dow industrials rising 14.57 points to the 3688.83 level, Transports and Utilities again heading south.

The Climax Indicator registered a very weak rise to +2, no OBV higher up designations recorded. And once again the Net Field Trend indicator remained unchanged at -13, clearly indicating the continuation of the bear market.

No shorting is being done right now due to the fact that the high/low indicator is showing much stronger numbers compared to the April 4th low. But there is nothing happening now to suggest more than further trendless backing and filling for the rest of April. Too many key indicators have broken down to suggest otherwise.

Johnson & Johnson was strong today following buy recommendations on *Wall Street Week*. The stock fell apart following our sell recommendation in January 1992 at the high of 58-5/8 when William O'Neil assigned it a high Earnings Per Share figure of 91. *Shaw Industries* collapsed today to 18-7/8. We got out of that stock at 40 in January 1992. It had a high Earnings Per Share number of 83 at the time. Keep these things in mind as we enter another corporate earnings season.

Comex Gold fell a sharp 6.90 today but the Gold Stock Index did a better relative job of holding its ground, falling 2.61 to the 121.03 level and off the lows of the day. Just about all the precious metal stocks we follow did close above the lows of the day. *ASA* was the biggest casualty, falling to 39-7/8. We were stopped out at 41. Tomorrow is critical as we get the inflation numbers this week.

April 12, 1994 - Tuesday Evening

The Dow closed down 7.14 at the 3681.69 level and again the Transports and Utilities closed lower. Like in a basketball game, the market seems to be playing for time but the shot clock is building up pressure that a definitive move will soon have to be made. Certainly there is nothing going on the upside here and a test of the lows cannot be long put off.

The high/low indicator today showed 26 highs and 97 lows and thus a successful test of the lows is still the probable outcome.

The Climax Indicator today moved down to -1. Again there were no true On-Balance Volume up designations and that underscores the negative trend of the cluster indicators, there being no up clusters at all. Again there was no change in the Net Field Trend indicator, staying at a very negative -13.

On the precious metal stocks, the Gold Stock Index closed down .04 at the 120.99 level. We were stopped out of *Newmont Gold* at 42-1/2 and *Pegasus Gold* at 17-1/2. Best positioned stocks appear to be *Battle Mountain* which went up today and *Lac Minerals*. But we are definitely on the defensive here and tomorrow is another test following release of the Consumer Price Index.

This is a bear market and no buying is being done, simply the awaiting of another opportunity for putting out a line of shorts. Definitive downside action might be postponed until late May.

April 13, 1994 - Wednesday Evening

As stated yesterday, the market had run out of time and a definitive move would have to be made. The move came today with the Dow down 50 at the worst but cutting that loss to 20.22 in the closing minutes, the Dow at 3661.47. Smaller and more normal changes were seen in the Transports and Utilities.

The high/low indicator continued to strongly suggest that any new Dow low will be widely non-confirmed by the new lows, staying far short of the 637 number recorded on April 4th. Today we had 13 highs and 123 lows. But a similar pattern in 1929 still produced large short sale profits and thus new short sales are being suggested for nervous traders. Furthermore, Karen's new count showed 196 stocks within a point of new highs and 720 within a point of new lows. Thus today's actual numbers provide no technical guarantees that lows will be successfully tested.

Market breadth on both the big board and the Nasdaq has been very weak and thus no reversal to the upside in the Dow will be valid until it is also seen in the breadth numbers.

The Climax Indicator eased down to -5, still far above the recent lows of last week. The Net Field Trend indicator fell to -14, losing a field in *Procter & Gamble.*

Here are the new short sale recommendations along with the suggested put options: *Solectron* SLR June 30, *Varian* VAR August 35, *Vodafone Group* VOD July 80, *Warner-Lambert* WLA July 65, *Wells Fargo* WFC July 145, *Wendys* WEN July 17-1/2, *XTRA* (XTR) June 40, and *Zurn Industries* (ZRN) July 25.

Golds moved lower but there were no fresh stop outs today. I think the September lows are going to hold. Stocks look like a fresh buy here.

April 14, 1994 - Thursday Evening

The Dow managed to eke out a miniscule gain today of 1.75 points, putting the average at the 3663.25 level. Transports plunged almost 10 points while utilities gained a third of a point.

But beneath the surface it became increasingly clear that the April 4th supports are quickly giving way. We are knocking on the door of new lows in the Transports, Utilities, both advance/decline lines and the number of stocks within a point of new lows. With the A/D line down again today, there are no technical guarantees that we won't surpass the April 4th count of 637 new lows.

Today we had 13 highs and 133 lows but that doesn't carry with it the usual degree of bullishness, now knowing there are 720 stocks within a point of new lows.

The Climax Indicator was only able to rise from -5 to -4 today and that is a very poor showing. Once again there are no true OBV up designations. And again the NFI remained at the low level of -14.

I have been wrong several times on *Wells Fargo* in the past but this time it looks like we can score big. The chart shows a double top in the 148 area. I would place a stop loss at 162. Supports to watch for are the 136 level and the 127 level. Breaking those levels, stock is then headed to 106.

The precious metal stocks looked much better today. There were again no stop outs. Group getting ready for next important upleg.

April 16, 1994 - Saturday Afternoon

Option expiration Friday did nothing for the bulls, the Dow falling 1.79 points to the 3661.46 level. Again the advance/decline line fell and brought new lows within one to two day reach.

The latest count of stocks within a point of new highs and lows showed further technical deterioration, stocks within a point of new highs contracting to a new low on this move of 153, and stocks within a point of new lows remaining at the very high level of 719. Again a continuing contraction of the number of actual lows cannot be guaranteed with so many stocks close to new lows.

The Climax Indicator rose from -4 to -3, again with a very bearish set of internal numbers: 2 true ups, 4 higher downs, 9 lower downs, and 8 lower ups. The Net Field Trend indicator improved from -14 to -13, *Allied-Signal* gaining 2 fields, *Alcoa* losing a field, *Exxon* gaining a field, and *General Electric* losing a field.

Among the new short sale recomnmendations, *Wells Fargo* appears the most promising. After rising on Friday to a high of 150-3/8, it fell 5/8ths to close down at 148-3/4. I have projected a fall to as low at 106 on this stock.

DSC Communications, Deere, Dow Chemical, Dow Jones, Dreyfus, Eaton Corp., and *Federal-Mogul* all look like good shorts. More on these later.

The Gold Stock Index plunged 5.08 points on Friday to the 114.10 level. Instead of dictating a bearish opinion, I strongly suspect that we are looking at a selling climax not unlike that of last September. A similar washout back then was immediately followed by a very strong 5-month upswing. On Friday we were only stopped out on *Placer-Dome* It wasn't a one-way street. *Lac Minerals* rose 3/8ths to 8-7/8 for instance. So I would ignore stop levels and buy into this weakness.

April 18, 1994 - Monday Evening

Being a major bear market, anything it takes to put the market lower will take place. Today it was the third Fed tightening action of the year that did it. That put the bond market into a shambles and pulled the rug out from under anything the stock market might have had in mind. The long bond fell 1-1/4 points to send the yield up to 7.40%. The Dow fell 41.05 points closing at the 3620.42 level.

While the industrial average is only 27 points away from the April 4th low, any vision of a successful test vanished as both advance/decline lines collapsed to new bear market lows. The Dow Transports also fell to a new 1994 low today. The high/low indicator showed 14 highs and 179 lows but I strongly suspect that we now have over 800 stocks within a point of new lows and thus those counting on a successful test of the April 4th low may shortly be very disappointed.

The Climax Indicator today fell to -8. There were no OBV true up designations. The Net Field Trend indicator remained unchanged at the revised figure of -13.

Among our new short sales, *Solectron, Vodafone, Wells Fargo, Wendys* and *Xtra* all started off the week with good declines.

Gold stocks again took hits but my conclusion remains the same. We are seen duplicating the washout of last September which within hours saw the start of a 5-month rally. *Pegasus* is the only stock that has violated the September low. I repeat my Saturday advice. Ignore stops and buy into current weakness.

(Continuation of Epilogue- Follows Feb. to April Commentaries)

2. *All Crashes Start As a Correction*

In the early days of the 1994 market downturn the bulls were totally confident that any downturn was a correction in a continuing bull market. Of course all crashes have to initially look like a correction and so the earliest descriptions of the 1994 downturn and the total ignorance on the part of the bulls as to what was to follow was understandable.

Like the July 1990 market top, the stock counting technique flashed the most reliable warnings of the developing technical disaster.

When the number of big board stocks within a point of new lows escalated to 582 on July 24, 1990, it was putting the big lie on the Dow which at that time was down 77 points off the bull cycle high. I was pleading with my letter subscribers to get their house in order. Less than two weeks later, the Kuwait invasion news sent the Dow on a decline that was to see a 635-point drop.

The warnings by March 1, 1994, similar to those of July 1990, were getting louder. Karen's count showed no less than 611 big board common stocks within a point or less of new 52-week lows. Making the comparison still more dramatic, the identical gurus who were caught 100% bullish in July 1990 at the top were the same ones preaching the bullish gospel in early 1994, one of the better known ones so positive that the decline would end soon that no defensive measures were taken.

While the advance/decline line was down 2,548 between the day of the Dow high in July 1990 and the 24th of that month, the advance/decline line in 1994 was already down 6,000 by March 3rd.

3. *The Mutual Fund Cover-Up*

We had only 35 funds in 1949 and it only required a small column to list all the closing bid and ask prices. My memories of this go back to the days of the old *New York World Telegram* when Ralph Hendershot was the financial editor. So over the past 45 years I have watched the number snowball all the way to over 4,000 various types of funds today, everybody getting into the act with most fund managers never having experienced a major bear market. I saw in this the most dangerous of parabolic curves.

Getting down to basics, what is a mutual fund? A mutual is a collection of stocks. The main advantage to owning shares in a mutual fund is that one acquires diversification among hundreds of stocks that the individual could never hope to privately have a stake in. But there is no reason for there being over 4,000 funds when 50 or 100 could provide the same protection of diversification. So again, why 4,000? There is only one possible answer. It comes down to one word: Greed. In forming a new fund there are new management fees but there are no new advantages to the public ownership. The same objectives can be achieved by a handful of funds. Seeing the parabolic proliferation of the equity funds, it was easy to predict the coming downfall in so many of them. One could try to make a case that a bull market justifies their existence, but few were aware of their future in a bear market.

Memories of the terminal proliferation of the investment trusts of the 1920's had long since faded, history showing that most of those had gone out of business by 1932. Burton Malkiel, in his *A Random Walk Down Wall Street*, reminds us of the Mates fund in the go-go years of the late 1960's. Mates was the hottest of the funds and between 1968 and 1974 it fell from $15 a share to $1. Mates liquidated and opened a singles bar in New York.

The funds in 1994 had most of the public's money at the top and in their heart of hearts the managers knew they had painted themselves into a corner, wanting to cut their personal losses but desperate now to keep the public fully invested in the fund shares. So the 1994 rout led the fund managers to fashion a litany of psychological persuasion to encourage the public to stay with the funds and not sell their shares. While this strategy of encouragement had a brief rallying effect, temporarily shoring up a few leaks, even King Canute couldn't hold back the tides in a bear market and there were no Canutes on Wall Street in 1994. While the waves would cast a few back on the shore, the technical undertow was too dangerous and too persistent for rallying attempts to have any lasting strength.

4. *How the 1994 Bear Market Was Signalled*

I have consistently underscored the high/low indicator as the most important of all technical indicators. I hold that a genuine bull market requires a constant expansion in the number of new stock highs and a constant contraction in the number of stock lows. I maintained a 100% bullish outlook in the 1990-92 portion of the bull cycle by simply following the steady expansion in the number of stock highs. Typically on the other side of the market were the fundamentalists, these being the economists and the media. Since we were going through a recession in 1991, economists and the media were bearish on stocks. Then a technical bell sounded. I heard it very clearly and correctly acted on it. The internal top of the bull cycle was signalled. The number of new stock highs peaked at 335 on December 31, 1991, never to see that number again in that cycle. I correctly began to exit the market in January 1992, the month that saw so many stocks reach their peak prices.

As we were getting out of the market, the fundamentalists were moving back in, erroneously led to believe that the popular Earnings Per Share ratings seen in *Investor's Business Daily* were a reliable guide to when to buy a stock. Zacks Investment Research was equally guilty in encouraging investment at the worst of times. So while the insiders were getting out of *U. S. Surgical* in January 1992 at 134-1/2 a share, others got sucked in at the top because it was assigned an Earnings Per Share rating of 99 and a Relative Strength rating of 95 right at the exact top, getting bullish fundamental endorsements at the very worst of times. Zacks Investment Research, in a January 1994 ad, stated that corporate earnings is the most powerful force driving any stock's price. Of course, nothing could be further from the truth. To support their erroneous claim, they show a chart of *U.S. Surgical* with their falling earnings estimate. But their chart started when the price of the stock was already down to 50. Where were they when the stock was at 134-1/2? My message for Zacks is simple. The most powerful force driving any stock's price is supply and demand, certainly not corporate earnings.

Stocks that peaked in January 1992 were not isolated examples. The high/low indicator had underscored the importance of those peaks. Since most brokerage firms recommend stocks at peak earnings, it was amusing throughout the 1992-93 period to see these firms reduce their original buy recommendations made at the peak to a hold rating. Nothing frustrates a customer more than to be put into a stock at the top and then told to hold it while it declines. But that is exactly the advice most people got on the stocks that peaked in January 1992 and later collapsed.

So right at the internal peak we see that brokerage firms were mostly recommending stocks that later declined. We saw that Louis Rukeyser's Elves recorded their peak +6 reading in January 1992 and we noted that he began his newsletter right near the time of the internal peak. I had also noted at that time that William O'Neil's New USA Mutual Fund was formed after most stocks had seen their peak prices.

Throughout the 1992-93 period my critics countered my negative stance by doing what they always do after most stocks have seen their highs. They leaned on the popular averages which always are the last to record their peak levels. My warnings mostly fell on deaf ears while the bearish evidence continued to build. Those analysts who merely leaned on the published number of actual stock highs and lows failed to see the vital transition showing the internal contraction in the number within a point of new 52-week highs and the rapid expansion in the number within a point or less of 52-week lows.

5. *There Is Little Relief From the Bear Market*

For awhile the bulls thought they would have the luxury of escaping the ravages of a bear market in U.S. stocks by simply directing most of their new buying into the foreign stock funds. Almost invariably when the public gets an idea most of its benefits have already been seen. Besides what we saw in our technique of counting stocks within a point or less of new 52-week highs and lows, we saw in January 1994 that the majority of new highs were increasingly showing up in the foreign stock funds and that raised the odds that the January high in the Dow was not only a high here, but also a global high.

John Bogle, founder of the Vanguard Funds, stated that 80% of all monies pouring into the funds in early 1994 was going into the foreign funds. Isn't that typical? It comes in right at the top. It added to the evidence that there was to be little relief from the developing bear market. All markets began to decline simultaneously.

6. *Deep Shadows*

Since the Dow Jones Averages are the property of Dow Jones and the *Wall Street Journal*, they have sought to keep the myth alive as long as possible that their averages and the market are one and the same. A perfect example of this was the market of April 19, 1994. On that day the big board advance/decline line plunged another 742 to a new bear market low and the Nasdaq advance/decline line plunged 857 to a new bear market low. But because the Dow-Jones Industrial average was only down 0.60, the Journal the next day headlined their market coverage by stating that stock prices had only slipped a fraction.

They didn't say that the Dow slipped a fraction but that stocks slipped a fraction. If the Dow and the market are the same then it could be shown that most stocks peaked on January 31, 1994 and only recently took a big plunge. Most advisors were not only caught off guard by the 1994 drop in the Dow, but their clients were under water all through 1993. I documented the fact that most stocks had peaked prior to January 1, 1993 just as they had in 1928 well before the 1929 crash. I stood virtually alone in getting people out of *Amgen* at 80, *Apple* at 67, *Glaxo* at 37, *Merck* at 57, *U.S. Surgical* at 134-1/2 back in 1992 at their exact peaks. The serious 1992-93 market dichotomy was recognized at the time it was happening and my followers were able to sidestep the horrendous declines those and hundreds of other stocks suffered in that 1992-93 period, declines that were ignored by those who relied on the Dow Averages for their market guidance.

7. *Now They Tell You That Cash Was King*

My market advice for investors throughout 1993 was to stay out of the market. I had to take a lot of heat for that advice. But it took until April 21, 1994 for the media to catch up with the truth. On that day appeared a major article in the *Wall Street Journal* by John Dorfman, summed up in the first seven words of the headline: *CASH BEAT STOCKS, BONDS IN PAST YEAR*

Wall Street didn't want you to know that. I didn't hear a single comment afterwards in the financial media about that article. And they never discussed the bearish dichotomy that I had documented throughout the 1992-93 period. And they never challenged those who used Earnings Per Share numbers that I had proved sucked in many investors right at the top in so many stocks. No, the media flashed no warnings when the investing public most needed them.

Their warnings always came late. The April 25, 1994 *Barron's* cover feature was *When Stocks Were Hot, Insiders Quickly Exited.* Howard R. Gold stated on the inside pages:

> "How toppy was the stock market? Just ask all the insiders who were selling out. The stock market's recent turbulence may have caught many investors by surprise, but not some of the biggest and shrewdest. Even as the market was roaring ahead late last year and early this year, the cognoscenti were quietly liquidating hundreds of millions of dollars in shares of such highflying stocks as *Snapple, Perrigo, First USA, AutoZone* and *Nextel Communications*. If mutual funds were willing to pay up for stocks, these insiders were more than willing to sell."

But *Barron's* runs the article on April 25th after the Dow is down 400 points.

8. *The Coming Mutual Fund Collapse*

With most mutual funds facing the major problem of a serious bear market, they were going to bend over backwards with their efforts to keep the public in the market. That entailed a great deal of jawboning. They preached the benefits of balanced funds, foreign funds, tax free municipals, dollar cost averaging, giving mutual fund shares as gifts, and always stressed the long-term goals of mutual fund investing. One fund went so far as to provide crayons and coloring books for young investors.

My dire forecast for the industry heavily depended on my knowledge of the parabolic curve. That had stood me in good stead in calling the top in gold and silver in January 1980 and again in calling the peak in UAL before the October 1989 mini -crash. All parabolics are followed by collapse.

9. *The Parabolic In Newsletters*

In parallel fashion, the proliferation in the number of market newsletters further underscored the pinnacle of the cycle.

10. *And Once Again the People Indicators*

For years I have urged my followers to keep a diary. Not only is it good advice in general, but it is particularly useful when following the stock market. The stock market is most rewarding to those who have a long memory. Thanks to Dan Dorfman being completely devoid of memory, that *USA Today* columnist and daily CNBC-TV commentator unwittingly handed me one of my most reliable people indicators on a silver platter. I called the indicator The Anderson Effect.

In the Dan Dorfman column which appeared in the April 29, 1994 edition of *USA Today* his title was *IDS PRO BETS DOW WILL CLIMB TO 4200.* The entire column was devoted to Peter Anderson's extremely bullish market forecast, a view shared by Dorfman. Peter Anderson runs IDS Advisory, with $10 billion in stocks. He was so bullish that his fund had no cash reserves.

The story gets better. Since my daily diary is replete with not only everything personal, it is probably the most complete data bank on the stock market including forecasts by others as well as newspaper clippings. In reviewing my July 1990 notes on that stock market peak, lo and behold I came across the Dan Dorfman *USA Today* column of July 6, 1990. His title was *BULL SEES BEST OF ALL WORLDS FOR STOCK PLAYERS.* You guessed it. That Dan Dorfman column was devoted to Anderson's bullish stock market forecast right at the top.

Anderson gave Dorfman his three top picks in that July 1990 interview and they were *Dayton Hudson, Loews,* and *Great Western Financial.* Checking those out in the M. C. Horsey chart book, here is what happened to those stocks between July 1990 and December 1990:

	July 1990	December 1990
Dayton-Hudson	79	47
Loews	120	76
Great Western Financial	21	8

So Peter Anderson's July 1990 forecast is a matter of record and that added considerable interest to his extremely bullish April 1994 forecast because I then had a new indicator to work with. Since market indicators are my business, then the Anderson Effect was germane to technical analysis and was just as valid as any other proven people indicator. We are all the beneficiaries of the fact that Dan Dorfman never researches his columns. Thus I thank him for contributing *The Anderson Effect*.

And a word on gold. The last paragraph in the April 29, 1994 Dorfman column thus took on special interest. Dorfman asked Anderson his view on gold. Anderson's answer was classic. He said "Fools gold. There's no world class political crisis and no inflation. And they are the gold sparks. Also, gold stocks are way ahead of the rise in the gold price. I definitely see them under-performing."

That was probably the best endorsement I was going to see on gold. And it pointed up a common denominator in all the stock market forecasts made in 1994 by the wrong-way bulls. All of them had missed the 1994 drop and they all harped on the *no-inflation.*

So Dan Dorfman put himself on record in April, 1994 as an extreme bull on stocks and a bear on gold, endorsing Anderson's views. Interestingly enough, the price of gold soared on May 6, 1994.

11. ***Barbarians At the Gate***

By May 1994 there were too many bulls counting on a big summer rally having already started. I told my letter subscribers to pay particular attention to the numbers we were getting on the stock count of big board stocks within a point or less of new 52-highs and lows. The bulls felt they had an adrenaline shot when the Fed hiked rates for the fourth time, the Dow rising 107 points that week. But there were still far too many big board stocks within a point or less of new lows. I saw these as the technical barbarians at the gate set to trigger a soaring number of new lows the next time the market stumbled.

I noted that stocks knocking on the doors of new lows had risen in number to as high as 814 on the May 13th count with actual lows at 115 while the count of May 17th reflecting the day of the almost 50-point rally on the Fed rate hike showed 755 stocks within a point of new lows with actual lows at 108. That was just one of several technical potholes that detracted from that upswing.

12. *Human Nature the Same For the Past 65 Years*

And in a final fitting tribute to the validity of the OBV indicators, I present here for the first time my Climax Indicator and Net Field Trend indicator readings for the period from May 31, 1929 through November 13, 1929 to prove that those OBV indicators peaked in July 1929 and got everybody out of the market before the great crash. Those exclusive numbers comprise the final table in the Appendix. Market students will find that table of extreme importance.

Section XII
APPENDIX

Appendix

The Paradox of the Two Black Pyramids

A technical mystery that continued to intrigue me all through the third bull phase of the 1990-94 bull cycle involved the Trendline *Short Range Oscillator.* That oscillator is charted on the back cover of Trendline's *Daily Action Stock Charts.* The glaring feature of the chart comprises two very prominent advances which are blacked in to form two pyramids. Those twin peaks represented the radically overbought markets of February 1991 and January 1992. The formation of the first black pyramid coincided with the heavy buying which was triggered by the Persian Gulf war. The second black pyramid formed the overbought market that followed the December 11, 1991 bottom. What fascinated me was the fact that all during the remainder of the 1990-94 bull cycle the Trendline *Short Range Oscillator* never again traced out another black pyramid despite a gain of over 600 points in the Dow.

Since the Trendline's oscillator is based on the *advance/decline line,* what was preventing the oscillator from duplicating the first two pyramids? Something was wrong and I was determined to find out what it was. I was convinced that it had something to do with the *dichotomy.*

The high/low indicator solved the mystery. In the 1992-93 period *we saw a better than 94% contraction in the number of new stock highs.* That strongly suggested to me that the next black pyramid would be an *inverted* one in which the Short Range Oscillator became extremely oversold and formed a downside pyramid representing a very large decline in the stock market.

The Search For the Third Black Pyramid

I had to do some detective work. First I had to reconstruct the Four Column numbers prior to the start of the black pyramid Persian Gulf war rally as well as the Four Column numbers prior to the second black pyramid December 1991 rally. If I could find a fit with the reverse numbers of the first two black pyramids *then I would have identified the start of that elusive third pyramid, the strong technical signal for an equal and opposite sharp drop of many hundreds of points in the Dow.*

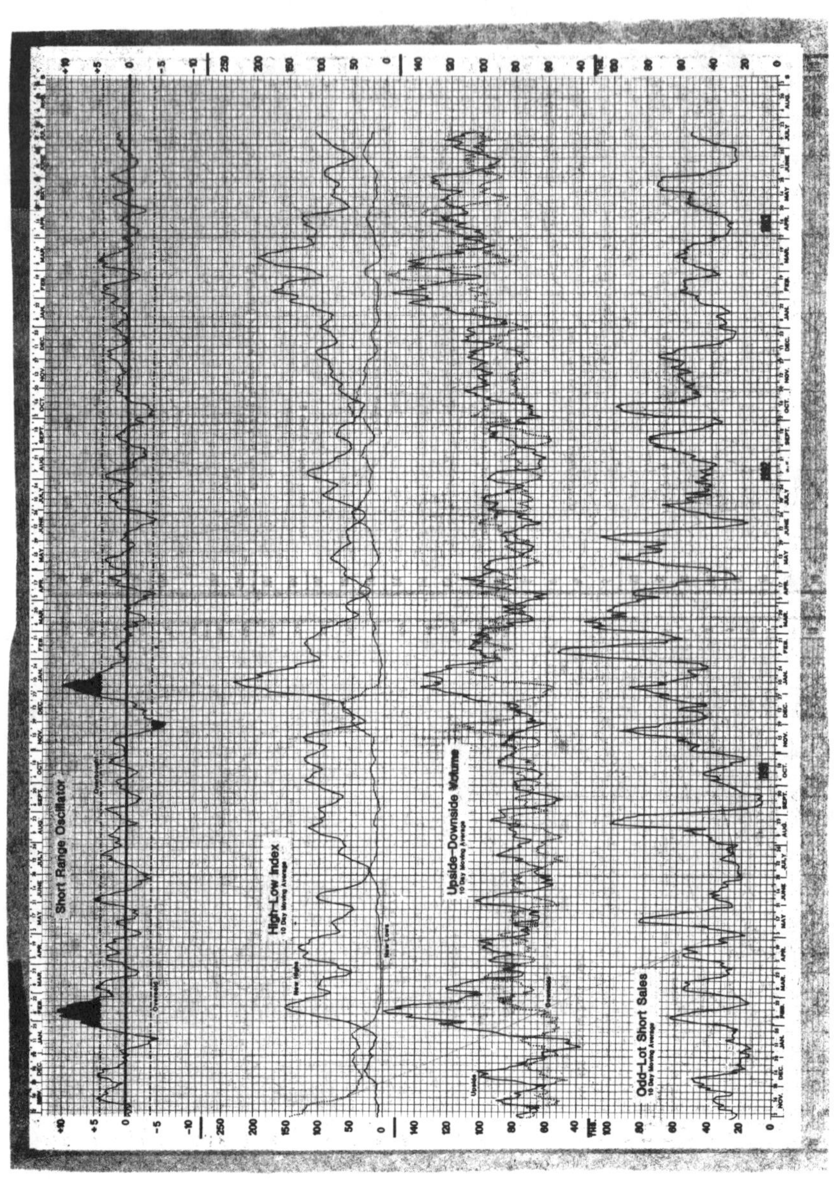

Going beyond just looking for a fit between the two sets of 4-column numbers and their reciprocals, I looked for a possible answer in their separate columns.

In my relentless search for the third and very elusive inverted black pyramid, I required the current series of 65-stock 4-column numbers to match either the reciprocal numbers preceding the first black pyramid or those preceding the second black pyramid.

Reciprocal				Actual Series Preceding Feb. 1994 Break			
Date	Dow	CLX	Four Columns	Date	Dow	CLX	Four Columns
11/29	2518.81	+14	12-8-2-12	12/20	3755.21	+8	11-2-8-7
11/30	2559.65	-28	2-17-13-0	12/21	3745.15	+1	6-4-9-8
12/3	2565.59	-27	4-12-21-2	12/22	3762.19	+16	16-5-3-8
12/4	2579.70	-40	2-11-32-1	12/23	3757.72	+8	11-7-3-7
12/5	2610.40	-42	2-10-36-2	12/27	3792.93	+15	14-2-4-7
12/6	2602.48	-23	6-8-25-4	12/28	3793.77	+15	15-7-3-10
12/7	2590.10	-5	6-2-14-5	12/29	3794.33	0	12-14-5-7
12/10	2596.78	-5	8-2-12-1	12/30	3775.88	-9	7-12-6-2
12/11	2586.14	+4	7-2-8-7	12/31	3754.09	-16	6-17-6-1
12/12	2622.28	-29	3-8-26-2	1/3	3756.60	-14	7-15-10-4
12/13	2614.36	-12	3-1-17-3	1/4	3783.90	+4	11-6-8-7
12/14	2593.81	0	4-5-12-13	1/5	3798.82	-3	12-12-12-9
12/17	2593.32	-2	3-5-12-12	1/6	3803.88	+1	14-7-13-7
12/18	2626.73	-20	1-6-18-3	1/7	3820.77	0	7-3-7-3
12/19	2626.73	-10	2-5-16-9	1/10	3865.51	+26	20-3-0-9
12/20	2629.51	-5	4-4-14-19	1/11	3850.31	-8	8-13-5-2
12/21	2633.66	-12	8-3-23-6	1/12	3848.63	-1	9-9-7-6
12/24	2621.29	+3	8-2-10-7	1/13	3842.43	-6	8-10-9-5
12/26	2637.13	-10	3-2-14-3	1/14	3867.20	+6	8-6-7-11
12/27	2625.50	+5	4-2-10-13	1/17	3870.29	0	10-8-9-7
12/28	2629.21	+6	2-3-9-16	1/18	3870.29	+5	14-7-11-9
12/31	2633.66	-7	0-7-10-10	1/19	3884.37	+6	15-6-7-4
1/2	2610.64	+14	5-2-17-18	1/20	3891.96	+8	14-5-5-4
1/3	2573.51	+19	10-4-6-19	1/21	3914.48	-4	13-9-11-3
1/4	2566.09	+10	9-5-19-15	1/24	3912.79	0	11-8-7-4
1/7	2522.77	+32	11-1-1-23	1/25	3895.34	-4	9-11-7-5
1/8	2509.41	+11	9-7-7-16	1/26	3908.00	+3	7-9-3-8
1/9	2470.31	+26	17-2-7-18	1/27	3926.30	+11	12-7-2-8
1/10	2498.76	-1	6-3-9-5	1/28	3945.43	+14	10-6-1-11
1/11	2501.49	+9	10-5-5-9	1/31	3978.36	+33	22-2-0-13
1/14	2483.91	+24	17-4-3-14	2/1	3964.01	+13	13-5-0-5
1/15	2490.59	+7	7-6-3-9	2/2	3975.54	+11	10-3-3-7
1/16	2508.91	-5	8-11-7-5	2/3	3967.66	-2	8-11-4-5
1/17	2623.51	-47	0-23-24-0	2/4	3871.42	-33	0-20-14-1

There were enough similarities here to see the February 4, 1994 break as an important kickoff on the downside, the opposite of the Persian Gulf war kickoff on the upside.

Now we will try the same exercise with the reciprocal of the second black pyramid.

Using the same technique of comparing the current readings with the *reciprocal* readings preceding the first and second black pyramids, I saw a comparison of current numbers to the reciprocal approach numbers leading up to the October 9, 1992 bottom as a legitimate exercise proving the validity of the January 31, 1994 top and the plunge that followed.

Date	Dow	CLX	Reciprocal Four Columns	Date	Dow	CLX	Actual Four Columns
9/14	3376.22	-26	4-14-19-3	1/10	3865.51	+26	20-3-0-9
9/15	3327.32	+7	8-3-4-3	1/10	3850.31	-8	8-13-5-2
9/16	3319.21	+10	12-4-7-9	1/12	3848.63	-1	9-9-7-6
9/17	3315.70	+10	11-2-5-6	1/13	3842.43	-6	8-10-9-5
9/18	3327.05	-7	15-4-11-3	1/14	3867.20	+6	8-6-7-11
9/21	3320.82	+2	5-4-5-6	1/17	3870.29	0	10-8-9-7
9/22	3280.85	+17	8-3-2-14	1/18	3884.37	+5	14-7-11-9
9/23	3278.69	+14	12-6-4-12	1/19	3884.37	+6	15-6-7-4
9/24	3287.87	-4	5-7-6-4	1/20	3891.96	+8	14-5-5-4
9/25	3250.30	+13	11-3-4-9	1/21	3914.48	-4	13-9-11-3
9/28	3276.26	-10	5-13-5-3	1/24	3912.79	0	11-8-7-4
9/29	3266.80	-5	7-11-6-5	1/25	3895.34	-4	9-11-7-5
9/30	3271.66	-2	9-12-8-9	1/26	3908.00	+3	7-9-3-8
10/1	3254.37	+19	11-5-3-16	1/27	3926.30	+11	12-7-2-8
10/2	3200.59	+32	16-1-1-18	1/28	3945.43	+14	10-6-1-11
10/5	3179.00	+33	23-4-3-17	1/31	3978.36	+33	22-2-0-13
10/6	3178.19	+12	13-3-6-8	2/1	3964.01	+13	13-5-0-5
10/7	3152.25	+24	17-1-2-10	2/3	3967.66	-2	8-1--4-5
10/8	3176.03	-1	9-8-5-3	2/4	3871.42	-33	0-20-14-1

Here the fit is excellent, even to the matching 33 readings. I was totally satisfied that from three standpoints (reciprocals of approaches to first and second black pyramids and the reciprocal approach to the October 1992 bottom) the January 31, 1994 top was of major significance as well as the decline that I expected would follow.

The last test was to check the pattern of the single columns. There again the available numbers here showed the technical intelligence of pattern recognition.

For the rest of the bull cycle I was looking for two elusive 4-column combinations, the reciprocals of January 16, 1991 and December 11, 1991. Those magic 65-stock 4-column combinations were:

8 - 11 - 7 - 5
15 - 8 - 6 - 6

It was my fervent belief that either of those combinations would be immediately followed by a break of several hundred points in the Dow.

I had believed that I finally saw the start of the elusive inverted third black pyramid on February 4, 1994.

The Paramount Communications Collapse

The *Paramount Communications* chart first caught my eye in November 1993. I saw the sharp rise from 59 to 83 on the titanic battle for control between *Viacom* and *QVC*. Right away I saw that something was wrong. Between September and November the stock had traded more shares than the total for the year up until the time the battle for control began. But, surprisingly, the stock literally went nowhere on that huge amount of volume. So I was looking at a classic case of stock churning. It was at that point that I predicted a coming collapse for the *Paramount* shares, recommending the shares as a short sale on any drop more than 5 points off the top. The short sale wasn't triggered until late December 1993 when the stock closed under the 78 level.

Here is how the stock looked in November 1993:

Paramount OBV
1993-94

Date	Price	Change	On-Balance Volume	
Oct. 28	80-3/8	-5/8	-1,300,000	
Oct. 29	80-5/8	+1/4	- 293,400	
Nov. 1	79-3/4	-7/8	-1,037,100	
Nov. 2	79-1/8	-5/8	-2,070,000	
Nov. 3	78-5/8	-1/2	-3.248,400	
Nov. 4	78-3/4	+1/8	-2,105,500	
Nov. 5	80-1/4	+1-1/2	263,700	UP
Nov. 8	82-1/8	+1-7/8	3,019,500	UP
Nov. 9	81	-1-1/8	275,900	

Nov. 10	80-1/2	-1/2	-1,263,200	
Nov. 11	82-1/2	+2	160,600	
Nov. 12	83	+1/2	2,350,900	
Nov. 15	80-1/8	-2-7/8	-347,300	
Nov. 16	78-5/8	-2-3/4	-3,378,000	DOWN
Nov. 17	77-1/2	-7/8	-7.445,400	DOWN
Nov. 18	77	-1/2	-10,329,700	DOWN
Nov. 19	76-3/8	-5/8	-14,847,900	DOWN
Nov. 22	79	+2-5/8	-7,091,500	
Nov. 23	76-1/4	-2-3/4	-9,836,700	
Nov. 24	80-1/8	+3-7/8	-6,292,800	Up
Nov. 26	79-7/8	-1/4	-8,083,800	
Nov. 29	78-1/2	-1-3/8	-9,704,500	
Nov. 30	78-3/4	+1/4	-8,387,000	
Dec. 1	78-7/8	+1/8	-7.720,200	
Dec, 2	79	+1/8	-6,768,100	
Dec. 3	79-3/8	+3/8	-5,871,000	Up
Dec. 6	79-1/4	Unch	-5,871.000	Up
Dec, 7	79-1/4	-1/8	-7,042,400	
Dec. 8	79-1/4	Unch	-7,042,400	
Dec. 9	82	+2-3/4	-3,617,200	Up
Dec. 10	81-1/8	-7/8	-6,210,000	
Dec, 13	80-3/8	-3/4	-7,718,000	Down
Dec. 14	81-1/8	+3/4	-5,229,000	
Dec. 15	81	-1/8	-7,243,300	
Dec. 16	81-1/4	+1/4	-6,345,500	
Dec. 17	81-5/8	+3/8	-4,869,200	Up
Dec. 20	82	+3/8	-2,950,300	UP
Dec. 21	80-1/4	-1-3/4	-6,091,700	
Dec. 22	79-5/8	-5/8	-8,041,100	DOWN
Dec. 23	78-5/8	-1	-9,806,600	DOWN
Dec. 27	78-1/8	-1/2	-11,256,100	DOWN
Dec. 28	77-7/8	-1/4	-12,650,300	DOWN
Dec. 29	77-7/8	Unch,	-12,650,000	DOWN
Dec, 30	77-1/2	-3/8	-13,329,300	DOWN
Dec. 31	77-3/4	+1/4	-12,212,100	
Jan. 3	78-1/4	+1/2	-11,447,600	
Jan. 4	77-1/2	-3/4	-12,651,400	
Jan. 5	78-1/4	+3/4	-11,062,800	Up
Jan. 6	78-1/2	+1/4	-9,977,800	Up
Jan. 7	79-1/4	+3/4	-8,278,900	Up

Jan. 10	77-3/8	-1-7/8	-9,788,200	
Jan. 11	77-3/8	Unch	-9,788,200	
Jan. 12	77-1/4	-1/8	-10,943,600	
		....		
Feb. 22	74-5/8	-3/8	-22,290,800	DOWN

Table 1
Dow 65 Stock 4-Column Analysis

Date	Dow	CLXCum.	CLX	Four Columns	True	EW
1993						
11/ 1	3692.61	+ 7	+ 7	9 - 7 - 3 - 8	+ 6	+ 5
11/ 2	3697.64	+ 4	+11	9 - 7 - 5 - 7	+10	+ 9
11/ 3	3661.87	-19	- 8	3 -10 -14 - 2	- 1	+ 6
11/ 4	3624.98	-31	-39	1 -11 -22 - 1	-22	- 5
11/ 5	3643.43	- 5	-44	4 - 4 - 9 - 4	-27	-10
11/ 8	3647.90	- 5	-49	7 - 6 - 8 - 2	-28	- 7
11/ 9	3640.07	-10	-59	7 - 6 -14 - 3	-35	-11
11/10	3663.55	+10	-49	8 - 2 - 8 -12	-35	-21
11/11	3662.43	- 3	-52	9 - 7 - 9 - 4	-35	-18
11/12	3684.51	+14	-38	10 - 3 - 4 -11	-29	-20
11/15	3677.52	+7	-31	9 - 4 - 8 -10	-28	-25
11/16	3710.77	+23	- 8	16 - 3 - 4 -14	-16	-24
11/17	3704.35	- 5	-13	6 -10 - 5 - 4	-15	-17
11/18	3685.34	- 2	-15	7 -12 - 3 - 6	-11	- 7
11/19	3694.01	- 2	-17	10 -11 - 5 - 4	- 6	+ 5
11/22	3670.25	- 8	-25	7 - 8 -11 - 4	-10	+ 5
11/23	3674.17	- 1	-26	4 - 7 - 6 - 8	-12	+ 2
11/24	3687.58	+11	-15	7 - 5 - 3 -12	- 8	- 1
11/26	3683.95	+13	- 2	8 - 3 - 2 -10	- 2	- 2
11/29	3677.80	+ 7	+ 5	11 - 9 - 3 - 8	+ 6	+ 7
11/30	3683.95	+ 5	+10	8 - 6 - 5 - 8	+ 3	+ 8
12/ 1	3697.08	+ 7	+17	9 -11 - 4 -13	+ 8	+11
12/ 2	3702.08	+ 9	+26	6 - 7 - 3 -13	+11	+ 8
12/ 3	3704.07	+ 4	+30	5 - 5 - 5 - 9	+11	+ 4
12/ 6	3710.21	+11	+41	9 - 4 - 4 -10	+16	+ 3
12/ 7	3718.88	+12	+53	7 - 7 - 0 -12	+23	+ 5
12/ 8	3734.53	+13	+66	7 - 4 - 2 -12	+28	+ 2
12/ 9	3729.78	+ 7	+73	11 - 7 - 3 - 6	+36	+11
12/10	3740.67	+ 6	+79	7 - 8 - 4 -11	+39	+11
12/13	3764.43	+12	+91	13 - 6 - 5 -10	+47	+15
12/14	3742.63	- 9	+82	10 -16 - 9 - 6	+48	+26
12/15	3716.92	- 8	+74	9 -18 - 8 - 9	+49	+36
12/16	3726.14	+ 2	+76	11 -10 - 8 - 9	+52	+40
12/17	3751.57	+10	+86	14 - 8 - 5 - 9	+61	+48
12/20	3755.21	+ 8	+94	11 - 2 - 8 - 7	+64	+46
12/21	3745.15	+ 1	+95	6 - 4 - 9 - 8	+61	+39
12/22	3762.19	+16	+111	16 - 5 - 3 - 8	+74	+49
12/23	3757.72	+ 8	+119	11 - 7 - 3 - 7	+82	+56
12/27	3792.93	+15	+134	14 - 2 - 4 - 7	+92	+61
12/28	3793.77	+15	+149	15 - 7 - 3 -10	+104	+70
12/29	3794.33	0	+149	12 -14 - 5 - 7	+111	+84
12/30	3775.88	- 9	+140	7 -12 - 6 -12	+112	+85
12/31	3754.09	-16	+124	6 -17 - 6 - 1	+112	+101
1994						
1/ 3	3756.60	-14	+110	7 -15 -10 - 4	+109	+109
1/ 4	3783.90	+ 4	+114	11 - 6 - 8 - 7	+112	+111
1/ 5	3798.82	- 3	+111	12 -12 -12 - 9	+112	+114
1/ 6	3803.88	+ 1	+112	14 - 7 -13 - 7	+113	+115
1/ 7	3820.77	0	+112	7 - 3 - 7 - 3	+113	+115
1/10	3865.51	+26	+138	20 - 3 - 0 - 9	+133	+129
1/11	3850.80	- 8	+130	8 -13 - 5 - 2	+136	+143
1/12	3848.63	- 1	+129	9 - 9 - 7 - 6	+138	+148
1/13	3842.43	- 6	+123	8 -10 - 9 - 5	+137	+152
1/14	3867.20	+ 6	+129	8 - 6 - 7 -11	+138	+148
1/17	3870.29	0	+129	10 - 8 - 9 - 7	+139	+149
1/18	3870.29	+ 5	+134	14 - 7 -11 - 9	+142	+150
1/19	3884.37	+ 6	+140	15 - 6 - 7 - 4	+150	+160

1/20	3891.96	+ 8	+148	14 - 5 - 5 - 4	+159	+170
1/21	3914.48	- 4	+144	13 - 9 -11 - 3	+161	+178
1/24	3912.79	0	+144	11 - 8 - 7 - 4	+165	+186
1/25	3895.34	- 4	+140	9 -11 - 7 - 5	+167	+194
1/26	3908.00	+ 3	+143	7 - 9 - 3 - 8	+171	+199
1/27	3926.30	+11	+154	12 - 7 - 2 - 8	+181	+208
1/28	3945.43	+14	+168	10 - 6 - 1 -11	+190	+212
1/31	3978.36	+33	+201	22 - 2 - 0 -13	+212	+223
2/ 1	3964.01	+13	+214	13 - 5 - 0 - 5	+225	+236
2/ 2	3975.54	+11	+225	10 - 3 - 3 - 7	+232	+239
2/ 3	3967.66	- 2	+223	8 -11 - 4 - 5	+236	+249
2/ 4	3871.42	-33	+190	0 -20 -14 - 1	+222	+254
2/ 7	3906.32	-14	+176	3 -12 - 9 - 4	+216	+256
2/ 8	3906.03	-14	+162	6 -12 - 8 - 0	+214	+266
2/ 9	3931.92	+ 3	+165	7 - 6 - 5 - 7	+216	+267
2/10	3895.34	-14	+151	5 -10 -11 - 2	+210	+269
2/11	3894.78	-10	+141	7 - 9 -10 - 2	+207	+273
2/14	3904.06	- 3	+138	5 - 5 - 8 - 5	+204	+270
2/15	3928.27	+ 2	+140	6 - 7 - 9 -12	+201	+262
2/16	3937.27	- 9	+131	6 -11 - 9 - 5	+198	+265
2/17	3922.64	-12	+119	4 -13 -13 -10	+189	+259
2/18	3887.46	-25	+94	1 -14 -17 - 5	+173	+252
2/22	3911.66	- 5	+89	3 - 7 - 9 - 8	+167	+245
2/23	3891.66	-14	+75	2 - 9 -13 - 6	+156	+237
2/24	3839,90	-39	+36	1 -15 -25 - 0	+132	+228
2/25	3838.78	-18	+18	3 - 8 -14 - 1	+121	+224
2/28	3832.02	-11	+7	5 - 8 -15 - 7	+111	+215
3/ 1	3809.23	-18	-11	5 - 6 -21 - 4	+95	+201
3/ 2	3831.74	-10	-21	7 - 6 -19 - 8	+83	+187
3/ 3	3824.42	-11	-32	5 - 7 -14 - 5	+74	+180
3/ 4	3832.30	+ 4	-28	10 - 2 -12 - 8	+72	+172
3/ 7	3856.22	+12	-16	9 - 4 - 6 -13	+75	+166
3/ 8	3851.72	+ 5	-11	7 - 7 - 7 -12	+75	+161
3/ 9	3853.41	+ 3	-8	3 - 4 - 6 -10	+72	+152
3/10	3830.62	-20	-28	3 -11 -13 - 1	+62	+152
3/11	3862.70	- 1	-29	5 - 3 - 9 - 6	+58	+145
3/14	3862.98	- 1	-30	6 - 6 -10 - 9	+54	+138
3/15	3849.59	- 3	-33	4 - 5 -14 -12	+44	+121
3/16	3848.15	+10	-23	6 - 4 - 6 -14	+44	+111
3/17	3865.14	+ 9	-14	8 - 8 - 6 -15	+46	+106
3/18	3895.65	+ 2	-12	15 -13 - 8 - 8	+53	+118
3/21	3864.85	-11	-23	6 -11 - 9 - 3	+50	+123
3/22	3862.55	+ 6	-17	9 - 3 - 7 - 7	+52	+121
3/23	3869.46	+ 1	-16	6 - 3 - 4 - 2	+54	+124
3/24	3821.09	-26	-42	3 -16 -14 - 2	+43	+127
3/25	3774.73	-30	-72	1 -20 -16 - 5	+28	+127
3/28	3762.35	-21	-93	1 -11 -14 - 3	+15	+122
3/29	3699.02	-42	-135	1 -18 -25 - 0	- 9	+116
3/30	3626.75	-48	-183	1 -17 -33 - 1	-41	+100
3/31	3635.96	-39	-222	0 -12 -27 - 0	-68	+85
4/ 4	3593.35	-47	-269	0 - 9 -38 - 0	-106	+46

Table 2
Current Cluster Analysis- 65 Stocks

Date	Dow	CLX	CLX Cum.	Four Columns	True	EW
1993						
11/ 1	3692.61	+27	+27	28 - 7 - 0 - 6	+28	+29
11/ 2	3697.64	+8	+35	8 - 4 - 0 - 4	+36	+37
11/ 3	3661.87	-10	+25	3 - 3 -10 - 0	+29	+33
11/ 4	3624.98	-26	- 1	0 - 4 -22 - 0	+ 7	+15
11/ 5	3643.43	-16	-17	3 - 0 -19 - 0	- 9	- 1

11/ 8	3647.90	-15	-32	4 - 0 -19- 0	-24	-16
11/ 9	3640.07	-18	-50	8 - 3 -23- 0	-39	-28
11/10	3663.55	-20	-70	16 - 3 -33- 0	-56	-42
11/11	3662.43	-32	-102	0 - 4 -28- 0	-84	-66
11/12	3684.51	- 3	-105	0 - 0 - 6- 3	-90	-75
11/15	3677.52	- 6	-111	7 - 3 -13- 3	-96	-81
11/16	3710.77	+16	-95	25 - 4 -12- 6	-83	-70
11/17	3704.35	-8	-103	6 - 5 - 9- 0	-86	-68
11/18	3685.34	+10	-93	13 - 3 - 3- 3	-76	-58
11/19	3694.01	+3	-90	13 - 7 - 3- 0	-66	-41
11/22	3670.25	+4	-86	15 - 5 -11- 5	-62	-37
11/23	3674.17	+3	-83	10 - 6 - 7- 6	-59	-34
11/24	3687.58	+1	-82	6 - 6 - 9-10	-62	-41
11/26	3683.95	+28	-54	4 - 0 - 0-24	-58	-61
11/29	3677.80	+41	-13	31 - 3 - 3-16	-30	-46
11/30	3683.95	+27	+14	16 - 4 - 0-15	-14	-41
12/ 1	3697.08	+12	+26	19 -13 - 6-12	- 1	-27
12/ 2	3702.08	+8	+34	10 -14 - 3-15	+ 6	-21
12/ 3	3704.07	+14	+48	12 - 5 - 5-12	+13	-21
12/ 6	3710.21	+18	+66	12 - 0 - 3- 9	+22	-21
12/ 7	3718.88	+11	+77	0 - 0 - 0-11	+22	-32
12/ 8	3734.53	+13	+90	3 - 0 - 0-10	+25	-39
12/ 9	3729.78	-5	+85	3 -12 - 3- 7	+25	-34
12/10	3740.67	+9	+94	7 - 3 - 7-12	+25	-43
12/13	3764.43	+18	+112	18 - 0 - 3- 8	+40	-36
12/14	3742.63	-13	+99	0 - 3 -10- 0	+30	-43
12/15	3716.92	+5	+104	21 - 6 -16- 6	+35	-38
12/16	3726.14	-19	+85	20 -13 -26- 0	+29	-31
12/17	3751.57	+10	+105	26 -13 - 6- 3	+49	- 1
12/20	3755.21	+2	+107	22 - 5 -21- 6	+50	- 1
12/21	3745.15	-12	+95	9 - 3 -21- 3	+38	-13
12/22	3762.19	+29	+124	16 - 0 - 4-17	+50	-18
12/23	3757.72	+19	+143	19 - 3 - 5- 8	+64	- 9
12/27	3792.93	+50	+193	48 - 4 - 0- 6	+112	+37
12/28	3793.77	+47	+240	48 - 5 - 6-10	+154	+74
12/29	3794.33	+31	+271	37 - 6 - 3- 3	+188	+111
12/30	3775.88	+5	+276	21 - 9 - 7- 0	+202	+134
12/31	3754.09	-22	+254	13 -20 -15- 0	+200	+152
1994						
1/ 3	3756.60	-28	+226	6 -12 -22- 0	+184	+148
1/ 4	3783.90	-24	+202	0 - 6 -18- 0	+166	+136
1/ 5	3798.82	-29	+173	12 - 7 -34- 0	+144	+121
1/ 6	3803.88	-26	+147	19 - 9 -36- 0	+127	+113
1/ 7	3820.77	-23	+124	4 - 8 -22- 3	+109	+100
1/10	3865.51	+23	+147	22 - 6 - 0- 7	+131	+121
1/11	3850.31	+2	+149	6 - 7 - 0- 3	+137	+131
1/12	3848.63	-5	+144	3 - 8 - 0- 0	+140	+142
1/13	3842.43	-23	+121	7 -21 -12- 3	+135	+129
1/14	3867.20	-12	+119	10 -10 -18- 6	+127	+125
1/17	3867.20	-13	+106	12 -11 -18- 4	+121	+126
1/18	3870.29	-22	+84	19 -12 -29- 0	+111	+128
1/19	3884.37	-13	+71	25 -18 -20- 0	+116	+151
1/20	3891.96	+12	+83	34 -12 -16- 6	+134	+175
1/21	3914.48	-17	+66	19 -21 -15- 0	+138	+200
1/24	3912.79	+19	+85	31 - 0 -12- 0	+157	+219
1/25	3895.34	-7	+78	15 - 8 -14- 0	+158	+228
1/26	3908.00	+4	+82	8 - 4 - 0- 0	+166	+240
1/27	3926.30	+13	+95	10 - 3 - 3- 9	+173	+241
1/28	3945.43	+13	+108	11 - 0 - 4- 6	+180	+242
1/31	3978.36	+22	+130	22 - 0 - 0- 0	+202	+264
2/ 1	3964.01	+19	+149	22 - 0 - 3- 0	+221	+283
2/ 2	3975.54	+26	+175	23 - 3 - 0- 6	+244	+303
2/ 3	3967.66	+21	+196	28 - 7 - 0- 0	+272	+338
2/ 4	3871.42	-10	+186	0 - 0 -10- 0	+262	+328

2/ 7	3906.32	-24	+162	0 - 9 -15 - 0	+247	+322
2/ 8	3906.03	-37	+125	0 -21 -16 - 0	+231	+327
2/ 9	3931.92	-22	+103	6 -14 -14 - 0	+223	+333
2/10	3895.34	-32	+71	0 -11 -21 - 0	+202	+323
2/11	3894.78	-20	+51	6 - 9 -17 - 0	+191	+321
2/14	3904.06	-11	+40	3 - 0 -14 - 0	+180	+310
2/15	3928.27	-6	+34	7 - 3 -11 - 1	+176	+308
2/16	3938.27	+7	+41	11 - 0 - 4 - 0	+183	+315
2/17	3922.64	-29	+12	9 -13 -21 - 6	+171	+310
2/18	3887.18	-44	-32	7 -11 -40 - 0	+138	+288
2/22	3911.66	-24	-56	8 - 7 -25 - 0	+121	+278
2/23	3891.68	-25	-81	12 -10 -27 - 0	+106	+273
2/24	3839.90	-46	-127	0 - 7 -39 - 0	+67	+241
2/25	3838.78	-37	-164	0 - 5 -32 - 0	+35	+214
2/28	3832.02	-38	-202	3 - 9 -32 - 0	+6	+194
3/ 1	3809.23	-38	-240	6 - 4 -40 - 0	-28	+164
3/ 2	3831.74	-47	-287	4 - 8 -43 - 0	-67	+133
3/ 3	3824.42	-34	-321	3 - 6 -31 - 0	-95	+111
3/ 4	3832.30	-27	-348	16 - 3 -40 - 0	-119	+90
3/ 7	3856.22	-2	-350	23 - 4 -21 - 0	-117	+96
3/ 8	3851.72	-15	-365	6 - 5 -19 - 3	-130	+85
3/ 9	3853.41	-12	-377	0 - 3 -16 - 4	-146	+68
3/10	3830.62	-31	-408	3 - 7 -27 - 0	-170	+51
3/11	3862.70	-18	-426	4 - 3 -22 - 3	-188	+33
3/14	3862.98	-14	-440	8 - 0 -26 - 4	-206	+11
3/15	3849.59	-12	-452	6 - 0 -24 - 6	-224	-13
3/16	3848.15	-11	-463	7 - 0 -25 - 7	-248	-38
3/17	3865.14	-12	-475	5 - 3 -30 -16	-267	-76
3/18	3895.94	-1	-476	16 - 4 -22 - 9	-273	-87
3/21	3864.85	-1	-477	14 - 8 -16 - 9	-275	-90
3/22	3862.55	-5	-482	21 - 3 -34 -11	-288	-111
3/23	3869.46	+13	-469	20 - 3 - 4 - 0	-272	-92
3/24	3821.09	+1	-468	6 - 0 - 5 - 0	-271	-91
3/25	3774.79	-12	-480	0 - 3 - 9 - 0	-280	-97
3/28	3762.35	-37	-517	0 -15 -22 - 0	-302	-104
3/29	3699.02	-77	-594	0 -18 -59 - 0	-361	-145
3/30	3626.75	-84	-678	0 -27 -57 - 0	-418	-175
3/31	3635.96	-77	-755	0 -19 -58 - 0	-476	-214
4/ 4	3593.35	-126	-881	0 -15 -111- 0	-587	-310

Table 3
Current Supercluster Analysis - 65 Stocks

1993	Dow	CLX	Cum.	4-Columns	True	EW
Nov. 1	3692.61	+51	+51	65 - 15 - 9 - 10	+56	+61
Nov. 2	3697.64	+64	+115	78 - 16 - 9 - 11	+125	+74
Nov. 3	3661.87	+71	+186	81 - 7 -10 - 7	+196	+145
Nov. 4	3624.98	+52	+238	75 - 8 -22 - 7	+249	+199
Nov. 5	3643.43	-12	+226	32 - 8 -36 - 0	+245	+203
Nov. 8	3647.90	-24	+202	26 - 8 -42 - 0	+229	+195
Nov. 9	3640.07	-21	+181	30 - 7 -44 - 0	+215	+188
Nov. 10	3663.55	-22	+159	32 - 3 -51 - 0	+196	+172
Nov. 11	3662.43	-21	+138	32 - 4 -49 - 0	+179	+159
Nov. 12	3684.51	-28	+110	17 - 4 -44 - 3	+152	+133
Nov. 15	3677.52	-14	+96	31 - 7 -47 - 9	+136	+115
Nov. 16	3710.77	+6	+102	39 - 4 -41 - 12	+134	+105
Nov. 17	3704.35	-5	+97	37 - 5 -42 - 9	+129	+96
Nov. 18	3685.34	+8	+105	40 - 3 -41 - 12	+128	+86
Nov. 19	3694.01	+1	+106	31 - 7 -32 - 9	+127	+83
Nov. 22	3670.25	+13	+119	40 - 5 -33 - 11	+134	+84
Nov. 23	3674.17	-3	+116	35 - 11 -36 - 9	+133	+85
Nov. 24	3687.58	+8	+124	40 - 17 -28 - 13	+145	+101
Nov. 26	3683.95	+19	+143	41 - 17 -32 - 27	+154	+100

Nov. 29	3677.80	+44	+187	56 - 14 -20 - 22	+190	+128
Nov. 30	3683.95	+42	+229	54 - 18 -20 - 26	+224	+154
Dec. 1	3697.08	+29	+258	36 - 17 -23 - 33	+237	+151
Dec. 2	3702.08	+40	+298	40 - 20 -23 - 43	+254	+145
Dec. 3	3704.07	+51	+349	51 - 14 -23 - 37	+282	+150
Dec. 6	3710.21	+21	+370	35 - 5 -17 - 26	+300	+147
Dec. 7	3718.88	+44	+314	33 - 5 -14 - 30	+319	+141
Dec. 8	3734.53	+43	+357	29 - 0 -14 - 28	+334	+128
Dec. 9	3729.78	+18	+375	10 - 7 -17 - 32	+327	+96
Dec. 10	3740.67	+21	+396	10 - 7 -16 - 34	+321	+63
Dec. 13	3764.43	+23	+419	21 - 4 -22 - 28	+320	+38
Dec. 14	3742.63	+5	+424	21 - 7 -17 - 8	+324	+41
Dec. 15	3716.92	+15	+439	37 - 5 -26 - 9	+335	+48
Dec. 16	3726.14	-3	+436	50 - 13 -40 - 0	+345	+71
Dec. 17	3751.57	+14	+450	61 - 20 -30 - 3	+376	+119
Dec. 20	3755.21	+13	+463	64 - 15 -45 - 9	+395	+144
Dec. 21	3745.15	+6	+469	53 - 15 -42 - 10	+406	+160
Dec. 22	3762.19	+20	+489	51 - 15 -33 - 17	+424	+176
Dec. 23	3757.72	+24	+513	55 - 14 -30 - 13	+449	+212
Dec. 27	3792.93	+64	+577	84 - 15 -22 - 17	+511	+272
Dec. 28	3793.77	+68	+645	91 - 12 -21 - 10	+581	+334
Dec. 29	3794.33	+79	+724	90 - 6 -18 - 13	+653	+399
Dec. 30	3775.88	+44	+768	75 - 15 -26 - 10	+702	+453
Dec. 31	3754.09	+25	+793	76 - 26 -32 - 7	+746	+516
Jan. 3	3756.60	-6	+787	52 - 26 -36 - 4	+762	+554
Jan. 4	3783.90	-24	+763	40 - 35 -29 - 0	+773	+600
Jan. 5	3798.82	-16	+747	41 - 17 -40 - 0	+774	+618
Jan. 6	3803.88	+1	+748	52 - 15 -39 - 3	+787	+643
Jan. 7	3820.77	-8	+740	50 - 11 -56 - 9	+781	+639
Jan. 10	3865.51	-29	+711	29 - 12 -56 - 10	+754	+614
Jan. 11	3850.31	-6	+705	24 - 10 -33 - 13	+74	+602
Jan. 12	3848.63	+14	+719	25 - 8 -13 - 10	+757	+612
Jan. 13	3842.43	-3	+716	29 - 21 -25 - 14	+761	+623
Jan. 14	3867.20	0	+716	27 - 22 -22 - 17	+766	+633
Jan. 17	3870.29	+8	+724	28 - 20 -19 - 19	+775	+643
Jan. 18	3870.29	-11	+713	40 - 18 -37 - 4	+778	+660
Jan. 19	3884.37	-6	+707	51 - 21 -40 - 4	+789	+688
Jan. 20	3891.95	-10	+697	54 - 18 -52 - 6	+791	+702
Jan. 21	3914.48	+25	+722	80 - 24 -34 - 3	+837	+769
Jan. 24	3912.79	+44	+766	78 - 6 -31 - 3	+884	+819
Jan. 25	3895.34	+25	+791	64 - 18 -24 - 3	+924	+874
Jan. 26	3908.00	+17	+808	59 - 15 -27 - 0	+956	+921
Jan. 27	3926.30	+20	+828	48 - 16 -24 - 12	+972	+949
Jan. 28	3945.43	+31	+859	49 - 8 -25 - 15	+996	+966
Jan. 31	3978/36	+23	+882	49 - 4 -28 - 6	+1017	+985
Feb. 1	3964.01	+34	+916	56 - 4 -31 - 13	+1042	+1001
Feb. 2	3975.54	+47	+963	62 - 10 -21 - 16	+1083	+1036
Feb. 3	3967.66	+54	+1017	55 - 10 -13 - 22	+1125	+1066
Feb. 4	3871.42	+30	+1047	48 - 3 -18 - 3	+1155	+1096
Feb. 7	3906.32	0	+1047	43 - 15 -31 - 3	+1167	+1120
Feb. 8	3906.03	-26	+1021	37 - 27 -39 - 3	+1165	+1142
Feb. 9	3931.92	-26	+995	32 - 23 -38 - 3	+1159	+1156
Feb. 10	3895.34	-27	+968	24 -17 -37 - 3	+1146	+1157
Feb. 11	3894.78	-30	+938	23 - 21 -35 - 3	+1134	+1163
Feb. 14	3904.06	-32	+906	17 - 18 -34 - 3	+1117	+1161
Feb. 15	3928.27	-20	+886	25 - 15 -33 - 3	+1109	+1165
Feb. 16	3938.27	-12	+874	24 - 6 -30 - 0	+1103	+1165
Feb. 17	3922.64	-31	+843	22 - 19 -43 - 9	+1082	+1154
Feb. 18	3887.18	-41	+802	20 - 17 -50 - 6	+1052	+1135
Feb. 22	3911.66	-57	+745	21 - 21 -63 - 6	+1010	+1108
Feb. 23	3891.68	-64	+681	25 - 22 -70 - 3	+965	+1082
Feb. 24	3839.90	-47	+634	22 - 11 -58 - 0	+929	+1057
Feb. 25	3838.78	-53	+581	19 - 8 -64 - 0	+884	+1020
Feb. 28	3832.02	-73	+508	10 - 14 -69 - 0	+825	+975
Mar. 1	3809.23	-71	+437	13 - 12 -72 - 0	+766	+928
Mar. 2	3831.74	-82	+355	11 - 13 -83 - 3	+794	+866

Mar. 3	3824.42	-78	+277	10 - 14 -77 - 3	+727	+810
Mar. 4	3832.30	-75	+202	23 - 16 -85 - 3	+665	+761
Mar. 7	3856.22	-60	+142	31 - 18 -76 - 3	+620	+731
Mar. 8	3851.72	-44	+98	24 - 11 -63 - 6	+581	+697
Mar. 9	3853.41	-20	+78	25 - 14 -41 - 10	+565	+685
Mar. 10	3830.62	-20	+58	24 - 12 -42 - 10	+547	+669
Mar. 11	3862.70	-11	+47	25 - 15 -34 - 13	+538	+662
Mar. 14	3862.98	-12	+35	26 - 7 -42 - 11	+522	+642
Mar. 15	3849.59	+11	+46	27 - 0 -33 - 17	+516	+619
Mar. 16	3848.15	+ 6	+52	30 - 0 -38 - 14	+508	+597
Mar. 17	3865.14	- 1	+51	25 - 3 -43 - 20	+490	+562
Mar. 18	3895.94	+13	+64	28 - 4 -33 - 22	+485	+529
Mar. 21	3864.85	+21	+85	38 - 8 -39 - 30	+484	+506
Mar. 22	3862.55	+6	+91	36 - 11 -47 - 28	+473	+478
Mar. 23	3869.46	+12	+103	42 - 12 -44 - 26	+471	+462
Mar. 24	3821.09	+28	+131	39 - 9 -15 - 13	+495	+482
Mar. 25	3774.79	+17	+148	31 - 6 -16 - 8	+510	+495
Mar. 28	3762.35	-26	+122	21 - 18 -38 - 9	+493	+487
Mar. 29	3699.02	-77	+45	13 - 21 -75 - 6	+431	+440
Mar. 30	3626.75	-95	-50	6 - 27 -80 - 6	+357	+387
Mar. 31	3635.96	-116	-166	7 - 40 -83 - 0	+281	+351
Apr. 4	3593.35	-155	-321	7 - 24 -138 - 0	+150	+244

Table 4
30 Industrial OBV Patterns Leading Up To 1994 Peak

The best way to understand OBV is to see it in action.

Allied Signal

11/ 1	72.63	96,696,700		Rising
11/ 2	73.25	97,004,900	Up	Rising
11/ 3	71.00	96,531,400		Rising
11/ 4	71.63	96,824,600		Rising
11/ 5	71	96,606,800		Rising
11/ 8	70.75	96,424,500	Down	Rising
11/ 9	71	96,690,900		Rising
11/ 10	71.88	96,985,100	Up	Rising
11/ 11	72.88	97,400,000	UP	Rising
11/ 12	73.25	97,731,600	UP	Rising
11/ 15	72.88	97,731,600	UP	Rising
11/ 16	72.88	97,731,600	UP	Rising
11/ 17	72.38	97,596,100		Rising
11/ 18	72.13	97,444,800		Rising
11/ 19	71.25	97,280,300		Rising
11/ 22	71	97,092.200		Rising
11/ 23	71.38	97,244,100		Rising
11/ 24	72.25	97,456,300		Rising
11/ 26	72.25	97,456,300		Rising
11/ 29	71.75	97,350,800		Rising
11/ 30	71.13	97,161,100		Rising
12/ 1	72.25	97,491,900	Up	Rising
12/ 2	73.00	97,649,600	Up	Rising
12/ 3	74.13	98,050,900	UP	Rising
12/ 6	75.25	98,580,700	UP	Rising
12/ 7	75.13	98.272,300		Rising
12/ 8	75.63	98,466,100		Rising
12/ 9	75.88	98,775,900	UP	Rising
12/ 10	75.75	98,584,500		Rising
12/ 13	74.88	98,306,300		Rising
12/ 14	75.13	98,663,500		Rising
12/ 15	75.13	98,663,500	UP	Rising
12/ 16	75.25	99,902,300	UP	Rising
12/ 17	77.25	100,422,300	UP	Rising

12/ 20	77.50	100,786,600	UP	Rising
12/ 21	77.75	101,014,000	UP	Rising
12/ 22	78.63	101,358,600	UP	Rising
12/ 23	79.13	101,844,800	UP	Rising
12/ 27	79.88	102,115,900	UP	Rising
12/ 28	79.88	102,115,900	UP	Rising
12/ 29	80.00	102,496,700	UP	Rising
12/ 30	80.00	102,496,700	UP	Rising
12/ 31	79.00	102,395,800		Rising
1/ 3	77.75	102,136,500		Rising
1/ 4	76.25	101,385,900		Rising
1/ 5	76.50	101,914,600		Rising
1/ 6	77.50	102,281,700		Rising
1/ 7	77.75	102,474,500		Rising
1/ 10	78.00	102,974,100	UP	Rising
1/ 11	78.25	103,230,000	UP	Rising
1/ 12	77.63	103,002,600		Rising
1/ 13	77.00	102,847,800		Rising
1/ 14	77.75	103,012,200		Rising
1/ 17	77.50	102,880,200		Rising
1/ 18	77.75	103,076,700	Up	Rising
1/ 19	78.38	103,244,900	UP	Rising
1/ 20	79.25	103,536,700	UP	Rising
1/ 21	79.00	103,127,700		Rising
1/ 24	79.00	103,127,700		Rising
1/ 25	77.88	102,860,900	Down	Rising
1/ 26	77.13	102,612,600	Down	Rising
1/ 27	78.00	102,761,400		Rising
1/ 28	78.38	102,925,100		Rising
1/ 31	78.63	103,068,700		Rising
2/ 1	79.75	103,539,200	UP	Rising
2/ 2	79.25	103,265,800		Rising
2/ 3	78.00	103,006,300		Rising
2/ 4	75.25	102,663,800		Rising
2/ 7	75.88	103,069,700		Rising
2/ 8	77.38	103,449,400		Rising
2/ 9	79.88	103,998,200	UP	Rising
2/ 10	78.88	103,586,700		Rising
2/ 11	79.38	103,884,500		Rising
2/ 14	78.00	103,703,500		Rising
2/ 15	79.75	103,954,700	Up	Rising
2/ 16	79.88	104,202,700	UP	Rising
2/ 17	80.00	104,648,600	UP	Rising
2/ 18	79.13	104,402,900		Rising
2/ 22	79.13	104,402,900		Rising
2/ 23	78.38	104,231,700		Rising
2/ 24	77.00	103,966,700		Rising
2/ 25	77.00	103,966,700		Rising
2/ 28	76.38	103,712,000		Rising
3/ 1	76.00	103,249,500	Down	Rising
3/ 2	75.50	102,039,700	Down	Doubtful
3/ 3	76.00	102,481,600		Doubtful
3/ 4	77.38	102,756,600		Doubtful
3/ 7	78.50	102,951,200		Doubtful
3/ 8	77.13	102,698,600		Doubtful
3/ 9	77.38	102,907,000		Doubtful
3/ 10	76.75	102,565,200	Down	Doubtful
3/ 11	77.88	102,848,500		Doubtful
3/ 14	77.38	102,522,400	Down	Doubtful
3/ 15	38.88	103,022,300	Up	Doubtful
3/ 16	38.25	102,640,700		Doubtful
3/ 17	38.50	103,155,400	Up	Doubtful
3/ 18	38.50	103,155,400	Up	Doubtful
3/ 21	38.63	103,551,400	Up	Doubtful
3/ 22	38.75	104,094,100	Up	Doubtful
3/ 23	39.13	104,594,700	Up	Doubtful

3/ 24	38.88	103,946,100		Doubtful
3/ 25	38.25	103,529,500		Doubtful
3/ 28	37.13	102,490,000	Down	Doubtful
3/ 29	36,50	101,861,100	DOWN	Falling
3/ 30	34.25	100,648,500	DOWN	`Falling
3/ 31	36.50	101,685,800		Falling
4/ 4	36.38	100,872,400		Falling
4/ 5	37.00	101,435,500		Falling
4/ 6	37.13	101,876,000	Up	Falling
4/ 7	36.13	101,459,000		Falling
4/ 8	36.13	101,459,000		Falling
4/ 11	36.75	101,934,300	Up	Falling
4/ 12	36.50	101,453,900	Down	Falling
4/ 13	35.50	101,083,300	Down	Falling
4/ 14	35.75	101,801,100		Falling
4/ 15	35.88	102,327,800	UP	Rising
4/ 18	34.50	101,427,800		Rising
4/ 19	34.13	100,092,600	DOWN	Doubtful

Alcoa

11/ 1	xd	67.75	55,756,400		Rising
11/ 2		68.00	56,223,300	UP	Rising
11/ 3		66.88	55,882,200		Rising
11/ 4		67.50	56,155,300		Rising
11/ 5		68.00	56,382,500	UP	Rising
11/ 8		68.13	56,507,200	UP	Rising
11/ 9		68.38	56,696,700	UP	Rising
11/ 10		69.75	56,992,300	UP	Rising
11/ 11		69.25	56,668,500		Rising
11/ 12		69.63	56,904,100		Rising
11/ 15		69.25	56,687,900		Rising
11/ 16		69.25	56,687,900		Rising
11/ 17		68.75	56,375,800	Down	Rising
11/ 18		68.50	56,263,600	Down	Rising
11/ 19		70.25	56,659,800		Rising
11/ 22		71.75	57,178,000	UP	Rising
11/ 23		72.13	57,413,900	UP	Rising
11/ 24		71.13	57,222,400		Rising
11/ 26		71.13	57,222,400		Rising
11/ 29		69.88	56,950,400		Rising
11/ 30		69.25	56,787,300		Rising
12/ 1		70.25	57,084,500		Rising
12/ 2		70.38	57,381,300		Rising
12/ 3		69.50	57,233,800		Rising
12/ 6		68.75	57,045,200		Rising
12/ 7		69.25	57,233,700		Rising
12/ 8		72.50	57,715,500	UP	Rising
12/ 9		71.50	57,334,200		Rising
12/ 10		72.38	57,487,900		Rising
12/ 13		73.63	57,925,000	UP	Rising
12/ 14		72.38	57,686,000		Rising
12/ 15		70.63	57,226,700	Down	Rising
12/ 16		70.25	56,845,000	Down	Rising
12/ 17		69.88	56,408,900	Down	Rising
12/ 20		69.63	55,832,900	DOWN	Doubtful
12/ 21		68.38	55,423,200	DOWN	Doubtful
12/ 22		68.50	55,800,000		Doubtful
12/ 23		68.25	55,646,600		Doubtful
12/ 27		68.63	55,818,800	Up	Doubtful
12/ 28		69.75	56,011,900	Up	Doubtful
12/ 29		69.38	55,834,200		Doubtful
12/ 30		69.38	55,834,200		Doubtful
12/ 31		69.38	55,834,200		Doubtful
1/ 3		70.63	56,100,800	Up	Doubtful
1/ 4		70.50	55,841,500		Doubtful

1/ 5	72.25	56,513,100	Up	Doubtful
1/ 6	71.88	56,132,900		Doubtful
1/ 7	72.38	56.418,400		Doubtful
1/ 10	74.13	56,857,500	Up	Doubtful
1/ 11	71.63	56,299,600		Doubtful
1/ 12	72.88	56,640,800		Doubtful
1/ 13	73.25	57,206,000	Up	Doubtful
1/ 14	73.00	57,053,400		Doubtful
1/ 17	74.25	57,395,900	Up	Doubtful
1/ 18	73.88	56,972,700	Down	Doubtful
1/ 19	74.88	57,392,100		Doubtful
1/ 20	74.38	57,042,700		Doubtful
1/ 21	73.88	55,126,600	DOWN	Falling
1/ 24	75.63	55,772,900		Falling
1/ 25	75.75	56,083,000		Falling
1/ 26	76.50	56,608,200		Falling
1/ 27	76.50	56,608,200		Falling
1/ 28	76.75	56,982,100		Falling
1/ 31	79.13	58,384,500	UP	Doubtful
2/ 1	79.38	59,653,300	UP	Doubtful
2/ 2	79.25	59,194,300		Doubtful
2/ 3	78.25	58,453,600		Doubtful
2/ 4	76.13	57,660,200		Doubtful
2/ 7	78.13	58,510,800		Doubtful
2/ 8	79.38	59,300,500		Doubtful
2/ 9	80.50	60,029,200	UP	Doubtful
2/ 10	79.25	59,160,600		Doubtful
2/ 11	78.13	58,827,200		Doubtful
2/ 14	78.38	59,330,400		Doubtful
2/ 15	78.13	58,933,800		Doubtful
2/ 16	79.63	59,224,300		Doubtful
2/ 17	78.75	58,822,700	Down	Doubtful
2/ 18	78.00	58,376,700	Down	Doubtful
2/ 22	77.00	58,105,800	Down	Doubtful
2/ 23	76.00	57,682,100	Down	Doubtful
2/ 24	76.25	58,046,300		Doubtful
2/ 25	76.25	58,046,300		Doubtful
2/ 28	75.25	57,537,100	Down	Doubtful
3/ 1	74.50	56,454,600	Down	Doubtful
3/ 2	76.50	57,056,800		Doubtful
3/ 3	74.88	56,644,500		Doubtful
3/ 4	75.13	56,924,800		Doubtful
3/ 7	75.50	57,163,400	Up	Doubtful
3/ 8	74.75	56,796,700		Doubtful
3/ 9	74.88	57,206,100	Up	Doubtful
3/ 10	73.13	56,627,900	Down	Doubtful
3/ 11	74.00	56,866,800		Doubtful
3/ 14	73.50	56,591,400	Down	Doubtful
3/ 15	73.63	56,925,400	Up	Doubtful
3/ 16	73.75	57,154,100	Up	Doubtful
3/ 17	75.50	57,443,600	UP	Rising
3/ 18	77.13	57,995,900	UP	Rising
3/ 21	77.13	57,995,900	UP	Rising
3/ 22	78.38	58,358,100	UP	Rising
3/ 23	78.75	58,686,700	UP	Rising
3/ 24	78.25	58,523,300		Rising
3/ 25	76.25	58,267,800		Rising
3/ 28	75.75	58,103,900		Rising
3/ 29	74.63	57,920,900		Rising
3/ 30	71.75	57,211,900		Rising
3/ 31	71.63	56,631,300		Rising
4/ 4	72.13	57,414,700		Rising
4/ 5	72.00	57,065,000		Rising
4/ 6	72.38	57,546,200	Up	Rising
4/ 7	72.38	57,546,200	Up	Rising
4/ 8	71.38	57,008,900	Down	Rising

4/ 11	71.63	57,405,400		Rising
4/ 12	71,63	57,405,400		Rising
4/ 13	69.50	57,106,200		Rising
4/ 14	69.42	56,841,500	Down	Rising
4/ 15	67.75	56,474,900	DOWN	Doubtful
4/ 18	66.38	56,037,500	DOWN	Doubtful
4/ 19	65.00	55,152,500	DOWN	Doubtful

American Express

11/ 1	31.75	154,318,400		Doubtful
11/ 2	31.75	154,318,400		Doubtful
11/ 3	30.50	152,515,900	Down	Doubtful
11/ 4	30.50	152,515,900	Down	Doubtful
11/ 5	30.88	153,722,500		Doubtful
11/ 8	30.63	151,642,000	Down	Doubtful
11/ 9	31.88	153,362,500		Doubtful
11/ 10	31.25	152,423,600		Doubtful
11/ 11	30.88	151,318,500	Down	Doubtful
11/ 12	31.13	152,799,600		Doubtful
11/ 15	31.75	153,517,500	Up	Doubtful
11/ 16	32.00	154,182,900	Up	Doubtful
11/ 17	31.00	153,088,600		Doubtful
11/ 18	30.75	151,869,000		Doubtful
11/ 19	30.75	151,869,000		Doubtful
11/ 22	29.75	150,185,200	DOWN	Falling
11/ 23	30.25	151,323,800		Falling
11/ 24	30.75	152,558,700		Falling
11/ 26	31.00	152,794,800		Falling
11/ 29	31.63	153,760.100		Falling
11/ 30	31.38	153,268,700		Falling
12/ 1	32.18	154,311,400	UP	Doubtful
12/ 2	32.25	155,000,600	UP	Doubtful
12/ 3	31.63	154,447,400		Doubtful
12/ 6	31.25	153,445,000		Doubtful
12/ 7	31.63	154,502,800		Doubtful
12/ 8	31.88	154,636,000		Doubtful
12/ 9	31.63	154,636,000		Doubtful
12/ 10	31.50	154,254,100		Doubtful
12/ 13	31.38	153,374,500	Down	Doubtful
12/ 14	31.25	152,516,400	Down	Doubtful
12/ 15	30.38	151,626,700	Down	Doubtful
12/ 16	30.13	149,750,800	DOWN	Doubtful
12/ 17	30.38	152,322,800		Doubtful
12/ 20	30.88	153,305,400		Doubtful
12/ 21	31.50	154,765,400		Doubtful
12/ 22	31.13	153,665,400		Doubtful
12/ 23	31.38	154,777,000	Up	Doubtful
12/ 27	31.88	155,583,600	UP	Doubtful
12/ 28	31.25	154,693,900		Doubtful
12/ 29	31.13	153,698,900		Doubtful
12/ 30	31.38	154,332,200		Doubtful
12/ 31	30.88	153,661,800	Down	Doubtful
1/ 3	29.63	151,987,000	Down	Doubtful
1/ 4	30.25	153,181,400		Doubtful
1/ 5	29.88	151,798,200	Down	Doubtful
1/ 6	29.25	147,643,200	DOWN	Doubtful
1/ 7	29.13	143,628,400	DOWN	Doubtful
1/ 10	29.50	147,699,900		Doubtful
1/ 11	30.75	152,927,400		Doubtful
1/ 12	30.63	148,972,700		Doubtful
1/ 13	31.25	151,151,100		Doubtful
1/ 14	32,13	153,020,800	Up	Doubtful
1/ 17	31.38	152,175,100		Doubtful
1/ 18	30.75	150,623,900		Doubtfui
1/ 19	30.13	148,593,900	Down	Doubtful

1/ 20	30.75	150,493,000		Doubtful
1/ 21	30.88	152,026,100		Doubtful
1/ 24	31.50	153,132,400	UP	Rising
1/ 25	32.75	160,211,500	UP	Rising
1/ 26	32,13	157,295,800		Rising
1/ 27	32.00	156,141,900		Rising
1/ 28	32.63	158,626,800		Rising
1/ 31	32.63	158,626,800		Rising
2/ 1	32.63	158,626,800		Rising
2/ 2	32.75	159,916,700		Rising
2/ 3	32.25	159,107,200		Rising
2/ 4	30.88	157,498,500		Rising
2/ 7	30.63	154,185,800	Down	Rising
2/ 8	30.75	156,650,000		Rising
2/ 9	30.38	154,561,900		Rising
2/ 10	30.38	154,561,900		Rising
2/ 11	31.25	155,811,700		Rising
2/ 14	31.00	154,887,900		Rising
2/ 15	30.63	153,367,800	Down	Rising
2/ 16	30.25	151,966,800	Down	Rising
2/ 17	30.00	149,696,600	Down	Rising
2/ 18	29.75	148,153,800	DOWN	Doubtful
2/ 22	30.25	149,387,000		Doubtful
2/ 23	30.38	150,517,200		Doubtful
2/ 24	29.38	148,964,600		Doubtful
2/ 25	29.38	148,964,600		Doubtful
2/ 28	29.25	147,687,700	DOWN	Doubtful
3/ 1	28.88	145,681,800	DOWN	Doubtful
3/ 2	28.75	142,723,600	DOWN	Doubtful
3/ 3	28.63	141,748,100	DOWN	Doubtful
3/ 4	28.50	140,299,200	DOWN	Doubtful
3/ 7	28.75	142,347,400		Doubtful
3/ 8	29.00	144,421,100		Doubtful
3/ 9	28.25	141,997,500		Doubtful
3/ 10	28.38	143,712,400		Doubtful
3/ 11	28.63	145,309,900	Up	Doubtful
3/ 14	28.88	147,442,300	Up	Doubtful
3/ 15	29.38	150,440,300	Up	Doubtful
3/ 16	30.50	152,861,600	Up	Doubtful
3/ 17	30.13	151,720,000		Doubtful
3/ 18	30.13	151,720,000		Doubtful
3/ 21	30.00	150,573,300		Doubtful
3/ 22	29.88	148,761,400		Doubtful
3/ 23	30.63	150,079,700		Doubtful
3/ 24	29.75	148,942,900		Doubtful
3/ 25	29.63	147,412,500	Down	Doubtful
3/ 28	29.38	146,027,700	Down	Doubtful
3/ 29	28.75	144,523,800	Down	Doubtful
3/ 30	28.00	142,304,300	Down	Doubtful
3/ 31	27.75	139,193,400	DOWN	Falling
4/ 4	27.25	137,422,900	DOWN	Falling
4/ 5	28.63	139,797,200		Falling
4/ 6	29.75	142,763,300		Falling
4/ 7	30.00	143,968.900		Falling
4/ 8	30.00	143,968,900		Falling
4/ 11	30.38	144,822,700		Falling
4/ 12	29.88	143,973,100		Falling
4/ 13	29.88	143,973,100		Falling
4/ 14	29.88	143,973,100		Falling
4/ 15	30.13	145,480,300	Up	Falling
4/ 18	30.00	144,098,800		Falling
4/ 19	30.25	145,646,600	Up	Falling

American Telephone

11/ 1	58.00	135,758,500		Falling

11/ 2	57.50	134,060,900	DOWN	Falling
11/ 3	56.88	131,577,500	DOWN	Falling
11/ 4	55.63	129,554,500	DOWN	Falling
11/ 5	56.13	131,709,400		Falling
11/ 8	55.88	130,148,300		Falling
11/ 9	55.88	130,148,300		Falling
11/ 10	55.38	127,101,800	DOWN	Falling
11/ 11	56.75	131,050,900		Falling
11/ 12	57.38	133,374,800	Up	Falling
11/ 15	56.75	131,482,700		Falling
11/ 16	56.88	133,497,200	Up	Falling
11/ 17	56.75	131,857,700		Falling
11/ 18	56.00	129,687,500	Down	Falling
11/ 19	56.25	132,898,100		Falling
11/ 22	55.88	131,153,500		Falling
11/ 23	55.88	131,153,500		Falling
11/ 24	55.38	129,579,600	Down	Falling
11/ 26	55.88	130,066,700		Falling
11/ 29	54.88	127,947,700	Down	Falling
11/ 30	54.63	124,975,900	DOWN	Falling
12/ 1	54.25	122,076,400	DOWN	Falling
12/ 2	54.50	124,170,400		Falling
12/ 3	54.50	124,170,400		Falling
12/ 6	55.13	126,083,000		Falling
12/ 7	55.25	128,049,400		Falling
12/ 8	55.38	129,529,700		Falling
12/ 9	54.88	128,306,700		Falling
12/ 10	54.75	126,984,100		Falling
12/ 13	54.75	126,984,100		Falling
12/ 14	54.63	125,457,600		Falling
12/ 15	55.00	127,562,300		Falling
12/ 16	55.00	127,562,300		Falling
12/ 17	54.63	124,288,000	Down	Falling
12/ 20	54.63	124,288,000	Down	Falling
12/ 21	54.63	124,288,000	Down	Falling
12/ 22	54.25	122,461,500	Down	Falling
12/ 23	54.38	124,790,700		Falling
12/ 27	54.50	125,836,300		Falling
12/ 28	54.00	124,165,300		Falling
12/ 29	53.25	122,194,500	Down	Falling
12/ 30	52.63	119,410,200	DOWN	Falling
12/ 31	52.50	116,483,600	DOWN	Falling
1/ 3	52.63	118,809,800		Falling
1/ 4	52.00	115,666,700	DOWN	Falling
1/ 5	52.63	120,573,000	Up	Falling
1/ 6	53.75	124.646.900	Up	Falling
1/ 7	54.63	127,656,800	Up	Falling
1/ 10	55.00	130,416,200	Up	Falling
1/ 11	54.88	128,110,600		Falling
1/ 12	54.13	125,706,700		Falling
1/ 13	54.13	125,706,700		Falling
1/ 14	54.50	127,562,600		Falling
1/ 17	54.88	129,465,400		Falling
1/ 18	55.00	131,745,100	Up	Falling
1/ 19	55.75	134,058,200	UP	Doubtful
1/ 20	56.25	136,323,400	UP	Doubtful
1/ 21	56.00	133,584,300		Doubtful
1/ 24	55.50	131,894,200		Doubtful
1/ 25	55.25	130,561,200		Doubtful
1/ 26	56.00	131,840,500		Doubtful
1/ 27	56.75	133,914,900		Doubtful
1/ 28	56.63	132,209,400		Doubtful
1/ 31	56.75	134,025,000	Up	Doubtful
2/ 1	56.25	132,749,300		Doubtful
2/ 2	56.63	134,152,800	Up	Doubtful
2/ 3	55.75	132,661,500	Down	Doubtful

2/ 4	54.88	130,450,800	Down	Doubtful
2/ 7	54.50	128,073,200	Down	Doubtful
2/ 8	54.50	128,073,200	Down	Doubtful
2/ 9	54.00	126,626,200	Down	Doubtful
2/ 10	54.00	126,626,200	Down	Doubtful
2/ 11	54,50	127,948,300		Doubtful
2/ 14	54.38	126,809,800		Doubtful
2/ 15	54.75	128,429.600	Up	Doubtful
2/ 16	54.63	127,303,500		Doubtful
2/ 17	54.25	125,575,900	DOWN	Falling
2/ 18	53.50	123,322,900	DOWN	Falling
2/ 22	53.50	123,322,900	DOWN	Falling
2/ 23	53.00	122,038,600	DOWN	Falling
2/ 24	52.38	119,636,400	DOWN	Falling
2/ 25	52.75	121,211,800		Falling
2/ 28	52.50	119,772,700		Falling
3/ 1	52.25	117,349,200	DOWN	Falling
3/ 2	51.75	113,845,000	DOWN	Falling
3/ 3	51.25	111,427,600	DOWN	Falling
3/ 4	51.38	114,158,000		Falling
3/ 7	51.63	116,109,400		Falling
3/ 8	50.88	113,395,300		Falling
3/ 9	51.13	115,725,000		Falling
3/ 10	51.13	115,725,000		Falling
3/ 11	50.88	113,336,900	Down	Falling
3/ 14	51.25	116,114,900	Up	Falling
3/ 15	52.38	119,051,800	Up	Falling
3/ 16	52.75	121,615,700	Up	Falling
3/ 17	53.50	124,330,000	Up	Falling
3/ 18	53.50	124,330,000	Up	Falling
3/ 21	53.63	125,888,200	Up	Falling
3/ 22	53.50	124,297,800		Falling
3/ 23	53.38	122,755,300		Falling
3/ 24	53.00	120,443,500		Falling
3/ 25	52.63 xd	120,443,500		Falling
3/ 28	52.75	121,908,800		Falling
3/ 29	51.75	120,677,800		Falling
3/ 30	51.75	120,677,800		Falling
3/ 31	51.25	118,608,800	Down	Falling
4/ 4	51.00	116,293,000	Down	Falling
4/ 5	52.00	118,692,100		Falling
4/ 6	51.25	116,309,400		Falling
4/ 7	50.88	114,299,800	Down	Falling
4/ 8	50.13	112,278,300	DOWN	Falling
4/ 11	50.00	110,263,500	DOWN	Falling
4/ 12	50.38	112,639,500		Falling
4/ 13	50.13	111,038,200		Falling
4/ 14	50.00	109,081,100	DOWN	Falling
4/ 15	50.00	109,081,100	DOWN	Falling
4/ 18	49.63	107,522,700	DOWN	Falling
4/ 19	50.63	109,664,300		Falling

Bethlehem Steel

11/ 1	16.63	68,226,200	Down	Rising
11/ 2	16.75	68,625,400		Rising
11/ 3	16.38	68,075,500	Down	Rising
11/ 4	16.75	68,498,700		Rising
11/ 5	16.25	68,104,200		Rising
11/ 8	16.50	68,523,300	Up	Rising
11/ 9	16.38	68,258,800		Rising
11/ 10	17.63	69,186,500	Up	Rising
11/ 11	17.50	68,810,600		Rising
11/ 12	18.00	69,356,000	Up	Rising
11/ 15	17.50	69,164,700		Rising
11/ 16	17.50	69,164,700		Rising

11/ 17	17.25	68,887,000		Rising
11/ 18	17.38	69,035,700		Rising
11/ 19	17.50	69,281,600		Rising
11/ 22	17.13	68,767,600	Down	Rising
11/ 23	16.75	68,412,500	Down	Rising
11/ 24	17.38	68,727,300		Rising
11/ 26	17.50	68,872,900		Rising
11/ 29	17.38	68,357,400	Down	Rising
11/ 30	17.38	68,357,400	Down	Rising
12/ 1	17.50	68,891,800	Up	Rising
12/ 2	17.88	69,304,700	Up	Rising
12/ 3	17.38	69,152,100		Rising
12/ 6	16,63	68,856,700		Rising
12/ 7	17.50	69,420,000	UP	Rising
12/ 8	17.88	70,470,000	UP	Rising
12/ 9	18.00	71,100,000	UP	Rising
12/ 10	18.13	71,559,600	UP	Rising
12/ 13	18.38	71,971,000	UP	Rising
12/ 14	18.13	71,160,100		Rising
12/ 15	18.13	71,160,100		Rising
12/ 16	18.00	70,484,500		Rising
12/ 17	18.50	71,071,300		Rising
12/ 20	18.50	71,071,300		Rising
12/ 21	18.50	71,071,300		Rising
12/ 22	19.00	71,715,000		Rising
12/ 23	18.50	71,312,600		Rising
12/ 27	18.50	71,312,600		Rising
12/ 28	19.00	71,618,300		Rising
12/ 29	19.88	72,857,900	UP	Rising
12/ 30	19.88	72,857,900	UP	Rising
12/ 31	20.38	73,467,700	UP	Rising
1/ 3	20.00	72,992,900		Rising
1/ 4	20.25	74,040,100	UP	Rising
1/ 5	20.00	73,073,800		Rising
1/ 6	20,50	74,049,100	UP	Rising
1/ 7	20.63	74,785,900	UP	Rising
1/ 10	21,13	76,185,700	UP	Rising
1/ 11	20.88	73,862,800		Rising
1/ 12	21.88	75,444,000		Rising
1/ 13	21.50	74,346,800		Rising
1/ 14	21.63	76,140,300	Up	Rising
1/ 17	22.13	76,821,100	UP	Rising
1/ 18	22.25	77,482,700	UP	Rising
1/ 19	22.25	77,482,700	UP	Rising
1/ 20	22.50	78,058,900	UP	Rising
1/ 21	23.63	78,957,900	UP	Rising
1/ 24	23.75	80,412,900	UP	Rising
1/ 25	21.63	78,729,500		Rising
1/ 26	23.25	81,485,400	UP	Rising
1/ 27	22.75	80,483,100		Rising
1/ 28	23.38	80,483,100		Rising
1/ 31	23.38	81,237,000		Rising
2/ 1	22.75	80,536,500		Rising
2/ 2	23.00	80,965,200		Rising
2/ 3	23.25	81,476,500	Up	Rising
2/ 4	23.00	79,832,800	Down	Rising
2/ 7	23.63	81,437,100		Rising
2/ 8	24.13	82,325,800	UP	Rising
2/ 9	23.50	80,031,700		Rising
2/ 10	23.63	82,018,300		Rising
2/ 11	23.00	81,562,600		Rising
2/ 14	22.50	81,219,600		Rising
2/ 15	22.25	80,475,900		Rising
2/ 16	22.75	81,055,800		Rising
2/ 17	23.00	81,443,500		Rising
2/ 18	22.75	80,831,000		Rising

2/ 22	22.63	80,129,800	Down	Rising
2/ 23	22.38	79,780,600	DOWN	Doubtful
2/ 24	22.38	79,780,600	DOWN	Doubtful
2/ 25	22.25	79,431,900	DOWN	Doubtful
2/ 28	21.75	78,904,300	DOWN	Doubtful
3/ 1	21.00	78,204,800	DOWN	Doubtful
3/ 2	20.38	77,209,300	DOWN	Doubtful
3/ 3	21.25	77,777,600		Doubtful
3/ 4	21.88	78,224.500		Doubtful
3/ 7	21.88	78,224,500		Doubtful
3/ 7	21.50	77,878,000		Doubtful
3/ 8	21.38	74,981,200	DOWN	Doubtful
3/ 9	21.63	75,957,100		Doubtful
3/ 10	22.00	77,438,300		Doubtful
3/ 11	21.88	76,959,900		Doubtful
3/ 14	21.88	76,959,900		Doubtful
3/ 15	21.50	76,742,300		Doubtful
3/ 16	21.50	76,742,300		Doubtful
3/ 17	21.88	77,046,100		Doubtful
3/ 18	21.50	75,743,400	Down	Doubtful
3/ 21	21.38	75,527,000	Down	Doubtful
3/ 22	22.13	76,098,000		Doubtful
3/ 23	22.75	76,700,500		Doubtful
3/ 24	22.38	76,419,100		Doubtful
3/ 25	20.88	75,669,800		Doubtful
3/ 28	20.88	75,669,800		Doubtful
3/ 29	20.50	75,158,200	Down	Doubtful
3/ 30	20.25	74,183,200	DOWN	Doubtful
3/ 31	19.88	73,180,500	DOWN	Doubtful
4/ 4	19.50	72,757,500	DOWN	Doubtful
4/ 5	20.75	73,602,500		Doubtful
4/ 6	21.38	74,238,000		Doubtful
4/ 7	21.63	74,615,000		Doubtful
4/ 8	20.75	74,007,800		Doubtful
4/ 11	20.75	74,007,800		Doubtful
4/ 12	20.88	74,255,600		Doubtful
4/ 13	20.88	74,255,600		Doubtful
4/ 14	21.63	75,031,300	Up	Doubtful
4/ 15	21.88	75,660,400	Up	Doubtful
4/ 18	20.88	75,387,400		Doubtful
4/ 19	20.13	74,196,900		Doubtful

Boeing

11/ 1	37.75	14,194,400		Falling
11/ 2	37.63	13,220,900	Down	Falling
11/ 3	37.75	13,919,500		Falling
11/ 4	37.38	13,196,600	Down	Falling
11/ 5	37.25	13,779,800		Falling
11/ 8	36.75	13,296,600		Falling
11/ 9	35.88	11,910,800	DOWN	Falling
11/ 10	35.50	10,548,500	DOWN	Falling
11/ 11	35.63	11,841,700		Falling
11/ 12	36.38	13,211,700		Falling
11/ 15	37.00	14,261,900	Up	Falling
11/ 16	37.63	15,136,300	Up	Falling
11/ 17	40.75	18,113,400	UP	Doubtful
11/ 18	39.13	15,423,000		Doubtful
11/ 19	38.50	14,145,500		Doubtful
11/ 22	38.75	15,418,400		Doubtful
11/ 23	39.00	16,253,600		Doubtful
11/ 24	38.50	15,866,800		Doubtful
11/ 26	38.75	16,136,400		Doubtful
11/ 29	39.13	17,007,000	Up	Doubtful
11/ 30	38.63	16,372,900		Doubtful
12/ 1	37.88	15,160,600	Down	Doubtful

12/ 2	37.88	15,160,600	Down	Doubtful
12/ 3	38.13	15,817,300		Doubtful
12/ 6	38.88	16,422,300		Doubtful
12/ 7	41.00	19,816,900	UP	Rising
12/ 8	39.63	17,276,300		Rising
12/ 9	39.88	18,253,300		Rising
12/ 10	40.00	19,168,200		Rising
12/ 13	41.13	20,530,200	UP	Rising
12/ 14	41.13	20,530,200	UP	Rising
12/ 15	42.75	23,187,300	UP	Rising
12/ 16	43.75	26,379,200	UP	Rising
12/ 17	44.38	29,135,300	UP	Rising
12/ 20	44.63	30,731,300	UP	Rising
12/ 21	43.88	29,338,200		Rising
12/ 22	43.63	28,124,100		Rising
12/ 23	43.75	28,861,800		Rising
12/ 27	44.25	29,457,100		Rising
12/ 28	43.63	28,725,600		Rising
12/ 29	43.13	28,269,700		Rising
12/ 30	43.13	28,269,700		Rising
12/ 31	43.25	28,724,400		Rising
1/ 3	43.63	29,601,300	Up	Rising
1/ 4	43.00	28,406.200		Rising
1/ 5	42.75	27,209,300	Down	Rising
1/ 6	43.25	28,419,100		Rising
1/ 7	42.88	27,475,300		Rising
1/ 10	42.75	26,526,700	Down	Rising
1/ 11	42.63	25,618,400	Down	Rising
1/ 12	42.88	26,709,400		Rising
1/ 13	42.88	26,709,400		Rising
1/ 14	44.38	28,178,700		Rising
1/ 17	44.50	28,901,200	Up	Rising
1/ 18	44.25	27,346,500		Rising
1/ 19	44.13	26,402,100		Rising
1/ 20	44.50	26,966,400		Rising
1/ 21	45.13	28,888,900		Rising
1/ 24	44.50	27,620,700		Rising
1/ 25	43.00	26,339,500	Down	Rising
1/ 26	42.75	25,406,200	DOWN	Falling
1/ 27	42.63	24,498,100	DOWN	Falling
1/ 28	42.63	24,498,100	DOWN	Falling
1/ 31	43.25	25,413,200		Falling
2/ 1	42.75	24,711,400		Falling
2/ 2	43.50	25,436,700	Up	Falling
2/ 3	42.88	24,256,000	DOWN	Falling
2/ 4	42.50	23,268,400	DOWN	Falling
2/ 7	42.50	23,268,400	DOWN	Falling
2/ 8	43.25	24,022,400		Falling
2/ 9	43.25	24,022,400		Falling
2/ 10	43.50	24,704,000		Falling
2/ 11	43.63	25,473,100	UP	Doubtful
2/ 14	44.63	26,934,700	UP	Doubtful
2/ 15	44.38	26,051,700		Doubtful
2/ 16	46.63	29,321,900	UP	Doubtful
2/ 17	47.75	33,357,000	UP	Doubtful
2/ 18	47.50	30,920,900		Doubtful
2/ 22	47.50	30,920,900		Doubtful
2/ 23	46.88	29,933,100		Doubtful
2/ 24	46.88	29,933,100		Doubtful
2/ 25	47.38	31,310,500		Doubtful
2/ 28	46.75	30,579,600		Doubtful
3/ 1	46.50	29,595,600	Down	Doubtful
3/ 2	46.75	30,627,700		Doubtful
3/ 3	46.25	29,448,100	Down	Doubtful
3/ 4	47.13	30,473,200		Doubtful
3/ 7	47.75	31,441,100	Up	Doubtful

3/ 8	47.00	30,674,600		Doubtful
3/ 9	46.75	30,060,400		Doubtful
3/ 10	46.88	30,608,300		Doubtful
3/ 11	47.63	31,244,000		Doubtful
3/ 14	47.88	32,287,000	Up	Doubtful
3/ 15	46.75	31,158,100		Doubtful
3/ 16	46.13	30,341,200		Doubtful
3/ 17	45.75	28,978,600	DOWN	Falling
3/ 18	47.00	30,585,100		Falling
3/ 21	46.00	29,914,400		Falling
3/ 22	46.00	29,914,400		Falling
3/ 23	46.25	30,290,500		Falling
3/ 24	46.38	31,066,900	Up	Falling
3/ 25	45.75	30,426,800		Falling
3/ 28	45.88	31,040,600		Falling
3/ 29	45.63	30,223,300	Down	Falling
3/ 30	45.38	29,162,600	Down	Falling
3/ 31	44.50	27,802,400	DOWN	Falling
4/ 4	44.25	26,857,200	DOWN	Falling
4/ 5	45.38	27,907,400		Falling
4/ 6	45.50	29,031,500		Falling
4/ 7	45.25	28,115,700		Falling
4/ 8	44.75	27,468,200		Falling
4/ 11	45.13	28,059,100		Falling
4/ 12	45.75	28,748,300		Falling
4/ 13	45.13	27,595,600		Falling
4/ 14	45.25	28,389,100		Falling
4/ 15	45.25	28,389,100		Falling
4/ 18	44.75	27,581,600	Down	Falling
4/ 19	45.38	28,549,900	Up	+Falling

Caterpillar Tractor

11/ 1	92.25	+6.519,500	UP	Doubtful
11/ 2	92.38	+6,891,200	UP	Doubtful
11/ 3	91.00	+6,377,500		Doubtful
11/ 4	89.63	+6,083,400		Doubtful
11/ 5	90.00	+6,686,700		Doubtful
11/ 8	91.38	+7,096,800	UP	Doubtful
11/ 9	90.00	+6,669.400		Doubtful
11/ 10	90.88	+7,010,300		Doubtful
11/ 11	90.38	+6,740,900		Doubtful
11/ 12	89.25	+5,821,500	Down	Doubtful
11/ 15	89.88	+6,391,400		Doubtful
11/ 16	88.75	+4,764,500	Down	Doubtful
11/ 17	88.00	+4,062,900	Down	Doubtful
11/ 18	85.88	+3,608,400	Down	Doubtful
11/ 19	85.50	+3,137,300	Down	Doubtful
11/ 22	83.50	+2,523,600	Down	Doubtful
11/ 23	83.63	+3,046,300		Doubtful
11/ 24	85.63	+3,379,200		Doubtful
11/ 26	85.63	+3,379,200		Doubtful
11/ 29	85.88	+3,798,900		Doubtful
11/ 30	85.25	+3,607,600		Doubtful
12/ 1	85.88	+3,906,200	Up	Doubtful
12/ 2	86.13	+4,164,000	Up	Doubtful
12/ 3	85.50	+3,920,200		Doubtful
12/ 6	85.88	+4.424,500	Up	Doubtful
12/ 7	84.00	+3,876,000	Down	Doubtful
12/ 8	85.13	+4,286,900		Doubtful
12/ 9	86.00	+4,552,100	UP	Doubtful
12/ 10	85.88	+4,289,400		Doubtful
12/ 13	85.50	+3,939,800		Doubtful
12/ 14	84.75	+3,619,700	DOWN	Doubtful
12/ 15	85.63	+4,001,100		Doubtful
12/ 16	86.25	+4,329,500		Doubtful

12/ 17		86.38	+4,622,700	UP	Doubtful
12/ 20		87.63	+4,847,900	UP	Doubtful
12/ 21		87.00	+4,681,800		Doubtful
12/ 22		87.38	+5,271,700	UP	Doubtful
12/ 23		87.88	+5,439,100	UP	Doubtful
12/ 27		90.00	+5,637,300	UP	Doubtful
12/ 28		90.38	+5,886,000	UP	Doubtful
12/ 29		90.50	+6,148,800	UP	Doubtful
12/ 30		90.13	+5,916,300		Doubtful
12/ 31		89.00	+5,726,700		Doubtful
1/ 3		89.38	+5,935,600		Doubtful
1/ 4		91.00	+6,283,800	UP	Doubtful
1/ 5		91.00	+6,283,800	UP	Doubtful
1/ 6		91.50	+6,584,200	UP	Doubtful
1/ 7		90.38	+6,255,500		Doubtful
1/ 10		90.50	+6,813,900	UP	Doubtful
1/ 11		90.63	+7,132,000	UP	Doubtful
1/ 12		90.63	+7.132,000	UP	Doubtful
1/ 13	xd	90.63	+7.362.600	UP	Doubtful
1/ 14		90.50	+7,041,300		Doubtful
1/ 17		92.50	+7,450,400	UP	Doubtful
1/ 18		92.75	+7,943,100	UP	Doubtful
1/ 19		93.63	+8,455,700	UP	Doubtful
1/ 20		94.00	+9,944,100	UP	Doubtful
1/ 21		98.63	+11,396,200	UP	Doubtful
1/ 24		100.25	+12,614,200	UP	Doubtful
1/ 25		98.63	+12,012,200		Doubtful
1/ 26		99.25	+12,595,300		Doubtful
1/ 27		101.50	+13,298,800	UP	Doubtful
1/ 28		103.63	+13,868,400	UP	Doubtful
1/ 31		104.13	+14,569,600	UP	Doubtful
2/ 1		105.63	+15,289,300	UP	Doubtful
2/ 2		104.63	+14,852,100		Doubtful
2/ 3		105.38	+15,222,900		Doubtful
2/ 4		102.50	+14,603,200	Down	Doubtful
2/ 7		105.25	+15,553,700	UP	Rising
2/ 8		108.00	+16,164,600	UP	Rising
2/ 9		108.88	+16,698,300	UP	Rising
2/ 10		106.13	+16,116,400		Rising
2/ 11		105.13	+15,458,500		Rising
2/ 14		106.00	+15,879,200		Rising
2/ 15		107.50	+16,255,400		Rising
2/ 16		107.38	+15,837,100		Rising
2/ 17		108.75	+16,432,600	Up	Rising
2/ 18		108.13	+15,845,600		Rising
2/ 22		110.63	+16,695,000	Up	Rising
2/ 23		110.63	+16.695,000	Up	Rising
2/ 24		108.63	+16,027,700		Rising
2/ 25		107.75	+15,621,000	Down	Rising
2/ 28		108.38	+15,896,700		Rising
3/ 1		108.88	+16,385,200		Rising
3/ 2		112.00	+17,008,900	UP	Rising
3/ 3		112.75	+17,819,300	UP	Rising
3/ 4		112.13	+17,305,400		Rising
3/ 7		114.13	+17,699,400		Rising
3/ 8		114.50	+18,323,600	UP	Rising
3/ 9		114.63	+18,816,600	UP	Rising
3/ 10		115.00	+19,302,000	UP	Rising
3/ 11		116.50	+19,909,900	UP	Rising
3/ 14		117.00	+20,286,400	UP	Rising
3/ 15		117.25	+20.646,400	UP	Rising
3/ 16		116.25	+20,359,600		Rising
3/ 17		119.50	+20,672,700	UP	Rising
3/ 18		119.13	+19,546,900	Down	Rising
3/ 21		118.38	+19,155,800	Down	Rising
3/ 22		118.75	+19,508,300		Rising

3/ 23		120.75	+20,100,700		Rising
3/ 24		116.88	+19,240,200		Rising
3/ 25		116.63	+18,787,100	Down	Rising
3/ 28		114.00	+18,051,700	Down	Rising
3/ 29		110.88	+17,538,600	Down	Rising
3/ 30		109.50	+16,388,400	Down	Rising
3/ 31		112.38	+17,151,600		Rising
4/ 4		113.25	+18,148,200		Rising
4/ 5		116.25	+18,827,600		Rising
4/ 6		120.00	+19,372,000		Rising
4/ 7		118.50	+18,760,800		Rising
4/ 8		117.38	+18,281,100		Rising
4/ 11		115.88	+18,001,400		Rising
4/ 12		114.75	+17,702,800		Rising
4/ 13		113.50	+17,257,100		Rising
4/ 14		112.13	+16,984,100		Rising
4/ 15		111.88	+16,560,400		Rising
4/ 18		110.63	+16,244,800	Down	Rising
4/ 19		108.38	+15,355,900	DOWN	Doubtful

Chevron

11/ 1		96.75	170,296,900		Rising
11/ 2		95.13	169,649,500		Rising
11/ 3		94.75	169,241,700	DOWN	Falling
11/ 4	xl	94.50	169,637,200		Falling
11/ 5		93.88	169,241,800		Falling
11/ 8		93.38	168,922,500	DOWN	Falling
11/ 9		92.50	168,394,400	DOWN	Falling
11/ 10		91.50	167,410,600	DOWN	Falling
11/ 11		90.13	166,967,700	DOWN	Falling
11/ 12		90.75	167,536,500		Falling
11/ 15		90.63	166,947,400	DOWN	Falling
11/ 16		90.00	166,174,300	DOWN	Falling
11/ 17		93.00	167,037,600		Falling
11/ 18		89.00	156,568,600	DOWN	Falling
11/ 19		89.88	158,138,400		Falling
11/ 22		89.63	157,378,500		Falling
11/ 23		89.75	158,068,800		Falling
11/ 24		89.75	158,068,800		Falling
11/ 26		85.50	157,196,700	Down	Falling
11/ 29		85.63	158,522,800	Up	Falling
11/ 30		86.88	159,558,000	Up	Falling
12/ 1		87.00	160,298,500	Up	Falling
12/ 2		86.13	159,523,500		Falling
12/ 3		86.38	160,139,500		Falling
12/ 6		86.63	160,643,800	Up	Falling
12/ 7		87.00	161,127,700	Up	Falling
12/ 8		86.00	160,652,500		Falling
12/ 9		86.00	160,652,500		Falling
12/ 10		86.63	161,218,100	Up	Falling
12/ 13		86.50	160,582,800	Down	Falling
12/ 14		85.50	159,824,300	Down	Falling
12/ 15		84.38	159,313,700	Down	Falling
12/ 16		84.25	158,709,200	Down	Falling
12/ 17		84.88	159,474,200		Falling
12/ 20		86.13	159,937,100		Falling
12/ 21		86.13	159,937,100		Falling
12/ 22		87.50	160,479,000		Falling
12/ 23		87.63	160,859,200		Falling
12/ 27		88.63	161,201,800		Falling
12/ 28		88.88	161,575,800	UP	Rising
12/ 29		88.00	160,979,800		Rising
12/ 30		88.13	161,477,900		Rising
12/ 31		87.13	161,118,300		Rising
1/ 3		88.00	161,920,200	UP	Rising

1/ 4	89.50	162,434,900	UP	Rising
1/ 5	90.75	163,475,500	UP	Rising
1/ 6	90.50	162,895,500		Rising
1/ 7	91.38	163,372,700		Rising
1/ 10	91.75	163,998,000	UP	Rising
1/ 11	90.75	163,523,000		Rising
1/ 12	89.88	162,823,100	Down	Rising
1/ 13	89.63	162,205,400	Down	Rising
1/ 14	89.88	162,809,600		Rising
1/ 17	89.88	162,809,600		Rising
1/ 18	89.38	162,292,500		Rising
1/ 19	90.00	162,949,400	Up	Rising
1/ 20	90.50	163,381,000	Up	Rising
1/ 21	91.38	164,407,900	UP	Rising
1/ 24	92.63	165,369,500	UP	Rising
1/ 25	92.50	164,897,200		Rising
1/ 26	92.00	164,282,400		Rising
1/ 27	91.75	163,781,300		Rising
1/ 28	91.75	163,781,300		Rising
1/ 31	93.38	164,210,800		Rising
2/ 1	93.25	163,697,900	Down	Rising
2/ 2	93.88	164,200,500		Rising
2/ 3	94.38	164,709,200	Up	Rising
2/ 4	92.63	164,182,100		Rising
2/ 7	92.50	163,475,900	DOWN	Falling
2/ 8	91.75	162,992,400	DOWN	Falling
2/ 9	92.25	163,556,500		Falling
2/ 10	91.38	163,152,700		Falling
2/ 11	90.25	162,524,400	DOWN	Falling
2/ 14	89.88	162,002,500	DOWN	Falling
2/ 15	89.88	162,002,500	DOWN	Falling
2/ 16	89.50	161,492,100	DOWN	Falling
2/ 17	89.00	160,504,100	DOWN	Falling
2/ 18	88.25	159,683,100	DOWN	Falling
2/ 22	88.88	160,195,300		Falling
2/ 23	88.63	159,935,400		Falling
2/ 24	87.25	159,460,200	DOWN	Falling
2/ 25	85.75	158,492,400	DOWN	Falling
2/ 28	86.63	158,955,700		Falling
3/ 1	85.13	158,326,000	DOWN	Falling
3/ 2	87.25	158,945,500		Falling
3/ 3	88.75	159,785,100	Up	Falling
3/ 4	88.25	158,970,100		Falling
3/ 7	87.63	158,386,700		Falling
3/ 8	87.75	158,880,900		Falling
3/ 9	87.75	158.880,900		Falling
3/ 10	87.88	159,392,000		Falling
3/ 11	88.00	160,008,200	Up	Falling
3/ 14	87.75	159,492,700		Falling
3/ 15	88.00	159,947,400		Falling
3/ 16	89.75	160,541,500	Up	Falling
3/ 17	91.50	161,239,500	Up	Falling
3/ 18	92.75	162,549,000	Up	Falling
3/ 21	90.88	161,953,200		Falling
3/ 22	90.88	161,953,200		Falling
3/ 23	91.00	162,249,200		Falling
3/ 24	90.63	161,722,400	Down	Falling
3/ 25	89.50	160,937,100	Down	Falling
3/ 28	88.25	159,951,200	Down	Falling
3/ 29	87.25	159,592,800	Down	Falling
3/ 30	83.75	158,880,200	Down	Falling
3/ 31	84.00	159,664,300		Falling
4/ 4	83.75	159,019,200		Falling
4/ 5	85.38	159,625,400		Falling
4/ 6	84.75	159,019,800		Falling
4/ 7	85.25	159,421,100		Falling

4/ 8		84.88	158,794,900	Down	Falling
4/ 11		86.00	159,369,800		Falling
4/ 12		86.38	159,760,300	Up	Falling
4/ 13		86.00	159,484,600		Falling
4/ 14		88.38	160,548,600	Up	Falling
4/ 15		90.63	161,626,300	Up	Falling
4/ 18		89.88	160,667,400		Falling
4/ 19		91.25	161,391,000		Falling

Coca Cola

11/ 1		43.13	121,926,800		Doubtful
11/ 2		42.63	120,684,000		Doubtful
11/ 3		42.00	119,102,800	DOWN	Doubtful
11/ 4		41.50	117,811,100	DOWN	Doubtful
11/ 5		41.50	117,811,100	DOWN	Doubtful
11/ 8		41.50	117,811,100	DOWN	Doubtful
11/ 9		41.13	116,244,400	DOWN	Doubtful
11/ 10		40.63	114,120,700	DOWN	Doubtful
11/ 11		40.13	112,221,700	DOWN	Doubtful
11/ 12		40.75	113,644,500		Doubtful
11/ 15		41.38	114,633,100		Doubtful
11/ 16		42.13	115,339,400		Doubtful
11/ 17		42.38	117,031,300		Doubtful
11/ 18		42.00	115,431,300		Doubtful
11/ 19		42.63	117,860,500	Up	Doubtful
11/ 22		42.13	116,213,199		Doubtful
11/ 23		42.25	117,196,300		Doubtful
11/ 24	xd	42.00	117,196,300		Doubtful
11/ 26		42.25	117,643,300		Doubtful
11/ 29		42.25	117,643,300		Doubtful
11/ 30		42.00	116,473,300		Doubtful
12/ 1		42.25	117,890,000	Up	Doubtful
12/ 2		42.50	118,452,800	Up	Doubtful
12/ 3		42.88	119,297,800	Up	Doubtful
12/ 6		43.50	120,867,600	Up	Doubtful
12/ 7		44.00	122,131,500	Up	Doubtful
12/ 8		43.75	120,636,900		Doubtful
12/ 9		43.63	119,031,100		Doubtful
12/ 10		43.50	118,075,900		Doubtful
12/ 13		43.75	119,006,100		Doubtful
12/ 14		43.25	117,403,600	Down	Doubtful
12/ 15		42.63	115,672,500	Down	Doubtful
12/ 16		43.38	117,155,500		Doubtful
12/ 17		42.63	114,510,100	Down	Doubtful
12/ 20		42.88	115,428,700		Doubtful
12/ 21		43.50	116,625,600		Doubtful
12/ 22		44.00	118,265,900	Up	Doubtful
12/ 23		43.50	116,752,200		Doubtful
12/ 27		44.25	117,672,600		Doubtful
12/ 28		44.63	119,163,400	Up	Doubtful
12/ 29		45.00	121,041,600	Up	Doubtful
12/ 30		44.88	120,007,700		Doubtful
12/ 31		44.63	119,091,600		Doubtful
1/ 3		44.50	117,737,400		Doubtful
1/ 4		44.13	116,612,600	Down	Doubtful
1/ 5		43.00	114,761,400	Down	Doubtful
1/ 6		42.13	112,005,600	DOWN	Falling
1/ 7		42.63	114,290,200		Falling
1/ 10		43.38	115,855,100		Falling
1/ 11		42.75	114,506,500		Falling
1/ 12		43.25	115,588,000		Falling
1/ 13		42.63	114,620.600		Falling
1/ 14		42.50	112,982,900	Down	Falling
1/ 17		41.63	111,681,500	DOWN	Falling
1/ 18		41.00	108,672,700	DOWN	Falling

1/ 19		41.50	110,395,300		Falling
1/ 20		41.38	109,250,300		Falling
1/ 21		41.25	106,906,700	DOWN	Falling
1/ 24		40.50	105,629,200	DOWN	Falling
1/ 25		40.75	107,041,800		Falling
1/ 26		41.00	108,461,000		Falling
1/ 27		41.75	110,263,600		Falling
1/ 28		41.25	108,211,500		Falling
1/ 31		40.88	106,167,800		Falling
2/ 1		41.50	107,989,700		Falling
2/ 2		41.50	107,989,700		Falling
2/ 3		41.75	109,597,600		Falling
2/ 4		40.75	107,697,700		Falling
2/ 7		40.75	107,697,700		Falling
2/ 8		40.25	106,266,700		Falling
2/ 9		40.50	107,585,500		Falling
2/ 10		40.75	108,920,900		Falling
2/ 11		41.50	110,376,800	Up	Falling
2/ 14		41.00	109,227,500		Falling
2/ 15		40.88	107,368,900		Falling
2/ 16		41.38	108,905,400		Falling
2/ 17		41.75	111,149,700	Up	Falling
2/ 18		41.50	108,955,300		Falling
2/ 22		42.50	110,895,500		Falling
2/ 23		42.63	112,568,000	Up	Falling
2/ 24		42.00	111,153,100		Falling
2/ 25		42.00	111,153,100		Falling
2/ 28		42.63	112,895,700	Up	Falling
3/ 1		42.38	111,255,600		Falling
3/ 2		42.13	109,655,000	Down	Falling
3/ 3		41.63	108,569,600	Down	Falling
3/ 4		41.63	108,569,600	Down	Falling
3/ 7		41.63	108,569,600	Down	Falling
3/ 8		41.00	107,582.900	Down	Falling
3/ 9	xd	40.88	109,011,800		Falling
3/ 10		40.75	107,874,700		Falling
3/ 11		40.88	108,967,100		Falling
3/ 14		41.63	110,338,400	Up	Falling
3/ 15		41.13	108,275,100		Falling
3/ 16		41.13	108,275,100		Falling
3/ 17		41.50	110,298,600		Falling
3/ 18		41.88	115,143,800	UP	Rising
3/ 21		42.00	116,378,200	UP	Rising
3/ 22		42.13	117,626,500	UP	Rising
3/ 23		41.88	116,582,000		Rising
3/ 24		41.88	116,582,000		Rising
3/ 25		41.75	115,643,900		Rising
3/ 28		42.13	116,511,100		Rising
3/ 29		41.88	115,080,000	Down	Rising
3/ 30		41.00	113,306,500	Down	Rising
3/ 31		40.63	111,185,600	Down	Rising
4/ 4		40.25	108,757,900	Down	Rising
4/ 5		40.50	111,443,000		Rising
4/ 6		41.00	113,326,600		Rising
4/ 7		41.25	114,771,300		Rising
4/ 8		41.13	113,692,100		Rising
4/ 11		40.38	112,238,600		Rising
4/ 12		39.75	110,517,400		Rising
4/ 13		40.50	111,587,500		Rising
4/ 14		39.38	110,116,800	Down	Rising
4/ 15		39.38	110,116,800	Down	Rising
4/ 18		39.38	110,116,800	Down	Rising
4/ 19		39.63	111,348,900		Rising

Disney

11/ 1	43.63	-21,078,700	Up	Doubtful
11/ 2	43.00	-22,769,100		Doubtful
11/ 3	42.38	-24,041,300		Doubtful
11/ 4	42.50	-22,576,900		Doubtful
11/ 5	41.63	-24,053,400	Down	Doubtful
11/ 8	41.38	-25,474,600	Down	Doubtful
11/ 9	41.25	-26,474,400	Down	Doubtful
11/ 10	41.13	-30,219,200	DOWN	Falling
11/ 11	40.38	-32,670,900	DOWN	Falling
11/ 12	40.13	-34,689,100	DOWN	Falling
11/ 15	40.00	-36,282,300	DOWN	Falling
11/ 16	40.00	-36,282,300	DOWN	Falling
11/ 17	39.25	-37,779,100	DOWN	Falling
11/ 18	39.38	-36,123,300		Falling
11/ 19	39.00	-38,383,300	DOWN	Falling
11/ 22	38.13	-40,287,000	DOWN	Falling
11/ 23	38.88	-38,785,900		Falling
11/ 24	39.00	-37,583,800		Falling
11/ 26	38.88	-38,009,800		Falling
11/ 29	39.38	-36,872,300	Up	Falling
11/ 30	39.88	-35,116,500	Up	Falling
12/ 1	40.75	-33,361,000	Up	Falling
12/ 2	41.38	-31,961,900	Up	Falling
12/ 3	41.25	-32,898,000		Falling
12/ 6	41.00	-33,868,200		Falling
12/ 7	41.50	-32,873,600		Falling
12/ 8	41.63	-31,328,800	Up	Falling
12/ 9	42.25	-29,519,500	Up	Falling
12/ 10	42.00	-30,296,000		Falling
12/ 13	42.50	-29,536,900		Falling
12/ 14	42.00	-30,757,200	Down	Falling
12/ 15	42.13	-29,917,900		Falling
12/ 16	42.50	-28,747,500	UP	Rising
12/ 17	43.38	-26,243,300	UP	Rising
12/ 20	43.00	-27,321,500		Rising
12/ 21	43.25	-26,429,200		Rising
12/ 22	44.50	-24,593,900	UP	Rising
12/ 23	44.75	-22,632,400	UP	Rising
12/ 27	44.38	-23,471,300		Rising
12/ 28	44.00	-24,733,700		Rising
12/ 29	43.88	-26,171,300		Rising
12/ 30	43.75	-27.082,600		Rising
12/ 31	42.63	-27,741,300	Down	Rising
1/ 3	42.13	-26,365,200		Rising
1/ 4	44.63	-24,607,400		Rising
1/ 5	44.88	-23,099,700		Rising
1/ 6	45.38	-20,814,100	UP	Rising
1/ 7	46.50	-18,290.700	UP	Rising
1/ 10	47.75	-15,113,200	UP	Rising
1/ 11	47.13	-17,323,100		Rising
1/ 12	46.63	-18,884,100		Rising
1/ 13	46.00	-20,107,100		Rising
1/ 14	47.63	-18,280,200		Rising
1/ 17	46.63	-19,244,400		Rising
1/ 18	46.88	-18,152,900	Up	Rising
1/ 19	46.13	-16,754,900	Up	Rising
1/ 20	47.38	-15,309,500	Up	Rising
1/ 21	47.50	-13,640,000	UP	Rising
1/ 24	46.88	-14,560,500		Rising
1/ 25	47.00	-12,799,000	UP	Rising
1/ 26	47.13	-11,776,800	UP	Rising
1/ 27	46.63	-12,948,400		Rising
1/ 28	47.13	-11,075,000	UP	Rising
1/ 31	47.25	-9,587.700	UP	Rising

2/ 1		47.13	-10,487,400		Rising
2/ 2		47.00	-11,528,800		Rising
2/ 3		46.88	-12,463,500		Rising
2/ 4		45.00	-14,299,800	Down	Rising
2/ 7		46.63	-12,486,800		Rising
2/ 8		45.63	-13,935,400		Rising
2/ 9		45.25	-15,483,400	Down	Rising
2/ 10		45.63	-14,219,400		Rising
2/ 11		45.88	-13,349,700		Rising
2/ 14		46.38	-12,349,000	Up	Rising
2/ 15		46.75	-11,417,200	Up	Rising
2/ 16		46.88	-10,710,800	Up	Rising
2/ 17		46.75	-11,864,600		Rising
2/ 18		45.38	-13,309,900		Rising
2/ 22		45.88	-12,016,000		Rising
2/ 23		46.63	-10,822,200		Rising
2/ 24		47.38	-9,403,300	UP	Rising
2/ 25		47.88	-8,111,900	UP	Rising
2/ 28		48.00	-6,417,800	UP	Rising
3/ 1		47.63	-7,536,800		Rising
3/ 2		46.75	-8,554,800		Rising
3/ 3		45.75	-9,589,100		Rising
3/ 4		46.13	-8,428,200		Rising
3/ 7		46.38	-7,783,800		Rising
3/ 8		46.38	-7,783,800		Rising
3/ 9		47.75	-6,596,600		Rising
3/ 10		46.88	-7,512,900		Rising
3/ 11		47.00	-6,811,300		Rising
3/ 14		45.88	-8,804,300	Down	Rising
3/ 15		46.00	-7,196,500		Rising
3/ 16		45.75	-8,040,700		Rising
3/ 17		45.75	-8,040,700		Rising
3/ 18		47.00	-5,492,400	UP	Rising
3/ 21		46.13	-6,352,700		Rising
3/ 22		46.75	-5,404,900	UP	Rising
3/ 23		46.25	-6,211,100		Rising
3/ 24		45.25	-7,244,800	Down	Rising
3/ 25		45.00	-7,973,500	Down	Rising
3/ 28		44.00	-9,295,400	DOWN	Doubtful
3/ 29		43.13	-10,571,000	DOWN	Doubtful
3/ 30		42.25	-12,311,600	DOWN	Doubtful
3/ 31		42.00	-14,440,300	DOWN	Doubtful
4/ 4		41.63	-16,159,100	DOWN	Doubtful
4/ 5		42.88	-14,881,500		Doubtful
4/ 6		42.38	-15,879,900		Doubtful
4/ 7		42.38	-15,879,900		Doubtful
4/ 8		41.75	-16,534,100	DOWN	Doubtful
4/ 11		42.25	-15,641,100		Doubtful
4/ 12		42.25	-15,641,100		Doubtful
4/ 13		41.75	-16,479,300		Doubtful
4/ 14		41.38	-17,396,800	DOWN	Doubtful
4/ 15		40.88	-18,658,400	DOWN	Doubtful
4/ 18		40.00	-19,866,400	DOWN	Doubtful
4/ 19		41.63	-18,038,100		Doubtful

DuPont

11/ 1		47.75	91,969,600	UP	Rising
11/ 2		48.25	92,872,600	UP	Rising
11/ 3		47.88	92,145,800		Rising
11/ 4		48.50	92,804,500		Rising
11/ 5		48.88	93,768,200	UP	Rising
11/ 8	xd	48.13	93,012,300		Rising
11/ 9		47.13	92,435,000		Rising
11/ 10		47.00	91,245,600	Down	Rising
11/ 11		46.50	90,610,400	Down	Rising

11/ 12	47.38	91,463,000		Rising
11/ 15	48.13	92,432,100		Rising
11/ 16	48.38	92,898,000		Rising
11/ 17	47.88	92,282,600		Rising
11/ 18	48.88	92,938,600	Up	Rising
11/ 19	49.00	94,212,500	UP	Rising
11/ 22	49.00	94,212,500	UP	Rising
11/ 23	48.63	93,293,000		Rising
11/ 24	48.25	92,874,600		Rising
11/ 26	48.13	92,602,100		Rising
11/ 29	48.00	92,148,800	Down	Rising
11/ 30	47.75	91,422,300	Down	Rising
12/ 1	47.75	91,422,300	Down	Rising
12/ 2	47.75	91,422,300	Down	Rising
12/ 3	47.75	91,422,300	Down	Rising
12/ 6	48.00	92.014,800		Rising
12/ 7	47.25	91,429,400		Rising
12/ 8	47.50	92,184,800	Up	Rising
12/ 9	46.75	91,526,900		Rising
12/ 10	47.25	92,304,400	Up	Rising
12/ 13	48.38	93,219,600	Up	Rising
12/ 14	49.13	94,423,100	UP	Rising
12/ 15	49.25	95,620,500	UP	Rising
12/ 16	49.63	96,348,200	UP	Rising
12/ 17	49.38	94,895,100		Rising
12/ 20	49.50	95,541,800		Rising
12/ 21	49.38	94,609,100	Down	Rising
12/ 22	49.50	95,170,400		Rising
12/ 23	49.00	94,743,600		Rising
12/ 27	49.75	95,170,200		Rising
12/ 28	49.63	94,729,500	Down	Rising
12/ 29	49.25	93,796,000	Down	Rising
12/ 30	48.75	93,317,200	Down	Rising
12/ 31	48.25	92,759,900	Down	Rising
1/ 3	49.50	93,737,900		Rising
1/ 4	51.00	95,074,700		Rising
1/ 5	51.88	96,945,300	UP	Rising
1/ 6	52.38	98,790,400	UP	Rising
1/ 7	51.25	97,832,300		Rising
1/ 10	52.38	98,774,000		Rising
1/ 11	52.00	97,676,400	Down	Rising
1/ 12	51.88	96,917,800	Down	Rising
1/ 13	51.13	96,313,300	Down	Rising
1/ 14	52.38	97,269,200		Rising
1/ 17	52.88	97,854,900		Rising
1/ 18	53.38	98,871,400	UP	Rising
1/ 19	53.63	99,721,600	UP	Rising
1/ 20	54.13	100,594,100	UP	Rising
1/ 21	54.75	102,811,400	UP	Rising
1/ 24	54.13	101,492,300		Rising
1/ 25	54.38	102,445,200		Rising
1/ 26	54.13	100,679,900	Down	Rising
1/ 27	55.13	102,236,000		Rising
1/ 28	55.38	103,440,100	UP	Rising
1/ 31	56.13	104,558,000	UP	Rising
2/ 1	56.50	105,862,400	UP	Rising
2/ 2	56.00	104,390,200		Rising
2/ 3	55.63	103,420,200		Rising
2/ 4	53.63	102,072,700		Rising
2/ 7	54.88	103,154,800		Rising
2/ 8	54.88	103,154,800		Rising
2/ 9	55.00	103,834,300		Rising
2/ 10	54.00	103,101,600		Rising
2/ 11	54.25	103,692,600		Rising
2/ 14	54.38	104,493,300	Up	Rising
2/ 15	55.00	105,430,200	Up	Rising

2/ 16	54.88	104,611,100		Rising
2/ 17	54.50	103,529,400		Rising
2/ 18	54.88	104,147,900		Rising
2/ 22	54.75	103,387,300	Down	Rising
2/ 23	54.63	101,892,700	Down	Rising
2/ 24	53.25	100,778,200	Down	Rising
2/ 25	53.50	101,450,300		Rising
2/ 28	53.25	100,758,100	Down	Rising
3/ 1	52.50	99,726,800	DOWN	Doubtful
3/ 2	52.00	98,083,000	DOWN	Doubtful
3/ 3	51.75	97,279,600	DOWN	Doubtful
3/ 4	52.63	98,123,200		Doubtful
3/ 7	53.00	98,680,000		Doubtful
3/ 8	52.88	98,060,100		Doubtful
3/ 9	53.63	99,015,900	Up	Doubtful
3/ 10	-55.00	100,444,700	Up	Doubtful
3/ 11	55.75	101,869,400	Up	Doubtful
3/ 14	56.25	102,748,200	Up	Doubtful
3/ 15	55.88	101,404,000		Doubtful
3/ 16	57.00	103,691,700	Up	Doubtful
3/ 17	58.63	105,427,200	Up	Doubtful
3/ 18	58.75	110,562,500	UP	Doubtful
3/ 21	57.88	109,040,800		Doubtful
3/ 22	57.50	107,704,300		Doubtful
3/ 23	58.00	108,660,100		Doubtful
3/ 24	56.75	106,833,200	Down	Doubtful
3/ 25	56.25	106,143,500	Down	Doubtful
3/ 28	56.88	106,950,000		Doubtful
3/ 29	54.50	106,002,000	Down	Doubtful
3/ 30	53.25	104,605,500	Down	Doubtful
3/ 31	53.00	102,938,200	Down	Doubtful
4/ 4	52.63	101,449,700	Down	Doubtful
4/ 5	54.13	103,019,400		Doubtful
4/ 6	54.13	103,019,400		Doubtful
4/ 7	55.25	104,156,900		Doubtful
4/ 8	56.50	105,634,600		Doubtful
4/ 11	57.00	106,885,900		Doubtful
4/ 12	57.00	106,885,900		Doubtful
4/ 13	56.25	105,895,000		Doubtful
4/ 14	56.88	106,588,200		Doubtful
4/ 15	57.00	107,988,300	Up	Doubtful
4/ 18	56.88	104,643,400	Down	Doubtful
4/ 19	56.63	102,443,600	Down	Doubtful

Eastman Kodak

11/ 1	61.75	140,030,400		Falling
11/ 2	61.88	142,205,200		Falling
11/ 3	62.13	144,365,200		Falling
11/ 4	61.13	143,396,000		Falling
11/ 5	61.13	143,396,000		Falling
11/ 8	62.00	144,510,800	Up	Falling
11/ 9	62.38	145,434,800	Up	Falling
11/ 10	62.75	146,437,300	Up	Falling
11/ 11	63.50	147,664,000	UP	Doubtful
11/ 12	62.88	146,397,300		Doubtful
11/ 15	63.00	147,027,900		Doubtful
11/ 16	63.00	147,027,900		Doubtful
11/ 17	61.50	146,290,600	Down	Doubtful
11/ 18	60.75	145,215,300	Down	Doubtful
11/ 19	61.00	146,495,100		Doubtful
11/ 22	62.25	147,664,600	UP	Rising
11/ 23	62.25	147,664,600	UP	Rising
11/ 24 xd	61.75	147,664,600	UP	Rising
11/ 26	61.38	147,456,900		Rising
11/ 29	61.38	147,456,900		Rising

11/ 30	60.88	146,566,700		Rising
12/ 1	61.88	148,022,900	UP	Rising
12/ 2	62.13	148,682,300	UP	Rising
12/ 3	62.25	149,244,400	UP	Rising
12/ 6	62.88	149,755,100	UP	Rising
12/ 7	61.38	148,204,600		Rising
12/ 8	62.50	149,232,300		Rising
12/ 9	63.13	150,406,400	UP	Rising
12/ 10	63.50	151,355,800	UP	Rising
12/ 13	64.00	152,281,900	UP	Rising
12/ 14	62.75	151,438,800		Rising
12/ 15	55.50	139,752,700	DOWN	Doubtful
12/ 16	54.25	133,635,700	DOWN	Doubtful
12/ 17	55.25	137,048,300		Doubtful
12/ 20	55.88	138,987,000		Doubtful
12/ 21	56.13	140,987,300		Doubtful
12/ 22	55.63	142,338,100		Doubtful
12/ 23	56.13	142,996,300		Doubtful
12/ 27	56.13	142,996,300		Doubtful
12/ 28	56.13	142,996,300		Doubtful
12/ 29	56.25	143,631,900		Doubtful
12/ 30	56.13	143,147,800		Doubtful
12/ 31	56.25	143,450,100		Doubtful
1/ 3	56.00	142,145,700	Down	Doubtful
1/ 4	45.88	144,522,800	Up	Doubtful
1/ 5	45.63	142,965,900		Doubtful
1/ 6	46.38	144,554,400	Up	Doubtful
1/ 7	46.25	143,254,300		Doubtful
1/ 10	46.75	144,419,500		Doubtful
1/ 11	46.00	143,179,400	Down	Doubtful
1/ 12	45.63	141,241,300	DOWN	Falling
1/ 13	45.63	141,241,300	DOWN	Falling
1/ 14	45.50	140,275,800	DOWN	Falling
1/ 17	46.00	141,143,100		Falling
1/ 18	44.00	139,011,200	DOWN	Falling
1/ 19	43.00	135,557,400	DOWN	Falling
1/ 20	42.50	132,122,800	DOWN	Falling
1/ 21	42.50	132,122,800	DOWN	Falling
1/ 24	42.25	130,963,400	DOWN	Falling
1/ 25	42.50	133,279,600		Falling
1/ 26	43.00	134,784,700		Falling
1/ 27	43.00	134,784,700		Falling
1/ 28	43.50	135,904,700		Falling
1/ 31	44.13	137,340,900		Falling
2/ 1	44.25	138,964,300		Falling
2/ 2	44.88	140,169,400		Falling
2/ 3	44.25	139,248,700		Falling
2/ 4	43.50	137,960,800		Falling
2/ 7	43.50	137,960,800		Falling
2/ 8	43.50	137,960,800		Falling
2/ 9	43.00	136,409,100		Falling
2/ 10	42.88	135,257,300		Falling
2/ 11	43.38	136,319,500		Falling
2/ 14	42.88	134,395,900	Down	Falling
2/ 15	43.00	135,584,600		Falling
2/ 16	42.75	134,444,900		Falling
2/ 17	42.63	133,414,400	Down	Falling
2/ 18	42.50	132,207,200	Down	Falling
2/ 22	42.00	130,925,800	DOWN	Falling
2/ 23	41.00	129,829,500	DOWN	Falling
2/ 24	41.50	131,851,700		Falling
2/ 25	42.38	133,949,300		Falling
2/ 28	43.00	135,594,900	Up	Falling
3/ 1	43.00	135,594,900	Up	Falling
3/ 2	44.25	138,272,000	Up	Falling
3/ 3	44.00	136,989,100		Falling

3/ 4		44.63	137,534,100		Falling
3/ 7		44.63	137,534,100		Falling
3/ 8		45.00	140,120,300	Up	Falling
3/ 9		44.88	139,131,200		Falling
3/ 10		44.38	137,483,800		Falling
3/ 11		44.63	138,322,100		Falling
3/ 14		45.00	139,362,900		Falling
3/ 15		45.00	139,362,900		Falling
3/ 16		45.13	140,260,800	Up	Falling
3/ 17		45.00	139,597,000		Falling
3/ 18		45.13	141,640,700	Up	Falling
3/ 21		45.25	142,606,600	Up	Falling
3/ 22		45.25	142,606,600	Up	Falling
3/ 23		45.13	141,389,800		Falling
3/ 24		45.00	140,801,900		Falling
3/ 25		44.75	140,293,300		Falling
3/ 28		45.00	141,227,200		Falling
3/ 29		44.75	139,323,700	Down	Falling
3/ 30		44.63	135,636,100	Down	Falling
3/ 31		44.38	131,380,200	Down	Falling
4/ 4		44.00	128,315,800	DOWN	Falling
4/ 5		43.88	126,440,400	DOWN	Falling
4/ 6		43.63	125,803,400	DOWN	Falling
4/ 7		43.38	125,278,400	DOWN	Falling
4/ 8		42.25	124,178,300	DOWN	Falling
4/ 11		42.88	124,998,900		Falling
4/ 12		42.88	124,998,900		Falling
4/ 13		43.13	126,009,700		Falling
4/ 14		42.50	125,637,000		Falling
4/ 15		42.50	125,637,000		Falling
4/ 18		42.38	124,962,100		Falling
4/ 19		42.00	124,331,400		Falling

Exxon

11/ 1		65.13	239,829,800	Down	Rising
11/ 2		65.00	238,829,900	Down	Rising
11/ 3		64.63	237,680,900	Down	Rising
11/ 4		64.63	237,680,900	Down	Rising
11/ 5	xd	64.25	238,771,400		Rising
11/ 8		64.00	238,202,300		Rising
11/ 9		63.88	237,415,700	Down	Rising
11/ 10		64.25	238,055,700		Rising
11/ 11		63.75	237,283,100	Down	Rising
11/ 12		63.38	236,254,900	DOWN	Doubtful
11/ 15		62.75	235,170,900	DOWN	Doubtful
11/ 16		62.75	235,170,900	DOWN	Doubtful
11/ 17		63.75	236,716,300		Doubtful
11/ 18		64.50	237,900.100		Doubtful
11/ 19		64.25	236,104,200		Doubtful
11/ 22		64.25	236,104.200		Doubtful
11/ 23		63.88	235,404,300		Doubtful
11/ 24		63.25	234,595,700	DOWN	Doubtful
11/ 26		61.75	233,556,800	DOWN	Doubtful
11/ 27		61.88	233,306,900		Doubtful
11/ 30		62.75	236,845,400		Doubtful
12/ 1		62.00	235,543,100		Doubtful
12/ 2		62.25	236,471,300		Doubtful
12/ 3		62.63	237,329,400	Up	Doubtful
12/ 6		62.75	238,180,200	Up	Doubtful
12/ 7		62.63	237,217,600		Doubtful
12/ 8		62.25	236,213,800		Doubtful
12/ 9		62.25	236,213,800		Doubtful
12/ 10		62.99	237,519,600		Doubtful
12/ 13		62.88	237,519,600		Doubtful
12/ 14		63.00	238,606,000	Up	Doubtful

12/ 15	63.13	239,917,100	Up	Doubtful
12/ 16	63.50	240,951,300	Up	Doubtful
12/ 17	64.00	243,226,000	UP	Doubtful
12/ 20	63.75	242,352,000		Doubtful
12/ 21	63.13	241,393,500		Doubtful
12/ 22	63.00	239,917,000		Doubtful
12/ 23	63.00	239,917,000		Doubtful
12/ 27	64.25	240,895,600		Doubtful
12/ 28	64.00	240,176,100		Doubtful
12/ 29	63.63	239,217,700	Down	Doubtful
12/ 30	63.63	239,217,700	Down	Doubtful
12/ 31	63.13	238,417,700	Down	Doubtful
1/ 3	63.75	240,043,800		Doubtful
1/ 4	64.25	241,215,500	Up	Doubtful
1/ 5	64.63	242,892,800	Up	Doubtful
1/ 6	64.25	241,564,100		Doubtful
1/ 7	63.75	240,507,900		Doubtful
1/ 10	64.63	241,624,200		Doubtful
1/ 11	64.50	240,248,500	Down	Doubtful
1/ 12	64.88	241,308,100		Doubtful
1/ 13	65.63	243.276,600	UP	Rising
1/ 14	64.75	241,694,700		Rising
1/ 17	65.00	242,354,100		Rising
1/ 18	64.88	241,375,200	Down	Rising
1/ 19	65.50	242,244,300		Rising
1/ 20	66.38	243,377,400	UP	Rising
1/ 21	66.13	241,433,900		Rising
1/ 24	66.13	241,443,900		Rising
1/ 25	66.25	242,585,200		Rising
1/ 26	66.13	241,488,000		Rising
1/ 27	65.13	240,343,800	DOWN	Doubtful
1/ 28	65.75	241,455,300		Doubtful
1/ 31	66.50	242,465,900		Doubtful
2/ 1	66.25	241,388,300		Doubtful
2/ 2	67.13	243,580,000	UP	Doubtful
2/ 3	67.00	241,994,000		Doubtful
2/ 4	65.50	241,013,000	Down	Doubtful
2/ 7	65.38	239,933,600	DOWN	Doubtful
2/ 8	65.38	239,933,600	DOWN	Doubtful
2/ 9	66.00	240,902,900		Doubtful
2/ 10	65.88	239,888,700	DOWN	Doubtful
2/ 11	66.50	240,687,000		Doubtful
2/ 14	66.25	239,737,200	DOWN	Doubtful
2/ 15	66.63	240,882,100	Up	Doubtful
2/ 16	66.75	241,828,300	Up	Doubtful
2/ 17	66.75	241,828,300	Up	Doubtful
2/ 18	66.13	240,354,200		Doubtful
2/ 22	66.63	241,047,800		Doubtful
2/ 23	66.50	240,273,900	Down	Doubtful
2/ 24	65.25	239,309,600	DOWN	Falling
2/ 25	65.50	240,526,300		Falling
2/ 28	64.88	239,580,900		Falling
3/ 1	64.88	239,580,900		Falling
3/ 2	65.88	241,007,800	Up	Falling
3/ 3	66.13	242,219,500	UP	Doubtful
3/ 4	65.25	241,533,700		Doubtful
3/ 7	65.25	241,533,700		Doubtful
3/ 8	65.38	242,363,000	UP	Doubtful
3/ 9	65.50	243,160,500	UP	Doubtful
3/ 10	64.88	242,349,700		Doubtful
3/ 11	65.25	243,525,700	UP	Doubtful
3/ 14	65.25	243,525,700	UP	Doubtful
3/ 15	64.75	242,571,600		Doubtful
3/ 16	64.88	243,720,900	UP	Doubtful
3/ 17	65.63	245,173,400	UP	Doubtful
3/ 18	65.88	248,979,000	UP	Doubtful

3/ 21	65.50	248,186,400		Doubtful
3/ 22	65.63	248,934,000		Doubtful
3/ 23	65.38	248,316,600		Doubtful
3/ 24	65.50	249,521,100	UP	Doubtful
3/ 25	65.50	249,521,100	UP	Doubtful
3/ 28	65.00	248,445,800		Doubtful
3/ 29	65.00	248,445,800		Doubtful
3/ 30	63.50	246,978,400	Down	Doubtful
3/ 31	62.88	245,041,700	Down	Doubtful
4/ 4	61.00	242,593,400	Down	Doubtful
4/ 5	61.13	245,606,500		Doubtful
4/ 6	61.13	245,606,500		Doubtful
4/ 7	61.25	247,149,100		Doubtful
4/ 8	61.00	245,215,700		Doubtful
4/ 11	61.63	246,186,900		Doubtful
4/ 12	61.63	246,186,900		Doubtful
4/ 13	61.75	247,050,800		Doubtful
4/ 14	62.88	248,534,400	Up	Doubtful
4/ 15	63.00	250,363,300	UP	Rising
4/ 18	62.25	249,243,600		Rising
4/ 19	63.13	248,242,700		Rising

General Electric

11/ 1	97.50	182,112,600	Up	Doubtful
11/ 2	97.13	181,160,000		Doubtful
11/ 3	96.38	180,144,400	DOWN	Falling
11/ 4	93.75	178,812,300	DOWN	Falling
11/ 5	94.13	180,192,300		Falling
11/ 8	93.75	179,362,400		Falling
11/ 9	94.50	180,518,000	Up	Falling
11/ 10	94.63	181,337,000	Up	Falling
11/ 11	93.88	180,471,400		Falling
11/ 12	93.88	180,471,400		Falling
11/ 15	94.25	181,499,400	Up	Falling
11/ 16	96.50	182,598,600	UP	Doubtful
11/ 17	96.63	183,646,500	UP	Doubtful
11/ 18	97.50	184,732,100	UP	Doubtful
11/ 19	98.25	186,281,600	UP	Doubtful
11/ 22	98.25	186,281,600	UP	Doubtful
11/ 23	98.50	187,695,300	UP	Doubtful
11/ 24	97.75	187,008,400		Doubtful
11/ 26	98.50	187,303,800		Doubtful
11/ 29	97.88	186,463,400	Down	Doubtful
11/ 30	98.38	187,080,500		Doubtful
12/ 1	98.63	188,925,100	UP	Rising
12/ 2	100.00	190,009,300	UP	Rising
12/ 3	100.13	191,381,300	UP	Rising
12/ 6	100.38	192,149,200	UP	Rising
12/ 7	99.75	191,305,900		Rising
12/ 8	100.38	192,092,700		Rising
12/ 9	101.00	193,653,400	UP	Rising
12/ 10	101.63	194,698,600	UP	Rising
12/ 13	101.00	193,826,300		Rising
12/ 14	102.38	195,168,000	UP	Rising
12/ 15	103.38	197,173,200	UP	Rising
12/ 16	103.50	198,577,200	UP	Rising
12/ 17	105.13	201,294,200	UP	Rising
12/ 20	104.25	200,311,300		Rising
12/ 21	105.38	201,561,400	UP	Rising
12/ 22	105.38	201,561,400	UP	Rising
12/ 23	106.13	202,900,500	UP	Rising
12/ 27	106.75	203,501,700	UP	Rising
12/ 28	106.50	202,505,400		Rising
12/ 29	106.50	202,505,400		Rising
12/ 30	105.88	201,650,900		Rising

12/ 31	104.88	200,969,600		Rising
1/ 3	104.00	199,683,700	Down	Rising
1/ 4	103.63	198,007,600	Down	Rising
1/ 5	103.00	196,698,100	Down	Rising
1/ 6	103.88	198,877,200		Rising
1/ 7	104.38	199,741,400		Rising
1/ 10	104.88	200,844,800		Rising
1/ 11	105.63	202,333,000		Rising
1/ 12	106.00	206,300,500	UP	Rising
1/ 13	105.25	205,186,600		Rising
1/ 14	106.75	206,871,100	UP	Rising
1/ 17	107.13	207,687,900	UP	Rising
1/ 18	108.38	209,072,800	UP	Rising
1/ 19	108.75	209,942,100	UP	Rising
1/ 20	108.50	208,844,000		Rising
1/ 21	108.00	207,080,000		Rising
1/ 24	107.75	206,222,700		Rising
1/ 25	107.00	205,163,000	Down	Rising
1/ 26	106.50	204,291,600	Down	Rising
1/ 27	108.25	205,262,300		Rising
1/ 28	107.88	203,986,900	Down	Rising
1/ 31	107.75	202,698,500	Down	Rising
2/ 1	106.88	201,792,400	Down	Rising
2/ 2	109.13	203,000,800		Rising
2/ 3	109.75	204,361,700		Rising
2/ 4	106.50	203,008,400		Rising
2/ 7	108.25	204,352,700		Rising
2/ 8	107.25	203,588,200		Rising
2/ 9	108.25	204,438,500	Up	Rising
2/ 10	106.50	203,695,500		Rising
2/ 11	107.25	204,299,200		Rising
2/ 14	108.13	205,100,000	Up	Rising
2/ 15	109.00	206,266,000	Up	Rising
2/ 16	108.88	205,424,500		Rising
2/ 17	109.13	206,650,000	Up	Rising
2/ 18	108.00	205,137,400	Down	Rising
2/ 22	108.00	205,137,400	Down	Rising
2/ 23	107.38	204,418,100	Down	Rising
2/ 24	105.38	203,205,400	Down	Rising
2/ 25	105.13	202,208,600	Down	Rising
2/ 28	105.38	202,964,000		Rising
3/ 1	105.63	204,202,700		Rising
3/ 2	105.75	205,553,100		Rising
3/ 3	105.00	204,650,600		Rising
3/ 4	104.88	203,575,400		Rising
3/ 7	105.75	204,327,300		Rising
3/ 8	105.00	203,496,900	Down	Rising
3/ 9	105.38	204,330,100	Up	Rising
3/ 10	104.50	203,463,200	DOWN	Falling
3/ 11	105.25	204,249,300		Falling
3/ 14	105.25	204,249,300		Falling
3/ 15	104.88	203,378,700	DOWN	Falling
3/ 16	103.75	202,316,600	DOWN	Falling
3/ 17	103.00	201,048,700	DOWN	Falling
3/ 18	104.50	204,435,900	UP	Doubtful
3/ 21	104.00	203,591,000		Doubtful
3/ 22	103.25	202,722,600		Doubtful
3/ 23	103.88	203,477,900		Doubtful
3/ 24	103.63	202,519,400	Down	Doubtful
3/ 25	102.13	201.641,700	Down	Doubtful
3/ 28	103.50	202,527,300		Doubtful
3/ 29	102.25	201,662,000		Doubtful
3/ 30	98.75	199,015,600	DOWN	Doubtful
3/ 31	100.00	201,312,900		Doubtful
4/ 4	98.00	198,603,700	DOWN	Doubtful
4/ 5	98.88	200,421,400		Doubtful

4/ 6	97.63	198,048,900	DOWN	Doubtful
4/ 7	98.25	199,305,700		Doubtful
4/ 8	97.25	198,153,500		Doubtful
4/ 11	98.38	199,219,800		Doubtful
4/ 12	99.25	200,062,700	Up	Doubtful
4/ 13	98.88	198,950,100		Doubtful
4/ 14	97.50	198,122,700	Down	Doubtful
4/ 15	96.75	196,571,000	DOWN	Falling
4/ 18	94.88	194,799,900	DOWN	Falling
4/ 19	95.50	196,413,200		Falling

General Motors

11/ 1	48.25	184,986,900		Rising
11/ 2	49.00	187,606,500	UP	Rising
11/ 3	49.25	192,256,800	UP	Rising
11/ 4	48.38	189,919,200		Rising
11/ 5	47.75	187,439,000		Rising
11/ 8	48.63	189,170,500		Rising
11/ 9	48.63	189,170,500		Rising
11/ 10	51.13	194,215,000	UP	Rising
11/ 11	50.75	188,747,600		Rising
11/ 12	51.13	191,502,500		Rising
11/ 15	51.50	193,359,000		Rising
11/ 16	52.75	197,416,600	UP	Rising
11/ 17	53.75	202,165,300	UP	Rising
11/ 18	54.63	206,763,800	UP	Rising
11/ 19	54.25	202,957,900		Rising
11/ 22	52.75	199,950,600		Rising
11/ 23	52.75	199,950,600		Rising
11/ 24	53.75	201,810,500		Rising
11/ 26	53.88	202,279,300		Rising
11/ 29	54.38	204,214,300		Rising
11/ 30	52.75	201,529,200		Rising
12/ 1	53.25	204,245,000	Up	Rising
12/ 2	53.50	205,820,200	Up	Rising
12/ 3	55	208,887,100	UP	Rising
12/ 6	54.75	206,370,500		Rising
12/ 7	54.50	204,499,300		Rising
12/ 8	55.25	207,347,100		Rising
12/ 9	56	210,898,800	UP	Rising
12/ 10	56.13	212,457,400	UP	Rising
12/ 13	56.13	212,457,400	UP	Rising
12/ 14	54.88	210,949,000		Rising
12/ 15	54.63	208,220,600		Rising
12/ 16	54.75	209,751,400		Rising
12/ 17	54.75	209,751,400		Rising
12/ 20	54.25	208,502,000		Rising
12/ 21	54.88	210,984,000	Up	Rising
12/ 22	55.63	213,239,600	UP	Rising
12/ 23	55.25	211,673,200		Rising
12/ 27	56.25	213,108,800		Rising
12/ 28	56.75	214,413,100	UP	Rising
12/ 29	56.00	213,189,600		Rising
12/ 30	55.63	212,370,000		Rising
12/ 31	54.88	211,519,900	Down	Rising
1/ 3	55.38	213,605,600		Rising
1/ 4	56.75	216,018,900	UP	Rising
1/ 5	56.88	218,459,700	UP	Rising
1/ 6	57.13	221,433,700	UP	Rising
1/ 7	57.88	224,021,300	UP	Rising
1/ 10	59.25	227,826,100	UP	Rising
1/ 11	59.50	231,537,100	UP	Rising
1/ 12	59.25	227,567,600		Rising
1/ 13	60.25	229,672,400		Rising
1/ 14	61.25	232,303,400	UP	Rising

1/ 17	60.75	231,004,800		Rising
1/ 18	62.13	234,219,700	UP	Rising
1/ 19	60.88	231,708,600		Rising
1/ 20	60.13	229,299,900	Down	Rising
1/ 21	60.88	232,046,500		Rising
1/ 24	60.13	230,398,800		Rising
1/ 25	59.25	228,448,700	Down	Rising
1/ 26	58.63	226,159,500	Down	Rising
1/ 27	59.88	228,725,400		Rising
1/ 28	59.25	226,662,300		Rising
1/ 31	61.25	229,439,700	Up	Rising
2/ 1	61.00	226,480,300	Down	Rising
2/ 2	61.50	228,697,000		Rising
2/ 3	63.00	232,919,600	UP	Rising
2/ 4	61.63	228,119,000		Rising
2/ 7	63.00	232,403,100		Rising
2/ 8	64.75	236,428,600	UP	Rising
2/ 9	64.25	233,247,700		Rising
2/ 10	62.50	225,482,100	DOWN	Doubtful
2/ 11	61.13	222,000,200	DOWN	Doubtful
2/ 14	61.75	224,810,500		Doubtful
2/ 15	61.63	222,109,900		Doubtful
2/ 16	61.00	219,821,600	DOWN	Doubtful
2/ 17	60.00	216,975,700	DOWN	Doubtful
2/ 18	59.75	214,329,400	DOWN	Doubtful
2/ 22	59.75	214,329,400	DOWN	Doubtful
2/ 23	59.88	216,722,000		Doubtful
2/ 24	59.00	214,118,000	DOWN	Doubtful
2/ 25	58.25	211,765,700	DOWN	Doubtful
2/ 28	58.25	211,765,700	DOWN	Doubtful
3/ 1	58.13	209,676,800	DOWN	Doubtful
3/ 2	60.50	214,600,400		Doubtful
3/ 3	60.50	214,600,400		Doubtful
3/ 4	62.00	217,607,200	Up	Doubtful
3/ 7	61.50	216,017,400		Doubtful
3/ 8	62.00	218,291,900	Up	Doubtful
3/ 9	62.63	220,082,000	Up	Doubtful
3/ 10	62.25	218,604,300		Doubtful
3/ 11	62.88	220,183,600	Up	Doubtful
3/ 14	62.75	219,023,100		Doubtful
3/ 15	61.50	217,610,500	Down	Doubtful
3/ 16	61.75	219,397,400		Doubtful
3/ 17	60.38	218,017,100		Doubtful
3/ 18	59.88	213,695,800	Down	Doubtful
3/ 21	59.63	211,904,000	Down	Doubtful
3/ 22	59.63	211,904,000	Down	Doubtful
3/ 23	60.50	213,723,800		Doubtful
3/ 24	58.33	210,289,500	Down	Doubtful
3/ 25	56.88	207,951,800	DOWN	Falling
3/ 28	57.38	210,705,900		Falling
3/ 29	56.00	208,516,500		Falling
3/ 30	54.25	204,172,000	DOWN	Falling
3/ 31	53.88	198,721,900	DOWN	Falling
4/ 4	55.00	202,755,000		Falling
4/ 5	57.25	206,918,100		Falling
4/ 6	58.75	211,569,700	Up	Falling
4/ 7	60.13	215,776,900	Up	Falling
4/ 8	57.75	212,689,300		Falling
4/ 11	58.00	214,349,400		Falling
4/ 12	57.38	212,974,300		Falling
4/ 13	57.00	210,597,600	Down	Falling
4/ 14	58.00	212,793,800		Falling
4/ 15	58.50	214,798,800	Up	Falling
4/ 18	56.88	212,638,500		Falling
4/ 19	55.25	208,538,600	DOWN	Falling

Goodyear

11/ 1	45.13	105,863,200		Doubtful
11/ 2	45.38	106,251,400		Doubtful
11/ 3	44.38	105,760,600		Doubtful
11/ 4	43.75	105,365,000	DOWN	Doubtful
11/ 5	43.25	104,931,300	DOWN	Doubtful
11/ 8	43.88	105,316,500		Doubtful
11/ 9	42.75	104,883,600	DOWN	Doubtful
11/ 10	43.50	105,395,900	Up	Doubtful
11/ 11	42.50	104,878,100	DOWN	Falling
11/ 12	42.63	105,360,100		Falling
11/ 15	41.50	104,846,800	DOWN	Falling
11/ 16	41.75	105,320,600		Falling
11/ 17	41.00	104,814,100	DOWN	Falling
11/ 18	42.13	105,337,800	Up	Falling
11/ 19	41.75	104,846,600		Falling
11/ 22	40.88	104,450,200	DOWN	Falling
11/ 23	41.50	104,889,100		Falling
11/ 24	41.75	105,401,100	UP	Doubtful
11/ 26	41.75	105,401,100	UP	Doubtful
11/ 29	42.38	105,743,500	UP	Doubtful
11/ 30	44.50	106,706,000	UP	Doubtful
12/ 1	45.38	107,592,400	UP	Doubtful
12/ 2	45.50	108,516,800	UP	Doubtful
12/ 3	45.38	107,854,600		Doubtful
12/ 6	45.88	108,396,200		Doubtful
12/ 7	46.25	109,145,900	UP	Doubtful
12/ 8	46.13	108,575,600		Doubtful
12/ 9	46.38	109,043,700		Doubtful
12/ 10	47.00	109,417,300	UP	Doubtful
12/ 13	47.00	109,417,300	UP	Doubtful
12/ 14	46.25	108,992,800		Doubtful
12/ 15	44.00	107,981,000	Down	Doubtful
12/ 16	43.63	107,481,100	Down	Doubtful
12/ 17	43.38	106,777,500	Down	Doubtful
12/ 20	44.00	107,213,600		Doubtful
12/ 21	43.88	106,892,200		Doubtful
12/ 22	44.50	107,146,000		Doubtful
12/ 23	44.75	107,409,100	Up	Doubtful
12/ 27	45.25	107,692,300	Up	Doubtful
12/ 28	45.75	107,875,500	Up	Doubtful
12/ 29	45.63	107,590,900		Doubtful
12/ 30	45.50	107,461,300		Doubtful
12/ 31	45.75	107,726,500		Doubtful
1/ 3	44.38	107,373,700	Down	Doubtful
1/ 4	44.50	107,874,800	Up	Doubtful
1/ 5	45.00	108,424,400	UP	Rising
1/ 6	46.00	108,871,100	UP	Rising
1/ 7	45.75	108,569,700		Rising
1/ 10	46.63	108,871,400	UP	Rising
1/ 11	46.38	108,422,000	Down	Rising
1/ 12	45.50	107,866,200	Down	Rising
1/ 13	45.00	107,529,800	Down	Rising
1/ 14	47.25	108,300,000		Rising
1/ 17	49.13	109,092,200	UP	Rising
1/ 18	47.00	108,485,300		Rising
1/ 19	47.50	108,986,400		Rising
1/ 20	47.63	109,334,100	UP	Rising
1/ 21	47.63	109,334,100	UP	Rising
1/ 24	48.00	109,702,500	UP	Rising
1/ 25	48.38	109,981,000	UP	Rising
1/ 26	47.75	109,702,500		Rising
1/ 27	48.50	110,099,200	UP	Rising
1/ 28	47.88	109,688,000	Down	Rising
1/ 31	48.38	110,296,200	UP	Rising

2/ 1	48.75	110,695,200		Rising
2/ 2	48.00	110,295,700		Rising
2/ 3	47.63	110,074,900		Rising
2/ 4	47.00	109,599,300	DOWN	Doubtful
2/ 7	46.38	109,011,600	DOWN	Doubtful
2/ 8	47.50	109,539,300		Doubtful
2/ 9	48.13	110,316,000		Doubtful
2/ 10	47.13	109,773,400		Doubtful
2/ 11	45.88	109,142,700		Doubtful
2/ 14	46.00	109,616,500		Doubtful
2/ 15	47.50	110,103,900		Doubtful
2/ 16	47.00	109,836,400		Doubtful
2/ 17	47.25	110,157,100	Up	Doubtful
2/ 18	46.63	109,874,500		Doubtful
2/ 22	46.25	109,610,799	Down	Doubtful
2/ 23	45.00	109,137,000	Down	Doubtful
2/ 24	44.25	108,592,200	DOWN	Falling
2/ 25	45.00	109,313,800		Falling
2/ 28	45.25	110,108,800		Falling
3/ 1	44.00	109,479,500		Falling
3/ 2	44.75	110,171,700	UP	Doubtful
3/ 3	44.25	109,789,100		Doubtful
3/ 4	44.00	109,267,500	Down	Doubtful
3/ 7	44.13	109,654,100		Doubtful
3/ 8	44.00	109,016,200	Down	Doubtful
3/ 9	44.50	109,474,700		Doubtful
3/ 10	44.00	109,036,800		Doubtful
3/ 11	44.25	109,445,800		Doubtful
3/ 14	45.13	109,756,800	Up	Doubtful
3/ 15	45.63	110,204,600	UP	Rising
3/ 16	45.00	109,898,100		Rising
3/ 17	45.63	110,357,500	UP	Rising
3/ 18	45.25	109,689,000	Down	Rising
3/ 21	44.63	109,296,400	Down	Rising
3/ 22	44.13	108,558,600	DOWN	Rising
3/ 23	43.75	108,144,200	DOWN	Rising
3/ 24	43.38	107,620,400	DOWN	Rising
3/ 25	41.75	107,144,200	DOWN	Rising
3/ 28	42.75	108,398,500		Rising
3/ 29	41.75	107,569,200		Rising
3/ 30	40.13	106,084,800	DOWN	Rising
3/ 31	40.50	106,851,300		Rising
4/ 4	39.50	105,888,900	DOWN	Rising
4/ 5	40.63	107,742,000	Up	Rising
4/ 6	40.50	106,539,500		Rising
4/ 7	40.50	106,539,500		Rising
4/ 8	41.75	107,310,900		Rising
4/ 11	41.50	106,726,000		Rising
4/ 12	40.88	106,242,300	Down	Rising
4/ 13	41.13	106,953,800		Rising
4/ 14	40.00	106,415,700		Rising
4/ 15	40.00	106,415,700		Rising
4/ 18	39.50	106,033,500	Down	Rising
4/ 19	38.88	105,422,900	DOWN	Rising

IBM

11/ 1	47.75	11,564,200		Rising
11/ 2	50.88	21,722,300	UP	Rising
11/ 3	50.75	16,547,900		Rising
11/ 4	49.75	13,524,600		Rising
11/ 5	49.88	16,824,200		Rising
11/ 8	50.25	18,705,100		Rising
11/ 9	49.13	16,187,300		Rising
11/ 10	49.88	18,244,000		Rising
11/ 11	52.00	21,927,400	UP	Rising

11/ 12	51.63	18,730,200		Rising
11/ 15	51.00	17,276,800		Rising
11/ 16	52.75	20,666,000		Rising
11/ 17	51.88	16,285,300	Down	Rising
11/ 18	52.75	18,720,400		Rising
11/ 19	51.88	16,388,700		Rising
11/ 22	52.00	18.984,000	Up	Rising
11/ 23	53.13	21,051,200	Up	Rising
11/ 24	55.00	25,235,800	UP	Rising
11/ 26	55.75	26,446,800	UP	Rising
11/ 29	54.38	23,958,900		Rising
11/ 30	53.88	21,982,100		Rising
12/ 1	53.13	19,596,800		Rising
12/ 2	53.75	21,462,600		Rising
12/ 3	53.50	19,702,900		Rising
12/ 6	53.75	21,459,600		Rising
12/ 7	53.75	21,459,600		Rising
12/ 8	53.88	22,460,600	Up	Rising
12/ 9	53.63	21,044,600		Rising
12/ 10	55.25	24,902,000	Up	Rising
12/ 13	57.38	29,783,100	UP	Rising
12/ 14	56.13	27,347,600		Rising
12/ 15	56.88	29,633,900		Rising
12/ 16	57.50	32,586,700	UP	Rising
12/ 17	59.75	38,352,500	UP	Rising
12/ 20	58.38	35,517,000		Rising
12/ 21	58.63	37,788,600		Rising
12/ 22	59.25	39,318,900	UP	Rising
12/ 23	58.63	37,995,600		Rising
12/ 27	59.13	39,407,300	UP	Rising
12/ 28	58.38	38,129,900		Rising
12/ 29	58.13	37,049,000	Down	Rising
12/ 30	57.00	35,386,200	Down	Rising
12/ 31	56.50	33,467,300	Down	Rising
1/ 3	57.63	34,898,100		Rising
1/ 4	59.00	36,744,900		Rising
1/ 5	59.50	39,314,900		Rising
1/ 6	58.50	36,935,100		Rising
1/ 7	58.88	38,393,700		Rising
1/ 10	59.25	40.128,700	UP	Rising
1/ 11	58.63	38,438,100		Rising
1/ 12	58.13	36,935,000	Down	Rising
1/ 13	58.75	38,739,200		Rising
1/ 14	58.63	37,153,200		Rising
1/ 17	57.50	35,625,100	Down	Rising
1/ 18	57.13	33,369,200	DOWN	Doubtful
1/ 19	56.00	31,409,700	DOWN	Doubtful
1/ 20	55.25	29,131,200	DOWN	Doubtful
1/ 21	55.25	29,131,200	DOWN	Doubtful
1/ 24	58.63	33,350,500		Doubtful
1/ 25	58.25	23,195,600	DOWN	Doubtful
1/ 26	56.38	19,106,000	DOWN	Doubtful
1/ 27	57.13	21,321,200		Doubtful
1/ 28	57.75	22,865,100		Doubtful
1/ 31	56.50	20,772,700		Doubtful
2/ 1	56.50	20,772,700		Doubtful
2/ 2	56.38	18,619,500	DOWN	Doubtful
2/ 3	55.75	16,855,700	DOWN	Doubtful
2/ 4	52.00	13,295,800	DOWN	Doubtful
2/ 7	54.25	17,414,600		Doubtful
2/ 8	53.63	15,405,800		Doubtful
2/ 9	53.13	13,426,700		Doubtful
2/ 10	52.88	11,861,100	DOWN	Doubtful
2/ 11	53.25	13,846,600		Doubtful
2/ 14	54.00	15,720,300		Doubtful
2/ 15	54.50	17,447,700	Up	Doubtful

2/ 16	54.63	18,943,400	Up	Doubtful
2/ 17	52.75	16,653,200		Doubtful
2/ 18	52.63	13,974,500		Doubtful
2/ 22	53.63	15,251,400		Doubtful
2/ 23	53.50	14,056,200		Doubtful
2/ 24	52.88	12,403,300	Down	Doubtful
2/ 25	52.88	12,403,300	Down	Doubtful
2/ 28	52.88	12,403,300	Down	Doubtful
3/ 1	53.63	14,438,200		Doubtful
3/ 2	53.00	11,716,100	DOWN	Falling
3/ 3	52.63	10,099,600	DOWN	Falling
3/ 4	52.63	10,099,600	DOWN	Falling
3/ 7	52.25	8,315,900	DOWN	Falling
3/ 8	54.75	12,960,400		Falling
3/ 9	55.38	16,700,500	Up	Falling
3/ 10	56.00	19,728,000	UP	Doubtful
3/ 11	55.88	18,039,700		Doubtful
3/ 14	57.50	20,955,700	UP	Doubtful
3/ 15	57.38	18,503,200		Doubtful
3/ 16	58.25	20,386,600		Doubtful
3/ 17	57.88	18,492.500	Down	Doubtful
3/ 18	57.13	15,236,300	Down	Doubtful
3/ 21	58.63	17,937,300		Doubtful
3/ 22	58.25	16,088,000		Doubtful
3/ 23	57.25	13,425,100	Down	Doubtful
3/ 24	56.38	11,384,200	Down	Doubtful
3/ 25	54.00	8,400,700	Down	Doubtful
3/ 28	52.63	5,044,200	DOWN	Doubtful
3/ 29	52.63	1,879,500	DOWN	Doubtful
3/ 30	53.50	6,012,000		Doubtful
3/ 31	54.63	9,472,400		Doubtful
4/ 4	53.00	6,707,400		Doubtful
4/ 5	53.38	9,046,500		Doubtful
4/ 6	53.13	7,116,500		Doubtful
4/ 7	53.13	7,116,500		Doubtful
4/ 8	52.50	5,817,400	Down	Doubtful
4/ 11	53.00	7,109,700		Doubtful
4/ 12	52.88	5,221.500	Down	Doubtful
4/ 13	52.38	1,725,400	DOWN	Doubtful
4/ 14	53.88	4,353,400		Doubtful
4/ 15	53.00	1,714,400	DOWN	Doubtful
4/ 18	53.63	4,834,400	Up	Doubtful
4/ 19	53.38	2,736,900		Doubtful

International Paper

11/ 1	61.75		80,985,400		Doubtful
11/ 2	62.63		81,526,700		Doubtful
11/ 3	61.50		81,076,800		Doubtful
11/ 4	61.13		80,864,600		Doubtful
11/ 5	61.75		81,130,200		Doubtful
11/ 8	62.13		81,412,300		Doubtful
11/ 9	61.50		81,171,400		Doubtful
11/ 10	62.63		81,534,500	Up	Doubtful
11/ 11	64.38		82,325,400	UP	Doubtful
11/ 12	65.88		83,347,000	UP	Doubtful
11/ 15	65.25	xd	82,966,400		Doubtful
11/ 16	66.00		83,458,800	UP	Doubtful
11/ 17	65.25		83,038,400		Doubtful
11/ 18	64.13		82,592,400	Down	Doubtful
11/ 19	65.13		83,223,300		Doubtful
11/ 22	65.00		82,860,200		Doubtful
11/ 23	65.25		63,158,900		Doubtful
11/ 24	65.63		83,374,000	Up	Doubtful
11/ 26	66.25		83,543,600	UP	Rising
11/ 29	66.50		83,887,600	UP	Rising

11/ 30	66.75	84,289,400	UP	Rising
12/ 1	67.50	84,681,600	UP	Rising
12/ 2	66.88	84,244.400		Rising
12/ 3	67.13	84,503,500		Rising
12/ 6	67.50	84,847,600	UP	Rising
12/ 7	67.88	85,138,700	UP	Rising
12/ 8	67.50	84,789,400		Rising
12/ 9	66.63	84,393,800		Rising
12/ 10	67.00	84,674,100		Rising
12/ 13	68.00	84,945,100		Rising
12/ 14	67.13	84,676,700		Rising
12/ 15	66.88	84,252,500	Down	Rising
12/ 16	66.25	84,012,800	Down	Rising
12/ 17	67.88	84,638,800		Rising
12/ 20	67.63	84,329,800		Rising
12/ 21	67.75	84,487,200		Rising
12/ 22	66.88	84,317,500	Down	Rising
12/ 23	66.88	84,317,500	Down	Rising
12/ 27	68.25	84,314,100		Rising
12/ 28	67.88	84,161,800		Rising
12/ 29	67.88	84,161,800		Rising
12/ 30	68.25	84,278,600		Rising
12/ 31	67.75	84,056,500	Down	Rising
1/ 3	68.00	84,314,300	Up	Rising
1/ 4	69.63	84,927,400	Up	Rising
1/ 5	72.38	86,400,800	UP	Rising
1/ 6	71.50	85,483,000		Rising
1/ 7	72.63	86,300,700		Rising
1/ 10	73.63	86,852,100	UP	Rising
1/ 11	72.88	86,276,700		Rising
1/ 12	72.25	85,507,900		Rising
1/ 13	71.50	84,995,500	Down	Rising
1/ 14	72.00	85,423,300		Rising
1/ 17	72.50	85,787,400		Rising
1/ 18	74.38	86,621.300		Rising
1/ 19	74.25	86,051,500		Rising
1/ 20	73.75	85,648,500		Rising
1/ 21	74.38	86,715,100	Up	Rising
1/ 24	74.88	87,628,000	UP	Rising
1/ 25	74.50	87,172,700		Rising
1/ 26	74.00	86,771,800		Rising
1/ 27	74.88	87,351,500		Rising
1/ 28	74.88	87,351,500		Rising
1/ 31	75.13	87,742,400	UP	Rising
2/ 1	76.13	88,233,600	UP	Rising
2/ 2	77.00	88,935,300	UP	Rising
2/ 3	77.13	89,478,000	UP	Rising
2/ 4	75.75	88,818,100		Rising
2/ 7	76.63	89,408,800		Rising
2/ 8	76.00	88,909,000		Rising
2/ 9	76.25	89,595,400	UP	Rising
2/ 10	76.25	89,595,400	UP	Rising
2/ 11	76.50	90,066,800	UP	Rising
2/ 14	75.75	89,469,000		Rising
2/ 15	75.50	88,956,500		Rsiing
2/ 16	75.50	88,956,500		Rising
2/ 17	74.50	88,373,700	Down	Rising
2/ 18	74.63	88,993,100		Rising
2/ 22	74.50	88,713,700		Rising
2/ 23	74.75	88,991,400		Rising
2/ 24	73.25	88,438,700	Down	Rising
2/ 25	73.50	88,656,900		Rising
2/ 28	72.63	88,373,300	Down	Rising
3/ 1	71.63	87,768,600	Down	Rising
3/ 2	71.38	87,127,900	Down	Rising
3/ 3	72.38	87,623,400		Rising

3/ 4	71.88	87,365,400		Rising
3/ 7	72.38	87,545,400		Rising
3/ 8	74.25	88,106,300	Up	Rising
3/ 9	71.50	87,290,100	Down	Rising
3/ 10	69.50	86,350,000	DOWN	Falling
3/ 11	69.88	86,848,900		Falling
3/ 14	69.75	86,375,000		Falling
3/ 15	69.13	85,848,200	DOWN	Falling
3/ 16	68.25	85,170,400	DOWN	Falling
3/ 17	69.13	85,540,300		Falling
3/ 18	70.25	86,708,000		Falling
3/ 21	68.63	86,230,300		Falling
3/ 22	69.13	86,717,100	Up	Falling
3/ 23	70.38	87,460,500	Up	Falling
3/ 24	69.50	87,066,100		Falling
3/ 25	68.38	86,671,700		Falling
3/ 28	68.88	87,242,400		Falling
3/ 29	68.50	86,797,200		Falling
3/ 30	68.50	86,797,200		Falling
3/ 31	67.88	86,014,300	Down	Falling
4/ 4	66.00	85,694,600	Down	Falling
4/ 5	67.00	86,028,900		Falling
4/ 6	67.13	86,505,200		Falling
4/ 7	66.13	85,725,400		Falling
4/ 8	65.63	84,572,800	DOWN	Falling
4/ 11	65.88	85,056,800		Falling
4/ 12	65.63	84,530,500	DOWN	Falling
4/ 13	65.25	83,986,500	DOWN	Falling
4/ 14	64.88	83,458,000	DOWN	Falling
4/ 15	64.38	82,944,100	DOWN	Falling
4/ 18	64.75	83,323,200		Falling
4/ 19	62.88	82,873,800	DOWN	Falling

McDonalds

11/ 1	57.00	43,595,700		Rising
11/ 2	56.75	43,134,500		Rising
11/ 3	55.25	42,586,700		Rising
11/ 4	54.25	41,954,900	Down	Rising
11/ 5	55.75	42,551,200		Rising
11/ 8	55.75	42,551,200		Rising
11/ 9	55.00	41,926,100	Down	Rising
11/ 10	55.25	42,461,400		Rising
11/ 11	55.38	43,173,100	Up	Rising
11/ 12	56.25	43,738,000	Up	Rising
11/ 15	55.25	43,277,700		Rising
11/ 16	57.00	43,796,600	Up	Rising
11/ 17	56.75	43,121,300	Down	Rising
11/ 18	56.75	43,121,300	Down	Rising
11/ 19	56.50	41,942,700	Down	Rising
11/ 22	55.63	41,295,300	DOWN	Falling
11/ 23	56.50	42,353,100		Falling
11/ 24	58.38	43,480,100		Falling
11/ 26	58.13	43,273,500		Falling
11/ 29	58.50	43,908,300	UP	Doubtful
11/ 30	58.63	44,625,400	UP	Doubtful
12/ 1	58.38	43,965,800		Doubtful
12/ 2	57.88	43,394,000		Doubtful
12/ 3	57.88	43,394,000		Doubtful
12/ 6	58.88	43,983,700		Doubtful
12/ 7	58.50	43,281,900	Down	Doubtful
12/ 8	57.88	42,627,500	Down	Doubtful
12/ 9	57.38	41,563,400	Down	Doubtful
12/ 10	56.88	41,156,200	DOWN	Doubtful
12/ 13	57.38	41,645,400		Doubtful
12/ 14	58.00	42,189,000		Doubtful

12/ 15	57.63	41,395,900		Doubtful
12/ 16	57.88	42,027,700		Doubtful
12/ 17	57.88	42,027,700		Doubtful
12/ 20	57.75	41,748,200		Doubtful
12/ 21	57.38	41,353,800	Down	Doubtful
12/ 22	57.50	41,855,800		Doubtful
12/ 23	56.88	41,470,800		Doubtful
12/ 27	56.50	41,107,500	DOWN	Doubtful
12/ 28	57.13	41,552,900		Doubtful
12/ 29	58.25	42,163,700	Up	Doubtful
12/ 30	57.63	41,802,300		Doubtful
12/ 31	57.00	41,513,200		Doubtful
1/ 3	56.25	40,881,400	DOWN	Falling
1/ 4	56.13	40,303,200	DOWN	Falling
1/ 5	55.50	38,904,600	DOWN	Falling
1/ 6	55.50	38,904,600	DOWN	Falling
1/ 7	57.13	39,775,000		Falling
1/ 10	58.25	40,707,700		Falling
1/ 11	58.00	39,785,800		Falling
1/ 12	58.00	39,785,800		Falling
1/ 13	57.00	39,204,500		Falling
1/ 14	57.25	39,814,700		Falling
1/ 17	56.88	39,438,100		Falling
1/ 18	57.50	40.400,100	Up	Falling
1/ 19	58.88	41,155,800	Up	Falling
1/ 20	58.88	41,155,800	Up	Falling
1/ 21	58.50	40,193,200		Falling
1/ 24	58.50	40,193,200		Falling
1/ 25	59.00	40,877,600		Falling
1/ 26	59.38	41,383,700	Up	Falling
1/ 27	60.00	42.158,200	Up	Falling
1/ 28	60.75	43,095,800	UP	Doubtful
1/ 31	60.75	43.095,800	UP	Doubtful
2/ 1	60.38	42,358,000		Doubtful
2/ 2	59.75	41,775,800		Doubtful
2/ 3	59.88	42,265,200		Doubtful
2/ 4	59.25	41,537,700	Down	Doubtful
2/ 7	59.63	42,323,100	Up	Doubtful
2/ 8	59.13	41,807,800		Doubtful
2/ 9	60.38	42,312,700		Doubtful
2/ 10	60.88	43,103,100	UP	Rising
2/ 11	60.88	43,103,100	UP	Rising
2/ 14	60.50	42,561,900		Rising
2/ 15	61.75	43,396,700	UP	Rising
2/ 16	61.13	42,712,300		Rising
2/ 17	61.75	43,673,800	UP	Rising
2/ 18	60.50	42,684,100	Down	Rising
2/ 22	60.88	43,471,000		Rising
2/ 23	60.38	42,684,000	Down	Rising
2/ 24	59.75	41,940,500	Down	Rising
2/ 25	60.25	42,376,000		Rising
2/ 28	60.63	43,082,500		Rising
3/ 1	61.00	43,894,000	UP	Rising
3/ 2	61.75	44,559,300	UP	Rising
3/ 3	61.38	44,065,400		Rising
3/ 4	61.88	44,832,000	UP	Rising
3/ 7	62.00	45,600,600	UP	Rising
3/ 8	61.25	45,103,900		Rising
3/ 9	61.13	44,740,000		Rising
3/ 10	60.50	44,258,200		Rising
3/ 11	61.50	44,617,100		Rising
3/ 14	61.75	45,059,700		Rising
3/ 15	60.50	44,371,200		Rising
3/ 16	59.88	43,725,600	Down	Rising
3/ 17	59.75	42,904.700	Down	Rising
3/ 18	60.88	44,860,700		Rising

3/ 21	60.25	44,305,200		Rising
3/ 22	61.00	44,883,900	Up	Rising
3/ 23	60.63	44,509,000		Rising
3/ 24	59.25	43,889,100	Down	Rising
3/ 25	58.38	43,121,400	Down	Rising
3/ 28	58.75	43,651,300		Rising
3/ 29	57.75	42,620,700	DOWN	Falling
3/ 30	55.75	40,641,400	DOWN	Falling
3/ 31	56.88	42,129,000		Falling
4/ 4	57.13	43,376,400		Falling
4/ 5	58.25	44,659,500	Up	Falling
4/ 6	57.75	43,736,700		Falling
4/ 7	57.38	43,257,000		Falling
4/ 8	57.25	42,757,700		Falling
4/ 11	56.88	42,381,100		Falling
4/ 12	56.25	41,991,000		Falling
4/ 13	57.25	42,572,000		Falling
4/ 14	57.00	41,993,600		Falling
4/ 15	56.38	41,122,100	Down	Falling
4/ 18	56.50	41,526,200		Falling
4/ 19	56.88	42,063,500		Falling

Merck

11/ 1	32.00	-57,395,700	DOWN	Doubtful
11/ 2	31.75	-59,811,800	DOWN	Doubtful
11/ 3	32.88	-52,105.900	UP	Doubtful
11/ 4	32.25	-55,099,400		Doubtful
11/ 8	32.18	-57,145,900		Doubtful
11/ 9	31.88	-63,059,000	DOWN	Doubtful
11/ 10	32.50	-58,446,700		Doubtful
11/ 11	32.50	-58,446,700		Doubtful
11/ 12	32.75	-55,248,600		Doubtful
11/ 15	32.75	-55,248,600		Doubtful
11/ 16	33.88	-47,666,200	UP	Doubtful
11/ 17	34.00	-42,267,700	UP	Doubtful
11/ 18	34.63	-33,671,900	UP	Doubtful
11/ 19	35.13	-27,684,600	UP	Doubtful
11/ 22	33.63	-33,334,300		Doubtful
11/ 23	34.25	-29,288,400		Doubtful
11/ 24	34.50	-26,014,800	UP	Doubtful
11/ 26	34.50	-26,014,800	UP	Doubtful
11/ 29	33.88	-28,899,500		Doubtful
11/ 30	34.25	-25,273,800	UP	Doubtful
12/ 1	34.00	-29,331,900	Down	Doubtful
12/ 2 xl	33.63	-29,331,900	Down	Doubtful
12/ 3	34.00	-25,746,600		Doubtful
12/ 6	34.25	-22,099,800	UP	Rising
12/ 7	34.13	-24,353,600		Rising
12/ 8	33.75	-26,015,200		Rising
12/ 9	33.13	-29,196,500		Rising
12/ 10	33.00	-33,703.600	DOWN	Doubtful
12/ 13	32.88	-36,416,800	DOWN	Doubtful
12/ 14	32.63	-38,529,500	DOWN	Doubtful
12/ 15	32.88	-34,946,700		Doubtful
12/ 16	33.13	-32,093,400		Doubtful
12/ 17	33.63	-27,301,100		Doubtful
12/ 20	33.88	-24,998,800		Doubtful
12/ 21	34.00	-22,353,800		Doubtful
12/ 22	34.13	-19,496,500		Doubtful
12/ 23	34.25	-16,350,900	UP	Doubtful
12/ 27	35.25	-12,668,600	UP	Doubtful
12/ 28	35.25	-12,668,600	UP	Doubtful
12/ 29	35.13	-15,728,800		Doubtful
12/ 30	34.75	-17,674,699		Doubtful
12/ 31	34.38	-19,721,300		Doubtful

1/ 3		35.25	-15,937,800		Doubtful
1/ 4		36.00	-12,241,000	UP	Doubtful
1/ 5		37.25	-1,115,000	UP	Doubtful
1/ 6		36.63	-5,062,200		Doubtful
1/ 7		37.18	-1,593,800		Doubtful
1/ 10		37.50	+1,461,000	UP	Doubtful
1/ 11		37.13	-1,047,100		Doubtful
1/ 12		36.63	-3.509,100		Doubtful
1/ 13		36.63	-3,509,100		Doubtful
1/ 14		36.50	-5,779,000	Down	Doubtful
1/ 17		36.50	-5,779,000	Down	Doubtful
1/ 18		36.63	-2,976,500		Doubtful
1/ 19		35.88	-7,576,300	Down	Doubtful
1/ 20		35.75	-10,499,600	Down	Doubtful
1/ 21		35.13	-13,919,900	Down	Doubtful
1/ 24		34.75	-16,937,000	Down	Doubtful
1/ 25		35.75	-12,833,900		Doubtful
1/ 26		35.88	-10,125,300		Doubtful
1/ 27		35.75	-11,949,100		Doubtful
1/ 28		36.00	-9,298,300	Up	Doubtful
1/ 31		36.50	-6,605,100	Up	Doubtful
2/ 1		36.25	-8,778,300		Doubtful
2/ 2		36.38	-6,886,700		Doubtful
2/ 3		36.50	-3,966,300	Up	Doubtful
2/ 4		35.13	-6,784,400		Doubtful
2/ 7		35.13	-6,784,400		Doubtful
2/ 8		34.50	-9.683,400	Down	Doubtful
2/ 9		34.88	-7,777,100		Doubtful
2/ 10		34.88	-7,777,100		Doubtful
2/ 11		34.88	-7,777,100		Doubtful
2/ 14		33.75	-11,330,900	Down	Doubtful
2/ 15		33.75	-11,330,900	Down	Doubtful
2/ 16		33.13	-14,857,500	Down	Doubtful
2/ 17		33.13	-14,857,500	Down	Doubtful
2/ 18		32.88	-18,067,400	DOWN	Falling
2/ 22		32.63	-21,169,200	DOWN	Falling
2/ 23		32.50	-24,371,100	DOWN	Falling
2/ 24		31.88	-28,123,300	DOWN	Falling
2/ 25		32.25	-25,717,200		Falling
2/ 28		32.38	-22,974,900		Falling
3/ 1		32.00	-25,822,400		Falling
3/ 2	xd	32.00	-22,880,000	Up	Falling
3/ 3		31.50	-27,410,200	Down	Falling
3/ 4		31.00	-30,420,700	DOWN	Falling
3/ 7		32.00	-26,639,700		Falling
3/ 8		31.75	-28,539,400		Falling
3/ 9		32.38	-25,867,600	Up	Falling
3/ 10		31.88	-28,361,700		Falling
3/ 11		32.13	-26,223,600		Falling
3/ 14		32.00	-27,721,700		Falling
3/ 15		31.63	-29,901,400	Down	Falling
3/ 16		31.25	-32,148,400	DOWN	Falling
3/ 17		31.50	-29,791,400		Falling
3/ 18		31.75	-24,313,700	UP	Doubtful
3/ 21		32.00	-22,251,300	UP	Doubtful
3/ 22		30.50	-27,093,300		Doubtful
3/ 23		30.13	-33,510,700	DOWN	Doubtful
3/ 24		30.25	-29,318,300		Doubtful
3/ 25		30.13	-31,371,100		Doubtful
3/ 28		30.38	-29,220,600	Up	Doubtful
3/ 29		30.13	-31,723,700	Down	Doubtful
3/ 30		29.50	-35,914,100	DOWN	Falling
3/ 31		29.75	-31,392,700		Falling
4/ 4		29.13	-36,097,900	DOWN	Falling
4/ 5		30.13	-32,786,400		Falling
4/ 6		29.63	-34,953,100		Falling

4/ 7	29.75		-32,829,700		Falling
4/ 8	30.00		-30,488,800	Up	Falling
4/ 11	29.63		-33,626,700		Falling
4/ 12	29.63		-33,626,700		Falling
4/ 13	29.38		-36,992,000	DOWN	Falling
4/ 14	29.00		-39,871,300	DOWN	Falling
4/ 15	28.38		-44,480,700	DOWN	Falling
4/ 18	28.75		-41,159,900		Falling
4/ 19	28.38		-45,800,200	DOWN	Falling

Minnesota Mining

11/ 1	104.50		52,845,000	Up	Rising
11/ 2	105.13		53,126,500	Up	Rising
11/ 3	104.25		52,775,500		Rising
11/ 4	103.25		52,496,500	DOWN	Rising
11/ 5	104.25		52,862,600		Rising
11/ 8	104.88		53,146,000	UP	Doubtful
11/ 9	106.13		53,506,000	UP	Doubtful
11/ 10	106.38		53,760,800	UP	Doubtful
11/ 11	106.13		53,553,200		Doubtful
11/ 12	105.25		53,265,600		Doubtful
11/ 15	105.50	xd	53,583,500		Doubtful
11/ 16	107.13		53,838,500	UP	Doubtful
11/ 17	107.50		54,147,600	UP	Doubtful
11/ 18	108.00		54,596,200	UP	Doubtful
11/ 19	110.13		55,303,700	UP	Doubtful
11/ 22	109.00		54,852,300		Doubtful
11/ 23	109.00		54,852,300		Doubtful
11/ 24	108.00		54,652,800		Doubtful
11/ 26	107.88		54,575,200		Doubtful
11/ 29	108.25		54,808,300		Doubtful
11/ 30	109.00		54,996,800		Doubtful
12/ 1	109.00		54,996,800		Doubtful
12/ 2	108.38		54,808,100		Doubtful
12/ 3	108.00		54,637,000		Doubtful
12/ 6	108.00		54,637,000		Doubtful
12/ 7	107.63		54,459,000	Down	Doubtful
12/ 8	108.25		54,692,800		Doubtful
12/ 9	108.13		54,468,000		Doubtful
12/ 10	108.00		54,310,500	Down	Doubtful
12/ 13	110.88		54,573,700		Doubtful
12/ 14	110.38		54,227,400	Down	Doubtful
12/ 15	111.75		54,701,500	Up	Doubtful
12/ 16	113.00		55,047,800	Up	Doubtful
12/ 17	112.25		54,323,800		Doubtful
12/ 20	112.00		54,035,600	DOWN	Falling
12/ 21	110.00		53,723,500	DOWN	Falling
12/ 22	110.38		53,953,900		Falling
12/ 23	108.88		53,721,900	DOWN	Falling
12/ 27	109.13		53,954,000	Up	Falling
12/ 28	108.25		53,782,200		Falling
12/ 29	108.75		53,996,200	Up	Falling
12/ 30	108.88		54,124,800	Up	Falling
12/ 31	108.75		53,972,100		Falling
1/ 3	106.88		53,645,300	DOWN	Falling
1/ 4	106.00		53,296,600	DOWN	Falling
1/ 5	105.75		52,934,600	DOWN	Falling
1/ 6	107.25		53,306,200		Falling
1/ 7	108.13		53,855,500		Falling
1/ 10	108.00		53,443,600		Falling
1/ 11	109.75		53,757,800		Falling
1/ 12	110.00		54,036,800	Up	Falling
1/ 13	110.50		54,350,000	UP	Doubtful
1/ 14	109.88		54,081,300		Doubtful
1/ 17	109.25		53.915,000		Doubtful

1/ 18	109.38		54,142,400		Doubtful
1/ 19	111.38		54,488,400	UP	Doubtful
1/ 20	111.13		54,220,900		Doubtful
1/ 21	112.38		55,004,700	UP	Doubtful
1/ 24	111.13		54,697,900		Doubtful
1/ 25	110.25		54,457,400		Doubtful
1/ 26	111.00		54,626,800		Doubtful
1/ 27	107.25		53,511,200	Down	Doubtful
1/ 28	107.50		54,751,000	Up	Doubtful
1/ 31	107.25		54,211,000		Doubtful
2/ 1	105.88		53,799,200		Doubtful
2/ 2	106.50		54,150,300		Doubtful
2/ 3	106.75		54,557,300		Doubtful
2/ 4	104.88		54,058,300		Doubtful
2/ 7	104.88		54,058,300		Doubtful
2/ 8	105.88		54,551,200		Doubtful
2/ 9	105.25		54,298,500		Doubtful
2/ 10	104.63		54,012,700	Down	Doubtful
2/ 11	104.88		54,214,000		Doubtful
2/ 14	105.88		54,630,700	Up	Doubtful
2/ 15	108.50		55,159,400	UP	Rising
2/ 16	109.50		55,498,200	UP	Rising
2/ 17	108.00		55,122,300		Rising
2/ 18	105.38		54,358,700		Rising
2/ 22	107.75		54,778,300		Rising
2/ 23	106.88		54,488,400		Rising
2/ 24	106.25		54,090,700	Down	Rising
2/ 25	105.75		53,751.100	DOWN	Doubtful
2/ 28	105.38		53,511,600	DOWN	Doubtful
3/ 1	103.50		52,966,700	DOWN	Doubtful
3/ 2	103.75		53,496,200		Doubtful
3/ 3	103.25		53,030,400		Doubtful
3/ 4	103.25		53,030,400		Doubtful
3/ 7	104.38		53,408,800		Doubtful
3/ 8	104.88		53,649,000	Up	Doubtful
3/ 9	105.75		53,948,700	Up	Doubtful
3/ 10	104.50		53,582,900		Doubtful
3/ 11	103.25		52,638,500	DOWN	Falling
3/ 14	102.88		52,220,000	DOWN	Falling
3/ 15	103.00		52,551,600		Falling
3/ 16	102.50		52,250,100		Falling
3/ 17	101.88		51,857,900	DOWN	Falling
3/ 18	103.00		53,078,700	Up	Falling
3/ 21	101.38		52,660,500		Falling
3/ 22	101.00		52,286,400		Falling
3/ 23	101.25		52,603,400		Falling
3/ 24	100.00		52,109,100	Down	Falling
3/ 25	100.00		52,109,100	Down	Falling
3/ 28	100.00		52,109,100	Down	Falling
3/ 29	98.38		51,411,400	DOWN	Falling
3/ 30	99.00		52,131,800		Falling
3/ 31	99.00		52,131,800		Falling
4/ 4	98.00		51,563,500		Falling
4/ 5	99.25		51,912,000		Falling
4/ 6	99.00		51,621,200		Falling
4/ 7	99.88		51,895,100		Falling
4/ 8	102.38		52,368,300	Up	Falling
4/ 11	51.63	split	53,125,300	Up	Falling
4/ 12	51.00		52,498,400		Falling
4/ 13	50.38		51,937,900		Falling
4/ 14	49.50		51,290,800	DOWN	Falling
4/ 15	48.75		50,321,500	DOWN	Falling
4/ 18	48.00		49,722,600	DOWN	Falling
4/ 19	47.75		48,809,000	DOWN	Falling

J. P. Morgan

11/ 1	71.50	22,013,300		Rising
11/ 2	70.75	21,571,500		Rising
11/ 3	69.75	20,932,200	Down	Rising
11/ 4	68.75	20,405,900	DOWN	Doubtful
11/ 5	69.88	20,944,500		Doubtful
11/ 8	70.63	21,256,800		Doubtful
11/ 9	70.88	21,582,300		Doubtful
11/ 10	70.50	21,071,700		Doubtful
11/ 11	70.00	20,317,300	DOWN	Doubtful
11/ 12	70.25	20,711,700		Doubtful
11/ 15	69.88	20,374,300		Doubtful
11/ 16	70.88	20,619,400		Doubtful
11/ 17	70.00	20,257,000	DOWN	Doubtful
11/ 18	70.00	20.257,000	DOWN	Doubtful
11/ 19	69.50	19,990,000	DOWN	Doubtful
11/ 22	69.00	19,624,400	DOWN	Doubtful
11/ 23	69.13	20,048,700		Doubtful
11/ 24	69.38	20,310,300		Doubtful
11/ 26	69.63	20,433,000		Doubtful
11/ 29	70.75	21,070,400	Up	Doubtful
11/ 30	70.88	21,382,900	Up	Doubtful
12/ 1	72.13	22,028,400	Up	Doubtful
12/ 2	72.25	22,309,,000	Up	Doubtful
12/ 3	72.00	22,007,500		Doubtful
12/ 6	72.13	22,438,100	Up	Doubtful
12/ 7	71.25	22,064,100		Doubtful
12/ 8	72.75	22,579,500	Up	Doubtful
12/ 9	71.88	22,231,400		Doubtful
12/ 10	71.13	21,848,300	Down	Doubtful
12/ 13	71.88	22,259,600		Doubtful
12/ 14	70.50	21,969,400		Doubtful
12/ 15	70.38	21,516,900	Down	Doubtful
12/ 16	71.63	21,889,400		Doubtful
12/ 17	72.50	22,456,400	Up	Doubtful
12/ 20	72.38	21,888,800		Doubtful
12/ 21	71.38	21,536,700		Doubtful
12/ 22	71.63	21,930,500		Doubtful
12/ 23	71.38	21,597,700		Doubtful
12/ 27	71.50	21,765,000		Doubtful
12/ 28	70.88	21,556,200	Down	Doubtful
12/ 29	70.63	21,230,300	DOWN	Falling
12/ 30	69.75	20,664,000	DOWN	Falling
1/ 3	69.38	20,379,600	DOWN	Falling
1/ 4	69.25	19,722,800	DOWN	Falling
1/ 5	68.75	18,726,300	DOWN	Falling
1/ 6	67.63	17,771,300	DOWN	Falling
1/ 7	69.13	18,892,600		Falling
1/ 10	69.00	18,300,800		Falling
1/ 11	69.25	18,904,200	Up	Falling
1/ 12	69.63	19,630,000	Up	Falling
1/ 13	70.38	20,746,800	Up	Falling
1/ 14	71.50	21,775,000	Up	Falling
1/ 17	70.88	21,306,600		Falling
1/ 18	71.00	21,987,400	Up	Falling
1/ 19	70.00	21,261,000	Down	Falling
1/ 20	70.00	21,261,000	Down	Falling
1/ 21	70.00	21,261,000	Down	Falling
1/ 24	69.63	20,934,500	Down	Falling
1/ 25	68.38	20,324,100	Down	Falling
1/ 26	69.75	20,854,800		Falling
1/ 27	70.38	21,279,500		Falling
1/ 28	71.13	21,896,500		Falling
1/ 31	71.75	22,363,600	UP	Rising

2/ 1	71.38	21,986,400		Rising
2/ 2	71.88	22,319,300		Rising
2/ 3	70.88	21,635,900	Down	Rising
2/ 4	68.50	21,279,600	Down	Rising
2/ 7	69.25	21,942,200		Rising
2/ 8	68.25	21,227,900	Down	Rising
2/ 9	68.88	21,781,200		Rising
2/ 10	68.50	21,444,200		Rising
2/ 11	68.38	21,199,800	Down	Rising
2/ 14	69.00	21,481,100		Rising
2/ 15	69.50	21,783,600	Up	Rising
2/ 16	68.75	21,439,900		Rising
2/ 17	68.13	20,864,600	DOWN	Falling
2/ 18	68.00	20,310,300	DOWN	Falling
2/ 22	68.75	20,610,400		Falling
2/ 23	68.63	20,183,100	DOWN	Falling
2/ 24	67.63	19,527,700	DOWN	Falling
2/ 25	68.38	19,889,100		Falling
2/ 28	68.13	19,554,100		Falling
3/ 1	67.50	18,958,100	DOWN	Falling
3/ 2	66.25	17,874,500	DOWN	Falling
3/ 3	66.88	18,656,200		Falling
3/ 4	66.13	17,816,900	DOWN	Falling
3/ 7	65.00	17,130,300	DOWN	Falling
3/ 8	65.00	17,130,300	DOWN	Falling
3/ 9	64.63	16,082,000	DOWN	Falling
3/ 10	64.38	15,267,300	DOWN	Falling
3/ 11	65.88	16,123,000		Falling
3/ 14	65.50	15,615,700		Falling
3/ 15	65.65	16,647,100	Up	Falling
3/ 16	66.00	17,272,900	Up	Falling
3/ 17	65.00	16,496,300		Falling
3/ 18	64.75	15,037,700	DOWN	Falling
3/ 21	65.25	15,400,100		Falling
3/ 22	65.38	15,918,900		Falling
3/ 23	64.75	15,556,900		Falling
3/ 24	64.25	14,841,200	DOWN	Falling
3/ 25	63.88	14,239,000	DOWN	Falling
3/ 28	63.63	13,909,200	DOWN	Falling
3/ 29	62.13	13,167,300	DOWN	Falling
3/ 30	60.50	12,099,300	DOWN	Falling
3/ 31	62.75	13,006,800		Falling
4/ 4	60.00	10,882,500	DOWN	Falling
4/ 5	60.50	11,705,900		Falling
4/ 6	62.25	12,682,000		Falling
4/ 7	63.50	13,347,000	Up	Falling
4/ 8	64.13	14,072,800	Up	Falling
4/ 11	63.88	13,323,300		Falling
4/ 12	63.50	12,948,200		Falling
4/ 13	62.75	12,407,100		Falling
4/ 14	62.50	11,863,500		Falling
4/ 15	63.63	12,793,800		Falling
4/ 18	63.25	12,407,200		Falling
4/ 19	62.88	11,925,800		Falling

Philip Morris

11/ 1	54.25	151,638,100	UP	Doubtful
11/ 2	53.75	149,275,600		Doubtful
11/ 3	53.75	149,275,600		Doubtful
11/ 4	52.63	147,610,600		Doubtful
11/ 5	55.50	150,919,200		Doubtful
11/ 8	54.75	148,471,000		Doubtful
11/ 9	55.75	152,633,200	UP	Doubtful
11/ 10	55.38	150,421,300		Doubtful
11/ 11	56.75	153,474,700	UP	Doubtful

11/ 12	59.00	158,804,100	UP	Doubtful
11/ 15	57.88	155,837,200		Doubtful
11/ 16	57.13	153,215,300		Doubtful
11/ 17	55.75	149,097,300	Down	Doubtful
11/ 18	55.00	146,635,500	Down	Doubtful
11/ 19	55.75	149,088,200		Doubtful
11/ 22	55.50	147,271,800		Doubtful
11/ 23	54.88	145,982,600	Down	Doubtful
11/ 24	55.50	148,092,200		Doubtful
11/ 26	56.38	149,036,300		Doubtful
11/ 29	55.63	147,663,300		Doubtful
11/ 30	56.00	149,251,700	Up	Doubtful
12/ 1	55.00	147,677,300		Doubtful
12/ 2	55.25	148,988,700		Doubtful
12/ 3	55.38	150,102,200	Up	Doubtful
12/ 6	55.50	152,324,200	Up	Doubtful
12/ 7	56.13	154,992,400	Up	Doubtful
12/ 8	56.00	152,246,300		Doubtful
12/ 9 xd	55.25	152,246,300		Doubtful
12/ 10	54.88	150,588,800		Doubtful
12/ 13	55.50	152,199,500		Doubtful
12/ 14	54.88	150,582,500	Down	Doubtful
12/ 15	54.50	149,245,900	Down	Doubtful
12/ 16	54.63	150,737,100		Doubtful
12/ 17	55.00	154,187,300	Up	Doubtful
12/ 20	54.63	151,931,500		Doubtful
12/ 21	55.13	153,701,000		Doubtful
12/ 22	55.63	155,539,100	UP	Rising
12/ 23	55.63	155,539,100	UP	Rising
12/ 27	55.88	156,645,800	UP	Rising
12/ 28	55.75	155,353,200		Rising
12/ 29	56.38	156,586,000		Rising
12/ 30	55.88	155,118,000	Down	Rising
12/ 31	55.63	153,848,800	Down	Rising
1/ 3	57.63	156,028,200		Rising
1/ 4	58.00	157,601.300	UP	Rising
1/ 5	58.25	159,423,100	UP	Rising
1/ 6	58.38	161,191,300	UP	Rising
1/ 7	58.50	162,285,300	UP	Rising
1/ 10	59.00	163,883,600	UP	Rising
1/ 11	58.38	162,176,600		Rising
1/ 12	58.13	160,344,300		Rising
1/ 13	57.75	159,196,600		Rising
1/ 14	57.63	157,980,400		Rising
1/ 17	56.63	156,483,600		Rising
1/ 18	57.38	158,159,700		Rising
1/ 19	57.63	159,298,900		Rising
1/ 20	57.75	160.165,900		Rising
1/ 21	57.38	158,549,400		Rising
1/ 24	57.63	160,431,000	Up	Rising
1/ 25	57.88	162,278,500	Up	Rising
1/ 26	59.25	165,565,600	UP	Rising
1/ 27	60.00	169,675,600	UP	Rising
1/ 28	59.88	167,648,800		Rising
1/ 31	60.25	169,825,300	UP	Rising
2/ 1	59.75	168,393,900		Rising
2/ 2	59.50	166,868,900	Down	Rising
2/ 3	60.13	169,212,500		Rising
2/ 4	59.88	165,652,300	Down	Rising
2/ 7	59.88	165,652,300	Down	Rising
2/ 8	58.75	162,885,100	Down	Rising
2/ 9	59.13	164,316,900		Rising
2/ 10	57.75	162,672,700	Down	Rising
2/ 11	57.50	161,310,600	Down	Rising
2/ 14	58.75	162,719,700		Rising
2/ 15	59.38	164,036,600		Rising

2/ 16	59.13	161,851,600		Rising
2/ 17	58.13	159,894,500	Down	Rising
2/ 18	57.88	158,452,300	Down	Rising
2/ 22	58.25	159,636,200		Rising
2/ 23	58.88	161,603,300		Rising
2/ 24	58.25	159,415,500		Rising
2/ 25	58.00	157,834,700	Down	Rising
2/ 28	56.00	153,566,200	DOWN	Doubtful
3/ 1	55.50	149,393,600	DOWN	Doubtful
3/ 2	55.63	152,466,700		Doubtful
3/ 3	54.88	150,889,300		Doubtful
3/ 4	54.88	150,889,300		Doubtful
3/ 7	56.88	154,489,400	Up	Doubtful
3/ 8	56.00	152,595,200		Doubtful
3/ 9	55.38 xd	154,293,000		Doubtful
3/ 10	54.88	152,777,200		Doubtful
3/ 11	55.25	154,162,200		Doubtful
3/ 14	56.13	156,880,000	Up	Doubtful
3/ 15	56.00	153,867,200		Doubtful
3/ 16	55.88	152,480,400	Down	Doubtful
3/ 17	54.88	150,523,300	Down	Doubtful
3/ 18	55.00	154,549,000		Doubtful
3/ 21	54.00	152,943,800		Doubtful
3/ 22	52.13	148,088,100	DOWN	Falling
3/ 23	52.88	150,970,700		Falling
3/ 24	52.25	148,608,800		Falling
3/ 25	51.50	147,014,300	DOWN	Falling
3/ 28	51.25	143,682,100	DOWN	Falling
3/ 29	50.00	141,173,000	DOWN	Falling
3/ 30	50.75	144,232,100		Falling
3/ 31	50.63	141,356,500		Falling
4/ 4	49.38	137,987,700	DOWN	Falling
4/ 5	49.00	135,180,100	DOWN	Falling
4/ 6	48.88	132,158,500	DOWN	Falling
4/ 7	50.88	134,507,400		Falling
4/ 8	49.13	132,217,900		Falling
4/ 11	48.13	132,217,900		Falling
4/ 12	48.00	127,940,500	DOWN	Falling
4/ 13	48.63	130,436,800		Falling
4/ 14	49.63	133,219,200		Falling
4/ 15	50.00	136,583,600	Up	Falling
4/ 18	50.13	138,311,600	Up	Falling
4/ 19	51.88	141,578,300	Up	Falling

Procter & Gamble

11/ 1	53.75	64,327,300		Rising
11/ 2	53.38	63,781,700		Rising
11/ 3	52.25	63,097,100		Rising
11/ 4	51.88	62,321,800		Rising
11/ 5	53.38	62,989,400		Rising
11/ 8	54.38	64,072,000		Rising
11/ 9	54.63	65,088,400		Rising
11/ 10	56.25	66,347,500	UP	Rising
11/ 11	55.63	65,459,800		Rising
11/ 12	56.25	66,331,500		Rising
11/ 15	56.25	66,331,500		Rising
11/ 16	57.00	67,064,800	UP	Rising
11/ 17	55.38	65,865,500		Rising
11/ 18	55.13	65,221,300	Down	Rising
11/ 19	55.75	66,212,800		Rising
11/ 22	55.88	67,104,000	UP	Rising
11/ 23	55.25	66,614,200		Rising
11/ 24	55.38	67,370,800	UP	Rising
11/ 26	55.63	67,500,700	UP	Rising

11/ 29	57.50	69,234,600	UP	Rising
11/ 30	56.75	68,628,100		Rising
12/ 1	56.63	67,793,400		Rising
12/ 2	56.63	67,793,400		Rising
12/ 3	57.00	68,337,300		Rising
12/ 6	57.00	68,337,300		Rising
12/ 7	57.88	69,177,500		Rising
12/ 8	57.63	68,526,900		Rising
12/ 9	57.13	67,502,800	Down	Rising
12/ 10	56.50	66,827,600	Down	Rising
12/ 13	57.00	67,448,700		Rising
12/ 14	56.88	66,935,000		Rising
12/ 15	55.75	65,991,900	Down	Rising
12/ 16	55.00	65,167,200	DOWN	Doubtful
12/ 17	55.25	66,831,300		Doubtful
12/ 20	55.50	67,511,600	Up	Doubtful
12/ 21	56.00	68,070,300	Up	Doubtful
12/ 22	57.00	68,681,300	Up	Doubtful
12/ 23	57.13	69,205,700	Up	Doubtful
12/ 27	58.25	69,869,600	UP	Doubtful
12/ 28	58.63	70,795,400	UP	Doubtful
12/ 29	58.75	71,577,600	UP	Doubtful
12/ 30	57.75	71,150,800		Doubtful
12/ 31	57.00	70,775,200		Doubtful
1/ 3	57.50	71,840,700	UP	Doubtful
1/ 4	56.63	71,238,000		Doubtful
1/ 5	56.13	69,982,500	Down	Doubtful
1/ 6	56.88	70,897,600		Doubtful
1/ 7	56.75	70,315,200		Doubtful
1/ 10	58.88	71,412,200	Up	Doubtful
1/ 11	58.50	70,671,600		Doubtful
1/ 12	58.50	70,671,600		Doubtful
1/ 13	57.00	69,835,200	DOWN	Falling
1/ 14	57.88	70,570,000		Falling
1/ 17	57.75	70,100,300		Falling
1/ 18	57.75	70,100,300		Falling
1/ 19	58.25	70,793,800	Up	Falling
1/ 20	59.25	71,811,200	UP	Doubtful
1/ 21	59.38	73,493,400	UP	Doubtful
1/ 24	58.25	72,712,100		Doubtful
1/ 25	57.63	71,832,200		Doubtful
1/ 26	58.63	72,616,600		Doubtful
1/ 27	58.63	72,616,600		Doubtful
1/ 28	59.75	73,583,300	UP	Doubtful
1/ 31	59.50	72,807,600		Doubtful
2/ 1	58.13	72,009,800		Doubtful
2/ 2	58.75	72,551,200		Doubtful
2/ 3	59.00	73,366,200		Doubtful
2/ 4	57.88	72,784,300		Doubtful
2/ 7	58.25	73,600,200	UP	Doubtful
2/ 8	57.00	73,015,900		Doubtful
2/ 9	59.25	74,040,500	UP	Doubtful
2/ 10	57.38	73,325,000		Doubtful
2/ 11	58.75	74,052,800	UP	Doubtful
2/ 14	58.50	73,485,300		Doubtful
2/ 15	58.88	74,065,700	UP	Doubtful
2/ 16	59.50	74,641,200	UP	Doubtful
2/ 17	58.25	73,028,300	Down	Doubtful
2/ 18	57.38	72,000,700	Down	Doubtful
2/ 22	59.00	72,743,900		Doubtful
2/ 23	58.38	72,122,600		Doubtful
2/ 24	57.00	71,491,700	Down	Doubtful
2/ 25	56.88	70,894,900	Down	Doubtful
2/ 28	57.50	71,525,100		Doubtful
3/ 1	57.00	70,919,200		Doubtful
3/ 2	57.88	71,689,100	Up	Doubtful

3/ 3		56.88	71,012,200		Doubtful
3/ 4		56.88	71,012,200		Doubtful
3/ 7		57.13	71,545,500		Doubtful
3/ 8		57.25	72,053,200	Up	Doubtful
3/ 9		57.00	71,341,800		Doubtful
3/ 10		56.38	70,859,400	DOWN	Falling
3/ 11		57.25	71,407,400		Falling
3/ 14		56.75	70,753,700	DOWN	Falling
3/ 15		56.00	69,882,300	DOWN	Falling
3/ 16		56.38	70,799,600		Falling
3/ 17		55.88	70,077,300		Falling
3/ 18		56.63	72,377,300	UP	Doubtful
3/ 21		56.00	71,807,500		Doubtful
3/ 22		56.00	71,807,500		Doubtful
3/ 23		55.00	71,059,500		Doubtful
3/ 24		53.75	69,841,900	DOWN	Doubtful
3/ 25		53.75	69,841,900	DOWN	Doubtful
3/ 28		54.25	70,816,300		Doubtful
3/ 29		53.50	69,950,700		Doubtful
3/ 30		53.13	68,969,900	DOWN	Doubtful
3/ 31		53.50	70,167,800		Doubtful
4/ 4		52.50	69,191,100		Doubtful
4/ 5		54.50	70,211,800	Up	Doubtful
4/ 6		53.63	69,477,600		Doubtful
4/ 7		53.88	70,383,500	Up	Doubtful
4/ 8		54.25	71,098,700	Up	Doubtful
4/ 11		54.13	70,508,100		Doubtful
4/ 12		53.88	69,921,800		Doubtful
4/ 13		53.75	68,845,500	DOWN	Falling
4/ 14		54.88	69,727,400		Falling
4/ 15		53.88	68,756,100	DOWN	Falling
4/ 18		53.25	68,012,800	DOWN	Falling
4/ 19		54.63	68,938,000		Falling

Sears

11/ 1		57.13	197,185,000	Down	Rising
11/ 2		57.75	198,271,900		Rising
11/ 3		57.25	198,271,900		Rising
11/ 4		57.63	198,702,700	Up	Rising
11/ 5		58.75	199,540,500	Up	Rising
11/ 8		58.38	199,088,500		Rising
11/ 9		57.50	198,596,200		Rising
11/ 10		57.63	199,242,000		Rising
11/ 11		56.50	198,440,700	Down	Rising
11/ 12		56.63	199,081,800		Rising
11/ 15		57.00	199,682,100	UP	Rising
11/ 16		58.50	200,233,200	UP	Rising
11/ 17		57.38	199,625,400		Rising
11/ 18		57.00	199,037,500		Rising
11/ 19		56.00	198,064,200	DOWN	Doubtful
11/ 22		54.25	196,838,700	DOWN	Doubtful
11/ 23	xd	53.88	197,538,800		Doubtful
11/ 24		55.00	198,279,700		Doubtful
11/ 26		56.00	198,552,900		Doubtful
11/ 29		53.75	196,371,000	DOWN	Doubtful
11/ 30		54.38	197,279,500		Doubtful
12/ 1		55.00	198,026,000		Doubtful
12/ 2		54.13	197,390,400		Doubtful
12/ 3		53.88	196,537,300		Doubtful
12/ 6		52.13	195,560,700	DOWN	Doubtful
12/ 7		54.25	196,993,600		Doubtful
12/ 8		54.88	198,043,400	Up	Doubtful
12/ 9		54.88	198,043,400	Up	Doubtful
12/ 10		55.00	198,839,200	Up	Doubtful

12/ 13	55.25	199,418,500	Up	Doubtful
12/ 14	55.63	199,894,300	Up	Doubtful
12/ 15	55.88	200,578,700	UP	Doubtful
12/ 16	55.50	199,852,200		Doubtful
12/ 17	55.38	198,860,400		Doubtful
12/ 20	54.88	198,375,900		Doubtful
12/ 21	53.63	197,435,800		Doubtful
12/ 22	52.50	195,852,600		Doubtful
12/ 23	52.38	192,939,600	DOWN	Doubtful
12/ 27	52.25	191,984,700	DOWN	Doubtful
12/ 28	51.88	190,509,700	DOWN	Doubtful
12/ 29	53.63	181,746,900		Doubtful
12/ 30	53.25	191,041,000		Doubtful
12/ 31	52.88	190,350,500	DOWN	Doubtful
1/ 3	51.25	189,008,200	DOWN	Doubtful
1/ 4	53.38	190,392,100		Doubtful
1/ 5	53.13	188,899,400	DOWN	Doubtful
1/ 6	53.25	190,171,100		Doubtful
1/ 7	52.63	189,281,800		Doubtful
1/ 10	53.38	189,913,400		Doubtful
1/ 11	52.75	189,328,900		Doubtful
1/ 12	52.25	188,561,400	DOWN	Doubtful
1/ 13	53.13	189,189,500		Doubtful
1/ 14	53.38	189,724,600		Doubtful
1/ 17	52.50	189,355,200		Doubtful
1/ 18	51.75	188,201,400	DOWN	Doubtful
1/ 19	50.88	186,700,900	DOWN	Doubtful
1/ 20	51.38	187,856,000		Doubtful
1/ 21	52.25	189,211,400		Doubtful
1/ 24	52.00	188,322,400		Doubtful
1/ 25	52.00	188,322,400		Doubtful
1/ 26	53.88	189,291,800	Up	Doubtful
1/ 27	54.63	189,188,900	Up	Doubtful
1/ 28	55.00	191,067,500	Up	Doubtful
1/ 31	54.88	190,352,900		Doubtful
2/ 1	53.75	189,365,600		Doubtful
2/ 2	51.25	182,497,400	DOWN	Falling
2/ 3	51.50	183,924,800		Falling
2/ 4	50.63	182,381,200	DOWN	Falling
2/ 7	51.00	184,171,600	Up	Falling
2/ 8	47.75	178,102,100	DOWN	Falling
2/ 9	49.00	181,827,800		Falling
2/ 10	49.00	181,827,800		Falling
2/ 11	48.38	180,708,200		Falling
2/ 14	47.88	179,159,000		Falling
2/ 15	46.75	176,057,600	DOWN	Falling
2/ 16	46.25	172,774,700	DOWN	Falling
2/ 17	46.00	170,679,300	DOWN	Falling
2/ 18	47.00	172,447,100		Falling
2/ 22	47.13	173,438,300		Falling
2/ 23	46.50	171,230,900		Falling
2/ 24	46.13	170,310,100	DOWN	Falling
2/ 25	46.38	171,173,700		Falling
2/ 28	45.63	170,083,400	DOWN	Falling
3/ 1	46.75	171,961,700	Up	Falling
3/ 2	47.75	173,907,700	Up	Falling
3/ 3	47.63	172,482,800		Falling
3/ 4	48.63	174,249,200	Up	Falling
3/ 7	49.13	175,036,500	Up	Falling
3/ 8	49.13	175,036,500	Up	Falling
3/ 9	49.00	174,267,000		Falling
3/ 10	48.25	173,765,900		Falling
3/ 11	48.50	174,311,800		Falling
3/ 14	47.75	173,344,300	Down	Falling
3/ 15	48.50	174,581,600	Up	Falling
3/ 16	48.63	175,299,800	UP	Rising

3/ 17	46.88	174,122,700		Rising
3/ 18	48.13	176,062,800	UP	Rising
3/ 21	47.88	175,170,500		Rising
3/ 22	47.38	174,406,900		Rising
3/ 23	46.63	173,415,900	Down	Rising
3/ 24	45.75	171,813,300	DOWN	Doubtful
3/ 25	46.00	172,684,900		Doubtful
3/ 28	45.38	171,813,400		Doubtful
3/ 29	43.25	170,118,300	DOWN	Doubtful
3/ 30	43.38	171,781,100		Doubtful
3/ 31	43.13	169,940,600	DOWN	Doubtful
4/ 4	44.25	171,464,800		Doubtful
4/ 5	46.63	173,253,900	Up	Doubtful
4/ 6	47.13	174,296,200	Up	Doubtful
4/ 7	47.50	175,300,800	Up	Doubtful
4/ 8	47.13	174,417,800		Doubtful
4/ 11	47.88	175,288,200		Doubtful
4/ 12	48.25	175,993,600	Up	Doubtful
4/ 13	47.63	175,192,200		Doubtful
4/ 14	46.50	174,414,600	Down	Doubtful
4/ 15	46.50	174,414,600	Down	Doubtful
4/ 18	44.63	173,567,100	Down	Doubtful
4/ 19	45.50	174,728,900		Doubtful

Texaco

11/ 1		67.50	173,580,700		Doubtful
11/ 2	xd	66.75	174,153,800		Doubtful
11/ 3		66.38	173,402,700	Down	Doubtful
11/ 4		65.00	172,058,000	DOWN	Doubtful
11/ 5		65.38	172,849,100		Doubtful
11/ 8		65.00	172,413,600		Doubtful
11/ 9		64.88	171,682,000	DOWN	Doubtful
11/ 10		65.75	172,368,500		Doubtful
11/ 11		65.13	171,692,000		Doubtful
11/ 12		65.63	172,097,200		Doubtful
11/ 15		64.88	171,573,500	DOWN	Doubtful
11/ 16		65.13	172,403,500	Up	Doubtful
11/ 17		66.63	173,656,400	Up	Doubtful
11/ 18		65.63	173,045,800		Doubtful
11/ 19		66.00	173,480,500		Doubtful
11/ 22		66.63	173,924,000	Up	Doubtful
11/ 23		66.13	173,463,100		Doubtful
11/ 24		65.50	173,027,500	Down	Doubtful
11/ 26		63.88	171,972,000	Down	Doubtful
11/ 29		63.50	169,853,400	DOWN	Falling
11/ 30		64.13	170,732,000		Falling
12/ 1		63.63	169,998,400		Falling
12/ 2		63.38	168,868,400	DOWN	Falling
12/ 3		62.50	168,320,100	DOWN	Falling
12/ 6		62.50	168,320,100	DOWN	Falling
12/ 7		62.88	168,951,900		Falling
12/ 8		62.88	168,951,900		Falling
12/ 9		62.88	168,951,900		Falling
12/ 10		64.38	169,581,300		Falling
12/ 13		63.88	168,538,300		Falling
12/ 14		63.25	167,773.800	DOWN	Falling
12/ 15		62.50	166,932,000	DOWN	Falling
12/ 16		62.50	166,932,000	DOWN	Falling
12/ 17		63.38	167,681,600		Falling
12/ 20		63.75	168,037,700		Falling
12/ 21		63.50	167,439,800		Falling
12/ 22		64.38	168,255,800	Up	Falling
12/ 23		64.00	167,584,500		Falling
12/ 27		64.38	168,255,800	Up	Falling
12/ 28		64.63	168,686,000	Up	Falling

12/ 29	65.00	169,313,400	Up	Falling
12/ 30	65.00	169,313,400	Up	Falling
12/ 31	64.75	168,692,600		Falling
1/ 3	65.50	169,404,700	Up	Falling
1/ 4	65.63	170,053,600	Up	Falling
1/ 5	66.38	171,704,900	Up	Falling
1/ 6	65.75	170,707,700		Falling
1/ 7	65.38	170,184,800		Falling
1/ 10	66.00	170,684,800		Falling
1/ 11	66.13	171,205,200		Falling
1/ 12	65.75	170,575,500		Falling
1/ 13	65.88	171,172,200		Falling
1/ 14	65.75	170,645,800		Falling
1/ 17	65.25	169,957,800	Down	Falling
1/ 18	65.13	169,282,900	Down	Falling
1/ 19	65.13	169,282,900	Down	Falling
1/ 20	65.75	169,717,100		Falling
1/ 21	65.50	169,075,500	Down	Falling
1/ 24	66.13	170,540,400	Up	Falling
1/ 25	65.63	169,958,200		Falling
1/ 26	65.63	169,958,200		Falling
1/ 27	66.00	170,340,300		Falling
1/ 28	66.75	170,804,600	Up	Falling
1/ 31	67.63	171,594,900		Falling
2/ 1	66.50	171,137,800	Up	Falling
2/ 3	67.75	171,696,000	Up	Falling
2/ 3	67.75	171,696,000	Up	Falling
2/ 4	66.75	171,164,900		Falling
2/ 7	66.63	170,684,700	Down	Falling
2/ 8	66.63	170,684,700	Down	Falling
2/ 9	67.00	170,973,200		Falling
2/ 10	66.50	170,700,200		Falling
2/ 11	66.88	170,922,200		Falling
2/ 14	66.75	170,460,100	Down	Falling
2/ 15	67.00	170,823,700		Falling
2/ 16	66.63	170,389,500	Down	Falling
2/ 17	66.88	171,042,200	Up	Falling
2/ 18	66.50	170,652,600		Falling
2/ 22	66.75	170,960,200		Falling
2/ 23	66.75	170,960,200		Falling
2/ 24	65.63	170,510,400	Down	Falling
2/ 25	65.00	170,102,400	DOWN	Falling
2/ 28	64.88	169,680,800	DOWN	Falling
3/ 1	64.75	169,236,700	DOWN	Falling
3/ 2	65.38	170,070,400		Falling
3/ 3	66.38	170,527,900		Falling
3/ 4	66.00	170,146,900		Falling
3/ 7	65.88	169,745,100		Falling
3/ 8	65.63	169,364,300		Falling
3/ 9	65.50	169,126,200	DOWN	Falling
3/ 10	66.00	169,765,200		Falling
3/ 11	66.13	170,436,200		Falling
3/ 14	65.38	169,978,900		Falling
3/ 15	65.38	169,978,900		Falling
3/ 16	65.38	169,978,900		Falling
3/ 17	66.00	171,158,800	UP	Doubtful
3/ 18	66.25	172,325,100	UP	Doubtful
3/ 21	66.38	172,618,100	UP	Doubtful
3/ 22	67.25	173,214,100	UP	Doubtful
3/ 23	66.38	172,994,700		Doubtful
3/ 24	65.50	172,330,800		Doubtful
3/ 25	65.88	172,936,300		Doubtful
3/ 28	64.75	172,093,000	Down	Doubtful
3/ 29	64.38	171,560,600	Down	Doubtful
3/ 30	63.13	170,866,900	Down	Doubtful
3/ 31	63.00	169,933,000	Down	Doubtful

4/ 4	62.25	167,892,000	DOWN	Doubtful
4/ 5	63.00	168,496,800		Doubtful
4/ 6	63.63	169,029,300		Doubtful
4/ 7	63.75	169,507,700		Doubtful
4/ 8	64.13	169,973,800		Doubtful
4/ 11	64.88	170,440,500		Doubtful
4/ 12	64.63	169,852,700		Doubtful
4/ 13	63.38	169,066,400		Doubtful
4/ 14	63.75	169,914,800		Doubtful
4/ 15	64.63	170,770,300	Up	Doubtful
4/ 18	64.13	170,192,300		Doubtful
4/ 19	63.88	169,633,800		Doubtful

Union Carbide

11/ 1	19.63	187,789,200		Doubtful
11/ 2	19.63	187,789,200		Doubtful
11/ 3	19.88	188,570,900		Doubtful
11/ 4	19.88	188,570,900		Doubtful
11/ 5	20.00	189,320,000	Up	Doubtful
11/ 8	19.88	188,943,000		Doubtful
11/ 9	20.00	189,700,700	Up	Doubtful
11/ 10	19.88	189,125,500		Doubtful
11/ 11	20.25	190,316,100	UP	Doubtful
11/ 12	20.50	191,404,900	UP	Doubtful
11/ 15	20.38	190,744,900		Doubtful
11/ 16	20.63	191,378,700		Doubtful
11/ 17	20.50	190,836,800		Doubtful
11/ 18	20.63	191,498,700	UP	Doubtful
11/ 19	20.88	192,330,400	UP	Doubtful
11/ 22	20.13	191,793,600		Doubtful
11/ 23	20.63	192,086,800		Doubtful
11/ 24	20.50	191,873,800		Doubtful
11/ 26	20.63	192,040,400		Doubtful
11/ 29	20.63	192,040,400		Doubtful
11/ 30	20.88	192,497,000	UP	Doubtful
12/ 1	20.63	191,868,600	Down	Doubtful
12/ 2	20.38	191,417,600	Down	Doubtful
12/ 3	20.75	191,851,400		Doubtful
12/ 6	20.88	192,612,300	UP	Rising
12/ 7	20.63	192,207,900		Rising
12/ 8	20.88	192,673,000	UP	Rising
12/ 9	21.50	193,717,100	UP	Rising
12/ 10	21.63	194,389,600	UP	Rising
12/ 13	22.38	195,488,900	UP	Rising
12/ 14	21.88	194,833,200		Rising
12/ 15	21.88	194,833,200		Rising
12/ 16	22.25	195,603,700	UP	Rising
12/ 17	21.38	194,608,100	Down	Rising
12/ 20	22.25	195,716,600	UP	Rising
12/ 21	22.13	195,103,800		Rising
12/ 22	22.50	195,636,700		Rising
12/ 23	22.25	194,764,800	Down	Rising
12/ 27	22.63	195,026,000		Rising
12/ 28	22.75	195,377,400		Rising
12/ 29	22.63	194,887,800		Rising
12/ 30	22.13	194,614,500	Down	Rising
12/ 31	22.38	194,991,300		Rising
1/ 3	22.63	196,281,800	UP	Rising
1/ 4	22.50	195,174,900		Rising
1/ 5	22.38	193,397,000	DOWN	Doubtful
1/ 6	22.00	192,668,000	DOWN	Doubtful
1/ 7	22.00	192,668,000	DOWN	Doubtful
1/ 10	22.13	193,380,100		Doubtful
1/ 11	22.25	194.283,000		Doubtful

1/ 12	22.38	194,867,500		Doubtful
1/ 13	22.88	195,616,100		Doubtful
1/ 14	23.13	196,743,200	UP	Doubtful
1/ 17	24.25	197,742,100	UP	Doubtful
1/ 18	24.50	199,715,700	UP	Doubtful
1/ 19	25.00	200,902,800	UP	Doubtful
1/ 20	24.88	199,903,900		Doubtful
1/ 21	24.25	198,816,400		Doubtful
1/ 24	24.75	199,503,000		Doubtful
1/ 25	24.38	198,924,000		Doubtful
1/ 26	24.25	198,229,000	Down	Doubtful
1/ 27	24.88	198,912,300		Doubtful
1/ 28	24.38	198,231,700		Doubtful
1/ 31	25.50	199,209,300	Up	Doubtful
2/ 1	24.63	198,296,400		Doubtful
2/ 2	25.75	198,980,900		Doubtful
2/ 3	25.63	198,327,500		Doubtful
2/ 4	24.13	197,310,600	DOWN	Falling
2/ 7	25.38	198,257,800		Falling
2/ 8	25.00	197,507,100		Falling
2/ 9	25.25	198,037,200		Falling
2/ 10	25.50	198,512,300	Up	Falling
2/ 11	24.50	197,993,600		Falling
2/ 14	25.00	198,335,000		Falling
2/ 15	24.88	197,936,000	Down	Falling
2/ 16	25.00	198,319,900		Falling
2/ 17	25.00	198,319,900		Falling
2/ 18	25.00	198,319,900		Falling
2/ 22	25.25	198,795,600	UP	Rising
2/ 23	24.88	198,233,700		Rising
2/ 24	24.25	197,349,500	DOWN	Doubtful
2/ 25	23.75	196,473,900	DOWN	Doubtful
2/ 28	23.88	197,338,400		Doubtful
3/ 1	24.00	198,274,800		Doubtful
3/ 2	24.50	198,955,700	UP	Doubtful
3/ 3	24.00	198,521,900		Doubtful
3/ 4	24.13	199,074,400	UP	Doubtful
3/ 7	24.00	198,546,100		Doubtful
3/ 8	23.88	197,980,500	Down	Doubtful
3/ 9	24.25	198,546,000		Doubtful
3/ 10	24.00	198,061,600		Doubtful
3/ 11	24.25	198,338,600		Doubtful
3/ 14	24.75	198,714,600	Up	Doubtful
3/ 15	24.50	198,210,500		Doubtful
3/ 16	25.38	198,796,300	Up	Doubtful
3/ 17	25.50	199,289,500	UP	Rising
3/ 18	25.88	200,197,900	UP	Rising
3/ 21	25.75	199,790,700		Rising
3/ 22	25.88	200,334,500	UP	Rising
3/ 23	26.00	200,743,400	UP	Rising
3/ 24	25.63	200,204,300		Rising
3/ 25	25.00	199,983,400		Rising
3/ 28	24.50	199,379,800	Down	Rising
3/ 29	24.25	199,027,900	Down	Rising
3/ 30	23.50	198,233,400	Down	Rising
3/ 31	22.50	197,374,200	DOWN	Doubtful
4/ 4	22.75	198,169,000		Doubtful
4/ 5	25.00	198,913,500		Doubtful
4/ 6	24.13	198,436,900		Doubtful
4/ 7	24.75	198,745,500		Doubtful
4/ 8	24.25	198,503,500		Doubtful
4/ 11	24.88	198,966,700	Up	Doubtful
4/ 12	25.38	199,485,300	Up	Doubtful
4/ 13	24.50	199,143,700		Doubtful
4/ 14	24.38	198,875,200		Doubtful
4/ 15	23.88	198,543,400		Doubtful

4/ 18		23.88	198,543,400		Doubtful
4/ 19		25.00	200,055,200	Up	Doubtful

United Technologies

11/ 1		61.75	62,370,200	Down	Rising
11/ 2		63.13	62,951,600	Up	Rising
11/ 3		63.13	62,951,600	Up	Rising
11/ 4		62.38	62,743,200		Rising
11/ 5		61.75	62,526,600		Rising
11/ 8		62.00	62,761,400		Rising
11/ 9		63.25	63,038,400	Up	Rising
11/ 10		63.13	62,800,500		Rising
11/ 11		64.13	63,178,200	Up	Rising
11/ 12		64.13	63,178,200	Up	Rising
11/ 15	xd	63.88	63,482,000	Up	Rising
11/ 16		65.75	63,999,800	UP	Rising
11/ 17		65.63	63,175,500		Rising
11/ 18		64.63	62,769,400	Down	Rising
11/ 19		62.88	62,088,800	DOWN	Doubtful
11/ 22		62.50	61,853,400	DOWN	Doubtful
11/ 23		61.88	61,453,800	DOWN	Doubtful
11/ 24		61.50	61,281,400	DOWN	Doubtful
11/ 26		61.63	61,322,000		Doubtful
11/ 29		61.34	61,549,100		Doubtful
11/ 30		61.88	61,746,400		Doubtful
12/ 1		61.50	61,389,300		Doubtful
12/ 2		62.13	61,509,100		Doubtful
12/ 3		62.00	61,265,400	DOWN	Doubtful
12/ 6		61.75	60,896,400	DOWN	Doubtful
12/ 7		62.00	61,164,400		Doubtful
12/ 8		62.88	61,453,600		Doubtful
12/ 9		62.75	61,125,500		Doubtful
12/ 10		62.25	60,783,000	DOWN	Doubtful
12/ 13		62.00	60,633,400	DOWN	Doubtful
12/ 14		61.88	60,402,400	DOWN	Doubtful
12/ 15		61.75	60,074,800	DOWN	Doubtful
12/ 16		61.88	60,232,900		Doubtful
12/ 17		61.75	59,859,800	DOWN	Doubtful
12/ 20		61.63	59,646,500	DOWN	Doubtful
12/ 21		61.50	59,238,200	DOWN	Doubtful
12/ 22		61.75	59,536,100		Doubtful
12/ 23		62.13	59,693,500		Doubtful
12/ 27		62.00	59,487,700		Doubtful
12/ 28		63.00	59,682,500		Doubtful
12/ 29		61.63	59,472,800	Down	Doubtful
12/ 30		61.75	59,674,900		Doubtful
12/ 31		62.00	59,798,700	Up	Doubtful
1/ 3		60.00	59,467.300	DOWN	Falling
1/ 4		60.75	59,894,200	UP	Doubtful
1/ 5		62.00	60,576,300	UP	Doubtful
1/ 6		61.88	60,395,300		Doubtful
1/ 7		62.88	60,581,100	UP	Doubtful
1/ 10		64.00	61,022,500	UP	Doubtful
1/ 11		63.75	60,831,000		Doubtful
1/ 12		64.63	61,229,100	UP	Doubtful
1/ 13		64.13	61,082,900		Doubtful
1/ 14		64.00	60,831,300		Doubtful
1/ 17		64.63	61,027,700		Doubtful
1/ 18		64.63	61,027,700		Doubtful
1/ 19		65.50	61,237,800	UP	Doubtful
1/ 20		65.38	60,223,100	Down	Doubtful
1/ 21		65.13	60,857,000	Down	Doubtful
1/ 24		64.00	60,595,500	Down	Doubtful
1/ 25		64.25	60,805,200		Doubtful

1/ 26		64.88	61,075,600		Doubtful
1/ 27		64.63	60,508,400	Down	Doubtful
1/ 28		65.00	60,750,600		Doubtful
1/ 31		67.38	61,317,200	UP	Rising
2/ 1		66.63	60,920,400		Rising
2/ 2		66.63	60,920,400		Rising
2/ 3		66.75	61,106,800		Rising
2/ 4		64.25	60,844,800	Down	Rising
2/ 7		64.63	61,143,000	Up	Rising
2/ 8		65.50	61,423,300	UP	Rising
2/ 9		65.50	61,750,900	UP	Rising
2/ 10		64.88	61,543,600		Rising
2/ 11		65.38	61,750,100		Rising
2/ 14		67.38	62,182,800	UP	Rising
2/ 15		68.38	62,635,800	UP	Rising
2/ 16		71.00	63,329,600	UP	Rising
2/ 17		70.63	62,016,300		Rising
2/ 18		69.63	61,337,400	Down	Rising
2/ 22		69.25	61,045,700	Down	Rising
2/ 23		67.50	60,708,400	DOWN	Doubtful
2/ 24		66.88	60,355,000	DOWN	Doubtful
2/ 25		66.50	59,967,700	DOWN	Doubtful
2/ 28		68.00	60,508,400		Doubtful
3/ 1		67.63	60,172,000		Doubtful
3/ 2		66.00	59,654,400	DOWN	Doubtful
3/ 3		66.13	60,203,500		Doubtful
3/ 4		67.63	60,632,600	Up	Doubtful
3/ 7		68.63	61,036,300	Up	Doubtful
3/ 8		68.38	60,796,400		Doubtful
3/ 9		68.25	60,623,600		Doubtful
3/ 10		67.75	60,396,000		Doubtful
3/ 11		69.75	60,840,300		Doubtful
3/ 14		69.75	60,840,300		Doubtful
3/ 15		68.00	60,654,000		Doubtful
3/ 16		68.00	60,654,000		Doubtful
3/ 17		68.38	60,916,200	Up	Doubtful
3/ 18		68.25	60,397,400	Down	Doubtful
3/ 21		68.25	60,397,400	Down	Doubtful
3/ 22		67.75	60,270,900	Down	Doubtful
3/ 23		68.00	60,438,100		Doubtful
3/ 24		68.00	60,438,100		Doubtful
3/ 25		66.50	60,149,900	Down	Doubtful
3/ 28		66.13	59,796,500	Down	Doubtful
3/ 29		64.88	59,558,700	DOWN	Falling
3/ 30		62.50	59,097,600	DOWN	Falling
3/ 31		62.13	58,487,400	DOWN	Falling
4/ 4		62.25	59,159,200		Falling
4/ 5		65.50	59,704,700		Falling
4/ 6		64.38	59,348,200		Falling
4/ 7		64.75	59,583,900		Falling
4/ 8		64.75	59,583,900		Falling
4/ 11		64.13	59,351,100		Falling
4/ 12		64.00	59,129,300	Down	Falling
4/ 13		64.25	59,455,800		Falling
4/ 14		64.75	59,875,800	Up	Falling
4/ 15		65.88	60,474,300	Up	Falling
4/ 18		64.50	59,863,700		Falling
4/ 19		63.63	59,233,400		Falling

Westinghouse

11/ 1	xd	14.25	35,697.600		Rising
11/ 2		14.25	35,697,600		Rising
11/ 3		14.13	34,903,000		Rising
11/ 4		14.00	33,629,800		Rising

11/ 5	14.00	33,629,800		Rising
11/ 8	14.00	33,629,800		Rising
11/ 9	14.00	33,629,800		Rising
11/ 10	14.00	33,629,800		Rising
11/ 11	14.00	33,629,800		Rising
11/ 12	14.00	33,629,800		Rising
11/ 15	14.00	33,629,800		Rising
11/ 16	13.63	32,530,100	Down	Rising
11/ 17	13.63	32,530,100	Down	Rising
11/ 18	13.38	31,857,000	DOWN	Doubtful
11/ 19	13.50	32,782,500		Doubtful
11/ 22	13.63	34,189,000		Doubtful
11/ 23	13.63	34,189,000		Doubtful
11/ 24	13.88	34,847,500	Up	Doubtful
11/ 26	14.25	35,224,000	Up	Doubtful
11/ 29	14.13	33,734,700		Doubtful
11/ 30	14.00	33,080,400		Doubtful
12/ 1	14.25	35,180,200		Doubtful
12/ 2	14.50	35,874,400	Up	Doubtful
12/ 3	14.25	35,226,100		Doubtful
12/ 6	14.00	34,682,200		Doubtful
12/ 7	14.00	34,682,200		Doubtful
12/ 8	14.00	34,682,200		Doubtful
12/ 9	14.13	35,436,700		Doubtful
12/ 10	13.88	34,968,600		Doubtful
12/ 13	14.00	35,534,000	Up	Doubtful
12/ 14	13.88	34,818,300	Down	Doubtful
12/ 15	13.75	33,864,600	Down	Doubtful
12/ 16	13.63	33,058,000	Down	Doubtful
12/ 17	13.88	34,070,000		Doubtful
12/ 20	13.88	34.070,000		Doubtful
12/ 21	13.88	34,070,000		Doubtful
12/ 22	13.88	34,070,000		Doubtful
12/ 23	14.13	34,978,200		Doubtful
12/ 27	14.00	34,093,600		Doubtful
12/ 28	14.13	34,680,300		Doubtful
12/ 29	14.25	35,505,100	Up	Doubtful
12/ 30	14.13	34,872,000		Doubtful
12/ 31	14.13	34,872,000		Doubtful
1/ 3	13.75	33,642,400	Down	Doubtful
1/ 4	14.13	35,124,500		Doubtful
1/ 5	13.75	33,272,900	Down	Doubtful
1/ 6	13.88	33,932,300		Doubtful
1/ 7	13.63	32,770,900	DOWN	Falling
1/ 10	14.13	34,812,100	Up	Falling
1/ 11	14.00	31,356,800	DOWN	Falling
1/ 12	13.63	27,476,500	DOWN	Falling
1/ 13	13.25	25,411,600	DOWN	Falling
1/ 14	13.13	23,289,500	DOWN	Falling
1/ 17	13.13	23,289,500	DOWN	Falling
1/ 18	13.38	24.546,600		Falling
1/ 19	14.00	26,244,200		Falling
1/ 20	13.88	24,756,700		Falling
1/ 21	13.63	23,260,700	DOWN	Falling
1/ 24	14.13	25,788,300		Falling
1/ 25	14.13	25,788,300		Falling
1/ 26	14.13	25,788,300		Falling
1/ 27	13.88	24,708,800		Falling
1/ 28	14.25	25,542,900		Falling
1/ 31	14.00	24,564,400	Down	Falling
2/ 1	14.00	24,564,400	Down	Falling
2/ 2	14.00	24,564,400	Down	Falling
2/ 3	14.00	24,564,400	Down	Falling
2/ 4	13.88	21,639,100	DOWN	Falling
2/ 7	14.25	23,506,900		Falling

2/ 8	14.25	23,506,900		Falling
2/ 9	15.13	26,651,100	Up	Falling
2/ 10	14.75	25,252,200		Falling
2/ 11	14.63	24,704,200		Falling
2/ 14	15.00	25,765,200		Falling
2/ 15	15.00	25,765,200		Falling
2/ 16	14.63	24.966,000		Falling
2/ 17	14.75	25,669,300		Falling
2/ 18	14.63	25,067,200		Falling
2/ 22	14.75	25,573,200		Falling
2/ 23	15.00	26,437,600	Up	Falling
2/ 24	14.88	25,626,100		Falling
2/ 25	14.63	25,140,400		Falling
2/ 28	14.38	24,383,400	Down	Falling
3/ 1	14.13	23,460,800	Down	Falling
3/ 2	14.38	24,205,200		Falling
3/ 3	14.63	25,392,100		Falling
3/ 4	14.50	24,178,300		Falling
3/ 7	14.13	23,530,600		Falling
3/ 8	13.88	22,252,600	Down	Falling
3/ 9	13.75	21.495,400	DOWN	Falling
3/ 10	13.63	20,555,100	DOWN	Falling
3/ 11	13.50	19,748,100	DOWN	Falling
3/ 14	13.13	18,624,300	DOWN	Falling
3/ 15	13.25	19,652,100		Falling
3/ 16	13.25	19,652,100		Falling
3/ 17	13.38	20,391,400		Falling
3/ 18	13.25	18,995,500		Falling
3/ 21	13.00	18,319,400	DOWN	Falling
3/ 22	13.13	18,903,600		Falling
3/ 23	13.13	18,903,600		Falling
3/ 24	13.13	18,903,600		Falling
3/ 25	13.00	18,423,800		Falling
3/ 28	12.88	16,637,200	DOWN	Falling
3/ 29	12.50	15.511,800	DOWN	Falling
3/ 30	12.13	14,281,800	DOWN	Falling
3/ 31	12.00	12,221,100	DOWN	Falling
4/ 4	11.88	10,190,300	DOWN	Falling
4/ 5	11.88	10,190,300	DOWN	Falling
4/ 6	11.63	9,213,900	DOWN	Falling
4/ 7	11.75	10,301,400		Falling
4/ 8	11.88	10,911,600		Falling
4/ 11	11.63	10,159,700		Falling
4/ 12	11.75	10,812,900		Falling
4/ 13	11.75	10,812,900		Falling
4/ 14	11.63	10,270,200		Falling
4/ 15	11.50	9,331,000	Down	Falling
4/ 18	11.13	8,327,000	DOWN	Falling
4/ 19	11.00	7,336,700	DOWN	Falling

Woolworth

11/ 1	22.75	30,558,700		Doubtful
11/ 2	22.75	30,558,700		Doubtful
11/ 3	22.63	30,233,000		Doubtful
11/ 4	21.88	29,494,800	DOWN	Doubtful
11/ 5	21.00	28,112,700	DOWN	Doubtful
11/ 8	21.00	28,112,700	DOWN	Doubtful
11/ 9	20.75	27,056,900	DOWN	Doubtful
11/ 10	20.88	27,618,400		Doubtful
11/ 11	21.13	28,433,400		Doubtful
11/ 12	22.13	29,060,400		Doubtful
11/ 15	22.50	29,532,800		Doubtful
11/ 16	22.38	29,022,900		Doubtful
11/ 17	22.63	29,319,700		Doubtful

11/ 18	22.63	29,319,700		Doubtful
11/ 19	22.50	28,787,200	Down	Doubtful
11/ 22	22.50	28,787,200	Down	Doubtful
11/ 23	22.38	28,417,600	Down	Doubtful
11/ 24	22.75	28,698,100		Doubtful
11/ 26	22.75	28,698,100		Doubtful
11/ 29	22.75	28,698,100		Doubtful
11/ 30	23.13	29,067,800		Doubtful
12/ 1	23.75	29,457,900	Up	Doubtful
12/ 2	23.50	28,939,900		Doubtful
12/ 3	23.25	28,656,700		Doubtful
12/ 6	23.63	29,141,100		Doubtful
12/ 7	24.13	29,970,400	Up	Doubtful
12/ 8	23.75	29,688,100		Doubtful
12/ 9	23.75	29,688,100		Doubtful
12/ 10	23.63	29,388,600		Doubtful
12/ 13	23.88	29,969,600		Doubtful
12/ 14	23.88	29,969,600		Doubtful
12/ 15	23.75	29,586,100		Doubtful
12/ 16	23.75	29,586,100		Doubtful
12/ 17	23.75	29,586,100		Doubtful
12/ 20	24.00	29,950,000		Doubtful
12/ 21	23.50	29,439,800	Down	Doubtful
12/ 22	23.50	29,439,800	Down	Doubtful
12/ 23	23.88	29,783,500		Doubtful
12/ 27	24.00	30,309,100	UP	Rising
12/ 28	24.00	30,309,100	UP	Rising
12/ 29	24.50	30,853,900	UP	Rising
12/ 30	24.63	31,210,700	UP	Rising
12/ 31	25.38	31,830,600	UP	Rising
1/ 3	26.13	32,367,800	UP	Rising
1/ 4	25.75	32,033,600		Rising
1/ 5	25.75	32,033,600		Rising
1/ 6	24.88	31,034,700		Rising
1/ 7	25.00	31,461,200		Rising
1/ 10	24.88	30,879,400	Down	Rising
1/ 11	24.88	30,879,400	Down	Rising
1/ 12	25.38	31,288,000		Rising
1/ 13	25.13	30,829,700	Down	Rising
1/ 14	25.63	31,341,900	Up	Rising
1/ 17	25.88	32,011,100	Up	Rising
1/ 18	25.50	31,432,900		Rising
1/ 19	25.38	30,866,400		Rising
1/ 20	25.63	31,284,600		Rising
1/ 21	25.63	31,284,600		Rising
1/ 24	25.63	31,284,600		Rising
1/ 25	25.50	31,015,100		Rising
1/ 26	25.50	31,015,100		Rising
1/ 27	25.75	31,253,500		Rising
1/ 28	26.00	31,827,300	Up	Rising
1/ 31	25.88	31,500,400		Rising
2/ 1	25.38	31,129,300		Rising
2/ 2	25.88	31,485,300		Rising
2/ 3	24.63	30,679,700	DOWN	Falling
2/ 4	24.13	30,053,900	DOWN	Falling
2/ 7	24.25	30,443,800		Falling
2/ 8	25.00	30,644,500		Falling
2/ 9	24.63	30,454,400		Falling
2/ 10	24.50	30,176,600		Falling
2/ 11	24.38	30,008,700	DOWN	Falling
2/ 14	24.63	30,198,100		Falling
2/ 15	24.50	29,918,100	DOWN	Faliing
2/ 16	24.25	29,639,900	DOWN	Falling
2/ 17	23.88	29,322,500	DOWN	Falling
2/ 18	24.00	29,550,000		Falling
2/ 22	23.88	29,195,600	DOWN	Falling

2/ 23	23.50	28,844,900	DOWN	Falling
2/ 24	22.88	28,534,400	DOWN	Falling
2/ 25	22.50	27,393,300	DOWN	Falling
2/ 28	22.00	26,619,900	DOWN	Falling
3/ 1	21.63	25,931,600	DOWN	Falling
3/ 2	21.50	25,100,400	DOWN	Falling
3/ 3	21.50	25,100,400	DOWN	Falling
3/ 4	20.75	24,257,800	DOWN	Falling
3/ 7	20.75	24,257,800	DOWN	Falling
3/ 8	20.75	24,257,800	DOWN	Falling
3/ 9	20.38	23,725,800	DOWN	Falling
3/ 10	20.25	23,046,700	DOWN	Falling
3/ 11	20.25	23,046,700	DOWN	Falling
3/ 14	20.25	23,046,700	DOWN	Falling
3/ 15	20.13	22,574,800	DOWN	Falling
3/ 16	19.25	21,926,900	DOWN	Falling
3/ 17	19.88	22,874,400		Falling
3/ 18	19.88	22,874,400		Falling
3/ 21	19.75	22,549,600		Falling
3/ 22	19.75	22,549,600		Falling
3/ 23	19.63	22,061,000		Falling
3/ 24	19.38	21,533,900	DOWN	Falling
3/ 25	19.13	20,976,000	DOWN	Falling
3/ 28	18.50	20,425,700	DOWN	Falling
3/ 29	18.00	19,866,800	DOWN	Falling
3/ 30	17.00	17,625,100	DOWN	Falling
3/ 31	15.13	13,114,900	DOWN	Falling
4/ 4	13.00	10,059,500	DOWN	Falling
4/ 5	14.75	15,380,800		Falling
4/ 6	13.88	10,973,800		Falling
4/ 7	14.88	12,726,000		Falling
4/ 8	15.00	15,507,700	Up	Falling
4/ 11	15.25	17,445,800	Up	Falling
4/ 12	15.25	17,445,800	Up	Falling
4/ 13	17.25	19,716,000	Up	Falling
4/ 14	16.50	17,823,900		Falling
4/ 15	17.00	18,539,000		Falling
4/ 18	16.50	17,894,300		Falling
4/ 19	16.13	17,169,800	Down	Falling

Table 5
Full Review of Key Indicators

May 31, 1929 Through November 13, 1929

Date	Dow	CLX	Cum.CLX	Four Columns	True	EW	NFI
5/31	297.41	+1	+1	1 - 0 - 0 - 0	+1	+1	+1
6/ 1	299.12	+1	+2	1 - 0 - 0 - 0	+2	+2	+1
6/ 3	304.20	+4	+6	4 - 0 - 0 - 0	+4	+4	+3
6/ 4	310.57	+6	+12	6 - 0 - 0 - 0	+12	+12	+5
6/ 5	307.68	+6	+18	6 - 0 - 0 - 0	+18	+18	+7
6/ 6	307.72	+3	+21	6 - 3 - 0 - 0	+24	+27	+8
6/ 7	307.46	+4	+25	8 - 4 - 0 - 0	+32	+39	+11
6/ 8	305.12	-3	+22	1 - 5 - 0 - 1	+33	+44	+11
6/10	303.27	-2	+20	6 - 7 - 1 - 0	+38	+56	+11
6/11	306.64	+4	+24	7 - 3 - 1 - 1	+44	+64	+12
6/12	306.68	0	+24	6 - 6 - 1 - 1	+49	+74	+13
6/13	313.05	+17	+41	14 - 1 - 0 - 4	+63	+85	+16
6/14	313.68	+13	+54	11 - 1 - 0 - 3	+74	+94	+16
6/15	314.26	+10	+64	8 - 1 - 0 - 3	+82	+100	+16
6/17	319.33	+23	+87	20 - 0 - 0 - 3	+102	+117	+17
6/18	319.67	+10	+97	10 - 4 - 0 - 4	+112	+127	+17
6/19	316.41	-5	+92	2 - 7 - 0 - 0	+114	+136	+17
6/20	317.73	+2	+94	5 - 2 - 1 - 0	+118	+142	+16

6/21	320.68	+9	+103	11 - 3 - 0 - 1	+129	+155	+17
6/22	322.23	+11	+114	10 - 1 - 0 - 2	+139	+164	+17
6/24	321.15	+2	+116	5 - 4 - 0 - 1	+144	+172	+17
6/25	326.16	+8	+124	9 - 4 - 0 - 3	+153	+182	+17
6/26	328.60	+10	+134	12 - 4 - 0 - 2	+165	+196	+18
6/27	328.91	+6	+140	9 - 5 - 0 - 2	+174	+208	+18
6/28	331.65	+9	+149	9 - 2 - 0 - 2	+183	+217	+18
6/29	333.79	+8	+157	8 - 2 - 0 - 2	+191	+225	+18
7/ 1	335.22	+7	+164	10 - 5 - 0 - 2	+201	+238	+18
7/ 2	340.28	+18	+182	15 - 0 - 2 - 5	+214	+246	+18
7/ 3	341.99	+12	+194	12 - 1 - 1 - 2	+225	+256	+19
7/ 5	344.27	+14	+208	15 - 2 - 0 - 1	+240	+272	+21
7/ 6	344.66	+6	+214	5 - 1 - 0 - 2	+245	+276	+20
7/ 8	346.55	+8	+222	10 - 2 - 0 - 0	+255	+288	+22
7/ 9	345.57	+5	+227	8 - 5 - 0 - 2	+263	+299	+22
7/10	343.30	-6	+221	3 - 8 - 1 - 0	+265	+309	+22
7/11	343.04	-2	+219	6 - 7 - 2 - 1	+269	+319	+19
7/12	346.37	+5	+224	8 - 2 - 1 - 0	+276	+328	+22
7/13	345.94	0	+224	3 - 1 - 2 - 0	+277	+330	+19
7/15	341.93	-4	+220	1 - 4 - 3 - 2	+275	+330	+18
7/16	344.24	+5	+225	4 - 4 - 1 - 6	+278	+331	+18
7/17	345.63	+12	+237	6 - 1 - 0 - 7	+284	+331	+19
7/18	344.59	+3	+240	4 - 2 - 1 - 2	+287	+334	+20
7/19	345.20	+4	+244	5 - 4 - 0 - 3	+292	+340	+20
7/20	345.87	+1	+245	5 - 4 - 1 - 1	+296	+347	+18
7/22	341.37	-11	+234	3 - 9 - 6 - 1	+293	+352	+14
7/23	345.48	+2	+236	2 - 2 - 1 - 3	+294	+352	+13
7/24	343.04	-8	+228	3 -11 - 2 - 2	+295	+362	+13
7/25	344.67	0	+228	3 - 6 - 1 - 4	+297	+366	+13
7/26	345.47	-1	+227	4 - 7 - 3 - 5	+298	+369	+13
7/27	343.73	-3	+224	2 - 4 - 2 - 1	+298	+372	+11
7/29	339.21	-11	+213	0 - 9 - 5 - 3	+293	+373	+11
7/30	343.12	+7	+220	1 - 1 - 0 - 7	+294	+368	+11
7/31	347.70	+16	+236	6 - 0 - 0 -10	+300	+364	+12
8/ 1	350.56	+12	+248	8 - 2 - 0 - 6	+308	+368	+13
8/ 2	353.08	+9	+257	8 - 4 - 1 - 6	+315	+373	+13
8/ 3	355.62	+8	+265	8 - 3 - 1 - 4	+322	+379	+14
8/ 5	352.50	-6	+259	2 - 5 - 3 - 0	+321	+383	+11
8/ 6	351.39	-3	+256	3 - 5 - 3 - 2	+321	+386	+11
8/ 7	348.44	-10	+246	3 - 5 - 8 - 0	+316	+386	+4
8/ 8	352.10	-1	+245	2 - 1 - 2 - 0	+316	+387	+4
8/ 9	337.99	-25	+220	0 - 12 -13 - 0	+303	+386	+2
8/10	344.84	0	+220	1 - 0 - 2 - 1	+302	+384	+2
8/12	351.13	+3	+223	4 - 5 - 2 - 6	+304	+385	+3
8/13	354.03	+5	+228	8 - 3 - 2 - 2	+310	+392	+5
8/14	354.86	+2	+230	7 - 4 - 4 - 3	+313	+396	+5
8/15	354.42	-1	+229	4 - 3 - 5 - 3	+312	+395	+4
8/16	361.49	+14	+243	11 - 0 - 2 - 5	+321	+399	+5
8/17	360.70	+9	+252	6 - 0 - 0 - 3	+327	+402	+5
8/19	365.20	+18	+270	10 - 0 - 0 - 8	+337	+404	+6
8/20	367.67	+15	+285	11 - 1 - 1 - 6	+347	+409	+8
8/21	365.55	+9	+294	9 - 1 - 0 - 1	+356	+418	+12
8/22	369.95	+11	+305	11 - 0 - 0 - 0	+367	+429	+12
8/23	374.61	+11	+316	13 - 3 - 1 - 2	+379	+442	+12
8/24	375.44	+8	+324	9 - 1 - 1 - 1	+387	+450	+12
8/26	374.46	+4	+328	7 - 1 - 3 - 1	+391	+454	+9
8/27	373.79	-1	+327	3 - 2 - 2 - 0	+392	+457	+9
8/28	372.06	-4	+323	2 - 4 - 3 - 1	+391	+459	+9
8/29	376.18	+6	+329	6 - 1 - 1 - 2	+396	+463	+10
8/30	380.33	+5	+334	9 - 5 - 0 - 1	+405	+476	+11
9/ 3	381.17	+8	+342	9 - 4 - 0 - 3	+414	+486	+11
9/ 4	379.61	+5	+347	7 - 4 - 0 - 2	+421	+495	+12
9/ 5	369.77	-15	+332	0 -11 - 4 - 0	+417	+502	+9
9/ 6	376.29	0	+332	3 - 2 - 1 - 0	+419	+506	+10
9/ 7	377.56	+4	+336	5 - 1 - 0 - 0	+424	+512	+11
9/ 9	374.93	-6	+330	3 - 8 - 1 - 0	+426	+522	+11

9/10	367.29	-15	+315	1 -14 - 3 - 1	+424	+533	+11
9/11	370.91	0	+315	2 - 5 - 0 - 3	+426	+537	+12
9/12	366.35	-18	+297	0 -17 - 1 - 0	+425	+553	+12
9/13	366.85	-7	+290	1 -10 - 2 - 4	+424	+558	+11
9/14	367.01	-6	+284	2 - 6 - 3 - 1	+423	+562	+10
9/16	372.39	+10	+294	3 - 1 - 1 - 9	+425	+556	+9
9/17	368.52	+2	+296	1 - 1 - 2 - 4	+424	+552	+9
9/18	370.90	+2	+298	0 - 4 - 2 - 8	+422	+546	+7
9/19	369.97	-6	+292	3 -10 - 2 - 3	+423	+554	+9
9/20	362.05	-19	+273	1 - 9 -11 - 0	+413	+553	+3
9/21	361.16	-16	+257	0 - 6 -10 - 0	+403	+549	0
9/23	359.00	-13	+244	1 - 6 -11 - 2	+393	+543	0
9/24	352.61	-23	+221	1 - 9 -15 - 0	+379	+538	-5
9/25	352.57	-14	+207	2 - 8 - 9 - 1	+372	+538	-5
9/26	355.95	-4	+203	2 - 4 - 4 - 1	+370	+539	-5
9/27	344.87	-16	+187	0 - 6 -10 - 0	+360	+535	-7
9/28	347.17	-10	+177	0 - 3 - 7 - 0	+353	+531	-7
9/30	343.45	-19	+158	0 - 8 -11 - 0	+342	+528	-7
10/1	342.57	-13	+145	0 - 6 -13 - 6	+329	+515	-7
10/2	344.50	-3	+142	0 - 2 - 6 - 5	+323	+506	-9
10/3	329.95	-23	+119	0 - 7 -16 - 0	+307	+497	-9
10/4	325.17	-22	+97	1 - 5 -20 - 2	+288	+481	-9
10/5	341.36	+3	+100	1 - 0 - 0 - 2	+289	+480	-9
10/7	345.72	+3	+103	2 - 0 - 2 - 3	+289	+477	-8
10/8	345.00	-1	+102	2 - 0 - 4 - 1	+287	+474	-8
10/9	346.66	+4	+106	3 - 0 - 2 - 3	+288	+472	-7
10/10	352.86	+14	+120	3 - 0 - 1 -12	+290	+462	-7
10/11	352.69	+3	+123	2 - 1 - 2 - 4	+290	+459	-7
10/14	350.97	0	+123	1 - 2 - 1 - 2	+290	+459	-7
10/15	347.24	+1	+124	0 - 0 - 3 - 4	+287	+452	-7
10/16	336.13	-11	+113	0 - 6 - 5 - 0	+282	+453	-7
10/17	341.86	+1	+114	0 - 1 - 4 - 6	+278	+444	-7
10/18	333.29	-12	+102	0 - 5 - 8 - 1	+270	+440	-10
10/19	323.87	-26	+76	0 -13 -13 - 0	+257	+440	-11
10/21	320.01	-17	+59	0 - 8 -12 - 3	+245	+433	-12
10/22	326.51	+5	+64	1 - 1 - 2 - 7	+244	+426	-12
10/23	305.85	-20	+44	0 - 2 -18 - 0	+226	+410	-18
10/24	299.47	-18	+26	1 - 0 -23 - 4	+204	+384	-23
10/25	301.22	-5	+21	1 - 0 - 6 - 0	+199	+379	-22
10/26	298.97	-4	+17	1 - 0 - 5 - 0	+195	+375	-22
10/28	260.64	-24	-7	0 - 2 -22 - 0	+173	+355	-22
10/29	230.07	-24	-31	0 - 0 -26 - 2	+147	+327	-23
10/30	258.47	+2	-29	0 - 0 - 0 - 2	+147	+325	-24
10/31	273.51	+2	-27	0 - 0 - 1 - 3	+146	+321	-24
11/ 4	257.68	-3	-30	0 - 1 - 2 - 0	+144	+320	-25
11/ 6	232.13	-8	-38	0 - 0 - 8 - 0	+136	+312	-24
11/ 7	238.19	-6	-44	0 - 0 - 6 - 0	+130	+306	-30
11/ 8	236.53	+1	-43	0 - 0 - 1 - 2	+129	+303	-25
11/11	220.39	-11	-54	0 - 3 - 8 - 0	+121	+298	-24
11/12	209.74	-25	-79	0 - 8 -17 - 0	+104	+289	-24
11/13	198.69	-27	-106	0 - 3 -24 - 0	+80	+268	-24

GLOSSARY

Accumulation - Following the valid assumption that volume precedes price, a stock is seen to be under accumulation when the OBV numbers are persistently trending higher.

Advance/Decline Line - A major technical indicator. It is simply a cumulative record of advancing stocks and declining stocks. For example, if on a given day there are 845 advancing stocks and 672 declining stocks then the advance/decline line, which is a measure of market breadth, rose by 173. The number 173 would be added to a previous cumulative record of market breadth.

Auction Market - Buyers attempt to buy at the lowest price and sellers attempt to sell at the highest price. No transaction occurs until the price satisfies both buyer and seller. The stock market is an auction market, bringing buyers and sellers together. A buyer alone can sell nothing. It takes two to tango - a balance, an equation. In the stock market they cannot both be right. The right side must beguile the wrong side into doing its bidding, giving the other what its wants on its terms, and that sets the stage for the eternal struggle - the game. We are constantly being pressured by the other side to balance the market equation on its terms. The pressures are often very subtle and close to being undetected and other times so obvious that their obviousness blinds the unsuspecting. The media is the unsuspecting too in these pressure tactics, always making it easier for the right side of the market equation to beat the wrong side. When one is caught up in the buying or selling of stocks it is so easy to forget that the stock market is an auction market. When you make your move based on certain motivations, examine the counter-motivations which make your move possible but not necessarily right.

Bar Chart - Prior to the use of my On-Balance Volume, the bar chart was the orthodox method of recording volume with a stock price chart, a series of vertical lines depicting daily volume. It is still being done and, while not the best way of showing volume in the most meaningful way, is nevertheless useful. One can see in a general way whether a stock is under accumulation but it is not accurate enough. Looking at the type of presentation one can only guess at possible accumulation or distribution trends. This writer has maintained that the only intelligent way to relate volume to price and identify accumulation or distribution is by On-Balance Volume.

Bathtub Analogy ™ - Used to depict the correct flow of money in the bull-bear cycle. At the beginning of the bull cycle the market bathtub is empty. The advance/decline line is at the bottom. The bathtub starts to refill with water, the first water entering the tub representing the smart money. The water level continues to rise until it crests, represented by the bull cycle peak in the advance/decline line. The last water to enter the tub is represented by the least informed money. Very late in the bull cycle the bathtub drain is opened, a fact which the uninformed money is generally unaware of. The smart money begins to make its exit and is the first water to leave the tub, first in and first out. The water level begins to recede as a majority of stocks have peaked and begin to work lower, represented by a declining advance/decline line as well as a downturn in the high/low indicator. The generally uninformed public, always mesmerized and misled by what the Dow Jones Industrial Average is doing, is not yet aware of the receding water level because the Dow is still making bull cycle highs. The popularly followed Dow is generally the last to rise and the last to fall, being the surface water, the last water in the tub. When the start of the bear cycle is at last recognized, the water level drops rapidly, and at the end of the bear cycle the water is sucked out of the tub rapidly, the smart money awaiting that sign as a signal that the tub is ready to be refilled again for another bath and a repetition of the complete cycle.

My buy signal in October 1987 following that crash was an excellent example of recognizing the Bathtub Analogy. At the tail end of the huge decline the water is sucked out of the tub rapidly. Nothing was more rapid than the 508-point drop in October 19, 1987 on super climax volume of over 600 million shares. That crash quickly emptied the bathtub and thus was the signal that the tub was ready to be refilled, the resumption of the bull cycle.

Bear Market - True bear markets tend to start "out of the blue" with the majority at a loss to explain the first downswing. Bear market means a declining market. A bear market is normally related to the bull market that it follows, thereby completing the entire bull-bear cycle, but it is absolutely no relation to the bull market which follows after that bear market is completed. That is a new ball game. Bear market may or may not be accompanied by the business recession. Bear market is a market term referring specifically to the opposite of a bull market. While varying greatly in terms of serverity and duration of the previous bull market, a bear market is obviously increasingly probable the older the previous bull market becomes. All market downturns after a bull cycle is over 20 months old are suspect and deserve close examination. Downturns after a bull cycle is 30 months old are extremely dangerous and very likely are the real thing. Bear markets are always shorter in duration than the bull cycle preceding them. In estimating their length, always keep the 4 to 4-1/2 year cycle in mind, major market bottoms very seldom being more than 4-1/2 years apart. A bull cycle lasting 33 months would therefore be expected to be followed by a bear market lasting from 15 to 21 months, but not beyond 21 months.

But a crash market automatically starts a new bull cycle, thereby contracting the length of the bear cycle it was in.

Bear Phases - Bull and bear markets tend to run in three distinct phases. The first bear phase outstanding characteristic is public disbelief in what is happening. The economy usually still looks strong, the news is generally bullish, and corporate earnings are usually still rising. However, the smart money has pulled the plug and is pessimistic while the public confidence in the market outlook in unimpaired. As the news worsens and the confident public begins to change their mind about the outlook, deciding to get out of many stocks, the market embarks on a very sharp rally lasting anywhere from a few weeks to a few months, the sharp rally characterizing the second phase of the bear market. Following a fresh collapse to new lows, the public confidence has by now completely eroded. The smart money, watching for such signs of collapse in the public confidence, now makes the key shift from their pessimism to confidence as prices now cascade lower into the super depressed bargain area. The public, having been fooled by the second phase, the "rally that fools the majority", is in no mood to expect any new rallies in the final bear market phase. Their first phase disbelief has been transformed in the third phase to belief, belief that everything is going to get worse. When the next rally comes it usually starts a new bull market but by that time that would be the last thing the public could believe, thus the disbelief attached to the next phase, the first bull market phase.

Bear Trap - Any technically non-confirmed move to the downside encouraging the bulk of the investing and speculating public to be bearish. The most important bear traps terminate bear markets. In any case, they precede strong rallies. The period following the 1987 crash was replete with bear traps, the most notable of these being the 1929-30 parallels which hooked the majority into viewing all post crash action as being merely a rally in a bear market.

Breakthrough (Breakout) - The terms breakthrough and breakout are interchangeable. This implies that either a stock price or average has moved above a previous high resistance level or has moved below a previous low support level. Such breakthroughs imply that the movement will be enhanced in the direction of the breakout on the physical principle of bodies in motion (momentum). The same terms apply to the more important On-Balance Volume movements through previous support or resistance levels on the demonstration that volume precedes price.

Bull Market - Any rising market might be called a bull market, but that would be a very loose definition. True bull markets imply a sweeping untrend embracing many months of duration with three definable phases. Like bear markets, bull markets very widely in scope and duration. However, a bull market has no relation to the bear market it follows, and thus there is little to go on at first in estimating its length or importance. Since the time span between major market tops is a complete variable, unlike the more predictable cyclicality of major bottoms, one has to depend heavily on the bull phase characteristics (see bull phases) to estimate the probable duration of a bull market. But we do know that bull markets last longer then bear markets, and any bull market worthy of the name is going to last one to two years longer with the accent on the "or longer".

Bull Phases - Running three phases, the first bull phase is characterized by public disbelief in what is happening, disbelief that stock prices can rise importantly in the face of all the obviously bad news and bad fundamentals. The smart money, having turned confident during the third phase of the preceding bear market, is now more confident than ever in the face of the pessimistic public, although the first bull phase the news is bad, and the public gapes in disbelief as prices climb a wall of worry. When the lagging fundamentals attempt to catch up and the public is told that there is light at the end of the tunnel, eliminating the earlier public disbelief in the rise, then the first bull phase is ending. The end is technically shown by a topping out in the number of new individual highs, a topping out by the advance/decline line, one Dow stock after another having recorded an On-Balance Volume peak and other deteriorating technical phenomena. Just when the public confidence is given a shot in the arm and a little belief in the rise begins to replace the widespread pessimism, the market goes into a decline. At this point it is possible to project an approximate duration of the bull market, multiplying the duration of the first phase by three and adding the total time span to the last recorded major bottom.

The outstanding characteristic of the second bull phase is the decline that fools the majority. The smart money, having taken the first easy profits at the end of the first phase, sells out to the public which has been fooled by the shot in the arm burst of confidence. They sit back awaiting the new buying opportunities on the wide second phase market decline. The public is still generally confused, getting whipsawed on the second phase decline. Fundamentals obviously get stronger and the media helps to blow this up to boom proportions.

Bull phase three is at hand. The outstanding characteristic of that phase is the public belief in what is happening. They now take over the bulk of the market buying as the smart money period of confidence comes to an end. When the next decline comes, it usually starts a bear market, but by that time it would be the last thing the public could believe, thus the disbelief attached to the next phase, the first bear market phase.

Bull Trap - Any technically non-confirmed move to the upside encouraging the bulk of the investing and speculating public to the bullish. The most important bull traps terminate bull markets. In any case, they precede declines.

Buying Climax - A climax implies an ending. A buying climax is associated with such a sharp price run-up, with everything so heavily one-sided on the rise, that a move in the opposite direction becomes inevitable. Such a climax may be of the one-day variety ending a very short-term swing, or it could be of intermediate or final significance ending months of advance, or even years of advance. All climaxes involved increased volume. While heavy volume is never a concern during the first two phases of a bull market, very heavy volume during the third phase is uninformed public buying, often ending in a buying climax. Beware of such climactic action late in a bull market.

Climax Indicator ™ - This is the net number of up and down OBV breakouts among the 30 Dow Jones industrial stocks. Each day all the up designations are counted and all the down designations are counted regardless of whether they are lower ups or higher ups or higher downs.

Clusters ™ - A group of up or down OBV designations with no opposite designations seen in between. The bigger the cluster the more important it is. For instance, a large cluster of up designations would generally suggest that the next down designation would be a constructive higher down rather than the negative lower down. Conversely, a large cluster of down designations would generally suggest that the next up designation would be a negative lower up designation rather than the constructive higher up. But lower ups are not to be feared coming off of a well documented market bottom. Single higher down designations following a cluster of ups are more bullish than a large cluster of higher down designations. A large cluster of higher downs can more easily lead toward a bearish abortion because obviously a large cluster of higher down designations sees a string of steadily lower OBV levels. Conversely, single lower up designations following a cluster of downs are more negative than a large cluster of lower ups. A large cluster of lower ups can more easily lead toward a bullish abortion because obviously a large cluster of lower ups can more easily lead toward a bullish abortion because obviously a large cluster of lower ups sees a string of steadily higher OBV levels which can bullishly abort to higher OBV up designations.

Declining Tops - A pattern of declining tops implies a loss of upside energy and an ultimate decline. Each peak is less than the previous one, showing increasing weakness. The pattern is significant both in terms of price and On-Balance Volume.

Distribution - Following the valid assumption that volume precedes price, a stock is seen to be under distribution when the OBV numbers are persistently trending lower.

Divisor - The key figure that determine the volatility of the Dow Jones Industrial Average. Every time one of the Dow industrial stocks splits or pays a stock dividend, the divisor on that average is lowered. At this writing, the divisor is an extremely low 0.3715, meaning that less than a 3/8th change in any Dow stock equated with a full point change in the average.

Early Warning Climax Indicator ™ - Here the number of true ups is added to the number of higher downs and the total number of true downs and lower ups is subtracted. This is deemed to be a significant improvement over the orthodox Climax Indicator because it contains the potentialities of change by putting the higher downs and lower ups in their positive and negative segment.

Field Trend ™ - On-Balance Volume records upside breakouts and downside breakouts. When those breakouts trace out a rising zig-zag there is then a rising field trend. When there is no evidence of a rising or falling zig-zag in the clusters of breakouts record a downward zig-zag, the field trend is said to be falling.

Gaps - A gap is created in the price movement of a stock when the opening price is considerably higher or lower than the intra-day highs or lows of the day before. Gaps can also occur during the day and these usually occur following a dramatic piece of news affecting the stock or the market. When a gap is filled on the upside it is seen to be very bullish. When a gap is filled on the downside it is seen to be very bearish.

High/Low Indicator - These are the two sets of numbers seen every day recording the number of stocks recording new 52-week highs and lows.

Higher Downs - If an OBV down designation is higher than a previous down designation it should always be circled for easy identification. These are always counted as technically bullish designations because any positive OBV trend shows higher ups and higher downs. They are also commonly associated with a negative or falling field trend which is potentially starting to turn positive.

Lower Ups - If an OBV up designation is lower than a previous up designation it should always be circled for easy identification. These are always counted as technically bearish designations because any negative OBV trend shows lower ups and lower downs. They are also commonly associated with a positive or rising field trend which potentially is starting to turn negative.

Momentum - This is the rate of acceleration in price or volume expansion, best noted by developing gaps in velocity figures or gaps in an On-Balance Volume series. Upside momentum is the greatest just short of price maturity, and downside momentum tends to reach a peak at or near an important bottom.

Net Field Trend ™ - Major indicator depicting the true volume trend of the 30 Dow Jones industrial stocks. It is simply the difference between the number of Dow industrial stocks in rising field trends and the number of Dow industrial stocks in falling field trends.

Net Field Trend Indicator ™ - The number of Dow industrial stocks show that they are in either rising, doubtful, or falling field trends. This is the net difference between the number of rising field trends and the number in falling field trends. If the number of rising field trends outnumber the falling field trends then the NFI is a positive number.

On-Balance Volume ™ - This is the term I gave my entire theory validating the proof that volume precedes price. On-Balance Volume is derived by simply adding the total volume of trading when the price of the stock closes up and subtracting the total volume of trading when the price of the stock closes down. These numbers each day are done on a cumulative continuing basis. When the price of the stock closes unchanged the OBV simply repeats the number from the day before. This is done because if the volume is unable to change the price of the stock, it isn't worth recording.

Overhead Supply - This is the total amount of shares traded in a stock at higher price levels through which the stock (after a decline) is trying to cut through on the recovery movement. Some chartists call it the high volume zone. High volume at higher prices presents a formidable resistance on recovery movements. To put is another way: too many people are waiting to move out of a stock the minute it returns to the higher levels at which they originally made their purchase. If a stock can cut back through overhead supply, it is a strongly bullish endorsement for a further upswing. Overhead supply can be measured, and when a decline has generated an equal number of shares with the overhead supply, then the decline is either over or just about to be terminated (overhead supply concept).

Range Indictor ™ - No market crash movement is possible until the market comes within range. When the Climax Indicator is at –20 or lower, then there is the technical potential for a crash move. Every day the range indictor can be determined as a worse case scenario counting up the potential number of OBV down designations. (both higher and lower downs).

Resistance - Any barrier to progress is resistance. Once a price support level is broken, that support level becomes the resistance point on the recovery movement. The theory of resistance holds true in OBV movements.

Rising Bottoms - The ability of a stock to turn up above each preceding important low point traces out a pattern of rising bottoms, a bullish formation. However, that is only half the formation. To be complete, there should also be an accompanying series of rising tops. Rising bottoms (by definition) precede rising tops and are thus the first technical requirement which must be met if a situation is to be termed a bullish one. The same formation should be looked for in OBV.

Rising Tops - This is the typical pattern best seen in the second and third phase bullish stock price movements. It must be seen in the first phase bullish OBV movements, otherwise the later bullish unfoldment will not be seen. Rising tops beget rising tops until third phase negative gravity takes over.

Selling Climax - This is a situation that occurs when a clear majority of all stocks reach an oversold condition simultaneously. Selling climaxes have the following characteristics: (1) Heavy volume, (2) decided plurality of declines over advances, (3) transactions reported long after they occur (the late tape), (4) strong price reversal occurring before the session has ended or the next day, and (5) the move accompanied by a large number of odd lot short sales.

Short Interest - The total number of shares sold short and reported by the New York Stock Exchange once a month. A large short interest is basically bullish but is largely tempered by the volume of trading. Viewing the short interest, the question that must be answered is: are the shorts right or wrong on the market? A mere quantity of shortsellers tells us nothing. Shortsellers are wrong as a group in a bull market and right as a group in a bear market. Therefore, we must ascertain the primary trend before we attempt to weigh the significance of the short interest. If the primary trend is judged to be bullish, then the short interest is significant, especially if it is rising in relation to the average daily volume. If the primary trend of the market is judged to be bearish, then a large short interest is of no help to the bulls because then the shorts are shorting with the trend, and there is no compulsion to cover their short sales. In a bull market there definitely is an increasing compulsion to cover, and that is a measurable bullish factor.

Support - Any barrier to decline is called support. Once a resistance level has been successfully penetrated by a stock advance, the retreat from that level is expected to meet support at the old resistance level. The theory of support also holds true in OBV movements.

True Climax Indicator ™ - The lower ups and higher downs are eliminated. The True CLX is simply the net number of true up designations and true down designations. It is an acid test of strength or weakness.

INDEX

A

B

G

H

I

J

K

L

M

N

O

P

R

S

W

Z

To Contact the Author:

The Granville Market Letter
Drawer 413006
Kansas City, Missouri 64141

Telephone 1-800-876-5388
or
1-816-474-5353